PREPARING FOR THE
NEW
SAT
MATHEMATICS

JOYCE BERNSTEIN, Ed. D.
Retired Curriculum Associate for Mathematics
East Williston Union Free School District
Old Westbury, New York

RICHARD J. ANDRES, Ph. D.
Retired Mathematics Teacher and SAT Instructor
Jericho High School
Jericho, New York

AMSCO

AMSCO SCHOOL PUBLICATIONS, INC.,

a division of Perfection Learning®

REVIEWERS

David J. Bruskewicz
Byram Hills High School
Byram Hills Consolidated School District
Armonk, NY

Patricia Williams
Westfield High School
Fairfax County Public Schools
Fairfax, VA

Michael Strada
Southern Regional High School
Southern Regional School District
Manahawkin, NJ

Kendra Hardy
Tunstall High School
Pittsylvania Country School District
Danville, VA

Cheryl LaBrecque
French American International School
Bay Area Private Schools
San Francisco, CA

Martine Richardson
Overlea High School
Baltimore County Public Schools
Baltimore, MD

Kristine Miller
Wachusett Regional High School
Wachusett Regional School District
Holden, MA

Please visit our Web sites at:
www.amscopub.com and *www.perfectionlearning.com*

When ordering this book, please specify:
Softcover ISBN: 978-1-63419-814-1 *or* **2679201**
eBook ISBN: 978-1-68240-453-9 *or* **26792D**

8 9 10 11 12 13 DR 23 22 21 20 19 18

Printed in the United States of America

Thanks to Peg and Marc for their
patience and encouragement.

Table of Contents

Introduction

You are reading this book because you are preparing to take the SAT. Luckily, you have been preparing for the SAT your whole life, whether you knew it or not. Your life experiences, the classes you've taken, the books you've read, and the daily problems you've solved are all a part of what you will bring with you on test day. Nonetheless, the SAT is an important test, and you need to prepare for it in order to get the best score you can. This book will help you get ready by providing lessons on important skills found on the SAT and by modeling SAT questions with complete, step-by-step answer explanations. In addition, you will find many practice problems and four full-length SAT Math Model Exams to rehearse your skills before test day. Using this book will help you be confident and prepared on test day.

The New SAT

In the spring of 2016, the College Board will release a new SAT. The revised version of the test sets a higher standard that is more closely aligned with your classroom learning, creating a bridge between your high school work and the academics you can expect in college.

The new SAT will consist of four components: a Reading Test, a Language and Writing Test, a Math Test, with No Calculator and Calculator sections, and an optional Essay-Writing Task. The test will now be scored on a scale of 400 to 1,600 points. The sections will be as follows:

- Evidence-Based Reading and Writing Test: 200 to 800 possible points.

- Math Test (No Calculator and Calculator sections): 200 to 800 possible points.

- Optional Essay Test: 2 to 8 possible points on each of three traits (reading, analysis, and writing). Your essay score will not affect your Writing Test score. The essay will be assessed according to your abilities to read and understand, analyze, and write about a passage.

This book will thoroughly prepare you to take the new SAT Math Test, both the No Calculator and Calculator sections. (To prepare for the Evidenced-Based Reading and Writing Sections as well as the Optional Essay Section, see our companion book, *Preparing for the SAT—Reading, Writing, and Language, and Essay,* which can be purchased at www.perfectionlearning.com.)

The New SAT Math Test

The new SAT Math Test has a focus on rigor and "math that matters," which is math that you can apply in solving substantive problems. In many cases, you will be required to demonstrate a capacity for sustained reasoning over multiple steps. For example, given a certain real-world context, which may be presented verbally, numerically, or graphically, you will be required to mathematically model the given issue and to carry out the needed mathematical procedures to arrive at a correct solution.

Additionally, the new SAT Math Test will ask multiple questions regarding a given scenario. These scenarios may come from the sciences, the humanities, work-force training programs, or other real-world contexts. This will emulate work that you will encounter in postsecondary courses. As an example, there could be a set of bio-statistic questions based on the comparative food sources, weights, and distances traveled by turtles in the Caribbean versus those in the Mediterranean. You might then be asked to examine ratios and/or percentages, or perhaps calculate and compare the mean, median, and mode of given data, or possibly look for some other mathematical patterns.

Finally, the mathematical practices emphasized on the new SAT Math Test include problem solving; modeling; using appropriate tools, such as your calculator, strategically; and looking for and making use of algebraic structure. Such practices are central to the demands of postsecondary work.

The Structure of the New SAT Math Test

The new SAT Math Test contains both multiple choice questions and student-produced response questions within two test sections: No Calculator Allowed and Calculator Allowed. The test will assess your mathematical reasoning and problem solving abilities across four content categories:

1. **Heart of Algebra**

   The focus here will be on demonstrating that you have a substantive command of algebraic structure. Questions from this content category will focus heavily on creating, evaluating, and reasoning with linear equations and systems of linear equations.

2. **Problem-Solving and Data Analysis**

   In this content category, expect questions involving quantitative literacy. You will be asked to demonstrate your ability to solve real-world problems by analyzing data presented as sample statistics, graphs, tables, and/or text summaries. This content category also tests your ability to use ratios, percentages, and proportional reasoning to solve problems in real-world contexts.

3. **Passport to Advanced Math**

   This section involves reasoning with more complex equations and functions in one variable as well as understanding and solving questions using the graphs of quadratic and other higher-order functions.

4. **Additional Topics in Math**

   In this brief section, you may be asked questions about geometry and trigonometry as well as the arithmetic of complex numbers.

The No Calculator section of the Math Test features 20 questions and is timed at 25 minutes. This section will contain questions from only 3 of the 4 content categories.

- Heart of Algebra: 8 questions
- Passport to Advanced Math: 9 questions
- Additional Topics: 3 questions

The Calculator section of the Math Test features 38 questions and is timed at 55 minutes. This section will contain questions from all 4 content categories.

- Heart of Algebra: 13 questions
- Problem-Solving and Data Analysis: 13 questions
- Passport to Advanced Math: 7 questions
- Additional Topics: 3 questions

The Calculator section of the Math Test will also include a single-scenario extended thinking question from the Problem Solving and Data Analysis category. This question will have two parts and may be numbered as 37 and 38 or 37a and 37b. It will require you to execute multiple steps to produce solutions. It may require you to make connections between and among the different parts of the problem such that your thought process itself will suggest a solution strategy.

Multiple Choice and Student-Produced Response Questions

As previously mentioned, the new SAT Math Test contains both multiple choice questions and student-produced response questions (also called gridded-response questions). Each multiple choice question is followed by four answer options. The answer choices usually include responses that result from common math errors, so be careful with your reasoning and your calculations. If you can eliminate obviously incorrect answer choices, your chances of selecting the correct answer from the remaining options will increase.

The student-produced response questions require you to enter your answer by marking the ovals in the special student-produced response grid. The grid will accommodate whole numbers, decimals, and fractions. Be aware that some of these questions have more than one correct answer. The machine scoring the test has been programmed to accept all correct answers for these questions. You only need to grid one correct answer. If there is more than one way to state the answer, such as a fraction or a decimal, you may grid in either. The machine will accept all correct equivalencies.

Specific rules govern how you enter your solution in an answer grid. If you have the right answer but grid it incorrectly, you will not receive credit.

- You may fill in the boxes above each column to help you fill in the corresponding ovals correctly. Answers written in the boxes will not be scored. Only the answer marked in the ovals in the grid will be scored. Fill in only one oval in any column. Completely darken the ovals.

- Four columns can be marked. Although you may start in any column, you should begin with the first column on the left. Columns not used should be left blank.

- All columns may be gridded with a digit or a decimal point. Columns 2 and 3 may also be gridded with a slash mark (/), which represents the separation of the numerator from the denominator in a fraction.

- Fractions do not need to be reduced unless they do not fit in the grid.

- You cannot grid a mixed number. Mixed numbers must be gridded as improper fractions or decimals. If the answer is $3\frac{1}{2}$ and you grid it as 31/2, the machine scoring the test will read it as $\frac{31}{2}$. Therefore, grid $3\frac{1}{2}$ as $\frac{7}{2}$ or 3.5.

- For repeating decimals, enter the most accurate value the grid will accommodate. You must use all four spaces for a repeating decimal. For example, grid in 0.6666 as .666 or .667. Less accurate values, such as 0.66 or 0.67, are not acceptable. Do not worry about rounding your answer as long as you fill in all the spaces.

- No student-produced response question has a negative answer.

- If the answer has a label, such as % or $, disregard the symbol when gridding in the answer.

Since the four-space, student-produced response grid is a special feature of the SAT, you can practice by completing the following grids. Fill in each grid with the number that appears above it.

1. 3.8   **2.** $\frac{7}{8}$ **3.** $4\frac{2}{5}$ **4.** $\frac{5}{10}$ **5.** 0.77777   **6.** 250   **7.** 0.05   **8.** 10%

(See p. 7 for the answers.)

Scoring

On the new SAT, you will earn points for questions answered correctly, but you will not lose points for questions that you answer incorrectly or leave blank. This means that you should definitely guess, even if you have no idea what the right answer is. If you are running out of time on a section, you should fill in answers even if you don't have time to read the questions.

On the No Calculator section of the Math Test, you'll find

15 multiple choice questions, each worth 1 point	15 points
5 grid-in responses questions, each worth 1 point	5 points
	20 points

On the Calculator section of the Math Test, you'll find

30 multiple choice questions, each worth 1 point	30 points
6 grid-in responses questions, each worth 1 point	6 points
1 extended thinking question set worth 2 points	2 points
	38 points

Preparing to Take the New SAT

Long-Term Preparation

The best way to prepare for the new SAT is to learn all you can from your classes in school. Whether it is for a class or on your own, it is important to:

- Read broadly. The more you read, the better your reading skills. This will help you on all the sections of the new SAT, including math.

- Read deeply and critically. Think about what the author (or the test question) is really saying or asking you.

- Expand your vocabulary. Mathematics is a language. In order to fully understand it, you need to become familiar with and understand its common terms.

Short-Term Preparation

If you will be taking the new SAT in the next few months, start practicing. Follow the **How to Use this Book** section at the end of this Introduction. It is important to:

- Learn the format of the test and the directions for each section so that there are no surprises on test day.

- Work through the lessons in this book, paying close attention to your weaker areas.

- Get help from someone who can explain concepts with which you are still struggling.

Before the Test

- Set up a study schedule. Devote a specific amount of time each day or week to work through this book.

- Don't cram. The new SAT assesses your ability to think critically about the structure of the mathematics in each problem. This test requires thorough preparation, which comes from extensive practice.

- Take care of yourself. A rested brain and a healthy body will serve you well on test day. It is important to get enough sleep, eat well, exercise, stay hydrated, and engage in other activities that contribute to your overall health and well-being.

- Manage anxiety. If test taking makes you nervous, practice ways of calming your brain. If you find yourself feeling stressed as you work through the lessons in this book, take a few deep breaths. If needed, take a break, go on a walk, or practice another way of managing your emotions. Taking the time before the test to find stress-management techniques that work for you will help you on test day.

On Test Day

- Allow for plenty of time to arrive at the testing center.

- Bring the necessary documents and identification.

- Wear a watch so that you can keep track of the time during the test. You will not be permitted to use your phone.

- Bring an approved calculator with fresh batteries for the calculator portion of the math test. Consult https://sat.collegeboard.org/register/calculator-policy for a list of approved calculator models.

- Bring water and a quiet snack in case you need them during the breaks.

Test-Taking Strategies

Here are some specific strategies to help you on the SAT Math Test. They are provided here in a single list, but they are also repeated throughout the book in solution explanations as appropriate.

- Substitute friendly numbers for variables in problems to help you determine the correct answer. While this method is extremely useful, it is possible to stumble upon a special case or make an arithmetic error, so choose your numbers wisely.

- Backfill. If the problem is simple enough and you want to avoid doing the more complex algebra, or if the problem presents a phrase such as $x = ?$, then fill in the answer choices that are given in the problem until you find the one that works. Obviously, one of them must be correct.

- Begin each problem by scanning the answer choices. Doing so will give you a sense of direction. That is, are you looking for fractions, decimals, percents, integers, squares, cubes, perimeters, areas, etc.? Immediately eliminate any answer choices that do not make sense.

- Do not waste time doing complex arithmetic or lengthy algebra. The questions on the new SAT Math Test make good use of algebraic structure. If you find yourself bogged down in a difficult computation, you have probably missed the point of the question.

- Fill in the information you know to help you find the unknown. In geometry problems where the figure is drawn to scale, do your work on the given figure. The picture itself provides visual information useful in solving the problem. On drawn-to-scale geometry figures, the angles and lines that "look" equal are equal. Draw in lines and angles, extend lines, and mark measurements in these diagrams. This will save you time and clarify the problem.

- If a figure is <u>not</u> drawn to scale, proceed with caution! If a geometry problem has these words of warning, you can usually assume that (a) the picture is misleading, (b) the answer choice closest to the given visual setup is probably incorrect, and (c) you should *redraw the figure accurately*.

- Test the extremes. If you are given a range of values, such as $4 < x < 9$, first test the extremes (4 and 9). The answer will become obvious.

- Look for patterns whenever possible. The new SAT Math Test makes use of pattern and structure.

- Do not be misled by generic answers. Answer choices such as "None of the above" or "It cannot be determined from the information given" or "All of the above" are only good choices if all the other options have been carefully eliminated.

- Do the math. This is the ultimate strategy. Do not search your mind for tricks, gimmicks, or math magic to solve problems. This is a math test. Use the knowledge you've gained in your classes and from this text to think through problems, determine a solution strategy, and carry out the math.

Timing and Pacing

- Work through all of the questions at a steady pace. Don't get stuck too long on any one question. It is better to gain points by getting the easier questions correct than to waste too much time struggling with a difficult question.

- Mark questions you found difficult and return to those if you have the time. You probably won't have time to check all of your answers, but go back to the difficult questions if you can.

- Check your answer sheet frequently to make sure you are in the right place. If you skip a question, be sure to skip that space on your answer sheet.

- Keep track of time. If you are running out of time, answer the easier questions first and then make an educated guess on the more difficult ones.

Stress Management

- Focus on what you do know, not what you don't know. When you read a question, ask yourself, "What do I know?" Use that knowledge as a jumping off point to quickly develop a solution strategy.

- Remember that on the new SAT you can answer some questions incorrectly and still do well overall.

- Stay positive. You have prepared, so be confident in your ability.

How to Use this Book

This book was developed to prepare you to do well on the new SAT Math Test. The College Board, developer of the SAT, has published a comprehensive list of all the mathematics you could possibly be tested over on the math section of the test. The lessons in this book explain all of these skills in clear, concise language using many examples. The lessons help you master the skills by providing isolated practice over specific objectives.

This book also provides practice with the format and types of questions found on the new SAT. You will become familiar with the way questions are worded so that you can more easily identify how to answer them on test day. All of the questions in this book have full solution strategies provided with test-taking tips embedded, as appropriate, to help you learn how to be a more effective test taker and avoid making errors.

Here are some steps for using this book:

1. Take the Diagnostic Test (pp. 8–32), score your test, and then consult the chart that correlates each question with a lesson in the book. Identify which skills you need to practice the most. Plan to spend more time working through those lessons.

2. Work through the lessons for the Heart of Algebra (pp. 43–156), Problem Solving and Data Analysis (pp. 157–280), Passport to Advanced Mathematics (pp. 281–406), and Additional Topics in Math (pp. 407–535) sections of this book. The lesson format for each of these is as follows:

    Explain: Summarizes skills taught in the lesson.

    Think It Through: Further explains the skills using example questions with full explanations and answers.

    Practice: Provides additional practice of skills directly related to the objective.

    Model SAT Questions: Simulates how the skills may appear on the new SAT Math Test. These questions may be multiple choice or student-produced response.

    SAT-Type Questions: Ends each lesson and provides targeted practice with the skills in the lesson. Again, these questions may be multiple choice or student-produced response.

3. At the end of each category, you will find a **Summary SAT-Type Test** for the topics in that category only. Be sure to take each of these practice tests and then use the correlation charts at the end of each category to help you evaluate what you know and what you still need to practice. Take the time to review the material in the lessons with which you had difficulty.

4. After completing the lessons in this book, take the full-length **SAT Math Model Exams** (pp. 537–654). These complete exams closely mirror the new SAT. Taking these tests under the time restraints, as shown at the beginning of each test, will help you learn to manage your time and build your confidence. You can grade your test and translate your raw score into what you would likely receive on the math section of the SAT (score conversion chart located on p. 40).

As you work through this book, keep a record of your scores on the opening Diagnostic Test, the four category SAT-Type Summary Tests, and the four full-length SAT Math Model Exams at the end of the book so that you can compare results and see the progress you've made.

Final Notes and Reminders

- The math covered on this exam is traditionally taught in the first three years of high school.

- All work must be done in your test booklet. No scrap paper is allowed.

- Although you can use a calculator on one section of the math test, using it for every question can steal far too much of your time. Be judicious in your calculator usage.

- It is advantageous to answer every question. You earn points for questions answered correctly, but you don't lose points for questions answered incorrectly. Skipping questions offers no advantage.

- Students who actively take the time to prepare for this standardized test can raise their scores. Scoring well on the SAT doesn't involve overnight clever tricks or magic gimmicks. Scoring well takes practice, practice, and more practice.

- You may take the SAT as many times as it is offered. Most students take it near the end of their junior year of high school (11th grade) and perhaps again in the early part of their senior year. An excellent way to prepare for this test is to take the real SAT test as only practice in March or April, just to get a feel for the actual conditions. This practice session is a great way to learn how to budget your time and energy as well as to remove the anxiety that naturally accrues from the lengthy run-up to this important test.

- Lastly, the SAT is published by the Educational Testing Service (ETS) under the sponsorship of the College Entrance Examination Board (the College Board). Your school guidance office should have the most recent SAT Preparation Guide, which will have all the information about registering for the exam. The College Board can be contacted through their web page, www.collegeboard.org or http://deliveringopportunity.org. The College Board can be reached by phone at 1-866-630-9305 (technical support) and 1-866-756-7346 (customer service).

Answers to grid exercises 1–8 on page 3

1. 3.8   2. $\frac{7}{8}$ 3. $4\frac{2}{5}$ 4. $\frac{5}{10}$ 5. 0.77777   6. 250   7. 0.05   8. 10%

To the Teacher

The educational focus of *Preparing for the New SAT Mathematics* makes it the perfect choice for use in the classroom. The five-section lesson structure: **Explain, Think It Through, Practice, Model SAT Questions, and SAT-Type Questions** provides a scaffolded, instructional approach to all of the skills outlined by the College Board on its test blueprint for the new SAT Math Test.

If you are an SAT tutor working with a classroom of students:

- Have students take the Diagnostic Test to identify areas for review to focus instruction.

- Use the Diagnostic Test correlation chart to create individual lesson plans for students.

- Encourage students to work individually on the lessons where they need review.

- Provide support if students struggle with a particular concept.

- Monitor formative assessments as students complete **SAT-Type Questions** at the end of each lesson. Revisit related **Think It Through**, **Practice**, and **Model SAT Questions** within the lesson to facilitate needed reviews of skills or concepts.

- Use the **Summary SAT-Type Tests** (summative assessments) to evaluate student progress.

- Review Test-Taking Strategies (pages 5–6) and administer classwide **SAT Math Model Exams 1–4**, adhering to the strict time restraints and other conditions reminiscent of the official test.

- Monitor and support students after each administration of the **SAT Math Model Exams** to review needed skills.

If you are a high school math teacher, the skills focus of this book makes it the perfect companion to your classroom textbook for:

- Providing targeted review and assessment.

- Familiarizing students with the format of SAT Math questions.

- Offering additional problem-solving practice in real-world contexts.

- Building mathematical fluency, conceptual understanding, and application.

Diagnostic Test Instructions

The following Diagnostic Test will assess your current knowledge of the topics tested on the new SAT Mathematics test. The questions on this Diagnostic Test match those you will encounter on the new SAT. Your results will help you focus your review and provide you with a benchmark against which you can measure your progress as you move through the lessons in this book.

Student Instructions

When you take this Diagnostic Test, as well as any of the other assessments in this book, you should:

- Take it under conditions as close as possible to the actual testing conditions.

- Sit in a quiet place where you will not be disturbed.

- Time yourself. You will have 55 minutes for the calculator-allowed section and 25 minutes for the no-calculator-allowed section.

- Give yourself a 3-minute break between the two sections.

After you complete the Diagnostic Test,

- Use the Answer Key with complete solutions found on pp. 33–39 to check your answers.

- Study the solutions to any questions you have missed.

- Use the correlation chart on pp. 41–42 to spot error trends and identify your areas of strengths and weaknesses for focused review.

    The correlation chart shows the category and lesson where you can find explanatory text and similar questions. Circle or highlight any questions you missed; then pay close attention to those lessons as you review the information in this book. For example, if you answer question number 1 incorrectly, pay close attention to the information in Category 1, Lesson 3, pp. 81 – 97.

- Determine your estimated SAT score by using the Score Conversion Chart on p. 40.

Answer Sheet

Diagnostic Test

Use a No. 2 pencil. Fill in the circle completely. If you erase, erase completely.
Incomplete erasures may be read as answers.

No Calculator

1 Ⓐ Ⓑ Ⓒ Ⓓ   6 Ⓐ Ⓑ Ⓒ Ⓓ   11 Ⓐ Ⓑ Ⓒ Ⓓ
2 Ⓐ Ⓑ Ⓒ Ⓓ   7 Ⓐ Ⓑ Ⓒ Ⓓ   12 Ⓐ Ⓑ Ⓒ Ⓓ
3 Ⓐ Ⓑ Ⓒ Ⓓ   8 Ⓐ Ⓑ Ⓒ Ⓓ   13 Ⓐ Ⓑ Ⓒ Ⓓ
4 Ⓐ Ⓑ Ⓒ Ⓓ   9 Ⓐ Ⓑ Ⓒ Ⓓ   14 Ⓐ Ⓑ Ⓒ Ⓓ
5 Ⓐ Ⓑ Ⓒ Ⓓ   10 Ⓐ Ⓑ Ⓒ Ⓓ   15 Ⓐ Ⓑ Ⓒ Ⓓ

16, 17, 18, 19, 20 — grid-in answer boxes

Calculator

1 Ⓐ Ⓑ Ⓒ Ⓓ   7 Ⓐ Ⓑ Ⓒ Ⓓ   13 Ⓐ Ⓑ Ⓒ Ⓓ   19 Ⓐ Ⓑ Ⓒ Ⓓ   25 Ⓐ Ⓑ Ⓒ Ⓓ
2 Ⓐ Ⓑ Ⓒ Ⓓ   8 Ⓐ Ⓑ Ⓒ Ⓓ   14 Ⓐ Ⓑ Ⓒ Ⓓ   20 Ⓐ Ⓑ Ⓒ Ⓓ   26 Ⓐ Ⓑ Ⓒ Ⓓ
3 Ⓐ Ⓑ Ⓒ Ⓓ   9 Ⓐ Ⓑ Ⓒ Ⓓ   15 Ⓐ Ⓑ Ⓒ Ⓓ   21 Ⓐ Ⓑ Ⓒ Ⓓ   27 Ⓐ Ⓑ Ⓒ Ⓓ
4 Ⓐ Ⓑ Ⓒ Ⓓ   10 Ⓐ Ⓑ Ⓒ Ⓓ   16 Ⓐ Ⓑ Ⓒ Ⓓ   22 Ⓐ Ⓑ Ⓒ Ⓓ   28 Ⓐ Ⓑ Ⓒ Ⓓ
5 Ⓐ Ⓑ Ⓒ Ⓓ   11 Ⓐ Ⓑ Ⓒ Ⓓ   17 Ⓐ Ⓑ Ⓒ Ⓓ   23 Ⓐ Ⓑ Ⓒ Ⓓ   29 Ⓐ Ⓑ Ⓒ Ⓓ
6 Ⓐ Ⓑ Ⓒ Ⓓ   12 Ⓐ Ⓑ Ⓒ Ⓓ   18 Ⓐ Ⓑ Ⓒ Ⓓ   24 Ⓐ Ⓑ Ⓒ Ⓓ   30 Ⓐ Ⓑ Ⓒ Ⓓ

31 32 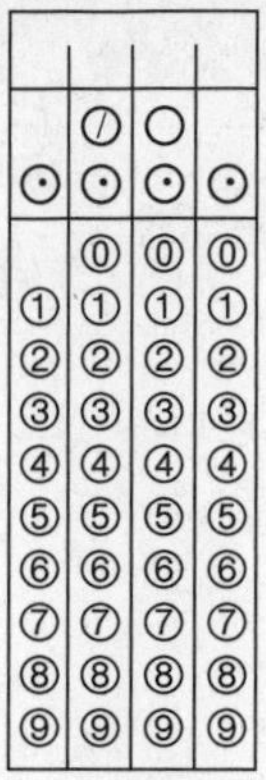 33 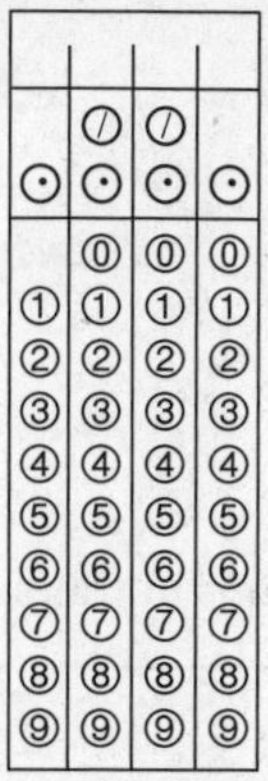 34

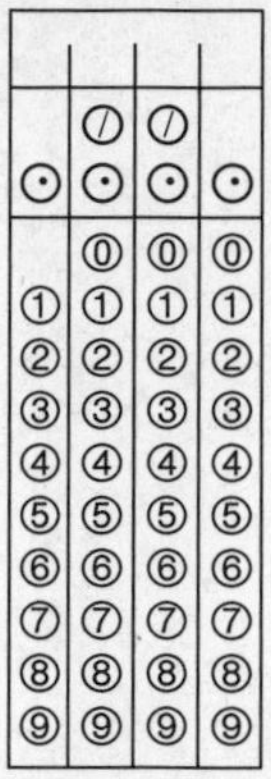

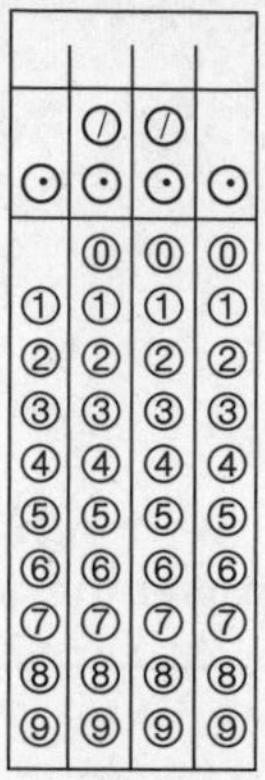

35 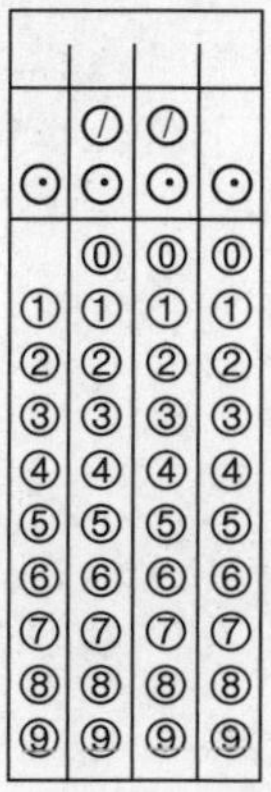 36 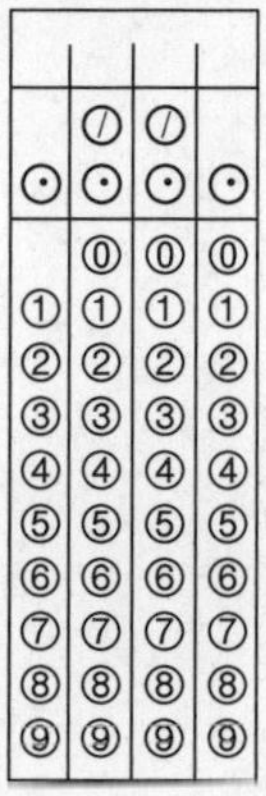 37 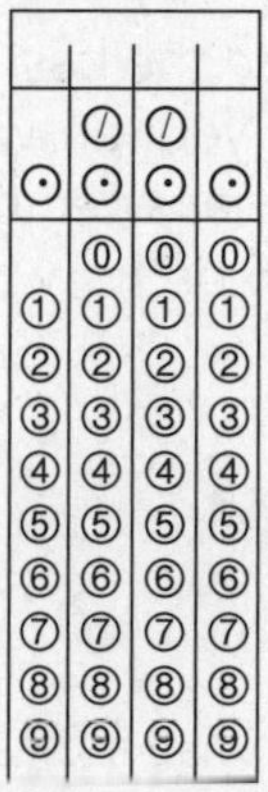 38

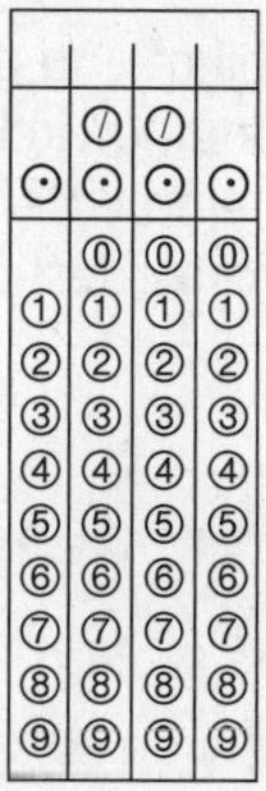

25 MINUTES, 20 QUESTIONS

NO CALCULATOR ALLOWED

Turn to the No Calculator section of your answer sheet to answer the questions in this section.

Directions

For questions 1–15, calculate the answer to each problem and choose the best option from the choices given. Bubble in the corresponding circle on your answer sheet. For the remaining questions, solve the problem and enter your answer in the grid on your answer sheet. Refer to the directions before question 16 on how to enter your answers in the grid.

Notes

1. The use of a calculator is <u>not</u> permitted on this test section.
2. All variables and expressions represent real numbers unless otherwise indicated.
3. Figures provided are drawn to scale unless otherwise noted.
4. All figures lie in a plane unless otherwise noted.
5. Unless otherwise noted, the domain of a given function f is the set of all real numbers x for which $f(x)$ is a real number.

Reference

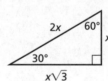

$A = \pi r^2$
$C = 2\pi r$

$A = lw$

$A = \frac{1}{2}bh$

$c^2 = a^2 + b^2$

Special Right Triangles

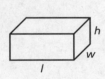

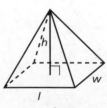

$V = lwh$

$V = \pi r^2 h$

$V = \frac{4}{3}\pi r^3$

$V = \frac{1}{3}\pi r^2 h$

$V = \frac{1}{3}lwh$

The number of degrees of arc in a circle is 360.
The number of radians of arc in a circle is 2π.
The sum of the measures in degrees of the angles of a triangle is 180.

CONTINUE

Which of the following x-values satisfy the inequality $\dfrac{7}{6}+\dfrac{x}{2}<x-\dfrac{1}{3}$?

A) $x<-4.5$

B) $x<\dfrac{5}{3}$

C) $x>3$

D) $x<3$

The algebraic expression $(2x+1)^2-2(2x^2-1)$ is equivalent to

A) $4x+3$

B) $2x+3$

C) 3

D) -1

The cost of an overseas telephone call is a cents for the first three minutes and b cents for each minute thereafter. If n is an integer greater than 3, which of the following is an expression for the cost of a call lasting n minutes?

A) $3a+b(n-3)$

B) $a+n(b-3)$

C) $a+b(n-3)$

D) $a+b(3-n)$

$$y-x=-2$$
$$y+8=x^2-4x$$

Based on the system of equations given above, what is one possible value of xy?

A) 3

B) -3

C) -6

D) -12

CONTINUE

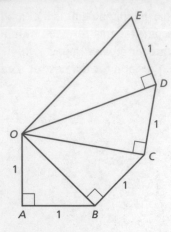

In the figure above with four right triangles, $OA = AB = BC = CD = 1$. What is the length of $\overline{OE}$?

A) $2\sqrt{2}$

B) $3\sqrt{3}$

C) $4\sqrt{3}$

D) $\sqrt{5}$

The expression $i^3 - i(2 - i)$ is equal to
$\left(\text{Note: } i = \sqrt{-1}\right)$

A) $1 + i$

B) $1 - i$

C) $-1 - 3i$

D) $1 + 3i$

The price of renting a lake house for the weekend varies inversely with the number of people renting the house. If it costs \$150 per person when 8 people rent the house, how much will it cost when 12 people rent the same house?

A) \$125 per person

B) \$100 per person

C) \$165 per person

D) \$85 per person

In the equation $x^2 - 14x + a = 0$, where a is a constant, the sum of the roots exceeds the product of the roots by 3. What is the value of a?

A) 17

B) 11

C) −11

D) −17

CONTINUE

Which is the solution to the following equation: $x^{-3} + 6 = 14$?

A) -2

B) $-\dfrac{1}{2}$

C) $\dfrac{1}{8}$

D) $\dfrac{1}{2}$

In the equation $A = p + prt$, solve for p.

A) $p = \dfrac{A}{2rt}$

B) $p = \dfrac{A}{1+rt}$

C) $p = \dfrac{A-p}{rt}$

D) $p = A - prt$

If the graphs of $y = 3^x$ and $y = 3^{-x}$ are drawn on the same set of axes, the graphs will intersect at a point that lies on which of the following lines?

A) $x = 0$

B) $y = 0$

C) $y = x$

D) $y = -x$

Given: $\overset{\frown}{AB}$ is the arc of a circle with center C, where the central angle $\angle ACB = 30°$. If the length of $\overset{\frown}{AB}$ is 6π, what is the area of sector ACB?

A) 108π

B) 72π

C) 36π

D) 9π

CONTINUE

If two lines with equations $y = m_1x + b_1$ and $y = m_2x + b_2$ intersect and form right angles, which of the following must be true?

A) $m_1 = m_2$

B) $b_1 = -\dfrac{1}{b_2}$

C) $m_1 = \dfrac{1}{m_2}$

D) $m_1 = -\dfrac{1}{m_2}$

Which of the following is the sum of the solutions to $|7x - 4| = 25$?

A) $-1\dfrac{1}{7}$

B) $\dfrac{8}{7}$

C) $\dfrac{29}{7}$

D) $7\dfrac{1}{7}$

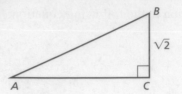

Note: Figure <u>not</u> drawn to scale.

In the given right triangle ABC, side length $BC = \sqrt{2}$. If $(\sin A)(\cos A)(\tan A) = \dfrac{1}{2}$, then the length of $\overline{AB}$ is

A) $\sqrt{2}$

B) 2

C) $2\sqrt{2}$

D) 4

CONTINUE

No Calculator Allowed

For the remaining questions, solve the problem and enter your answer in the answer grid. Instructions for entering your answer in the grid are described below.

1. It is not required that you write your answer in the boxes at the top of the grid, but it is suggested.

2. Do not mark more than one circle in each column.

3. There are no negative answers in this portion of the test.

4. If the problem has more than 1 correct answer, grid only 1 of those answers.

5. Grid fractions as proper or improper fractions only.

6. Decimal answers must fill the entire grid.

Examples

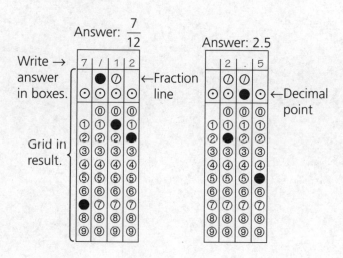

No Calculator Allowed

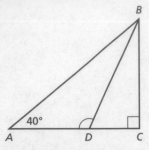

Note: Figure <u>not</u> drawn to scale.

In the figure above, $BC \perp AC$ and $\overline{BD}$ bisects $\angle ABC$. If the measure of $\angle BAD$ is 40°, what is the measure of $\angle ADB$?

$$5x + y = 15$$
$$3x + y = 11$$

If (x, y) is the solution to the system of equations above, what is the value of x?

If the graph of the equation $(x - 2)^2 + y^2 = 25$ passes through the point $(7, a)$, what is the value of a?

CONTINUE

No Calculator Allowed

x	f(x)	g(x)
0	1	2
1	5	4
2	3	1
3	4	0
4	0	5
5	2	3

In the table above, the functions f and g are defined for only the six values of x as shown. If $g(k) = 0$, what is the value of $g(f(k))$?

Find the solution of $2 + h = \sqrt{10 - h}$.

STOP

If you finish before time is called, you may check your work on this section only.
Do not turn to any other section.

No Calculator Allowed

55 MINUTES, 38 QUESTIONS

CALCULATOR ALLOWED

Turn to the Calculator section of your answer sheet to answer the questions in this section.

Directions

For questions 1–30, calculate the answer to each problem and choose the best option from the choices given. Bubble in the corresponding circle on your answer sheet. For the remaining questions, solve the problem and enter your answer in the grid on your answer sheet. Refer to the directions before question 31 on how to enter your answers in the grid.

Notes

1. The use of a calculator is permitted on this test section.
2. All variables and expressions represent real numbers unless otherwise indicated.
3. Figures provided are drawn to scale unless otherwise noted.
4. All figures lie in a plane unless otherwise noted.
5. Unless otherwise noted, the domain of a given function f is the set of all real numbers x for which $f(x)$ is a real number.

Reference

$A = \pi r^2$
$C = 2\pi r$

$A = lw$

$A = \frac{1}{2}bh$

$c^2 = a^2 + b^2$

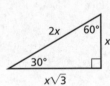

Special Right Triangles

$V = lwh$

$V = \pi r^2 h$

$V = \frac{4}{3}\pi r^3$

$V = \frac{1}{3}\pi r^2 h$

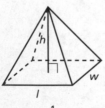

$V = \frac{1}{3}lwh$

The number of degrees of arc in a circle is 360.
The number of radians of arc in a circle is 2π.
The sum of the measures in degrees of the angles of a triangle is 180.

CONTINUE

Calculator Allowed

Which of the following equations represents a line that is parallel to the line with the equation $y + 2 = 2x$, if the parallel line passes through the origin?

A) $y = 2x$

B) $y = -\dfrac{1}{2}x - 2$

C) $y = -2x$

D) $y = \dfrac{1}{2}x - 2$

Which of the following has two real number values that must be restricted from the domain when evaluating the given expression?

A) $\dfrac{4}{x^2 + 1}$

B) $(x - 3)(x + 3)$

C) $\dfrac{9}{x^2}$

D) $\dfrac{6}{x+1} + \dfrac{3}{x}$

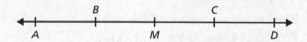

In the given number line, point M is the midpoint of both $\overline{BC}$ and $\overline{AD}$. The coordinates of points B and C are 3 and 8, respectively. If the distance AD is 13 units, then the coordinate of point D is

A) 10

B) 11

C) 12

D) 13

If $a^x \cdot a^5 = a^{15}$ and $(a^3)^y = a^{12}$, what is the value of $x + y$?

A) 7

B) 12

C) 14

D) 19

CONTINUE

Which of the following represents the radian measure of an angle formed by the minute and the hour hand of a clock at 2:30?

A) $\dfrac{2\pi}{3}$

B) $\dfrac{5\pi}{12}$

C) $\dfrac{7\pi}{12}$

D) $\dfrac{23\pi}{18}$

What is k, the constant of variation, if y varies directly as x and $y = 12$ when $x = 3$?

A) 60

B) 36

C) 12

D) 4

Ashley bought $4n$ articles for c cents each. When she sold $3n$ of the articles she noticed that she had recovered her initial investment. Express in terms of c the amount she charged for each article.

A) $\dfrac{3}{7}c$

B) $\dfrac{3}{4}c$

C) c

D) $\dfrac{4}{3}c$

The chemical compound calcium chloride, $CaCl_2$, is used as a road deicer. The density of $CaCl_2$ is 2.24 g/cm³. If the mass of calcium chloride in a small tank is 50,000 grams, what is the volume of the substance in the tank in cubic meters? $\left(\text{Density} = \dfrac{\text{mass}}{\text{volume}} \right)$

A) 0.125 m³

B) 0.02 m³

C) 20 m³

D) 12.5 m³

CONTINUE

Calculator Allowed

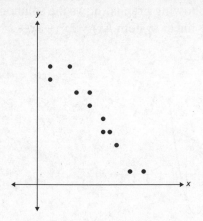

Select the most reasonable choice for for the equation of the line of best fit for the scatterplot above.

A) $y = 3.5x + 103$

B) $y = 3.5x - 100$

C) $y = -3.5x + 103$

D) $y = -3.5x - 100$

The table below shows the math and foreign language enrollment among eleventh grade students at Springfield High School. What is the probability that a randomly selected eleventh grade student from this high school who is enrolled in Pre-Calculus is also enrolled in Latin?

	Latin	Other Language	Total
Pre-Calculus	24	240	264
Other math	3	33	36
Total	27	273	300

A) 1%

B) 9%

C) 11%

D) 80%

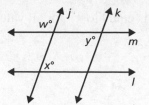

In the figure above, line l is parallel to line m and line j is parallel to line k. If $x° + y° = 120°$, what is the degree measure of w?

A) 60°

B) 80°

C) 100°

D) 120°

A local fitness center wants to know which types of equipment are used most frequently. A survey sent to randomly selected members asking what single piece of equipment they use most frequently while at the center yielded the following summarized results:

Equipment Type	Number of Respondents
Treadmill	78
Stationary Bike	52
Elliptical	37
Free Weights	30

Based on the results above, which of the following can be inferred about the entire population of fitness center members?

A) Very few fitness center members use the free weights and they should be eliminated.

B) Treadmills are the most popular equipment type.

C) If you use the fitness center's free weights, you will also use the elliptical.

D) Among all members, exactly 15 fewer people use the elliptical than the stationary bike.

CONTINUE

13

Which of the following is equal to $k^{\frac{3}{2}}$ for all values of k?

A) $\sqrt{k^{\frac{1}{3}}}$

B) $\sqrt{k^3}$

C) $\sqrt[3]{k^{\frac{1}{2}}}$

D) $\sqrt[3]{k^2}$

14

If rain falls at the rate of x centimeters per minute, how many hours will it take for n centimeters to fall?

A) $\dfrac{n}{60x}$

B) $\dfrac{x}{60n}$

C) $\dfrac{60n}{x}$

D) $\dfrac{60x}{n}$

15

Write an equation of a circle with diameter endpoints located at $(0, 5)$ and $(0, 1)$.

A) $x^2 + (y-5)^2 = 4$

B) $(x-5)^2 + (y-1)^2 = 4$

C) $x^2 + (y-3)^2 = 4$

D) $(x-1)^2 + (y-3)^2 = 4$

16

Which of the following graphs shows the solution to the quadratic-linear system $f(x) = 2x^2 + 3x - 2$ and $g(x) = \dfrac{1}{2}x + 3$?

A)

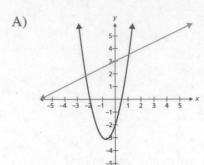

B)

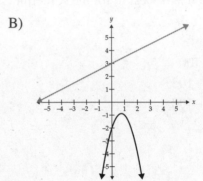

C)

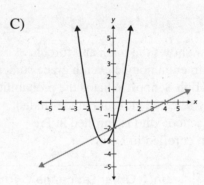

D)

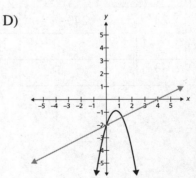

CONTINUE

Calculator Allowed

A 4-centimeter diameter of an engine part cannot differ from its specification by more than 0.05 centimeters. If the variable n represents the measured diameter of the engine part, which of the following statements reflects the restriction on n?

A) $n - 4 \geq 0.05$

B) $4 - n \geq 0.05$

C) $|n - 0.05| \leq 4$

D) $|4 - n| \leq 0.05$

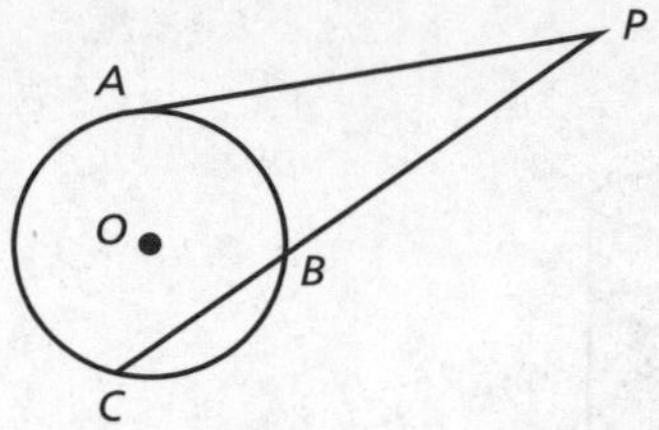

Note: Figure not drawn to scale.

In circle O, above, secant $\overline{PBC}$ and tangent $\overline{PA}$ are drawn. If $m\widehat{AB} = 52°$ and $m\widehat{BC} = 150°$, what is $m\angle P$?

A) 53°

B) 78°

C) 106°

D) 158°

The higher the price a jeweler charges for a school ring, the fewer rings he will sell. After experimenting with different prices in different schools, the jeweler found the following linear relationship between s, the selling price, and q, the quantity sold:

$$q = -2s + 576$$

Find the whole dollar selling price that results in the maximum profit for the jeweler if it costs him $12.50 to produce each ring.

A) $150

B) $290

C) $213

D) $165

The vertex of a parabola defined as $f(x) = x^2 - 4x + 3$ has coordinates $(2, -1)$. Which of the following are the coordinates of the vertex of the parabola defined by $g(x)$ where $g(x) = f(x + 2)$?

A) $(4, -1)$

B) $(2, -3)$

C) $(0, -1)$

D) $(2, 1)$

CONTINUE

The figures above show the height of water in two right circular cylinders, A and B. The base area of container A is 12π square inches and the base area of cylinder B is 16π square inches. The water from A is to be poured into container B until the volume of water in both containers is equal. After the transfer, what will be the height (in inches) of the water in container B?

A) 3.5 inches

B) 3.75 inches

C) 4 inches

D) 4.25 inches

The expression $\dfrac{3}{8+2i}$ is equivalent to

$\left(\text{Note: } i = \sqrt{-1}\right)$

A) $\dfrac{12+3i}{68}$

B) $\dfrac{2-i}{5}$

C) $\dfrac{3}{8-2i}$

D) $\dfrac{12-3i}{34}$

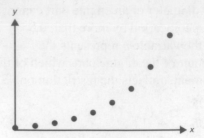

The scatterplot above shows change in population for a small bacteria culture. Which statement best describes the graph?

A) Linear growth

B) Linear decay

C) Exponential decay

D) Exponential growth

If it takes 8 volunteers 3 hours to deliver gifts to children in the hospital, how many hours would it take 10 volunteers to deliver the same number of gifts?

A) 2 hours and 20 minutes

B) 2 hours and 24 minutes

C) 2 hours and 28 minutes

D) 2 hours and 32 minutes

CONTINUE

Calculator Allowed

The results of testing a new medication on 1,000 people with a certain disease found that 480 of the patients showed improvement when they used the medication. Assume these 1,000 people can be regarded as a random sample from the population of all people with this disease. The margin of error for the study is 5 percentage points.

Which of the following is the most reasonable inference to make based on the information above?

A) It would be reasonable to think that more than half the people with this disease would not improve because $\frac{480}{1,000} < 0.50$.

B) It would be reasonable to think that less than half the people with this disease would improve because $\frac{480}{1,000} - 0.025 < 0.50$.

C) It would be reasonable to think that about half the people with this disease would improve because $\frac{480}{1,000} + 0.05 > 0.50$.

D) It would be reasonable to think that less than half the people with this disease would improve because $\frac{480}{1,000} + 0.025 < 0.50$.

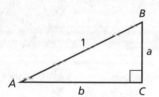

Given the right triangle ABC, above, the expression $(\sin A)(\sin A)$ is equivalent to

A) $1 + a^2$
B) $1 - a^2$
C) $1 - b^2$
D) $1 + b^2$

The entrance fees for an amusement park are $14.50 for children and $20 for adults. During a 3-hour period a total of 258 children and adults entered the park and the park collected admission fees of $4,071. Solving which of the following systems of equations gives the number of children, c, and the number of adults, a, that entered the park during those three hours?

A) $\begin{cases} a+c = 4,071 \\ 14.50c+20a = 258 \end{cases}$

B) $\begin{cases} a+c = 258 \\ 14.50c+20a = \dfrac{4,071}{2} \end{cases}$

C) $\begin{cases} a+c = 258 \\ 14.50c+20a = 4,071 \end{cases}$

D) $\begin{cases} a+c = 258 \\ 14.50c+20a = 4,071 \cdot 2 \end{cases}$

For the years 2001 to 2016, the function $V(p) = 0.225p + 45,000$ expresses the expected number of registered voters, V, in a certain district in terms of the population, p, of the district. The district population was 220,000 in 2001. If the population increases to 270,000 in 2016, what is the increase in the expected number of registered voters in the district from the year 2001 to the year 2016?

A) 11,250
B) 50,000
C) 94,500
D) 105,750

CONTINUE

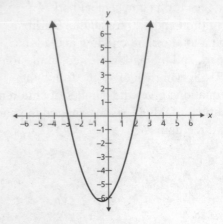

What function is represented by the graph above?

A) $f(x) = x^2 - x - 6$

B) $f(x) = x^2 + x - 6$

C) $f(x) = x^2 - x + 6$

D) $f(x) = x^2 + x + 6$

The governor of a large southern state wanted to quickly and inexpensively determine the approximate number of residents in her state who are older than 50. Which technique for gathering that data would be best to use?

A) Survey

B) Observation

C) Experiment

D) Census

CONTINUE

Calculator Allowed

For the remaining questions, solve the problem and enter your answer in the answer grid. Instructions for entering your answer in the grid are described below.

1. It is not required that you write your answer in the boxes at the top of the grid, but it is suggested.

2. Do not mark more than one circle in each column.

3. There are no negative answers in this portion of the test.

4. If the problem has more than 1 correct answer, grid only 1 of those answers.

5. Grid fractions as proper or improper fractions only.

6. Decimal answers must fill the entire grid.

Examples

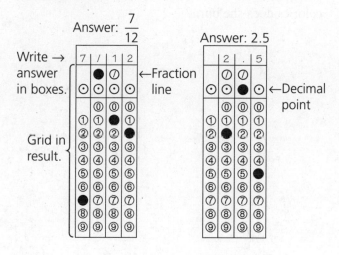

Answer: $\frac{7}{12}$

Write → answer in boxes.
←Fraction line

Grid in result.

Answer: 2.5
←Decimal point

Acceptable ways to grid $\frac{2}{3}$ are:

Answer: 201 – either position is correct

CONTINUE

Calculator Allowed

If the arithmetic mean of the numbers $x, x + 1$, $x + 4, 3x$, and $4x$ is 11, what is the median of these numbers?

Type of Exercise	Calories Burned (per minute)
Hitting golf balls at a driving range	7.5
Playing singles tennis	10
Swimming at an indoor pool	12

The table above shows Lowri's weekly exercise. She spends twice as much time playing tennis as hitting golf balls and twice as much time hitting golf balls as swimming. If she spends a total of 210 minutes exercising each week, how many calories does she burn?

CONTINUE

Calculator Allowed

If $(x + 2)^2 = (x - 5)^2$, what is the value of $x^2 - 1$?

A solution is made by mixing x amount of concentrate with water. To the nearest hundredth, how many liters of this concentrate should be mixed with 3 liters of water so that 28 percent of the solution is concentrate?

A grocery store's demand function for bananas is $y = D(p) = -p^2 - 5p + 600$ where $D(p) =$ the number of pounds of bananas sold and $p =$ the price in dollars for a pound of bananas. If the store receives a shipment of 500 pounds of bananas for the coming week, what is the highest price the grocer could charge per pound and be reasonably sure of selling all the bananas before the next weekly shipment arrives?

If $\frac{1}{2}x = a = \frac{2}{3}y$ and $x + y = na$, what is the value of n?

CONTINUE

Questions 37 and 38 refer to the following information.

Arline is traveling on a vacation from New York, New York to London, England. She is planning on making most of her foreign purchases using her credit card, but will also need some cash. Prior to leaving, Arline visited a local branch of her bank to convert 400 US dollars to British pounds using the daily foreign exchange rate. For this service the bank charged a 1.5% conversion fee. While in London, Arline knows that when she purchases items with her credit card, her bank will convert the price in pounds to the equivalent price in US dollars using the daily foreign exchange rate. The bank will also charge Arline a fee of 2% of the purchase price for the conversion.

After returning home from her trip, Arline discovered that she had 151 British pounds left in her wallet. She took those pounds back to the bank to be exchanged for US dollars, again paying a 1.5% bank conversion fee. If the daily foreign exchange rate was 0.755 pounds per dollar before she left and after she returned, how much money did Arline pay out in fees for the two bank conversions on that sum of cash? (Round your answer to the nearest penny.)

37

In London Arline purchased a tea set for 350 pounds. Later in her hotel room, Arline viewed her credit card statement online and saw that the bank charged her card $556.99 for the tea set, which included the 2% conversion fee. What was the foreign exchange rate in pounds per US dollar that the bank used for her purchase? (Round your answer to the nearest hundredth of a pound.)

· ▲ ·

STOP

If you finish before time is called, you may check your work on this section only.
Do not turn to any other section.

Diagnostic Test Answer Key

1. (C)   Multiply the given inequality by the common denominator of all the fractions, 6. Then, $7 + 3x < 6x - 2$. Collect the like terms and solve to see that $9 < 3x$ and $3 < x$.

2. (A)   Expand $(2x + 1)^2 - 2(2x^2 - 1)$ so that $(2x + 1)(2x + 1) - 4x^2 + 2$. FOIL the binomials and $4x^2 + 4x + 1 - 4x^2 + 2$. Collecting the like terms, $\cancel{4x^2} + 4x + 1 - \cancel{4x^2} + 2 = 4x + 3$.

3. (C)   Represent the cost for the first 3 minutes as a. The remaining minutes are represented by $(n - 3)$ and they cost b cents each, which is $b(n - 3)$ for all the remaining minutes. Sum the two representations and the total cost is $a + b(n - 3)$.

4. (A)   Begin by solving each equation for y. For the first equation, $y - x = -2$ becomes $y = x - 2$ and $y + 8 = x^2 - 4x$ is $y = x^2 - 4x - 8$. Now set the two equations equal to each other and solve for the variable x. So $x - 2 = x^2 - 4x - 8$ and $0 = x^2 - 5x - 6$. Factoring, $0 = (x - 6)(x + 1)$ and $x = 6$ or $x = -1$. If $x = 6$ then $y = x - 2 = 6 - 2 = 4$. One solution set is $(6, 4)$. If $x = -1$, then $y = -1 - 2 = -3$; the other solution set is $(-1, -3)$. The product $xy = 6 \cdot 4 = 24$, which is not an answer choice, or $-1(-3) = 3$, which is choice A.

5. (D)   To solve this problem, we must use the Pythagorean theorem 4 times with great care. Triangle OAB is an isosceles right triangle with hypotenuse $OB = \sqrt{2}$. Then

$$OC = \sqrt{\left(\sqrt{2}\right)^2 + 1^2} = \sqrt{2 + 1} = \sqrt{3}$$

$$OD = \sqrt{\left(\sqrt{3}\right)^2 + 1^2} = \sqrt{3 + 1} = \sqrt{4} = 2$$

$$OE = \sqrt{2^2 + 1^2} = \sqrt{4 + 1} = \sqrt{5}$$

6. (C)   Distribute through the parenthesis to find that $i^3 - i(2 - i) = i^3 - 2i + i^2$. Recall that $i^2 = -1$ and that $i^3 = -i$. Substituting those values and simplifying, $-i - 2i - 1 = -3i - 1$, which we can write as $-1 - 3i$.

7. (B)   Inverse variation can be expressed by the equation $y = \dfrac{k}{x}$. For this problem, $150 = \dfrac{k}{8}$, and $k = 1,200$. Now find the cost per person to rent the lake house if 12 people are staying: $y = \dfrac{1200}{12} = \$100$.

8. (B)   Recall that in a quadratic equation, the coefficient b is the negative of the sum of the roots, and the constant term is the product of the roots. For this equation, $b = -14$, so we know the sum of the roots must be 14. We are told that $14 = a + 3$. So $a = 14 - 3 = 11$.

9. (D)   Subtract 6 from both sides of the given equation so that $x^{-3} = 8$. Rewrite the problem as $\dfrac{1}{x^3} = \dfrac{8}{1}$ so that the exponent becomes positive. Now find the reciprocals of both fractions and $\dfrac{x^3}{1} = \dfrac{1}{8}$. Finish by taking the cube root of both sides $\sqrt[3]{x^3} = \sqrt[3]{\dfrac{1}{8}}$; $x = \dfrac{1}{2}$.

10. (A) The intersection of these two typical exponential equations occurs at the point (0, 1). This point is on the *y*-axis, which has the linear equation $x = 0$.

11. (B) Manipulate the given equation so it is solved for *p* rather than *A*. Begin by factoring *p* out of the terms on the right-hand side. Then, $A = p + prt$ becomes $A = p(1 + rt)$. Now divide both sides by $(1 + rt)$ and $\dfrac{A}{1+rt} = p$.

12. (A) Since the central angle $\angle ACB = 30°$, the angle measure is $\dfrac{1}{12}$ of the degree measure of a circle. The length of $\overarc{AB}$ is 6π, which is also $\dfrac{1}{12}$ of the circumference of the circle. This means the circle's circumference is $12(6\pi) = 72\pi$. Using the formula $2\pi r = 72\pi$, $r = 36$, and the area of the circle is $\pi r^2 = \pi 36^2 = 1,296\pi$. The area of the sector *ACB* is $\dfrac{1}{12}(1296\pi) = 108\pi$.

13. (D) Since the two lines intersect and form right angles, they are perpendicular lines. The slopes of perpendicular lines are negative reciprocals of each other. Of the available answer choices, $m_1 = -\dfrac{1}{m_2}$.

14. (B) Since $|7x - 4| = 25$, either $7x - 4 = 25$ or $7x - 4 = -25$. Solve each equation. If $7x - 4 = 25$, then $7x = 29$ and $x = 4\dfrac{1}{7}$. If $7x - 4 = -25$, then $7x = -21$ and $x = -3$. The sum of $4\dfrac{1}{7}$ and $-3 = 1\dfrac{1}{7}$ or $\dfrac{8}{7}$.

15. (B) Use the figure and trigonomic ratios to find that $\sin A = \dfrac{\text{opposite}}{\text{hypotenuse}} = \dfrac{\sqrt{2}}{AB}$, $\cos A = \dfrac{\text{adjacent}}{\text{hyptenuse}} = \dfrac{AC}{AB}$, and $\tan A = \dfrac{\text{opposite}}{\text{adjacent}} = \dfrac{\sqrt{2}}{AC}$. We know that $(\sin A)(\cos A)(\tan A) = \dfrac{1}{2}$, so $\dfrac{\sqrt{2}}{AB} \cdot \dfrac{AC}{AB} \cdot \dfrac{\sqrt{2}}{AC} = \dfrac{1}{2}$. Simplifying, $\dfrac{\sqrt{4}}{(AB)^2} = \dfrac{1}{2}$ and $\dfrac{2}{(AB)^2} = \dfrac{1}{2}$. Cross-multiply and solve: $(AB)^2 = 4$ and $AB = 2$.

16. (115) Recall that the sum of degree measures of the angles in a triangle is 180°. For triangle *ABC*, $m\angle ABC + 40° + 90° = 180°$, so $m\angle ABC = 50°$. Since $\overline{BD}$ bisects $\angle ABC$, $m\angle ABD = 25°$. For triangle *ABD*, $\angle A + \angle ABD + \angle ADB = 40 + 25 + \angle ADB = 180°$ and $m\angle ADB = 180 - 65 = 115°$.

17. (2) Notice that both equations have 1 as the coefficient for *y*. Subtract the second equation from the first:

$$\begin{array}{r} 5x + y = 15 \\ -3x - y = -11 \\ \hline 2x = 4 \end{array}$$

and $x = 2$.

18. (0) Recognize that in this case $a = y$, so substitute $x = 7$ into the given equation and solve for *y*. If we do so, $(7 - 2)^2 + a^2 = 25$, $5^2 + a^2 = 25$, and $a^2 = 25 - 25$. Hence, $a^2 = 0$ and $a = 0$.

19. (5) Reading the table, $g(k) = 0$, yields $k = 3$. Then $f(k) = f(3) = 4$, and $g(f(3)) = g(4) = 5$.

20. (1) Begin solving for *h* by squaring both sides of the equation: $(2 + h)^2 = \left(\sqrt{10-h}\right)^2$. Expanding, $4 + 4h + h^2 = 10 - h$. Collecting the like terms we see that $h^2 + 5h - 6 = 0$. Now factor $(h + 6)(h - 1) = 0$ and solve for *h* so that $h = -6$ or $h = 1$. Before bubbling in an answer, substitute

your answers back into the original equation to make sure neither is extraneous. Substituting 1 for h yields $3 = \sqrt{9} = 3$, a true statement. So $h = 1$ is a solution. Substituting –6 for h, we have $2 + -6 = \sqrt{10 - (-6)}$ which is $-4 = \sqrt{16}$ and $-4 = 4$, a false statement. The solution $h = -6$ is an extraneous root.

Calculator Allowed

1. **(A)** Parallel lines have equal slopes, so manipulate the given equation into slope-intercept form such that $y = 2x - 2$. The slope of this line is $m = 2$ and the slope of the line parallel to this will also be 2. Put this information and the given point into point-slope form and $y - 0 = 2(x - 0)$ which simplifies into $y = 2x$.

2. **(C)** First determine the midpoint of $\overline{BC}$ which is $\frac{3 + 8}{2} = 5.5$. We know half the length of $\overline{AD}$ is 6.5. Thus, $5.5 + 6.5 = 12$, the coordinate of point D.

3. **(D)** Values are restricted from the domain when their inclusion results in an undefined output. For choice A, we can substitute any real number for x, square it, and add 1 without resulting in a zero denominator. The domain of B is all real numbers, and for choice C, any real number can be squared. The number 0 would be restricted from the domain of C, but the question asks which of the expressions has two values to restrict from the domain. For answer choice D, we must restrict $x = -1$ and $x = 0$ from the domain because either of those values will result in a zero denominator. Division by 0 is undefined.

4. **(C)** Using the rules of exponents, $a^x \cdot a^5 = a^{15}$ means the sum of the exponents is 15, so $x + 5 = 15$, and $x = 10$. In $(a^3)^y = a^{12}$, the product of the exponents equals 12; thus, $3(y) = 12$ and $y = 4$. The value of $x + y = 10 + 4 = 14$.

5. **(C)** Consider that there are 12 arcs, one for each hour, on a circular clock. Each arc measures $\frac{360°}{12} = 30°$. At 2:30, the minute hand is at the 6th hour mark and the hour hand is midway between the 2- and the 3-hour marks. Hence, half an arc plus 3 arcs, from the 3 to the 6, is $15° + 90° = 105°$. Converting that measurement to radian measure, we have $105° \cdot \frac{\pi}{180°} = \frac{7\pi}{12}$.

6. **(D)** The number of articles, $4n$, multiplied by the cost of each article, c, provides the total cost, $4nc$. Since Ashley recovered the total cost, her charge per item can be found by $\frac{\text{total cost}}{\text{number of items}}$. Substituting the values from the problem and simplifying, $\frac{4nc}{3n} = \frac{4}{3}c$.

7. **(D)** Direct variation obeys the relationship $y = kx$. Substituting the values from the problem, $12 = 3k$ and $k = 4$.

8. **(B)** Using the given formula, density $= \frac{\text{mass}}{\text{volume}}$ and $2.24 = \frac{50,000}{x}$. Solving for x, $2.24x = 50,000$, so that $x = 22321.43$ cubic cm. The question asks for the volume in cubic meters: $\frac{22,321.43 \text{ cm}^3}{1} \cdot \frac{1 \text{ m}^3}{1,000,000 \text{ cm}^3} \approx 0.02 \text{ m}^3$.

9. (C) The points appear to form a line with a negative slope, so eliminate answer choices A and B. The y-intercept will be positive, so choice D is not correct.

10. (B) The total number of students enrolled in Pre-Calculus is 264. Of those 264 students, 24 are enrolled in Latin. Dividing $\frac{24}{264} = 0.0\overline{9}$, which we can round to approximately 9%.

11. (D) We know that the measures of angles x and y are equal, so each angle measures $\frac{120}{2} = 60°$. The measure of the angle vertical to angle w is $180° - 60° = 120°$, so the measure of angle w is 120°.

12. (B) The survey asked which single piece of equipment each randomly selected member uses most frequently; therefore, choice C can be eliminated. Sample results will not exactly mirror the results of the entire population, so answer choice D is incorrect. Choice A draws a specific conclusion, so choice B is best.

13. (B) We can rewrite $k^{\frac{3}{2}}$ as $k^{3 \cdot \frac{1}{2}} = \left(k^3\right)^{\frac{1}{2}} = \sqrt{k^3}$.

14. (A) Let $z =$ the number of minutes it will take for n cm of rain to fall and set up a proportion: $\frac{x\ \text{cm}}{1\ \text{min}} = \frac{n\ \text{cm}}{z\ \text{min}}$. Solve this proportion for z so that $z\ \text{min} = \frac{n}{x}$. The problem asks how many hours it will take, so change the units of z to hours by dividing by 60: $\frac{n}{x} \div 60$ is $\frac{n}{x} \cdot \frac{1}{60} = \frac{n}{60x}$.

15. (C) Use the midpoint formula to determine the center, M, of the circle. Then $M = \left(\frac{0+0}{2}, \frac{5+1}{2}\right) = (0, 3)$. Calculate the length of the circle's radius using the coordinates of the center and one point. So $(0-0)^2 + (5-3)^2 = r^2$ and $r^2 = 4$. The equation of the circle is $x^2 + (y - 3)^2 = 4$.

16. (A) To solve this problem, you must verify the graph matches the functions in the question. It is easier to check the linear function first. We can eliminate choices C and D because the y-intercept is incorrect. Examine the quadratic function. The coefficient of the squared term is positive, so the parabola should open up. Of the remaining choices, A is correct.

17. (D) Whether the diameter n is larger or smaller than 4 centimeters, the absolute value of the difference between the actual measurement and 4 must be a positive number that is less than or equal to 0.05 centimeters.

18. (A) The profit on the sale of q items is the amount of money taken in from sales less the cost of production. Let $P =$ total profit be defined as the quantity (q) · selling price (s) – quantity (q) · production cost per item. We can substitute $-2s + 576$ for q and \$12.50 for the production cost per item. Then $P = (-2s + 576)s - [(-2s + 576)(12.50)]$. Distributing, $-2s^2 + 576s - [-25s + 7200]$ which becomes $-2s^2 + 576s + 25s - 7200$. Collecting the like terms, $-2s^2 + 601s - 7200$. This function has a maximum and the price at which the rings should be sold to ensure the maximum profit is $s = \frac{-b}{2a} = \frac{-601}{2(-2)} = 150.25$. Round to the nearest dollar and $s = \$150$.

19. (A) We know that $m\angle P = m\widehat{AC} - m\widehat{AB}$. Since the circle contains 360°,

$m\widehat{AC} = 360 - (52 + 150) = 360 - 202 = 158°$. Substitute this value into

the formula above and $m\angle P = \frac{1}{2}(158 - 52) = \frac{1}{2}(106) = 53°$.

20. (C) The function $f(x + 2)$ transforms the parabola $f(x)$ by shifting its given vertex two units to the left so that the new vertex is $(2 - 2, -1) = (0, -1)$.

21. (B) First determine the present volumes of the containers in terms of π. Container A has $12\pi \cdot 6 = 72\pi$ cubic inches of water and container B has $16\pi \cdot 3 = 48\pi$ cubic inches of water. Now find the average of the

volumes $= \frac{72\pi + 48\pi}{2} = \frac{120\pi}{2} = 60\pi$. Each container will have 60π cubic

inches of water after the transfer. The new volume of container B is found by solving $16\pi \cdot h = 60\pi$ for $h = 3.75$ inches.

22. (D) Simplify the expression by multiplying both the numerator and the

denominator by the conjugate of the denominator. So $\frac{3}{8 + 2i} \cdot \frac{8 - 2i}{8 - 2i}$

becomes $\frac{3(8 - 2i)}{(8 + 2i)(8 - 2i)}$ and $\frac{24 - 6i}{64 - 16i + 16i - 4i^2}$. Simplifying,

$\frac{24 - 6i}{64 - 4(-1)} = \frac{24 - 6i}{68} = \frac{12 - 3i}{34}$.

23. (D) The graph is clearly not linear so eliminate answer choices A and B. The graph shows a curve that grows as the x-values increase, so this can only be exponential growth.

24. (B) The more volunteers there are, the less time it will take to deliver the gifts; therefore, there is an inverse relationship between number of volunteers and number of hours needed to complete the job. Use the formula for

inverse variation, $y = \frac{k}{x}$, to determine k, the constant of variation. Then

$3 = \frac{k}{8}$ and $k = 24$. The amount of time needed for 10 volunteers to

deliver the gifts is $y = \frac{24}{10} = 2.4$ hours. Notice that the answer choices

are not formatted in this fashion. Convert 0.40 of an hour into minutes: $(0.40)(6) = 24$ minutes. It will take 10 volunteers 2 hours and 24 minutes to deliver the gifts.

25. (C) Begin by calculating the sample proportion as $\frac{480}{1,000} = 0.48$. We know

the margin of error is ± 0.05 so the actual proportion of all patients with this disease who would show improvement on this medication is between $0.48 - 0.05 = 0.43$ and $0.48 + 0.05 = 0.53$. Examine the answer choices. Choice A does not take into account the margin of error, so eliminate it. Choices B and D do not reflect the correct margin of error. The best

answer is C because $\frac{480}{1,000} \approx 0.50$, and this is within the margin of error.

26. (C) In a right triangle $\sin = \dfrac{\text{opposite side}}{\text{hypotenuse}} = \dfrac{a}{1} = a$. So $(\sin A)(\sin A) = a^2$, but none of the answers reflect this. How else can we express a^2? Recall that the Pythagorean theorem relates the lengths of the legs of right triangle to the length of its hypotenuse: $a^2 + b^2 = c^2$. Applying this theorem to the given triangle, $a^2 + b^2 = 1$, and solving for a^2, we have $a^2 = 1 - b^2$.

27. (C) Since c represents the number of children and a represents the number of adults, the total number of people entering the park for that 3-hour period is $a + c = 258$. The amount of money collected for admission fees during that time is $14.50c + 20a = 4{,}071$.

28. (A) Substitute 220,000 for p in the given function $V(p) = 0.225p + 45{,}000$. Then $V(220{,}000) = 0.225(220{,}000) + 45{,}000 = 49{,}500 + 45{,}000 = 94{,}500$. Substituting 270,000 in the same function, $V(270{,}000) = 0.225(270{,}000) + 45{,}000 = 60{,}750 + 45{,}000 = 105{,}750$. The increase is the difference between $V(270{,}000)$ and $V(220{,}000)$ which is $105{,}750 - 94{,}500 = 11{,}250$.

29. (B) The graph crosses the x-axis at $(-3, 0)$ and $(2, 0)$. Therefore, we know that $x = -3$ and $x = 2$ are the zeros of the function. Working backwards to create the function itself, $(x + 3)(x - 2) = 0$, and FOILing, $x^2 + x - 6 = 0$. Transferring this to function notation, $f(x) = x^2 + x - 6$.

30. (A) The only choices to consider are a survey or a census; the other answer choices make no sense in this context. Since we need to know the answer to the question quickly and not spend a lot of money, the best choice is a survey.

31. (9) To find the value of the variable x, add x, $x + 1$, $x + 4$, $3x$, and $4x$, divide by 5, and set equal to the given mean 11. Doing so, $\dfrac{10x + 5}{5} = 11$. Solving, $10x + 5 = 55$, $10x = 50$, and $x = 5$. The numbers in this set are 5, 6, 9, 15, and 20. The median number is 9.

32. (2010) Let g = the time spent hitting golf balls, let t = the time spent playing tennis, and let s = the time spent swimming. We know that $2g = t$, $\dfrac{g}{2} = s$, and that $g + t + s = 210$. Substituting for t and s, $g + 2g + \dfrac{g}{2} = 210$. Now solve for g: $2g + 4g + g = 420$, $7g = 420$, and $g = 60$. Lowri spends 60 minutes hitting golf balls, $2(60) = 120$ minutes playing tennis, and $\dfrac{60}{2} = 30$ minutes swimming each week. To find the total number of calories burned, use the chart and sum $60(7.5) + 120(10) + 30(12) = 2{,}010$ calories.

33. $\left(\dfrac{5}{4} \text{ or } 1.25\right)$ Expand $(x + 2)^2 = (x - 5)^2$ into $x^2 + 4x + 4 = x^2 - 10x + 25$. Collect the like terms and solve to see that $14x = 21$ and $x = 1.5$. Use this value in the equation $x^2 - 1$ so that $(1.5)^2 - 1 = 1.25$, which is equivalent to $\dfrac{5}{4}$ if you worked the problem using fraction notation rather than decimal notation.

34. (7.81) Set the given function, $D(p) = -p^2 - 5p + 600$, equal to 500. Then $500 = -p^2 - 5p + 600$. Subtract 500 from each side and simplify so that $p^2 + 5p - 100 = 0$. Using the quadratic formula, $p = \dfrac{-5 \pm \sqrt{(-5)^2 - 4(1)(-100)}}{2}$.

Simplify and $p = \dfrac{-5 \pm \sqrt{25 + 400}}{2} = \dfrac{-5 \pm \sqrt{425}}{2} = \dfrac{-5 + 20.62}{2}$. Finishing,

$p = \$7.81$. Note that in this context we are ignoring $p = \dfrac{-5 - 20.62}{2}$ as that

will lead to a negative answer. Prices cannot be negative.

35. (1.17) Let $x =$ the amount of concentrate to be used. Then $x + 3 =$ the total amount of liquid, concentrate and water, in the solution. Hence, $\dfrac{\text{concentrate}}{\text{total liquid}} = \dfrac{x}{x + 3} = 28\%$ which we can express as $\dfrac{x}{x + 3} = \dfrac{28}{100}$.

Cross-multiply and solve to find that $100x = 28x + 84$, $72x = 84$ and $x = 1.1\overline{6} = 1.17$ liters.

36. $\left(\dfrac{7}{2} \text{ or } 3.5\right)$ Rewrite $\dfrac{1}{2}x = a = \dfrac{2}{3}y$ as $\dfrac{1}{2}x = a$ and $a = \dfrac{2}{3}y$. Now solve each of these

equations for x and y, respectively. Then $x = 2a$ and $y = \dfrac{3}{2}a$. Substitute

x and y in the equation $x + y = na$, so that $2a + \dfrac{3}{2}a = na$. Now divide all

terms by a to see that $2 + \dfrac{3}{2} = n$ and $n = 3.5$.

37. (0.64) Let $x =$ the daily foreign exchange rate for British pounds to US dollars. So 100% of the US dollar price + 2% conversion fee is $1.02x = 556.99$ and $x = \$546.0686$. Now we know the amount the tea set cost in US dollars. We can set up a proportion to solve for the daily foreign exchange rate,

d: $\dfrac{d}{1} = \dfrac{350}{546.0686}$. Solving, $546.0686d = 350$ and $d = 0.6409$ pounds.

Alternately, consider that since $556.99 is 102% of the price in British pounds, we can solve for the exchange rate directly using this proportion:

$\dfrac{350}{556.99} = \dfrac{d}{1.02}$. Doing so, $357 = 556.99d$, and $d = 0.6409$. The instructions

state we must round to the nearest hundredth, so $d = 0.64$.

38. (6) Arline is paying the bank fee twice; once when she converts her money from US dollars to British pounds and again when she converts her money back from British pounds to US dollars. Use the given exchange rate to

determine how much 151 British pounds is in US dollars. So $\dfrac{151}{x} = \dfrac{0.755}{1}$

and $x = \$200$. Multiply 1.5% and $200, then double the result and $(2)(0.015)(200) = \$6$.

Score Conversion Chart

Use the chart below to convert your raw score on any of the assessments in this book into an estimated scaled score. **The conversions in the chart below are <u>estimates only</u>.** Visit <u>https://collegereadiness.collegeboard.org/about/scores</u> for more information and the latest scoring conversions.

How to use this chart:

On the new SAT, you will only gain points for the questions you answer correctly; you will not lose points for questions answered incorrectly or for those questions you skipped or did not have time to answer. After completing and correcting your assessment, award yourself 1 point per question answered correctly on both sections of the math test. Sum the total points you earned to calculate your raw score. Use the chart below to convert that raw score into an estimated SAT score.

Raw Score	Scaled Score		Raw Score	Scaled Score
0	200			
1	200		31	570
2	210		32	580
3	230		33	580
4	250		34	590
5	270		35	600
6	290		36	610
7	300		37	620
8	320		38	630
9	330		39	630
10	340		40	640
11	350		41	650
12	370		42	660
13	380		43	670
14	390		44	680
15	400		45	680
16	420		46	690
17	430		47	700
18	440		48	700
19	450		49	710
20	460		50	720
21	470		51	730
22	480		52	740
23	490		53	750
24	500		54	760
25	510		55	770
26	520		56	780
27	530		57	790
28	540		58	800
29	550			
30	560			

Correlation Chart

Diagnostic Test – No Calculator Allowed

Use the correlation chart below to determine which lessons to focus on as you prepare for the SAT Math Test.

(The no calculator portion of the SAT Math Exam will not contain items from Problem Solving and Data Analysis category.)

Question Number	Heart of Algebra	Problem Solving & Data Analysis	Passport To Advanced Math	Additional Topics in Math	Pages to Study
1	Lesson 2				57 – 80
2			Lesson 2		298 – 315
3	Lesson 1				43 – 56
4			Lesson 6		359 – 373
5				Lesson 2	426 – 451
6				Lesson 7	506 – 513
7	Lesson 5				112 – 119
8			Lesson 4		327 – 342
9			Lesson 1		281 – 297
10			Lesson 5		343 – 358
11	Lesson 2				57 – 80
12				Lesson 3	452 – 473
13	Lesson 3				81 – 97
14	Lesson 2				57 – 80
15				Lesson 4	474 – 488
16				Lesson 2	426 – 451
17	Lesson 4				98 – 111
18				Lesson 6	502 – 505
19			Lesson 7		374 – 388
20			Lesson 3		316 – 326
Total Correct	_____ / 7		_____ / 7	_____ / 6	NA

Correlation Chart

Diagnostic Test – Calculator Allowed

Use the correlation chart below to determine which lessons to focus on as you prepare for the SAT Math Test.

Question Number	Heart of Algebra	Problem Solving & Data Analysis	Passport to Advanced Math	Additional Topics in Math	Pages to Study
1	Lesson 3				81 – 97
2	Lesson 6				120 – 138
3			Lesson 2		298 – 315
4			Lesson 1		281 – 297
5				Lesson 5	489 – 501
6	Lesson 2				57 – 80
7	Lesson 5				112 – 119
8		Lesson 2			177 – 187
9		Lesson 3			188 – 200
10		Lesson 5			215 – 230
11				Lesson 2	426 – 451
12		Lesson 8			252 – 264
13			Lesson 1		281 – 297
14	Lesson 1				43 – 56
15				Lesson 6	502 – 505
16			Lesson 6		359 – 373
17	Lesson 2				57 – 80
18			Lesson 5		343 – 358
19				Lesson 3	452 – 473
20			Lesson 7		374 – 388
21				Lesson 1	407 – 425
22				Lesson 7	506 – 513
23		Lesson 4			201 – 214
24	Lesson 5				112 – 119
25		Lesson 7			246 – 251
26				Lesson 4	474 – 488
27	Lesson 4				98 – 111
28	Lesson 3				81 – 97
29			Lesson 5		343 – 358
30		Lesson 8			252 – 264
31		Lesson 6			231 – 245
32	Lesson 4				98 – 111
33			Lesson 3		316 – 326
34			Lesson 4		327 – 342
35		Lesson 1			157 – 176
36	Lesson 4				98 – 111
37		Lesson 1			157 – 176
38		Lesson 1			157 – 176
Total Correct	_____ / 11	_____ / 11	_____ / 9	_____ / 7	NA

CATEGORY 1

Heart of Algebra

LESSON 1:

Representing Relationships Between Quantities and Creating Algebraic Expressions

- Simplifying and Evaluating Algebraic Expressions

- Formulas and Absolute Value

- Representing Relationships Using Algebraic Language

- Finding Equivalent Expressions

Explain **Simplifying and Evaluating Algebraic Expressions**

Algebraic expressions contain numbers, variables, and the symbols for the operations. Since algebraic expressions themselves represent numbers, they can be added, subtracted, multiplied, and divided. Some examples of algebraic expressions are:

$$x + 7, \quad 3x - 1, \quad y^2 - ab, \quad \frac{b}{r}, \quad \frac{\sqrt{a}}{2}, \quad 6(2x - y^3), \quad \frac{a - b}{c}$$

Like terms are terms that contain the same variables with corresponding variables having the same exponents. You can combine only like terms.

Simplify: $3x^2 - 2x - 2x^2 + 5x - 4$

$$3x^2 - 2x - 2x^2 + 5x - 4$$
$$x^2 + 3x - 4$$

The **distributive property** allows you to distribute multiplication over addition or subtraction:

$$8(4x + 7) = (8)(4x) + (8)(7) \qquad -5x(y - 1) = (-5x)(y) + (-5x)(-1)$$

$$= 32x + 56 \qquad\qquad\qquad = -5xy + 5x$$

To **evaluate** an algebraic expression, substitute the numerical value of the variable into the expression. Then evaluate the resulting numerical expression.

Evaluate $5 + 3a^3$ when $a = 2$.

Substitute in 2 for a in the expression and evaluate, using the order of operations:

$$5 + 3a^3 = 5 + 3(2)^3$$

$$= 5 + 3(8) = 5 + 24 = 29$$

Think It Through

Example 1

Simplify $5x^2 - 3x + 2x^2 - 4x + 9$.

A) 9

B) $7x^2 + x + 9$

C) $3x^2 - 7x + 9$

D) $7x^2 - 7x + 9$

Solution

Rewrite the problem so the like terms are grouped together. Then $5x^2 - 3x + 2x^2 - 4x + 9 = 5x^2 + 2x^2 - 3x - 4x + 9$. Now combine like terms and the simplified expression is $7x^2 - 7x + 9$.

Answer: D

Example 2

Evaluate $x + 3(x - 1)$ for $x = 2$.

A) 1

B) 3

C) 5

D) 7

Solution

Substitute the value 2 for x and $x + 3(x - 1)$ becomes $2 + 3(2 - 1)$. Use the order of operations to simplify and $2 + 3(1) = 2 + 3 = 5$.

Answer: C

Practice Simplifying and Evaluating Algebraic Expressions

Answers begin on page 655.

1. Simplify $2x^3 - 4x + 8 - x^3 + 5x - 15$.

    A) $x^3 + x - 7$

    B) $3x^3 + x - 15$

    C) $x^3 - x - 7$

    D) $x^3 + x + 15$

2. Simplify $-2(3y - 1) + y + 1$.

    A) $-6y - 1$

    B) $-5y - 1$

    C) $-6y + 3$

    D) $-5y + 3$

3. Evaluate $(a + b)^2(a - c)$ when $a = -1$, $b = -2$, and $c = 1$.

A) −4

B) −6

C) −9

D) −18

4. Evaluate $a - c(b + c)$ when $a = 1$, $b = 2$, and $c = -1$.

A) 2

B) 1

C) −1

D) −2

5. In the figure below, segment $\overline{PR}$ is divided into 2 segments. The length of $\overline{PQ}$ is $x + y$, and the length of $\overline{QR}$ is $x - y$. If $\overline{PQ}$ is twice as long as $\overline{QR}$ and $x = 15$, then what is the length of $\overline{PR}$?

Note: Figure not drawn to scale.

A) 5

B) 20

C) 25

D) 30

6. If $2c = -1$, then $(4 - 4c)^2 =$

A) 6

B) 36

C) 4

D) 2

7. What is the result when $10x - 7$ is subtracted from $9x - 15$?

A) $x + 8$

B) $x + 22$

C) $-x - 8$

D) $-x + 8$

8. What does $5(x + y) - (5x - y)$ equal?

A) $4y$

B) $6y$

C) $10x - 6y$

D) $10x - 4y$

Model SAT Questions

1. If $a = b = -1$, what is the value of $(a - b)(a + b)$?

A) −1

B) 0

C) 1

D) 2

Strategy: Substitute −1 for *a* and for *b* in the expression and then evaluate. So $(a - b)(a + b)$ is $(-1 - (-1))(-1 + -1)$ which simplifies to $(0)(-2) = 0$. Alternately, you can FOIL the binomials prior to substituting in the values. If you do so, $(a - b)(a + b)$ becomes $a^2 - b^2$ and $(-1)^2 - (-1)^2 = 0$. Select answer choice B.

2. If $x = 10^2$, what is the value of $(4 + x)(4 - x)\left(\dfrac{1}{x}\right)$?

A) 168.1

B) −99.84

C) −159

D) 152

Strategy: Substitute 10^2 for *x* in $(4 + x)(4 - x)\left(\dfrac{1}{x}\right)$. Then $(4 + 10^2)(4 - 10^2)\left(\dfrac{1}{10^2}\right) =$ $(104)(-96)\left(\dfrac{1}{100}\right) = -99.84$. This is answer choice B.

3. If $\dfrac{a}{b} = k$ and $ab \neq 0$, then $\dfrac{a+b}{a}$ is equal to

   A) $\dfrac{k}{k+1}$

   B) $\dfrac{k+1}{k-1}$

   C) $\dfrac{k+1}{k}$

   D) $k+1$

Strategy: Consider that $\dfrac{a+b}{a} = \dfrac{a}{a} + \dfrac{b}{a}$ and $\dfrac{a}{a} + \dfrac{b}{a} = 1 + \dfrac{b}{a}$. Now, since $\dfrac{a}{b} = \dfrac{k}{1}$, $\dfrac{b}{a} = \dfrac{1}{k}$. So $1 + \dfrac{b}{a} = 1 + \dfrac{1}{k}$. This is not listed as one of the answer choices, so simplify by rewriting the fraction. The common denominator is k, and $1 + \dfrac{1}{k} = \dfrac{k}{k} + \dfrac{1}{k}$, which becomes $\dfrac{k+1}{k}$. Select answer choice C.

4. If $a = 3$, $b = -5$, and $c = 3$, what is the value of $(a+b)^c$?

   A) 5

   B) 8

   C) −6

   D) −8

Strategy: Substitute 3 for a, −5 for b, and 3 for c. Then $(a+b)^c = (3+(-5))^3 = (-2)^3 = -8$. Choose answer D.

Explain Formulas and Absolute Value

A rule or relationship among terms that is expressed using mathematical symbols is a **formula**. There are many real-world formulas found throughout geometry, statistics, physics, and other science fields. We can evaluate any formula for any of the variables it contains so long as we are given values for all the other variables in the formula.

The **absolute value** of any given number, n, is its distance from 0 on the number line. Since absolute value represents distance, its value will always be positive or 0. Absolute value is symbolized by $|n|$. If n is negative then $|-n|$ is a positive number. On the SAT, the absolute value is always the nonnegative choice of n or $-n$. Note: if n is a negative number then $|n| = -n$. For example, if $n = -3$, then $|-3| = -(-3) = 3$.

Example 1

The formula $F = \dfrac{9}{5}C + 32$ converts temperatures from degrees Celsius to degrees Fahrenheit. Find the Fahrenheit temperature, F, when the Celsius temperature $C = -20°$.

A) 0° F
B) −4° F
C) 4° F
D) 12° F

Solution

Substitute −20 in for the variable C and $F = \dfrac{9}{5}C + 32$ becomes $F = \dfrac{9}{5}(-20) + 32 = -36 + 32 = -4°$.

Answer: B

Example 2

The height, h, of a projectile with initial vertical velocity v, at time t after launch, is given by the formula $h = -\dfrac{1}{2}gt^2 + vt$. Find the height, in meters, at time $t = 2$ seconds when $g = 32$ m/s^2 and $v = 50$ m/s.

A) 8 meters
B) 16 meters
C) 36 meters
D) 72 meters

Solution

Substitute the given values for g, t, and v. Then $-\dfrac{1}{2}gt^2 + vt$ is $-\dfrac{1}{2}(32)(2^2) + 50(2) = -16(4) + 100 = 36$ m.

Answer: C

Example 3

Which of the following has the least value if $a = -1$ and $b = -2$?

A) $|a + b|$
B) $|a - b|$
C) $|a| + |b|$
D) $|a| - |b|$

Solution

We must substitute in the given values in each of the answer choices to see which yields the smallest value. For A, $|a + b|$, $|(-1) + (-2)| = |-3| = 3$. Answer choice B is $|a - b| = |(-1) - (-2)| = |-1 + 2| = |1| = 1$. So far, answer choice B is the smallest. Check answer C and $|a| + |b|$ is $|-1| + |-2|$, which is the same as $1 + 2 = 3$. Choice D is $|a| - |b|$ and $|-1| - |-2| = 1 - 2 = -1$. This is the smallest value.

Answer: D

Example 4

The area of a trapezoid with height h, upper base b, and lower base B is given by the formula $A = \dfrac{h(b+B)}{2}$. What is the area of a trapezoid, in square inches, when $h = 4''$, $b = 6''$, and $B = 7''$?

A) 52 inches²

B) 26 inches²

C) 15.5 inches²

D) 12 inches²

Solution

Substitute the values into the given formula. Then $A = \dfrac{h(b+B)}{2} = \dfrac{4(6+7)}{2} = $ 26 inches².

Answer: B

Example 5

The area of the cross section of a ring with outer radius R and inner radius r is given by $A = \pi\left(R^2 - r^2\right)$. What is the area of a ring with outer radius 9 and inner radius 5? Use the approximation $\pi = \dfrac{22}{7}$.

A) $12\dfrac{4}{7}$ units²

B) $50\dfrac{2}{7}$ units²

C) 176 units²

D) 1232 units²

Solution

Simply substitute the given values for R and r into the formula. Then the area of the cross section is $\pi\left(R^2 - r^2\right) = \dfrac{22}{7}\left(9^2 - 5^2\right)$. Continuing, $\dfrac{22}{7}(81 - 25) = \dfrac{22}{7}(56) = 8(22) = $ 176 units².

Answer: C

Practice Formulas and Absolute Value

Answers begin on page 655.

1. The formula for the area of a kite with diagonals d_1 and d_2 is $A = \dfrac{d_1 \cdot d_2}{2}$. Find the area of a kite with diagonals of lengths $\sqrt{2}$ and $\sqrt{8}$.

2. Which of the following expressions has the same value as $\dfrac{|-6|}{-2} - \dfrac{|4-7|}{6}$?

A) $\dfrac{-2|-3|}{3} + 4|3-1|$

B) $\dfrac{-|9-5|}{8} + \dfrac{|1-7|}{2}$

C) $\dfrac{-|2-4|}{4} + \dfrac{-3|2-5|}{3}$

D) $\dfrac{|-9|}{3} - \dfrac{|2-8|}{3}$

1. The measure of an interior angle of a regular polygon with n sides can be represented as $\dfrac{180n - 360}{n}$ degrees. Find the degree measure of an interior angle of a regular hexagon.

   A) 60°

   B) 80°

   C) 120°

   D) 150°

Strategy: We know that a hexagon has 6 sides, so $n = 6$. Then $\dfrac{180n - 360}{n} = \dfrac{180 \cdot 6 - 360}{6} = \dfrac{1080 - 360}{6} = \dfrac{720}{6} = 120°$. Select answer choice C.

Explain ## Representing Relationships Using Algebraic Language

The language of algebra is symbolic. For many problems on the SAT, you will be given a scenario in words and you will need to translate it into an algebraic expression or equation as part of completing the problem task. It is important that you are able to translate from words into algebra fairly quickly or you will lose valuable time on the test. The table below is a guide to translating words into symbolic algebra.

Key Words	Symbol	English and Algebra Translations
Signs of Operations		
sum, add, increase, more than, plus, increased by, greater, exceeded by, and	+	f increased by 10 $\quad f + 10$ the sum of x and 9 $\quad x + 9$
difference, subtract, take away, minus, decrease, fewer, less, less than, decreased by, diminished by	−	4 less y $\quad 4 - y$ 32 fewer CDs than Abdul's $\quad A - 32$
multiply, of, product, times, square of a number, the number squared, a number times itself	$\cdot$ n^2	the product of 4 and t $\quad 4 \cdot t$ or $4t$ One-half of the pumpkin weighs 3 pounds $\quad \dfrac{1}{2}p = 3$ 6 times the square of a number $\quad 6 \cdot n^2$
divide, quotient, into, for, per, divided by	÷	500 divided into 4 parts $\quad 500 \div 4$ Sue cut a 24-inch board into 8 pieces. $\quad 24 \div 8$

Example

Translate "the difference between 10 times the square of a number and the number itself" into algebraic language.

A) $10(n^2 - n)$

B) $\dfrac{10n^2}{n}$

C) $10n^2 - n$

D) $10n - n^2$

Solution

Let n = the number. Then 10 times the square of a number translates as $10n^2$. The words "the difference" indicate subtraction; in this case, we are subtracting n. The correct expression is $10n^2 - n$.

Answer: C

Practice Representing Relationships Using Algebraic Language

Answers begin on page 655.

Express each statement by means of operators, variables, and numbers.

1. The difference between the square root of a number n and the number n squared.

   A) $\sqrt{n} - n$

   B) $\sqrt{n - n^2}$

   C) $\sqrt{n} - n^2$

   D) $n^2 - \sqrt{n}$

2. The sum of a and b decreased by their product.

   A) $ab - (a - b)$

   B) $a + b - ab$

   C) $a + b + ab$

   D) $a + b - \dfrac{a}{b}$

3. The product of m and n divided by three times their difference.

   A) $mn - 3(m - n)$

   B) $\dfrac{mn}{3(m - n)}$

   C) $\dfrac{m}{n} - 3(m - n)$

   D) $\dfrac{m + n}{3(m - n)}$

4. Three times the difference of a and b divided by twice their sum.

   A) $\dfrac{3(a - b)}{2(a + b)}$

   B) $\dfrac{2(a + b)}{3(a - b)}$

   C) $3(a - b) - 2(a + b)$

   D) $\dfrac{3a - b}{2a + b}$

1. A quality control inspector took a sample of x items from a production line and found that d of the items were defective. Which of the following could be the expression for the fraction of the sample that was <u>not</u> defective?

   A) $\dfrac{d}{x}$

   B) $\dfrac{x-d}{d}$

   C) $\dfrac{x-d}{x}$

   D) $\dfrac{d-x}{x}$

Strategy: The number of non-defective items is represented by the expression $x - d$. The total number of items taken from the production line is x. The fraction of the items that were not defective is $\dfrac{x-d}{x}$. This is answer choice C.

2. When twice the sum of $-4x + 6$ and $6x - 4$ is subtracted from $8x + 6$, the result is

   A) $12x + 10$

   B) $-4x - 2$

   C) $4x + 2$

   D) $4x + 8$

Strategy: First, calculate twice the sum of $-4x + 6$ and $6x - 4 = 2(-4x + 6 + 6x - 4)$, which becomes $2(2x + 2) = 4x + 4$. Now subtract $4x + 4$ from $8x + 6$. That is, $8x + 6 - (4x + 4) = 8x + 6 - 4x - 4 = 4x + 2$. This is answer choice C.

3. During its second year of operation, the Coastal Construction Company produced 3,000 more units of affordable housing than it produced in its first year, when it produced c units. The company earns a profit of p dollars for each unit produced. Which of the following represents the total profit made by the Coastal Construction Company in its first two years?

   A) $3{,}000p$ dollars

   B) $6{,}000p$ dollars

   C) $(3{,}000 + 2c)p$ dollars

   D) $(6{,}000 - c)p$ dollars

Strategy: During its first year of operation, Coastal Construction Company produced c units. In the second year of the operation, they produced $c + 3{,}000$ units. So, during the first two years, they produced $c + c + 3{,}000 = 2c + 3{,}000$ units of affordable housing. The profit was p dollars per unit, or $(3{,}000 + 2c)p$. Select answer choice C.

Finding Equivalent Expressions

Two expressions are equivalent if you can manipulate the terms of one expression by any of a combination of distributing a factor over a sum or difference, simplifying a fractional expression, and combining like terms so both expressions are represented identically.

Think It Through

Example

Which of the following expressions is equivalent to $4a^2b + c - 2(a^2b + c)$?

A) $2a^2b - c$

B) $2a^2b + 2c$

C) $2a^2b + 3c$

D) $2a^2b + 6c$

Solution

Notice that you can distribute the -2 through the parentheses. Start there.

$4a^2b + c - 2(a^2b + c)$ Distribute the -2.

$4a^2b + c - 2a^2b - 2c$ Combine like terms.

$2a^2b - c$

Answer: A

Practice   **Finding Equivalent Expressions**

Answers begin on page 656.

1. $m^2n - 4m^2 + 3mn^2 - (-m^2n + 3mn^2 - 2m^2)$

   Which of the following is equivalent to the expression above?

   A) $7m^2 + mn^2$

   B) $2m^2n - 6m^2$

   C) $2m^2n - 2m^2$

   D) $2m^2n - 2m^2 + 6mn^2$

2. $\dfrac{3x^2y + 6xy - 9xy^2}{3}$

   Which of the following is equivalent to the expression above?

   A) $x^2y + 2xy + 3xy^2$

   B) $-2x^2y + 2xy$

   C) $-2x^2y - 2xy$

   D) $x^2y + 2xy - 3xy^2$

SAT-Type Questions

Answers begin on page 656.

1. If $a = 2$, $b = -3$, and $c = 4$, find the value of $(ab)^c$.

   A) $-1,296$

   B) -648

   C) 1

   D) $1,296$

2. If $-1 < w < 0$, then which of the following statements is true?

   A) $w < w^2 < w^3$

   B) $w^2 < w < w^3$

   C) $w < w^3 < w^2$

   D) $w^3 < w^2 < w$

3. If k is an odd integer, which of the following represents an even integer?

   A) $3k$

   B) k^3

   C) $k^2 + 1$

   D) $k + 2$

4. If the volume of a right circular cylinder is expressed by the formula $V = \pi r^2 h$, for which of the following values r (radius) and h (height) is the volume 24π cubic units?

   A) $r = 2, h = 3$

   B) $r = 2, h = 6$

   C) $r = 2, h = 12$

   D) $r = 8, h = 3$

5. In the figure below, what is the length of $\overline{PS}$ in terms of x?

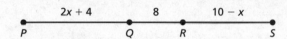

   A) $14 - x$

   B) $x + 22$

   C) $3x + 22$

   D) $3x + 2$

6. What is the result when $3 - 2x$ is subtracted from the sum of $x + 3$ and $5 - x$?

   A) $5 + 2x$

   B) $-5 - 2x$

   C) $5 - 2x$

   D) $-5 + 2x$

7. Anton sells used cars. His base salary is $800 a week and he receives a 12% commission on each sale. Represent Anton's total salary for the week if he had d dollars of sales.

   A) $800 + 12d$ dollars

   B) $800 + 0.12d$ dollars

   C) $812d$ dollars

   D) $800.12d$ dollars

8. Hayley is staying at a hotel that charges $125.99 per night. A local tax of 8.25% is applied to the room rate. A $10.00 charge is added for a parking space for each night. There is no tax on the parking space charge. Hayley is arriving with a car. Which of the following represents Hayley's total charge for a stay of n nights?

A) $n(125.99 \cdot 1.0825 + 10)$

B) $n(125.99 \cdot 1.0825) + 10$

C) $n(1.0825 \cdot 135.99)$

D) $n(125.99 + 1.0825 \cdot 10)$

9. If $x = y = -1$, what is the value of $3(x + y) - (3x - y)$?

A) -8

B) -4

C) -3

D) -2

10. If $x = -3$, $y = 2$, and $z = 3$, find the value of xy^z.

A) -216

B) -24

C) -18

D) 216

11. If $x = -2$, which of the following is <u>not</u> an expression for zero?

A) $\dfrac{0}{x}$

B) $x^2 - 4$

C) $x + (-x)$

D) $x - 2$

12. If $\dfrac{x}{y} = m$ and $xy \neq 0$, then $\dfrac{x - y}{x}$ is equal to

A) $m - 1$

B) $\dfrac{m - 1}{m}$

C) $\dfrac{m}{m - 1}$

D) $\dfrac{m - 1}{m + 1}$

13. Three friends contributed x dollars <u>each</u> to buy a present costing d dollars. However, if d dollars was less than the total amount of money they had collected, then the refund, in dollars, for <u>each</u> of the three friends could be represented as

   A) $\dfrac{3x-d}{3}$

   B) $\dfrac{3d-x}{3}$

   C) $\dfrac{x-3d}{3}$

   D) $\dfrac{d-3x}{3}$

14. If $|x-5|<4$, which of the following is a possible value of x?

   A) 0

   B) 1

   C) 4

   D) 9

Student-Produced Response Questions

15. If $a=6$ and $b=4$, find the value of $\dfrac{a-b}{a+b}$.

16. If $w=3$, $x=4$, $y=-3$, and $z=-4$, find the value of $\dfrac{x-w}{y-z}$.

17. If $j = 2$, $k = -2$, $m = 1$ and $n = -1$, find the value of $\left(\dfrac{m}{j}\right)^{kn}$.

18. If $p = 3$, $q = 3$, $r = 5$, and $s = 4$, find the value of $\left(\dfrac{r+s}{p}\right)^{q}$.

LESSON 2:

Creating and Solving Linear Equations and Inequalities; Literal Equations and More on Absolute Value

- ☐ **Creating and Solving Equations**
- ☐ **Literal Equations**
- ☐ **Absolute Value Equations**
- ☐ **Creating and Solving Linear Inequalities**
- ☐ **Solving Absolute Value Inequalities**

Explain Creating and Solving Equations

An **equation** is a statement of equality between two expressions. The solution to an equation is a value of the **variable** (a letter used to represent a number) that makes the equation true. To find the solution, work to get the variable alone on one side of the equation and a number on the other side of the equation. Remember, to maintain the balance of an equation, you must perform the same operation on both sides. On the SAT, you will be asked to create and solve equations.

Think It Through

Example 1

A local public access television station provides time slots for programming in 15-minute intervals. If the station only operates between the hours of 6 am and 6 pm, which of the following equations represents the total number of 15-minute time slots, s, available on Thursdays and Fridays?

A) $4 \cdot 48 = s$

B) $2(12 \cdot 4) = s$

C) $48s = 4$

D) $2\left(\dfrac{s}{4}\right) = 48$

Solution

Since the station operates 12 hours per day, and each hour has four 15-minute time slots available, the total number of time slots for one day is $12 \cdot 4 = s$.

For two days, the number of time slots is $2(12 \cdot 4) = s$.

Answer: B

Example 2

Solve: $5x - 3 = 27$.

A) −6

B) −5

C) 5

D) 6

Solution

Begin isolating the variable by adding 3 to both sides. Then

$$5x - 3 = 27$$
$$\underline{+3 = 3}$$

$$\frac{\cancel{5}x}{\cancel{5}} = \frac{30}{5} \qquad \text{Divide both sides of the equation by 5.}$$

$$x = 6$$

You can check your answer by substituting it back into the equation for x and seeing if a true statement results. Does $5(6) - 3 = 27$? Yes, $27 = 27$.

Answer: D

Example 3

Solve: $4x + 7 = 10 + x$.

A) 1

B) $\dfrac{3}{4}$

C) $\dfrac{3}{17}$

D) −1

Solution

When variables exist on both sides of the equation, we must manipulate the terms so one side of the equal sign has all the variable terms and the other side has the constants. For this problem,

$4x + 7 = 10 + x$ Subtract x from each side.

$\underline{-x = -x}$

$3x + 7 = 10$ Subtract 7 from each side.

$\underline{-7 = -7}$

$$\frac{\cancel{3}x}{\cancel{3}} = \frac{3}{3} \qquad \text{Divide both sides by 3.}$$

$$x = 1$$

Answer: A

Example 4

Solve: $5(a - 2) = 8a + 11$.

A) 7

B) 5

C) −7

D) −5

Solution

In this problem, we must distribute the 5 through the parentheses before we can start isolating the variable a. So $5(a - 2) = 8a + 11$ becomes $5a - 10 = 8a + 11$ and

$5a - 10 = 8a + 11$	Subtract $5a$ from both sides.
$\underline{-5a \qquad = -5a}$	
$-10 = 3a + 11$	Subtract 11 from each side.
$\underline{-11 = \qquad -11}$	
$\dfrac{-21}{3} = \dfrac{3a}{3}$	Divide both sides by 3.
$-7 = a$	

Answer: C

Example 5

Solve: $\dfrac{3}{4}x - 5 = \dfrac{2}{3}x + 4$.

Solution

When a problem involves fractional terms, you have the option of working with the fractions as they are, or you can multiply every term of the equation by the least common multiple (LCM) of the denominators. Multiplying through by the LCM will eliminate the fractions. For this problem, the LCM of 3 and 4 is 12.

$$12\left(\frac{3}{4}x - 5 = \frac{2}{3}x + 4\right) \qquad \text{Multiply through by the LCM.}$$

$9x - 60 = 8x + 48$ Subtract $8x$ from both sides.

$-8x = -8x$

$x - 60 = 48$ Add 60 to each side.

$+60 = +60$

$x = 108$

Bubble in 108 on the answer grid.

Answer: 108

Example 6

Solve for x: $4(x - 3) + x + 3 = 2(x - 3) + 3(x - 1)$.

A) No solution

B) Infinitely many solutions

C) 12

D) 9

Solution

Begin this problem by distributing through the parentheses as needed.

$4(x - 3) + x + 3 = 2(x - 3) + 3(x - 1)$ Distribute.

$4x - 12 + x + 3 = 2x - 6 + 3x - 3$ Combine like terms.

$5x - 9 = 5x - 9$

Notice that when we combine the like terms, we have like expressions on each side of the equal sign. No matter what value we use for the variable, a true statement will always result. When this happens, there are infinitely many solutions to the equation. Note that if a false statement had resulted, there would be no solution to the equation.

Answer: B

Example 7

When 6 times the number n is added to 11, the result is 53. What number results when 3 times n is added to 4?

A) 7

B) 53

C) 25

D) 31

Solution

For this problem, we must both create and solve an equation, and then use that solution in a second equation. The phrase "6 times the number n" is $6n$. Add 11 and set the expression equal to 53 to get $6n + 11 = 53$. Solving, $6n = 42$ and $n = 7$. Then $3n + 4$ is $3(7) + 4 = 25$.

Answer: C

Practice Creating and Solving Equations

Answers begin on page 657.

1. Solve for x: $4x - (7 - 2x) = 1 + 2x + 8$.

   A) $\dfrac{1}{4}$

   B) 4

   C) 8

   D) 12

2. Solve for the value of a: $\dfrac{1}{3}(6a - 15) = (a - 2) + 2$.

3. Solve for the value of m: $0.04(12) + 0.01m = 0.02(12 + m)$.

4. Find the equation that is equivalent to $24p = 54q + 36$.

   A) $4p = 8q + 6$

   B) $4p = 9q + 12$

   C) $4p = 9q + 6$

   D) $-20p = 36$

5. One of the requirements for becoming an associate scientist in a certain lab is the ability to accurately process 100 specimen slides per hour. Ibragim can currently process 65 slides per hour and believes that with practice he can increase his processing speed by 2 slides per hour each week. Which of the following represents the number of slides per hour that Ibragim believes he will be able to process w weeks from now?

   A) $2 + 65w$

   B) $100 + 2w$

   C) $100 - 65w$

   D) $65 + 2w$

1. If $\dfrac{3}{x} - 2 = \dfrac{2}{x}$, what is the value of x?

   A) $-\dfrac{5}{2}$

   B) $-\dfrac{1}{2}$

   C) $\dfrac{1}{2}$

   D) $\dfrac{5}{2}$

Strategy: Given $\dfrac{3}{x} - 2 = \dfrac{2}{x}$, multiply each term by the common denominator x.

Then $x\left(\dfrac{3}{x} - 2 = \dfrac{2}{x}\right)$, and $3 - 2x = 2$. Collect the like terms and solve for the variable

to see that $-2x = -1$ and $x = \dfrac{1}{2}$. This is answer choice C.

2. If $5x + 3 = 23$, then $x - \dfrac{1}{2} =$

   A) $3\dfrac{1}{2}$

   B) 4

   C) $4\dfrac{1}{2}$

   D) 7

Strategy: Begin by solving $5x + 3 = 23$ for x. Then $5x = 20$ and $x = 4$. Substitute

$x = 4$ into $x - \dfrac{1}{2}$ and see that $4 - \dfrac{1}{2} = 3\dfrac{1}{2}$. This is answer choice A.

3. If $3x - 7 = 5$, then $9x - 21 =$

   A) 3
   B) 4
   C) 10
   D) 15

Strategy: This problem can be solved as we did in problem #2 above, or we can recognize that the second expression, $9x - 21$, can be rewritten in terms of the first expression $3x - 7$:

$$9x - 21 = 3(3x - 7)$$
$$= 3(5)$$
$$= 15$$

Select answer choice D.

4. For what value of x is $2(x+3)+4x$ equal to $3(2x+1)$?

A) Infinitely many values exist.

B) No such value exists.

C) 2

D) 0

Strategy: We must begin by distributing the terms through the parentheses as needed.

$2(x+3)+4x = 3(2x+1)$	Distribute.
$2x+6+4x = 6x+3$	Combine like terms.
$6x+6 = 6x+3$	Subtract $6x$ from each side.
$6 = 3$	

This is a false statement. When a false statement results, it means there is no value of x that makes the given equation true. Choose answer B.

5. Given $\dfrac{x+3}{2}+2x = \dfrac{3}{2}-\dfrac{x-27}{5}$, what is the value of x?

Strategy: In this problem, it is easiest to eliminate the fractions by multiplying through by the LCM of the denominators. So

$10\left(\dfrac{x+3}{2}+2x = \dfrac{3}{2}-\dfrac{x-27}{5}\right)$	Multiply through by the LCM, 10.
$5(x+3)+20x = 15-2(x-27)$	Distribute.
$5x+15+20x = 15-2x+54$	Collect the like terms.
$25x+15 = -2x+69$	Add $2x$ to both sides.
$\underline{+2x \qquad = +2x}$	
$27x+15 = 69$	Subtract 15 from each side.
$\underline{-15 = -15}$	
$\dfrac{27x}{27} = \dfrac{54}{27}$	Divide both sides by 27.
$x = 2$	

Bubble in 2 on your answer grid.

```
 2
       ⑦ ⑦
 ⊙  ⊙  ⊙  ⊙
    ⓪ ⓪ ⓪
 ① ① ① ①
 ● ② ② ②
 ③ ③ ③ ③
 ④ ④ ④ ④
 ⑤ ⑤ ⑤ ⑤
 ⑥ ⑥ ⑥ ⑥
 ⑦ ⑦ ⑦ ⑦
 ⑧ ⑧ ⑧ ⑧
 ⑨ ⑨ ⑨ ⑨
```

Explain Literal Equations

Literal equations are equations with several variables. The equation $ax + b = cx - d$ is an example of a literal equation. You can solve for any one of the variables by following the same procedures you would use in solving equations with one variable.

Think It Through

Example

Solve the following literal equation for m: $P = L + \dfrac{a}{x} m$

A) $\dfrac{x(P + L)}{a}$

B) $\dfrac{x(P - L)}{a}$

C) $\dfrac{a(P - L)}{x}$

D) $ax(P - L)$

Solution

We want to manipulate the equation to isolate m rather than P. Begin by

subtracting L from both sides so that $P - L = \dfrac{a}{x} m$. Now we can multiply every

term by x so that $Px - Lx = am$. Finish by dividing both sides by a: $\dfrac{Px - Lx}{a} = m$

or $\dfrac{x(P - L)}{a} = m$.

Answer: B

1. If $k + m^2 = k + n^2$, then what is the value of m?

   A) n only

   B) $-n$ only

   C) n or $-n$

   D) 0

Strategy: Isolate the term m^2 by subtracting k from both sides. Then $m^2 = n^2$. Take the square root of both terms and $m = \pm n$. Select answer choice C.

2. If $D - m = mrx$, then $m =$

   A) $\dfrac{rx}{D}$

   B) $\dfrac{D}{rx}$

   C) $\dfrac{D}{2rx}$

   D) $\dfrac{D}{1+rx}$

Strategy: Begin by adding m to both sides so all the terms with an m are on the same side of the equal sign. Then $D - m = mrx$ becomes $D = m + mrx$. Factor out the m on the right-hand side: $D = m(1 + rx)$. Finish by dividing both sides by $(1 + rx)$ and $m = \dfrac{D}{1+rx}$. Pick answer choice D.

3. Solve for x: $\dfrac{1}{a} - \dfrac{1}{x} = \dfrac{1}{b}$.

   A) $a - b$

   B) $\dfrac{ab}{b-a}$

   C) $\dfrac{b-a}{ab}$

   D) $\dfrac{-ab}{b-a}$

Strategy: Multiply each term by the common denominator, abx:

$\cancel{a}bx \dfrac{1}{\cancel{a}} - ab\cancel{x}\dfrac{1}{\cancel{x}} = \dfrac{1}{\cancel{b}}a\cancel{b}x$ becomes $bx - ab = ax$. Rearrange the equation so that $bx - ax = ab$. Now factor out x, and $x(b - a) = ab$. Divide by $(b - a)$ to see $x = \dfrac{ab}{b-a}$.

This is answer choice B.

The absolute value of any real number is the distance between that number and zero on the number line. Symbolically, the absolute value of x is written as $|x|$. The formal definition of this concept is: If $x \geq 0$, then $|x| = x$, and if $x < 0$, then $|x| = -x$. For all real values of x, $|x|$ is nonnegative. We briefly discussed this concept in Lesson 1. In this lesson, we extend our knowledge of absolute value to solving absolute value equations.

Think It Through

Example

Find the value of x given $|x + 5| = 12$.

A) 7 or −7
B) 7 or −17
C) 17 or −17
D) 7 or 17

Solution

Recall the formal definition of absolute value: If $x \geq 0$, then $|x| = x$, and if $x < 0$, then $|x| = -x$. When solving an equation involving absolute value, we don't know if $x \geq 0$ or if $x < 0$; therefore, we must take both possibilities into account by solving two equations. Then $|x + 5| = 12$ becomes $x + 5 = 12$ or $x + 5 = -12$, and $x = 7$ or $x = -17$. It is essential to check both values in the original equation since the actual solution may have two values, one value, or no values. If $x = 7$, then $|x + 5| = 12$ is $|7 + 5| = 12$ and $|12| = 12$. If $x = -17$, $|x + 5| = 12$ is $|-17 + 5| = 12$ and $|-12| = 12$. Both are true statements, so both solutions are correct.

Answer: B

Practice Absolute Value Equations

Answers begin on page 658.

1. If $|x + 4.3| = 9$, what are the possible values of x?

   A) 4.7 and −4.7
   B) 4.7 and −5.7
   C) 4.3 and −13.3
   D) 4.7 and −13.3

2. If $|x - 2| = 3$, what are the possible values of x?

   A) −1 and 5
   B) −5 and −1
   C) 1 and 5
   D) 1 and −5

1. If $|121 - g| = 6$, what is one possible value of $\dfrac{g+1}{2}$?

   A) 58

   B) 63

   C) 60

   D) 56

Strategy: We begin by writing two equations and solving. Then $121 - g = 6$ or $121 - g = -6$.

$121 - g = 6$	$121 - g = -6$
$-g = 6 - 121$	$-g = -6 - 121$
$g = -6 + 121 = 115$	$g = 6 + 121 = 127$

Remember that it is essential to check both values in the original equation since the actual solution may have two values, one value, or no values.

If $g = 115$:	If $g = 127$:
$|121 - 115| = 6$	$|121 - 127| = 6$
$|6| = 6$	$|-6| = 6$

True statements result and both values are solutions. Then, if $g = 115$, $\dfrac{g+1}{2}$ is $\dfrac{115+1}{2} = 58$. Stop and select answer choice A.

2. Solve for x: $2x - |x + 2| = 11$.

   A) -3

   B) 13

   C) -3 and 13

   D) 3 and 13

Strategy: When solving an absolute value equation, we want the absolute value isolated on one side of the equal sign. If this is not the case in a given equation, then first we must make it so by using known equation-solving procedures. So rewrite $2x - |x + 2| = 11$ as $-|x + 2| = 11 - 2x$, then multiply by -1 and $|x + 2| = -11 + 2x$. Now write and solve two equations: $x + 2 = -11 + 2x$ or $x + 2 = -(-11 + 2x)$.

$x + 2 = -11 + 2x$	$x + 2 = -(-11 + 2x)$
$-x = -13$	$x + 2 = 11 - 2x$
$x = 13$	$3x = 9$ and $x = 3$

Check both values:

If $x = 13$:	If $x = 3$:
$2x - |x + 2| = 11$	$2x - |x + 2| = 11$
$2(13) - |13 + 2| = 11$	$2(3) - |3 + 2| = 11$
$26 - 15 = 11$	$6 - 5 = 1$
$11 = 11$	$1 \neq 11$, thus $x \neq 3$

A true statement results only when $x = 13$. Choose answer B.

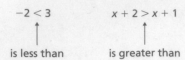

An **inequality** states that one quantity is less than or greater than another.

$$-2 < 3 \qquad\qquad x + 2 > x + 1$$

is less than   is greater than

Two other inequality symbols are ≤ (less than or equal to) and ≥ (greater than or equal to).

The transitive property of inequality states that if $a < b$ and $b < c$, then $a < c$. For example, since $-2 < 3$ and $3 < 15$, then $-2 < 15$. The transitive property is true for all the inequality symbols.

To solve inequalities, we follow the same procedures we use for equation solving. Remember that adding or subtracting across an inequality symbol <u>does not</u> change the direction of the symbol. Multiplying or dividing a positive number across an inequality symbol <u>does not</u> change the direction of the symbol. However, multiplying or dividing by a negative number across an inequality symbol <u>does</u> change the direction of the symbol.

Statements such as $-2 < x \le 1$ are called **compound inequalities**. These inequalities are conjunctions of two or more inequalities and are read beginning with the variable, "x is greater than -2 but less than or equal to 1." For this inequality, x can be any value between -2 and 1, including 1, but <u>not</u> including -2. This solution is graphed on a number line below.

Recall that to solve compound inequalities, we must work with all three sections of the inequality at the same time. The goal is to end up with a single variable between the inequality symbols and expressions or constants on each end. Consider the compound inequality $-3 < 2x + 5 \le 15$ and solve for x.

$-3 < 2x + 5 \le 15$ Subtract 5 from all three sections.

$\underline{-5 < \qquad -5 \le -5}$

$\dfrac{-8}{2} < \dfrac{2x}{2} \le \dfrac{10}{2}$ Divide all three sections by 2.

$-4 < x \le 5$

Compound inequalities such as $-4 < x \le 5$ may also be written using the word *and*: $x > -4$ and $x \le 5$.

Additionally, remember that compound inequalities using the word *or* are graphed as rays opening in opposite directions. The graph of $x < 2$ <u>or</u> $x > 6$ is shown below.

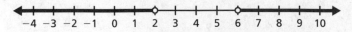

Note that inequalities including the term <u>or</u> cannot be expressed as compound inequalities.

Example 1

Given $\frac{x}{2}+1>0$ and $2x-3<7$, solve for x.

A) $-2<x<5$

B) $x>-2$ or $x<5$

C) $2<x<5$

D) $x>2$ and $x<5$

Solution

Solve each inequality separately:

$\frac{x}{2}+1>0$ and $2x-3<7$

$\frac{x}{2}>-1$ and $2x<10$

$x>-2$ and $x<5$

This answer can be restated as the compound inequality $-2<x<5$.

Answer: A

Example 2

Solve for x if $-(x-2)>3$.

A) $x>5$

B) $x<-5$

C) $x>1$

D) $x<-1$

Solution

There are several ways in which we might start solving this inequality. One method is to distribute the negative sign through the parentheses so that $-(x-2)>3$ becomes $-x+2>3$. Then, subtracting 2 from both sides, $-x>1$. Recall that if both sides of an inequality are multiplied or divided by a negative number, we reverse the direction of the inequality. Thus $x<-1$.

Answer: D

Example 3

If the sum of two integers x and k is less than x, which of the following must be true?

A) $k<0$

B) $k>0$

C) $x<0$

D) $x+k<0$

Solution

First, we must create the inequality $x+k<x$. Collect the like terms and $k<x-x \Rightarrow k<0$.

Answer: A

Answers begin on page 658.

1. Solve the inequality $3x - 8 < 1$.

   A) $x > 3$

   B) $x > -3$

   C) $x < 3$

   D) $x < -3$

2. Solve the inequality $-5x + 1 > -9$.

   A) $x < 2$

   B) $x > 2$

   C) $x < -2$

   D) $x > -2$

3. Solve the inequality $1 < 2a + 3 < 7$.

   A) $a > -1$ or $a < 2$

   B) $-1 > a > 2$

   C) $-1 < a < 2$

   D) $-1 > a < 2$

Model SAT Questions

1. If $-2x > -x + 10$, which of the following numbers is <u>not</u> a solution?

   A) -24

   B) -22

   C) -12

   D) -5

Strategy: Solve the inequality:

$-2x > -x + 10$ Add x to both sides.
$\underline{+x > +x}$

$\dfrac{-x}{-1} > \dfrac{10}{-1}$ Divide both sides by -1. Don't forget to reverse the inequality sign.

$x < -10$

Examine the answer choices. Only -5 is not less than -10. Select choice D.

2. Let a and b be positive integers. If $a > b$, which of the following expression(s) must be true?

   I. $a^2 > b^2$

   II. $a - b < 0$

   III. $-2a > -2b$

   A) None

   B) I only

   C) I and II only

   D) III only

Strategy: Check each of the inequalities. For statement I, choose values for a and b. If $a = 5$ and $b = 3$, $a^2 > b^2$ becomes $5^2 > 3^2$, which is $25 > 9$. This is true, so statement I is true. We can choose numbers to test statement II or notice that adding b to each side yields $a < b$. But the problem gives $a > b$, so statement II is false. Eliminate choice C. We already know statement I is true. We can stop here and select answer choice B since there is no answer choice with statements I and III.

3. If $-17 \leq 3a - 5 < 16$, what is the greatest possible integer value of $2a + 3$?

    A) 16

    B) −1

    C) 15

    D) 0

Strategy: Solve the compound inequality by adding 5 to all three parts and then dividing all three pieces by 3. Then, $-17 \leq 3a - 5 < 16$ is $-12 \leq 3a < 21$, and $-4 \leq a < 7$. The greatest possible intege solution to the compound inequality is 6. Then $2(6) + 3 = 15$; this is answer choice C.

4. Pili is shipping boxes of chocolate to her customers. Each box of chocolate weighs 6.2 ounces, and the shipping box weighs 10.5 ounces. Pili will pay $4.95 in shipping costs if the total weight of her package is 36 ounces or less. What is the maximum number of boxes of chocolate Pili can ship in one box without going over the weight limit?

    A) 6

    B) 4

    C) 8

    D) 10

Strategy: Write the inequality that represents this situation. Let b = the number of boxes of chocolate Pili can ship at the given charge. Then $6.2b + 10.5 \leq 36$. Solving for the variable, $6.2b \leq 25.5$ and $b \leq 4.11$. The maximum number of boxes of chocolate Pili can ship is 4. Select answer choice B.

· · · · · · · **Explain** **Solving Absolute Value Inequalities** · · · · · · · · · · · · · · · · ·

The statement $|x| < k$ is equivalent to $x < k$ and $x > -k$ (where $k > 0$). This is usually expressed as the compound inequality $-k < x < k$, or in set notation $\{x: -k < x < k\}$ and read as "the set of all x such that x is greater than $-k$ and less than k". A real-world example of this concept is tolerance levels found in manufacturing processes. For example, if the distance between two drilled holes on a blueprint for a metal bracket is listed as 2.400 inches and the tolerance allowed is ±0.015 inches, this means that the acceptable distance, d, between the holes can be represented as $|d - 2.400| \leq 0.015$. To solve this statement for the endpoints of the tolerance interval, we use the compound inequality $-0.015 \leq d - 2.400 \leq 0.015$ and solve for d. Add 2.400 to each term, so that $2.385 \leq d \leq 2.415$, or $\{d: 2.385 \leq d \leq 2.415\}$.

The distance between the two holes should be between 2.385 inches and 2.415 inches, inclusive. If the distance is greater or less, then the item is rejected.

The statement $|x| > k$ is equivalent to saying that $x > k$ <u>or</u> $x < -k$ (where $k \geq 0$). Once again, in this type of inequality, it is only necessary that x satisfy one of the two conditions to be in the solution set.

Think It Through

Example 1

Solve the inequality $|2x - 3| < 9$.

A) $\{x: -3 \leq x \leq 6\}$
B) $\{x: -3 < x < 6\}$
C) $\{x: 3 < x < 6\}$
D) $\{x: -3 \leq x \leq 6\}$

Solution

Write the problem as two inequalities, $2x - 3 < 9$ and $2x - 3 > -9$. These two inequalities can be written as the compound inequality $-9 < 2x - 3 < 9$. Solving simultaneously, add 3 to all the terms so that $-6 < 2x < 12$ and divide all terms by 2, so $-3 < x < 6$. All the answer choices are given in set notation, so $\{x: -3 < x < 6\}$.

Answer: B

Example 2

Solve for x in the absolute value inequality $|2x - 1| \geq 7$.

A) $x \geq 4$ or $x \leq -3$
B) $\{x: -3 \leq x \leq 4\}$
C) $-3 < x < 4$
D) $x \leq -3$

Solution

This problem is of the form $|x| \geq k$, so

$$2x - 1 \geq 7 \qquad \text{or} \qquad 2x - 1 \leq -7$$
$$2x \geq 8 \qquad\qquad\qquad 2x \leq -6$$
$$x \geq 4 \qquad\qquad\qquad x \leq -3$$

The result can written as $x \geq 4$ or $x \leq -3$.

We could check these solution ranges by substituting a value less than -3, say -4, and a value greater than 4, say 5. Then

$$|2x - 1| \geq 7 \qquad\qquad |2x - 1| \geq 7$$
$$|2(-4) - 1| \geq 7 \qquad\qquad |2(5) - 1| \geq 7$$
$$|-9| \geq 7 \qquad\qquad\qquad |9| \geq 7$$
$$9 \geq 7 \qquad\qquad\qquad 9 \geq 7$$

Both values return true statements.

Answer: A

Answers begin on page 658.

1. Match the graph below with the correct inequality.

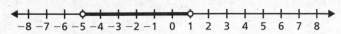

A) $|2x+4| < 6$

B) $|2x+4| > 6$

C) $|2x+4| < 8$

D) $|2x+4| > 8$

2. Match the graph below with the correct inequality.

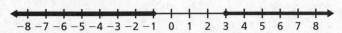

A) $-1 < x < 3$

B) $-1 \le x \le 3$

C) $x < -1$ or $x > 3$

D) $x \le -1$ or $x \ge 3$

3. Which choice is equivalent to $|x| < 5$?

A) $x < 5$

B) $x > -5$

C) $-5 \le x \le 5$

D) $-5 < x < 5$

4. Which of the given choices is equivalent to $|x+3| > 6$?

A) $x > 3$ or $x < -3$

B) $x < -3$ and $x > 3$

C) $x < 3$ and $x < -3$

D) $x > 3$ or $x < -9$

Model SAT Questions

1. Which of the following is equivalent to $|x-7| < 5$?

A) $x < 12$

B) $2 < x < 12$

C) $x < -2$ or $x > 12$

D) $-12 < x < 2$

Strategy: Express $|x-7| < 5$ as the two the cases $x - 7 < 5$ and $x - 7 > -5$. Then solve each case. For $x - 7 < 5$, $x < 12$, and for $x - 7 > -5$, $x > 2$. As a compound inequality, we write $2 < x < 12$. This is answer choice B.

2. Which of the following is equivalent to $|8 - 6m| > 4$?

A) $m < \dfrac{2}{3}$ or $m > 2$

B) $m > \dfrac{2}{3}$ or $m > 2$

C) $m < 2$ or $m > \dfrac{2}{3}$

D) $-\dfrac{2}{3} < m < 2$

Strategy: Rewrite $|8-6m| > 4$ as two cases: $8 - 6m > 4$ or $8 - 6m < -4$. Then solve each inequality. For $8 - 6m > 4$, $-6m > -4$, and $m < \dfrac{2}{3}$. For $8 - 6m < -4$, $-6m < -12$, and $m > 2$. Select answer choice A.

3. The design for various city sewer pipes allows for pipes of diameter d, ranging from 24 to 32 inches. Any pipes more or less than these diameters are rejected. Which of the following represents the correct inequality by which a pipe is judged to be acceptable?

A) $|d-28| \le 4$

B) $|d-4| \le 28$

C). $|d+4| \le 32$

D) $|d+24| \le 32$

Strategy: To determine the absolute value inequality, we need to calculate the tolerance interval. Find the average of the endpoints 24 and 32. Then $\frac{24+32}{2} =$ 28 inches. Now find the difference between 28 and $24 = 4$. The tolerance is 28 ± 4 inches. So the difference between any diameter, d, and 28 can be no more than 4. This is represented by answer choice A.

SAT-Type Questions

Answers begin on page 658.

1. If $33mn + 10 = 38mn$, then what is the value of $-\frac{3}{2}mn$?

A) -6

B) -3

C) $-\frac{5}{2}$

D) 3

2. If $\frac{7x+9n}{5} = x$, then what is $4x$ in terms of n?

A) $-18n$

B) $\frac{-18}{5}n$

C) $-\frac{9}{5}n$

D) $9n + 7$

3. Given $\frac{5x}{3} - \frac{3x}{2} - x = 5$, what is the value of $x + x^2$?

A) 6

B) 30

C) 36

D) 42

4. What is the sum of the solutions to the equation $|-5x - 5| = 45$?

   A) -18

   B) -9

   C) -2

   D) 2

5. -12 and 24 are solutions to which of the following equations?

   A) $|-x - 6| = 18$

   B) $|-x + 6| = 30$

   C) $|x + 6| = 6$

   D) $|x - 6| = 18$

6. Which of the following represents the solution to this compound inequality:
   $\dfrac{x}{2} > 2$ or $-3(x - 2) > 0$?

   A) $x > 4$ or $x < 2$

   B) $x < 4$ or $x < 2$

   C) $x > 2$ or $x < 4$

   D) No solution

7. If 6 more than x is less than 9, or 3 less than x is greater than 7, which of the following is <u>not</u> a solution to this compound inequality?

   A) -3

   B) 0

   C) 7

   D) 11

8. The solution of $\left|\dfrac{3}{4}x + 2\right| - 1 > 3$ is

   A) $x > \dfrac{8}{3}$ or $x < -8$

   B) $-8 < x < \dfrac{8}{3}$

   C) $\dfrac{8}{3} < x < 8$

   D) $x < \dfrac{8}{3}$ or $x > 8$

9. Given $\dfrac{1}{2}k - 4 = -1 + 2k$, what is the value of k^{-k}?

   A) $-\dfrac{1}{2}$

   B) 4

   C) 2

   D) $\dfrac{1}{4}$

10. If $\dfrac{ax}{w-a} = 1$, and x and w are both positive, then

    A) $a = \dfrac{x}{w+1}$

    B) $a = \dfrac{x-1}{w}$

    C) $a = \dfrac{w}{x+1}$

    D) $a = \dfrac{x+1}{w}$

11. If $a = bc$, $\dfrac{1}{2}b = r$, and $c = 8r$, then, in terms of a, what does r equal?

    A) $\dfrac{a}{4}$

    B) $\sqrt{\dfrac{a}{4}}$

    C) $\dfrac{\sqrt{a}}{4}$

    D) $\dfrac{\sqrt{a}}{16}$

12. The solution of $\left|\dfrac{1-5x}{3}\right| \geq 7$ is

    A) $x \geq -4$ or $x \leq 4.4$
    B) $x \leq -4$ or $x \geq 4.4$
    C) $-4 \leq x \leq 4.4$
    D) $4 \leq x \leq 4.4$

13. The solution of $\left|\dfrac{3}{2}x - 13\right| \geq 2$ is

    A) $-10 \leq x < 7\dfrac{1}{3}$

    B) $7\dfrac{1}{3} \leq x \leq 10$

    C) $-7\dfrac{1}{3} \leq x \leq 10$

    D) $x \leq 7\dfrac{1}{3}$ or $x \geq 10$

14. Given $x - 1 > 3$ and $-2x < -8$, which of the following is the solution to this compound inequality?

    A) $x > -2$
    B) $x > -4$
    C) $x > -2$ and $x < -4$
    D) No solution

15. Which of the given equations has no solution?

    A) $2x + 4 = 2(x + 4)$

    B) $4(2x + 6) = 2(4x + 12)$

    C) $3(x + 1) = 2x + 3$

    D) $x = 0$

16. What is the product of the solutions to the equation $\left| \dfrac{k}{3} + 6 \right| = 4$?

    A) 24

    B) 30

    C) 48

    D) 180

17. What is the smaller solution to the equation $\left| 18 - \dfrac{x}{4} \right| = 4$?

    A) 10

    B) 14

    C) 22

    D) 56

18. If $a = \dfrac{x}{1 - x}$, which of the following represents x in terms of a?

    A) a

    B) $\dfrac{a}{a - 1}$

    C) $\dfrac{a}{1 - a}$

    D) $\dfrac{a}{a + 1}$

19. If $\dfrac{x^2}{6} = 4p$, what is the value of $12p$?

    A) $\dfrac{x^2}{3}$

    B) $\dfrac{x^2}{2}$

    C) x^2

    D) $2x^2$

20. What is the positive difference between the solutions to the equation $\left| 2 + \dfrac{p}{3} \right| = 5$?

    A) 10

    B) 12

    C) 18

    D) 30

21. The solution of $\left|\dfrac{3-x}{5}\right| \geq 4$ is

    A) $x \leq -17$ or $x \geq 23$

    B) $x \leq 23$ or $x \geq -17$

    C) $x \leq -17$ and $x \geq 23$

    D) $-17 \leq x \leq 23$

22. The solution of $\left|\dfrac{2}{3}a + 14\right| < 2$ is

    A) $-24 < a < -18$

    B) $-18 < a < 24$

    C) $18 < a < 24$

    D) $-16 < a < -12$

23. Which equation has infinitely many solutions?

    A) $\dfrac{x}{2} = 2x$

    B) $3x + 1 = 3x - 1$

    C) $4x - 10 = 2(2x - 4) - 2$

    D) $x + 1 = 3x - 2$

24. Which of the following represents the solution to the following compound inequality: $4x \geq -x + 5$ and $6 \geq 4x - 3$?

    A) $x \leq 2.25$

    B) $-1 \leq x \leq 2$

    C) $1 \leq x \leq 2.25$

    D) $-2.25 \leq x \leq 1$

25. Which of the following is the graph of the solution to $-x \geq 4$ or $2x - 1 \geq 7$?

    A)

    B)

    C)

    D)

26. If $7^b = 343$, what is the value of $8b + 1$?

27. Solve for m: $\dfrac{5m}{2} - 12 = \dfrac{m}{3} + 1$.

28. Solve for a: $0.25(a + 32) = 3.2 + a$.

29. If w weeks and 3 days is equal to 241 days, what is the value of w?

30. When 5 times the number y is added to 14, the result is 4. What number results when 3 times y is added to 6?

Linear Functions

▪ **Creating, Evaluating, and Interpreting Linear Functions**

▪ **Slope, Parallel Lines, and Perpendicular Lines**

• • • • • • **Explain** **Creating, Evaluating, and Interpreting** • • • • • • • • • • • • • •
Linear Functions

In mathematics, a **function** is a rule that assigns each number in the **domain** to a number in the **range**. The numbers in the domain are the values of the independent variable x. The numbers in the range to which each value of x is paired are designated by the dependent letter y or by $f(x)$. A function is usually designated by the letter f, although other letters such as g and h are sometimes used. The notation $f(x)$ is read "f of x" and the ordered pairs (x, y) can be written as $(x, f(x))$.

While an equation does not have to be linear to be a function, this lesson will focus on straight lines. The domain of a linear function is all real numbers. The range of a linear function is all real numbers except when the equation is of the form $f(x) = c$, where c is a constant. In this case, the range of the function is only the number c. For other functions, the domain and/or the range can be restricted. On the SAT, you may be asked to create a linear function, to evaluate a linear function, or to interpret the meaning of a linear function as a whole. You may also be asked to interpret the meaning of a single term of the linear function in context of a real-world situation.

Definitions

The **domain** of a function is the set of x values for which a function is defined.

The **range** of a function is the set of all the values of y that can be produced by that function.

• • • • • • **Think It Through** •

Example 1

If $g(x) = 2x + \dfrac{1}{2}$, what is the value of $g(3) + g(-1)$?

A) 11

B) 9

C) 5

D) 8

Solution

In this problem, we need to evaluate the given function at $x = 3$ and at $x = -1$ and then sum the results. So, $g(3) = 2(3) + \dfrac{1}{2} = 6\dfrac{1}{2}$ and $g(-1) = 2(-1) + \dfrac{1}{2} = -1\dfrac{1}{2}$. Thus, $g(3) + g(-1) = 6\dfrac{1}{2} + \left(-1\dfrac{1}{2}\right) = 5$.

Answer: C

Example 2

The students in the Eastern High School marching band are arranged in 3 rows. Each row contains a certain number of students standing side by side plus two flag bearers. Write a linear function in two variables that represents the total number of students in the marching band if x is the number of students standing side by side in one row.

A) $f(x) = 3x^2 + 2$

B) $f(x) = 3^2(x) + 2$

C) $f(x) = 3x + 6$

D) $f(x) = 9x$

Solution

Immediately eliminate answer choice A as it is not a linear function. Then since x = number of students standing side-by-side in one row, $3x$ is the number of students standing side-by-side in the entire formation. In each row there are two flag bearers, so in three rows there are $2(3) = 6$ flag bearers. Let $f(x)$ = total number of students and the function modeling this situation is $f(x) = 3x + 6$.

Answer: C

Example 3

If $f(x) = x + 2$, what is the value of $f(x - 2)$?

A) $x - 2$

B) x

C) $x + 2$

D) 2

Solution

When we evaluate a function, we replace x in the original function with the new term or expression. So, $f(x - 2) = (x - 2) + 2$. Then $x - 2 + 2$ is x.

Answer: B

Example 4

A school fundraising event is selling used music CDs. The function that reflects the price of each CD at the fundraiser is $f(x) = 0.50x + 2$, where x represents the original price of the CD. Which of the following is the best interpretation of the term $0.50x$?

A) The final cost of each CD is half of what it cost new.

B) The original price of the CD is divided in half.

C) The original price of the CD is increased by 50%.

D) Each CD is $2.00 more than double the original price.

Solution

One way to determine the best interpretation of the term $0.50x$ is to choose a value for x and solve for $f(x)$. Pick a friendly number like $10. If $x = 10, then $f(10) = 0.50(10) + 2 \Rightarrow 5 + 2$. Stop here. The original price of the CD went from $10 new to $5 and $5 is half of $10. The best interpretation is B.

Answer: B

Answers begin on page 661.

Questions 1 – 3 refer to the following information.

The function f is defined as $f(x) = 2x + 5$. Find the value for each of the following:

1. $f(7) =$

2. $f(0) =$

3. $f(-2.5) =$

4. A garden has room for 5 rows of flowers. There are four additional flowers, one in each corner of the arrangement. Write a function to describe the total number of flowers in the garden plot if each row has x flowers.

   A) $f(x) = (5 + 4)x$

   B) $f(x) = 5x + 4$

   C) $f(x) = 6x - 4$

   D) $f(x) = 5x + 20$

5. It costs a certain amount of money to prepare a book for sale. Suppose the linear function that represents the total revenue gained from the sale of the book is $f(n) = 3n - 3{,}000$, where n represents the number of copies sold. Which of the following is the best interpretation of the function $f(n)$?

   A) It cost $3.00 per copy to prepare each book for sale and the company earned $3,000 from the book sales.

   B) The company spent $3,000 preparing the book for sale, which cost $3.00 per copy, so they sold 100 books.

   C) The book is sold for $3.00 per copy and the company gains a profit of $3,000 from the sales of the book.

   D) The company invested $3,000 in preparing the book for printing. The difference between the sale price of each copy and the cost to print each copy is $3.00.

1. A local fitness club charges a $50 sign-up fee and then $25 per month. Express the cost of using the fitness club as a function of m, where m represents the number of months the member participates.

    A) $f(m) = 25 + 50m$

    B) $f(m) = 50 + 25m$

    C) $f(m) = 75$

    D) $f(m) = 25m - 50$

Strategy: Each month the member will pay $25, so we can represent that term as $25m$. The $50 sign-up fee is a one-time cost, so $f(m) = 50 + 25m$. This is answer choice B.

2. If $f(x) = 2x + 3$, for what value of a is it true that $3f(a) = f(4a)$?

    A) 1.5

    B) 2

    C) 3

    D) 4.5

Strategy: Convert $f(x)$ into $f(a)$ so that $f(a) = 2a + 3$. Then $3f(a) = 3(2a + 3) = 6a + 9$ and $f(4a) = 2(4a) + 3 = 8a + 3$. Set $3f(a) = f(4a)$ and $6a + 9 = 8a + 3$. Collect the like terms and solve for a to find that $6 = 2a$ and $a = 3$. Select answer choice C.

3. A newly released song had an original rating of 23 points on a musical survey chart. Each week after the song was released, its rating fell by the same number of points such that the equation that represents the song's point rating during any given week is $h(w) = 23 - 2w$, where w is the number of weeks since the song's release. Which of the following is the best interpretation of the term $-2w$?

    A) The song's point rating fell by 2 points every week after it was released.

    B) The point rating for the song increased by 2 points every week after it was released.

    C) The song had a point rating of -2 three weeks after it was released.

    D) Not very many people liked the song 5 weeks after it was released.

Strategy: Since w represents the number of weeks since the song was released, $-2w$ tells us the rating fell 2 points each week after the release. This is answer choice A.

4. If $g(x) = \frac{1}{3}x + 16$, what is the value of x when $g(x) = 19$?

Strategy: In this case, we are substituting for $g(x)$ rather than x. Then $19 = \frac{1}{3}x + 16$; solving for x, $3 = \frac{1}{3}x$ and $x = 9$. Bubble in 9 on the answer grid.

· · · · · **Explain** **Slope, Parallel Lines, and Perpendicular Lines** · · · · · · · · · ·

Thus far, we have examined linear functions as a whole. In this section, we will narrow our focus to one particular part of a linear function: the slope. Broadly, the **slope** of a linear function is the steepness of the line. More specifically, slope of a line is its vertical change of the line divided by its horizontal change. You may recall from math class that the formula for slope is $\dfrac{\text{rise}}{\text{run}} = \dfrac{\text{the change in } y}{\text{the change in } x} = \dfrac{y_2 - y_1}{x_2 - x_1}$. Slope can also be considered the rate of change of the variables. For example, in model problem #3 on the previous page, the rate of change was −2 points per week.

The slope of a line graphed on the coordinate plane can be positive, negative, 0, or undefined.

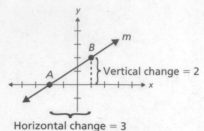

Horizontal change = 3

Slope of line $m = \frac{2}{3}$.

Uphill lines have positive slope.

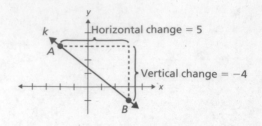

Slope of line $k = -\frac{4}{5}$.

Downhill lines have negative slope.

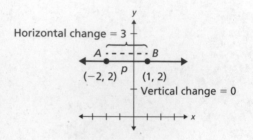

Slope of line $p = 0$.
Horizontal lines have 0 slope.

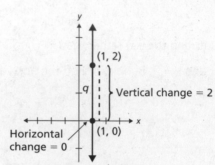

Slope of line q is undefined.
Vertical lines have an undefined slope.

When we write a linear equation, it is generally presented in slope-intercept form which is $y = mx + b$. We can also express this type of equation in function notation, $f(x) = mx + b$. In either case, m is the slope of the line and b is the value of the y-intercept. Note that linear equations can also be presented in standard form, $ax + by = c$, or point-slope form, $y - y_1 = m(x - x_1)$. On the SAT, you will be expected to recognize and answer questions about linear equations in any of the given forms.

Sometimes we graph more than one equation on a single xy-plane. When we do so, this is called a system of linear equations. We will discuss systems in significantly more detail in Lesson 4, but here we want to define two special kinds of lines that are graphed together: parallel lines and perpendicular lines.

Lines that are parallel have the same slope. Parallel lines never intersect.

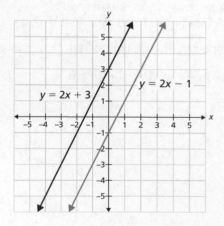

Lines that are perpendicular have slopes that are negative reciprocals of each other. The product of the slopes of perpendicular lines is −1. Perpendicular lines create 90° angles at their point of intersection.

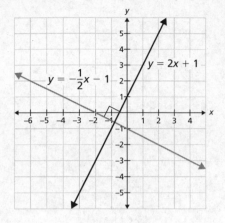

Think It Through

Example 1

The slope of the line in the graph below is

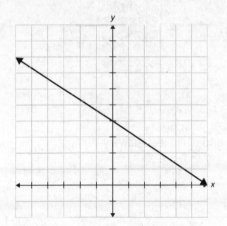

A) Positive
B) Negative
C) 0
D) Undefined

Solution

Graphs are always read from left to right. The line is sloping downhill, so the slope is negative.

Answer: B

Example 2

What is the slope of the line defined by the point $(4, -1)$ and the equation $mx - 3y = 11$?

Solution

Use the given point to determine the value of m. Then $m(4) - 3(-1) = 11$, $4m + 3 = 11$, and $m = 2$. But note that the given equation is not in slope-intercept form, so we must manipulate it a bit to solve for the slope. Then $mx - 3y = 11$ becomes $-3y = -mx + 11$, and dividing by 3, $y = \dfrac{mx}{3} - \dfrac{11}{3}$. Substitute in the value for m and $y = \dfrac{2}{3}x - \dfrac{11}{3}$. The slope of the line is $\dfrac{2}{3}$.

Answer: $\dfrac{2}{3}$

Example 3

In the figure below, line r intersects the x- and y-axes at $(x, 0)$ and $(0, y)$ respectively. What is the slope of line r?

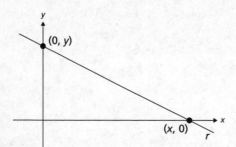

A) $\dfrac{x}{y}$

B) $-\dfrac{x}{y}$

C) $\dfrac{y}{x}$

D) $-\dfrac{y}{x}$

Solution

Use the formula for the slope of a line: $\frac{y_2 - y_1}{x_2 - x_1}$. Let $(x_1, y_1) = (0, y)$ and let $(x_2, y_2) = (x, 0)$. Then $\frac{0 - y}{x - 0} = -\frac{y}{x}$.

Answer: D

Example 4

Find the value of a so that the slope, m, of the line through (3, 5) and (4, a) is 2.

Solution

Again, we are going to use the formula for the slope of a line:
$m = \frac{y_2 - y_1}{x_2 - x_1}$. Let $(x_1, y_1) = (3, 5)$ and let $(x_2, y_2) = (4, a)$. So, $\frac{a - 5}{4 - 3} = 2$,
$a - 5 = 2$, and $a = 7$. Bubble in 7 on your answer grid.

Answer: 7

Example 5

Which of the given lines is parallel to $2y = 3x + 4$?

A) $6y = 3x - 4$
B) $2y = x + 2$
C) $4y = 6x - 1$
D) $y = 3x + 4$

Solution

Parallel lines have the same slope. Solve $2y = 3x + 4$ for y so it is in slope-intercept form. Dividing all the terms by 2, $y = \frac{3}{2}x + 2$ and $m = \frac{3}{2}$. Look at the answer choices to see which equation has slope $m = \frac{3}{2}$. Immediately eliminate choice D as its slope is $m = 3$. Examine the other choices. Answer A will have a slope of $m = \frac{1}{2}$, as will answer choice B. The answer must be C, but quickly check by dividing all the terms in choice C by 4; $m = \frac{6}{4} = \frac{3}{2}$.

Answer: C

Answers begin on page 661.

1. Find the slope of line k.

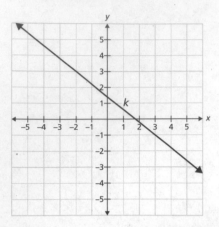

   A) $m = \dfrac{4}{5}$

   B) $m = -\dfrac{4}{5}$

   C) $m = \dfrac{5}{4}$

   D) $m = -\dfrac{5}{4}$

2. Find the slope of the line passing through point $P(-3, 4)$ and point $Q(4, 4)$.

3. Find the value of a so that the slope m of the line through $(-2, 6)$ and $(1, -3a)$ is -2.

4. What is the slope of the line perpendicular to the line $mx + 4y = 17$ if $mx + 4y = 17$ contains the point $\left(\dfrac{1}{3}, 4\right)$?

5. Find the slope of the line passing through point $C(1, 4)$ and point $D(1, -4)$.

   A) $m = 0$

   B) $m = \text{Undefined}$

   C) $m = 8$

   D) $m = -8$

1. The line $y = mx + 10$, where m is a constant, is graphed in the xy-plane. If the line contains the point (a, b), where $a \neq 0$ and $b \neq 0$, what is the slope of the line in terms of a and b?

   A) $\dfrac{b+10}{a}$

   B) $\dfrac{b-10}{a}$

   C) $\dfrac{a-b}{10}$

   D) $\dfrac{a+10}{b}$

Strategy: Substitute the point (a, b) into the given equation and solve for m, the slope. Then $b = ma + 10$, $b - ma = 10$, and $m = \dfrac{b-10}{a}$. This is answer choice B.

2. Which of the following represents a line that is perpendicular to the line with equation $y = -2x + 5$?

   A) $2y - x = 12$

   B) $y = -2x + 9$

   C) $2y - \dfrac{1}{2}x = 6$

   D) $2x + 2y = 12$

Strategy: A line perpendicular to $y = -2x + 5$ will have slope $m = \dfrac{1}{2}$. Eliminate answer choice B as it has the same slope as the given equation. Look at answer choice A. If we manipulate the formula so it is in slope-intercept form, $2y - x = 12$ becomes $2y = x + 12$, and, dividing all the terms by 2, $y = \dfrac{1}{2}x + 6$. Select choice A.

3. A line in the xy-plane passes through the origin and has slope $m = \dfrac{1}{4}$. Which of the following points lies on the line?

   A) $(0, 4)$

   B) $(1, 4)$

   C) $(4, 1)$

   D) $(8, 3)$

Strategy: First, determine the equation of the line. Because we are told the slope and a point, it is easiest to use point-slope form. Then $y - 0 = \dfrac{1}{4}(x - 0)$ and $y = \dfrac{1}{4}x$. Clearly, $(0, 4)$ is not correct. In this case, if $x = 1$, $y = \dfrac{1}{4}$, so choice B is also incorrect. When $x = 4$, $y = \dfrac{1}{4}(4)$ and $y = 1$. Select choice C.

4. Line p in the xy-plane contains points from each of quadrants I, III, and IV, but no points from quadrant II. Which of the following must be true?

A) The slope of line p is undefined.

B) The slope of line p is positive.

C) The slope of line p is negative.

D) The slope of line p is 0.

Strategy: Think through the question. A line running through all the quadrants but II cannot have a negative slope. Eliminate choice C. Lines with undefined or 0 slopes cannot run through three quadrants, so also eliminate answer choices A and D. Select answer choice B.

5. The graph of a linear function f has intercepts at $(c, 0)$ and $(0, d)$ in the xy-plane. If $c + d = 0$ and $c \neq d$, which of the following is true about the slope of the graph of f?

A) It is positive.

B) It equals 0.

C) It is undefined.

D) It is negative.

Strategy: Remember that the value of the slope is given by the formula

$m = \dfrac{y_2 - y_1}{x_2 - x_1}$. Let (x_1, y_1) be $(c, 0)$ and let (x_2, y_2) be $(0, d)$ and $m = \dfrac{d - 0}{0 - c} = -\dfrac{d}{c}$. But

we also know that $c + d = 0$ so $c = -d$. We can substitute $c = -d$ into the slope $-\dfrac{d}{c}$,

which becomes $\dfrac{-d}{-d} = 1$. The slope of the line is positive. Choose answer A.

SAT-Type Questions

Answers begin on page 662.

1. Which of the following is the general equation of the family of linear equations perpendicular to $6y = 4x - 3$?

A) $2y = 3x + k$

B) $2y = -3x + k$

C) $3y = 2x + k$

D) $3y = -2x + k$

2. If $f(x) = 2x + 5$, then what is the value of $f(-9) - f(0)$?

A) -23

B) -18

C) -13

D) -10

3. If the given table provides the values of a linear function f for certain values of x, which of the following defines $f(x)$?

x	−1	0	1	2
$f(x)$	3	1	−1	−3

A) $f(x) = -x + 1$

B) $f(x) = -x + 2$

C) $f(x) = -2x + 1$

D) $f(x) = -2x + 2$

4. Isaac's gas tank holds 19 gallons of gas at the beginning of his trip south. If he drives at the rate of 50 mph, he gets 25 miles to the gallon. Which of the following functions f models the number of gallons of gas remaining in his tank h hours after his trip begins?

A) $f(h) = 19 - \dfrac{50}{25h}$

B) $f(h) = \dfrac{25h - 19}{50}$

C) $f(h) = 19 - \dfrac{50h}{25}$

D) $f(h) = 19 - \dfrac{25h}{50}$

5. Which equation describes a line that is parallel to the line $5y = 25.5x + 105$?

A) $10y = 51x + 120$

B) $25y = 0.5x + 120$

C) $51y = 10x + 120$

D) $25.5y = 25x + 120$

6. In the figure below, what is the slope of line m?

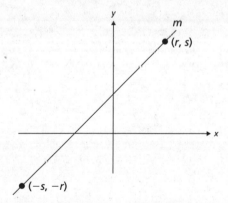

A) $-\dfrac{s}{r}$

B) $\dfrac{r}{s}$

C) $\dfrac{s}{r}$

D) 1

7. Eight values for x and the function f are given. If the function h is defined by $h(x) = f(2x - 3)$, what is the value of $h(4)$?

x	$f(x)$
1	–6
2	4
3	0
4	3
5	–2
6	4
7	–5
8	8

A) –2

B) 3

C) 5

D) 6

8. The cost of a family membership for the municipal pool is $10 for each member of the family plus $30 for a parking permit. Express this cost as a function of p, the number people in a family using a single car.

A) $f(p) = 40p$

B) $f(p) = 10p + 30$

C) $f(p) = 30p + 10$

D) $f(p) = 10p + 1$

9. Points on the line $3x + y = 1$ lie in which of the quadrants?

A) I and III only

B) I and IV only

C) I, II, and IV

D) I, III, and IV

10. If $P(x)$ equals the sale price of a $100 item offered at a discount of $x\%$, then a sale price of $80 can be expressed as

A) $P(80)$

B) $P(20)$

C) $P(100) - P(80)$

D) $100 - P(20)$

11. If a rectangle $ABCD$ is drawn in the xy-coordinate plane, as shown below, what is the product of the slopes of the sides $\overline{AB}$, $\overline{BC}$, $\overline{CD}$, and $\overline{DA}$?

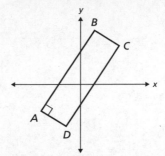

A) -1

B) $-\dfrac{1}{2}$

C) $\dfrac{1}{2}$

D) 1

12. The profit function f expressed as $f(x) = 4x - 80$ represents the profit for x items that are manufactured. How many items must be sold to break even?

A) 20 items

B) 40 items

C) 76 items

D) 80 items

13. The total daily profit P, in dollars, from making and selling x number of large salted bagels is given by the function $P(x) = 7x - (5x + b)$, where b is a constant. If 300 bagels were made and sold Saturday for a total profit of $250, what is the value of b?

A) 250

B) 300

C) 325

D) 350

14. If the graphs of $y = mx + b$ and $y = cx + d$ are perpendicular, which of the given statements is true?

A) $m = c$

B) $mc > 0$

C) $mc = -1$

D) $m = c^2$

15. Cilla produces custom-made picture frames. The function $C = f(n)$ represents the cost C of making n picture frames. If Cilla sells her frames at 60% above cost plus an additional 6% sales tax, which of the following represents her total income, including the sales tax, each week?

A) $1.066f(n)$

B) $0.6f(n)$

C) $1.66f(n)$

D) $1.696f(n)$

Student-Produced Response Questions

16. If $f(x) = 5x + 14$, what is $2f(2) - f(2)$?

17. The linear function $C(t) = p + ant$ models the cost for four college sophomores to purchase a car and gasoline for a three-year period. In this function, t is the number of years, p is the purchase price of the car, a is the average cost of gasoline per gallon, and n is the average number of gallons purchased per year. If $p = \$29,000$, $a = \$3.85$ per gallon, and $n = 832$ gallons per year, what is the cost (to the nearest dollar) for each student during the three years of ownership?

18. The equation of line n is $y = 3x + 8$. If line r is parallel to line n and the equation for line r is $y = mx + 16$, what is the value of m?

19. If the function f is defined by $f(x) = \frac{1}{12}x + 4$ and $f(a) = 6$, what is the value of a?

20. The monthly fee for an online movie service is $10.99. The cost of viewing regular movies online is included with the monthly fee, but there is an additional fee of $0.85 per movie to rent premium movies online. For one month, Isla's membership and premium movie rental fees were $23.74. How many premium movies did Isla rent online that month?

LESSON 4:

Systems of Equations and Systems of Inequalities

- Solving Systems of Linear Equations in Two Variables
- Solving Systems of Linear Inequalities in Two Variables

Explain Solving Systems of Linear Equations in Two Variables

A **system of equations** is a group of two or more equations with the same set of variables that are graphed on the same xy-plane. Systems can contain linear equations, nonlinear equations, or some combination of both linear and nonlinear equations. The solution or solutions to a system of equations indicates the point or points where all the lines or curves intersect.

In this lesson, we will discuss solving systems of only linear equations. The basic principle behind solving a system is to work to first eliminate one variable, and then use the value you obtain to solve for the other variable. The method you use to eliminate a variable depends upon the equations.

Set of Equations	Method	Solution
$x + y = 15$ (1) $y = 2x$ (2)	**Substitution** Since $y = 2x$, *substitute* $2x$ for y in equation (1).	$x + y = 15$ (1) $x + 2x = 15$ $3x = 15$ $x = 5$ Substitute 5 for x in equation (2), and solve for y: $y = 2x$ (2) $y = 2(5)$ $y = 10$
$x + y = 10$ (1) $x - y = 4$ (2)	**Addition** Adding the two equations will eliminate one of the variables.	$x + y = 10$ $\underline{x - y = \ \ 4}$ $2x \ \ = 14$ $x = 7$ Substitute 7 for x in either equation, and solve for y: $x + y = 10$ (1) $7 + y = 10$ $y = 3$
$x + y = 9$ (1) $x + 2y = 11$ (2)	**Subtraction** Subtracting the two equations will eliminate one of the variables.	$x + y = 9$ $\underline{-x - 2y = -11}$ $-y = -2$ $y = 2$ Substitute 2 for y in either equation and solve for x: $x + y = 9$ (1) $x + 2 = 9$ $x = 7$

Note that systems of equations can have one solution, no solutions, or an infinite number of solutions.

Example 1

Which of the following ordered pairs (x, y) satisfies the system of equations below?

$x = 14 - 2y$
$3x - 4y = 2$

A) $(4, 6)$
B) $(6, 4)$
C) $(-4, 22)$
D) $(22, -4)$

Solution

Examine the structure of the given system and notice that in the first equation, x is represented in terms of y. Substitute $14 - 2y$ for x in the second equation. Then

$3(14 - 2y) - 4y = 2$	Distribute.
$42 - 6y - 4y = 2$	Combine like terms.
$42 - 10y = 2$	
$42 - 2 = 10y$	
$40 = 10y$	Solve for y.
$4 = y$	

Look at the answer choices. Only choice B has a y-value of 4. You can stop here and select answer B.

Answer: B

Example 2

If (x, y) is the solution to the system of equations below, what is the value of x?

$x + y = 8$
$x - y = 2$

Solution

The equations are already in standard form, and the y terms have opposite signs. If we add the equations together, we can solve for x directly:

$x + y = 8$
$\underline{x - y = 2}$ Add the columns.

$\dfrac{2x}{2} = \dfrac{10}{2}$ Divide both sides of the equation by 2.

$x = 5$

Bubble in 5 on your answer grid.

Example 3

In the system of equations below, k is a constant and x and y are variables. For what value of k will the system of equations have no solution?

$5y - 30x = 4$

$9y - kx = -8$

A) 54

B) $\dfrac{8}{9}$

C) 6

D) $\dfrac{2}{3}$

Solution

Recall from Lesson 3 that a system of linear equations will have no solution when they represent parallel lines. The equations of parallel lines have the same slope. We are looking for the value of k that will make both of the given equations have the same slope. Manipulate both equations from standard form into slope-intercept form. Then

$5y - 30x = 4$ $9y - kx = -8$

$5y = 30x + 4$ $9y = kx - 8$

$y = 6x + \dfrac{4}{5}$ $y = \dfrac{kx}{9} - \dfrac{8}{9}$

Now set the slope terms equal to each other and solve: $\dfrac{6}{1} = \dfrac{k}{9}$, $k = 54$.

Answer: A

Answers begin on page 663.

For questions 1 – 5, solve each of the given systems.

1. $y = 2x$
    $x + y = 9$

    A) $(-6, -3)$
    B) $(-3, -6)$
    C) $(6, 3)$
    D) $(3, 6)$

2. $y = 2x$
    $3x + 2y = 28$

    A) $(8, 4)$
    B) $(4, 8)$
    C) $(-8, -4)$
    D) $(-4, -8)$

3. $x + y = 5$
    $2x - y = 7$

    A) $(4, 1)$
    B) $(1, 4)$
    C) $(-4, -1)$
    D) $(-1, -4)$

4. $x - 3y = 1$
    $2x + 3y = 20$

    A) $(-2, -7)$
    B) $(-7, -2)$
    C) $(2, 7)$
    D) $(7, 2)$

5. $2x + 3y = 2$
    $4x + 3y = 3$

    A) $\left(\dfrac{1}{2}, \dfrac{1}{3}\right)$

    B) $\left(\dfrac{1}{3}, \dfrac{1}{2}\right)$

    C) $\left(2, -\dfrac{3}{4}\right)$

    D) $\left(2, \dfrac{3}{4}\right)$

Model SAT Questions

1. The graph of a line in the xy-plane has slope $m = -\dfrac{1}{2}$ and contains the point $(0, 5)$. The graph of a second line in the same coordinate plane passes through the points $(1, -3)$ and $(2, -1)$. If the two lines intersect at the point (a, b), what is the value of $a + b$?

    A) 4
    B) 5.5
    C) 1
    D) 7

Strategy: First we must determine the equations of the lines described. A line with slope $-\dfrac{1}{2}$ and point $(0, 5)$, which is the y-intercept, has an equation of $y = -\dfrac{1}{2}x + 5$. To calculate the equation of the second line, find the slope using the given points. Then $m = \dfrac{y_2 - y_1}{x_2 - x_1} = \dfrac{-1 - (-3)}{2 - 1} = 2$. Now use one of the given points to find the y-intercept. So, $y - (-3) = 2(x - 1)$ and $y + 3 = 2x - 2$. Solving for y, $y = 2x - 5$.

The two equations are $y = -\frac{1}{2}x + 5$ and $y = 2x - 5$. Both equations are equal to y, so set them equal to each other and solve for x: $-\frac{1}{2}x + 5 = 2x - 5$. Multiplying through by 2 to eliminate the fraction, $-x + 10 = 4x - 10$, $-5x = -20$, and $x = 4$. Solving for the y-coordinate, $y = 2(4) - 5 = 3$. The point of intersection is $(a, b) = (4, 3)$ and $4 + 3 = 7$. This is answer choice D.

2. In the system of equations below, a and b are constants. If the system has infinitely many solutions, what is the value of ab?

$ax + by = 6$
$6x + 9y = 18$

Strategy: For a system to have infinitely many solutions, both the slope term and the y-intercept in both equations must be alike. Examine the second equation. It is set equal to 18 while the first equation is set equal to 6. Recall that 18 divided by 3 is 6. This means that equation #1 is equation #2 divided by 3. Then $ax + by = 6$ becomes $2x + 3y = 6$ and $2(3) = 6$. Bubble in 6 on your answer grid.

3. Alannis has twelve pieces of U.S. paper currency that is a mixture of tens and twenties. In total she has $200 in value. How many of each bill does she have?

    A) 4 tens and 8 twenties

    B) 6 tens and 6 twenties

    C) 7 tens and 5 twenties

    D) 8 tens and 4 twenties

Strategy: We must create the system of equations that fits this scenario. Let $x =$ the number of \$10 bills and let $y =$ the number of \$20 bills. Then $x + y = 12$ since she has twelve pieces of U.S. paper currency. We also know the total value of currency is \$200. So, $10x + 20y = 200$. This system is most easily solved by substitution if we manipulate $x + y = 12$ into $x = 12 - y$. Then $10(12 - y) + 20y = 200$, $120 - 10y + 20y = 200$, and $120 + 10y = 200$. Solving for y, $y = \dfrac{200 - 120}{10} = 8$. Alannis has eight \$20 bills. We can solve for x in the traditional way or we can reason that Alannis must have four \$10 bills. Select answer choice A.

4. In the system of linear equations below, c and d are constants. If the system has infinitely many solutions, what is the value of $\dfrac{d}{c}$?

   $3x + 12y = 18$
   $cx + dy = 6$

   A) $\dfrac{1}{4}$

   B) 4

   C) 2

   D) 1

Strategy: Notice that in the first listed equation, the sum 18 is 3 times the sum in the second equation, 6. Multiply the second equation by 3 to get $3cx + 3dy = 18$. Since the right-hand sides of both equations are equal, equate each term to solve for both c and d. Then $3cx = 3x$ and $3dy = 12y$. Simplify by dividing both sides of $3cx = 3x$ by $3x$ and $3dy = 12y$ by $3y$. Then $c = 1$ and $d = 4$; $\dfrac{d}{c} = \dfrac{4}{1} = 4$. Alternately, since a system with infinitely many solutions contains two equal equations, use $3x + 12y = 18$ and reason that $\dfrac{d}{c} = \dfrac{12}{3} = 4$. Select answer choice B.

5. A group of families is going to see a movie. The adult tickets cost \$13.75 each and the children's tickets cost \$9.50 each. If the total cost of the movie tickets was \$161.75 for 13 people, how many adults were in the group?

   A) 4

   B) 13

   C) 9

   D) 5

Strategy: Write a system of linear equations and solve. Let $a =$ the number of adults in the group and let $c =$ the number of children in the group. Then $a + c = 13$ and $13.75a + 9.50c = 161.75$. This system is most easily solved using substitution. Solve $a + c = 13$ for c and $c = 13 - a$. Then $13.75a + 9.50c = 161.75$ becomes $13.75a + 9.50(13 - a) = 161.75$. Distributing, $13.75a + 123.50 - 9.50a = 161.75$. Collect the like terms and solve for a so $4.25a = 38.25$, and $a = 9$. This is answer choice C.

Explain   Solving Systems of Linear Inequalities in Two Variables

Linear inequalities in two variables are usually written in one of the following forms:

$Ax + By > C$
$Ax + By \geq C$
$Ax + By < C$
$Ax + By \leq C$

Like systems of linear equations, systems of linear inequalities contain at least two inequalities in like variables. Systems of linear inequalities in two variables contain more than one inequality. Remember that the solution to an inequality is a set of numbers rather than a single number. Similarly, the solution of a system of linear inequalities in two variables is any ordered pair (x, y) that produces a true statement when the values of x and y are substituted into each inequality in the system. The methods we reviewed for solving linear equations can be used to solve linear inequalities.

Think It Through

Example 1

In the xy-plane, if a point with coordinates (a, b) lies in the solution set of the system of inequalities below, what is the maximum possible value of b?

$y \leq 2x - 1$
$y \leq -x + 8$

A) $b = 3$
B) $b = 4$
C) $b = 5$
D) $b = 6$

Solution

The solution to the system of equations is most easily found using the substitution method. Both inequalities have the variable y on the left-hand side, so $2x - 1 = -x + 8$. Then $3x = 9$ and $x = 3$. Using either inequality, find that $y = 5$. Since both inequalities include a less than sign ($<$), 5 is the largest possible value of b. You can also graph these two inequalities on your calculator to determine the largest value of b.

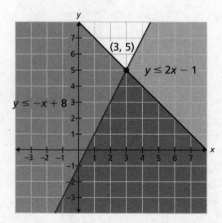

Answer: C

Example 2

A delivery truck must travel over a bridge in a small town with a weight limit of 50,000 pounds. The truck itself weighs 13,500 pounds and its cargo consists of large boxes weighing either 50 pounds or 75 pounds. The cargo space of the truck can carry a maximum of 55 boxes. Which of the following systems of inequalities represents the number of 50-pound and 75-pound boxes the truck can carry and still be allowed to travel over the bridge?

A) $\begin{cases} x - y \leq 55 \\ 50x + 75y \leq 36{,}500 \end{cases}$

B) $\begin{cases} x + y \leq 55 \\ 50x + 75y \leq 36{,}500 \end{cases}$

C) $\begin{cases} x + y \leq 55 \\ 50x + 75y \leq 50{,}000 \end{cases}$

D) $\begin{cases} x + y \leq 55 \\ 50x - 75y \leq 50{,}000 \end{cases}$

Strategy: The cargo truck can only carry 55 boxes. If we let $x =$ the number of 50-pound boxes and let $y =$ the number of 75 pound boxes, then $x + y \leq 55$. The bridge the truck must travel over can support no more than 50,000 pounds and the truck itself weighs 13,500 pounds. Then letting the variables remain defined as above, $50x + 75y \leq 50{,}000 - 13{,}500$ which simplifies into $50x + 75y \leq 36{,}500$.

Answer: B

•••••• Practice **Solving Systems of Linear Inequalities in Two Variables** •••••••••••••

Answers begin on page 664.

1. Which of the given ordered pairs is in the solution set of:

   $y \geq 2x + 10$

   $y > 4x$

   A) $(-1, -4)$
   B) $(1, 4)$
   C) $(-10, -40)$
   D) $(10, 40)$

2. Which ordered pair is in the solution set of:

   $y \leq x + 1$

   $y \geq -2x - 5$

   A) $(-2, 6)$
   B) $(-4, 0)$
   C) $(2, 6)$
   D) $(0, 6)$

3. Which of the following systems of inequalities is represented by the shaded regions of the graph below?

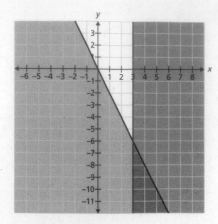

A) $\begin{cases} y \leq -2x \\ x \leq 3 \end{cases}$

B) $\begin{cases} y \leq -2x \\ x \geq 3 \end{cases}$

C) $\begin{cases} y \geq -2x \\ x \geq 3 \end{cases}$

D) $\begin{cases} y \geq -2x \\ x \leq 3 \end{cases}$

4. Which of the following points satisfies the system of linear inequalities below?

$x + y < 3$
$x - 3y > 10$

A) $(10, -1)$
B) $(1, 3)$
C) $(-0.5, -5)$
D) $(-1, -3)$

5. In which quadrant of the xy-coordinate system would the solution to the system of inequalities, $x > 0$ and $y < 0$, be found?

A) Quadrant I
B) Quadrant II
C) Quadrant III
D) Quadrant IV

6. In the xy-plane, if a point with coordinates (a, b) lies in the solution set of the system of inequalities below, what is the minimum possible value of b?

$y \geq x + 1$
$y \geq -2x - 11$

A) $b = 4$
B) $b = 3$
C) $b = -3$
D) $b = -4$

Model SAT Questions

1. Graphite tennis racquets can be bought for $150 and aluminum tennis racquets for $100. The specialty store *Point-Set-Match* wants to order no more than $900 worth of tennis racquets, and plans to order more aluminum racquets than graphite ones. Which of the following systems of inequalities can represent the possible combinations of graphite racquets (x) and aluminum racquets (y) that can be ordered?

A) $\begin{cases} y > x \\ 150x + 100y < 900 \end{cases}$

B) $\begin{cases} y > x \\ 150x + 100y \leq 900 \end{cases}$

C) $\begin{cases} y < x \\ 150x + 100y \geq 900 \end{cases}$

D) $\begin{cases} y \geq x \\ 150x + 100 \leq 900 \end{cases}$

Strategy: The store plans to order more aluminum rackets than graphite rackets, so eliminate choices C and D. Represent the cost of x graphite rackets as 150x and represent the cost of y aluminum rackets as 100y. The total cost of the racquets is then 150x + 100y. The store wants to spend no more than $900, so 150x + 100y ≤ 900. This is choice B.

2. If the system of inequalities $y \geq 2x + 1$ and $y \leq 2x$ are graphed in the xy-plane, which quadrant contains no solutions to the system?

    A) Quadrant I

    B) Quadrant II

    C) There are solutions in all four quadrants.

    D) There are no solutions in any of the four quadrants.

Strategy: Examine the slopes of the given inequalities. They are both $m = 2$, so the boundaries of these inequalities run parallel to each other. The inequality $y \geq 2x + 1$ will have shading above the line but the inequality $y \leq 2x$ will have shading below the inequality line. There will not be overlap between the shaded areas, so this system of inequalities has no solution. You can verify this using your graphing calculator. The best answer is choice D.

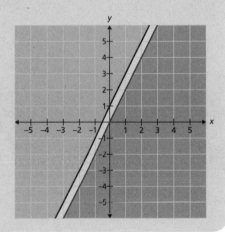

SAT-Type Questions

Answers begin on page 665.

1. Which of the following ordered pairs (x, y) satisfies the system of equations below?

    $x + 3y = 0$

    $2x + 5y = 3$

    A) $(-3, 9)$

    B) $(9, -3)$

    C) $(3, -1)$

    D) $(-9, 3)$

2. The graph of a line in the xy-plane has slope $m = 3$ and contains the point $(1, 7)$. The graph of a second line passes through the points $(-4, 2)$ and $(2, 5)$. If the two lines intersect at the point (p, q), what is the value of $p + q$?

    A) 4

    B) 7

    C) −2

    D) 2

3. The Stuffed Animal Toy Company needs 2.5 yards of brown cloth to make a monkey and 6 yards of brown cloth to make a bear. The monkey's arms, legs, and tail require a total of 4 yards of flexible plastic tubing, while the bear's legs require only 2 yards of plastic tubing. The toy company has 352 yards of brown cloth and 460 yards of plastic tubing in stock. If m = the number of monkeys and b = the number of bears, then the number of the two types of stuffed animals that can be made without buying more cloth or tubing can be determined by which of the following systems of inequalities (where $m \geq 0$ and $b \geq 0$)?

A) $\begin{cases} 4m + 2b \leq 352 \\ 2.5m + 6b \leq 460 \end{cases}$

B) $\begin{cases} 2.5m + 4b \leq 352 \\ 2m + 6b \leq 460 \end{cases}$

C) $\begin{cases} 2.5m + 6b \leq 352 \\ 4m + 2b \leq 460 \end{cases}$

D) $\begin{cases} 2.5m + 2b \leq 352 \\ 4m + 6b \leq 460 \end{cases}$

4. Which of the given sets of inequalities describes the shaded area of the graph?

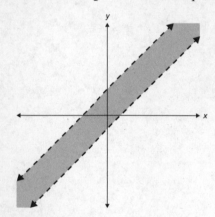

A) $\begin{cases} y > x - 1 \\ y < x + 2 \end{cases}$

B) $\begin{cases} y < x - 1 \\ y > x + 2 \end{cases}$

C) $\begin{cases} y < x - 1 \\ y \geq x + 2 \end{cases}$

D) $\begin{cases} y > -1 \\ y < 2 \end{cases}$

5. The difference between two numbers is 4. If twice the larger number x is equal to three more than three times the smaller number y, what are the numbers written as an ordered pair (x, y)?

A) $(-5, -1)$

B) $(-1, -5)$

C) $(9, 5)$

D) $(5, 9)$

6. In a vegetable store, a customer paid \$8.80 for 3 pounds of tomatoes and 5 pounds of potatoes. A second customer paid \$15.15 for 7 pounds of tomatoes and 6 pounds of potatoes. What is the positive difference in the price per pound of tomatoes and potatoes?

   A) \$0.40

   B) \$1.35

   C) \$2.21

   D) There is not enough information to answer this question.

7. Find the solution set for the system:

   $4(x + 1) = 2y$

   $2x = y - 2$

   A) No solution.

   B) Infinitely many solutions.

   C) $(1, 4)$

   D) $(2, 6)$

8. The perimeter of a rectangular garden is 320 yards. If the length is 8 yards less than 3 times the width, what are the dimensions of the garden?

   A) length = 119 yards, width = 41 yards

   B) length = 118 yards, width = 42 yards

   C) length = 116 yards, width = 44 yards

   D) There is not enough information to answer this question.

9. The Key Club has 20 cups of flour to make cookies and tarts. A tray of cookies requires 2 cups of flour; a tray of tarts requires 1 cup of flour. It takes one-half hour to make a tray of cookies and 45 minutes to make a tray of tarts. The club has access to only one oven. The total supply of cookies and tarts must be produced in 8 hours. Which system of inequalities describes the constraints faced by the Key Club if c represents the number of trays of cookies and t represents the number of trays of tarts?

   A) $\begin{cases} \dfrac{c}{2} + 45 \le 8 \\ 2c + t \le 20 \end{cases}$

   B) $\begin{cases} \dfrac{c}{2} + \dfrac{3t}{4} \le 8 \\ c + t \le 20 \end{cases}$

   C) $\begin{cases} \dfrac{c}{2} + 45t \le 8 \\ c + 2t \le 20 \end{cases}$

   D) $\begin{cases} \dfrac{c}{2} + \dfrac{3t}{4} \le 8 \\ 2c + t \le 20 \end{cases}$

10. Find the solution set for the system:

$3x + 6 = 2y$

$6(x + 6) = 4y$

A) No solution.

B) Infinitely many solutions.

C) $(2, 6)$

D) $(4, 9)$

Student-Produced Response Questions

11. If $0.005 \leq x \leq 0.5$ and $0.01 \leq y \leq 0.10$, then what is the largest value of $\dfrac{x}{y}$?

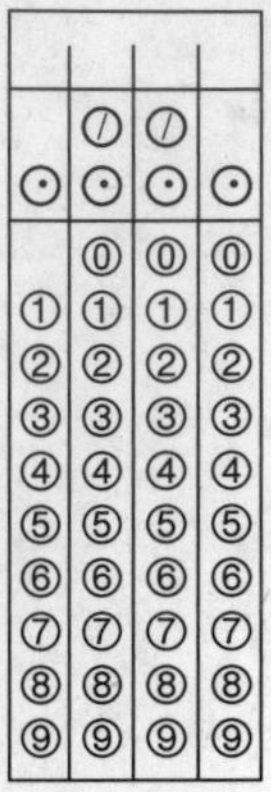

12. What is the value of y where the boundaries of these two inequalities intersect?

$y \geq 3x - 2$

$y \geq \dfrac{3}{2}x + 4$

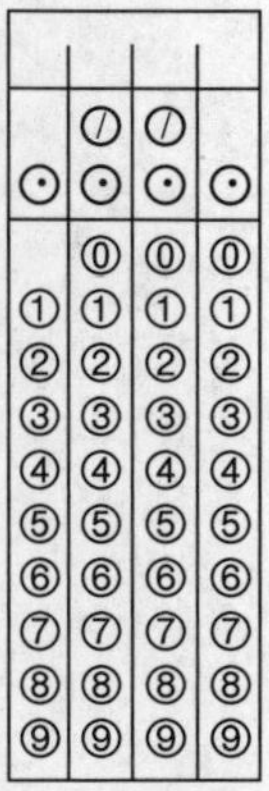

13. The difference between two numbers is 24, and the sum of those numbers is 48. What is the product of these numbers?

14. If (x, y) is the solution to the system of equations below, what is the value of x?

$$4x + y = 12$$
$$2x - \frac{1}{2}y = 2$$

15. Mrs. Kellen's most recent math test consisted of 50 questions. Some of the questions were worth 2 points and the rest of the questions were worth 3 points. If there were 115 points available on the test, how many questions were worth 2 points?

Explain Direct and Inverse Variation Equations and Computation

Two special types of functions are called **direct variation** and **inverse variation**.

Direct variation is a function in which the ratio between a number, y, in the range, and the corresponding number, x, in the domain, is the same for all pairs of the function. Another way of stating this is that direct variation is a relationship between two variables in which one of the variables is a constant multiple of the other. We say that y varies in proportion with x, or that y is directly proportional to x. Let $y = f(x)$. Then, if $f(a_1) = b_1$ and $f(a_2) = b_2$, it follows that $\dfrac{b_1}{a_1} = \dfrac{b_2}{a_2}$.

The equation for direct variation is $\dfrac{y}{x} = k$ or $y = kx$, where k is the value of the ratio of the two proportional quantities x and y, and is called the **constant of proportionality**. Note that in direct variation, the cross-products for $\dfrac{y_1}{x_1} = \dfrac{y_2}{x_2}$ are equal. For example, if $f(4) = 3$ and $f(8) = 6$, then $\dfrac{3}{4} = \dfrac{6}{8}$. We can verify by cross-multiplication that the proportion is true: $3 \cdot 8 = 4 \cdot 6 \Rightarrow 24 = 24$.

In **inverse variation**, as one variable changes, the other changes proportionally to the *inverse* of the first. We say that y varies inversely with x. We can model this relationship with the equation $y = \dfrac{k}{x}$, where k is the **constant of variation**. Then $xy = k$ for all points (x, y) on the graph of the function.

Think It Through

Example 1

If y varies directly as x, and $y = 8$ when $x = 1$, what is the value of y when $x = 4$?

Solution

To solve, set up a proportion: $\frac{y}{x} \Rightarrow \frac{8}{1} = \frac{y}{4}$. Cross-multiply and $y = 32$.

We can check our answer by substitution: $\frac{8}{1} = \frac{32}{4}$, $1 \cdot 32 = 8 \cdot 4$

and $32 = 32$.

Answer: 32

Example 2

If a weight of 15 ounces attached to the end of a spring stretches that spring 5 inches, what weight would stretch the spring 12 inches if the elongation, *E*, is directly proportional to the weight, *W*?

Solution

The elongation of the spring is directly proportional to the amount

of weight attached to it. So, $\frac{E_1}{W_1} = \frac{E_2}{W_2}$ and $\frac{5 \text{ inches}}{15 \text{ ounces}} = \frac{12 \text{ inches}}{W_2}$.

Cross-multiply so that $5W_2 = 12(15)$ which becomes $5W_2 = 180$.

Then $W_2 = 36$ ounces.

Answer: 36

Example 3

What would be the constant of variation, *k*, if *y* varies inversely with *x*, and $y = 10$ when $x = 1.4$?

Solution

Simply substitute the known values into the formula for inverse variation.

Then $10 = \dfrac{k}{1.4}$ and $k = 14$.

Answer: 14

$$
\begin{array}{|c|c|c|c|}
\hline
1 & 4 & & \\
\hline
\end{array}
$$

Example 4

Using the information in Example 3, find the value of x when $y = 21$.

Solution

We again substitute in the equation $y = \dfrac{k}{x}$. Then $21 = \dfrac{14}{x}$ and $x = \dfrac{14}{21}$ which reduces to $\dfrac{2}{3}$.

Answer: $\dfrac{2}{3}$

$$
\begin{array}{|c|c|c|c|}
\hline
2 & / & 3 & \\
\hline
\end{array}
$$

Answers begin on page 667.

1. If y varies directly as x and $y = 0.5$ when $x = 6$, what is the value of x when $y = 3$?

4. If a varies directly as b and $a = 4$ when $b = 9$, what is the value of b when $a = 6$?

2. If b varies inversely as h and $b = 8$ when $h = 9$, what is the value of b when $h = 6$?

5. If x varies directly as the square of y and $x = 12$ when $y = 4$, what is the value of x when $y = 6$?

3. If x varies inversely as y and $x = 12$ when $y = 8$, what is the value of x when $y = 10$?

6. If a varies directly as the square of x and $a = 45$ when $x = 3$, what is the constant of proportionality?

1. In a freshwater lake, the increase in water pressure varies directly with the increase in water depth. If a scuba diver feels 21.65 pounds per square inch of pressure at a depth of 50 feet, how deep is he when the pressure is 38.97 pounds per square inch?

   A) 48.9 feet

   B) 65 feet

   C) 90 feet

   D) 100 feet

Strategy: Immediately eliminate answer choice A; since the pressure increased from 21.65 lb/in² to 38.97 lb/in², the diver must be at a depth of more than 50 feet. Now set up a proportion that reflects the direct variation relationship among the variables: $\dfrac{21.65}{50} = \dfrac{38.97}{d}$. Cross-multiply and $21.65d = 1948.50$, $d = 90$ feet. This is answer choice C.

2. The number of days needed to complete a job varies inversely with the number of people working on the job if all the people work at the same rate. If 15 people can dig a trench in 3 days, how fast can 9 people dig the same-sized trench?

Strategy: This is an inverse variation problem, so $xy = k$. In this case, $15 \cdot 3 = k$ and $k = 45$. Divide 45 by 9 and you obtain the answer 5. It will take 9 people 5 days to dig the same-sized trench. Bubble in 5 on your answer grid.

3. If a varies inversely as the square of b and directly as c, and $a = 4$ when $b = 4$ and $c = 8$, then what is the value of a when $c = 18$ and $b = 6$?

   A) 2

   B) 4

   C) 6

   D) 8

Strategy: Pay close attention to the wording of this problem. Since a varies inversely as the square of b and directly as c we can write $a = \dfrac{ck}{b^2}$. Substituting in the given values, $4 = \dfrac{8k}{4^2}$ which becomes $4 = \dfrac{k}{2}$ and $k = 8$. But ultimately we need to know the value a when $c = 18$ and $b = 6$. Using the value of k, $a = \dfrac{18 \cdot 8}{6^2} = \dfrac{144}{36} = 4$. Select answer choice B.

SAT-Type Questions

Answers begin on page 667.

1. Which of the following tables does <u>not</u> represent direct variation?

   A)

x	1	2	5
y	5	10	25

   B)

A	1	$\frac{1}{2}$	$\frac{1}{3}$
B	2	1	1

   C)

R	−5	3	7
S	10	−6	−14

   D)

q	$\frac{1}{4}$	$\frac{1}{3}$	$\frac{1}{2}$
r	$\frac{1}{2}$	$\frac{2}{3}$	1

2. Every year a band is paid \$450 to play at the county fair. Let r represent the amount each member receives and let n represent the number of members in the band. The inverse variation relationship between r and n is best represented as

   A) $\dfrac{450}{r} = \dfrac{1}{n}$

   B) $r + n = 450$

   C) $\dfrac{n}{r} = 450$

   D) $rn = 450$

3. If it takes 4 construction workers 3 hours to pave a playground, how many hours will it take 8 construction workers to complete the same task?

   A) 0.25 hours

   B) 0.5 hours

   C) 1.5 hours

   D) 6 hours

4. If a teacher can score 4 SAT essays in 1 hour and 15 minutes, how long will it take the teacher to score 100 essays?

    A) 25 hours

    B) 31.25 hours

    C) 75 hours

    D) 90.25 hours

5. Which of the following equations does <u>not</u> represent direct variation?

    A) $y = 5x$

    B) $y = \dfrac{1}{3}x$

    C) $xy = 8$

    D) $\dfrac{y}{x} = 13$

6. Which of the following tables represents y varying directly with x?

    A)

x	y
3	5
4	6
5	7

    B)

x	y
3	5
4	4
5	3

    C)

x	y
3	9
4	16
5	25

    D)

x	y
3	6
4	8
5	10

7. The minimum stopping distance for a moving car is calculated to be directly proportional to the square of the car's speed. If a certain car has a stopping distance of 44 feet when traveling at 30 mph, what will be the stopping distance for the same car traveling at 45 mph?

    A) 31 feet

    B) 66 feet

    C) 99 feet

    D) 97 feet

Student-Produced Response Questions

8. A mass of 50 kilograms causes a wooden beam to bend 6 centimeters. If the amount of bending varies directly with the object's mass, what mass will cause the beam to bend 8.7 centimeters?

9. The price of a diamond varies directly as the square of its weight. If a diamond weighing 1.8 carats costs $5,253 what is the cost of a diamond of similar quality weighing 1.2 carats? Round to the nearest dollar.

10. The electrical resistance of a given wire varies directly as the length. What is the resistance of 300 feet of that wire having 0.00027 ohms of resistance per foot?

LESSON 6:

Understanding and Interpreting the Algebraic Connections Between Linear Equations and Their Graphical Representations

- The *xy*-plane; Distance and Midpoint Formulas

- More on Functions; Other Graphical Representations

Explain The *xy*-Plane; Distance and Midpoint Formulas

We have referred to the *xy*-plane and coordinate pairs in previous lessons. In this lesson, we will formally define these terms and discuss the connection between a linear equation and its graph. The **xy-plane**, also known as the **coordinate plane**, is a 2-dimensional space that contains **coordinate axes**, which are perpendicular lines of reference for labeling points in a plane. The horizontal number line is called the *x*-axis and the vertical number line is the *y*-axis. The two axes intersect at the point (0, 0), which is called the **origin**. The coordinates of a point in the plane are an ordered pair of numbers (*x*, *y*). These ordered pairs can also be called **coordinate pairs**. In the illustration below, (–4, 2), (5, 2), (–4, –3), and (3, –3) are all coordinate pairs.

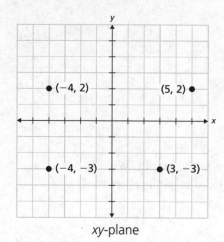

xy-plane

On the SAT, you will be expected to not only generate linear functions within contexts, but you will also be asked to select the appropriate graph based on a description of the function. You may also have to determine the key features of the graph from its equation or you may be given a graph and be required to connect it to the correct equation. The SAT may also ask you to determine how a graph might be impacted by a change in its equation. We have already touched on some of these tasks in previous lessons and we will briefly revisit these topics in subsequent lessons where appropriate.

Questions about linear equations and the *xy*-plane can be asked in several different ways. To ensure you are thoroughly prepared for the SAT exam, we will now review the distance and midpoint formulas and demonstrate how the formulas are connected to these types of questions.

To find the length of the line segment connecting two given points, with coordinates (x_1, y_1) and (x_2, y_2), in the *xy*-plane, use the distance formula $d = \sqrt{(x_2 - x_1)^2 + (y_2 - y_1)^2}$. Note that you can also determine the distance between two points in the *xy*-plane using the Pythagorean theorem. This is discussed in more detail in Category 4.

The midpoint formula is $(\bar{x}, \bar{y}) = \left(\dfrac{x_1 + x_2}{2}, \dfrac{y_1 + y_2}{2} \right)$. This formula will generate the point

that divides the line segment defined by its two end points, with coordinates (x_1, y_1) and (x_2, y_2), into two equal parts. Notice that with this formula, you are finding the average of the *x*- and *y*-coordinates. The horizontal lines over the *x* and *y* are read as "*x*-bar" and "*y*-bar."

Think It Through

Example 1

Find the distance between the points (–6, 2) and (1, 5).

A) $\sqrt{10}$
B) 10
C) $\sqrt{58}$
D) 58

Solution

Utilize the distance formula. Let $(x_1, y_1) = (-6, 2)$ and let $(x_2, y_2) = (1, 5)$. Then
$d = \sqrt{\left(1 - (-6)\right)^2 + (5 - 2)^2}$ which becomes $\sqrt{7^2 + 3^2}$. Simplifying, $\sqrt{49 + 9} = \sqrt{58}$.

Answer: C

Example 2

Find the midpoint of (–2, 5) and (8, –1).

A) (3, 2)
B) (10, 6)
C) (5, 3)
D) (4, 2)

Solution

Use the midpoint formula: $(\bar{x}, \bar{y}) = \left(\dfrac{x_1 + x_2}{2}, \dfrac{y_1 + y_2}{2} \right)$. Then
$\left(\dfrac{-2 + 8}{2}, \dfrac{5 + (-1)}{2} \right) = \left(\dfrac{6}{2}, \dfrac{4}{2} \right)$. Simplifying, the midpoint of the line
segment connecting (–2, 5) and (8, –1) is (3, 2).

Answer: A

Example 3

Find the endpoint *B* of $\overline{AB}$ when *A* is (–2, 8) and the midpoint *M* is (4, 11).

A) (1, 9.5)
B) (8, 12)
C) (1, 14)
D) (10, 14)

Solution

Because the midpoint of a line segment is a bisector, the absolute value of the distance from one endpoint to the midpoint is the same as the absolute value of the distance from the midpoint to the subsequent endpoint. To find the coordinates of the other endpoint, use the *loop* method. Draw the line segment and count from the known endpoint to the midpoint for the *x*-coordinates and repeat the pattern to find the other endpoint *x*-coordinate. Then count from the known endpoint to the midpoint for the *y*-coordinates and repeat the pattern to find the other endpoint *y*-coordinate.

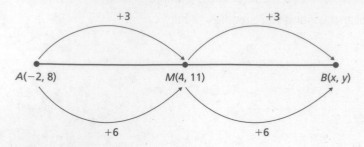

Thus, $x = 4 + 6 = 10$ and $y = 11 + 3 = 14$.
The coordinates of the endpoint B are $(10, 14)$.

Answer: D

· · · · · **Practice** **The *xy*-Plane; Distance and Midpoint Formulas** · · · · · · · ·

Answers begin on page 668.

1. Find the distance between the points $(1, -1)$ and $(4, -5)$.

2. Find the distance between $(-14, -1)$ and $(-2, -6)$.

3. Find the midpoint between $(-4, 4)$ and $(4, 0)$.

   A) $(0, 0)$
   B) $(0, 2)$
   C) $(4, 2)$
   D) $(8, -4)$

4. Find the endpoint B of $\overline{AB}$ when A is $(1, 3)$ and the midpoint M is $(3, 0)$.

   A) $(5, 1.5)$
   B) $(4, -2)$
   C) $(5, -3)$
   D) $(7, -3)$

Questions 1 and 2 refer to the following graph.

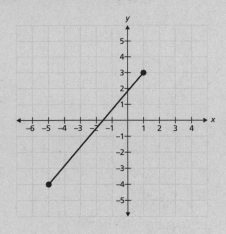

1. What is the product of the coordinates of the midpoint of the given line segment?

Strategy: First determine the coordinates of the endpoints from the graph. They are (1, 3) and (–5, –4). So, $(\bar{x}, \bar{y}) = \left(\dfrac{1+(-5)}{2}, \dfrac{3+(-4)}{2}\right)$ and $\left(\dfrac{-4}{2}, \dfrac{-1}{2}\right) = \left(-2, -\dfrac{1}{2}\right)$. The product of the coordinates of the midpoint is 1. Bubble in 1 on your answer grid.

2. What is the slope of the given line segment?

Strategy: We already know the coordinates of the endpoints, so substitute them into the slope formula from Lesson 3. Then $m = \dfrac{-4-3}{-5-1} = \dfrac{7}{6}$. Grid in $\dfrac{7}{6}$ on your bubble sheet.

3. Suppose that a line segment has endpoints $A(1, 3)$ and $B(x, y)$. If the midpoint M has coordinates of $(x + 3A, y + 2A)$, what are the coordinates of B?

A) $(4, 9)$

B) $(13, 11)$

C) $(9, 17)$

D) $(7, 15)$

Strategy: In this question, we need to determine the relationship between x and A and y and A. Begin by using the midpoint formula $\dfrac{1+x}{2} = x + 3A$ and $\dfrac{3+y}{2} = y + 2A$. Now solve each of the equations for A. For $\dfrac{1+x}{2} = x + 3A$, $1 + x = 2x + 6A$, and $A = \dfrac{1-x}{6}$. The equation $\dfrac{3+y}{2} = y + 2A$ becomes $3 + y = 2y + 4A$, and $A = \dfrac{3-y}{4}$. Since both equations are now set equal to A, we can set them equal to each other. Then $\frac{1-x}{6} = \frac{3-y}{4}$ and $6(3 - y) = 4(1 - x)$.

Distributing through the parentheses yields $18 - 6y = 4 - 4x$. Collect all the variables on the left-hand side of the equation and all of the constants on the right-hand side so that $4x - 6y = -14$. Divide through by -2 and $3y - 2x = 7$. Now test each of the given coordinates in the equation to see which one produces a true statement. For $(4, 9)$, $3(9) - 2(4) \neq 7$. Move to choice B; $3(11) - 2(13) = 7$. Stop here and pick answer B.

4. Examine the graph given below.

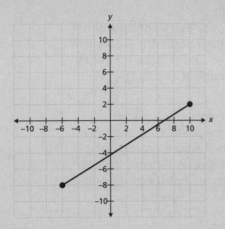

If a line perpendicular to this segment is drawn through the midpoint, which of the following answer choices is the equation of that line?

A) $8y = 5x + 1$

B) $8x - 5y = 1$

C) $5y = -8x + 1$

D) $1 = 8x + 5y$

Strategy: We need to determine both the midpoint and the slope of the line segment in the graph. The endpoints of the segment are $(-6, -8)$ and $(10, 2)$, so the midpoint is $(\overline{x}, \overline{y}) = \left(\frac{(-6)+10}{2}, \frac{(-8)+2}{2} \right)$ which becomes $\left(\frac{4}{2}, -\frac{6}{2} \right) = (2, -3)$.

Then the slope is $m = \frac{2-(-8)}{10-(-6)} = \frac{10}{16} = \frac{5}{8}$. Remember from Lesson 3 in this category that the slopes of lines that are perpendicular to each other are negative reciprocals.

The slope of the line perpendicular to this line segment is $-\frac{8}{5}$, and the equation can be determined by the point-slope equation $y - (-3) = -\frac{8}{5}(x - 2)$. Simplifying a bit, $y + 3 = -\frac{8}{5}x + \frac{16}{5}$ and $y = -\frac{8}{5}x + \frac{1}{5}$. Notice that none of the answer choices are given in this form, so multiply both sides by 5 to find $5y = -8x + 1$. This is answer choice C.

In Category 1, Lesson 3, we defined the term *function* and explained *domain* and *range* within the context of mathematics. We stated that all linear equations are functions, but that an equation does not have to be linear to be a function. It can sometimes be difficult to quickly determine if an equation is a function just by looking at the equation itself. But, because a function pairs every member of the domain with exactly one member of the range, it is easy to tell from a graph if an equation is a function or not. All functions pass the **vertical line test**. That is, if you construct a vertical line through the graph of the function at any *x* value in the domain, that line crosses the graph at only a single point.

Additionally, functions that pair each element of the range with exactly one member of the domain are **one-to-one** functions. One-to-one functions pass both the vertical line test and what is known as the **horizontal line test**. If you construct a horizontal line through any *y* value of the range, the line crosses the graph at exactly one point. All linear functions are one-to-one functions.

In the figures below, both graphs A and B are functions. A vertical line placed anywhere along the graph intersects the graph in exactly one place. Graph A passes the vertical line test but fails the horizontal line test. It represents a function, but it is not one-to-one function. Graph B, a linear function, is one-to-one. Graph C fails the vertical line test and is therefore not a function. Graphs that are not functions cannot be one-to-one functions.

Graph A   Graph B   Graph C

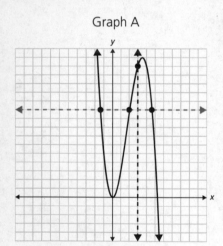
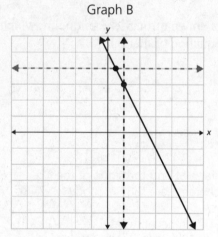
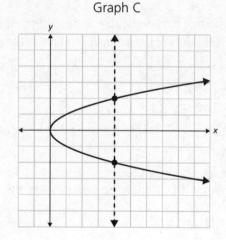

As we stated previously, along with knowing if a graph represents a function or not, on the SAT you will be expected to generate linear functions within contexts. The SAT may also ask you to determine how a graph might be impacted by a change in its equation. You may also need to select the appropriate graph based on a description of the function, determine the key features of the graph from its equation, or you may be given a graph and be required to connect it to the correct equation. In the previous section, we focused on the distance and midpoint formulas in relation to this objective. Here we will address some of the other forms these questions may take on the SAT. If you would like additional practice beyond this lesson, questions similar to this are briefly addressed in Category 2, Lesson 4.

Example 1

Which of the following graphs does <u>not</u> represent a function?

A)

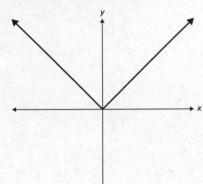

B)

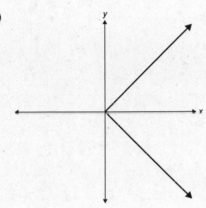

C)

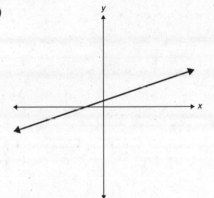

D)

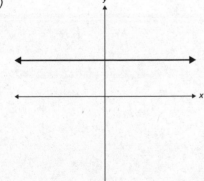

Solution

Test each of the given graphs using the vertical line test. Only graph B fails:

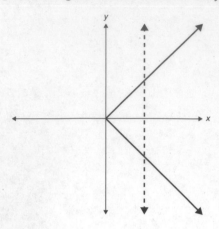

Answer: B

Example 2

Which of the following functions generated this graph?

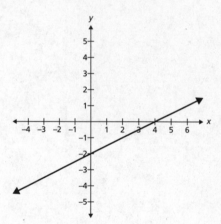

A) $f(x) = \dfrac{1}{2}x + 4$

B) $f(x) = \dfrac{1}{2}x - 2$

C) $f(x) = x^2 - 5$

D) $f(x) = 2x - 2$

Solution

There are several ways we could solve this problem. Logically, we can immediately eliminate answer choices A and C, as choice A has the wrong *y*-intercept and choice C is not a linear function. To determine if the slope of the given line is $\dfrac{1}{2}$ or 2, we could pick two points and calculate the slope or recall that the greater the slope, the greater the steepness of the line. The slope of a line where $m = 2$ would be greater than what is shown here. The answer must be choice B. Note that if this type of question appears on the calculator portion of the exam, you can very quickly check each equation using your graphing calculator.

Answer: B

Example 3

If the function f has a negative slope, a negative x-intercept, and a negative y-intercept, which of the following could represent the graph of f(x)?

A)
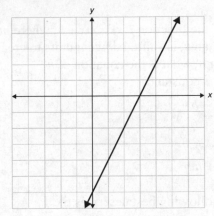

B)
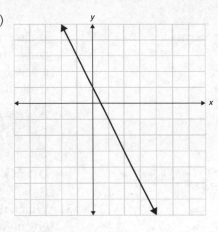

C)
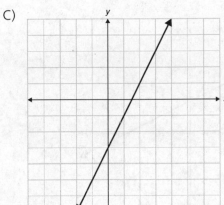

D)
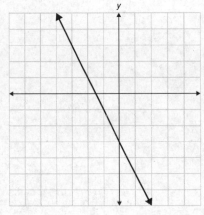

Solution

We are looking for a graph with a negative slope. This eliminates answer choices A and C as their slopes are both positive. We also need the graph to have negative x- and y-intercepts. The only remaining graph that fits this description is answer choice D.

Answer: D

Example 4

If function f has slope $m = 3$ and contains the point (–3, 2) and function g has slope $m = 3$ and contains the point (–3, 6) and these functions are graphed on the same xy-plane, which of the following is true about the relationship between functions f and g?

A) Function g is function f shifted up 4 units.

B) Function f is perpendicular to function g.

C) The functions f and g intersect at point (x, y).

D) Function f and function g have an infinite number of solutions.

Solution

Recall that the graphs of linear functions that share identical slope values are parallel. Eliminate answers B and C as parallel lines will not intersect. Functions f and g cannot be the same line if they have different y-coordinate values for the same x-coordinate value, so choice D is not correct. The answer is choice A. You can verify this by determining the equation of each function and then graphing them, either by hand or on your calculator, or by comparing the y-intercepts of each function.

Answer: A

Answers begin on page 668.

1. Which of the following graphs represents a function?

A)

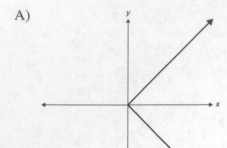

B)

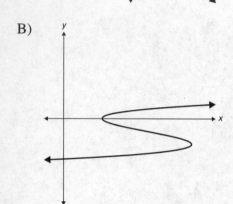

C)

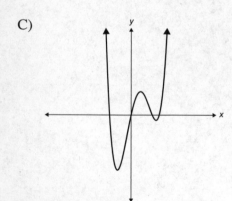

D)

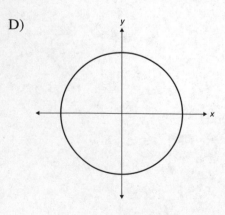

2. If the graph of the function $f(x) = mx + b$, where m and b are constants, is shifted down a units to create a new function h, what is the equation of h? (Note that a is a constant.)

A) $h(x) = mx - b + a$

B) $h(x) = mx + b - a$

C) $h(x) = ax + b$

D) $h(x) = ax + mb$

3. Which of the following best describes the given graph?

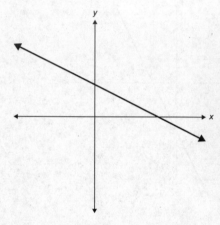

A) Positive slope; y-intercept of $(0, 2)$.

B) Negative slope; x-intercept of $(4, 2)$.

C) Negative slope; x-intercept of $(4, 0)$.

D) Positive slope; y-intercept of $(0, 4)$.

4. Which of the given graphs does <u>not</u> represent a function?

A)

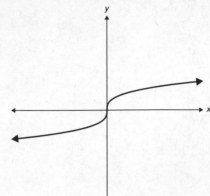

B)

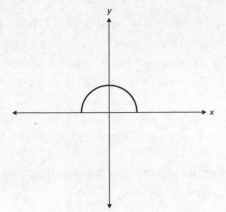

C)

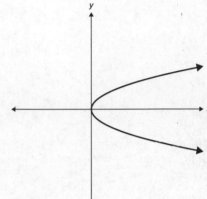

D)

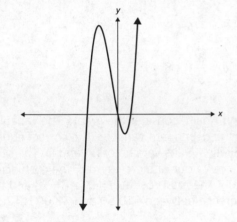

Questions 1 and 2 refer to the following information.

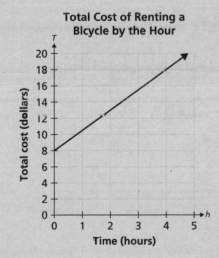

Total Cost of Renting a Bicycle by the Hour

The graph above displays the total cost, T, in dollars, of renting a bicycle for h hours.

1. What does the T-intercept represent in the graph?

   A) The initial cost of renting the bicycle.
   B) The total number of bicycles rented on any given day.
   C) The average number of hours a person rents a bicycle.
   D) The increase in the cost to rent the bicycle per hour of rental.

Strategy: Consider the graph. At time $h = 0$, the cost to rent a bicycle is $8.00. Thus, the T-intercept is the initial cost of renting the bicycle. Select choice A.

2. Which of the following represents the relationship between T and h?

   A) $h = 5T$
   B) $T = 2.50h + 8$
   C) $T = \dfrac{5}{8}h + 8$
   D) $h = \dfrac{8}{5}T + 8$

Strategy: Again, consider the graph. The variable h is the independent variable and T is the dependent variable. The correct equation will likely be of the form "$T =$". Eliminate answer choices A and D. The slope of answer choice B indicates that for every hour of bicycle rental, the cost increases by $2.50. Is this verified by the graph? The total cost at $h = 0$ is $T = $8 and the total cost at $h = 1$ is $T = $10.50. The difference between $10.50 and $8.00 is $2.50. Answer choice B is correct.

3. Which of the following graphs shows a one-to-one function?

   A)

   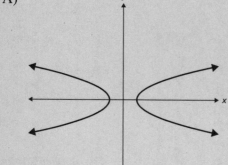

   B)

   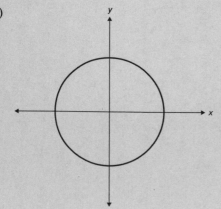

C)

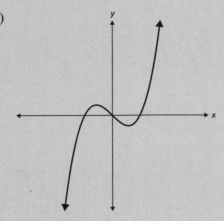

D)

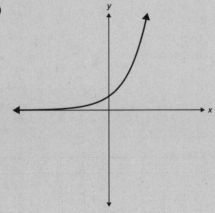

Strategy: Graphs A and B are not functions as they fail the vertical line test. Graph C is a function, but it is not a one-to-one function as it fails the horizontal line test. Only graph D passes both the vertical line test and the horizontal line test. Select answer choice D.

 SAT-Type Questions

Answers begin on page 669.

1. What are the coordinates of the midpoint of the line segment with endpoints $(-5, -2)$ and $(3, -2)$?

    A) $(-1, -2)$
    B) $(-1, -1)$
    C) $(1, -1)$
    D) $(1, 2)$

Questions 2–4 refer to the following information.

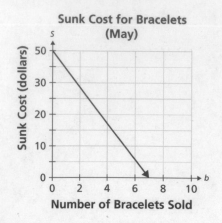

Leda decided to make and sell bracelets at a local farmer's market. She invested a certain amount of money in supplies and she sells each of her bracelets for a set price. The graph above displays the number of bracelets Leda must sell to recoup her sunk cost. She will recoup this sunk cost when $S = 0$.

2. In this graph, what does the S-intercept represent?

   A) The amount Leda must charge per bracelet.
   B) The total number of bracelets Leda sold in her first month of business.
   C) The amount of money Leda spent on supplies that month.
   D) There is not enough information to answer this question.

3. Which of the following represents the linear relationship between S and b?

   A) $S = 50 - 7b$
   B) $S = 7b + 50$
   C) $b = 50S$
   D) $S = 50b - 7$

4. Suppose that Leda sells 15 bracelets on her first morning in the farmer's market. What is her profit?

   A) $55
   B) $105
   C) $7.00
   D) $30.00

5. Which one of the following graphs does not represent a function?

A)

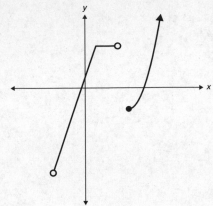

B)

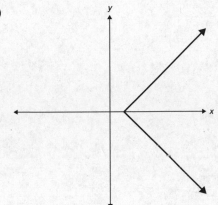

C)

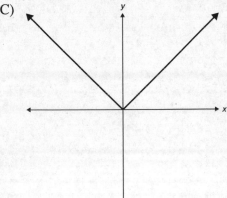

D)

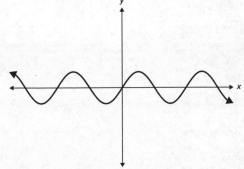

6. If the coordinates of two adjacent corners of a square are at $A(4, 2)$ and $B(7, 6)$, what is the length of a side of the square?

    A) 2.5
    B) 5
    C) $5\sqrt{2}$
    D) $5\sqrt{3}$

7. Which of the following graphs represents a one-to-one function?

    A)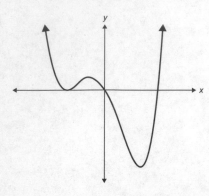

    B)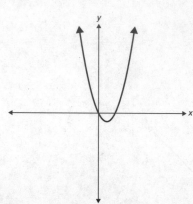

    C)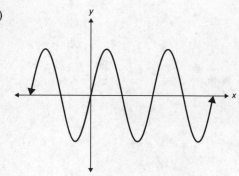

    D)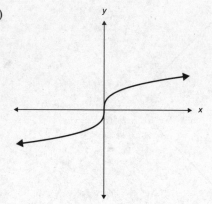

8. Examine the graph below.

    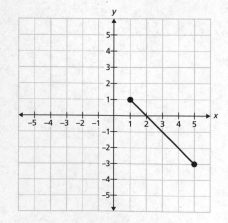

    If a line perpendicular to this segment is drawn through one of the endpoints, which of the following could be the equation of that line?

    A) $x - y = 2$
    B) $-y = 2x + 4$
    C) $y - x = -8$
    D) $4x - y = 7$

9. If the function g, which has slope $m = -4$ and contains the point $(1, -3)$, and the function h, which has slope $m = \frac{1}{4}$ and contains the point $(1, 1)$, are both graphed on the same xy-plane, which of the following is <u>not</u> true about the relationship between functions g and h?

A) Function h is function g shifted down 4 units.
B) Function g is perpendicular to function h.
C) The functions g and h intersect at point (x, y).
D) Function g is not parallel to function h.

10. Which of the following graphs does <u>not</u> represent a function?

A)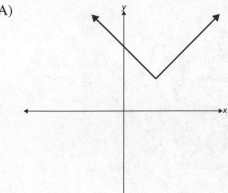

B)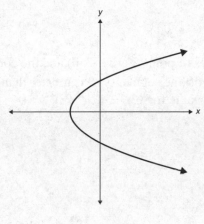

C)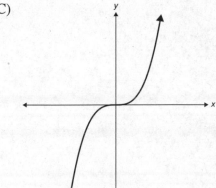

D)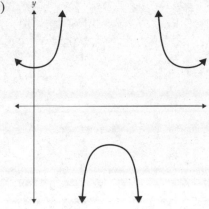

Student-Produced Response Questions

11. What is the product of the coordinates of the midpoint of the line segment defined by the endpoints $A(1, 2)$ and $B(6, 10)$?

12. If one endpoint of a line segment $\overline{AB}$ is (−5, 2), and the midpoint is (2, −5) what is the *x*-coordinate of the other endpoint?

13. In the *xy*-plane, the coordinates of point *A* are (−2, 0) and the coordinates of point *B* are (1, *y*). If the slope of line segment $\overline{AB}$ is greater than 0.4 but less than 0.5, what is one possible value for *y*?

Summary SAT-Type Test

· · · · · **Multiple Choice** ·

Calculators Allowed

Answers begin on page 670.

1. If the points $(2, 3)$ and $(5, y)$ lie on a line whose slope is $m = -\dfrac{7}{6}$, what does y equal?

    A) $y = -6.5$

    B) $y = -0.5$

    C) $y = 0.5$

    D) $y = 6.5$

2. If $\dfrac{a}{b}$ is a fraction greater than 1, which of the following expressions must be a fraction less than 1?

    A) $\sqrt{\dfrac{a}{b}}$

    B) $\dfrac{a}{0.5b}$

    C) $\dfrac{b^2}{a}$

    D) $\dfrac{b}{a}$

3. For what value of n is $|-n - 2| + 3$ equal to 2?

    A) $n = -1$

    B) $n = -\dfrac{2}{3}$

    C) $n = 1$

    D) No value of n makes this statement true.

4. Given the relation $\{(5, 2), (3, 5), (6, 2), (k, 4)\}$, which value of k will result in the relation not being a function?

    A) 1

    B) 2

    C) 3

    D) 4

5. Desserts on a restaurant's adult menu cost $6 each and on the child's menu they cost $3 each. If 160 desserts were sold on Sunday for a total of $816, how many adults ordered dessert?

   A) 27
   B) 48
   C) 112
   D) 136

6. For the system of inequalities shown below, which of the following relationships between a and b must be true?

   $$y < 2x - a$$
   $$y > 2x - b$$

   A) $a > b$
   B) $b > a$
   C) $a = b$
   D) $|a| = |b|$

7. If $(a + b)^2 < 11$, which of the following ordered pairs, (a, b), does not satisfy this inequality?

   A) $(3, 0)$
   B) $(-2, 5)$
   C) $(-2, -1)$
   D) $(1, -5)$

8. If $x = \dfrac{1}{3}$, what is the value of $\dfrac{1}{x} + \dfrac{1}{x-1}$?

   A) $-\dfrac{2}{3}$

   B) $\dfrac{2}{3}$

   C) 1
   D) 1.5

9. If $\dfrac{1}{4}x + \dfrac{1}{5}y = 3$, what is the value of $\dfrac{5x + 4y}{12}$?

   A) $\dfrac{1}{5}$

   B) $\dfrac{1}{4}$

   C) 5
   D) 6

10. A freight elevator is carrying boxes of construction material. The boxes weigh either 30 pounds or 55 pounds. Let x be the number of 30 pound boxes and let y be the number of 55 pound boxes that the elevator is carrying. The maximum weight the elevator can hold is 2,000 pounds. The maximum number of boxes the freight elevator can fit is 60. Which of the following systems of inequalities represents the situation described?

A) $\begin{cases} 30x + 55y \le 2,000 \\ x + y \le 60 \end{cases}$

B) $\begin{cases} \dfrac{x}{30} + \dfrac{y}{55} \le 2,000 \\ x + y \le 60 \end{cases}$

C) $\begin{cases} x + y \le 2,000 \\ 30x + 55y \le 2,000 \end{cases}$

D) $\begin{cases} 30x + 55y \le 60 \\ x + y \le 2,000 \end{cases}$

11. If $6x = 14$, what is the value of $9x^2$?

A) 7

B) 21

C) 49

D) 147

12. If $4x - y = 2y + 8$ and $x + 6y = 5$, what is the value of x?

A) $x = -\dfrac{3}{7}$

B) $x = \dfrac{7}{3}$

C) $x = -\dfrac{4}{7}$

D) $x = \dfrac{7}{4}$

13. A local campaign to stock a food pantry for homeless adults was kicked off by a donation of $10,000 on January 1, 2010. Every month after that date, the fundraisers met their goal of collecting $1,000. If m represents the number of months since January 1, 2010, which of the following represents the number of months the charity was able to declare a cumulative income of at least $25,000?

A) $25,000 - 1,000 \le m$

B) $10,000 + 1,000m \ge 25,000$

C) $25,000 \ge 10,000m$

D) $25,000 \le 10,000m$

14. If Adrian is a years old and Bobby is b years old, which of the following represents Adrian's age when Bobby was x years old?

A) $a - b + x$

B) $a - b - x$

C) $a + b - x$

D) $b - a + x$

15. If the system of inequalities $y > 2x + 1$ and $y > \dfrac{x}{2} + 4$ is graphed, which quadrant contains no solution to the system?

A) Quadrant I

B) Quadrant II

C) Quadrant III

D) Quadrant IV

16. Line l in the xy-plane contains points from each of quadrants II and III, but no points from quadrants I or IV. Which of the following must be true?

A) The slope of line l is undefined.

B) The slope of line l is zero.

C) The slope of line l is positive.

D) The slope of line l is negative.

17. Which of the following expressions is equal to 0 for some value of z?

A) $|z - 1| + 1$

B) $|1 - z| + 1$

C) $|z - 1| - 1$

D) $|z + 1| + 1$

18. Lines a and b intersect at the point $(1, 4)$ in the xy-coordinate plane. Lines a and m intersect at the point $(2, 7)$. Which of the following is an equation for line a?

A) $y = 3x - 1$

B) $y = 3x - 4$

C) $y = 3x + 1$

D) $y = 3x + 3$

19. If the number n is 18 less than $2a$, and a is 3 more than n, what is the value of n?

A) $n = 15$

B) $n = 12$

C) $n = 6$

D) $n = 4$

20. What is the product ab, if $(1, 5)$ and $(3, 11)$ are members of the function $y = 2ax + b$?

A) 6

B) 3

C) 2

D) 1.5

21. A scout troop is estimating the number of badges, b_e, its 32 members will earn during the next year. The troop would like their estimate to be within 12 badges of the number of badges actually earned. During the year, the troop earns b_a badges. Which of the following inequalities represents the relationship between the troop's estimate and the actual number earned if their estimate is within the stated tolerance?

A) $b_e - b_a \leq 12$

B) $|b_e + b_a| \leq 12$

C) $|b_e - b_a| \leq 12$

D) $b_e > 12 + b_a$

22. The frequency of a vibrating string on a certain musical instrument varies inversely to the length of the string. If a string of m inches vibrates at a frequency of 78 hertz and the same type of string at 6 inches in length vibrates at a frequency of 117 hertz, what is the value of m?

A) 4 inches

B) 9 inches

C) 36 inches

D) 1,521 inches

23. If $ar^n - rx = 0$, then an expression for x in terms of a, n, and r is

A) $x = ar^n$

B) $x = ar^{n+1}$

C) $x = \dfrac{ar^n}{r}$

D) $x = ar^n - 1$

24. Given the formulas $S = \dfrac{1}{2}gt^2$ and $V = gt$ where g is a constant, which of the following expresses S as a function of V?

A) $S = \dfrac{V^2}{2g}$

B) $S = \dfrac{V^2}{2g^3}$

C) $S = \dfrac{2V^2}{g^3}$

D) $S = \dfrac{2V^2}{g}$

25. The intensity, I, of light is inversely proportional to the square of the distance, d, from the light source. If k is a positive constant of proportionality then the intensity, I, can be represented by which of the following?

A) kd^2

B) $\dfrac{k}{d}$

C) $\dfrac{k}{d^2}$

D) $\left(\dfrac{k}{d}\right)^2$

26. In the xy-plane, point A has coordinates $(6, -6)$ and point B has coordinates (x, y). The midpoint of AB is $(2, -1)$. What are the coordinates of B?

A) $(-2, 4)$

B) $(2, -4)$

C) $(4, -3.5)$

D) $(8, -7)$

27. If $y = \dfrac{-3x}{2}$ and $2x - \dfrac{15x}{2} = -11$, what is the sum $2x + y$?

A) -1

B) 1

C) 2

D) 3

28. In the xy-plane, the line represented by the equation $3x + y = 5$ is perpendicular to the line with the equation $y = mx + b$, where m and b are constants. What is the value of m?

A) -3

B) $-\dfrac{1}{3}$

C) $\dfrac{1}{3}$

D) 3

29. In the xy-plane, if a point with coordinates (a, b) lies in the solution set of the system of inequalities below, what is the maximum possible value of b?

$$y \le -10x + 2000$$

$$y \le 40x$$

A) 40

B) 160

C) 320

D) $1,600$

30. Which of the following best describes the given graph?

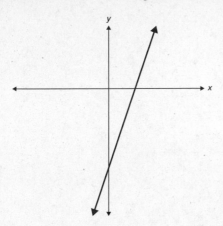

A) Positive slope; y-intercept of $(0, 5)$.

B) Negative slope; x-intercept of $(1.5, -5)$.

C) Negative slope; x-intercept of $(1.5, 0)$.

D) Positive slope; y-intercept of $(0, -5)$.

Student-Produced Response Questions

31. If $2x + y = -3$ and $x + 2y = 18$, then $2x + 2y =$

32. It took 12 people 5 hours to take down a tubular scaffolding around a private home. If 4 more people had been hired to work at the same pace, how much less time would it have taken?

33. If $-\dfrac{10}{3} < -3x + 2 < -\dfrac{9}{4}$, what is one possible value of $9x - 6$?

34. Olja walks at least 8 dogs and at most 12 dogs each morning. Based on this information, what is a possible number of mornings it could take Olja to walk 24 dogs?

35. If a line that is perpendicular to this line segment is drawn through the segment's midpoint, what is the slope of the line?

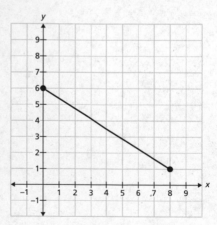

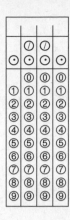

36. If y is directly proportional to x^2 and $y = \dfrac{1}{4}$ when $x = \dfrac{1}{3}$, what is the positive value of x when $y = \dfrac{9}{4}$?

Questions 37 and 38 refer to the following information.

The subscription price for Monster online streaming service is $10.50 each month for the basic plan. The extra charge for each premium video downloaded is $3.50. The subscription price for Zombie online streaming service is $25.00 per month. The extra charge for each premium video downloaded is $2.00.

37. Melanija subscribes to Monster streaming service and her cousin Nassim subscribes to Zombie streaming service. They want to download the same premium videos so they can share comparisons of the productions. What is the greatest number of videos each cousin can download so Melanija's expenses are less?

38. Melanija and Nassim were both born during the month of June. During her birthday month, Monster charged Melanija half price for her basic service. Nassim's birthday special from Zombie was 2 free premium downloads. If the cousins want to make identical orders during their birthday month, what is the greatest number of videos each cousin can download so Melanija's expenses are less?

⊘	⊘		
⊙	⊙	⊙	⊙
	⓪	⓪	⓪
①	①	①	①
②	②	②	②
③	③	③	③
④	④	④	④
⑤	⑤	⑤	⑤
⑥	⑥	⑥	⑥
⑦	⑦	⑦	⑦
⑧	⑧	⑧	⑧
⑨	⑨	⑨	⑨

Summary SAT-Type Test

• • • • • **Multiple Choice** •

No Calculator Allowed

Answers begin on page 674.

1. If $6 - x > 0$ and $5x + 2 > -8$, then x could equal any of the following except

   A) 5
   B) 2
   C) 0
   D) −2

2. All of the following equations are examples of a direct variation <u>except</u>

   A) $y = 13x$
   B) $y = \dfrac{x}{3}$
   C) $2y = mx$
   D) $xy = k$

3. A line in the xy-plane has y-intercept $(0, -1)$ and has a slope of $m = \dfrac{1}{3}$. Which of the following points lies on the line?

   A) $(-3, 0)$
   B) $(6, 1)$
   C) $(1, 3)$
   D) $(6, 2)$

4. Which of the following represents a number n such that one third of its square root is 3?

   A) $\dfrac{\sqrt{3}}{3}$
   B) $3\sqrt{3}$
   C) 27
   D) 81

5. If $x < -3$ or $x > 3$, then which of the following must also be true?

   I. $x^2 > 3$
   II. $|x| > 3$
   III. $x^3 > 3$

   A) I only
   B) I and II only
   C) I and III only
   D) II and III only

6. Dr. Jeffrey is a physician who volunteers in a clinic. Each day, he treats the same number of patients per hour. The number of patients, P, he has left to see on any given day is given by the equation $P = 28 - 4h$ where h is the number of hours he has already worked that day. Which of the following statements best describes the meaning of the term -4 in the equation $P = 28 - 4h$?

A) The number of patients Dr. Jeffrey will see in 4 hours.

B) The number of patients who are rescheduled for another day.

C) The number of patients Dr. Jeffrey sees in a day.

D) The number of patients Dr. Jeffrey sees in one hour.

7. Rita worked 8 hours over the weekend and earned r dollars per hour. Carlos worked 6 hours over the weekend and earned c dollars per hour. Which of the following represents the total amount of money, in dollars, earned by Rita and Carlos?

A) $14rc$

B) $48rc$

C) $8r + 6c$

D) $6r + 8c$

8. In the system of linear equations below, a is a constant. If the system has no solution, what is the value of a?

$$\frac{1}{4}x - \frac{1}{2}y = 8$$
$$ax - 3y = 10$$

A) $a = \dfrac{3}{2}$

B) $a = \dfrac{2}{3}$

C) $a = -\dfrac{2}{3}$

D) $a = -\dfrac{3}{2}$

9. Consider the given values in tables (a) and (b). If m_1 is the rate of change for (a) and m_2 is the rate of change for (b), find the product $m_1 \cdot m_2$.

(a)

x	y
−3	6
0	4
6	0

(b)

x	y
5	2
6	1
7	0
8	−1

A) $-\dfrac{5}{3}$

B) $-\dfrac{2}{3}$

C) $\dfrac{1}{3}$

D) $\dfrac{2}{3}$

10. The points $(2, 3)$, $\left(3, \dfrac{4}{3}\right)$, $\left(4, \dfrac{3}{4}\right)$, and $(6, n)$ lie on the graph of a function.

If y is inversely proportional to the square of x, what is the value of n?

A) $n = \dfrac{1}{6}$

B) $n = \dfrac{1}{4}$

C) $n = \dfrac{1}{3}$

D) $n = \dfrac{2}{3}$

11. Which of the following graphs is <u>not</u> a representation of a function?

A)
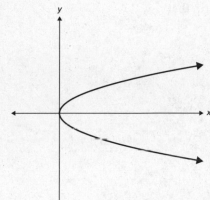

B)
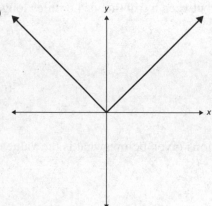

C)
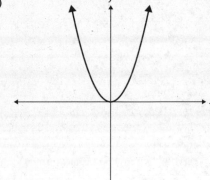

D)
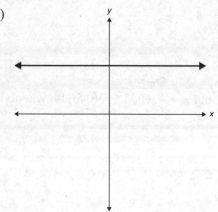

A) Graph A
B) Graph B
C) Graph C
D) Graph D

12. In the given equation, what is the value of k?

$$\frac{4(k+3)-5}{6} = \frac{12-(3-k)}{9}$$

   A) $-\dfrac{3}{10}$

   B) $\dfrac{11}{13}$

   C) 1

   D) $\dfrac{12}{5}$

13. The cost, C, of a taxi cab ride longer than $m-1$ miles and shorter than or equal to m miles is given by the equation $C = 4 + 2.5m$. Based upon this formula, what is the difference in cost between a trip that is 4.6 miles long and a trip that is 2.8 miles long?

   A) $2.50

   B) $4.40

   C) $5.00

   D) $9.00

14. Based on the system of equations given below, what is the value of the product xy?

$$3x - y = y + 8$$
$$x + 4y = 5$$

   A) 1.5

   B) 2.5

   C) 3.5

   D) 6

15. If x varies directly as $2n + 1$, and $n = 4$ when $x = 6$, find n when $x = 18$.

   A) $n = 12$

   B) $n = 13$

   C) $n = 14$

   D) $n = 27$

16. If $\dfrac{1}{3}x + \dfrac{1}{2}y = 8$, what is the value of $2x + 3y$?

17. At a school bake sale, plates of cookies sold for $5.00 and plates of brownies sold for $8.00. Altogether, the sale raised $500. If at least 25 plates of brownies were sold, what is one possible number of plates of cookies sold?

18. According to the system of equations below, what is the value of x?

$$x + y = -4$$
$$4x + y = 5$$

19. In the figure of rectangle *RAMD*, below, the point $(x, 4)$ lies on the diagonal (not shown) that connects point *R* to point *M*. What is the value of *x*?

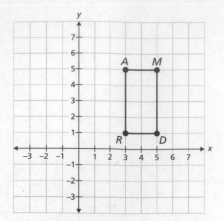

20. Find the distance between the points $(-3, 4)$ and $(5, -2)$.

Correlation Chart

Summary SAT-Type Test—Heart of Algebra (Calculators Allowed)

Use the chart below to mark the questions you found difficult to determine which lessons you need to review.

Question Number	Lesson 1 (p. 43 – 56)	Lesson 2 (p. 57 – 80)	Lesson 3 (p. 81 – 97)	Lesson 4 (p. 98 – 111)	Lesson 5 (p. 112 – 119)	Lesson 6 (p. 120 – 138)
1						
2						
3						
4						
5						
6						
7						
8						
9						
10						
11						
12						
13						
14						
15						
16						
17						
18						
19						
20						
21						
22						
23						
24						
25						
26						
27						
28						
29						
30						
31						
32						
33						
34						
35						
36						
37						
38						
Total Correct	____ / 5	____ / 11	____ / 4	____ /10	____ / 4	____ / 4

Correlation Chart

Summary SAT-Type Test—Heart of Algebra (No Calculators Allowed)

Use the chart below to mark the questions you found difficult to determine which lessons you need to review.

Question Number	Lesson 1 (p. 43 – 56)	Lesson 2 (p. 57 – 80)	Lesson 3 (p. 81 – 97)	Lesson 4 (p. 98 – 111)	Lesson 5 (p. 112 – 119)	Lesson 6 (p. 120 – 138)
1						
2						
3						
4						
5						
6						
7						
8						
9						
10						
11						
12						
13						
14						
15						
16						
17						
18						
19						
20						
Total Correct	____ / 2	____ / 5	____ / 3	____ / 5	____ / 3	____ / 2

Problem Solving and Data Analysis

LESSON 1:

Solving Problems Using Ratios, Proportions, and Percent

- Ratios
- Proportions
- Percent

Explain Ratios & Proportions

A **ratio** is a fraction that compares two quantities.

If there are 3 boys to every 2 girls in class, the ratio is 3 to 2. This can be written as 3:2 or $\frac{3}{2}$.

The ratio $\frac{3}{2}$ is in simplest form; actual quantities could be $\frac{6}{4}$ or $\frac{90}{60}$ or $\frac{3N}{2N}$.

A **proportion** is an equation that states that two ratios are equal. Proportions can be expressed using colon notation or fractional notation.

$$3:2 = 6:4 \text{ or } \frac{3}{2} = \frac{6}{4}$$

If there is an unknown quantity in a proportional relationship, you must cross multiply and divide to find the unknown number.

Example 1

Five of the 12 members of the chess club are female and the rest are male. What is the ratio of female chess club members to male chess club members?

Solution

We know that 5 members are female and the total membership is 12. Thus, there are $12 - 5 = 7$ male members. The ratio of female to male members is 5:7, or $\frac{5}{7}$.

Example 2

Solve for x: $\frac{3}{8} = \frac{x}{120}$

Solution

Original Problem: $\frac{3}{8} = \frac{x}{120}$

Cross Multiply: $8x = 3 \times 120$

Simplify: $8x = 360$

Divide to solve for x: $\frac{8x}{8} = \frac{360}{8}$

$x = 45$

Example 3

A child's fire truck has two gear belts, one in the front and one in the back. When the front gear belt turns 5 times, the rear gear belt turns 8 times. If the front belt turns 800 times, what is the number of times the rear belt turns?

A) 500

B) 1,280

C) 4,000

D) 6,400

QUICK TIP

Some questions on the SAT will ask you to compare one ratio or proportional relationship to another.

Solution

Set up the proportion. Let x = unknown quantity.

$$\frac{\text{front belt}}{\text{rear belt}} \rightarrow \frac{5}{8} = \frac{800}{x} \leftarrow \frac{\text{front belt}}{\text{rear belt}} \leftarrow \text{Note that the labels are aligned.}$$

Cross Multiply. $\quad 5x = 8 \cdot 800$

$\quad\quad\quad\quad\quad\quad 5x = 6,400$

Divide both sides by 5. $\quad \frac{5x}{5} = \frac{6,400}{5}$

$\quad\quad\quad\quad\quad\quad x = 1,280$

Answer: B

Example 4

An oil tank is $\frac{3}{5}$ filled in 6 minutes. Which of the following is the only suitable equation to use to find the number of minutes it takes to fill the entire tank?

A) $\frac{3}{5}x = 6$

B) $6x = \frac{3}{5}$

C) $6 = \frac{3}{5x}$

D) $\frac{1}{6} = \frac{3}{5x}$

Solution

This question does not ask us to solve the proportion; it only asks us to set up the proportion. We know that $\frac{3}{5}$ of the tank is filled in 6 minutes. So:

$$\frac{\frac{3}{5}\text{tank}}{6\,\text{minutes}} = \frac{1\,\text{tank}}{x\,\text{minutes}}.$$ Note the label alignment.

Cross multiply and find $\frac{3}{5}x = 6$

Answer: A

QUICK TIP

For other problems on the SAT, you will need to select the correct equation from a list of choices.

Example 5

If it takes $\frac{1}{6}$ of a day to fill $\frac{2}{3}$ of a pool with water, what part of a day will it take to fill the entire pool?

Solution

$$\frac{\frac{2}{3}\text{pool}}{\frac{1}{6}\text{day}} = \frac{1\,\text{pool}}{x\,\text{days}}$$ Note that the labels are again aligned.

Cross multiply. $\frac{2}{3}x = \frac{1}{6}$. Multiply both sides by $\frac{3}{2}$ to eliminate the fractional coefficient.

$$\frac{3}{2} \cdot \frac{2}{3}x = \frac{3}{2} \cdot \frac{1}{6}$$

$$x = \frac{1}{4} \text{ or } x = 0.25$$

QUICK TIP

Remember that on the SAT, you can answer in fractional or equivalent decimal form.

Example 6

The directions on a box of pancake mix call for $1\frac{1}{3}$ cups of mix and 1 cup of water to make enough pancakes to serve 2 people. Which proportion would be used to find the number of cups of pancake mix necessary to serve 5 people?

A) $\dfrac{2\frac{1}{3}}{2} = \dfrac{x}{5}$

B) $2\frac{1}{3} \cdot 2 = 5x$

C) $\dfrac{1\frac{1}{3}}{2} = \dfrac{x}{5}$

D) $1\frac{1}{3} \cdot 2 = 5x$

Solution

Set up a proportion, making sure like labels are in the same position for both ratios.

$$\frac{1\frac{1}{3} \text{ cups mix}}{2 \text{ people}} = \frac{x \text{ cups mix}}{5 \text{ people}}$$

Answer: C

Practice Ratio & Proportion

Answers begin on page 677.

1. If the ratio of a to b is 3:4, and the ratio of c to b is 9 to 10, what is the ratio of a to c?

A) $\dfrac{3}{5}$

B) $\dfrac{27}{45}$

C) $\dfrac{5}{6}$

D) $\dfrac{6}{5}$

2. The proportion $y:7 = 5:3$ is the same as which of the following?

A) $y:3 = 5:7$
B) $y:3 = 7:5$
C) $5:y = 3:7$
D) $5:y = 7:3$

3. If $\dfrac{3}{5}x = \dfrac{6}{4}y$, then $\dfrac{x}{y} =$

A) $\dfrac{9}{20}$

B) $\dfrac{4}{3}$

C) $\dfrac{5}{2}$

D) $\dfrac{20}{9}$

4. If $\dfrac{7}{3} = \dfrac{1}{m}$ and $\dfrac{1}{m} = R$, then $\dfrac{1}{R} =$

A) $\dfrac{3}{7}$

B) 1

C) 2

D) $\dfrac{7}{3}$

5. If $\dfrac{7}{10} = \dfrac{1}{a}$ and $\dfrac{1}{a} = b$, then $\dfrac{1}{b} =$

A) $\dfrac{7}{10}$

B) 1

C) 2

D) $\dfrac{10}{7}$

6. At a cost of s stickers for c cents, how many stickers can be bought for d dollars?

A) $\dfrac{100sd}{c}$

B) $\dfrac{sd}{c}$

C) $\dfrac{sd}{100c}$

D) $1000cds$

Model SAT Questions

1. Each country has a flag designed to a specific height:length ratio. The United States of America has a height:length ratio of 10:19. Which flag size shown below could be the measurements of a United States flag?

   A) 2.0 feet: 2.8 feet

   B) 2.0 feet: 3.0 feet

   C) 2.0 feet: 3.4 feet

   D) 2.0 feet: 3.8 feet

Strategy: The ratio 10:19 does not have units on it, but the answer choices are marked in feet. We can use cross multiplication to compare the ratios, but it is faster to notice that 10 is slightly more than half of 19. Similarly, 2.0 feet is slightly more than half of 3.8 feet. Answer choice D is correct.

2. An aspect ratio of an image is the ratio of its width to its height. High-definition televisions use an aspect ratio of 1.78:1. The following answer choices are television screen sizes rounded to the nearest inch. Which one could be a high-definition television?

   A) 8 inches × 4 inches

   B) 34 inches × 16 inches

   C) 49 inches × 28 inches

   D) 60 inches × 40 inches

Strategy: Notice that 1.78 is almost twice as much as 1. Scan the answer choices for a ratio in which the first value is almost twice as large as the second value. Choice C is the only possible answer.

Explain Percents

Percent is a certain amount out of 100. The symbol for percent is %. For ease of calculation, percent is often written as a ratio or as an equivalent decimal.

For example, 5% means 5 out of 100 and can be expressed as 5%, $\dfrac{5}{100}$, or 0.05.

It is unlikely that the SAT will ask you to calculate a percentage directly; however, you may be asked to calculate a percentage from a table or other data presentation. You may also be asked to determine the percentage increase or decrease or to use a given percentage to figure another number. For continuity, we will first provide a brief review of simple percent problems before moving to problems similar to what you will see on the SAT.

Think It Through

Example 1

Find 6% of 25.

Solution

Change 6% to a decimal and multiply: $0.06 \times 25 = 1.5$

Answer: 1.5

Example 2

5 is what percent of 25?

Solution

Write the problem as a ratio and then simplify.

$$\frac{5}{25} = \frac{1}{5} = 0.20 = 20\%$$

Answer: 20%

Example 3

20% of what number is 5?

Solution

Use a proportion to solve:

$$\frac{20}{100} = \frac{5}{x}$$

$$20x = 500$$

$$x = 500 \div 20 = 25$$

Answer: 25

Practice Percents I

Answers begin on page 677.

1. What is 18% of 350?

2. What percent of 350 is 63?

3. 63 is 18% of what number?

4. What is $37\frac{1}{2}\%$ of 64?

5. What percent of 40 is 14?

6. 40 is 25% of what number?

7. 48 is what percent of 32?

8. $\frac{1}{4}\%$ of what number is 10?

9. What is 125% of 200?

10. $33\frac{1}{3}\%$ of what number is 6?

11. What is 0.8% of 200?

12. What percent of 150 is 3?

162 Problem Solving and Data Analysis • Lesson 1

Example 1

If $m = 2a$ and a is 20% of b, then m is what percent of b?

A) 2%

B) 4%

C) 20%

D) 40%

Solution

a is 20% of b means $a = 0.20b$.

Substitute $0.20b$ for a in the equation.

$m = 2a$

$m = 2(0.20b)$

$m = 0.40b = 40\%$ of b

Answer: D

Example 2

At South High School, the ratio of male students to female students is 5 to 3. What percent of the students at South High School are female?

A) 37.5%

B) 40%

C) 45%

D) 20%

Solution

Out of every 8 students at South High School, 5 are male and 3 are female. Then:

$$\frac{3}{8} = 0.375 = 37.5\%$$

Answer: A

Example 3

If Harri is 20% faster than Preeti, then what percent slower is Preeti than Harri?

A) $12\frac{1}{2}\%$

B) 15%

C) $16\frac{2}{3}\%$

D) 20%

Solution

Translate the words.

Harri is 20% faster than Preeti   →   Harri = Preeti + 20% of Preeti

Substitute in a friendly number for Preeti's rate.

Let's use 10. $= 10 + 0.20(10)$

$$= 10 + 2$$

$$= 12$$

Since Harri's rate, 12, is 2 more than Preeti's rate, 10, the problem reduces to finding what percent 2 is of 12:

$\dfrac{2}{12} = \dfrac{1}{6} = 0.166$ $= 16\dfrac{2}{3}\%$, which is answer choice C.

Answer: C

Example 4

Viktor must practice his clarinet for t minutes. After Viktor practiced for d minutes he stopped. What percent of his practice did he <u>not</u> finish?

A) $\dfrac{100(t-d)}{t}\%$

B) $\dfrac{t}{100(t-d)}\%$

C) $\dfrac{100(t-d)}{d}\%$

D) $\dfrac{100(1-d)}{t}\%$

Solution

Translate problem into a fraction:

$$\dfrac{\text{time practiced}}{\text{total practice}} = \dfrac{t-d}{t}$$

Percents are always based on the number 100, so multiply the fraction you developed above by 100 to convert it to a percent:

$$\dfrac{100(t-d)}{t}\%$$ This is answer choice A.

Answer: A

• • • • • **Practice** **Percents II** •

Answers begin on page 678.

1. If 8 is 8% of N, then what does N equal?

   A) 1

   B) 8

   C) 80

   D) 100

2. A high school summer camp enrolled 60 juniors and 30 seniors. Twenty percent of the junior and 40 percent of the senior campers passed the ropes course on the first try. What percent of the campers passed the ropes course on the first try?

   A) 24%   C) $36\dfrac{2}{3}\%$

   B) $26\dfrac{2}{3}\%$ D) 54%

3. If Jasmyn is $33\frac{1}{3}\%$ richer than Gohar, then Gohar is what percent poorer than Jasmyn?

A) 30%

B) $22\frac{1}{2}\%$

C) 25%

D) 20%

4. If 150% of J is equal to half of K, and $K \neq 0$, then $\dfrac{J}{K}$ is

A) $\dfrac{1}{5}$

B) $\dfrac{1}{3}$

C) 3

D) 5

5. If 30% of all male students attended the basketball game and 50% of the student population is male, then what percent of the student population are males who attended the basketball game?

A) 15%

B) 20%

C) 40%

D) 80%

Think It Through

Examples 1 and 2 refer to the following information.

The table below shows the Fall 2014 enrollment of 639 students in mathematics classes at a local community college.

	College Algebra	Calculus I	Calculus II	Total
Freshmen	107	57	13	177
Sophomores	84	61	67	212
Juniors	52	32	72	156
Seniors	13	33	48	94
Total	256	183	200	639

QUICK TIP

There will be some SAT problems that require you to calculate a percentage from a table or graph.

Example 1

About what percentage of Sophomore and Junior students are enrolled in Calculus I?

A) 34%

B) 25%

C) 29%

D) 31%

Solution:

To solve this, we must extract the pertinent information from the table. There are $61 + 32 = 93$ sophomore and junior students enrolled in Calculus I, and there are $212 + 156 = 368$ sophomore and junior students enrolled in math classes. Divide 93 by 368 to find 0.253, or about 25%.

Answer: B

Example 2

In the spring of 2014, there were 752 students enrolled in a mathematics course at this community college. If 38% of the students were taking College Algebra, about how many more students took College Algebra in the spring of 2014 than in the fall of 2014?

A) 30 students
B) 256 students
C) 286 students
D) 49 students

Solution:

First, determine the number of students enrolled in College Algebra in the spring of 2014 by multiplying 0.38 by 752 = 285.76. Then, subtract from that number the total number of students enrolled in College Algebra in the fall of 2014: 285.76 − 256 = 29.76, or about 30 students.

Answer: A

Example 3

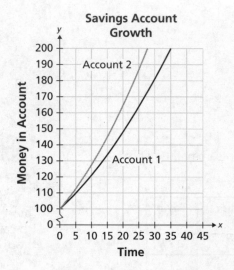

An investor places $100 into each of two different savings accounts that each earn a different amount of compound interest. The investor does not withdraw or deposit any additional money over the life of the investments. The amount of money in each account as a function of time is shown above. Which of the following is a correct statement about the data above?

A) At time $t = 0$, the amount of money in Account 1 is equal to the amount in Account 2.
B) At time $t = 5$, Account 1 has about 10% more money than Account 2.
C) At time $t = 10$, Account 2 has about 50% more money than Account 1.
D) For the first 15 units of time, the amount of money in Account 1 is increasing more quickly than the amount in Account 2.

Solution:

Although you can check all of the statements B, C, and D, statement A is clearly the only correct one as the original problem stated the investor placed $100 into each of the accounts to start. Thus, at time $t = 0$, both accounts had the same balance.

Answer: A

Questions 1 and 2 refer to the following information.

The chart below shows the number of high school students in each grade taking an elective art class. No student is enrolled in more than one course.

	Studio	Ceramics	Pottery	Photography	Total
Grade 9	250	12	2	36	300
Grade 10	15	42	51	59	167
Grade 11	0	56	64	80	200
Grade 12	0	79	82	85	246
Total	265	189	199	260	913

1. About what percent of students taking art in grades 9 and 10 are taking Pottery or Photography?

    A) 13%
    B) 32%
    C) 50%
    D) 69%

Strategy: Begin the problem by summing the number of students in grades 9 and 10 that are taking pottery or photography: $2 + 51 + 36 + 59 = 148$ students. Then divide that sum by the total number of 9th and 10th graders enrolled in an elective art class: $148 \div (300 + 167) = 0.317$, or about 32%.

2. According to data collected on past students, about 45% of students who enroll in an elective art class in grade 9 go on to enroll in another elective art class in grade 10. If this statistic is true, about how many of this year's 10th graders took an elective art class in grade 9?

    A) 90
    B) 95
    C) 135
    D) 75

Strategy: Multiply the total number of 10th graders enrolled in an elective art class by 45%: $167 \cdot 0.45 = 75.15$, or about 75 students. This is answer choice D.

3. If $J = 4L$ and $L = 20\%$ of M, then J is what percent of M?

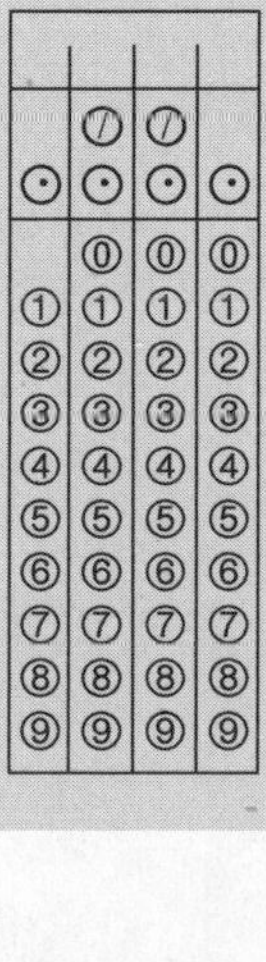

4. If $\dfrac{3}{4}A = \dfrac{2}{3}B$, then what is the value of $\dfrac{B}{A}$?

Question 5 refers to the following graph.

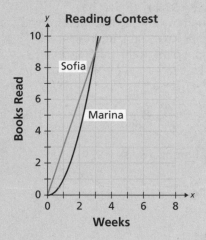

5. Two siblings, Marina and Sofia, competed to read the most books over the summer break. After two weeks, what percent of the total number of books read were completed by Marina?

Strategy: Read the graph by moving 2 units to the right on the horizontal axis to reflect the number of weeks stated in the problem. Reading off the vertical axis at $x = 2$, Marina read 4 books while Sofia read 6 books. Thus, Marina read $4 \div (4 + 6) = 0.40 = 40\%$ of the total books read.

Explain Other Types of Percent Problems

Percent change problems measure the percentage by which a certain number has increased or decreased over time. It is useful for understanding how a value changed over a set time period. Finding percent change is a three-step process. First, find the change; that is, the increase or decrease. Then, make a fraction, placing the difference in the numerator and the *original amount* in the denominator. Lastly, change the fraction to a decimal and then to a percent:

To find percent change: $100\left(\dfrac{\text{the difference}}{\text{the original amount}}\right)$.

The SAT may also contain **sale price** problems. These types of problems ask you to calculate the sale price of an item in a store:

- Find the amount of the discount by multiplying the regular price by the rate of discount.

- Subtract the amount of the discount from the regular price.

    Example   What is the sale price of a $15 shirt at a 20% discount?

    $15 × 20% = $15 × 0.20 = $3.00

    Sale Price: $15 − $3.00 − $12

Finally, some SAT problems may ask you to calculate **simple interest**. Remember that the simple interest formula is $I = Prt$, where P is the principal, r is the interest rate as a decimal, and t is the time over which the money is invested. To find the simple interest on a given amount of principal, multiply the principal times the rate (written as a decimal) times the number of periods.

QUICK TIP

In addition to those previously described, there are a few other types of percent problems that may appear on the SAT.

Think It Through

Example 1

The price of chocolate candy increases from $2.00 per pound to $2.50 per pound. What is the percent increase?

Solution

$2.50 − $2.00 = $0.50 ← the difference

$$\frac{\text{the difference}}{\text{the original amount}} = \frac{0.50}{2.00} = \frac{50}{200} = \frac{1}{4}$$

$\dfrac{1}{4} = 0.25 = 25\%$ increase

Example 2

Vahan works a 40-hour week, Monday to Friday. Occasionally, she is asked to work on Sunday and is paid twice her regular wage per hour. If Vahan works 4 hours on Sunday, by what percent are her wages for the week increased?

A) 10%

B) 15%

C) 20%

D) 25%

Solution

Choose easy values to substitute into the problem. Assume Vahan traditionally earns $10 per hour, or 40 × $10 = $400 for the week. If she works 4 hours on Sunday, she earns 4 × $20 = $80 additional dollars.

$$100\left(\frac{\text{difference}}{\text{original amount}}\right) = 100\left(\frac{80}{400}\right) = 20\%$$

Answer: C

Example 3

After a 10% sale, a sweater cost $48.60. What was the original price of the sweater?

Solution

The sale price, $48.60, is 90% of the original price, so $48.60 = 0.9 · original price.

The original price $= \dfrac{\$48.60}{0.90} = \$54$

Example 4

To encourage his child to save money, a father opened a pretend bank account for him. Money left in the account earned $\frac{1}{2}$% interest each month it was left in the "bank." If the child left $10 in the bank for 6 months, how much money would be in his account?

A) $10.30

B) $13.30

C) $13.00

D) $3.30

Solution

To find the total amount in the account, multiply the initial deposit by the interest rate as a decimal, and then multiply that product by the length of time the money was in the account. So, 10 · 0.005 · 6 = 0.30. This is the interest earned. Add the interest to the $10 initial deposit, and the child has $10.30 in his account.

Answers begin on page 678.

1. The price of a share of stock decreases from $25 a share to $18 a share. Find the percent decrease.

2. The regular price of a coat is $89. What is the sale price after a 20% discount?

3. The Pollitts bought their home for $170,000 and sold it for $340,000. Find the percent increase.

4. Find the interest on $2,700 for 6 months at 6% annual interest rate.

5. The sale price of an item is $25.50. If the rate of discount is 15%, what was the regular price of the item?

•••• Model SAT Questions ••

1. Gia went to the movies with her 7-year-old daughter and her 70-year-old mother. Movie tickets are half-price for children under 12 years old, and there is a 25% discount for senior citizens. If Gia's $8.00 ticket was the regular retail price, what percent of the full retail price did Gia pay for the three tickets?

   A) 60%

   B) 66.$\overline{6}$%

   C) 70%

   D) 75%

Strategy: First determine how much Gia paid for all three admissions. The child's ticket was sold at a 50% discount, and 0.5 × $8.00 = $4.00. The senior's ticket was sold for 75% of the regular price, and 0.75 × $8.00 = $6.00. In total, the three tickets cost $4.00 + $6.00 + $8.00 = $18.00. Then, full retail price is 3 × $8.00 = $24.00, so $\frac{18}{24} = 0.75$ or 75%, answer choice D.

2. A family club keeps a small amount of money on hand for members to borrow for short periods of time. The simple interest charged is $7\frac{1}{2}$%. Stephen borrowed $5,000 for 3 months. How much, to the nearest dollar, was he required to pay back at the end of 3 months?

Strategy: Find the simple interest on $5,000 at 7.5% for 0.25 years using the formula *I = Prt*. Then, *I* = $5,000 · 0.075 · 0.25 = $93.75. Before rounding, Stephen must repay $5,000 + $93.75 = $5,093.75. To answer an SPR question on the SAT, we must round and eliminate the dollar sign and the comma.

Answers begin on page 678.

1. Raven went on a diet and charted her progress. The graph below shows her weekly weight loss. What was the percent decrease in Raven's weight from week 1 to week 5?

   A) 8%

   B) 9%

   C) 7%

   D) 10%

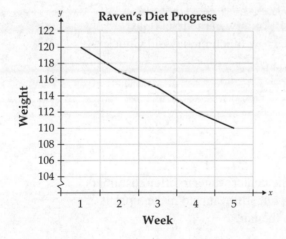

2. A family wants to buy a large high-definition television for their living room. The width:height ratio for a high-definition TV is 1.78:1. Their height clearance is 3 feet. What choice shows the maximum width of a TV fitting in this space?

   A) 1.6 feet

   B) 1.7 feet

   C) 5.3 feet

   D) 5.4 feet

3. Berko is paid time and a half for all work in excess of 36 hours per week. If he works 40 hours in one week, by what percent are his regular wages for the week increased?

A) 6%

B) $16\frac{2}{3}\%$

C) 20%

D) $33\frac{1}{3}\%$

4. The chart below shows height to width ratios for the flags of Central American countries.

Country	Aspect Ratio
Costa Rica and Nicaragua	3:5
Guatemala	5:8
Honduras	1:2
Panama	2:3

The height to width ratio for the United States flag is 10:19. Which country shown above has a flag height to width ratio closest to the ratio used for the United States flag?

A) Costa Rica and Nicaragua

B) Honduras

C) Guatemala

D) Panama

5. The ratio of Andrew's hourly wage to Bob's hourly wage is 2:3. The ratio of Bob's hourly wage to Chuck's hourly wage is 9:4. Andrew earned $600 last week and worked twice as many hours as Chuck. How much money did Chuck earn last week?

A) $100

B) $400

C) $300

D) $200

6. A first-edition comic book costs a dealer $60. If the dealer wants to offer customers a discount of 10% off the price marked on the tag but still wants to make a profit of 20% over cost, what price should be placed on the tag?

A) $64.80

B) $72

C) $79.90

D) $80

Student-Produced Response Questions

7. Meike purchased a $10 item at a hardware store to be used for a painting project. He later found an online coupon for the store that would allow him to save 20% on all purchases during a certain time period. Meike went back to the hardware store during the time the coupon could be used and bought a paint roller for $10.00, a paintbrush for $7.00, painter's tape for $6.50, and epoxy glue for $5.25. If the prices listed above were the amounts before the coupon was applied, what percent did Meike save on all the supplies for his painting project? Round to the nearest whole percent, if needed.

8. A church fund loans money to its members at the rate of 6% annual interest on the original loan principal. Unice borrowed $2,400 in January and paid back $1,000 by the end of June. In December of that year, she paid off the loan. To the nearest dollar, how much did Unice pay to close out of the loan at the end of the year?

9. A merchant is selling a new line of watches. He prices the watches at $120 and runs a 10% off sale. During the sale, he made a profit of 20% on the watches. How much did the merchant pay for each watch?

10. To make the school basketball team, Selena has to take at least 20 free throws and successfully make 60% of her shots. So far, Selena has taken 15 shots and has been successful 4 times. What is the minimum number of total shots Selena must take to qualify for the team?

LESSON 2:

Solving Measurement, Unit Rate, and Density Problems

- Measurement
- Unit Rates
- Density

Explain Measurement

Measurement problems, in which units of measure must be converted, are often seen on the SAT as real-world application problems for ratio and proportion. The table below shows common length, mass, and capacity conversion factors for both the English and metric systems.

Definition

Measurement is the act of comparing an unknown size to an established standard.

Measurements

Table of Measures

Length	Weight (Mass)	Liquid (Capacity)

Customary System:
1 foot (ft.) = 12 inches (in.)
1 yard (yd.) = 36 inches
    1 yard = 3 feet
1 mile (mi.) = 5,280 feet
	1 pound (lb.) = 16 ounces (oz.)
	1 ton (T) = 2,000 pounds
		1 cup (c.) = 8 fluid
		    ounces (fl. oz.)
		1 pint (pt.) = 2 cups
		1 quart (qt.) = 2 pints
		1 gallon (gal.) = 4 quarts

Metric System: 1 meter (m) = 1,000 millimeters (mm) 1 meter = 100 centimeters (cm) 1 kilometer (km) = 1,000 meters	1 gram (g) = 1,000 milligrams (mg) 1 kilogram (km) = 1,000 grams	1 liter (L) = 1,000 milliliters (mL) 1 kiloliter (kL) = 1,000 liters
Area		
1 square foot (sq. ft.) = 144 square inches (sq. in.) 1 square yard (sq. yd.) = 9 square feet		
Time		
1 minute (min.) = 60 seconds (sec.) 1 hour (hr.) = 60 minutes 1 day = 24 hours 1 week = 7 days 1 year = 365 days (except for leap year)	1 month ≈ 30 days 1 year = 52 weeks 1 year = 12 months	

To convert from **larger** units to **smaller** units, find the conversion factor and multiply. To convert from **smaller** units to **larger** units, find the conversion factor and divide. Be sure to include labels. If your labels cancel properly, your problem setup is correct.

To convert from one square measure to another, make sure to square the conversion factor. To convert from one cubic measure to another, make sure to cube the conversion factor.

Example 1

How many cartons, each containing 12 ounces of candy, are required to complete an order for 3 pounds of candy? (1 pound = 16 ounces)

A) 2

B) 4

C) 6

D) 8

Solution

$$\frac{3 \text{ lbs}}{1} \times \frac{16 \text{ ounces}}{1 \text{ lb}} \times \frac{1 \text{ carton}}{12 \text{ ounces}} = 4 \text{ cartons}$$

Answer: B

Example 2

A small lot measured 200 cm × 200 cm. Find the area of the lot in square meters.

A) 0.004 m²

B) 4 m²

C) 0.4 m²

D) 40,000 m²

Solution

From the table on page 177, 100 cm = 1 m. Therefore, (100 cm)² = (1 m)² or 10,000 cm² = 1 m².

Then, 200 cm × 200 cm = 40,000 cm² and $\frac{40,000 \text{ cm}^2}{1} \times \frac{1 \text{ m}^2}{10,000 \text{ cm}^2} = 4 \text{ m}^2$.

Answer: B

Explain Scale Drawings

A specific type of measurement conversion problem often seen on the SAT is that of the relationship between a scale model and the true object it represents. A **scale model** reflects the real object or surface, but all the real-life dimensions have been reduced or enlarged by the same scale factor. The scale factor is the ratio of any two corresponding lengths between the model and the real object or surface;

mathematically, one ratio is: $\dfrac{\text{scale drawing measure}}{\text{actual measure}}$.

To solve scale model problems, set up a proportion that compares the scale factor ratio to the ratio of the model dimension compared to the actual dimension. It is essential that the units of corresponding measurements are the same.

Example 1

A scale drawing of a car shows 1 inch = 4 feet. If the actual car is 18 feet 6 inches long, how long is the car in the scale drawing?

A) 74.4 inches

B) 74 inches

C) 4.65 inches

D) 4.625 inches

Solution:

Set up a proportion: $\dfrac{\text{scale drawing (1 inch)}}{\text{actual (4 feet)}} = \dfrac{\text{drawing (} x \text{ inches)}}{\text{actual (18.5 feet.)}}$.

Note that the length of the actual car is converted to feet, so that the unit of measurement for the actual object matches the unit in the given scale. Then,

$$\frac{1}{4} = \frac{x}{18.5}$$

$4x = 18.5$ Cross multiply

$x = 4.625$ inches   Solve for x

Answer: D

Example 2

On a scale drawing, 5 centimeters represent 20 meters. How many centimeters represent 8 meters 4 centimeters? (100 centimeters = 1 meter)

A) 2.01

B) 2.1

C) 32.16

D) 32.2

Solution

8 meters 4 centimeters = (8 × 100 centimeters) + 4 centimeters

$$= 804 \text{ centimeters} - 8.04 \text{ meters}$$

Set up a proportion.

$$\frac{5 \text{ centimeters}}{20 \text{ meters}} = \frac{x \text{ centimeters}}{8.04 \text{ meters}}$$

$$x = \frac{(5)(8.04)}{20} = 2.01 \text{ centimeters}$$

Answer: A

Answers begin on page 679.

1. Convert 3 feet to inches.

   A) 12
   B) 24
   C) 36
   D) 48

2. Convert 10 yards to inches.

   A) 720
   B) 360
   C) 120
   D) 90

3. Convert 45 square feet to square yards.

   A) 5 yd^2
   B) 9 yd^2
   C) 135 yd^2
   D) 405 yd^2

4. Convert 2 miles per hour to feet per second.

5. Architects are planning to build a skyscraper that is 1,440 feet tall. They are creating a model that is 1 yard high. Which of the following scales best describes the model?

   A) 1 inch = 35 feet
   B) 1 inch = 40 feet
   C) 1 inch = 45 feet
   D) 1 inch = 50 feet

Model SAT Questions

1. One side of a 3-kilometer stretch of highway in Ontario will be decorated with a border of bricks, each of which is 500 millimeters long. How many bricks will be needed?

   A) 6,000
   B) 15,000
   C) 600,000
   D) 1,500,000

Strategy: 1 kilometer = 1,000 meters and 1 meter = 1,000 millimeters. Therefore, 1 kilometer = 1,000 × 1,000 = 1,000,000 millimeters and 3 kilometers = 3,000,000 millimeters. Since each brick is 500 millimeters long, there will be $\frac{3,000,000}{500}$ = 6,000 bricks. This is answer choice A.

2. A scale model of a rectangular baseball field is 40 inches long and has an area of 1,200 square inches. The width of the actual field is 150 yards. What is the area of the actual field?

   A) 800 yd^2

   B) 8,000 yd^2

   C) 30,000 yd^2

   D) 3,000,000 yd^2

Strategy: The width of the scale model is $\dfrac{\text{area}}{\text{length}} = \dfrac{1{,}200}{40} = 30$ inches. Knowing the width of the actual field and the scale model, set up a proportion to find the length of the actual field, x. This proportion will place the actual field dimensions in the numerators and the model dimensions in the denominators: $\dfrac{x \text{ yd}}{40 \text{ in}} = \dfrac{150 \text{ yd}}{30 \text{ in}}$.

Cross multiply and divide to find that $x = (40 \cdot 150) \div 30 = 200$ yds. Then, the area of the actual field is length × width = $200 \cdot 150 = 30{,}000$ yd^2. Answer choice C is correct.

Explain Unit Rate

A **unit rate** is the ratio of two measurements in which the second measurement is 1.

Examples of unit rate situations include:

- cost per unit weight, such as dollars per 1 ounce
- distance per unit time, such as kilometers per 1 hour
- job done per unit time, such as fences painted per 1 hour
- population density, number of residents per single unit of defined area

On the SAT, unit rates are often part of larger problems.

Think It Through

Example 1

Jordan reads fiction at a rate of 3,000 words in a quarter of an hour. What is Jordan's reading rate in words per minute?

A) 12,000 words per minute

B) 750 words per minute

C) 200 words per minute

D) 20 words per minute

Solution

The units of measure must appear in the fractions so they can be canceled.

$$\frac{3000 \text{ words}}{\frac{1}{4} \text{ hour}} \times \frac{1 \text{ hour}}{60 \text{ minutes}} = \frac{3000 \text{ words}}{15 \text{ minutes}} = 200 \text{ words per minute}$$

Answer: C

Example 2

A car drove 300 miles in four hours. How fast was the car traveling in miles per hour?

Solution

Note that when we set up the problem, the needed units are already in the correct positions:

$$\frac{300 \text{ miles}}{4 \text{ hours}} = 75 \text{ miles per hour.}$$

Example 3

The chart below shows estimated population and area for four European countries and the United States. Which country has a population density closest to the United States?

Country	Land Area (mi²)	Population Estimate
United States	3,794,101	318,906,617
France	210,026	63,970,000
Germany	137,886	80,781,000
Italy	116,336	60,762,320
Portugal	35,556	10,562,178

A) France

B) Germany

C) Italy

D) Portugal

Solution

Divide each population by the corresponding land area to determine the population density.

United States: $\dfrac{318,906,617}{3,794,101} = 84.05$

France: $\dfrac{63,970,000}{210,026} = 304.58$

Germany: $\dfrac{80,781,000}{137,886} = 585.85$

Italy: $\dfrac{60,762,320}{116,336} = 522.30$

Portugal: $\dfrac{10,562,178}{35,556} = 297.06$

Portugal's population density is closest to the population density in the United States.

Answer: D

Answers begin on page 680.

1. Lugus can walk 6 km in 3 hours. At that rate, how many hours will it take him to walk 8 km?

2. Michael read 10 books in 5 weeks. At that rate, how many weeks will it take him to read 25 books?

3. Johannes can prepare dinner for 4 people for $15. How much money will it cost to prepare dinner for 10 people?

    A) $22.50
    B) $30.00
    C) $35.00
    D) $37.50

4. Which of the countries listed below has the lowest population density?

Country	Population	Land Area (mi²)
Barbados	256,000	170
Belgium	10,827,519	11,787
Benin	8,935,000	43,484
Bermuda	65,000	20

    A) Barbados
    B) Belgium
    C) Benin
    D) Bermuda

Explain Density

Density is the ratio of mass per unit volume. Scientists usually measure mass in grams (g) and the volume in 1 cm³, which is equivalent to 1 mL.

Think It Through

Example

A rectangular solid rock with a mass of 60 grams takes up a volume of 30 cm³. What is the density of the rock?

A) 0.5 grams per cm³
B) 2 grams per cm³
C) 90 grams per cm³
D) 180 grams per cm³

Solution

Density is $\dfrac{\text{mass}}{\text{unit volume}} = \dfrac{60 \text{ grams}}{30 \text{ cm}^3} = 2$ grams per cm³. Answer choice B is correct.

Answers begin on page 680.

1. A liquid weighing 306 grams completely fills a graduated cylinder that has a capacity of exactly 22.5 mL. Calculate the density of the liquid.

    A) 0.074 g/mL

    B) 13.600 g/mL

    C) 74 g/mL

    D) 13,600 g/mL

2. The density of ethyl alcohol is 0.789 g/mL. What is the mass of the ethyl alcohol that exactly fills a 200.0 mL container?

    A) 394.5 grams

    B) 278.9 grams

    C) 253.5 grams

    D) 157.8 grams

Model SAT Questions

1. A skater can travel at a speed of 12 miles per hour. At that rate, how many minutes will it take him to travel 3,696 feet?

Strategy: The first step is to find the speed in feet per minute.

$$\frac{12 \text{ miles}}{1 \text{ hour}} \cdot \frac{1 \text{ hour}}{60 \text{ minutes}} \cdot \frac{5,280 \text{ feet}}{1 \text{ mile}} = \frac{1056 \text{ feet}}{\text{minute}}.$$ Then, set up a proportion to find

the time it will take him to travel the given distance: $\frac{1056 \text{ feet}}{1 \text{ minute}} = \frac{3,696 \text{ feet}}{x \text{ minutes}}$.

Cross multiply and divide to find that $x = 3,696 \div 1,056 = 3.5$ minutes.

2. A solid that measures 3.0 cm by 6.0 cm by 6.0 cm has a mass of 120 grams. What is the density of the solid?

   A) 0.9 cm^3/gram

   B) 8 grams/cm

   C) 1.11 grams/cm^3

   D) 120 grams/108 cm^3

Strategy: Density is mass per single unit of volume, so this eliminates choice D. We know that the mass of the solid is 120 grams, and we can calculate the solid's volume as 6.0 cm $\cdot$ 6.0 cm $\cdot$ 3.0 cm = 108 cm^3. So,

$\text{Density} = \dfrac{\text{mass}}{\text{volume}} = \dfrac{120 \text{ grams}}{108 \text{ cm}^3} \approx 1.11$ grams/cm^3. This is answer choice C.

3. The density of the chemical element palladium is 12 g/cm^3. A certain rectangular block of palladium weighing 216 grams has a base area that is 12 cm^2. What is the height of the block?

   A) 1.5 cm

   B) 3.0 cm

   C) 4.0 cm

   D) 9.0 cm

Strategy: Set up a proportion to find the volume of the block. $\dfrac{12 \text{ grams}}{1 \text{ cm}} = \dfrac{216 \text{ grams}}{V \text{ cm}}$.

Cross multiply and divide to find that $V = 216 \div 12 = 18$ cm^3. Let h be the block's height. Then, $18 = 12h$ and $h = 1.5$ cm. The correct answer choice is A.

SAT-Type Questions

Answers begin on page 680.

1. A scale drawing of a playground shows 1 inch = 10 feet. If the actual playground is 50 yards long, how long is the playground in the scale drawing?

   A) 5 inches

   B) 10 inches

   C) 12 inches

   D) 15 inches

2. If a single ounce of silver costs $5.50, how much money is needed to buy $2\frac{1}{2}$ pounds of silver?

   A) $88

   B) $176

   C) 200

   D) $220

3. The density of lead is 11.39 grams/cm^3. What is the mass of a cube of lead, if each side measures 6 cm?

    A) 18.96 grams

    B) 2460.24 grams

    C) 410.04 grams

    D) 68.34 grams

4. Water flows into a 500-liter tank, filling 10% of the capacity in 1 minute. What is the rate of flow in kiloliters per hour?

    A) 3 kiloliters per hour

    B) 4 kiloliters per hour

    C) 5 kiloliters per hour

    D) 6 kiloliters per hour

5. If Juanita can make 10 centerpieces in 15 minutes, how many hours will it take her to make 960 centerpieces?

    A) 6 hours

    B) 11.25 hours

    C) 22.5 hours

    D) 24 hours

6. The chart below shows population and land area for Guadeloupe, Israel, Jamaica, and Malta. Which country has the lowest population density?

Country	Population	Land Area (square miles)
Guadeloupe	403,355	640
Israel	8,320,122	967
Jamaica	2,711,476	640
Malta	416,055	3,421

    A) Guadeloupe

    B) Israel

    C) Jamaica

    D) Malta

7. Carl is 6 feet 4 inches tall. His son is three-quarters as tall. What is the difference in their heights?

    A) 1 foot 6 inches

    B) 1 foot 7 inches

    C) 4 feet 6 inches

    D) 4 feet 10 inches

8. The element Krypton, abbreviated Kr, is used as a gas in fluorescent lights. The density of Kr is 0.00373g/cm^3. If the mass of a tank of Kr is 9.0×10^2 grams, what is the volume of the tank, measured in cubic meters?

    A) 2.413×10^{-1} m^3

    B) 2.413 m^3

    C) 2.413×10^3 m^3

    D) 2.413×10^5 m^3

9. A road crew can pave 1.5 miles of road in an eight-hour shift. If they were stopped after two hours because of weather conditions, how many feet of road did they pave? (5,280 feet = 1 mile)

A) 440 feet

B) 780 feet

C) 1,980 feet

D) 1,760 feet

10. A structure shaped like a cylinder has a base with area 60π square feet and a volume of 240π cubic feet. The scale model of the cylinder has a height of 12 inches. What is the volume of the scale model?

A) 3.75π ft^3

B) 15.0π ft^3

C) 45π ft^3

D) 60π ft^3

Student-Produced Response Questions

11. Louis built a wall using bricks that are each 4 inches high. He used a 1-inch layer of cement between each row of bricks. If his wall is 7 feet 10 inches tall, how many rows of bricks are in Louis's wall?

12. Alyssa has some containers that each hold one gallon of liquid. She used these containers to dispose of waste from the chemistry laboratory. She collected 3 quarts 1 pint of liquid from the first table, 4 quarts from the second table, 2 quarts from the third table, and 3 quarts 1 pint from the fourth table. What is the least number of containers Alyssa needed to collect the waste from all the tables? (4 quarts = 1 gallon, 2 pints = 1 quart)

LESSON 3:

Describing and Interpreting Scatterplots

- **Scatterplots**
- **Linear Patterns in Scatterplots, Lines of Best Fit, & Correlation**
- **Non-linear Behavior in Scatterplots**

Scatterplots relate two sets of data on a graph. Both the vertical and horizontal axes show numeric data.

Explain Linear Patterns in Scatterplots, Lines of Best Fit, & Correlation

When you look at numeric data that reflects real-world events, the data are often expressed as ordered pairs of variables. Often a pattern can be recognized that is close enough to a line that we can use a linear relationship to help us describe how the variables are related. We can create a picture of this relationship with a scatterplot. Scatterplots created on a graphing calculator look like the images shown below. The data are entered as a pair of lists. Each observation of the data is considered as an ordered pair and is graphed as a dot. The horizontal axis is used to scale the independent variable, and the vertical axis is used to scale the dependent variable. Data that appear to be linear have a **linear correlation** and can be approximated by a **line of best fit**. The line of best fit will have a slope and y-intercept that helps us to predict the changes in the *dependent variable*, or the y-values, from changes in the *independent variable*, or the x-values.

- The slope tells us how much the y-value of the line of best fit changes with a one-unit change in the x-value.

- The sign of the slope tells us whether y gets larger or smaller as x gets larger. The slope of the line will depend on whether the correlation is positive or negative.

- The y-intercept helps us to understand the predicted value of y when x is zero.

One of three situations will occur:

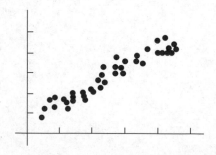

Definitions

Linear correlation is a tendency for two variables to change together in a linear fashion.

A **line of best fit** is a line on a graph that shows the general pattern the dots form.

1. The dots move from the lower left to the upper right. We say the variables in the two lists are **positively correlated**. We can imagine a line of best fit graphed through the scatterplot. **The slope of the line of best fit would be positive**. We can estimate the slope of the line of best fit by looking at the steepness of the line. A slope close to 1 would occur if the scatterplot points appear to move right at the same pace as they move up. If the points appear to move up faster than they move right, the slope would be more than 1. Likewise, if the points appear to move right faster than they move up, the slope would be still positive, but less than 1.

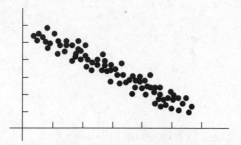

2. The dots move from the upper left to the lower right. We say the variables in the two lists are **negatively correlated**. We can again imagine a line of best fit graphed through the scatterplot. **The slope of the line of best fit would be negative**. We can estimate the slope of the line of best fit by looking at the steepness of the line. A slope close to −1 would occur if the scatterplot points appear to move right at the same pace as they move down. If the points appear to move down faster than they move right, the slope would be less than −1. Likewise, if the points appear to move right faster than they move down, the slope would be still negative, but greater than −1.

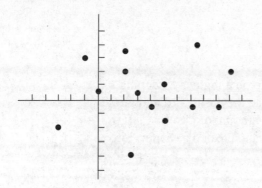

3. The dots do not appear in a linear pattern. We say there is **no correlation** in the data and we do not look for a line of best fit.

<u>Note:</u> The best-fitting straight line that minimizes the sum of the squares of the differences between the actual data values and the values predicted by the line is called the *least squares line*. While graphing calculators allow us to graph the least squares line using the linear regression feature, the SAT does not require students to do so.

Example

Which statement is true about the data collected in the following scatterplot?

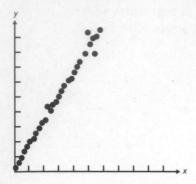

A) There is positive correlation and the slope of the line of best fit is close to 1.

B) There is positive correlation and the slope of the line of best fit is greater than 1.

C) There is positive correlation and the slope of the line of best fit is less than 1.

D) There is negative correlation and the slope of the line of best fit is close to −1.

Solution

The dots move from lower left to upper right. The graph moves up faster than it moves right, so the slope of the line of best fit is greater than 1.

Answer: B

Model SAT Questions

1. Matthew and his sister Merab took a long car trip on a highway, keeping to a fairly constant speed. Every 5 miles, Merab read the dashboard and wrote down the total number of miles traveled and the amount of gasoline left in the tank. She entered the data into her computer and created a scatterplot. Which description would fit her scatterplot?

   A) Weak positive linear correlation

   B) Strong positive linear correlation

   C) Weak negative linear correlation

   D) Strong negative linear correlation

   Strategy: The number of miles will increase at a fairly constant rate, while the amount of gasoline remaining will decrease at a fairly constant rate. This will show as a strong negative linear correlation, choice D.

2. A study showed the effects of cigarette smoking on lung cancer mortality rates.

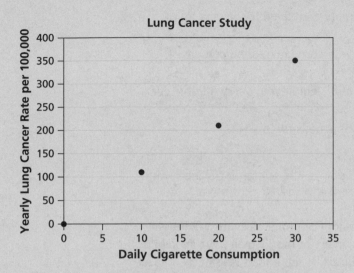

Which of the following statements is the best interpretation of the scatterplot above?

A) If you do not smoke, you cannot get lung cancer.

B) If you do smoke, you will get lung cancer.

C) There is a strong positive linear correlation between number of cigarettes smoked per day and the risk of getting lung cancer.

D) If you smoke less than 10 cigarettes per day, you will not get lung cancer.

Strategy: Scatterplots are collections of data, not rules. The data here forms a fairly straight line with a positive slope. All we can tell from this scatterplot is that there is a strong positive linear correlation between number of cigarettes smoked per day and the risk of getting lung cancer, answer choice C.

3. The scatterplot below compares employment status and car ownership in several counties.

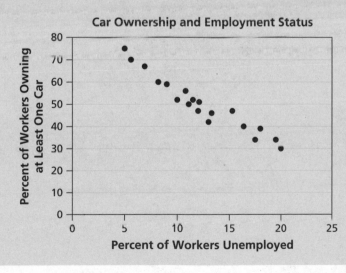

Which of the following statements is the best interpretation of the scatterplot above?

A) The rate of unemployment is negatively correlated to the percent of workers owning at least one car.

B) The rate of unemployment is positively correlated to the percent of workers owning at least one car.

C) If every eligible car owner in a county is employed, every eligible car owner would own at least one car.

D) The line of best fit for this scatterplot is not straight.

Strategy: Look at the direction of the plotted points. The scatterplot is linear with a negative slope, showing negative correlation. This is answer choice A.

4. The scatterplot below compares hand span in centimeters against height in centimeters for a group of 17 men. How many of the 17 men have an actual height that is lower than the height predicted by the line of best fit by at least 15 centimeters?

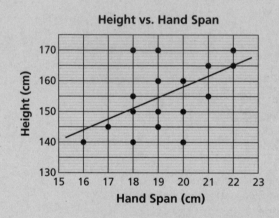

A) 1
B) 2
C) 3
D) 4

Strategy: One man, whose hand span is 20 cm and whose height is 140 cm, fits these criteria. Select answer choice A.

Questions 5 and 6 use the scatterplot below, which compares the total grams of fat to the total number of calories for some common fast food items.

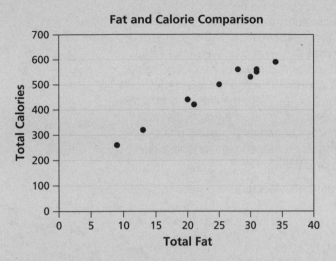

Fat and Calorie Comparison

5. Which equation is the best estimate for the line of best fit for this data?

   A) $y = 13x$
   B) $y = 150x + 13$
   C) $y = 13x + 150$
   D) $y = 153x$

Strategy: Without wasting time to find the y-intercept, see that it must be greater than 0. This eliminates answer choices A and D. Find $\frac{y_2 - y_1}{x_2 - x_1}$ for several pairs of values, such as $\frac{530 - 420}{30 - 21} = \frac{110}{9} = 12.222$. The closest slope shown is 13. Choice C, $y = 13x + 150$, is the only valid answer.

6. Which of the following is the best interpretation of the y-intercept?

   A) It helps the reader predict the total calories that food with no fat will have.
   B) It helps the reader estimate calories for food very low in fat.
   C) It tells the reader that it is unlikely that food will have no fat.
   D) It tells the reader that all food must have at least about 150 grams of fat in a serving.

Strategy: The y-intercept helps the reader think about food with no fat or very little fat because the y-intercept tells you the behavior when $x = 0$. Select answer choice B.

On the SAT, scatterplots for **non-linear behavior,** or behavior that does not approximate a straight line, will model quadratic or exponential behavior. If the graph is strictly increasing or decreasing, and the ratio between successive values of the dependent variable is nearly the same each time the independent variable is changed by a set amount, the behavior shown is **exponential**. If the ratio between the values of the dependent variable increases with distance from the minimum or maximum value, then the behavior shown is **quadratic**. Graphs of quadratic functions are symmetric with respect to a vertical *line of symmetry*. The point (x, y) where the line of symmetry intersects the graph is referred to as the *turning point,* or *vertex*. If a graph shows a turning point, the graph is quadratic. If the graph does not show a turning point, it might be necessary to see if the ratio between progressive dependent variable values remains the same or if the ratios steadily increase or decrease.

Inferential questions related to linear and non-linear behaviors require a deeper understanding of scatterplot representations.

Model SAT Questions

Questions 1 and 2 refer to the following information.

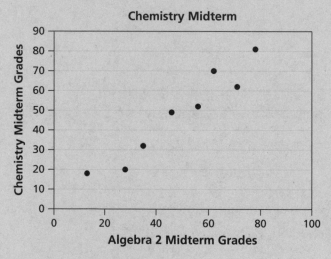

1. The scatterplot above shows the test results for eight students taking both Algebra 2 and Chemistry. Which is the best choice below for line of best fit?

   A) $y = 2x$

   B) $y = -x$

   C) $y = x$

   D) $y = x + 10$

Strategy: Study the plotted points. The data appears to be linear, and the slope of the line of best fit will be positive and close to 1. The change in Chemistry midterm grade values is similar to the change in Algebra 2 midterm grade values. The y-intercept for this line will be fairly close to 0. Thus, the best choice is C, $y = x$.

2. Ava was home sick during midterms week and took both exams when she returned to school. If Ava earned a 50 on her Algebra 2 exam, which score is most likely for her Chemistry exam?

   A) 30

   B) 50

   C) 70

   D) 90

Strategy: The grades for Algebra 2 and Chemistry appear to be similar, so use the line $y = x$ as a guide for the line of best fit. Using the line $y = x$ as a guide for predicting Ava's chemistry score, the closest dependent variable (y) value choice to 50 is the independent variable (x) value 50. Answer choice B is correct.

3. The following scatterplot shows the effect of blood alcohol level on relative risk of an accident.

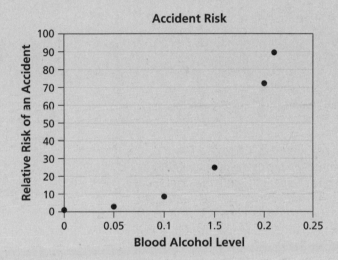

Which statement describes the data?

   A) The behavior is exponential with a minimum relative risk at the 0% blood alcohol level.

   B) The behavior is exponential with a minimum relative risk at the 0.05% blood alcohol level.

   C) The behavior is quadratic with a minimum relative risk at the 0% blood alcohol level.

   D) The behavior is quadratic with a minimum relative risk at the 0.05% blood alcohol level.

Strategy: The ratio of successive dependent variable values appears to be about 2.5 for all pairs of successive dependent values. Since the pairs increase at a constant ratio, the graph is exponential. The minimum value is at a 0% blood alcohol level, so select answer A.

4. The following scatterplot shows the interest-driven growth of a child's bank account over ten years.

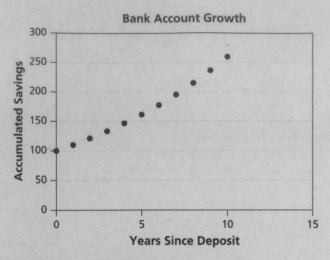

Bank Account Growth

Which statement is not supported by the scatterplot?

A) The initial investment was $100.

B) The growth was constant over time.

C) The growth was exponential for the first 10 years.

D) This graph cannot be extended beyond quadrant 1.

Strategy: Visually, you can see that the graph is exponential. Choose a few successive dependent variable values to mathematically prove this; you will find that the ratio is always close to 1.1. This eliminates choice B. Clearly the domain of the function is restricted to non-zero values, so eliminate choice D. The y-intercept tells us that $100 was in the account at time 0; this eliminates choice A. The graph is exponential so eliminate choice C and select choice B. Exponential growth is not constant over time.

SAT-Type Questions

Answers begin on page 682.

1. Which equation is most likely the equation for the line of best fit shown in the scatterplot below?

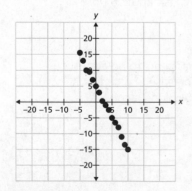

A) $y = 2x + 5$

B) $y = -2x + 5$

C) $y = -2x - 4$

D) $y = 2x - 4$

2. The scatterplot below shows the cucumber yield as measured in kg/m² for a range of rainfall amounts measured in millimeters.

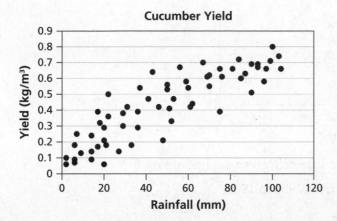

Cucumber Yield

Which of the following statements is <u>not</u> a correct interpretation of this scatterplot?

A) A farmer can predict his crop precisely by measuring rainfall.

B) There is a positive linear correlation between rainfall and cucumber yield.

C) The y-intercept shows the expected cucumber yield if there is no rain.

D) The line of best fit is meaningless outside the first quadrant.

3. The scatterplot below compares average speed, measured in miles per hour, to the average fuel consumption, measured in miles per gallon, for a new sport utility vehicle.

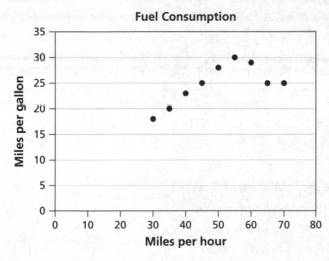

Fuel Consumption

Which of the following statements is best supported by the data in the scatterplot?

A) The slower the car is driven, the less gas per mile is used for all speeds.

B) The faster the car is driven, the less gas per mile is used for all speeds.

C) If the car is driven at 100 mph, the car will use fuel at a rate of 20 miles per gallon.

D) The graph is quadratic, except at high speeds.

4. The following scatterplot shows the number of students enrolled in United States elementary schools from 1990–2000.

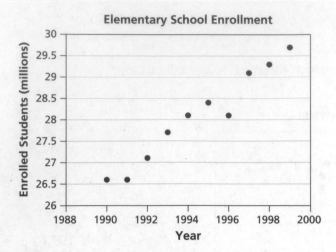

Which of the following is the most accurate statement about the line of best fit?

A) The slope changes to a negative value from 1995 to 1996.
B) The slope is zero from 1990 to 1991.
C) The slope increases over time.
D) The slope is constant over time.

5. The scatterplot below shows the number of sales per month for a new camera store. Which of the following statements best describes the sales growth for the first 6 months of operation?

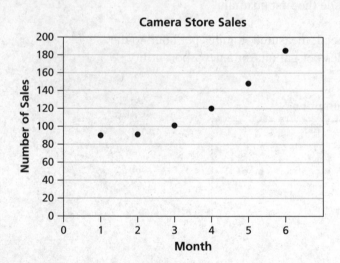

A) The scatterplot shows strong linear growth of sales after a flat start.
B) The scatterplot shows weak linear growth for the first 6 months.
C) The scatterplot shows exponential growth for the first 6 months.
D) The scatterplot shows quadratic growth for the first 6 months.

6. The scatterplot below shows the number of new employees hired by ABC Electronics in its first four years of business. Which of the following descriptions best fits ABC Electronics' hiring trend?

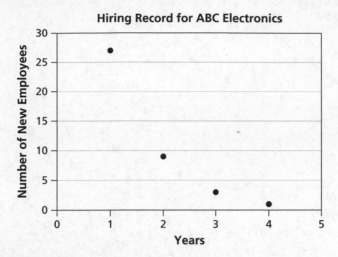

A) Linear behavior, negative slope
B) Exponential behavior, growth
C) Exponential behavior, decline
D) Quadratic behavior, decline

Student-Produced Response Questions

7. The scatterplot below records the hand span and height, measured in centimeters, of a group of volunteers. A line of best fit is drawn. How many volunteers were more than 10 centimeters taller than the height predicted by the line of best fit?

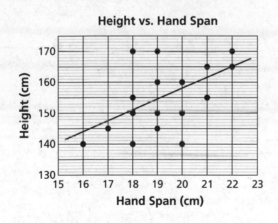

8. The scatterplot below compares hours spent studying and grades received on a final exam. What grade is predicted for a student who studied for 4 hours?

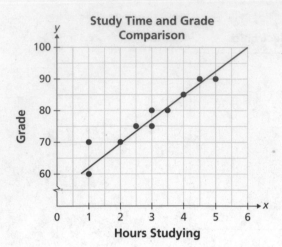

Study Time and Grade Comparison

LESSON 4:

Comparing Linear Growth with Exponential Growth

▪ **Linear Behavior**

▪ **Exponential Behavior**

· · · · · · **Explain** **Linear Behavior** ·

Recall that for linear behavior, the parent function is $f(x) = x$. **Linear functions** have a constant rate of growth, m, which is the slope of the line. As the value of x increases by one unit, the value of $f(x)$ increases by m. Thus, $f(x+1) - f(x) = m$.

The most general form of the linear function is $f(x) = mx + b$, where m is the slope of the line and b is the line's y-intercept. The slope (m) is the change in y with respect to x. For any two points (x_1, y_1) and (x_2, y_2), the slope is calculated using the formula $m = \dfrac{y_2 - y_1}{x_2 - x_1}$. If a line's slope is positive, the graph extends from lower left to upper right. If the slope is negative, the graph of the line extends from upper left to lower right. Remember, the greater the absolute value of the slope, the steeper the graph of the line. If the slope is zero, the line is parallel to the x-axis. In this case, the y-intercept is the y-coordinate of the intersection between the line and the y-axis.

Compare the graphs below. For each of these graphs, $|m| = 2$. The "steepness" is the same. The sign of the slope determines left to right orientation, and the y-intercept determines the vertical placement of the line.

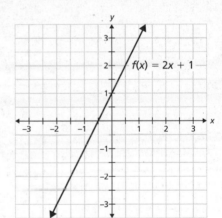
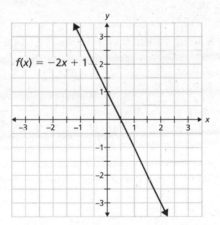

On the SAT, you may be asked to identify the correct linear equation from a table of (x, y) coordinates. You may also be asked to select the correct graph based on its described properties.

Example 1

Which of the given functions is represented in the table below?

x	f(x)
1	2
2	5
3	8
4	11

A) $f(x) = 3x$

B) $f(x) = x + 3$

C) $f(x) = 3x - 1$

D) $f(x) = 3x - 2$

Solution

The rate of change from one $(x, f(x))$ pair to the next is constant, so by definition, the function is linear. Notice that all the answer choices are linear, so none of them can be eliminated, but we can see that they are all given in the form $f(x) = mx + b$, so we need to find the slope and the y-intercept for the equation defined by the table.

The table shows that as x-values increase by 1, $f(x)$ increases by 3, so the slope is $\frac{3}{1}$, or 3. Now find the y-intercept. Extend the table to find the y-value when $x = 0$. Following the pattern, $f(0) = f(1) - 3 = 2 - 3 = -1$. Then, $f(x) = 3x - 1$.

Answer: C

Example 2

Which of the following graphs represents a linear function with a positive slope and a y-intercept of 5?

A)

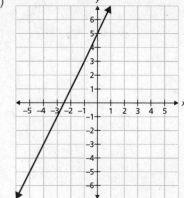

B)

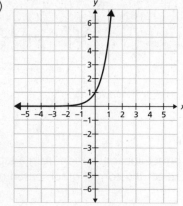

C)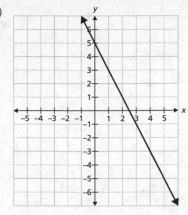

D)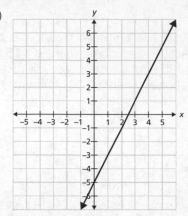

Solution

Answer choice B is not linear, so eliminate it. Answer choice D has a *y*-intercept of −5, and it can also be eliminated. Between choices A and C, only A has a slope that extends from the lower left to the upper right, indicating that it is positive.

Answer: A

Example 3

Which type of function is defined by the data in the table below?

x	f(x)
1	−1.1
2	−2.5
3	−3.9
4	−5.3

A) Exponential growth
B) Exponential decay
C) Linear growth
D) Linear decline

Solution

The difference in successive pairs of dependent variable values is constant, meaning the behavior is linear. The $f(x)$ values are decreasing, showing linear decline.

Answer: D

Example 4

Geno is starting a window-washing business. He has decided to charge a $5.00 flat fee and $0.50 per window. Which of the following equations can Geno use to determine the amount of money to collect from each customer?

A) $f(x) = 0.50^x + 5$
B) $f(x) = 5x + 0.50$
C) $f(x) = 0.50x + 5$
D) $f(x) = 0.50x - 5$

Solution

In this situation, the amount of money Geno will collect from each customer will vary only by the number of windows he washes because everyone is charged a $5.00 flat fee. Thus, $0.50 represents m, or the change in the total cost of each job for each additional window washed. The only answer choices where $0.50 represents m are C and D. Since the $5.00 flat fee is added to each job, select C.

Answer: C

Model SAT Questions

1. Which of the given functions represents the following data table?

n	$f(n)$
1	−1
2	−4
3	−7
4	−10

   A) $f(n) = 3n - 4$
   B) $f(n) = -3n + 2$
   C) $f(n) = 3^n - 4$
   D) $f(n) = 3^{n-1} - 1$

Strategy: The difference in successive pairs of $f(n)$ values is constant, so the function is linear. This eliminates answer choices C and D. Try substituting in values from the chart for choices A and B. A: $f(1) = 3(1) - 4 = -1$, but $f(2) = 3(2) - 4 = 2$. You could stop here and select answer choice B, but to be sure, try B: $f(1) = -3(1) + 2 = -1$, $f(2) = -3(2) + 2 = -4$. Stop here. Choice B is correct.

2. Categorize the data in the table below:

x	$f(x)$
1	1.2
2	2.5
3	3.8
4	5.1

   A) Exponential growth
   B) Exponential decay
   C) Linear growth
   D) Linear decline

Strategy: Find the difference in successive pairs of dependent variable values: $2.5 - 1.2 = 1.3$, $3.8 - 2.5 = 1.3$, and $5.1 - 3.8 = 1.3$. These differences are constant and the values are increasing, which indicates linear growth.

An **exponential function** has a constantly increasing rate of growth; this differs from a linear function. The parent function for exponential growth, $f(x) = b^x$, tells us that as x grows by one unit, the value of $f(x)$ increases by a constant rate, b. So,

$$\frac{f(x+1)}{f(x)} = b$$

The most general form of the exponential function is $f(x) = ab^x$. We will refer to a as the coefficient and b as the base.

Compare the graphs of the functions $f(x) = 2^x$ and $g(x) = 3^x$ (below) and see that both the functions have a y-intercept equal to 1, but the function with the larger base grows more quickly in the first quadrant.

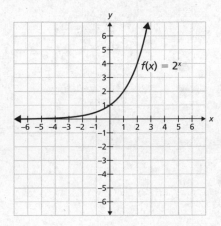
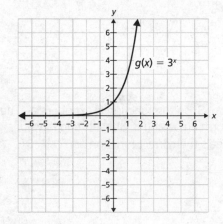

Now compare the graphs of the functions $f(x) = 2^x$ and $h(x) = 3 \cdot 2^x$. The graph of the function $h(x)$ has a y-intercept equal to 3, which is the coefficient, and it grows 3 times as fast as the function $f(x)$.

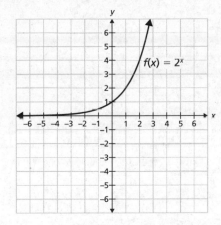
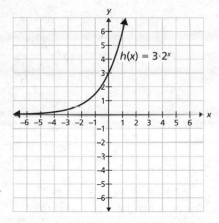

Like the linear behavior portion of this lesson, SAT questions with regard to exponential behavior may ask you to identify the correct exponential equation from a table of (x, y) coordinates or to select the correct graph based on its described properties.

Example 1

Which of the given functions is represented in the table below?

x	f(x)
0	1
1	3
2	9
3	27

A) $f(x) = 3^x + 1$

B) $f(x) = 3^x$

C) $f(x) = x^3$

D) $f(x) = 3x + 1$

Solution

The $f(x)$ values increase by a constant ratio, 3, so the function is exponential. The only answer choices given in exponential form are A and B. Substituting in values for x and solving for $f(x)$ immediately reveals the correct function as $f(x) = 3^x$.

Answer: B

Example 2

Categorize the data in the table below:

x	f(x)
1	0.25
2	0.75
3	2.25
4	6.75

A) Exponential growth

B) Exponential decay

C) Linear growth

D) Linear decline

Solution

Begin by determining if the function is linear or exponential. The dependent variable values do not increase by a constant rate but by a constant ratio of 3, thus the function is exponential. The dependent variable values are increasing, so this is an example of exponential growth.

Answer: A

Example 3

Which of the following best describes this graph?

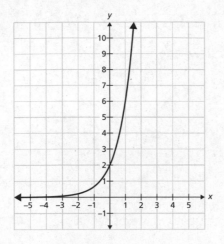

A) Linear, increasing, slope = 0.25, *y*-intercept = 2
B) Exponential, decreasing, *y*-intercept = 1
C) Exponential, increasing, *y*-intercept = 2
D) Linear, decreasing, slope = 0.25, *y*-intercept = 1

Solution

The graph shows a curve rather than a line, so the graph is exponential. This eliminates answer choices A and D. The *y*-intercept is 2, and the graph is increasing.

Answer: C

Model SAT Questions

1. A workout goal for a young athlete, Kia, included increased repetitions of a required exercise for 4 days. The routine called for the following schedule:

Day	Repeats
1	1
2	3
3	9
4	27

   Kia wanted to continue increasing her workout repetitions for a 7-day week following the pattern shown in the table. How many exercise repetitions would she do on day 7?

Strategy: Check to see how the number of exercises each day is growing. Since each day's repetition number is three times the prior day, this pattern is exponential growth.

Day	Repeats
1	$1 = 3^0$
2	$3 = 3^1$
3	$9 = 3^2$
4	$27 = 3^3$

You know for day n, the number of repetitions is 3^{n-1}. On day $n = 7$, the number of repetitions is $3^{7-1} = 3^6 = 729$.

Answer:

2. Which function represents the following data table?

x	f(x)
1	2
2	4
3	8
4	16

A) $f(x) = 2x$

B) $f(x) = 2x + 6$

C) $f(x) = 2^{x-1}$

D) $f(x) = 2^x$

Strategy: The dependent values are growing at a constant ratio rather than a constant rate; you know this means the function is exponential. Eliminate answer choices A and B. Now, substitute values into C and D to find which function is correct. For C, $f(1) = 2^{1-1} = 2^0 = 1$. So, C is not correct. Check answer D to be sure: $f(1) = 2^1 = 2$, and $f(2) = 2^2 = 4$. Stop checking and select answer D.

SAT-Type Questions

Answers begin on page 682.

1. Which of the following graphs represents the function $f(x) = 0.5x - 1$?

A)

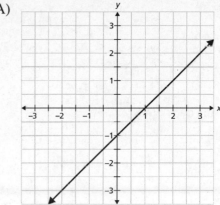

B)

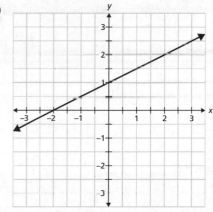

C)

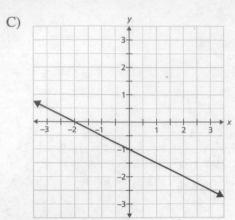

D)

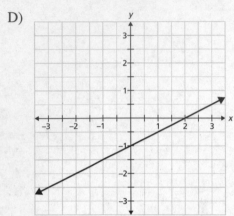

Use the following information for problems 2 and 3:

Flavio picks fruit on his family farm to earn extra money. Last weekend, his dad gave him a choice in payment options:

Option 1: $0.01 if Flavio picks 1 full basket of fruit, $0.02 if he picks 2 full baskets, $0.04 if he picks 3 full baskets, and so on, doubling the payment with each basket filled.

Option 2: $10 for agreeing to help pick fruit and, starting with the fifth basket, $10 for each basket he picks.

2. How much money will Flavio earn if he chooses Option 1 and fills 15 baskets?
    A) $75
    B) $150
    C) $163.84
    D) $327.68

3. How much money will Flavio earn if he chooses Option 2 and fills 15 baskets?
    A) $150
    B) $120
    C) $110
    D) $50

4. Scientists use carbon-14 dating when they estimate the time period to which ancient artifacts belong. The graph below models radioactive decay of carbon-14, comparing percentage of original mass to time, measured in thousands of years.

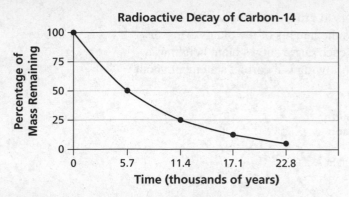

Radioactive Decay of Carbon-14

Which type of function is shown on the graph?

A) Linear increasing

B) Linear decreasing

C) Exponential increasing

D) Exponential decreasing

5. The table below shows the average yearly balance in a savings account where interest is compounded annually. No money is deposited or withdrawn after the initial amount is deposited.

Year	Balance
0	$200.00
5	$210.20
10	$220.92
15	$232.19
20	$244.04
25	$256.49

Which type of function would best model the given data?

A) A linear function with a negative rate of change

B) A linear function with a positive rate of change

C) An exponential decay function

D) An exponential growth function

6. The table below represents the function $f(x)$:

x	f(x)
2	5
4	17
6	65

Which equation represents $f(x)$?

A) $f(x) = 3^x - 4$

B) $f(x) = 2^x + 1$

C) $f(x) = 10x - 5$

D) $f(x) = 4x + 1$

7. A botanist places two plants in separate pots to grow. After the initial
    measurement ($t = 0$), the botanist measures the heights of the plants every day.
    The data were fit by smooth curves where each curve shows plant height as a
    function of time, in weeks. Which of the following is a correct statement about
    the data collected?

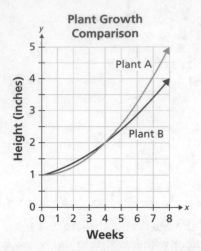

A) The heights of both plants were the same throughout the study.

B) For the first 4 weeks, plant A grew faster than plant B.

C) For the second 4 weeks, plant A grew faster than plant B.

D) There were no intervals for which the rate of growth for both plants was
the same.

8. A scientist recorded the growth of two colonies of bacteria in two separate petri
    dishes. After the initial placement ($t = 0$), the scientist measures and records the
    area covered by the bacteria every hour. The data were fit by a smooth curve
    as shown below, where each curve represents the area covered by bacteria as a
    function of time, in hours. Which of the following is a correct statement about
    the data shown in the graph?

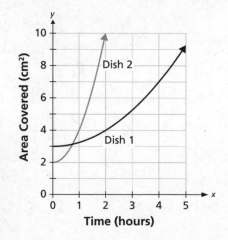

A) At time 0, the bacteria in Dish 1 covered twice as much area as the bacteria
in Dish 2.

B) At the measurement for hour 2, the bacteria in Dish 1 covered 40% of the
area covered by the bacteria in Dish 2.

C) For the first 5 hours, the bacteria in Dish 1 grew at a constant rate.

D) For the first 5 hours, the bacteria in Dish 2 grew at a constant rate.

9. Which is the graph of $f(x) = 3^x$?

A)

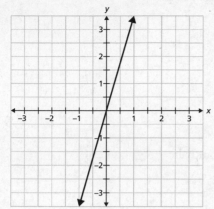

B)

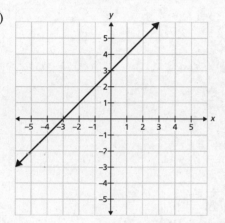

C)

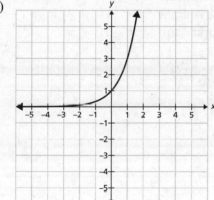

D)

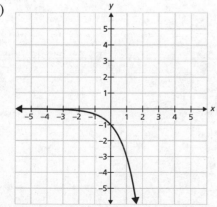

Student-Produced Response Questions

10. The chart below shows a pattern to be used for adding beads in a costume design.

Row	Number of Beads
1	3
2	9
3	15
4	21

Maria wanted to continue this pattern for 10 rows. How many beads would she use for row 10?

11. A card shop manager wanted to encourage students to work over a school holiday, so he offered them a bonus for each day of the holiday they worked. Part of the bonus schedule is shown in the table below. The pattern continues, with the bonus doubling for each additional day a student worked. If a student worked for 10 days, what is the bonus he will receive?

Number of Days	Bonus
1	$1
2	$2
3	$4
4	$8

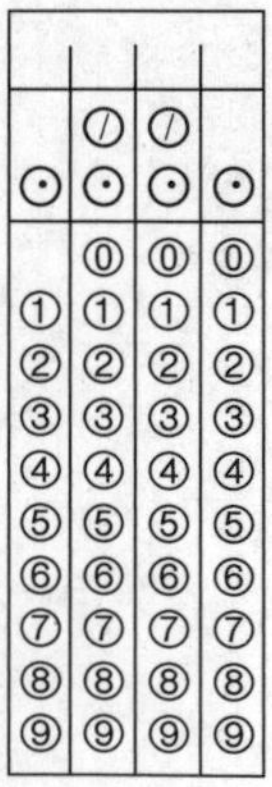

Summarizing Categorical Data and Relative Frequencies; Calculating Conditional Probability

- Two-Way Frequency Tables
- Two-Way Relative Frequency Tables
- Completing a Two-Way Frequency Table
- Association and Independence

· · · · · · **Explain** Two-Way Frequency Tables and · · · · · · · · · · · · · · · · ·
Two-Way Relative Frequency Tables

A **categorical variable** is a variable that can only take on a limited number of values. For example, a person's dessert choice or a student's grade in school are categorical variables. The values are always treated as non-numeric—even if grade levels are listed as 9, 10, 11, and 12—as the values cannot be used for mathematical calculations. **Bivariate data** is data collected on two variables. Bivariate categorical data is often displayed in **two-way frequency tables,** such as the one below, which shows relationships among two categorical variables: gender and elective course preference.

	Art Studio	Band	Technology	Total
Males	8	18	20	46
Females	22	22	10	54
Total	30	40	30	100

To be successful on the SAT, it is important to master two-way frequency table vocabulary:

Joint Frequencies: Entries in the body of the table, not along the border.
Marginal Frequencies: Totals in the last row and final column.
Total Frequency: The total number surveyed (lower right-hand value).

On the SAT, you may be asked to determine conditional relative frequency, which is also known as (aka) **conditional probability**, from a two-way frequency table. Conditional relative frequency is the ratio of a joint frequency and a related marginal frequency. For example, in order to find the conditional relative frequency that if you are a female you are enrolled in the Technology course,

the ratio would be $\dfrac{\text{joint frequency for females and Technology}}{\text{females}}$.

$Conditional\ Relative\ Frequency\ (aka)\ Conditional\ Probability = \dfrac{\text{joint frequency}}{\text{marginal frequency}}$.

A **two-way relative frequency table**, such as the one on the next page, converts all the values in the two-way frequency table to their **relative frequency** or **relative marginal frequency** equivalents.

$Relative\ Frequency = \dfrac{\text{joint frequency}}{\text{total frequency}}$

$Relative\ Marginal\ Frequency = \dfrac{\text{marginal frequency}}{\text{total frequency}}$

This is the <u>relative frequency</u> table for the two-way frequency table shown on the previous page.

	Art Studio	Band	Technology	Total
Males	0.08	0.18	0.20	0.46
Females	0.22	0.22	0.10	0.54
Total	0.30	0.40	0.30	1.00

Note that in a relative frequency table, all entries are decimals. The lower right total frequency entry is 1.00 since $\frac{\text{total frequency}}{\text{total frequency}} = 1$.

Think It Through

Examples 1 through 5 refer to the table shown above and repeated here.

	Art Studio	Band	Technology	Total
Males	8	18	20	46
Females	22	22	10	54
Total	30	40	30	100

Example 1

What is the joint frequency for a female choosing Art Studio as her elective?

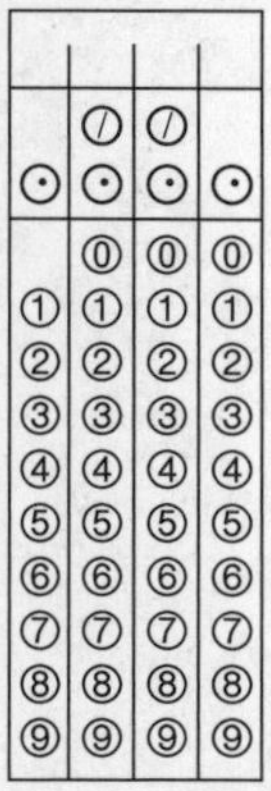

Solution

Joint frequencies are taken from the body of the table. The data in the cell intersecting the female row and the Art Studio column shows 22.

Answer: 22

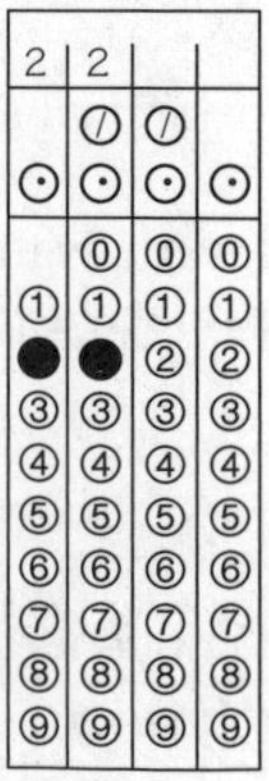

Example 2

What is the marginal frequency that a survey respondent is taking Art Studio?

Solution

Marginal frequencies are taken from the last row or final column. The total for Art Studio is 30.

Answer: 30

Example 3

What is the probability that a student chooses the Technology elective, given that the student is a male?

A) $\dfrac{20}{30}$

B) $\dfrac{20}{46}$

C) $\dfrac{30}{100}$

D) $\dfrac{10}{54}$

Solution

The question refers to males only. The marginal frequency for males is 46. The joint frequency for males and Technology is 20. Thus, the conditional relative

frequency is $\dfrac{20}{46}$.

Answer: B

Example 4

Find the relative frequency for a student selecting Art Studio to be male.

A) $\dfrac{8}{30}$

B) $\dfrac{8}{46}$

C) $\dfrac{30}{100}$

D) $\dfrac{46}{100}$

Solution

The question refers to students enrolled in Art Studio. The marginal frequency for Art Studio is 30, and the joint frequency for Art Studio and males is 8.

The conditional frequency is $\dfrac{8}{30}$.

Answer: A

Example 5

Find the relative marginal frequency that a student selects Band as an elective.

Solution

Use the relative marginal frequency formula: $\dfrac{\text{marginal frequency}}{\text{total frequency}} =$

$\dfrac{40}{100} = 0.40$.

Answer: 0.40

Model SAT Questions

Questions 1 and 2 use the following two-way frequency table.

A local police department kept track of speeding tickets issued over a certain time period. They separated first-time offenders from repeat-offenders and then separated the data by gender.

	Males	Females	Total
First-time	30	20	50
Repeat	25	5	30
Total	55	25	80

1. What is the conditional probability that a speeder is a first-time offender, given that he is a male?

    A) 0.375
    B) $0.\overline{54}$
    C) 0.60
    D) 0.875

Strategy: Reading from the males column, there were 30 first-time offenders of the 55 males receiving a ticket. So, $\dfrac{30}{55} = .\overline{54}$, which is choice B.

2. What is the conditional probability that a speeder is a male, given he is a first-time offender?

    A) 0.375
    B) $0.\overline{54}$
    C) 0.60
    D) 0.875

Strategy: Using the first-time offender row, of the 50 people ticketed, 30 were male. Thus, $\dfrac{30}{50} = 0.60$. Select answer choice C.

3. Mehtap had a two-way frequency table showing hair color for males and females in her class. What is the conditional relative frequency for a student being male given he has blond hair?

	Brown Hair	Blond Hair	Red Hair	Total
Male	25	20	5	50
Female	55	5	10	70
Total	80	25	15	120

    A) 0.20
    B) 0.80
    C) 20
    D) 40

The conditional relative frequency for students with blond hair being male is $\dfrac{20}{25} = 0.80$, which is answer choice B.

4. The two-way frequency table shown below reflects data for a study on citizens' opinions about highway improvement budgeting.

	Increase Spending	Keep Spending the Same	Decrease Spending	Total
Urban Resident	300	300	600	1,200
Suburban Resident	300	300	200	800
Total	600	600	800	2,000

Which of the following facts is <u>not</u> supported by the data in the table?

A) The conditional probability for urban residents preferring an increase in spending is 0.25.

B) The marginal probability that a subject's preference is to keep spending the same is 0.30.

C) The conditional probability that a subject who wants a decrease in spending is a suburban resident is 0.25.

D) The marginal probability that a subject interviewed is an urban resident is 12%.

Strategy: The conditional probability for urban residents preferring an increase in spending is $\frac{300}{1200} = 0.25$, so answer choice A is eliminated. The marginal probability that a subject's preference is to keep spending the same is $\frac{600}{2,000} = 0.30$; this eliminates answer choice B. The conditional probability that a subject who wants a decrease in spending is a suburban resident is $\frac{200}{800} = 0.25$, so not answer choice C. You can stop and select answer choice D, but check to be sure. The marginal probability that a subject interviewed is an urban resident is $\frac{1,200}{2,000} = 60\%$, not 12%.

······ Explain **Completing a Two-Way Frequency Table** ·············

When not all the data is given in a two-way frequency table, it is sometimes possible to complete the chart. Since the only arithmetic in the chart is addition, you can work backward and fill in single missing values in rows and columns.

Example

The two-way frequency table below, showing preferences for musical entertainment, is missing data. Complete the table and calculate the conditional probability that a female responding to this survey prefers ballet.

	Opera	Ballet	Jazz Concert	Total
Males	2		30	40
Females	8		32	
Total		48	62	120

Solution

Work backward and fill in missing cells needed to find the answer requested. The number of males requesting ballet is $40 - (2 + 30) = 8$. Then the number of females requesting ballet is $48 - 8 = 40$. The total number of females is $120 - 40 = 80$, or $8 + 40 + 32 = 80$.

The conditional probability that a female prefers ballet is $\frac{40}{80}$.

Answer: $\frac{1}{2}$ or 0.50

Explain Association and Independence

Just as we created a relative frequency table based on the total frequency, we can find the **conditional relative frequencies** for rows and columns.

The table shown at the beginning of this lesson is repeated here:

	Art Studio	Band	Technology	Total
Males	8	18	20	46
Females	22	22	10	54
Total	30	40	30	100

Use the end-of-row totals to find the row conditional relative frequencies for males and females. The corresponding <u>row</u> conditional frequency table is:

	Art Studio	Band	Technology	Total
Males	$\frac{8}{46} \approx 0.17$	$\frac{18}{46} \approx 0.39$	$\frac{20}{46} \approx 0.43$	$\frac{46}{46} = 1$
Females	$\frac{22}{54} \approx 0.41$	$\frac{22}{54} \approx 0.41$	$\frac{10}{54} \approx 0.19$	$\frac{54}{54} = 1$
Total	$\frac{30}{100} = 0.30$	$\frac{40}{100} = 0.40$	$\frac{30}{100} = 0.30$	$\frac{100}{100} = 1$

Use the end-of-column totals to find the column conditional relative frequencies for Art Studio, Band, and Technology. The corresponding <u>column</u> conditional frequency table is:

	Art Studio	Band	Technology	Total
Males	$\frac{8}{30} \approx 0.27$	$\frac{18}{40} = 0.45$	$\frac{20}{30} \approx 0.67$	$\frac{46}{100} = 0.46$
Females	$\frac{22}{30} \approx 0.73$	$\frac{22}{40} = 0.55$	$\frac{10}{30} \approx 0.33$	$\frac{54}{100} = 0.54$
Total	$\frac{30}{30} = 1$	$\frac{40}{40} = 1$	$\frac{30}{30} = 1$	$\frac{100}{100} = 1$

We can use these frequencies to determine whether one category influences the result for the other category.

We say there is an **association** between two categorical variables if the row conditional relative frequencies (or column conditional relative frequencies) are markedly different for the rows (or columns) of the table. If there is association, the joint relative frequencies for one categorical variable depend on the values of the second categorical variable.

In the table above, elective choice is associated with gender. If you compare the side-by-side column values, there are significant differences among the columns. Likewise, if you compare the left-to-right row values, there are significant differences among the rows. Therefore, gender and elective course choice are associated, and we can say that gender influences selection of elective courses.

If the row conditional relative frequencies or column conditional relative frequencies are very similar, we say the variables are independent. Given the two-way frequency table below and the corresponding row relative frequencies, we see the row values, while not identical, are very similar.

Two-Way Frequency Table

	Chocolate	Vanilla	Total
Males	19	41	60
Females	25	49	74
Total	44	90	134

Row Relative Frequency Table

	Chocolate	Vanilla	Total
Males	$\frac{19}{60} \approx 0.32$	$\frac{41}{60} \approx 0.69$	$\frac{60}{60} = 1$
Females	$\frac{25}{74} \approx 0.34$	$\frac{49}{74} \approx 0.66$	$\frac{74}{74} = 1$
Total	$\frac{44}{134} \approx 0.32$	$\frac{90}{134} \approx 0.67$	$\frac{134}{134} = 1$

The row relative frequency table reveals that ice cream flavor choice is not dependent upon gender. We say the gender and ice cream flavor choice variables are **independent**.

· · · · · · **Think It Through** ·

Example

A school district ran a survey to help plan next year's school calendar. Specifically, the district had to decide between two long vacations or three short vacations throughout the school year. The data collection method separated families in which at least one parent did not work outside the home from families where all parents living in the home worked outside the home.

	Two Vacations	Three Vacations	Total
Stay-at-Home-Parent	240	650	890
No Stay-at-Home-Parent	410	325	735
Total	650	975	1,625

Part 1

What is the conditional probability that a family requesting two vacations had a stay-at-home parent?

A) 240
B) 0.27
C) 0.37
D) 0.63

Solution

Conditional probability is calculated by dividing the joint frequency by the marginal frequency. The denominator is the marginal frequency for requestors of two vacations. The numerator is the joint frequency for two vacations and a stay-at-home parent: $\frac{240}{650} \approx 0.37$.

Answer: C

Part 2

Are family career responsibilities and vacation choices associated?

A) Yes, because the row conditional relative frequencies and column conditional frequencies are different with each row and column.

B) No, because the row conditional relative frequencies and column conditional frequencies are different with each row and column.

C) Yes, because there are more families with stay-at-home parents than families without stay-at-home parents.

D) No, because there are more families with stay-at-home parents than families without stay-at-home parents.

Solution

Calculate the row conditional relative frequencies. Note that the results would be the same if the column conditional relative frequencies were calculated instead. It is not necessary to worry about the total marginal calculations.

	Two Vacations	Three Vacations	Total
Stay-at-Home-Parent	$\frac{240}{890} \approx 0.27$	$\frac{650}{890} \approx 0.73$	890
No Stay-at-Home-Parent	$\frac{410}{735} \approx 0.56$	$\frac{325}{735} \approx 0.44$	735
Total	650	975	1,625

Because the row conditional relative frequencies are markedly different for the two rows, family career responsibilities and vacation choices are associated.

Answer: A

SAT-Type Problems

Answers begin on page 683.

1. The public library had a used book "giveaway" in which residents could take home and keep one book weeded from the library collection. The books were classified as Historical Fiction, Mystery, or Fantasy. Part of the data collected on which books were selected by which gender is shown below.

	Historical Fiction	Mystery	Fantasy	Total
Females		40	42	120
Males	50	25		
Total	88		47	

Which of the following statements is best supported by the data in the table?

A) The marginal relative frequency for Fantasy preference is $\frac{42}{47}$.

B) The marginal relative frequency for males is $\frac{3}{5}$.

C) The marginal relative frequency for males is $\frac{2}{5}$.

D) The marginal relative frequency for not choosing Mystery is $\frac{3}{4}$.

2. The following two-way table shows the results of a survey looking for a relationship between students who are in the school band and students who are on the math team.

	In School Band	Not in School Band	Total
On Math Team	40	20	
Not on Math Team	10	80	
Total			

Which of the following statements is best supported by the data?

A) The relative frequency of math team members is 0.40; math team membership and school band membership are not associated.

B) The relative frequency of math team members is 0.40; math team membership and school band membership are associated.

C) The conditional relative frequency of a school band member also being a math team member is 0.40; math team membership and school band membership are not associated.

D) The conditional relative frequency of a school band member also being a math team member is 0.40; math team membership and school band membership are associated.

3. A calculus teacher provided her students with a review sheet for a cumulative assessment. After grading the tests, the teacher surveyed her classes on use of the review sheet as a study tool. Her two-way frequency table is shown below.

	Used review sheet	Did not use review sheet	Total
Passed assessment	35	10	45
Did not pass assessment	3	12	15
Total	38	22	60

Based on the data in the table above, which of the following is the most accurate statement?

A) Use of the review sheet is independent of passing the assessment.

B) The marginal frequency of students passing the assessment is 22, and use of a review sheet is associated with passing the assessment for all students.

C) The marginal frequency of students not using the review sheet is 22, and use of the review sheet is associated with passing the assessment for this teacher's students.

D) The conditional relative frequency of students who did not pass the assessment and who did not use the review sheet is 0.20, and use of the review sheet is independent of passing the assessment.

4. An exit survey at a supermarket recorded the number of shoppers who brought their own reusable bags and shoppers who purchased pet food.

	Bought pet food	Did not buy pet food	Total
Reusable bags	24	50	74
Disposable bags	36	75	111
Total	60	125	185

Which of the following statements is best supported by the data in the table?

A) The conditional relative frequency for shoppers who buy pet food using disposable bags is the same as the conditional relative frequency for shoppers who do not buy pet food using disposable bags. The purchase of pet food and type of bag used are associated.

B) The conditional relative frequency for shoppers buying pet food using disposable bags is the same as the conditional relative frequency for shoppers not buying pet food using disposable bags. The purchase of pet food and type of bag used are not associated.

C) The marginal relative frequency for reusable bags is the same as the conditional relative frequency for shoppers buying pet food using disposable bags. The purchase of pet food and type of bag used are associated.

D) The marginal relative frequency for reusable bags is the same as the marginal relative frequency for buying pet food. The purchase of pet food and type of bag used are not associated.

Use the two-way frequency table below to answer question 5.

A survey was conducted to ask residents if they wanted to continue the current town schedule for street cleaning. The survey results are shown below.

	Fewer days	Same schedule	More days	Total
Male	25	50	75	150
Female	140	100	60	300
Total	165	150	135	450

5. What is the difference between the conditional relative frequencies for females wanting fewer days of street cleaning and females wanting more days of street cleaning?

   A) $\dfrac{1}{9}$

   B) $\dfrac{8}{45}$

   C) $\dfrac{1}{3}$

   D) $\dfrac{4}{15}$

6. A survey among high school students asked about changing the start time for school to one hour later than the current start time. Students were also asked if they had an after-school job. A portion of the survey results are shown below.

	Keep start time	Start 1 hour later	Total
Has an after-school job			200
Does not have an after-school job	30		300
Total		350	

   Which of the following statements is best supported by the data in the table?

   A) The conditional relative frequency for students having a job after school who want to start school one hour later is $\dfrac{2}{5}$, and there is an association between employment after school and desired start time for school.

   B) The conditional relative frequency for students having a job after school who want to start school one hour later is $\dfrac{2}{5}$, and there is not an association between employment after school and desired start time for school.

   C) The conditional relative frequency for students having a job after school who want to start school one hour later is $\dfrac{4}{25}$, and there is an association between employment after school and desired start time for school.

   D) The conditional relative frequency for students having a job after school who want to start school one hour later is $\dfrac{4}{25}$, and there is not an association between employment after school and desired start time for school.

7. A middle school statistics project used height, in inches, and eye color as part of its data collection project. Part of the survey results are shown below.

	Brown eyes	Blue eyes	Total
Over 65 inches		4	24
65 inches or shorter	80		
Total		20	

Which statement is best supported by the data in the table?

A) The categories measured are independent variables.
B) The categories measured are associated variables.
C) Most students surveyed had brown eyes and were taller than 65 inches.
D) There is not enough information provided to complete the two-way table.

Use the two-way frequency table below to answer question 8.

A group of young campers was given a choice between participating in archery or relay races. The completed two-way table below shows their preferences.

	Archery	Relay Races	Total
Girls	45	15	60
Boys	60	20	80
Total	105	35	140

8. Which of the following statements are supported by the data in the table?

1. Gender and sports preference are associated variables.
2. Gender and sports preference are independent variables.
3. The conditional relative frequency for boys to prefer relay races is 0.25.
4. The conditional relative frequency for girls to prefer relay races is $\dfrac{3}{28}$.

A) 1 and 3
B) 2 and 3
C) 1 and 4
D) 2 and 4

9. A survey asked students about their favorite literature genre. The results were separated by grade level, as displayed in the table below:

	Drama	Mystery	History	Total
Grade 9	70	82	98	250
Grade 10	84	80	101	265
Grade 11	60	95	85	240
Grade 12	52	73	110	235
Total	266	330	394	990

Which grade level had the highest percentage of students saying they most enjoy Mystery?

A) Grade 9
B) Grade 10
C) Grade 11
D) Grade 12

10. The table below shows the responses from a sample of a doctor's patients regarding their preference about a change from hours on one weekend day to hours one weekday evening. The doctor has about 2,000 patients, evenly divided between male and female.

	Weekend	Weekday Evening	Total
Males	150	50	200
Females	50	100	150
Total	200	150	350

Which of the following statements is best supported by the data in the table?

A) The marginal probability for weekend preference is approximately 0.57, and gender and time preference are associated.

B) The marginal probability for weekend preference is approximately 0.57, and gender and time preference are independent.

C) The conditional probability for those males preferring weekend is 0.70, and gender and time preference are associated.

D) The conditional probability for those males preferring weekend is 0.70, and gender and time preference are independent.

Student-Produced Response Questions

Use the two-way frequency table below to answer questions 11 through 14.

A school population consists of 4,480 students. The table below shows the results of a survey asking some students in grades 9, 10, 11, and 12 their opinion about cancelling classes for one day and instead holding a day of community service.

	Regular School Day	Day of Community Service	Total
Grade 9	65	75	140
Grade 10	60	60	120
Grade 11	100	50	150
Grade 12	75	75	150
Total	300	260	560

11. What is the marginal frequency for grade 11?

12. What is the joint frequency for grade 10 students preferring a day of community service?

13. What is the conditional probability that a 10th grader would prefer a regular school day?

14. What is the conditional relative frequency that a student who prefers a regular school day is in grade 12?

Working with Measures of Center and Spread

- Charts and Graphs to Represent Data
- Measures of Center
- Measures of Spread

····· **Explain** **Charts and Graphs to Represent Data** ·············

Often, data is represented in graphs rather than in lists. A "picture" of the data is sometimes easier to understand. The most commonly used graphs are described below.

Frequency tables are two-column tables showing data values in size order in the left column and frequency in the right column.

The frequency of a particular data value is the number of times the data value occurs. For example, if 4 students have a score of 100 on a mathematics examination, the score of 100 is said to have a frequency of 4.

For grouped data, if six students have scores ranging from 91 to 100 in mathematics, then the score range from 91 to 100 is said to have a frequency of 6.

Test Scores	Frequency
91–100	6
81–90	5
71–80	4
61–70	5
51–60	2
41–50	1
31–40	0
21–30	2

A **histogram**, often used to display grouped data, is shown below, representing the same data seen in the frequency table above. A histogram is similar to a vertical bar graph, but there are no gaps between the bars. The widths of the bars are all equal and represent equal intervals. The frequency for each interval is represented by the height of its bar.

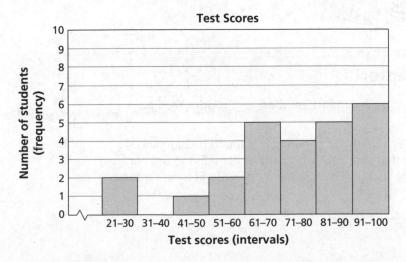

The charts show that 2 scores had values from 21 to 30, no scores had values from 31 to 40, 1 score had a value from 41 to 50, and so on. Note that we do not have exact values for any one score.

While frequency histograms are often used for large amounts of grouped data, **dot plots** are a good way to examine the shape of the data when the population or sample set is small. Unlike a histogram, the data values are not grouped. The picture below shows a dot plot.

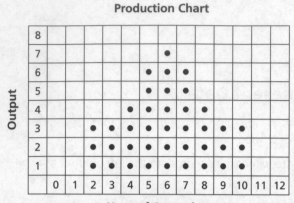

Production Chart

This dot plot shows there was no output of product until the 2ⁿᵈ hour. During the 2ⁿᵈ hour, 3 units of output were completed. During the 3ʳᵈ hour, 3 units of output were completed. During the 4ᵗʰ hour, 4 units of output were completed. During the 5ᵗʰ hour, 6 units of output were created, and so on.

A **pie chart** or **circle graph** uses "slices" to show relative sizes of data compared to the whole. The entire pie or circle represents 100% of the data.

Comparing the frequency table to the pie chart, absolute values can be displayed, percent can be displayed, or both can be displayed.

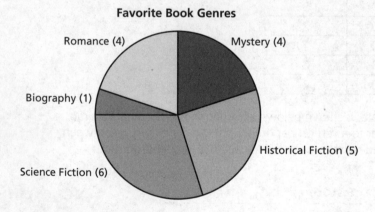

Favorite Book Genres

Explain **Measures of Center**

There are three measures of central tendency: **mean**, **median**, and **mode**. Each plays a role in describing and comparing data.

The **mean**, represented by the symbol $\bar{x}$, of a set of numbers is found by summing the numbers in the set and then dividing that sum by the quantity of items in the set. For example, the mean of the set of numbers 70, 75, 82, 88, and 95 is found by using the formula:

$$\bar{x} = \frac{\text{sum}}{\text{quantity}} = \frac{70+75+82+88+95}{5} = 82$$

232 Problem Solving and Data Analysis • Lesson 6

On the SAT, the data for finding the mean of a set may sometimes be presented in a frequency table.

Scores	Frequency
70	5
80	7
82	9
90	8

For this table, there are 5 scores of 70, 7 scores of 80, 9 scores of 82, and 8 scores of 90.

The sum is $(70 \cdot 5) + (80 \cdot 7) + (82 \cdot 9) + (90 \cdot 8) = 2368$

The quantity is the sum of the frequencies: $5 + 7 + 9 + 8 = 29$

$$\bar{x} = \frac{\text{sum}}{\text{quantity}} = \frac{2368}{29} \approx 81.7$$

The mean is the best measure of center for data that is roughly symmetric about the mean, as is shown in the histogram below. Notice that the amount of data that lies below the mean is the same as the amount of data above the mean.

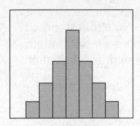

Another measure of central tendency is the median. The **median** is the middle value in a set when the numbers are arranged in order, either from least to greatest or from greatest to least. If there is an even quantity of values in the set, the median is the mean of the two middle values—and not necessarily a value in the number set.

- The median of 2, 4, $\boxed{6}$, 9, 20 is 6

- The median of 2, 4, $\boxed{6, 9}$, 20, 30 is $\frac{6+9}{2} = 7.5$ or $7\frac{1}{2}$

The median is the best measure of center for skewed data as shown in the graphs below. Notice that data can be skewed to the left or skewed to the right.

Skewed Left   **Skewed Right**

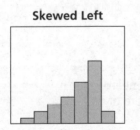 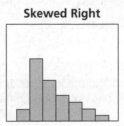

On the SAT, you may be asked questions regarding the relative positions of the mean and the median within a data set. It will be helpful to become familiar with the following facts:

- For symmetric data, the mean and the median are the same value.

- For skewed data, the mean is typically toward the direction of the skew, relative to the median.

  ○ If the data is left-skewed, the mean is smaller than the median.

  ○ If the data is right skewed, the mean is greater than the median.

The final measure of central tendency is the mode. The **mode** is the value or values that appear most often in a set. There may be no mode (each value appears the same number of times), one mode, or more than one mode.

The mode of the set 1, 2, 3, 4, 4, 5, 6 is 4.

The modes of the set 1, 3, 5, 5, 6, 7, 7, 8 are 5 and 7. This set is bimodal, having two modes.

The set 1,1, 2, 2, 5, 5, 8, 8 has no mode.

Explain Measures of Spread

While measures of center tell us where data is clustered, measures of spread help us quantify the variance in a data set. Although there are other measures of spread, the only measures found on the SAT are range and standard deviation.

The **range** is the difference between the highest and lowest values in a set of data. The range of the set 5, 10, 15, 20, 20, 30 is $30 - 5 = 25$.

The **standard deviation** is a measure of spread or variation in terms of each number's deviation from the mean. While the formula for standard deviation is not required for the SAT, it is helpful to know that it is based upon the sum of the squares of the differences between each data value and the mean of the data values. The greater the spread of the data, the greater the value of the standard deviation. Note that standard deviation is appropriate <u>only</u> when the data values are somewhat normally distributed; i.e., the data is mound-shaped and symmetric about the mean. For normal distributions, approximately $\frac{2}{3}$ of the data will fall within one standard deviation from the mean, $\frac{1}{3}$ above the mean, and $\frac{1}{3}$ below the mean, as shown the on the normal distribution below. Two data sets with the same range can have very different standard deviations, and two data sets with the same standard deviation can have very different ranges.

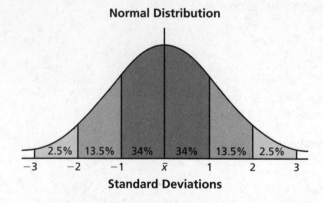

Normal Distribution

Standard Deviations

Recall that the standard deviation formula is built around the mean. Since the mean is not a good measure of skewed data, standard deviation is not a good measure of variance of skewed data (see skewed data graphic).

Example 1

The chart below represents the grades Mr. Lesser's class received on their final exam. To the nearest integer, what is the class mean?

Grades	Frequency
75	5
80	7
85	9
90	8
95	4
100	3

A) 60

B) 85

C) 86

D) 88

Solution

First, multiply each grade by its frequency, since that is how many students received a particular grade:

$5 \cdot 75 = 375$ $7 \cdot 80 = 560$ $9 \cdot 85 = 765$

$8 \cdot 90 = 720$ $4 \cdot 95 = 380$ $3 \cdot 100 = 300$

Sum the results:

$$375 + 560 + 765 + 720 + 380 + 300 = 3{,}100$$

Then divide by the number of grades in the class, the frequency total.

$$\bar{x} = \frac{3100}{36} = 86.111\ldots$$

Answer: C

Example 2

For the numbers 4, 11, 8, 9, and 8, which of the following is true?

A) median < mode < mean

B) median > mode > mean

C) mode = mean = median

D) mode > median > mean

Solution

Find the median, mean, and mode and compare. To find the median, arrange the numbers from least to greatest:

$$4, 8, 8, 9, 11$$

The median is 8.

The mean is $\dfrac{4+11+8+9+8}{5} = \dfrac{40}{5} = 8$.

The mode is 8, the most frequent number.

Answer: C

Example 3

The dot plots below show production results for 4 machines producing identical items. For which machine is the median significantly greater than the mean?

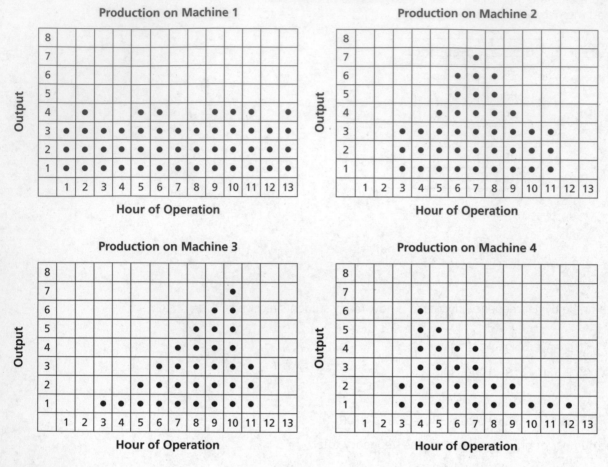

A) Machine 1
B) Machine 2
C) Machine 3
D) Machine 4

Solution

If the median is greater than the mean, the data must be skewed. This eliminates answer choices A and B. For skewed data, the mean is on the tail side of the median. When the median is greater than the mean, the mean is to the left of the median, and the data is skewed left.

Answer: C

Answers begin on page 686.

1. For a set of three positive fractions, mean = median = $\frac{1}{2}$. If the smallest fraction is $\frac{5}{12}$, what is the largest fraction?

    A) $\frac{7}{12}$ C) $\frac{5}{9}$

    B) $\frac{6}{11}$ D) $\frac{8}{13}$

2. The 2006 – 2010 American Community Survey collected data on the number of vehicles per household. The results of this survey are shown below for the United States as a whole and for the cities Dallas, TX; New York, NY; and Jackson, WY.

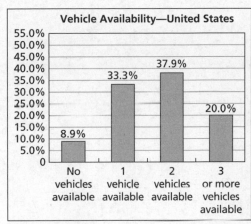

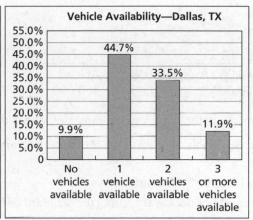

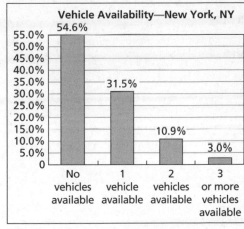

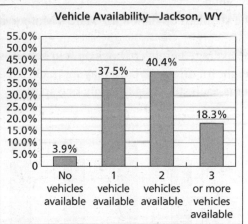

For which of the graphs above can we not measure spread using standard deviation?

A) United States

B) New York

C) Dallas

D) Jackson

3. If $m > 0$, what is the mean of $2m + 3$, $3m - 1$, and $7m - 5$?

   A) $6m + 3$

   B) $4m + 3$

   C) $4m - 1$

   D) $3m$

4. An investigator surveyed employees about their annual salaries in two different factories in the same town. The results are reported below via dot plots:

   Terry's Tools

   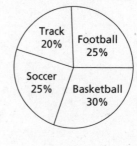

Under $30,000	$30,000 to $39,999	$40,000 to $49,000	$50,000 to $59,000	At least $60,000

   Marc's Motors

Under $30,000	$30,000 to $39,999	$40,000 to $49,000	$50,000 to $59,000	At least $60,000

   Which of the following statements is the most valid comparison of the data?

   A) The median salary for Terry's Tools is higher than the median salary for Marc's Motors.

   B) The mean salary for both factories is the same.

   C) Because the range for both sets of data is the same, the standard deviation for both sets of data is the same.

   D) It is appropriate to find the standard deviation for Marc's Motors' data only.

5. The graphs below describe the average heights of boys on four school sports teams. What is the average height for all of the boys playing track, soccer, basketball, and football? Assume each student plays only one sport.

   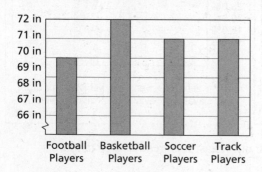

   A) 70.95 inches

   B) 71 inches

   C) 71.05 inches

   D) 71.10 inches

Questions 6 and 7 refer to the following information.

The bar chart below shows the number of volunteer hours completed by members of the junior class during the last week.

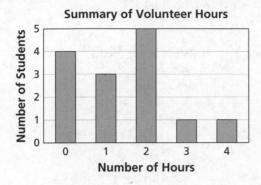

Summary of Volunteer Hours

6. What is the range for this data?

    A) 5

    B) 4

    C) 3

    D) 2

7. What is the median number of volunteer hours completed by the junior class?

    A) 1

    B) 1.5

    C) 2

    D) 2.5

Model SAT Questions

1. Anton has grades of 87, 83, 74, and 89 on four of his five tests. What grade must Anton earn on his fifth test so that the mean of all his test scores will be 85?

    A) 88

    B) 90

    C) 92

    D) 93

Strategy: Let x represent the fifth test score. Then $\dfrac{87+83+74+89+x}{5}=85$

and $333+x=85\cdot5$. Solving the equation for x, $x=425-333=92$. Select answer choice C.

2. In a class of 28 students, a certain number of students earned a mean of 76 on a recent exam and the rest of the students earned a mean of 88. Which of the following must be true about the entire class's mean test score, m?

    A) $m < 76$

    B) $88 > m$

    C) $m = 88$

    D) $76 < m < 88$

3. The mean of P and Q is 20. The mean of R, S, and T is 60. What is the mean of $P, Q, R, S,$ and T?

   A) 55

   B) 44

   C) 40

   D) 33

Strategy: The sum of P and Q is $2(20) = 40$. The sum of R, S, and T is $3(60) = 180$. The sum of P, Q, R, S, and T is $40 + 180 = 220$. The average is sum ÷ number = $220 ÷ 5 = 44$. The correct answer is B.

4. A data set is normally distributed with a mean of 50 and a standard deviation of 5. Which statement is true?

   A) All of the data lies between 40 and 60.

   B) About $\frac{2}{3}$ of the data is less than 55.

   C) About 47.5% of the data lies between 40 and 50.

   D) About $\frac{2}{3}$ of the data is greater than 45.

Strategy: Using the diagram on page 234 as a reference, about 68% of the data lies within 1 standard deviation from the mean, with 34% on either side of the mean. About 95% of the data lies within 2 standard deviations from the mean, with 47.5% on either side of the mean. Use this knowledge to check the choices. Since 1 standard deviation is 5, two standard deviations = 10. Thus the range 40 to 60 includes all data from 2 standard deviations below the mean to 2 standard deviations above the mean, or $2 \times 47.5\% = 95\%$ of the data, so answer choice A is not true. Look at B. The data points less than 55 include the lower 50% of the scores plus the 34% within 1 standard deviation above the mean. $50\% + 34\% = 84\%$. Since $\frac{2}{3} \approx 67\%$, answer choice B is also not true. Move to answer choice C. Since the mean is 50, and 40 is 2 standard deviations below the mean, the data between 40 and 50 is 47.5% of the data set. This is a true statement. Stop checking and select answer choice C.

Answers begin on page 686.

1. The mean of a set of test scores is 73. If a score of 75 is added to the set and a new mean is calculated, which of the following would be true?

    A) The new mean is greater than 73.
    B) The new mean is 73.5.
    C) The new mean is less than 73.
    D) The effect on the new mean cannot be determined.

2. The mean of A and B is 10. The mean of X, Y, and Z is 20. What is the mean of A, B, X, Y, and Z?

    A) 15
    B) 16
    C) 18
    D) 19

3. Set A has a standard deviation of 6. Set B has a standard deviation of 9. Based on this information, which of the following statements must be true?

    A) The range for set A and set B is the same.
    B) Set A is larger than set B.
    C) The mean of set B is 1.5 greater than the mean of set A.
    D) The data in set A varies less than the data in set B.

4. The mean grade on a test taken by 15 students was 70. When one more student took the test, the mean for all tests was raised to 71. What score did the last student to take the test earn?

    A) 80
    B) 82
    C) 84
    D) 86

5. The mean of four unique positive even integers is 12. What is the greatest possible value for the largest integer in this set?

    A) 6
    B) 12
    C) 36
    D) 42

6. Of five exam scores, three had the values 80, 78, and 91. If the mean of the set of five scores is 85, what is the mean of the remaining two scores?

    A) 88
    B) 87
    C) 86
    D) 85

7. Papa Bear, Mama Bear, and Baby Bear have an average weight of 330 pounds. If Mama Bear weighs the same as the mean, and Papa Bear weighs 20 pounds more than 7 times as much as Baby Bear, what is Papa Bear's weight?

    A) 560 pounds
    B) 580 pounds
    C) 80 pounds
    D) 365 pounds

8. Assume there are two data sets, A and B, with no repeating values. In set A, there are 12 values and the mean is equal to the median. Set B contains all the values in set A, as well as four additional data values, each of which is greater than any of the values in set A. Based on these facts, which of the following statements is true?

    A) Both the mean and the median are greater in set B than in set A, with the median increasing more than the mean.
    B) Both the mean and the median are greater in set B than in set A, with the mean increasing more than the median.
    C) Both the mean and the median are greater in set B than in set A, with the mean increasing 4 times as much as the median.
    D) Both the mean and the median are greater in set B than in set A, with the median increasing 4 times as much as the mean.

Questions 9 and 10 refer to the following information.

The heights below were reported for 100 students in a high school orchestra (note that heights are approximately normally distributed).

Height	Quantity
4'10"	4
4'11"	4
5'0"	10
5'1"	12
5'2"	20
5'3"	20
5'4"	16
5'5"	6
5'6"	4
5'7"	4

9. What is the range, in inches, for the data collected?

    A) 7
    B) 8
    C) 9
    D) 11

10. Which is the best description for heights falling within approximately one standard deviation from the mean?

   A) 4'11" to 5'2"

   B) 5'0" to 5'2"

   C) 5'1" to 5'4"

   D) 5'2" to 5'3"

Student-Produced Response Questions

11. The bar graph below represents the grades that students in Mr. Crisci's class received on an exam. What is the median score?

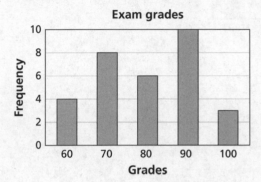

12. The grades on Ms. Abidor's algebra test were 50, 60, 72, 74, 76, 80, 92, 95, 60, 87, 90, 92, and 95. Nia took the test later, and the class median score did not change. What was Nia's score?

13. The graph below shows the number of stamps bought by Adrian, an avid stamp collector, in each of four years. She also bought stamps in 1993 and 1994 (not shown in this chart). If the average (arithmetic mean) for all six years is the same as the average for the first four years, what is the total number of stamps she bought in 1993 and 1994?

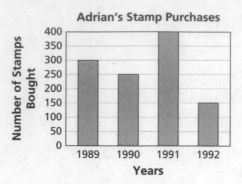

14. The average of 3 test scores is twice the median. If the median is 12 and the lowest score is 7, what is the highest score?

15. The mean grade on a quiz taken by 8 students was 85. Valentino took the test late.
His score raised the class average to 86. What was his score?

LESSON 7:

Making Inferences About Population Parameters Based on Sample Data

- **Population Parameters and Sample Statistics**
- **Confidence Level**
- **Confidence Interval**
- **Margin of Error**

Statistics is a problem-solving process consisting of formulating questions that can be answered with numerical data. This process includes designing and implementing a plan to collect, organize, analyze, and interpret the data in the context of the original question(s).

Explain Population Parameters and Sample Statistics

If a study requires information about every member of a **population**, a **census** is conducted. A census is a collection of data that includes every person or every situation in the population. A numerical measure collected from the census is called a **parameter**. Population proportion and population mean are parameters. However, it is often impossible or impractical to conduct a census. A population typically contains too many individuals to study, so an investigation is often restricted to one or more samples drawn from the population. A well–chosen **sample** will contain reliable information about a particular population parameter. The relation between the sample and the population must be such as to allow true inferences to be made about a population from that sample. For example, an election poll does not contain all voters. The data comes from only a sample of the voters. However, a well-planned election poll can be used to predict voting proportions for the entire population. A measure collected from a sample is called a sample **statistic**. Sample proportion and sample mean are examples of sample statistics.

When we report the results of a statistical analysis, it is important to state how confident we are that our sample statistic is close to the population parameter. A **confidence interval** is an interval of values of a sample statistic that is likely to contain the actual population parameter. The **confidence level** is the percentage of sample values (often 95% or 99%) that are expected to fall within the upper and lower bounds of the confidence interval. A **margin of error** gives the same information as the confidence interval. It shows the maximum expected difference between the population parameter and the sample statistic estimating that parameter. For example, if a survey predicted, with 95% certainty, that if an election were held at this time, candidate A would receive within 5% of 70% of the votes, the prediction would be qualified by stating that the results are 95% certain (confidence level) that the candidate would receive between 65% and 75% (confidence interval) of the votes. Another way to state the prediction is that there is a 95% certainty that candidate A would receive a 70% ± 5% (margin of error) of the votes. For example, if a poll made the following predictions with 95% certainty, both bullets give us the same information.

- Candidate A is predicted to receive 80% of the votes with a margin of error of ±5%.

- Candidate A is predicted to receive between 75% and 85% of the votes.

It makes sense that the statistician would be more certain of results stated with a larger confidence interval or greater margin of error and less certain of results with a narrower confidence interval or smaller margin of error. Depending on the requirements for the study, a narrower margin of error may be desired, even if the result is a lesser confidence level, or a higher confidence level may be desired, even if the result is a wider margin of error.

The formulae for confidence interval and margin of error calculations are related to the size of the sample. The larger the sample size is, the smaller the variability and the smaller the confidence interval or margin of error. Duplicate studies are repeated with a larger sample size when the confidence interval or margin of error in the first study is too large. When the sample size is large, we can assume the sample statistic is approximately normal. Therefore, the confidence level is about 95% that the population parameter will fall within two standard deviations of the sample statistic. A confidence level of 95% is typical for large samples.

Think It Through

Example 1

A local politician conducted a survey and reported that 80% of those who responded want to build a new park. The survey reports a 6% margin of error and a confidence level of 95% that the result reflects the desires of the entire community. Which statement best describes these results?

A) The politician can be 95% confident that between 77% and 83% of the population wants to build a new park.

B) The politician can be 89% confident that between 77% and 83% of the population wants to build a new park.

C) The politician can be 95% confident that at most 86% of the population wants to build a new park.

D) The politician can be 95% confident that between 74% and 86% of the population wants to build a new park.

Solution

We are told the confidence level is 95%, so eliminate choice B. The margin of error describes a confidence interval of all values between 80% − 6%, or 74%, and 80% + 6%, or 86%, which is choice D.

Answer: D

Example 2

The results of testing a new medication on 500 people with a certain disease found that 235 of the patients showed improvement when they used the medication. Assume these 500 people can be regarded as a random sample from the population of all people with this disease. The margin of error for the study is about 0.04, or 4%.

Which of the following is the most reasonable inference to make based on the information above?

A) It would be reasonable to think that more than half the people with this disease would not improve because $\frac{235}{500} < 0.50$.

B) It would be reasonable to think that less than half the people with this disease would improve because $\frac{235}{500} - 0.02 < 0.50$.

C) It would be reasonable to think that more than half the people with this disease would improve because $\frac{235}{500} + 0.04 > 0.50$.

D) It would be reasonable to think that less than half the people with this disease would improve because $\frac{235}{500} + 0.20 < 0.50$.

Solution

Calculate the sample proportion $\frac{235}{500} = 0.47$. We know the margin of error is ± 0.04, so the actual proportion of all patients with this disease who would show improvement on this medication is between 0.43 and 0.51 (0.47 ± 0.04). Examine the answer choices. Choice A does not take into account the margin of error, so eliminate it. Choices B and D do not reflect the correct margin of error. The answer must be C.

Answer: C

Example 3

An educational research group studied a new program designed to help first-graders pass the state examination in reading. The research showed, with 95% confidence, that 70% of students using this program would pass the state examination. The margin of error was 12%. In order to show a smaller margin of error, what measure might be taken?

A) The research group could decrease the required confidence level.
B) The research group could ignore the initial study and duplicate it with the same number of pupils at a different school.
C) The research group could increase the confidence level.
D) The research group could reduce the sample size by 12%.

Solution

Lowering the confidence level reduces the margin of error.

Answer: A

Example 4

A pre-election poll showed that the Green Party candidate would receive between 43% and 53% of the vote with a confidence level of 90%. The campaign committee wanted a smaller confidence interval. What measure might be taken?

A) The poll-takers could duplicate the poll, decreasing the sample size.
B) The poll-takers could duplicate the poll, increasing the sample size.
C) The poll-takers could select a different sample of the same size.
D) The poll-takers could increase the margin of error.

Solution

The confidence interval is related to the sample size. Increasing the sample size decreases the confidence interval.

Answer: B

1. A community conducted a survey and reported that 60% of the sample that responded wants to extend the school year by two weeks. The survey is reported with a 6% margin of error and a confidence level of 90%. Which statement best estimates the desire of the entire community?

    A) We can be 90% confident that between 57% and 63% of the population wants a longer school year.

    B) We can be 90% confident that between 54% and 66% of the population wants a longer school year.

    C) We can be 84% confident that between 57% and 63% of the population wants a longer school year.

    D) We can be 84% confident that 60% of the population wants a longer school year.

Strategy: Answer choices C and D do not report the correct confidence interval, so eliminate those. Calculating the interval of 60% with a 6% margin of error gets the prediction to be between 54% and 66%. This is answer choice B.

2. A state election ballot included a proposal to increase technology subsidies to K-12 schools. A pre-election survey of 500 urban residents found that 300 were in favor of the subsidies. The margin of error was about 0.04, or 4%. A pre-election survey of 500 rural residents found that 255 were in favor of the subsidies. The margin of error was about 0.04, or 4%. How can the proportions of people who preferred the proposal be compared?

    A) In urban areas, the proportion in favor of the plan is 0.60 ± 0.04, or from 0.56 to 0.64. In rural areas, the proportion in favor of the plan is 0.51 ± 0.04, or 0.47 to 0.55. The proportion of urban residents in favor of the plan appears to be higher.

    B) In urban areas, the proportion in favor of the plan is 0.60 ± 0.04, or from 0.56 to 0.64. In rural areas, the proportion in favor of the plan is 0.51 ± 0.04, or 0.47 to 0.55. The proportion in the two groups is close enough to be called the same.

    C) In urban areas, the proportion in favor of the plan is 0.40. In rural areas, the proportion in favor of the plan is 0.49. The proportion of rural residents in favor of the plan appears to be higher.

    D) The sample sizes in the study are too small to use to draw conclusions on a statewide issue.

Strategy: Eliminate answer choice D immediately as the sample sizes are quite large. Then calculate the sample proportions in favor of the plan: in urban areas, the proportion in favor of the plan is 300 out of 500 or 60%. In rural areas, the proportion in favor of the plan is 255 out of 500 or 51%. This rules out answer choice C. To determine which of choices A or B is correct, calculate the confidence intervals. For urban areas, 0.60 ± 0.04, or from 0.56 to 0.64. For rural areas, $0.51 \pm 0.04 = 0.47$ to 0.55. The proportion of urban residents in favor of the plan appears to be higher. There is no overlap in the confidence interval. The correct answer is choice A.

Answers begin on page 687.

1. Statistics can best be defined as the study of:

   A) Categorical data

   B) Random samples

   C) Numerical data

   D) Election polls

2. A principal conducted a survey of students about planting a new garden on the school lawn. He reported that 75% of students responding to the survey were in favor of planting the new garden. The survey results were reported with a 5% margin of error and a confidence level of 90% that the result reflects the entire student population. Which statement best estimates the population proportion that is in favor of planting the new garden?

   A) There is a 90% confidence that between 70% and 80% of the population wants to plant a new garden.

   B) There is an 85% confidence that between 70% and 80% of the population wants to plant a new garden.

   C) There is a 95% confidence that at most 80% of the population wants to plant a new garden.

   D) There is a 95% confidence that between 70% and 80% of the population wants to plant a new garden.

3. A school nurse conducted a survey asking all of the grade 12 students taking a foreign language class to self-report their height and weight. The results revealed that three-fourths of the grade 12 students enrolled in foreign language classes were overweight. The nurse reported these findings with a 4% margin of error and a confidence level of 90%. Based on this, which of the following statements about the school's grade 12 population is most accurate?

   A) We can be 90% confident that between 73% and 77% of students in the grade 12 class are overweight.

   B) We can be 86% confident that between 73% and 77% of students in the grade 12 class are overweight.

   C) We can be 90% confident that between 71% and 79% of students in the grade 12 class are overweight.

   D) We can be 86% confident that between 71% and 79% of students in the grade 12 class are overweight.

4. A medical study tested the efficacy of a new drug for acid reflux. The test showed improvement for 75% of the people taking the drug. The confidence level was reported at 90% and the margin of error was 10%. The researchers would like a smaller margin of error. What measure might they take?

   A) They could decrease the sample size.

   B) They could find another independent sample of the same size and hope for better results.

   C) They could decrease the required confidence level.

   D) They should choose a different way to select sample subjects.

5. A principal randomly selected 50 freshman students to complete a survey as they entered the school media center. She asked each of the 50 students to estimate how many minutes they spend using the school's media center each week. The results showed the sample mean was 145 minutes. The confidence interval for this estimate was the range 138 to 152 minutes. In order to replicate the survey and get a smaller confidence interval, how would you modify the sample?

   A) Randomly select 200 students as they enter the media center and repeat the survey.
   B) Randomly select 200 students as they leave the cafeteria and repeat the survey.
   C) Randomly select 25 students as they enter the media center and repeat the survey.
   D) Randomly select 60 students as they leave the cafeteria and repeat the survey.

6. A researcher randomly selected 50 residents in a large senior center to complete a survey about the number of times they each take prescribed medication each week. The mean number of doses in the sample was 70. The margin of error for this estimate was 5.2 doses. In order to replicate the survey and get a smaller margin of error, how could you modify the sample size?

   A) Randomly select another 50 residents from the center and repeat the study.
   B) Randomly select 60 customers as they leave the pharmacy and repeat the study.
   C) Randomly select 200 residents from the center and repeat the study.
   D) Randomly select 200 customers as they leave the pharmacy and repeat the study.

7. A large bowl contains 5,000 lollipops of assorted strawberry, lime, and grape flavors. Kepa wants an estimate of the proportion of lollipops in the bowl that are strawberry by taking several sample groups from the bowl. Which of the following statements about Kepa's sampling method is true?

   A) It is important that all of his samples are the same size.
   B) All samples the same size will have the same proportion of strawberry lollipops.
   C) The larger the sample, the larger the margin of error.
   D) The larger the sample, the smaller the margin of error.

8. Volunteers helped the school librarian to purge outdated books. They reported to the librarian that they had taken 500 books off the shelves and randomly wrapped them for disposal by size rather than by subject. The books were taken from the science section, the history section, and the biography section. The science chairperson wanted an estimate of the proportion of books that were science books. He unwrapped several packs of books and recorded the percent in each pack that were science books.

   Which of the following statements about this sampling method is true?

   A) If he picked the smallest packs of books, the margin of error would be smaller.
   B) If he picked the biggest packs of books, the margin of error would be smaller.
   C) It is important that the sample packs he opened were not next to each other.
   D) All packs with the same number of books would have the same number of science books.

No Student-Produced Response Questions for this Lesson.

LESSON 8:

Data Collection, Justifying Conclusions, and Making Inferences

- ■ **Analyzing Data Collection Methods**
- ■ **Justifying Conclusions**
- ■ **Evaluating Reports to Make Inferences**

· · · · · · **Explain** **Analyzing Data Collection Methods** · · · · · · · · ·

A statistical study is a four-step process:

1. The study begins by asking a question that can be answered with data.

2. The second step is the collection of the data, using the type of study that is most appropriate.

3. The third step is organization and analysis of the data.

4. The fourth step is to arrive at a conclusion in the context of the original question.

We have briefly discussed step 1 in a previous lesson. In this lesson, we will discuss steps 2 and 3. On the SAT, it will be important to be able to differentiate between the types of data collection methods and understand the appropriateness and pitfalls of each type. The three types of data collection methods we will examine are surveys, observational studies, and experimental studies.

- **Surveys** involve gathering information from subjects using a questionnaire. Surveys are often used because they can reach a large number of people and can gather information across a wide range of variables. The data collected is easy to organize because the responses are all in the same format. Responses to questions can be a simple yes or no. Responses can also involve choosing a number on a Likert scale. The scale usually has five choices ranging from strongly agree to strongly disagree. Surveys can be anonymous, offering the respondent confidentiality. A pitfall of surveys is that response is voluntary. Certain subgroups of the population may be less likely or more likely to respond. If the survey is written in English, residents with limited English language skills are unlikely to respond. People with strong feelings about an issue are more likely to respond than people who are not as interested. Surveys are the least effective data collection method. However, they are often used to learn about social and political opinions.

> **Definition**
>
> A **Likert scale** assigns a numerical value to an attribute that is not necessarily numerical. This allows for statistical analysis of data.

- **Observational studies** are not as easy to administer as surveys; however, they are more effective. Observational studies observe subjects as they are, without any manipulation from the researcher. A pitfall of observational studies is that the researcher must have the ability to interpret and record what she observes without changing the behavior of those she is observing.

In both observational studies and surveys, there is no interaction between the subjects and the researcher.

- **Experimental studies** are the best data collection method, involving treatments, procedures, or programs that are deliberately imposed on subjects in order to discover a possible change in the variable being measured. The researcher has control over some aspects of the sample, such as selecting the sample pool or forming the treatment groups. The researcher gathers data on the effects of some process or intervention. For example, if a researcher wants to test the effect of a new medication, she might design an experiment to compare the effects of the new medication to one currently used. She would make certain that one treatment is not favored over the other. She might enlist patients from a sample of local people using the current medication or look for participants elsewhere. After gathering participants, she would then randomly assign half of them to receive the new medication and half to receive the currently accepted medication. Random assignment is essential. While experimental studies are the best type of data collection method, pitfalls do exist. For example, this type of data collection method is time-consuming, expensive, and complicated.

There are benefits and drawbacks to all data collection methods, and there are instances when a data collection method is chosen due to extenuating circumstances. For example, there are times when a survey is done, even when an observational study may produce more descriptive data, simply because managing the observation is time-consuming or complicated. Also, you might choose an observational study, even if an experimental study would give more informative results, because of budgeting issues. Keep in mind that it is not moral for the researcher to subject participants to a situation that is physically harmful or unethical or illegal. A researcher could not complete an experimental study finding a relationship between eating foods high in fat and heart disease because that would be unethical. The researcher could, however, conduct an observational study to answer the question.

Once a researcher has chosen a data collection method, a participant sample needs to be selected because it is unlikely the researcher can conduct a census. There are several techniques for choosing participants, but it is important to understand the likely biases associated with various methods.

- In a **self-selected sample**, individuals volunteer to be part of the sample. These samples have obvious built-in biases. People who volunteer are more likely to have strong feelings in favor of or against an initiative.

- In a **convenience sample**, individuals who are easy to access are selected. An example is choosing the first *n* individuals to arrive at a location. Clearly, this method of sampling may lead to the selection of participants who are not representative of the population. For example, students who arrive at school very early may be more likely to be on the same bus route or more likely to come for before-school tutoring or clubs and thus are not representative of the entire student body.

- In a **simple random sample**, each member of the population has an equal chance of being selected. Often, a random number generator, such as the one found on your calculator, is used to select participants. Random samples are the most likely to be unbiased. Common forms of random sampling include:

  ○ **systematic random sample**, where members of the population are arranged in numeric or alphabetic order. The first subject is chosen by selecting a random starting point and then, starting with that subject, every *n*th member of the population is chosen. For example, the researcher could use a random number generator to choose the first subject and then every tenth member of the population after that first subject.

  ○ **stratified sample**, where individuals are put into groups that share a common characteristic, such as gender or grade level, and then participants are selected from each group using a simple sampling method. For example, in conducting a school survey, we could randomly select five students from each homeroom in the school.

  ○ **cluster sample**, where individuals are put into groups and then all members of some of the groups are selected using a simple sampling method. For example, in conducting a school survey, we could randomly select ten homerooms and then include all students in each of these homerooms.

Example 1

Which technique for gathering data is most appropriate for studying the effect of zinc supplements in reducing the severity of the common cold?

A) Survey
B) Observational Study
C) Experimental Study
D) Census

Solution

An experimental study allows the researcher to alter a single variable (zinc supplement or no zinc supplement) to study its effect on participants.

Answer: C

Example 2

Researchers want to know what proportion of the student body enjoys listening to baseball games on the radio. You have to choose from four ways to gather your data. Which is the most appropriate data collection method for gaining accurate information?

A) Pick a random sample of students and ask them the question, "Do you enjoy listening to baseball games on the radio?" and record their answers.
B) Pick a random sample of students and observe their activities during times baseball games are broadcast.
C) Pick a random sample and form three subgroups from the sample. One subgroup will listen to baseball games, the second will listen to news, and the third group will listen to music. After listening to the genres, you will collect data on the feelings of the people listening to each category.
D) Ask members of the junior varsity baseball team if they enjoy listening to baseball games on the radio.

Solution

Answer choice C does not clearly answer the question, which is limited to interest in baseball broadcasts. Choice D would provide clearly biased data. Choices A and B would provide useful data, but observational studies are more reliable than surveys.

Answer: B

Example 3

A principal of a high school with 2,000 students wants to survey about 150 students to determine the most popular school assembly programs. Which sampling procedure would create a stratified sample?

A) Select the first 150 students who enter school on Monday morning.
B) List the students alphabetically from 1 to 2,000 and select 150 students using a random number generator.
C) Select some homerooms and survey all students in these homerooms.
D) Divide 150 by the number of homerooms, record the quotient, and then use a random sampling method to select that number of students from each homeroom.

Solution

Answer choice A is a convenience sample, and choice B is systemic random sample. Option C is a cluster sample. Option D is a stratified sample.

Answer: D

Practice Analyzing Data Collection Methods

Answers begin on page 688.

1. Researchers wanted to check claims that a vitamin supplement encouraged height growth. To do this, they measured the increase in height of 100 children whose parents reported that they took the vitamin supplement and 100 children whose parents reported that they did not take the supplement. Which technique describes the study?

   A) Survey
   B) Observational Study
   C) Experimental Study
   D) Census

2. Sampling is used to choose

   A) an entire population.
   B) a fair representation of a group.
   C) a small number of people.
   D) sports statistics.

3. A high school principal wanted parent opinion about setting rules for allowing students to drive to school. The principal selected his sample by using an alphabetical school household list and randomly picking one of the first 5 households and then every tenth household after that. He then recorded the parent/guardian responses as "happy to allow their student to drive to school," "unwilling to allow their student to drive to school," or "indifferent." He reported his results to the superintendent of schools. Based on this information, which of the following is true of the principal's sample?

   A) It represented the entire parent population.
   B) It was large enough to provide meaningful data.
   C) It was unbiased.
   D) All of A, B, and C

4. The high school athletic director interviewed every member of a varsity team about the possibility of practice during school breaks. Which technique describes his study?

   A) Survey
   B) Observational Study
   C) Experimental Study
   D) Census

Model SAT Questions

1. A researcher wants to know the effect of sleeping no more than two hours each night. Which technique would be best for her data collection?

   A) Survey of a sample of people with sleep disorders.
   B) Observation of a sample of people who report sleeping no more than two hours each night.
   C) Experiment in which half the subjects are only allowed two hours of sleep each night.
   D) Experiment in which half the subjects are given medication to keep them awake.

Strategy: Answer choices C and D are unethical. You cannot deprive people of sleep or give them medication to keep them awake for the purpose of depriving them of sleep. A survey of those with sleep disorders is unlikely to produce the desired results, since there are those people whose disordered sleep involves sleeping too much and they would need to be included in the sample. Thus answer choice B is the best.

The design of a research study and the selection of participants is just one part of statistical research. Any conclusions drawn from collected data must show care in avoiding bias and must make certain that any "cause and effect" findings are valid and not influenced by lurking variables.

Explain Justifying Conclusions

Researchers must be careful to avoid misleading results.

Samples must be chosen to avoid **bias**. Bias is the tendency to favor the selection of certain members of the population. A sample must fairly represent the entire population being studied. For example, the sample for a study of residents' satisfaction with spending town money to improve a local park should represent all people in the town, not just those who use the park. People dissatisfied with the park or those who are uninterested in park facilities may not visit it at all, but their opinions should be included, since they would be in the population paying for improvements. In contrast, the sample for a study of community pool users' satisfaction with lifeguard services at the facility should be limited to people who use the facility.

Unless the study is an experiment, no cause-and-effect can be established. Surveys and observations can only establish an association. However, when studying variables that appear to have a strong association, researchers must be careful to account for any lurking variable(s). A **lurking variable** is one that causes two other variables to have what appears to be a high correlation even though there is no real direct relationship between the two variables. A common example of a lurking variable is that ice cream sales and the number of drowning accidents are positively related. Therefore, can it be concluded that ice cream sales cause drowning accidents? No, of course not. The lurking variable here is time of year. More ice cream is sold in the summer than in the winter, and there is more opportunity for drowning in the summer than in the winter.

Think It Through

Example 1

A suburban board of education wanted to find out the community feeling among eligible voters about increasing property taxes to pay for new school classroom equipment, such as electronic white boards, tablets, and other associated technology. Which sample would provide the least bias?

A) Parents of kindergarten students

B) Parents of high school seniors

C) Shoppers leaving the community supermarket

D) Participants in a senior citizen breakfast

Solution

Parents of kindergarten students may be very likely to want new computers. Their children have many years left in the district, so they will have a great deal of bias. Parents of high school seniors may feel that their families will no longer benefit from school improvement. Senior citizens may have limited resources and likely have no children in school. Shoppers leaving the community supermarket are likely the least biased group of these options. They may contain members of families with school-aged children and members of families with no school-aged children.

Answer: C

Example 2

Which of the following data collections is most likely to have a faulty conclusion caused by a lurking variable?

A) Data about gas mileage and car weight, including factors such as car type, size of motor, and tire pressure.

B) Data about the risk of heart attack and age, including activity level, race, gender, and presence of diabetes in the participants.

C) Data showing the increased damage to property as a result of the number of firefighters sent to fight the fire.

D) Data showing the risk of obesity based upon dietary habits, including factors such as medical records showing metabolism and parent problems with obesity.

Solution

Choice C ignores the fact that a bigger fire typically results in sending more firefighters. The other choices attempt to identify and account for lurking variables.

Answer: C

Practice Justifying Conclusions

Answers begin on page 688.

1. A sample must be selected to determine the favorite activities of people in a particular town. Which of the following samples is the most representative and unbiased?

   A) Tenth-grade students
   B) Women
   C) People at a beach
   D) People shopping in a supermarket

2. Which study is most likely to be free of lurking variables?

   A) A study linking cell phone use to lung cancer
   B) A study linking plant growth to nourishment and light
   C) A study linking favorite ice cream flavor to grade in school
   D) A study linking increased life expectancy, based upon number of cars in the household

3. Which study is most likely to be free of bias?

   A) A restaurant gets customer opinion about the new menu by having the chef visit tables and record responses.
   B) An employer conducts private interviews with a sample of his staff, asking if they are happy with their job.
   C) A booth is up in the supermarket with a man offering free cheese samples and asking each customer the same opinion question about the cheese.
   D) In a random sample of city residents, a survey asks if they are in favor of a new tax to provide renovation of the senior citizen center. The amount of the tax is not stated. The header of the survey page shows an elderly man with a cane.

1. Which of the following data collections is <u>least</u> likely to have a faulty conclusion caused by a lurking variable?

   A) Data collected about the current mathematical ability of juniors in high school and each student's final grade in last year's math class

   B) Data about 100 people's salaries and their respective heights

   C) Data collected about K-12 students' reading abilities and their shoe size

   D) Data collected about the number of minutes the average person spends using their cell phone in a certain country compared with the average life expectancy of a person in that same country

Strategy: If you look at answer choices B, C, and D, you can determine the lurking variables. In B, the lurking variable is gender. Men are taller, so any salary difference could be attributable to gender rather than height. Answer C's lurking variable is age. The older the student, the better the average reading ability. The lurking variable in D is affluence; the richer the country, the more people who will be able to afford cell phones and thus spend more time on them. The only logical answer choice is A.

2. A sample must be selected to determine the favorite activities of people in a particular town. Which of the following samples is the most representative and unbiased?

   A) Using the fourth name in the phone book and then every 12th name

   B) Women involved in the Chamber of Commerce

   C) Spectators at the Memorial Day parade

   D) People shopping in a local discount store

Strategy: Choice A is a systemic random sample, designed to guard against bias.

Explain Evaluating Reports to Make Inferences

Often, data is collected from a sample in order to make inferences about the larger population. This data may be presented in text summaries, which are used to describe simple results, or via tables, charts, and graphs. These pictorial methods of data display are a convenient way of summarizing results. While they show an easy-to-read "picture" of the data, all summaries must be read carefully. It is important to practice reading data reports displayed using various presentations in order to make inferences about the data (for a review of different types of graphical displays, see page 231).

Definition

An **inference** is conjecturing a conclusion about a given population based on results observed through random sampling.

Example 1

An elementary school principal conducted a survey to gather evidence about which holiday pie is the favorite among the 500 fourth grade students in his school. He went to Ms. Widyn's classroom and surveyed her students. The results are shown below.

Pie Flavor	Frequency
Apple	12
Cherry	8
Pecan	4
Pumpkin	6

Which of the following can be inferred about the entire population of fourth graders?

A) More than half of the students want apple pie.

B) About twice as many students prefer apple pie as prefer either pecan pie or pumpkin pie.

C) More students prefer apple pie than other pie flavors listed.

D) The sum of the number of students who like cherry pie and like pecan pie is exactly the same as the number of students who like apple pie.

Solution

Choice A is incorrect as the sample shows less than half the students wanting apple pie. Moving to answer choice B, we see it is incorrect, since 12 students prefer apple pie and 10 students prefer either pecan pie or pumpkin pie, and 12 is not twice 10. We also know that choice D is incorrect because it is unlikely the population will have the same proportions as the sample. Only answer choice C is correct.

Answer: C

Example 2

The bar chart below shows the results of a survey of people leaving a municipal parking lot who were asked about their car types. The survey will be used by a local used car dealer to help him plan the assortment of cars he has available for potential customers in this neighborhood.

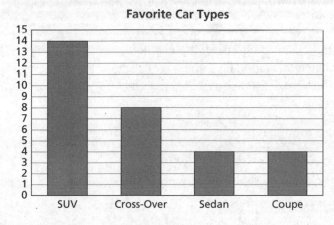

What information can the car dealer infer from this survey?

A) Only females will want sedans or coupes.

B) All families with children will want cross-overs.

C) Exactly half as many people will want sedans as want cross-overs.

D) Most people will want either SUVs or cross-overs.

Solution

This chart gives no information describing the respondents, so eliminate choices A and B. Survey proportions will not be exact matches for population proportions; this rules out choice C. The chart shows an overwhelming preference for SUVs and cross-overs.

Answer: D

Model SAT Questions

1. The following chart shows the number of students in Mrs. Neiffer's 7th period freshman math class who were born during each month of the year.

Month	Number of Students	Month	Number of Students
January	4	July	0
February	3	August	2
March	1	September	4
April	6	October	1
May	4	November	1
June	6	December	3

Which of the following can be inferred about the entire population of freshmen at this school?

A) None of the freshmen in the school have a birthday in July.

B) The month with the least number of students born in it is November.

C) More than half of the freshmen will have a birthday during the first six months of the year.

D) About 15% of the students will have a birthday in December.

Strategy: It is unlikely that none of the freshmen in the school have a birthday in July, so eliminate answer choice A. We also know that choice B is incorrect because it is unlikely the population will have the same proportions as the sample. Quick mental math shows that answer choice D is also incorrect. Select answer choice C.

2. Warwick is a clothing buyer for a large retail chain. He is surveying people about their favorite type of women's top. The information he gathers will be used to assist him in his buying decisions for next season's stock. The results of his survey are shown in the bar graph below.

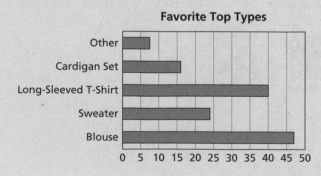

Favorite Top Types

What information can Warwick infer from this survey?

A) All females will want blouses next season.

B) Warwick should buy more long-sleeved t-shirts and blouses than the other types of tops.

C) Warwick shouldn't buy any cardigan sets.

D) The most common size among people who buy women's tops at this store is medium.

Strategy: We cannot determine the sizes of women's tops to buy from this information, so eliminate answer choice D. Some people did prefer cardigan sets, so eliminate answer choice C. Not all the people who responded to the survey chose blouses, and we don't know the gender of the people who responded, so answer choice A is not correct. Select answer choice B.

SAT-Type Questions

Answers begin on page 688.

1. The local parks department wanted to get an idea about improvement preferences from members of the community who use the park. On a weekday morning, the following data was collected at the park:

Improvement Chosen	Number of Responders
New swing sets	25
New tennis courts	50
New bicycle path	48

Which of the following can be inferred about the entire population of park users based on the data collected?

A) Most people want new tennis courts.

B) More than half of the community wants new tennis courts.

C) About twice as many people prefer a bicycle path to new swing sets.

D) Fewer than 50 park users want either a new bicycle path or new swing sets.

2. An environmental protection group wanted to understand the fish population in a protected state freshwater lake. Members of the group spent one day capturing fish and recording the number of each species. Their results are below:

Species	Number of Fish Caught
Largemouth Bass	33
White Catfish	30
Pirate Perch	30
Blotted Sunfish	10

Based on the chart for question 2, which of the following can be inferred about the entire fish population of the lake?

A) Largemouth bass are the most populous species in the lake.

B) The population of white catfish and pirate perch are similar in size.

C) There are 20 less blotted sunfish than pirate perch in the entire fish population.

D) The populations of largemouth bass and pirate perch are identical.

3. A statistics student wanted to estimate the number of red marbles in a tank of 1,000 marbles. The following table represents the results of several samples she took.

Sample Number	Sample Size	Number of Red Marbles in Sample	Percent of Red Marbles in Sample
1	5	2	40%
2	12	4	33.3%
3	16	4	25%
4	20	5	25%
5	24	6	25%
6	25	6	24%
7	30	8	26.7%
8	32	8	25%

Which statement describes the best estimate of all the red marbles in the tank?

A) The average of all sample percentages is 28%, so there are about 280 red marbles in the tank.

B) The larger the sample, the better the estimate so, giving more weight to the larger samples than the smaller ones, there appear to be about 250 red marbles in the tank.

C) Since samples must include at least 10% of the population, it is impossible to estimate the number of red marbles from the data in the table.

D) A valid study has at least 10 samples, thus it is impossible to estimate the number of red marbles from the data in the table.

4. From a high school student body of 3,600 students, a random sample of 800 students was selected and surveyed about moving the start of the school day from 7:30 am to 9:00 am. All 800 students provided a definitive response. If 300 students answered that they did not want to change the start time for the school day, which of the following is a valid statement about the entire student body?

A) About 1,350 students would probably like to start school later.

B) About 2,250 students would probably like to start school later.

C) About 300 students would probably like to start school later.

D) Not enough students were surveyed to make a prediction.

Student-Produced Response Questions

5. A local health organization surveyed a small group of residents about their habits for engaging in regular cardiovascular exercises. Of the 40 people surveyed, 12 said that they exercise regularly; the number of minutes those 12 adults exercise and the frequency of that exercise per week is shown below. The population of the area served by this health organization has about 5,000 adults.

Respondent No.	Minutes per Exercise Session	Frequency of Exercise per Week
1	45	6
2	30	7
3	60	7
4	60	2
5	40	5
6	60	5
7	45	3
8	45	4
9	30	5
10	20	7
11	30	6
12	60	5

Use the data in the table to predict about how many adults in the area served by this health organization engage in cardiovascular exercise routines lasting at least 30 minutes, at least 5 days each week.

Questions 6 and 7 refer to the following information.

A scout troop plans to bake cookies for an elementary school fundraiser. The troop surveyed a random sample of 30 families out of the 2,700 families with students in the school to see if the family would be likely to buy cookies, and, if so, to select a cookie type and to say how many boxes they would buy.

Of the 30 families surveyed, 15 indicated that they would buy cookies. The data collected is listed below.

Family No.	Cookie Type	Number of Boxes
1	S'mores	4
2	Vanilla Wafer	6
3	S'mores	3
4	Peanut Butter Clusters	2
5	Mint	5
6	Vanilla Wafer	4
7	Mint	2
8	Mint	5
9	Chocolate Chip	4
10	S'mores	8
11	Peanut Butter Clusters	1
12	S'mores	3
13	Chocolate Chip	5
14	Mint	2
15	Chocolate Chip	6

6. About how many families from the school population would be likely to buy chocolate chip cookies?

7. The cookies will cost $3.50 per box. About how much money can the scouts anticipate earning from cookie sales?

Multiple Choice

Calculator Allowed

Answers begin on page 689.

1. Many states require a valid social security card for all drivers moving into the state who want to get a new drivers' license. An advocacy group claimed that people are more likely to have a passport than their actual social security card. A survey was conducted to see how many newly arrived residents to certain states possessed a passport; the results are shown in the table below.

	Has a Passport	Does Not Have a Passport	Did Not Respond	Total
New York	20,114	8,015	2,965	31,094
Pennsylvania	15,987	12,005	1,994	29,986
Connecticut	12,639	15,552	800	28,991
Rhode Island	8,004	2,864	867	11,735
Total	56,744	38,436	6,626	101,806

According to the table, from which state did the greatest percentage of people report that they have a passport?

A) New York

B) Pennsylvania

C) Connecticut

D) Rhode Island

2. The two-way frequency table below shows the results of a survey about elective course preferences. Which statement about gender and elective preference is supported by the data?

	Art	Music	Technology	Total
Male	50	35	100	185
Female	48	36	90	174
Total	98	71	190	359

A) They are associated because the conditional frequencies, column by column, are not the same.

B) They are independent because the conditional frequencies, column by column, are nearly the same.

C) They are associated because the conditional frequencies, column by column, are nearly the same.

D) They are independent because the conditional frequencies, column by column, are not the same.

3. A population that initially had 20 members doubles every 20 years. Which graph represents this population growth?

A)
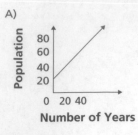

B)
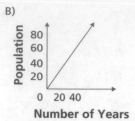

C)
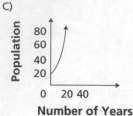

D)
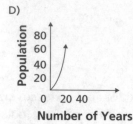

4. A student wants to determine the most liked teacher in his high school. Which type of study would be the most practical way to answer his question?

A) Experiment
B) Survey
C) Observation
D) Intuition

5. A scale drawing of a floor plan for a new living room is 5 inches long and 3 inches wide. If the actual living room is 44 feet long, what is the actual area of the room?

A) 8.8 yd²
B) 26.4 ft²
C) 129.0$\overline{6}$ yd²
D) 1161.6 yd²

6. A data set has a mean of 50 and a standard deviation of 10. Which statement is true?

A) All of the data lies between 30 and 70.

B) About $\frac{2}{3}$ of the data is less than 60.

C) About 47.5% of the data lies between 50 and 70.

D) About $\frac{2}{3}$ of the data is greater than 40.

7. A medical study tested a new drug for asthma relief. The test showed, with 95% confidence, that 85% of people taking the drug would show improvement. The margin of error was 7%. If the researchers want a smaller margin of error, what measure might they take?

A) They could reduce the sample size.
B) They could increase the sample size.
C) They could find another independent sample of the same size and hope for better results.
D) They should choose a different way to select sample subjects.

8. The scatterplot below represents the midterm chemistry grades for 40 students compared to the time those students spent playing video games.

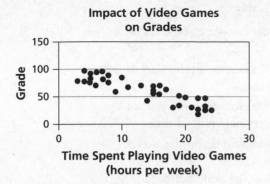

Impact of Video Games on Grades

Which statement best describes the graph?

A) There is a negative linear correlation between time spent playing video games and grades on the midterm.

B) There is a positive linear correlation between time spent playing video games and grades on the midterm.

C) There is a strong non-linear correlation between time spent playing video games and grades on the midterm.

D) There is not enough data to describe the relationship between time spent playing video games and grades on the midterm.

9. Four friends, Febe, Lupa, Michel, and Rian, were traveling through Europe when the currency exchange rate was $1.16 = 1 Euro. The friends ate lunch in a local restaurant and agreed to split the cost of the meal equally. If the total bill was 43.45 Euros, how much did the lunch cost each person in U.S. dollars? Round to the nearest penny, if needed.

A) $10.86
B) $9.36
C) $12.60
D) $11.52

10. The density of corn syrup is 38 grams/cm³. If 456 grams of corn syrup will fill a rectangular solid container with a base 3 cm × 2 cm, what is the height of the container in centimeters?

A) 12 cm
B) 6 cm
C) 3 cm
D) 2 cm

11. The half-life of a particular isotope is represented by the function $g(t) = 500(0.5)^t$ where $g(t)$ represents the number of milligrams of the isotope at time t. In the function $g(t)$, which of the following statements is true?

A) 500 represents the number of milligrams of the isotope at time t, and 0.5 represents the rate of decline.

B) 500 represents the number of milligrams of the isotope at the start of the observation, and 0.5 represents the rate of decline.

C) 500 represents the number of milligrams of the isotope at the start of the observation, and 0.5 represents the rate of every half-unit of time.

D) Eventually, the graph representing this function will lie on the x-axis.

12. Which type of function is represented by the data in the table below?

x	$f(x)$
1	4
2	2
3	1
4	0.5

A) Exponential growth

B) Exponential decay

C) Linear growth

D) Linear decline

13. Data set A and data set B are normally distributed. Both sets have a mean of 60. Data set A has a standard deviation of 30, but data set B has a standard deviation of 60. Which statement below is most accurate?

A) All of the data in set A falls within two standard deviations from the mean, and all of the data in set B falls within one standard deviation from the mean.

B) All of the data in set A falls within one standard deviation from the mean, and all of the data in set B falls within two standard deviations from the mean.

C) 95% of data set A values, represented by x, fall in the range of $0 < x < 120$; 95% of data set B values, represented by y, fall in the range $-60 < y < 180$.

D) 99% of data set A values, represented by x, fall in the range $0 < x < 120$; 99% of data set B values, represented by y, fall in the range $-60 < y < 180$.

14. A principal of a high school with 2,150 students wants to survey about 175 students to determine the most popular electives. Which procedure would create a systematic random sample?

A) Select the first 175 students who sign up for a charity walk.

B) From an alphabetical list of all students, start with the tenth student and then select every twelfth student until 175 students are selected.

C) Choose the first student to enter the school cafeteria and then continue to select every fifth student until 175 students have been selected.

D) From each alphabetized homeroom list, use a random number generator to select the same number of students from each homeroom so that about 175 students are selected.

15. The scatterplot below is data taken from eight students who are in both the Concert Orchestra and the School Literary Society.

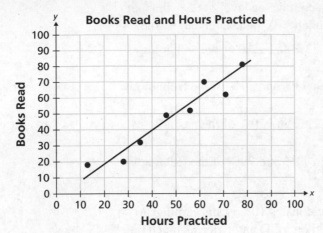

How many students practiced more than the number of hours predicted by the line of best fit?

A) 0

B) 3

C) 4

D) 7

16. The two-way frequency table below shows the results of a survey of freshmen regarding their summer plans.

	Travel	Camp	Work	Total
Male	4	25	30	59
Female	6	30	28	64
Total	10	55	58	123

What is the relative marginal frequency for plans to travel?

A) $\dfrac{4}{59}$

B) $\dfrac{10}{59}$

C) $\dfrac{59}{123}$

D) $\dfrac{10}{123}$

17. By surveying a sample of students taking Technology, the principal found that three-quarters of the students would like the school to offer a course in robotics. She reported with a 4% margin of error and a confidence level of 95% that her results reflect the desires of all technology students. Which statement is true?

A) There is a 95% confidence that between 73% and 77% of the technology students want a robotics course.

B) There is a 97.5% confidence that between 73% and 77% of the technology students want a robotics course.

C) There is a 95% confidence that between 71% and 79% of the technology students want a robotics course.

D) There is a 97.5% confidence that between 71% and 79% of the technology students want a robotics course.

18. Charlie received $150 at his weekend job. He donates 10% of his earnings to charity each time he is paid. He also spent $20 on a CD and twice as much on a present for his brother. He saved one-third of the rest. What is the ratio of his savings to his donations?

A) 10:3

B) 5:3

C) 1:5

D) 3:10

19. The town council wants to know the percentage of voters in the town who are in favor of improving a municipal playground. What is the population for this study?

A) The number of adults who live in the town.

B) The number of people who answered a survey mailed to all households.

C) All parents of children living in the town.

D) All eligible voters in the town.

20. The following 28 test scores were recorded:

Score	Quantity
100	2
95	4
90	6
85	2
80	3
75	7
70	4

Which statement about the test scores listed above is accurate?

A) The mode is 7 and the median is 85.

B) The mode is 7 and the median is 77.5.

C) The mode is 75 and the median is 82.5.

D) The mode is 75 and the median is 85.

21. Describe the pattern of the data shown in the scatterplot below.

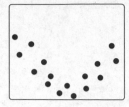

    A) Quadratic

    B) Negative linear

    C) Positive linear

    D) Exponential

22. The two-way frequency table below shows the results of a survey of people regarding the sport they most enjoy watching on television.

	Baseball	Basketball	Football	Total
Male	40	62	30	132
Female	60	90	45	195
Total	100	152	75	327

What is the conditional probability that a randomly selected female most enjoys watching football?

    A) $\dfrac{3}{13}$

    B) $\dfrac{4}{13}$

    C) $\dfrac{100}{327}$

    D) $\dfrac{5}{22}$

23. Data set A is normally distributed, with a mean of 120 and a standard deviation of 15. Which of the following statements regarding data set A is most accurate?

    A) All of the data lies between 90 and 150.

    B) About $\dfrac{2}{3}$ of the data are less than 135.

    C) About 47.5% of the data lies between 120 and 150.

    D) About $\dfrac{2}{3}$ of the data are greater than 105.

24. A school board wanted to review the use of school buses by primary grade children. The district called 60 families to ask if their student(s) rode the morning school bus. Of the 60 families surveyed, 15 said that their children use the bus. There are about 800 families with children in the primary grades in this district. Predict the number of families that make use of the school bus in the morning.

    A) 15

    B) 60

    C) 200

    D) 300

25. A school club collected 560 cans in the first 4 weeks of a charity drive. If the club continues to collect at the same rate, in how many more weeks will the class collect more than 1,200 cans?

A) 4

B) 5

C) 8

D) 9

26. A speed-reader can read x words in m minutes. How many hours will it take her to read y words?

A) $\dfrac{ym}{60x}$

B) $\dfrac{xy}{60m}$

C) $\dfrac{60m}{xy}$

D) $\dfrac{60xy}{m}$

27. Which of the following graphs represents an increasing exponential function with a y-intercept of $\dfrac{3}{2}$?

A)

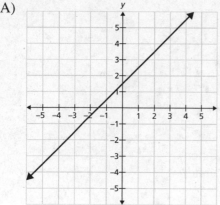

B)

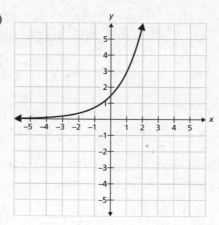

C)

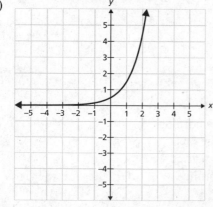

D)

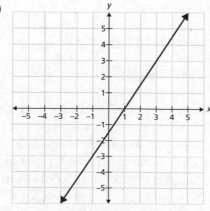

28. The table below shows book genre preferences for members of the library book club.

	Mysticism	Romance	Science Fiction	Total
Male	3	3	6	12
Female	4	6	0	10
Total	7	9	6	22

What is the conditional probability that a randomly selected male student does not choose a preference for Romance?

A) $\dfrac{1}{4}$

B) $\dfrac{3}{4}$

C) $\dfrac{2}{5}$

D) $\dfrac{13}{22}$

29. The table below shows the quiz scores for 59 students taking Discrete Mathematics. What is the median score?

Score	Frequency
0	0
1	0
2	3
3	5
4	6
5	8
6	8
7	8
8	7
9	6
10	8

A) 8

B) 7

C) 6

D) 5

30. The results of testing a new treatment on 250 people with a certain allergy found that 118 of the patients showed improvement in symptoms when they used the treatment. Assume these 250 people can be regarded as a random sample from the population of all people with this allergy. The margin of error for the study is about 0.04, or 4%. Which of the following is the most reasonable inference to make based on the given information?

A) It would be reasonable to think that more than half the people with this

allergy would improve because $\dfrac{118}{250} + 0.04 > 0.50$.

B) It would be reasonable to think that more than half the people with this

allergy would not improve because $\dfrac{118}{250} < 0.50$.

C) It would be reasonable to think that less than half the people with this allergy

would improve because $\dfrac{118}{250} - 0.20 < 0.50$.

D) It would be reasonable to think that less than half the people with this allergy

would improve because $\dfrac{118}{250} + 0.20 < 0.50$.

Student-Produced Response Questions

31. The following partial two-way table describes favorite ice cream flavors for students in a certain homeroom.

	Rocky Road	Peanut Brittle	Mocha Fudge	Mint Chip	Total
Male		5	6	4	20
Female	3			1	
Total		13	6	5	

If a student who named their favorite ice cream flavor as Rocky Road is chosen at random, what is the conditional probability that student is female?

32. The athletic director for a school with 3,000 students conducted a survey of one physical education class to find out which after-school, non-varsity physical fitness activities students would like to have offered. Of the 25 students in the class, 15 said they would participate in some form of physical fitness activity. The table shows the data for those 15 students.

Activity	Times per week
Weight Room	3
Treadmill	3
Tennis	2
Weight Room	5
Tennis	2
Tennis	5
Tennis	3
Weight Room	1
Tennis	5
Weight Room	2
Treadmill	2
Weight Room	5
Weight Room	2
Treadmill	3
Treadmill	2

Use the data above to predict how many students in the school would like to play tennis more often than 1 day per week.

33. Find the next term in the sequence below.

3, 9, 27, 81,...

34. If the density of copper is 8.96 g/cm³, and if the density of benzene is 0.8786 g/cm³, what mass of copper will have the same volume as 15 grams of benzene? Express your answer in grams.

35. Kohen delivers newspapers to earn extra money. As an incentive to carry a larger route, his manager gave him an unusual option. Kohen will earn $0.50 if he delivers 10 papers, $1.00 if he delivers 20 papers, $2.00 if he delivers 30 papers, and so on, doubling his pay with every 10 papers. How much money will Kohen earn if he delivers 70 papers?

36. The scatterplot below shows the observed ages and weights of boys visiting a certain pediatrician's office. The line of best fit is drawn. How many boys weighed more than the expected weight shown by the line of best fit?

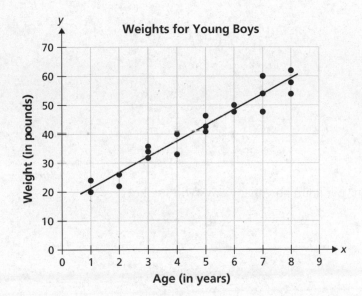

Weights for Young Boys

37. Mr. Bourne owns a 15,000-gallon swimming pool that he keeps filled to capacity. Due to its size, at the end of the season Mr. Bourne will need to drain the pool according to city regulations. The city code states that the maximum rate of drainage is 12 gallons per minute and the maximum time the drainage system can operate in one day is 6 hours.

PART 1

If Mr. Bourne's pool has a drainage system that measures the drainage rate in cubic feet (ft^3) per hour (1 ft^3 = 7.48 gallons), what is the maximum number of cubic feet Mr. Bourne can drain per hour and still be within the limits set by the city? Round to the nearest ft^3 per hour, if needed.

PART 2

If Mr. Bourne sets the drainage rate at 90 ft^3 per hour, how many days will it take him to fully drain his pool?

Correlation Chart

Summary SAT-Type Test—Problem Solving & Data Analysis (Calculators Allowed)

Use the chart below to mark the questions you found difficult to determine which lessons you need to review.

Question Number	Lesson 1 (p. 157–176)	Lesson 2 (p. 177–187)	Lesson 3 (p. 188–200)	Lesson 4 (p. 201–214)	Lesson 5 (p. 215–230)	Lesson 6 (p. 231–245)	Lesson 7 (p. 246–251)	Lesson 8 (p. 252–264)
1	○							
2					○			
3				○				
4								○
5	○							
6						○		
7							○	
8			○					
9	○							
10		○						
11				○				
12	○							
13						○		
14	○							
15			○					○
16					○			
17							○	
18	○							
19							○	
20						○		
21			○					
22	○							
23						○		
24								○
25	○							
26								
27				○				
28					○			
29						○		
30								○
31	○							
32								○
33				○				
34		○		○				
35	○							
36			○					
37a	○							
37b	○							
Total Correct	___ / 6	___ / 4	___ / 4	___ / 6	___ / 5	___ / 5	___ / 3	___ / 5

CATEGORY 3
Passport to Advanced Math

LESSON 1:

Creating Equivalent Expressions Involving Rational Exponents and Radicals

- **Integer Exponents and Rules for Operations**
- **Radicals and Fractional Exponents**
- **Operations on Terms with Radicals**

· · · · · **Explain** **Integer Exponents and Rules for Operations** · · · · · · · · · ·

A number that can be expressed by means of a base and an **exponent** is called a **power**. A power is a term or a factor of a term that can be written as the product of equal factors. The **base** is one of the equal factors. The exponent is the number of times the base is used as a factor.

Remember that in a power, it's Base^{Exponent}

We say that the exponent raises the base to a power. For example:

$4^3 = (4)(4)(4)$	base = 4	exponent = 3	power = 4^3 = 64	four to the third power, or four cubed
$10\omega^2$	base = ω	exponent = 2	power = ω^2	ten times ω **squared**, or ten times ω to the second power
$6j$	base = j	exponent = 1	power = j^1 or j	6 times j to the first power

We've shown examples of positive exponents, but an exponent may also be negative or zero:

- A *negative* exponent can be written as a unit fraction with a positive exponent in the denominator:

$$10^{-2} = \frac{1}{10^2} = \frac{1}{100} \qquad m^{-n} = \frac{1}{m^n}$$

- The exponent *zero* has a special meaning. Any number to the zero power equals 1:

$$10^0 = 1 \qquad 4^0 = 1 \qquad 1{,}000{,}000{,}000{,}000^0 = 1 \qquad m^0 = 1$$

We can simplify terms involving powers using the rules outlined above. We can also create equivalent expressions involving exponents by following the operational rules below.

Rules for Operations on Terms with Exponents

Operation	Rule	Examples
Addition and subtraction $x^n + x^m = x^n + x^m$ $x^n - x^m = x^n - x^m$	Like bases with unlike exponents *cannot* be added or subtracted unless they can be evaluated first.	$2^2 + 2^3 = 4 + 8 = 12$ $3^3 - 3^2 = 27 - 9 = 18$ $a^2 + a^3 = a^2 + a^3$ $a^3 - a^2 = a^3 - a^2$
Multiplication $x^n \cdot x^m = x^{n+m}$	To multiply powers of like bases, add the exponents.	$3^4 \cdot 3^5 = 3^9$ $a^2 \cdot a^3 = a^{2+3} = a^5$ $a^{-4} \cdot a^5 = a^{-4+5} = a^1 = a$
Division $\dfrac{x^n}{x^m} = x^{n-m}, \; x \neq 0$	To divide powers of like bases, subtract the exponent of the divisor from the exponent of the dividend.	$\dfrac{4^7}{4^5} = 4^{7-5} = 4^2$ $\dfrac{a^5}{a^2} = a^{5-2} = a^3$ $\dfrac{a^3}{a^8} = a^{3-8} = a^{-5} = \dfrac{1}{a^5}$ $\dfrac{a^7}{a^7} = a^{7-7} = a^0 = 1 \; if \; a \neq 0$
Raising a power to a power $\left(x^m\right)^n = x^{mn}$	To raise a term with an exponent to some power, multiply the exponents.	$\left(5^2\right)^3 = 5^{2 \cdot 3} = 5^6$ $\left(a^4\right)^3 = a^{4 \cdot 3} = a^{12}$
Raising a fraction to a power $\left(\dfrac{x}{y}\right)^n = \dfrac{x^n}{y^n}$	To raise a fraction to a power, raise the numerator and the denominator to that power.	$\left(\dfrac{3}{5}\right)^2 = \dfrac{3^2}{5^2} = \dfrac{9}{25}$ $\left(\dfrac{a}{b}\right)^7 = \dfrac{a^7}{b^7}$

QUICK TIP

When an exponent is negative or 0, we have special rules for simplifying:

$$x^1 = x$$
$$x^0 = 1, \; x \neq 0$$
$$x^{-n} = \frac{1}{x^n}$$
$$1^n = 1$$

QUICK TIP

Note that the number zero raised to the zero power (0^0) is undefined.

QUICK TIP

Sometimes when adding or subtracting unlike bases, you can try to rewrite the exponents so they have the same base: $2^6 + 8^2$ is the same as $2^6 + (2^3)^2$.

Operation	Rule	Examples
Raising a product to a power $(xy)^n = x^n y^n$	To raise a product to a power, raise each factor to that power.	$(5 \cdot 2)^3 = 5^3 \cdot 2^3 = 1{,}000$ $(4a)^2 = 4^2 \cdot a^2 = 16a^2$ $(ab)^5 = a^5 b^5$

Note that all the examples so far have involved positive bases. Working with negative bases is similar, but some care must be taken to ensure the final simplification has the correct sign.

Here are some useful points to remember about working with negative bases:

- $-x^n$ means $-(x^n)$. For example: $-3^2 = -(3^2) = -9$ and $-3x^2 = -3(x^2)$

- $(-x)^n$ means $(-x)^n$. For example: $(-3)^2 = (-3)(-3) = 9$

- When a negative base is raised to an *even* power, the result becomes positive. For example: $(-2)^4 = (-2)(-2)(-2)(-2) = +16$

- When a negative base is raised to an *odd* power, the result remains negative. For example: $(-2)^3 = (-2)(-2)(-2) = -8$

Think It Through

Example 1

Which expression is equal to 10,000?

A) 100^3

B) $(5^4)(2^4)$

C) $(10^2)(50^2)$

D) $(2)(250^2)$

Solution

We know that $10{,}000 = 10^4$, but that is not one of the answer choices.
Examine the choices that are given: A, C, and D are clearly greater than 10,000.
Check choice B. It is an application of the rule for raising a product to a power;
$(5^4)(2^4) = (5 \cdot 2)^4 = 10^4$.

Answer: B

Example 2

Simplify the expression $(x^2 y^2)^2$.

A) $(xy)^8$

B) $(xy)^6$

C) $x^4 y^4$

D) $x^2 y^4$

Solution

For this example, we need to utilize the rule for raising a power to a power:

$(x^2 y^2)^2 = (x^{2 \cdot 2} y^{2 \cdot 2}) = x^4 y^4$.

Answer: C

Example 3

Given that the expression in the denominator is not equal to zero, which expression is equivalent to $\dfrac{-2a^{-2}b^0c^{-3}}{10a^{-5}b^{-2}c}$?

A) $\dfrac{-a^3b^2}{5c^2}$

B) $\dfrac{-a^3b^3}{5c^4}$

C) $\dfrac{a^3b^2}{5c^4}$

D) $\dfrac{-a^3b^2}{5c^4}$

Solution

One way to think about this problem is to break the large fraction into its respective parts. Then, $\dfrac{-2a^{-2}b^0c^{-3}}{10a^{-5}b^{-2}c} = \dfrac{-2}{10} \cdot \dfrac{a^{-2}}{a^{-5}} \cdot \dfrac{b^0}{b^{-2}} \cdot \dfrac{c^{-3}}{c}$. Now simplify each fraction using the division of like bases with unlike exponents rule: $\dfrac{a^{-2}}{a^{-5}} = a^{-2-(-5)} = a^{-2+5} = \dfrac{a^3}{1}$, $\dfrac{b^0}{b^{-2}} = \dfrac{b^2}{1}$, and $\dfrac{c^{-3}}{c} = c^{-3-(1)} = \dfrac{c^{-4}}{1}$. Of course, $\dfrac{-2}{10} = \dfrac{-1}{5}$. Now, put all the pieces together and finish simplifying by removing the negative exponents: $\dfrac{-2a^{-2}b^0c^{-3}}{10a^{-5}b^{-2}c} = \dfrac{-1a^3b^2}{5c^4}$.

Answer: D

•••••• Practice   **Integer Exponents and Rules for Operations** ••••••••••••

Answers begin on page 693.

1. What is the value of $2^{-3} + 2^{-2}$?

   A) $\dfrac{1}{64}$

   B) $\dfrac{1}{32}$

   C) $\dfrac{1}{2}$

   D) $\dfrac{3}{8}$

2. What is the value of $3^3 \cdot 3^2$?

   A) 3
   B) 35
   C) 243
   D) 729

3. What is the value of $4^2 + 4^3$?

   A) 20
   B) 80
   C) 600
   D) 1024

4. Given that the expression in the denominator is not equal to zero, which expression is equivalent to $\dfrac{\left(-9a^2b^2\right)^2}{\left(3a^3b\right)^3}$?

   A) $\dfrac{-3}{a^5b}$

   B) $\dfrac{3}{a^5b}$

   C) $\dfrac{3b}{a^5}$

   D) $\dfrac{-3b}{a^5}$

5. What is the value of $\dfrac{5^4}{5^2}$?

   A) 5

   B) 25

   C) $\dfrac{1}{5}$

   D) $\dfrac{1}{25}$

6. What is the value of $(3^3)^2$?

   A) 15

   B) 81

   C) 243

   D) 729

7. What is the value of $10^0 \cdot 10^3$?

   A) 0

   B) $\dfrac{1}{1,000}$

   C) 1

   D) 1,000

Model SAT Questions

1. If $\left(m^{5x}\right)^3 = m^{30}$, what is the value of x?

   A) 0.5

   B) 2

   C) 5

   D) 22

Strategy: In this problem we must solve for the unknown, x, which is in the exponent. We are able to set the exponential expression on the left-hand side of the equation equal to the exponential expression on the right-hand side of the equation because the bases are like. Then, $3 \cdot 5x = 30$, $15x = 30$, and $x = 2$. The correct answer is B.

2. Given that $x^{-5} \neq 0$, which of the following expressions is equivalent to $\dfrac{27x^{-7}}{9x^{-5}}$?

   A) $\dfrac{3}{x^2}$

   B) $3x^2$

   C) $\dfrac{3}{x^{35}}$

   D) $\dfrac{3}{x^{-2}}$

Strategy: Think of the original expression as $\dfrac{27}{9} \cdot \dfrac{x^{-7}}{x^{-5}}$. Then, $\dfrac{27}{9} = 3$ and we can simplify the exponents on the variables using the division rule: $\dfrac{x^{-7}}{x^{-5}} = x^{-7-(-5)} = x^{-7+5} = x^{-2}$. The expression $3x^{-2}$ is not one of the answer choices. Simplify the negative exponent and the expression becomes $\dfrac{3}{x^2}$.

This is answer choice A.

The **square root** of a number is a value that, when multiplied by itself, returns the original number. For example, $\sqrt{49} = 7$ because $7 \cdot 7 = 49$. The square root of n is written as $\sqrt{n}$ or radical n, where n is called the **radicand** and the symbol $\sqrt{}$ is called the **radical sign**. Every positive number has two different square roots. They are positive and negative numbers with the same absolute value. The positive value is called the **principal square root**. For example, while $\sqrt{9}$ is both $+3$ and -3, the principal square root of 9 is 3.

QUICK TIP

Unless stated otherwise, it is the principal square root that is the intended solution.

$$\sqrt{b} = x \text{ if and only if } x \geq 0 \text{ and } x^2 = b.$$

A number by which a square root is multiplied is called the *coefficient*. Thus, the product of 4 and $\sqrt{5}$ is written $4\sqrt{5}$ where the number 4 is the coefficient and the number 5 is the radicand.

A number that is the square of a rational number is called a **perfect square**. Consider the following examples:

$$11^2 = 121 \qquad \sqrt{121} = 11 \qquad 121 \text{ is a perfect square}$$
$$16^2 = 256 \qquad \sqrt{256} = 16 \qquad 256 \text{ is a perfect square}$$
$$\left(\frac{2}{3}\right)^2 = \frac{4}{9} \qquad \sqrt{\frac{4}{9}} = \frac{2}{3} \qquad \frac{4}{9} \text{ is a perfect square}$$

Points to Remember

- The square root of every perfect square is a rational number.

- The square root of every number that is not a perfect square is irrational.

- For every non-negative real number n: $\left(\sqrt{n}\right)^2 = \sqrt{n^2} = n$.

- The square root of a negative number does not exist in the set of real numbers.

The radicand is often referred to as the "square root" symbol; however, it can be used to describe any root. Next we consider nth roots.

The nth root of a number is a number whose nth power equals the original number. For example, $\sqrt[4]{81} = 3$ because $3^4 = 81$. The symbol $\sqrt[n]{b}$ means the nth root of b. In this notation, b is the *radicand* and n is called the **index**.

$$\sqrt[3]{27} = 3 \qquad 3 \cdot 3 \cdot 3 = 27$$
$$\sqrt[4]{\frac{1}{16}} = \frac{1}{2} \qquad \frac{1}{2} \cdot \frac{1}{2} \cdot \frac{1}{2} \cdot \frac{1}{2} = \frac{1}{16}$$
$$\sqrt[5]{32} = 2 \qquad 2 \cdot 2 \cdot 2 \cdot 2 \cdot 2 = 32$$

QUICK TIP

Remember that when the index is 3, we refer to the root as the cube root.

Points to Remember

- Finding the nth root of a number is the inverse operation of raising a number to the power n. In general, the nth root of b is x (written as $\sqrt[n]{b} = x$) if and only if $x^n = b$.

- When no index appears, the index is 2 and the operation is square root.

- If the *index n is even*, the operation is closed in the set of real numbers for all non-negative real numbers only. When we multiply an even number of identical values together, the product is always non-negative.

- If the *index n is odd*, the operation is closed regardless of the sign of the radicand. For example, $\sqrt[3]{8} = 2$ and $\sqrt[3]{-8} = -2$. In other words, with an odd index, the root always has the same sign as the radicand.

Similar to how we simplified expressions involving integer exponents, we can simplify expressions involving radicals. Note that a radical is only considered simplified when the integer remaining under the radical has no factor, other than 1, that has an integer nth root. Also, the final simplified expression has no radical in the denominator (if there is a denominator). Generally, for all counting numbers n, $\sqrt[n]{a \cdot b} = \sqrt[n]{a} \cdot \sqrt[n]{b}$ and $\sqrt[n]{\dfrac{a}{b}} = \dfrac{\sqrt[n]{a}}{\sqrt[n]{b}}$. If n is even, a and b must be non-negative.

On the SAT, if the choices provided show no radical sign in the denominator, multiply both the numerator and the denominator by the radical expression in the denominator.

For example, $\dfrac{\sqrt{2}}{\sqrt{3}}$ can be rewritten without a radical in the denominator by multiplying numerator and denominator by $\sqrt{3}$: $\dfrac{\sqrt{2} \cdot \sqrt{3}}{\sqrt{3} \cdot \sqrt{3}} = \dfrac{\sqrt{6}}{\sqrt{9}} = \dfrac{\sqrt{6}}{3}$. This process is called "rationalizing the denominator."

From earlier in this lesson, we know that $\left(\sqrt[n]{x^1}\right)^n = x$ and $\left(x^{\frac{1}{n}}\right)^n = x^{\frac{n}{n}} = x^1 = x$.

Therefore, we can see the relationship between radical expressions and expressions containing fractional exponents. The basic building block for conversions between radical expressions and expressions containing fractional exponents is the relationship $\sqrt[n]{x^1} = x^{\frac{1}{n}}$.

Think It Through

Example 1

Find the principal square root of $0.64a^2b^4$.

A) $0.08ab^3$

B) $0.08ab^2$

C) $0.8ab^3$

D) $0.8ab^2$

Solution

We are being asked to simplify $\sqrt{0.64a^2b^4}$. Using the idea $\sqrt[n]{a \cdot b} = \sqrt[n]{a} \cdot \sqrt[n]{b}$, we can think of $\sqrt{0.64a^2b^4}$ as $\sqrt{0.64} \cdot \sqrt{a^2} \cdot \sqrt{b^4}$. Then, $\sqrt{0.64} = 0.8$. This eliminates answer choices A and B. Find the roots of the variables: $\sqrt{a^2} = a$ and $\sqrt{b^4} = b^2$.

Answer: D

Example 2

Simplify $16^{\frac{3}{2}}$.

A) 24

B) 64

C) 512

D) 4,096

Solution

We can think of $16^{\frac{3}{2}} = \left(16^{\frac{1}{2}}\right)^3 = \left(\sqrt{16}\right)^3 = 4^3 = 64$. Alternately,

$16^{\frac{3}{2}} = \sqrt[2]{16^3} = \sqrt[2]{4096} = 64$.

Answer: B

Example 3

Completely simplify $\sqrt{18x^3y^2}$.

A) $3x^2y^2\sqrt{2x}$

B) $9x^2y^2\sqrt{2x}$

C) $3xy\sqrt{2x}$

D) $3xy\sqrt{2}$

Solution

There are several ways to go about simplifying this expression. One way would be to again utilize this idea $\sqrt[n]{a \cdot b} = \sqrt[n]{a} \cdot \sqrt[n]{b}$, and break up the expression. Then, $\sqrt{18x^3y^2} = \sqrt{18} \cdot \sqrt{x^3} \cdot \sqrt{y^2}$, and $\sqrt{18} = \sqrt{9 \cdot 2} = \sqrt{9} \cdot \sqrt{2} = 3\sqrt{2}$. This eliminates choice B. Begin simplifying the variables. So, $\sqrt{x^3} = \sqrt{x \cdot x \cdot x} = x\sqrt{x}$ and $\sqrt{y^2} = y$. Then, putting it all together, the answer is $3xy\sqrt{2x}$. You could also think of this problem as $\sqrt{18x^3y^2} = \sqrt{9x^2y^2 \cdot 2x} = \sqrt{9x^2y^2} \cdot \sqrt{2x} = 3xy\sqrt{2x}$.

Answer: C

• • • • • Practice Radicals and Fractional Exponents • • • • • • • • • • • •

Answers begin on page 693.

1. Completely simplify $125^{\frac{2}{3}}$.

   A) 81

   B) 50

   C) 25

   D) 10

2. Completely simplify $16^{\frac{3}{4}}$.

   A) 8

   B) 64

   C) 512

   D) 4,096

3. Completely simplify $\sqrt{24x^4yz^5}$.

   A) $2x^2y^2\sqrt{8yz}$

   B) $2xy\sqrt{6yz}$

   C) $4x^2y^2\sqrt{6yz}$

   D) $2x^2z^2\sqrt{6yz}$

4. Completely simplify $\sqrt{\dfrac{a^2b^6}{c^2}}$.

   A) $\dfrac{ab^2}{c}$

   B) $\dfrac{ab^3}{c}$

   C) $\dfrac{a^2b^6}{c^2}$

   D) ab^3c

1. Which equation below is <u>not</u> true?

   A) $\left(\sqrt{x^2 y}\right)^2 = x^2 y$

   B) $\left(2\sqrt[3]{xy^4}\right)^6 = 2x^2 y^8$

   C) $\left(3\sqrt{a^4 z^2}\right)^4 = 81a^8 z^4$

   D) $\left(3\sqrt[3]{a^2 b^4}\right)^3 = 27a^2 b^4$

Strategy: A quick mental check of answer choice A shows the equation to be true. Looking at the left-hand side of answer choice B, you know that $2^6 = 64$, but the right-hand side of that equation has a coefficient of 2 rather than 64. Stop checking and select B.

2. Simplify $\sqrt[3]{16x^6 yz^4}$.

   A) $x^2 yz\sqrt[3]{2z}$

   B) $2x^2 yz\sqrt[3]{2z}$

   C) $x^2 z\sqrt[3]{2yz}$

   D) $2x^2 z\sqrt[3]{2yz}$

Strategy: The index of the root is 3 rather than 2, so we need to find any factors of 16 that are perfect cubes and convert the variable exponents to numbers divisible by 3. Then, $\sqrt[3]{16x^6 yz^4} = \sqrt[3]{8x^6 z^3 \cdot 2yz} = \sqrt[3]{8x^6 z^3} \cdot \sqrt[3]{2yz} = 2x^2 z\sqrt[3]{2yz}$.
This is answer choice D.

3. Simplify $\dfrac{2}{5}\sqrt{\dfrac{3c^2 d}{2m^2 n}}$.

   A) $\dfrac{2c\sqrt{6dn}}{10mn}$

   B) $\dfrac{2c\sqrt{6dn}}{20mn}$

   C) $\dfrac{12cdn}{10mn}$

   D) $\dfrac{2cdn\sqrt{6}}{10mn}$

Strategy: This problem is less difficult than it appears. Begin by

multiplying the coefficient by the square root: $\dfrac{2}{5}\sqrt{\dfrac{3c^2 d}{2m^2 n}} = \dfrac{2\sqrt{3c^2 d}}{5\sqrt{2m^2 n}}$. Then,

$\dfrac{2\sqrt{c^2 \cdot 3d}}{5\sqrt{m^2 \cdot 2n}} = \dfrac{2\sqrt{c^2}\sqrt{3d}}{5\sqrt{m^2} \cdot \sqrt{2n}} = \dfrac{2c\sqrt{3d}}{5m\sqrt{2n}}$. But this is not one of the answer choices.

Remove the radical from the denominator:
$\dfrac{2c\sqrt{3d} \cdot \sqrt{2n}}{5m\sqrt{2n} \cdot \sqrt{2n}} = \dfrac{2c\sqrt{6dn}}{5m\sqrt{4n^2}} = \dfrac{2c\sqrt{6dn}}{5m \cdot 2n} = \dfrac{2c\sqrt{6dn}}{10mn}$. Select answer choice A.

Now that we have reviewed simplifying terms with rational exponents and radicals, we can review how to operate on radicals.

Rules for Adding and Subtracting Radicals

- Like radicals have the same index and the same radicand. Only like radicals can be added or subtracted.

- If the indices are different, the radicals cannot be added or subtracted.

- If the radicands are different, try to simplify by factoring to see if the radicands can be made to be the same.

- Finally, add or subtract the coefficients.

Rules for Multiplying Radicals

- The radicands do not need to be the same.

- Write the factors under one radical sign.

- Multiply.

- If possible, simplify the product.

Think It Through

Example 1

Find the sum of $3\sqrt{7}$ and $4\sqrt{112}$.

A) $7\sqrt{119}$

B) $19\sqrt{7}$

C) $35\sqrt{7}$

D) $67\sqrt{7}$

Solution

Begin the problem by noting that you can further simplify $4\sqrt{112}$. Quick trials will show that the largest perfect square that is a factor of 112 is 16. Remember, though, that you cannot add or subtract radicals unless their indexes and radicands are exactly the same. Thus, the problem gives you a hint that $\sqrt{112}$ must be able to be expressed as something times $\sqrt{7}$. Try to work with that information. Then, $4\sqrt{112} = 4\sqrt{16} \cdot \sqrt{7} = 4 \cdot 4\sqrt{7} = 16\sqrt{7}$. Now we can sum the terms: $3\sqrt{7} + 4\sqrt{112} = 3\sqrt{7} + 16\sqrt{7} = 19\sqrt{7}$.

Answer: B

Example 2

Find the product of $8\sqrt{32}$ and $4\sqrt{8}$.

A) 64

B) 128

C) 256

D) 512

Solution

Remember from the reading above that you do not need to have like radicals when multiplying. So, $8\sqrt{32} \cdot 4\sqrt{8} = (8 \cdot 4)\sqrt{32 \cdot 8} = 32\sqrt{256} = 32 \cdot 16 = 512$.

Answer: D

Practice **Operations on Terms with Radicals**

Answers begin on page 693.

1. Find the sum: $3\sqrt{48} + 11\sqrt{75}$.

   A) $14\sqrt{123}$

   B) $9\sqrt{3}$

   C) $67\sqrt{3}$

   D) $25\sqrt{3}$

2. Find the difference: $\sqrt{96} - \sqrt{54}$.

   A) $\sqrt{6}$

   B) $7\sqrt{6}$

   C) $\sqrt{42}$

   D) $\sqrt{21}$

3. Find the completely simplified product: $\sqrt{3m} \cdot \sqrt{8m}$.

   A) $2m\sqrt{8}$

   B) $m\sqrt{24}$

   C) $24m^2$

   D) $2m\sqrt{6}$

4. Find the quotient: $\sqrt{14m^4} \div \sqrt{6m^2}$.

   A) $\dfrac{m^2}{3}\sqrt{21}$

   B) $\dfrac{m}{3}\sqrt{21}$

   C) $\dfrac{m^2}{9}\sqrt{21}$

   D) $\dfrac{m}{9}\sqrt{21}$

Model SAT Questions

1. Simplify: $\sqrt{8}\left(\sqrt{117} - \sqrt{13}\right)$.

   A) $4\sqrt{26}$

   B) $8\sqrt{26}$

   C) $2\sqrt{22}$

   D) $4\sqrt{22}$

Strategy: Begin by distributing the $\sqrt{8}$ through the parentheses: $\sqrt{8}\left(\sqrt{117} - \sqrt{13}\right) = \sqrt{936} - \sqrt{104}$. Then, look for perfect square factors within each of the roots. Remember that you cannot add or subtract radicals unless their indexes and radicals match. The largest perfect square factor of 936 is 36 and the largest perfect square factor of 104 is 4. Now, $\sqrt{936} - \sqrt{104} = \sqrt{36 \cdot 26} - \sqrt{4 \cdot 26} = 6\sqrt{26} - 2\sqrt{26} = 4\sqrt{26}$. Select answer choice A.

2. $7\sqrt{12} + 7\sqrt{108} =$

    A) $7\sqrt{120}$
    B) $28\sqrt{3}$
    C) $56\sqrt{3}$
    D) $168\sqrt{3}$

Strategy: Like previous problems, you must rewrite this problem so the radicals are the same: $7\sqrt{12} + 7\sqrt{108} = 7\sqrt{12} + 7\sqrt{9 \cdot 12} = 7\sqrt{12} + 7\sqrt{9} \cdot \sqrt{12} = 7\sqrt{12} + 7 \cdot 3\sqrt{12} = (7 + 21)\sqrt{12} = 28\sqrt{12}$. But $28\sqrt{12}$ is not one of the answer choices, so keep simplifying: $28\sqrt{4} \cdot \sqrt{3} = (28 \cdot 2)\sqrt{3} = 56\sqrt{3}$. The correct answer is choice C.

3. $\sqrt{4} + 2\sqrt{50} - 3\sqrt{32} =$

    A) $4\sqrt{16}$
    B) $4\sqrt{2}$
    C) $2 - 2\sqrt{2}$
    D) 0

Strategy: Simplify the root of the perfect square and rewrite the other radicals so their radicands are the same. Then, $\sqrt{4} + 2\sqrt{50} - 3\sqrt{32} = 2 + 2\sqrt{25} \cdot \sqrt{2} - 3\sqrt{16} \cdot \sqrt{2} = 2 + 10\sqrt{2} - 12\sqrt{2}$. Combine the terms with the radicals to find $2 - 2\sqrt{2}$. This is answer choice C.

4. Simplify $3\sqrt{32} - 2\sqrt{18} + 2\sqrt{54}$

    A) $6\left(\sqrt{2} + \sqrt{6}\right)$
    B) $12\sqrt{2}$
    C) $6\left(\sqrt{6} - \sqrt{2}\right)$
    D) $30\sqrt{2} + 18\sqrt{6}$

Strategy: Rewrite the radicals: $3\sqrt{32} - 2\sqrt{18} + 2\sqrt{54} = 3\sqrt{16} \cdot \sqrt{2} - 2\sqrt{9} \cdot \sqrt{2} + 2\sqrt{9} \cdot \sqrt{6} = (3 \cdot 4)\sqrt{2} - (2 \cdot 3)\sqrt{2} + (2 \cdot 3)\sqrt{6} = 12\sqrt{2} - 6\sqrt{2} + 6\sqrt{6}$. Then, combine like terms and completely simplify to find $6\left(\sqrt{2} + \sqrt{6}\right)$. Select answer choice A.

Answers begin on page 694.

1. Simplify $\sqrt[3]{\dfrac{a^4b^3}{16c^4}}$.

   A) $\dfrac{ab\sqrt[3]{4ac^2}}{4c^3}$

   B) $\dfrac{ab\sqrt[3]{ac^2}}{c^2}$

   C) $\dfrac{2ab\sqrt[3]{ac^2}}{4c^2}$

   D) $\dfrac{ab\sqrt[3]{4ac^2}}{4c^2}$

2. $3a\sqrt{6a^9} + 3\sqrt{54a^{11}} =$

   A) $72a^5\sqrt{a}$

   B) $6a^5\sqrt{6a}$

   C) $12a^5\sqrt{6}$

   D) $12a^5\sqrt{6a}$

3. Simplify: $\dfrac{2}{3}\sqrt{\dfrac{128a^4b}{8a^5}}$

   A) $\dfrac{8\sqrt{ab}}{3a}$

   B) $\dfrac{16\sqrt{ab}}{3a}$

   C) $\dfrac{4\sqrt{ab}}{a}$

   D) $\dfrac{8\sqrt{ab}}{a}$

4. Which statement is equivalent to $-4^2x^3x^2$?

   A) $-16x^5$

   B) $-16x^6$

   C) $16x^5$

   D) $16x^6$

5. Find the value of x that makes $5^{31} = 5^{3x} \cdot 5^7$ true.

   A) 13

   B) 12

   C) 8

   D) 9

6. Simplify $\sqrt[3]{54x^4y^3z^8}$.

   A) $xz^2\sqrt[3]{54xz^2}$

   B) $3xyz^2\sqrt[3]{2xz^2}$

   C) $18xz^2\sqrt[3]{xz^2}$

   D) $3xz^2\sqrt[3]{2xz^2}$

7. $9\sqrt{3m^9} - 3m^4\sqrt{27m} =$

   A) 0

   B) 6

   C) $6\sqrt{3m}$

   D) $6m^2\sqrt{3m}$

8. $2y^3\sqrt{18x^5} + 2\sqrt{18x^5y^6} - 2x\sqrt{12x} =$

   A) $-4x\sqrt{3x}$

   B) $12x^2y^3\sqrt{2x} - 4x\sqrt{3x}$

   C) $6x^4y^3\sqrt{2x} + 6x^2y^3\sqrt{2x} - 4x\sqrt{3x}$

   D) $6x^2y^3\sqrt{2x} + 6x^2y^4\sqrt{2x} - 4x\sqrt{3x}$

9. Simplify $\dfrac{\sqrt{5x^4y^9}}{\sqrt{32x^7y^{22}}}$.

   A) $\dfrac{\sqrt{10xy}}{8x^3y^8}$

   B) $\dfrac{\sqrt{5}}{8x^2y^7}$

   C) $\dfrac{\sqrt{10xy}}{8x^2y^7}$

   D) $\dfrac{\sqrt{5}}{8x^3y^8}$

10. Given that the expression in the denominator is not equal to zero, which expression is equivalent to $\dfrac{-6x^5z^2}{2x^2z^3}$?

   A) $-3x^{10}z^{-1}$

   B) $-3x^2$

   C) $\dfrac{-3x^3}{z}$

   D) $\dfrac{-3x^3}{-z}$

11. Simplify $\sqrt[3]{\dfrac{16a^4d^3}{3a}}$.

A) $\dfrac{2ad\sqrt[3]{6}}{3}$

B) $\dfrac{2ad\sqrt[3]{18}}{3}$

C) $\dfrac{4ad\sqrt[3]{2}}{3}$

D) $\dfrac{2ad\sqrt[3]{18}}{9}$

12. Given that the expression in the denominator is not equal to zero, which expression is equivalent to $\dfrac{(a^2b^{-1})^3}{(a^3b^2)^2}$?

A) $\dfrac{1}{b^{12}}$

B) $\dfrac{1}{b^7}$

C) $\dfrac{-1}{b^{12}}$

D) $\dfrac{-1}{b^7}$

13. Simplify $\sqrt{\dfrac{2x^2z}{3a^2b}}$.

A) $\dfrac{2x\sqrt{z}}{3ab}$

B) $\dfrac{xb\sqrt{6z}}{3ab}$

C) $\dfrac{x\sqrt{6zb}}{3b}$

D) $\dfrac{x\sqrt{6zb}}{3ab}$

14. Given that the expression in the denominator is not equal to zero, which expression is equivalent to $\dfrac{2\left(x^{-2}y^{-2}\right)^2}{4x^{-4}}$?

A) $\dfrac{1}{2y^4}$

B) $\dfrac{1}{y^4}$

C) $\dfrac{2x^2}{y^2}$

D) $\dfrac{x^2}{2y^2}$

Student-Produced Response Questions

15. Find the value of x that makes the statement $\left(k^{3x+2}\right)^2 = k^{28}$ true.

16. What is the value of $\dfrac{1}{4^2} + \dfrac{1}{2^2}$?

17. What is the value of $\dfrac{6^6}{6^4}$?

18. What is the value of $3^{-1} + 3^{-2}$?

```
┌───┬───┬───┬───┐
│   │ ⊘ │ ⊘ │   │
│ ⊙ │ ⊙ │ ⊙ │ ⊙ │
├───┼───┼───┼───┤
│   │ ⓪ │ ⓪ │ ⓪ │
│ ① │ ① │ ① │ ① │
│ ② │ ② │ ② │ ② │
│ ③ │ ③ │ ③ │ ③ │
│ ④ │ ④ │ ④ │ ④ │
│ ⑤ │ ⑤ │ ⑤ │ ⑤ │
│ ⑥ │ ⑥ │ ⑥ │ ⑥ │
│ ⑦ │ ⑦ │ ⑦ │ ⑦ │
│ ⑧ │ ⑧ │ ⑧ │ ⑧ │
│ ⑨ │ ⑨ │ ⑨ │ ⑨ │
└───┴───┴───┴───┘
```

LESSON 2:

Operating on Polynomial and Rational Expressions

☐ **Simplifying Rational Expressions**

☐ **Adding and Subtracting Polynomial Expressions with Rational Coefficients**

☐ **Multiplying Polynomial Expressions with Rational Coefficients**

☐ **Dividing Polynomial Expressions with Rational Coefficients**

☐ **Adding and Subtracting Rational Expressions**

☐ **Multiplying and Dividing Rational Expressions**

Explain **Simplifying Rational Expressions**

A rational expression is said to be in simplest form if its numerator and denominator have no common factors other than 1 or −1. To reduce a rational expression to simplest form, factor both the numerator and denominator and divide each of them by their greatest common factor. When a rational expression is simplified, or reduced, it is understood that the simplified form of the expression is equivalent to the original expression only for those values for which the original expression was defined.

Definition

A **rational number** is one of the form $\dfrac{a}{b}$, where a and b are both integers and $b \neq 0$. Similarly, a **rational expression** is a fraction of the form $\dfrac{polynomial_1}{polynomial_2}$, where $polynomial_2 \neq 0$.

Think It Through

1. For what value or values is the following expression undefined?

   $$\frac{x^2 - 3x + 2}{x^2 - 25}$$

   A) 1 and 2
   B) −1 and −2
   C) 5
   D) 5 and −5

Solution

Since division by 0 is undefined, the expression will be undefined where the denominator is equal to 0. To solve this problem, set the denominator of the fraction equal to zero and solve for the unknown. There are two solution strategies for this problem. We could factor the perfect square binomial: $x^2 - 25 = 0$, $(x + 5)(x - 5) = 0$, and $x = \pm 5$. Alternately, we could isolate the variable and take its square root: $x^2 - 25 = 0$, $x^2 = 25$, $\sqrt{x^2} = \sqrt{25}$, and $x = \pm 5$.

Answer: D

---

2. Simplify: $\dfrac{7x - x^2}{x^2 - 10x + 21}$.

A) $\dfrac{x}{x-3}$

B) $\dfrac{x}{3-x}$

C) $\dfrac{7x}{x-3}$

D) $\dfrac{7x}{3-x}$

Solution

For this question, we must completely simplify the expressions in both the numerator and the denominator. From the numerator we can remove a common factor of x, and we can use trinomial factoring for the denominator:

$\dfrac{7x - x^2}{x^2 - 10x + 21} = \dfrac{x(7-x)}{(x-7)(x-3)}$. Notice that we have $(7 - x)$ in the numerator but an $(x - 7)$ in the denominator. If those were the same, we could cancel the

common factor. If we factor -1 out of the numerator, this is will change the signs: $\dfrac{-x(x-7)}{(x-7)(x-3)}$. Now we can cancel the common factor of $(x - 7)$ and we are left

with $\dfrac{-x}{x-3}$. But this is not an answer option, so we must rearrange the expression. Divide the numerator and the denominator by -1 to find $\dfrac{x}{3-x}$.

Answer: B

•••••• Practice **Simplifying Rational Expressions** •••••••••••••••

Answers begin on page 695.

1. For what value or values is the following fraction undefined?

$\dfrac{x-4}{x^2-6x}$

A) $x = 0, x = 4, x = 6$

B) $x = 4$

C) $x = 6$

D) $x = 0, x = 6$

2. Completely simplify the expression $\dfrac{10 - 2x}{x^2 - 25}$.

A) $\dfrac{-2}{x+5}$

B) $\dfrac{-2}{x-5}$

C) $\dfrac{-2}{5-x}$

D) $\dfrac{2}{5+x}$

3. Completely simplify the expression $\dfrac{x^3 - 16x}{x^3 + 12x^2 + 32x}$.

A) $\dfrac{-1}{2}$

B) $\dfrac{x-4}{x+8}$

C) $\dfrac{x+4}{x+8}$

D) $\dfrac{x(x-4)}{x+8}$

Adding and Subtracting Polynomial Expressions with Rational Coefficients

Addition and subtraction of polynomial expressions with rational coefficients relies on two important mathematical properties: the commutative property of addition and the distributive property. To add polynomials, we use the commutative property to rearrange the expressions so like terms are beside each other before combining the like terms. To subtract polynomials, use the distributive property to change every sign of every term in the subtracted polynomial and then combine like terms.

QUICK TIP

The commutative property states that we can add terms in any order we wish since $a + b = b + a$.

Think It Through

Example 1

Find the sum of the expressions $\left(\frac{5}{2} + \frac{1}{2}\right)x^2 + \left(\frac{3}{2} - \frac{7}{2}\right)x - 7$, $\frac{1}{2}x^2 + \frac{1}{3}x + 5$, and $\frac{5}{2}x^2 - \frac{5}{6}x - \frac{1}{4}$.

A) $6x^2 - \frac{2}{5}x - 2\frac{1}{4}$

B) $3x^2 + \frac{5}{2}x + 2\frac{1}{4}$

C) $3x^2 - \frac{1}{3}x + 4\frac{3}{4}$

D) $6x^2 - \frac{5}{2}x - 2\frac{1}{4}$

QUICK TIP

The distributive property allows us to multiply each term in a set of parentheses by a term outside the parentheses.

Solution

Begin by simplifying within the parentheses of the first addend:

$\left(\frac{5}{2} + \frac{1}{2}\right)x^2 + \left(\frac{3}{2} - \frac{7}{2}\right)x - 7 = \frac{6}{2}x^2 + \frac{-4}{2}x - 7$. While we could simplify the

fractional coefficients to integers, the terms in the other addends contain fractions, so it will be easier if all the numbers are in the same notation. Now we can use the commutative property to rearrange the problem and

find $\frac{6}{2}x^2 + \frac{1}{2}x^2 + \frac{5}{2}x^2 + \frac{-4}{2}x + \frac{1}{3}x - \frac{5}{6}x - 7 + 5 - \frac{1}{4}$. Recall the rules for adding

and simplifying fractions: $\frac{12}{2}x^2 - \frac{5}{2}x - 2\frac{1}{4} = 6x^2 - \frac{5}{2}x - 2\frac{1}{4}$.

Answer: D

Example 2

Completely simplify the following expression:
$(-1.5x^2 + 3.2x - 1.8) - (4.5x^2 - 3.2x - 2.4)$.

A) $-6x^2 + 6.4x + 0.6$

B) $6x^2 + 6.4x + 0.6$

C) $-6x^2 + 0.6$

D) $-6x^2 - 4.2$

Solution

Rewrite, removing the parentheses and distributing the negative sign through the second set of parentheses. This will change the sign on every term in the second polynomial. So, $-1.5x^2 + 3.2x - 1.8 - 4.5x^2 + 3.2x + 2.4$. Now use the commutative property to seat like terms next to each other and $(-1.5 - 4.5)x^2 + (3.2 + 3.2)x + (-1.8 + 2.4) = -6x^2 + 6.4x + 0.6$.

Answer: A

Answers begin on page 696.

1. Find the sum: $\left(\dfrac{5}{2}x^2 + \dfrac{3}{2}x - 5\right) + \left(\dfrac{x^2}{2} - \dfrac{7}{2}x - 2\right)$.

   A) $3x^2 + 2x - 7$

   B) $2x^2 - 2x - 7$

   C) $3x^2 - 2x - 7$

   D) $2x^2 + 2x - 7$

2. Find the sum:
   $\left(-1.2x^2 + 3.4x - 1.6\right) + \left(2.3x^2 - 4.1x - 1.2\right)$.

   A) $1.1x^2 - 0.7x + 2.8$

   B) $1.1x^2 - 0.7x - 2.8$

   C) $1.1x^2 + 0.7x - 2.8$

   D) $1.1x^2 - 0.7x - 0.4$

3. Find the difference:
   $\left(7.1x^2 - 6.4x + 1.9\right) - \left(-2.3x^2 + 3.8x - 1\right)$.

   A) $9.4x^2 - 4.1x + 2.9$

   B) $9.4x^2 + 4.1x + 2.9$

   C) $9.4x^2 + 10.2x + 2.9$

   D) $9.4x^2 - 10.2x + 2.9$

4. Find the difference: $\left(2.1x^2 + 4\right) - \left(2.8x^2 + 3x - 1.3\right)$.

   A) $-0.7x^2 - 3x + 5.3$

   B) $-0.7x^2 - 3x + 2.7$

   C) $-0.7x^2 + 3x + 5.3$

   D) $0.7x^2 - 3x + 5.3$

5. Find the difference: $7.1x^2 - 3.2 - [x - (2.5x^2 + 1)]$.

   A) $9.6x^2 - x - 2.2$

   B) $9.6x^2 - x - 0.2$

   C) $9.6x^2 + x - 2.2$

   D) $9.6x^2 - 0.7x - 2.2$

Explain **Multiplying Polynomials with Rational Coefficients**

There are many techniques for multiplying polynomials. A product is formed from pairing every term in the first polynomial with every term in the second polynomial the combining any like terms. One quick and easy way is to set up a physical diagram.

Think It Through

Example

Find the product: $\left(x^2 + 2x + 3\right) \cdot (x - 2)$

A) $x^3 + 2x^2 - x - 6$

B) $x^3 - 2x^2 - x - 6$

C) $x^3 + x - 6$

D) $x^3 - x - 6$

Solution

Set up a table, using the polynomial terms as the row and column headers.

	x^2	$2x$	3
x	x^3	$2x^2$	$3x$
-2	$-2x^2$	$-4x$	-6

Now carefully combine like terms: $x^3 + (2-2)x^2 + (3-4)x - 6 = x^3 - x - 6$.

Answer: D

Model SAT Questions

1. Find the product: $\left(\dfrac{1}{2}x^3 + \dfrac{1}{6}x^2 + 2\right) \cdot \left(\dfrac{1}{3}x^2 - \dfrac{1}{2}x - \dfrac{1}{2}\right)$.

A) $\dfrac{1}{6}x^5 - \dfrac{7}{36}x^4 - \dfrac{1}{12}x^3 + \dfrac{1}{12}x^2 + x - 1$

B) $\dfrac{1}{6}x^5 - \dfrac{1}{4}x^4 - \dfrac{1}{3}x^3 + \dfrac{1}{12}x^2 + x - 1$

C) $\dfrac{1}{6}x^5 - \dfrac{7}{36}x^4 - \dfrac{1}{3}x^3 + \dfrac{7}{12}x^2 - x - 1$

D) $\dfrac{1}{6}x^5 - \dfrac{7}{36}x^4 - \dfrac{1}{12}x^3 + \dfrac{7}{12}x - 1$

Strategy: Set up a table, using the polynomial terms as the row and column headers. The order of the terms does not matter.

	$\dfrac{1}{3}x^2$	$-\dfrac{1}{2}x$	$-\dfrac{1}{2}$
$\dfrac{1}{2}x^3$	$\dfrac{1}{6}x^5$	$-\dfrac{1}{4}x^4$	$-\dfrac{1}{4}x^3$
$\dfrac{1}{6}x^2$	$\dfrac{1}{18}x^4$	$-\dfrac{1}{12}x^3$	$-\dfrac{1}{12}x^2$
2	$\dfrac{2}{3}x^2$	$-x$	-1

Now carefully combine like terms. You might cross off the terms as you combine them so you don't forget or double count any.

$$\dfrac{1}{6}x^5 + \left(\dfrac{1}{18} - \dfrac{1}{4}\right)x^4 + \left(-\dfrac{1}{12} - \dfrac{1}{4}\right)x^3 + \left(\dfrac{2}{3} - \dfrac{1}{12}\right)x^2 - x - 1 =$$

$$\dfrac{1}{6}x^5 - \dfrac{7}{36}x^4 - \dfrac{1}{3}x^3 + \dfrac{7}{12}x^2 - x - 1.$$

The correct answer is choice C.

2. Find a polynomial that, when multiplied by $3x^2 - 2x + 1$, gives the product $3x^3 - 5x^2 + 3x - 1$.

A) $x - 1$
B) $x + 1$
C) $3x + 1$
D) $3x - 1$

Strategy: The unknown polynomial must be of the form $ax + b$ because the greatest exponent in the product, 3, is one degree more than the greatest exponent in the known factor. Go back to the general form $ax + b$. You know $a \cdot 3 = 3$ so $a = 1$. Now look at the constant term: $b \cdot 1 = -1$, so $b = -1$. The polynomial is $x - 1$. This is answer choice A.

· · · · · · **Explain** **Dividing Polynomial Expressions with Rational Coefficients** · · · · · · · ·

There are a few different types of polynomial division. Generally, solving these problems requires you to set up a long division format, making sure to include placeholders for missing exponent terms. For example, the quotient $\dfrac{x^3 - 4x - 21}{x + 3}$ should be set up as $x + 3 \overline{)x^3 + 0x^2 - 4x - 21}$. The procedure for determining the solution to this type of problem is exactly the same as the procedure for dividing integers and will be fully explained in the Model SAT Questions section. Note that the divisor in this example problem is a binomial. If the divisor is a monomial, though, you can handle the problem a bit more simply.

· · · · · · **Think It Through** ·

Example

Find the quotient: $\dfrac{2x^4 + 8x^2 - 4x}{2x}$

A) $x^3 + 4x - 2$
B) $x^3 + 4x^2 - 2$
C) $x^2 + 4x^2 - 2$
D) $x^3 + 4x + 2$

Solution

Since the divisor is a monomial, rethink the problem as $\dfrac{2x^4}{2x} + \dfrac{8x^2}{2x} - \dfrac{4x}{2x} =$

$\dfrac{2x^{4^3}}{2x_1} + \dfrac{8^4 x^2}{2x_1} - \dfrac{4^2 x}{2x_1} = x^3 + 4x - 2.$

Answer: A

Answers begin on page 696.

1. Find the quotient: $\dfrac{3x^2 + 6x + 9}{3}$.

   A) $3x + 2$

   B) $3x^2 + 2x + 3$

   C) $x^2 + 2x + 3$

   D) $x^2 + 2x + 6$

2. Find the quotient: $\dfrac{12x^4 - 3x^2 + 6x}{3x}$.

   A) $4x^3 - x - 2$

   B) $4x^3 - x + 2$

   C) $4x^3 + x + 2$

   D) $4x^2 - x + 2$

Model SAT Questions

1. Find the quotient: $\dfrac{x^3 + 7x^2 - 6x + 16}{x + 8}$.

   A) $x^2 + x + 2$

   B) $x^2 + x + 2 + \dfrac{1}{x + 8}$

   C) $x^2 - x + 2$

   D) $x^2 - x + 2 + \dfrac{1}{x + 8}$

Strategy: Repeat the following steps until finished:

Divide the first term of the dividend into the first term of the divisor. Write the quotient term above, aligning the terms by exponent. Multiply the divisor by the quotient term and align the product under the dividend, aligning the terms by exponent. Subtract. Bring down the next quotient term. Repeat the process until there are no more terms to bring down. If there is a remainder, R, write $\dfrac{R}{\text{divisor}}$ on the quotient line. If there is no remainder in any of the answer choices, the faster approach is to test each answer choice, multiplying it by the divisor, stopping when you see the dividend.

$$
\begin{array}{r}
x^2 - x + 2 \\
x + 8 \overline{)\, x^3 + 7x^2 - 6x + 16} \\
-(x^3 + 8x^2) \\
\hline
-x^2 - 6x \\
-(-x^2 - 8x) \\
\hline
2x + 16 \\
-(2x + 16) \\
\hline
0
\end{array}
$$

2. Find the quotient: $\dfrac{x^3-1}{x-1}$.

   A) x^2+x+1

   B) x^2-x+1

   C) x^2+x-1

   D) x^2+2x+1

Strategy: We begin this problem by setting up the division. Note that the dividend is missing the terms x^2 and x. We will need to insert these terms prior to carrying out the division. Then,

$$
\begin{array}{r}
x^2+x+1 \\
x-1{\overline{\smash{\big)}\,x^3+0x^2+0x-1}} \\
\underline{-\left(x^3-x^2\right)} \\
-x^2+0x \\
\underline{-\left(-x^2-x\right)} \\
x-1 \\
\underline{-\left(x-1\right)} \\
0
\end{array}
$$

Important pattern: Model SAT question 2 contains a pattern worth memorizing. For any counting number n,

$\dfrac{x^n-1}{x-1}=x^{n-1}+x^{n-2}+\ldots+x+1$. Thus, in the problem $\dfrac{x^3-1}{x-1}$, $n=3$ and $\dfrac{x^3-1}{x-1}=$

$x^{3-1}+x^{3-2}+1=x^2+x+1$.

3. Find the quotient: $\dfrac{x^3+1}{x+1}$.

   A) x^2-2x+1

   B) x^2+2x+1

   C) x^2-x+1

   D) x^2+x+1

Strategy: Note that this problem is very similar to the previous Model SAT problem, but the divisor here is $x+1$ rather than $x-1$. Like question 2, we can use polynomial division to solve this problem or we can make use of a second important pattern.

For any counting number n, $\dfrac{x^n+1}{x+1}=x^{n-1}-x^{n-2}+\ldots-x+1$. Unlike the previous

pattern, this pattern has alternating signs. Thus, in the problem $\dfrac{x^3+1}{x+1}$, $n=3$ and

$\dfrac{x^3+1}{x+1}=x^{3-1}-x^{3-2}+1=x^2-x+1$.

Adding and subtracting rational expressions is similar to adding and subtracting fractions. First, you must make sure the denominators are alike. Then you can sum the numerators, carry the same denominator into the answer, and simplify if needed.

Think It Through

Example 1

Find the sum of $\dfrac{6x}{x^2+3} + \dfrac{2x+1}{x^2+3}$.

A) $\dfrac{9x}{x^2+3}$

B) $\dfrac{8x+1}{x^2+3}$

C) $\dfrac{8x+1}{2x^2+6}$

D) $\dfrac{9x}{2x^2+6}$

Solution

In this problem, the denominators are the same, so we can sum the numerators.

We find that $\dfrac{6x}{x^2+3} + \dfrac{2x+1}{x^2+3} = \dfrac{8x+1}{x^2+3}$.

Answer: B

Example 2

Find the sum and simplify: $\dfrac{3x+5}{x^2-5x-24} + \dfrac{4}{x^2-5x-24}$.

A) $\dfrac{3}{x-8}$

B) $\dfrac{3}{x+3}$

C) $\dfrac{3x+9}{x^2-29}$

D) $\dfrac{3x+9}{x^2-10x}$

Solution

Begin by noting the form of the original denominators and the form of the answer choices. The original denominator is a trinomial, but the answer choices all have binomials in their denominators. This indicates that we will have to factor the denominator at some point. Now, add the numerators:

$\dfrac{3x+5}{x^2-5x-24} + \dfrac{4}{x^2-5x-24} = \dfrac{3x+9}{x^2-5x-24}$. We see that we can factor a 3 out of the

numerator and factor the denominator: $\dfrac{3(x+3)}{(x+3)(x-8)} = \dfrac{3}{x-8}$.

Answer: A

Example 3

Subtract and simplify: $\dfrac{2y^2+2y}{y^2-y-56}-\dfrac{y^2+35}{y^2-y-56}$.

A) $\dfrac{2y^2+y+35}{y^2-y-56}$

B) $\dfrac{3y^2+35}{y^2-y-56}$

C) $\dfrac{y+5}{y-8}$

D) $\dfrac{y-5}{y-8}$

Solution

Combine the numerators, being careful to appropriately distribute the negative

sign: $\dfrac{2y^2+2y-y^2-35}{y^2-y-56}=\dfrac{y^2+2y-35}{y^2-y-56}$. Factor both the numerator and the

denominator and then simplify to find $\dfrac{\cancel{(y+7)}(y-5)}{\cancel{(y+7)}(y-8)}=\dfrac{y-5}{y-8}$.

Answer: D

Practice Adding and Subtracting Rational Expressions

Answers begin on page 696.

Questions 1–4. Perform the indicated operation and simplify if possible.

1. $\dfrac{m^2}{m^2-m}-\dfrac{3m-2}{m^2-m}=$

   A) $\dfrac{m+2}{m}$

   B) $\dfrac{m-2}{m}$

   C) $\dfrac{m+1}{m}$

   D) $\dfrac{m-1}{m}$

2. $\dfrac{3}{a^2-a-6}-\dfrac{a}{a^2-a-6}=$

   A) $\dfrac{1}{a+2}$

   B) $\dfrac{1}{2+a}$

   C) $\dfrac{-1}{a-2}$

   D) $\dfrac{-1}{a+2}$

3. $\dfrac{d^2+2d}{2d+10}+\dfrac{4d+5}{2d+10}=$

   A) $\dfrac{d+1}{2}$

   B) $\dfrac{d+5}{2}$

   C) $\dfrac{d+1}{10}$

   D) $\dfrac{7d+5}{2d+10}$

4. $\dfrac{k^3-k^2-2k}{2k^2-4k}+\dfrac{k^3+k^2-6k}{2k^2-4k}=$

   A) k^2-2

   B) k

   C) $k+2$

   D) $k-2$

On the SAT, it is likely that you will be asked to work with expressions that do not have like denominators. We will review how to solve these types of problems now.

1. Perform the indicated operation and simplify: $\dfrac{3}{x^2+5x-14} - \dfrac{2}{x^2+8x+7}$.

    A) $\dfrac{1}{x^2-x-2}$

    B) $\dfrac{1}{x^2+x-2}$

    C) $\dfrac{x+7}{x-2}$

    D) $\dfrac{x+7}{x^2-x-2}$

Strategy: Begin by rewriting the terms in fully factored form:
$\dfrac{3}{x^2+5x-14} - \dfrac{2}{x^2+8x+7} = \dfrac{3}{(x+7)(x-2)} - \dfrac{2}{(x+7)(x+1)}$. Create a common denominator by combining the factored denominators. In this case, the common denominator is $(x+7)(x-2)(x+1)$. Then, create equivalent fractions by multiplying each numerator by the binomial(s) missing from its denominator. Then, $\dfrac{3(x+1)}{(x+7)(x-2)(x+1)} - \dfrac{2(x-2)}{(x+7)(x-2)(x+1)}$.
Distribute through the parenthesis, combine the numerators and simplify if possible: $\dfrac{3x+3}{(x+7)(x-2)(x+1)} - \dfrac{2x-4}{(x+7)(x-2)(x+1)} = \dfrac{\cancel{x+7}}{\cancel{(x+7)}(x-2)(x+1)} = \dfrac{1}{(x-2)(x+1)} = \dfrac{1}{x^2-x-2}$.

2. Perform the indicated operation and simplify: $\dfrac{y+2}{y^2-y-2} + \dfrac{1}{3y+3}$.

    A) $\dfrac{4}{3y+1}$

    B) $\dfrac{4}{3y-6}$

    C) $\dfrac{4(y+2)}{3(y-2)(y+1)}$

    D) $\dfrac{4}{3}$

Strategy: Rewrite the terms in factored form: $\dfrac{y+2}{y^2-y-2} + \dfrac{1}{3y+3} = \dfrac{y+2}{(y-2)(y+1)} + \dfrac{1}{3(y+1)}$. Then, you must create a common denominator and equivalent fractions. The common denominator is $3(y-2)(y+1)$. Now, $\dfrac{3(y+2)}{3(y-2)(y+1)} + \dfrac{y-2}{3(y-2)(y+1)} = \dfrac{3y+6}{3(y-2)(y+1)} + \dfrac{y-2}{3(y-2)(y+1)}$. Combine numerators and simplify if possible: $\dfrac{3y+6+y-2}{3(y-2)(y+1)} = \dfrac{4y+4}{3(y-2)(y+1)} = \dfrac{4\cancel{(y+1)}}{3(y-2)\cancel{(y+1)}} = \dfrac{4}{3(y-2)} = \dfrac{4}{3y-6}$.

Multiplying two rational expressions is similar to multiplying two rational numbers. First, factor the numerator and the denominator. Then, simplify the numerator and the denominator by canceling out all the common factors. Lastly, we multiply the remaining factors in the numerators and denominators.

Dividing two rational expressions is similar to dividing two rational numbers. Multiply the dividend by the reciprocal of the divisor, following the rules for multiplication.

Remember that the denominator must not equal zero.

Think It Through

Example 1

Find the product: $\dfrac{4x^4}{49y^2} \cdot \dfrac{35y}{16x^3}$.

A) $\dfrac{x}{4y}$

B) $\dfrac{5}{28y}$

C) $\dfrac{5x}{28y}$

D) $\dfrac{x}{2y}$

Solution

There are several ways to solve this problem. One way we can begin is to rewrite

the multiplication bit. So, $\dfrac{4x^4}{49y^2} \cdot \dfrac{35y}{16x^3} = \dfrac{4x^4 \cdot 5 \cdot 7y}{4 \cdot 4x^3 \cdot 7 \cdot 7y^2}$. Now it is a little easier to

see what factors can be canceled: $\dfrac{\cancel{4}x^4 \cdot 5 \cdot \cancel{7}y}{\cancel{4} \cdot 4x^3 \cdot \cancel{7} \cdot 7y^2} = \dfrac{x^4 \cdot 5y}{4x^3 \cdot 7y^2}$. We can use the

"division of like bases with unlike exponents" rules from lesson 1 to simplify the

variables and find that the answer is $\dfrac{5x}{28y}$.

Answer: C

Example 2

Find the quotient: $\dfrac{4x^4y^2}{3y} \div \dfrac{x^2y}{6xy^3}$.

A) $4x^3y^3$

B) $8x^3y^3$

C) $\dfrac{2x^5}{9y}$

D) $\dfrac{x^5}{3y}$

Solution

From fraction rules, remember that to divide, we must multiply the dividend, $\dfrac{4x^4y^2}{3y}$, by the reciprocal of the divisor, $\dfrac{6xy^3}{x^2y}$. Then, $\dfrac{4x^4y^2}{3y}\cdot\dfrac{6xy^3}{x^2y}=$

$\dfrac{4x^{4^2}y^2}{\cancel{3}\,y}\cdot\dfrac{\cancel{6}^2xy^3}{x^2y}=8x^3y^3$.

Answer: B

Practice   Multiplying and Dividing Rational Expressions

Answers begin on page 697.

1. Find the product: $\dfrac{3a^3}{14b^2}\cdot\dfrac{7b^4}{6a}$.

    A) $\dfrac{3a^2b^2}{4}$

    B) $\dfrac{a^2b^2}{2}$

    C) $\dfrac{a^2b^2}{4}$

    D) $\dfrac{3a^2b^2}{2}$

2. Find the product: $\dfrac{x^2-4}{2}\cdot\dfrac{4x}{x+2}$.

    A) $2x(x-2)$

    B) $2(x+2)$

    C) $x-2$

    D) $x+2$

3. Find the quotient: $\dfrac{8x^3z^2}{3y^3}\div\dfrac{4xz}{3y}$.

    A) $\dfrac{2x^4z^3}{y^4}$

    B) $\dfrac{6x^4z^3}{y^4}$

    C) $\dfrac{2x^2}{y^2}$

    D) $\dfrac{2x^2z}{y^2}$

Model SAT Questions

1. Find the product: $\dfrac{x^2-25}{2x+10}\cdot\dfrac{4x+12}{x^2-2x-15}$.

    A) 0

    B) 2

    C) $\dfrac{2(x+3)}{(x-3)}$

    D) $\dfrac{2(x-5)}{x+5}$

Strategy: Rewrite the numerator and denominator of this problem in fully factored form:

$\dfrac{x^2-25}{2x+10}\cdot\dfrac{4x+12}{x^2-2x-15}=\dfrac{(x+5)(x-5)}{2(x+5)}\cdot\dfrac{4(x+3)}{(x-5)(x+3)}$. Now cancel the common factors

to find that $\dfrac{\cancel{(x+5)}\,\cancel{(x-5)}}{2\cancel{(x+5)}}\cdot\dfrac{4\cancel{(x+3)}}{\cancel{(x-5)}\,\cancel{(x+3)}}=\dfrac{4}{2}=2$.

2. Find the quotient: $\dfrac{x^2-64}{x^2+8x} \div \dfrac{8x-64}{4x+4}$.

   A) $\dfrac{x+1}{2x}$

   B) $\dfrac{x+1}{x}$

   C) $\dfrac{(x+1)(x+8)}{x(x-8)}$

   D) $\dfrac{x(x+1)}{2}$

Strategy: Recall from fraction rules that to divide two fractions, you have to multiply the dividend by the reciprocal of the divisor. Thus, $\dfrac{x^2-64}{x^2+8x} \div \dfrac{8x-64}{4x+4} =$ $\dfrac{x^2-64}{x^2+8x} \cdot \dfrac{4x+4}{8x-64}$. Now fully factor all the pieces and cancel the common factors:

$$\dfrac{x^2-64}{x^2+8x} \cdot \dfrac{4x+4}{8x-64} = \dfrac{\cancel{(x+8)}\,\cancel{(x-8)}}{x\cancel{(x+8)}} \cdot \dfrac{4(x+1)}{8\cancel{(x-8)}} = \dfrac{4(x+1)}{8x} = \dfrac{x+1}{2x}.$$

SAT-Type Questions

Answers begin on page 697.

1. Find the product: $\dfrac{x^2-x-12}{x^2+x-20} \cdot \dfrac{x^2+11x+30}{x^3+9x^2+18x}$.

   A) $\dfrac{x+6}{x(x-6)}$

   B) $\dfrac{x+5}{x-5}$

   C) 1

   D) $\dfrac{1}{x}$

2. Find the polynomial that, when multiplied by $2x^2-4x+1$, gives the product $4x^3-12x^2+10x-2$.

   A) $2x^2-2$

   B) $2x^2+2$

   C) $2x-2$

   D) $2x+2$

3. Simplify: $\dfrac{x^3+2x^2-2x-4}{x+2}$

   A) x^2-2

   B) x^2+x-2

   C) x^2-x+2

   D) x^2+2

4. Perform the indicated operation and simplify: $\dfrac{6}{x^2+4x+3}+\dfrac{3}{x^2+7x+12}$.

A) $\dfrac{9}{x^2+5x+4}$

B) $\dfrac{9}{x^2-5x+4}$

C) $\dfrac{1}{x+4}$

D) $\dfrac{1}{x+3}$

5. Find the quotient: $\dfrac{z^3-36z}{3z-18}\div(z^2-2z-48)$.

A) $\dfrac{1}{3(z-8)}$

B) $\dfrac{z}{3(z-8)}$

C) $\dfrac{z}{3}$

D) $\dfrac{z}{z-8}$

6. Which answer choice provides the complete list of values of m for which the equation $\dfrac{m^2+4m+3}{6m+6}\div\dfrac{m^2+3m}{6m}=1$ is valid?

A) All the real numbers except $m=-1$.
B) All the real numbers except $m=0$.
C) All the real numbers except $m=-1$ and $m=0$.
D) All the real numbers except $m=-3$, $m=-1$, and $m=0$.

7. Find the product in simplest form: $\dfrac{7-x}{x^3-49x}\cdot\dfrac{x^2+10x+21}{3+x}$.

A) $-\dfrac{1}{x}$

B) $\dfrac{7-x}{x(x-7)}$

C) $\dfrac{3+x}{x(x+3)}$

D) $\dfrac{(3+x)(7-x)}{(x+3)(x-7)}$

8. Find the product of $(1.5x-1)$ and $(x^2-2.5x+1)$.

A) $1.5x^3-4.75x^2+4-x+1$
B) $1.5x^3-4.75x^2+4x-1$
C) $1.5x^3-2.75x^2+4x-1$
D) $1.5x^4-4.75x^3+4x-1$

9. Find the product: $\left(\dfrac{2}{3}x+\dfrac{1}{3}\right)\left(\dfrac{1}{2}x^2+\dfrac{1}{4}x+1\right)$.

A) $\dfrac{1}{3}x^3+\dfrac{1}{3}x^2+\dfrac{3}{4}x+\dfrac{1}{3}$

B) $\dfrac{1}{3}x^3+\dfrac{1}{3}x^2+\dfrac{2}{3}x+\dfrac{1}{3}$

C) $\dfrac{1}{3}x^3+\dfrac{1}{12}x^2+\dfrac{3}{4}x+\dfrac{1}{3}$

D) $\dfrac{1}{3}x^3+\dfrac{1}{2}x^2+\dfrac{3}{4}x+\dfrac{1}{3}$

10. Find the polynomial that, when multiplied by $\dfrac{1}{3}x-\dfrac{2}{3}$, gives the product $\dfrac{1}{6}x^2-\dfrac{2}{9}x-\dfrac{2}{9}$.

A) $\dfrac{1}{2}x-\dfrac{1}{3}$

B) $\dfrac{1}{4}x+\dfrac{1}{3}$

C) $\dfrac{1}{2}x+\dfrac{1}{3}$

D) $\dfrac{1}{6}x+\dfrac{1}{3}$

11. If the length of a rectangle is equal to $\dfrac{x+1}{x+2}$ and the area of the rectangle is $\dfrac{4x+4}{2x+4}$, find the width of the rectangle.

A) 1

B) 2

C) $\dfrac{x+2}{x+1}$

D) 4

12. Simplify: $\dfrac{x^3-3x^2+6x-2}{x-1}$.

A) x^2-2x+4

B) $x^2-2x-4+\dfrac{1}{x-1}$

C) $x^2-2x+4+\dfrac{2}{x-1}$

D) $x^2-2x+8+\dfrac{1}{x-1}$

13. Completely simplify: $\dfrac{x-3}{x^2-1}+\dfrac{3}{x-1}-\dfrac{4}{2x+2}$.

A) $\dfrac{2}{x+1}$

B) $\dfrac{2}{x-1}$

C) $\dfrac{4}{x+1}$

D) $\dfrac{4}{x-1}$

14. Perform the indicated operation and simplify: $\dfrac{x}{x^2+9x+18}-\dfrac{3}{x^2+3x}$.

A) $\dfrac{1}{x}$

B) $\dfrac{x+6}{x(x-6)}$

C) $\dfrac{x-6}{x(x+6)}$

D) $\dfrac{x(x+6)}{(x-6)}$

15. Subtract: $\dfrac{1}{a^2-a-6}-\dfrac{1}{2a^2-7a+3}$.

A) $\dfrac{1}{a^2-3a+2}$

B) $\dfrac{1}{2a^2-3a+2}$

C) $\dfrac{1}{2a^2+3a+2}$

D) $\dfrac{1}{2a^2+3a-2}$

16. Add: $\dfrac{1}{2-x}+\dfrac{2}{x-2}$.

A) $\dfrac{2}{x-2}$

B) $\dfrac{1}{x-2}$

C) $\dfrac{-2}{2-x}$

D) $\dfrac{-1}{x+2}$

17. The product of $\dfrac{x^2-9}{3-x}$ and $\dfrac{4x+16}{x^2+7x+12}$ is

A) -4.

B) -1.

C) 1.

D) 4.

18. Subtract: $\dfrac{x}{x^2-4x+3}-\dfrac{x}{x^2+2x-3}$.

A) $\dfrac{-3x}{(x+2)(x-4)(x-1)}$

B) $\dfrac{3x}{(x+3)(x-3)(x-1)}$

C) $\dfrac{6x}{(x+2)(x-4)(x-1)}$

D) $\dfrac{6x}{(x+3)(x-3)(x-1)}$

19. Completely simplify: $\dfrac{1}{x}+\dfrac{1}{x-2}-\dfrac{2}{x^2-2x}$.

A) $\dfrac{1}{x}$

B) $\dfrac{1}{x-2}$

C) $\dfrac{2}{x}$

D) $\dfrac{2}{x-2}$

20. Subtract: $\dfrac{2}{a^2-4}-\dfrac{1}{a^2+2a}$.

A) $\dfrac{1}{a^2-2a}$

B) $\dfrac{1}{a^2-2a+1}$

C) $\dfrac{a}{a^2-2a+1}$

D) $\dfrac{a-2}{a^2-2a+1}$

No Student-Produced Response Questions for this lesson.

LESSON 3:

Solving Radical and Rational Equations

■ Solving Radical Equations

■ Solving Radical Equations with Extraneous Roots

■ Solving Rational Equations

Explain Solving Radical Equations

A **radical equation** is an equation with at least one radical expression containing a variable under the radical symbol. To solve a radical equation, use the following power rule:

If $x = y$ and n is a positive integer, then $x^n = y^n$.

Also recall that $\left(\sqrt[n]{x}\right)^n = x$.

Think It Through

Example 1

Solve $\sqrt{x+2} = 3$.

A) 5
B) 7
C) 9
D) 10

Solution

The index on the root is not named, so by convention it is 2. Eliminate the square root sign from the equation by squaring both sides:

$$\left(\sqrt{x+2}\right)^2 = 3^3$$
$$x + 2 = 9$$
$$x = 7$$

Answer: B

Example 2

Solve $2\sqrt{m+11} = \sqrt{12m+4}$.

A) 4
B) 5
C) 24
D) 37

Solution

Here we have variables on both sides of the equation, both of them underneath root signs. To solve, we start by squaring both sides of the equation:

$$\left(2\sqrt{m+11}\right)^2 = \left(\sqrt{12m+4}\right)^2$$

$$4(m + 11) = 12m + 4$$

$$4m + 44 = 12m + 4$$

$$\underline{-4m \qquad\qquad -4m}$$

$$44 = 8m + 4$$

$$\underline{-4 \qquad\quad -4}$$

$$40 = 8m$$

$$5 = m$$

Answer: B

Answers begin on page 701.

Practice Solving Radical Equations

1. Solve: $\sqrt{3m+4} = 2\sqrt{m}$

3. Solve: $\sqrt{13+x} = 2\sqrt{1+x}$

2. Solve: $4\sqrt{2x-6} = \sqrt{13x-1}$

4. Solve: $2\sqrt{8x+1} = \sqrt{33x+1}$

1. If $3\sqrt{2x+1}=15$, then what is the value of x?

   A) 7
   B) 10
   C) 12
   D) 15

Strategy: Before we can remove the radical sign, we can eliminate its coefficient by dividing both sides by 3. Then, $\sqrt{2x+1}=5$, $\left(\sqrt{2x+1}\right)^2=5^2$, and $2x+1=25$. Solve for x to find $x=12$. Select answer choice C.

2. If $\sqrt{5x-1}+2=10$, then what is the value of $x+7$?

   A) 20
   B) 6
   C) 25
   D) 13

Strategy: Begin by subtracting 2 from each side of the equation to isolate the radical sign. Then, $\sqrt{5x-1}=8$, $\left(\sqrt{5x-1}\right)^2=8^2$, and $5x-1=64$. Solve for the unknown to find that $x=13$. But be careful! The question asks for the value of $x+7$. So, $13+7=20$. Select answer choice A.

Explain Solving Radical Equations with Extraneous Roots

A "solution" obtained through calculation that does not work when substituted into the original equation is called an extraneous solution. Radical equations with square roots often have extraneous solutions because through the process of solving these equations we must square both sides of the equation, which is a process that is not a "reversible" operation. For example, $(-2)^2=4$, but $\sqrt{4}=2$. We can't recapture the −2. This is why it is so important to check proposed solutions in the original equation to verify the solution is not an extraneous solution.

Think It Through

Example

Solve for x: $\sqrt{3x+1}=x-3$.

A) 8
B) 1
C) −8
D) −1

Solution

We begin this problem by squaring both sides of the equation to eliminate the square root sign.

$$\left(\sqrt{3x+1}\right)^2 = (x-3)^2$$

$3x + 1 = x^2 - 6x + 9$ Expand.

$x^2 - 9x + 8 = 0$ Combine like terms and set the equation equal to zero.

$(x - 8)(x - 1) = 0$ Factor.

$x = 8$ and $x = 1$ Set each factor equal to zero and solve for x.

Now we must check each solution in the original equation to see if a true statement results.

If $x = 8$, then: $\sqrt{3 \cdot 8 + 1} = 8 - 3$, $\sqrt{25} = 5$, $5 = 5$. This is a true statement, so $x = 8$ is a solution.

If $x = 1$, then: $\sqrt{3 \cdot 1 + 1} = 1 - 3$. Stop here as you can see the right side of the equation will be negative. The result of taking an even root of a number cannot be negative. This is a false statement; therefore, $x = 1$ is an extraneous root. The only true solution for this equation is $x = 8$.

Answer: A

Model SAT Questions

1. Solve $\sqrt{x+2} + 4 = x$.

   A) $\{4, 7\}$

   B) $\{2, 7\}$

   C) 4

   D) 7

Strategy: Rewrite so the radical expression is alone on the left side of the equation: $\sqrt{x+2} = x - 4$. Now begin isolating the variable by squaring both sides of the equation:

$$x + 2 = (x - 4)^2$$

Expand: $x + 2 = x^2 - 8x + 16$

Simplify: $0 = x^2 - 9x + 14$

Factor: $0 = (x - 7)(x - 2)$.

Therefore $x = 7$ or $x = 2$.

Check both solutions in the original equation.

$\sqrt{x+2} = x - 4$	$\sqrt{x+2} = x - 4$
$\sqrt{x+2} + 4 = x$	$\sqrt{x+2} + 4 = x$
Substitute 7	Substitute 2
$\sqrt{7+2} + 4 = 7$	$\sqrt{2+2} + 4 = 4$
$\sqrt{9} + 4 = 7$	$\sqrt{4} + 4 = 4$
$3 + 4 = 7$ True	$2 + 4 = 4$ False

Therefore, 2 is an extraneous root and must be rejected.

2. If $-1+\sqrt{5-x} = x$, what is $x + 5$?

 A) 1

 B) 6

 C) $\{1, 6\}$

 D) 2

Strategy: Begin by noticing the question is asking for a single solution to the equation $x + 5$, so eliminate answer choice C. From here, you can solve the radical equation for x and check the solutions and then solve $x + 5$, or you can solve the simple equation for x and check the given answer values in the radical equation.

The second method might be faster here, so if $x + 5 = 1$, then $x = -4$. If $x = -4$, then $-1+\sqrt{5-(-4)} = -4$, $-1+\sqrt{9} = -4$. Stop checking here because this is clearly a false statement. Move to the next answer choice. If $x + 5 = 6$, then $x = 1$. If $x = 1$, then $-1+\sqrt{5-1} = 1$, $-1+\sqrt{4} = 1$, $-1+2 = 1$, and $1 = 1$. This is a true statement. Stop checking answers and select answer choice B.

Explain Solving Rational Equations

A **rational equation** is an equation in which one or more of the terms is fractional. One way to solve such an equation is to multiply both sides by the least common denominator of all fractions and rational expressions that appear in the equation. Then, solve the resulting equation for the variable. As always, it is important to check for extraneous roots when needed.

Think It Through

Example 1

Solve $\dfrac{1}{x} + \dfrac{1}{3} = \dfrac{3}{2x} - 1$.

Solution

Determine the least common denominator, $6x$, and then multiply both sides of the

equation by that denominator. So, $\dfrac{6x}{1}\left(\dfrac{1}{x} + \dfrac{1}{3} = \dfrac{3}{2x} - 1\right)$. Note that our goal here is to eliminate the denominators. Simplify to find that $\dfrac{6x}{x}+\dfrac{6x}{3}=\dfrac{18x}{2x}-6x$, and $6+2x=9-6x$. Finally, solve for x: $8x=3$, $x=\dfrac{3}{8}$.

Answer:

Example 2

Solve for x: $\dfrac{x}{x-2}+\dfrac{1}{x-6}=\dfrac{4}{x^2-8x+12}$.

A) $\{6, -1\}$

B) $\{-6, 1\}$

C) -1

D) $\{6, 1\}$

Solution

Begin by noticing that $(x-2)(x-6)=x^2-8x+12$, so your common denominator is already worked out for you. Then multiply each side of the equation by that common denominator to find that $(x-2)(x-6)\cdot\left(\dfrac{x}{x-2}+\dfrac{1}{x-6}=\dfrac{4}{x^2-8x+12}\right)=$ $x(x-6)+1(x-2)=4$. Distribute and collect the like terms: $x(x-6)+1(x-2)=4$, $x^2-6x+x-2=4$, $x^2-5x-6=0$. Factor and solve for the unknowns: $(x-6)(x-1)=0$, and $x=6$, $x=1$. Quickly check to make sure neither answer is an extraneous solution; if $x=6$, then the fraction $\dfrac{1}{x-6}$ is undefined. So, the only answer is $x=-1$, which is answer choice C.

Practice Solving Rational Equations

Answers begin on page 701.

1. Solve for a: $9-\dfrac{2}{a}=5$.

  A) $\dfrac{1}{2}$

  B) $-\dfrac{1}{2}$

  C) 2

  D) -2

2. Solve for x: $\dfrac{3}{x}+\dfrac{1}{2}=\dfrac{11}{5x}$.

  A) $\dfrac{5}{8}$

  B) $-\dfrac{5}{8}$

  C) $\dfrac{8}{5}$

  D) $-\dfrac{8}{5}$

3. Solve for x: $\dfrac{x}{2} = \dfrac{3}{2x+1}$.

   A) $\{-1, 2\}$

   B) $\left\{-2, \dfrac{3}{2}\right\}$

   C) -2

   D) $\dfrac{3}{2}$

4. Solve for m: $\dfrac{8}{m+3} = \dfrac{m-1}{4}$.

   A) $\{5, 7\}$

   B) $\{-5, -7\}$

   C) $\{5, -7\}$

   D) $\{-5, 7\}$

Model SAT Questions

1. What is the solution to the equation $\dfrac{2}{x+5} + \dfrac{20}{x^2-25} = 1$?

   A) 7

   B) -5

   C) $\{-5, 7\}$

   D 5

Strategy: Begin by factoring the second denominator, $\dfrac{2}{x+5} + \dfrac{20}{(x+5)(x-5)} = 1$.

Now, it is clear that the common denominator is $(x+5)(x-5)$. So,

$$(x+5)(x-5) \cdot \left(\dfrac{2}{x+5} + \dfrac{20}{(x+5)(x-5)} \right) = 1 \cdot (x+5)(x-5)$$

$$\cancel{(x+5)}(x-5) \cdot \dfrac{2}{\cancel{x+5}} + \cancel{(x+5)}\,\cancel{(x-5)} \dfrac{20}{\cancel{(x+5)}\,\cancel{(x-5)}} = 1 \cdot (x+5)(x-5)$$

$$2(x-5) + 20 = (x+5)(x-5)$$

$$2x - 10 + 20 = x^2 - 25$$

$$2x + 10 = x^2 - 25$$

$$x^2 - 2x - 35 = 0$$

$$(x-7)(x+5) = 0$$

$$x - 7 = 0 \qquad x + 5 = 0$$

$$x = 7 \qquad x = -5$$

Since we have variables in the denominator, it is important to check for extraneous roots.

$\dfrac{2}{x+5} + \dfrac{20}{x^2-25} = 1$

$\dfrac{2}{x+5} + \dfrac{20}{x^2-25} = 1$

$x = 7$

$x = -5$

$\dfrac{2}{7+5} + \dfrac{20}{7^2-25} = 1$

$\dfrac{2}{-5+5}$ Stop here! Denominators cannot $= 0$.

$$\frac{2}{12}+\frac{20}{49-25}=1$$

$$\frac{1}{6}+\frac{20}{24}=1$$

$$\frac{1}{6}+\frac{5}{6}=1$$

$1 = 1$. Therefore, 7 is a root. The correct answer is A.

2. What is one possible solution to the equation $\dfrac{4}{x-1}+\dfrac{3}{x}=3$?

Strategy: Notice that the wording of the question suggests there is more than one viable solution to this problem. Begin by multiplying through by the least common denominator, $x(x-1)$. Then, $\left(x(x-1)\right)\left(\dfrac{4}{x-1}+\dfrac{3}{x}=3\right)$ becomes $4x+3(x-1)=3x(x-1)$. Distribute, combine like terms, and set the equation equal to zero: $3x^2-10x+3=0$. Now factor and solve each binomial. Check each answer to make sure it is valid. Bubble in 3 or $\dfrac{1}{3}$.

Answers begin on page 702.

1. If $\sqrt{6b+4} = 20$, then what is the value of b?

    A) 66

    B) 64

    C) 62

    D) 60

2. Solve for x: $\dfrac{1}{2} + \dfrac{2}{x-2} = \dfrac{5}{x-1}$.

    A) $\{3, 6\}$

    B) $\{-3, -6\}$

    C) 3

    D) -6

3. Solve for x: $\dfrac{4}{x} - \dfrac{10}{x(2-x)} = \dfrac{5}{x-2}$.

    A) -2

    B) 2

    C) No solution

    D) $(-2, 2)$

4. If $\sqrt{3x+3} = 3\sqrt{x-1}$, then what is the value of x^2?

    A) 1

    B) 9

    C) 16

    D) 4

5. If $\dfrac{2}{p+3} + \dfrac{4}{p} = \dfrac{6}{2p+6}$, what is the value of p?

    A) 4

    B) -4

    C) 8

    D) -8

6. If $2\sqrt{6x} = \sqrt{4x^2}$, what is the value of x?

    A) 0

    B) $\{0, -6\}$

    C) -6

    D) $\{0, 6\}$

7. Solve for b: $\dfrac{2b}{5+b} - \dfrac{1}{5-b} = \dfrac{10}{b^2-25}$.

    A) 5

    B) $\left\{-\dfrac{1}{2}, 5\right\}$

    C) $-\dfrac{1}{2}$

    D) No solution

8. Solve for x: $\dfrac{4}{x-5} - \dfrac{2}{x+5} = \dfrac{2}{x}$.

A) $\dfrac{2}{5}$

B) $-\dfrac{5}{3}$

C) -5

D) No solution

Student-Produced Response Questions

9. If $3\sqrt{2x+1} = 15$, then what is the value of x?

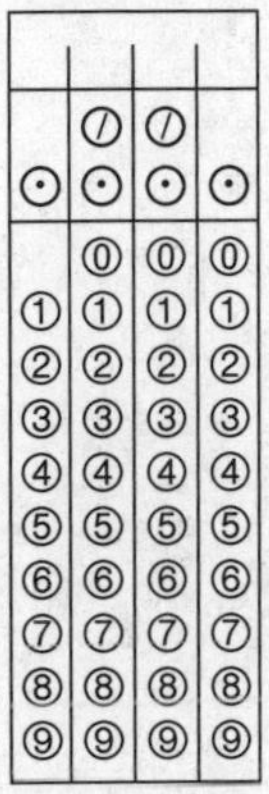

10. Solve for x: $\dfrac{2x+3}{x+9} = \dfrac{x+5}{x+9}$.

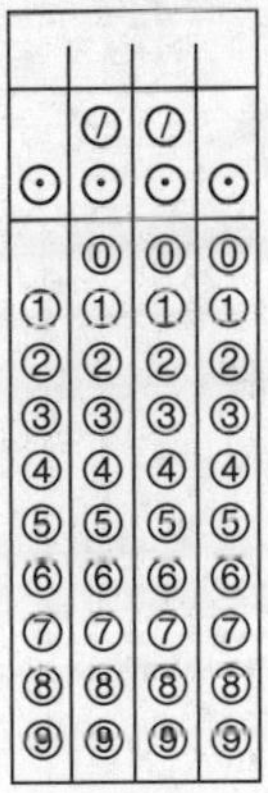

11. If $\sqrt{20x} = 2\sqrt{4x+5}$, then what is the value of x?

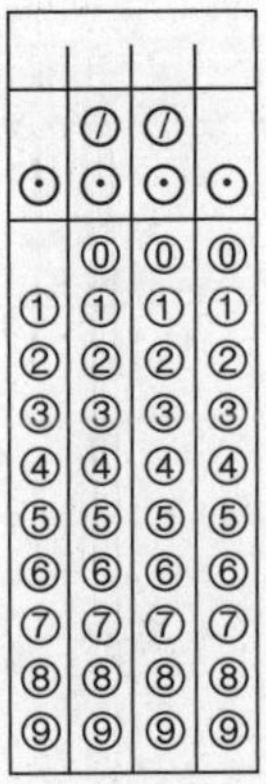

12. If $\sqrt{x} + 6 = x$, then $\sqrt{x}$ has what value?

13. If $5\sqrt{5x-1} = 7\sqrt{2x+5}$, then what is the value of $x + 2$?

14. Solve for x: $\dfrac{4x+3}{x-6} + \dfrac{x-4}{6-x} = \dfrac{44}{2x-12}$.

LESSON 4:

Creating, Analyzing, Interpreting, and Solving Nonlinear Equations

- Solving Quadratic Equations

- Creating, Analyzing, and Interpreting Quadratic Equations

- Creating, Analyzing, and Interpreting Exponential Equations

Explain Solving Quadratic Equations

A **quadratic equation** equates a second-degree polynomial, such as $f(x) = x^2 - 2x - 8$, to zero. The standard form of a quadratic equation is $ax^2 + bx + c = 0$. This lesson reviews algebraic strategies for finding solutions to quadratic equations. The solutions, known as roots of the equation or zeroes of the polynomial, tell us the point or points at which the function's graph touches the x-axis. We can algebraically locate the roots of a quadratic equation either by factoring or by using the quadratic formula.

1. **Factoring**. When we factor a quadratic equation, we are looking to find the two binomials we multiply together to make the quadratic trinomial. Thus, if we are factoring the trinomial $x^2 - 7x + 10 = 0$, the factored equation becomes $(x - 2)(x - 5) = 0$. By setting each binomial equal to 0 and solving, we find the roots $x = 2$ and $x = 5$.

2. **The quadratic formula**, $x = \dfrac{-b \pm \sqrt{b^2 - 4ac}}{2a}$, where a, b, and c are the

   coefficients of the quadratic equation, $ax^2 + bx + c = 0$, always works. Thus, for $x^2 - 7x + 10 = 0$, $a = 1$, $b = -7$, and $c = 10$. Substitute in these values

   and $x = \dfrac{-(-7) \pm \sqrt{(-7)^2 - 4 \cdot 1 \cdot 10}}{2} = \dfrac{7 \pm \sqrt{49 - 40}}{2} = \dfrac{7\sqrt{9}}{2} = \dfrac{7 \pm 3}{2}$.

   So again, $x = \dfrac{7+3}{2} = 5$ and $x = \dfrac{7-3}{2} = 2$.

   This second method, using the quadratic formula, $x = \dfrac{-b + \sqrt{b^2 - 4ac}}{2a}$, is an

   algebraic way for finding the roots. It's just one alternative to tracing the curve of the parabola on the calculator and reading the roots when the trace crosses the x-axis.

Think It Through

Example 1

What is the smallest root of the equation $x^2 - x - 12 = 0$?

A) −4

B) −3

C) 3

D) 4

Solution

Find the roots by factoring and then setting the factors equal to zero. Remember that when we factor a trinomial, we are looking to find the two binomials we multiply together that result in the given trinomial. Thus,

$(x^2 - x - 12) = (x - 4)(x + 3)$.

$x - 4 = 0 \qquad\quad x + 3 = 0$

$x = 4 \qquad\qquad x = -3$

The smaller solution is -3.

Answer: B

Example 2

To the nearest hundredth, what is the difference between the zeroes of the function $f(x) = 2x^2 - 9x - 3$?

Solution

Always keep in mind that when we are finding the zeroes of a function, we are locating the point or points at which the function's graph touches the x-axis. To find the zeroes for this quadratic, we could try to factor, but that can be challenging when the coefficient of the leading term is a number other than 1. Rather than waste time, go directly to using the quadratic formula. Then, substitute the coefficient values for $a = 2$, $b = -9$, and $c = -3$ into the quadratic formula:

$$x = \frac{-9 \pm \sqrt{9^2 - 4(2)(-3)}}{2 \cdot 2} = \frac{-9 \pm \sqrt{81 + 24}}{4}$$

$$x = \frac{9 \pm \sqrt{105}}{4} = \text{two possibilities} = (1)\ \frac{9 + \sqrt{105}}{4} = 4.81$$

$$\text{and (2)}\ \frac{9 - \sqrt{105}}{4} = -0.31$$

The distance between the roots 4.81 and −0.31, which is the difference between the zeroes, equals $4.81 - (-0.31) = 5.12$.

Answer: 5.12

Answers begin on page 703.

1. Which of the following answer choices gives the roots of the quadratic equation $x^2 - 13x - 30 = 0$?

   A) $\{-15, -2\}$
   B) $\{-15, 2\}$
   C) $\{15, -2\}$
   D) $\{15, 2\}$

2. What are the roots of $x^2 + 5x = 6$?

   A) $\{-1, 6\}$
   B) $\{1, -6\}$
   C) $\{2, -3\}$
   D) $\{2, 3\}$

3. For which equation is the solution set $\{3, 4\}$?

   A) $x^2 + 3x + 4 = 0$
   B) $x^2 - 7x + 12 = 0$
   C) $x^2 + 12x + 7 = 0$
   D) $x^2 - 9x = 16$

4. For which equation is the solution set $\{-8, 2\}$?

   A) $x^2 + 6x - 16 = 0$
   B) $x^2 + 6x - 10 = 0$
   C) $x^2 - 12x - 64 = 0$
   D) $x^2 - 16x + 6 = 0$

Model SAT Questions

1. Find the smaller root of the equation $\dfrac{x}{2} = \dfrac{2}{x}$.

   A) 2
   B) 0
   C) −2
   D) −4

Strategy: Although this does not look like a quadratic equation on its face, remember from Lesson 1 in Category 2 that we can cross-multiply two fractions that are set equal to each other. If we do so here, we find $x^2 = 4$. Subtract 4 from each side of the equation and then factor using the difference of squares: $x^2 - 4 = 0$, $(x - 2)(x + 2) = 0$. Solving for the roots, we see that $x = \pm 2$. The smaller root is −2. Select answer choice C.

2. Find the distance between the roots of the equation $\dfrac{x+5}{3} = \dfrac{10}{x-8}$.

   A) 3
   B) 7
   C) 10
   D) 17

Strategy: Again, before we can think about solving for the roots of this equation, we must modify it so it is in the correct form. Cross-multiply to find that $(x+5)(x-8) = 30$. Expand, combine the like terms, and set the equation equal to 0 to see that $x^2 - 3x - 70 = 0$. Now factor and solve for the roots: $(x+7)(x-10) = 0$, $(x+7) = 0$, $(x-10) = 0$, $x = -7$, $x = 10$. The distance is $10 - (-7) = 17$. This is answer choice D.

3. Solve the following equation: $\dfrac{x}{x+2} = \dfrac{3}{x} + \dfrac{4}{x(x+2)}$.

   A) 5

   B) 2

   C) −2

   D) −5

Strategy: Remember from Lesson 3 in this Category that we can clear the denominators in a rational equation by multiplying all the terms in the equation by the least common denominator. Then, $x(x+2)\left(\dfrac{x}{x+2} = \dfrac{3}{x} + \dfrac{4}{x(x+2)}\right)$ becomes $x^2 = 3(x+2) + 4$. Distribute and combine the like terms to find $x^2 = 3x + 10$. Set the polynomial equal to zero by subtracting $3x$ and 10 from both sides and then $x^2 - 3x - 10 = 0$. Now factor and solve: $(x-5)(x+2) = 0$. So, $x = 5$ and $x = -2$. However, we must reject $x = -2$ as a solution because replacing x with −2 creates terms that have zero value denominators, making the fractions undefined. Answer choice A is correct.

· · · · · · **Explain** **Creating, Analyzing, and Interpreting** · · · · · · · · · · · · · · · ·
                         Quadratic Equations

On the SAT, you may be asked to solve for the roots of quadratic equations directly, as we did in the previous section, or you may be asked to create a quadratic equation that represents a real-world scenario. One of the most common examples of quadratics in the real world is projectile motion. Projectile motion problems may be expressed in vertex form, $h(t) = k(t - \text{time at maximum height})^2 + \text{maximum height}$, which is generalized as $f(x) = a(x - h)^2 + k$. The advantage of vertex form is that it highlights the quadratic's vertex (h, k). This is especially useful for projectile motion as the object has a maximum height k at time h.

Another example of quadratics in the real world is the distance formula,

$\text{Distance} = \text{rate} \cdot \text{time}$, which can also be written as $\text{time} = \dfrac{\text{distance}}{\text{rate}}$ and as

$\text{rate} = \dfrac{\text{distance}}{\text{time}}$. These relationships may appear in problems requiring you to create

an equation, or you may be asked to interpret the meaning of a term in a written equation related to these concepts. Other examples of quadratics in the real world include determining the price a product should sell for and maximizing the area of a shape.

Note that it is important to be able to choose and produce equivalent forms of quadratic expressions to reveal and explain properties of a quantity.

Example 1

Marko traveled 105 miles in 2 hours on a car trip. He traveled 15 miles on local roads at a speed of x mph and 90 miles on the highway at a rate that was 30 mph faster than on local roads. Which equation can be used to find both rates of speed for Marko's trip?

A) $\dfrac{x}{15} + \dfrac{x+30}{90} = 2$

B) $\dfrac{15}{x+30} + \dfrac{90}{x} = 2$

C) $\dfrac{15}{x} + \dfrac{90}{x+30} = 2$

D) $\dfrac{30}{15} + \dfrac{x}{90} = 2$

Solution

Quickly scan the answer choices and realize that since they are all equal to 2 (which is the time of the trip in hours), the fractions on the left-hand side of the equation

must be in this form: $\text{time} = \dfrac{\text{distance}}{\text{rate}}$ to be correct. This eliminates answer choices

A and D. Only choice C correctly relates the distances to their given rates: distance 15 is tied to rate x and distance 90 is tied to rate $x + 30$.

Answer: C

Example 2

Papers need to be sorted for a school project. Simon sorts three times as fast as Haley, and together, they complete the task in 2 hours.

The equation $\dfrac{3}{x} + \dfrac{1}{x} = \dfrac{1}{2}$ represents the problem described above. Which of the

following describes what the expression $\dfrac{3}{x}$ represents in this equation?

A) The time, in hours, that it takes Simon to complete $\dfrac{1}{2}$ the job.

B) The portion of the job that Simon would complete alone in 1 hour.

C) The portion of the job that Haley would complete alone in 1 hour.

D) The time, in hours, it would take Haley to complete the entire job.

Solution

The entire job is completed in 2 hours; therefore, $\dfrac{1}{2}$ of the job is completed in

1 hour. Thus, the addends show the portion each person will complete in 1 hour.

From the problem description, Simon is 3 times as fast. So, $\dfrac{3}{x}$ shows Simon's work in 1 hour.

Answer: B

Example 3

If the expression $\dfrac{16x^2}{4x+1}$ is written in the equivalent form $\dfrac{1}{4x+1}+A$, what is A in terms of x?

A) $16x$
B) $16x-1$
C) $4x+1$
D) $4x-1$

Solution

There are multiple strategies you could use to solve this problem. The shortest route is to use the structure to rewrite the numerator of the expression $\dfrac{16x^2}{4x+1}$

as $\dfrac{\left(16x^2-1\right)+1}{4x+1}$ in order to create a term that is both divisible by $4x+1$

and is the difference of squares. Then, $\dfrac{\left(16x^2-1\right)+1}{4x+1}=\dfrac{(4x+1)(4x-1)+1}{4x+1}=$

$\dfrac{\cancel{(4x+1)}(4x-1)}{\cancel{4x+1}}+\dfrac{1}{4x+1}=4x-1+\dfrac{1}{4x+1}$. You could also use the division of polynomials to find the solution.

Answer: D

Example 4

A football is kicked upward. Its maximum height of 60 feet occurs after 4 seconds. Which function models this behavior?

A) $h(t)=-16(t+4)+60$
B) $h(t)=-16(t-4)^2+60$
C) $h(t)=-16(t-4)+60$
D) $h(t)=-16(t+4)^2+60$

Solution

Examine the answer choices. You know you are looking for a quadratic in the general form $f(x)=a(x-h)^2+k$, where the football will have a maximum height k at time h. Answer choice B is the only correct choice.

Answer: B

Creating, Analyzing, and Interpreting Quadratic Equations

Answers begin on page 703.

1. Dawn rode a bicycle 1 mile to a friend's house, traveling at x mph. She and her friend then drove to the grocery store, a distance of 12 miles, traveling at a rate 25 miles per hour faster than Dawn traveled by bicycle. If the entire trip took $\frac{3}{4}$ of an hour, which equation describes the trip?

A) $\dfrac{1}{x}+\dfrac{12}{x+25}=\dfrac{3}{4}$

B) $\dfrac{1}{x+25}+\dfrac{12}{x}=\dfrac{3}{4}$

C) $\dfrac{x+25}{x}+\dfrac{x^2}{x}=\dfrac{3}{4}$

D) $\dfrac{12}{x}+\dfrac{1}{25}=\dfrac{3}{4}$

2. Costumes are needed for the school play. Students Luke and Sead work together at the same speed. So do Jala and Sam. Jala and Sam together work at a speed that is double that of Luke and Sead together. Altogether, it takes the pairs 8 days to make all of the costumes.

If the equation $\dfrac{2}{x}+\dfrac{1}{x}=\dfrac{1}{8}$ represents the problem described above, what does the term $\dfrac{1}{2x}$ represent?

A) The time, in days, that it takes Jala and Sam to complete the job.

B) The portion of the job that Jala and Sam would complete alone in 1 day.

C) The portion of the job that Luke and Sead would complete in 1 day.

D) The portion of the job Luke would complete in 1 day.

3. If the expression $\dfrac{25x^2}{5x-1}$ is written in the equivalent form $\dfrac{1}{5x-1}+D$, what is D in terms of x?

A) $5x+1$

B) $5x-1$

C) $25x-1$

D) $25x+1$

4. A ball is kicked upward. Its maximum height of 40 feet occurs after 2.5 seconds. Which function models this behavior?

A) $h(t)=-16(t+2.5)+40$

B) $h(t)=-16(t-2.5)+40$

C) $h(t)=-16(t-2.5)^2+40$

D) $h(t)=-16(t+2.5)^2+40$

1. Joakim paid $8.25 for x pounds of candy. Antonia bought $x+1$ pounds of candy at the same price per pound and paid $9.50. Which equation could be used to find the price per pound for the candy?

A) $8.25x=9.50(x+1)$

B) $8.25x=\dfrac{x+1}{9.25}$

C) $\dfrac{8.25}{x}=\dfrac{9.5}{x+1}$

D) $x(x+1)=(8.95)(9.5)$

Strategy: The cost of $8.25 is associated with x pounds of candy, and $x+1$ pounds of candy is associated with $9.50. Then, the cost per pound is $\dfrac{\text{total cost}}{\text{number of pounds}}$, so $\dfrac{8.25}{x}=\dfrac{9.5}{x+1}$. This is answer choice C.

2. Two students, Jian and Emilia, volunteered to work on a memorial garden. Jian works at half the speed of Emilia. Altogether, it takes them 10 days to complete the work.

The equation $\frac{4}{x} + \frac{2}{x} = \frac{1}{5}$ represents the problem described above. Which of the following describes what the expression $\frac{2}{x}$ represents in this equation?

A) The time, in days, that is takes Jian and Emilia to complete the job.
B) The portion of the job that Jian would complete alone in 2 days.
C) The portion of the job that Emilia would complete alone in 2 days.
D) The portion of the job that Jian would complete working alone for 10 days.

Strategy: The entire job is completed in 10 days. Therefore, $\frac{1}{5} = \frac{2}{10}$ is how much of the job is completed in 2 days. The addends show the portion each person will complete in 2 days. Jian would complete $\frac{2}{x}$ in one day. This is answer choice B.

$\cdots\cdots$ Explain **Creating, Analyzing, and Interpreting Exponential Equations** $\cdots\cdots\cdots\cdots$

Many real-world problems involve a quantity (some value) growing or decaying exponentially over a period of time. Typically, *exponential growth* focuses on populations, financial investments, or biological entities growing in size, while *exponential decay* is often found in the diminishing price of a product (as in the yearly loss of the value of a car, called depreciation), or the steady decrease in a population, or the radioactive decay of isotopes.

> In general, these exponential functions are in the form $f(t) = ab^t$, where a and b are real numbers, and where $a \neq 0$, and $b \neq 1$, and t represents time.
>
> Initially $t = 0$, $f(0) = ab^0 = a(1) = a$, so the quantity a is called the *initial value* and b is called the *growth factor*.

On the SAT, you may be asked to create, manipulate, or interpret the meaning of an exponential equation in the context of a real-world scenario. This is very similar to the work you completed earlier in this lesson with quadratic equations. Commonly, we use the following exponential equations for growth and decay.

If $b > 1$, then there is exponential growth. To calculate exponential growth, we use the **exponential growth model**.

$$A = a(1 + r)^t$$
$$A = \text{future value}$$
$$a = \text{initial value}$$
$$r = \text{growth rate}$$
$$b \text{ is } (1 + r) = \text{growth factor}$$
$$t = \text{time}$$

If $0 < b < 1$, then there is exponential decay. To calculate exponential decay, we use the **exponential decay model**.

$$A = a(1 - r)^t$$

A = future value

a = initial value

r = decay rate

b is $(1 - r)$ = decay factor

t = time

Think It Through

Example 1

An entrepreneur finds an investment opportunity that turns his $10,000 investment into approximately $12,000 in two years. Over the two years, what was the annual rate of return on his initial investment?

A) 9%

B) 9.5%

C) 10.1%

D) 10.5%

Solution

Use the exponential growth model, $A = a(1+r)^t$, and substitute in the known values. The initial value is 10,000, r is the growth rate, 2 is the time, and 12,000 is the future value. Then, $12,000 = 10,000(1+r)^2$. Dividing both sides by 10,000, you are left with $(1+r)^2 = 1.2$. Take the square root of each side to find $\sqrt{(1+r)^2} = \sqrt{1.2}$. Now $1+r \approx 1.095$ and $r = .095$ or 9.5%.

Answer: B

Example 2

Two years ago, Marc paid $450 for a baseball signed by Andy Pettitte. The value of the card grew by 6% each year. If Marc sells the ball 5 years from now, what percent profit will he make?

A) 25%

B) 50%

C) 75%

D) 100%

Solution

Begin by determining the worth of the card today. The card was purchased 2 years ago and will be sold 5 years from now. That's 7 years of value growth. Utilize the exponential growth formula, $A = a(1+r)^t$, and substitute in the known values. So, $A = 450(1+.06)^7$ and $A = \$676.63$. From Lesson 1 of Category 2, subtract the current value from the original value, then divide that difference by the original value and multiply the result by 100 to determine the percentage increase of the card's value and thus the percent profit. Thus, $100 \cdot \left(\dfrac{676.63 - 450}{450} \right) = 50.36\%$ or about 50% growth.

Answer: B

Example 3

If a rubber ball is dropped from a height of 90 meters and, on each bounce, it rebounds two-thirds of the distance from which it fell, how many meters does it fall on the second descent?

A) 10 meters

B) 30 meters

C) 40 meters

D) 60 meters

Solution

This is an exponential decay model. The initial height is 90 meters and the decay

rate is $\frac{1}{3}$. Then, $A = 90\left(1 - \frac{1}{3}\right)^1 = 60$ meters.

Answer: D

Practice Creating, Analyzing, and Interpreting Exponential Equations

Answers begin on page 704.

1. Find the approximate value of a $2,000 initial investment that pays 6% interest, compounded quarterly, at the end of 3 years.

    A) $2,391

    B) $2,382

    C) $2,375

    D) $2,360

2. The concentration of a certain medication in a person's bloodstream decreases exponentially by 25% every hour. If the initial concentration of the medication was 1.5 mg per liter, what is the approximate time when the medication's concentration is reduced by 50%?

    A) 2.2 hours

    B) 2.4 hours

    C) 2.6 hours

    D) 2.6 hours

Model SAT Questions

1. Half-life is the period in which radioactive material is reduced by one-half. Material X has a half-life of 80 years. Which of the following equations will yield the amount of material X left after 400 years if the initial amount was 1,000 grams?

    A) $A = 1,000(0.50)^{80}$

    B) $A = 500(0.50)^{80}$

    C) $A = 500^5$

    D) $A = 1,000(0.50)^5$

Strategy: In an exponential decay problem, t is given by the quotient of the amount of time that has passed and the half-life of the material. For this problem,

$t = \dfrac{400}{80} = 5$. Then, the initial value is 1,000 and the rate of decay is 0.50.

So, $A = 1000(0.50)^5$; this is answer choice D.

2. A bacteria culture doubles every 15 minutes. After one and one-half hours, there were approximately 32,000 bacteria present. How many bacteria were initially in the culture?

A) 98

B) 500

C) 1,000

D) 11,314

Strategy: For this problem, we will need to work backwards. Let x be the initial amount of bacteria in the culture. The number of doubling times is $t = 1.5\left(\dfrac{60}{15}\right) = 6$. Then, using the exponential growth formula, $x(2.00)^6 = 32,000$, and $x = \dfrac{32,000}{2^6} = 500$. This is answer choice B.

SAT-Type Questions

Answers begin on page 704.

1. Find the solution set for $\dfrac{x+2}{2} = \dfrac{1}{x+3}$.

A) $\{1, 4\}$

B) $\{2, 3\}$

C) $\{-1, -4\}$

D) $\{-2, -3\}$

2. The difference in the average speed of two cars is 10 miles per hour. The slower car takes 1 hour longer to travel 240 miles than the faster car takes to travel 250 miles. Which equation will help you find the speeds of the cars?

A) $\dfrac{250}{t} - \dfrac{240}{t} = 10$

B) $\dfrac{250}{t-1} - \dfrac{240}{t+1} = 10$

C) $\dfrac{250}{t} - \dfrac{240}{t+1} = 10$

D) $\dfrac{250}{t} - \dfrac{240}{t-1} = 10$

3. Which expression is equivalent to $\dfrac{x^2 - 3x}{x-1}$?

   A) $x - 2 - \dfrac{2}{x-1}$

   B) $x - 2 + \dfrac{4}{x-1}$

   C) $x - 2 + \dfrac{1}{x-1}$

   D) $x - 2 + \dfrac{2}{x-1}$

4. Find the solution set for $\dfrac{5}{x+3} + \dfrac{5}{(x+2)(x+3)} = 1$.

   A) $\{-3, 3\}$

   B) $\{3\}$

   C) $\{-3\}$

   D) $\left\{\dfrac{5}{3}\right\}$

5. Find the solution set for $\dfrac{x}{x-2} + \dfrac{1}{x+2} = \dfrac{x+6}{x^2-4}$.

   A) $\{2, -4\}$

   B) $\{-2, 4\}$

   C) $\{-4\}$

   D) $\{4\}$

6. Find the approximate value of a $2,000 investment paying 5% interest compounded semi-annually, at the end of 3 years.

   A) $2,320

   B) $2,310

   C) $2,300

   D) $2,990

7. If the expression $\dfrac{81x^2}{9x+1}$ is written in the equivalent form $\dfrac{1}{9x+1} + K$, what is K in terms of x?

   A) $9x + 1$

   B) $9x - 1$

   C) $81x$

   D) $81x - 1$

8. Michael biked uphill, a distance of 2 miles, traveling at x mph. He completed the remaining 4 miles biking on level ground, traveling at a rate 5 miles per hour faster than he did on the hill. The entire trip took one and one-half hours. Which equation describes the trip?

A) $\dfrac{2}{x} + \dfrac{4}{x+5} = \dfrac{3}{2}$

B) $\dfrac{2}{x+5} + \dfrac{4}{x} = \dfrac{3}{2}$

C) $\left(\dfrac{3}{2}\right) + \left(\dfrac{2}{x}\right) + \left(\dfrac{3}{2}\right) + \left(\dfrac{4}{x+5}\right) = 1$

D) $\dfrac{x}{2} + \dfrac{x+5}{4} = \dfrac{3}{2}$

9. The number of donations to the town library has grown exponentially. In the year 2010, there were 240 donations. In the year 2011, there were 288 donations. Using this information, approximately how many donations were made in 2014?

A) 496

B) 498

C) 500

D) 502

10. Find the solution set for $\dfrac{x-1}{4} = \dfrac{12}{x+1}$.

A) $\{-7, 7\}$

B) $\{1, -1\}$

C) $\{1\}$

D) $\{7\}$

11. Find the solution set for $\dfrac{3x+4}{3} = \dfrac{3}{3x-4}$.

A) $\left\{\dfrac{4}{3}, -\dfrac{4}{3}\right\}$

B) $\left\{\dfrac{3}{4}, -\dfrac{3}{4}\right\}$

C) $\left\{\dfrac{3}{5}, -\dfrac{3}{5}\right\}$

D) $\left\{\dfrac{5}{3}, -\dfrac{5}{3}\right\}$

12. It takes 18 minutes less time to travel 60 miles by car at night than by day because the difference in traffic patterns allows the speed to be 10 miles per hour faster. Which equation can be used to find the average speed in the daytime?

A) $\dfrac{60}{t-18} + \dfrac{60}{t} = \dfrac{1}{6}$

B) $\dfrac{60}{t-18} - \dfrac{60}{t} = \dfrac{1}{6}$

C) $\dfrac{60}{t-18} = \dfrac{60}{t} + 10$

D) $\dfrac{60}{t-18} + \dfrac{60}{t} = 10$

13. Find the solution set for $\dfrac{5x+2}{8} = \dfrac{4}{5x-2}$.

A) $\left\{ \dfrac{6}{5}, -\dfrac{6}{5} \right\}$

B) $\left\{ \dfrac{5}{6}, -\dfrac{5}{6} \right\}$

C) $\left\{ -\dfrac{2}{5} \right\}$

D) $\left\{ \dfrac{2}{5} \right\}$

14. Ruth drove for 60 miles at a certain speed. Then, she increased her speed 5 mph and drove another 60 miles. The entire trip took $1\dfrac{1}{2}$ hours. Which of the following equations would help you find the rate at which Ruth drove initially?

A) $\dfrac{2x+5}{60} = \dfrac{3}{2}$

B) $60\left(\dfrac{1}{x} + \dfrac{1}{x+5} \right) = \dfrac{3}{2}$

C) $\dfrac{60}{2x+5} = \dfrac{3}{2}$

D) $\dfrac{60}{x} + \dfrac{65}{x+5} = \dfrac{3}{2}$

Student-Produced Response Questions

15. What is one possible solution to the equation $\dfrac{x-4}{2} = \dfrac{4}{x-6}$?

16. Margie walks 3 miles to the park and returns home on roller skates. Her roller skating speed is 4 miles per hour faster than her walking speed. The total round-trip time is 2 hours. Find Margie's skating speed in miles per hour.

17. The cost, c, for maintenance on an antique car increases by 5% each year. If Jose paid $200 for initial maintenance, then the charge x years later can be given by the function $c(x) = 200(n)^x$. What is the value of n?

18. A tank contains 225 gallons of oil. If 20% of the remaining oil is released each time the valve is opened, how much oil will remain in the tank after it is opened 4 times? Round to the nearest tenth of a gallon, if needed.

LESSON 5:

The Meaning of the Terms in Nonlinear Expressions; Relationships Between the Polynomial Zeros and Factors

- **Quadratic Definitions and End Behavior**
- **End Behavior for Exponential Functions**
- **Relationship Between Zeros and Factors of a Polynomial Function**

· · · · · · **Explain** **Quadratic Definitions and End Behavior** · · · · · · · · · · ·

Quadratic functions have the general form $f(x) = ax^2 + bx + c$, and appear as **parabolas** when graphed. In this section, we will learn how the terms of the function enable us to describe the parabola's behavior. We will use the function $f(x) = x^2 + 2x - 8$ to define the important terms and properties of a quadratic equation.

In a parabola, the **vertex** (also known as the turning point) is either the minimum or maximum value, depending on which way the parabola opens. The x-coordinate of the turning point is calculated by the formula $x = \dfrac{-b}{2a}$. The y-coordinate is found by substituting the x-coordinate value into the original function. In our example, $f(x) = x^2 + 2x - 8$, $x = \dfrac{-2}{2(1)} = -1$, and $y = f(-1) = (-1)^2 + 2(-1) - 8 = -9$. Thus, the turning point is located at $(-1, -9)$. Related to the vertex, the **axis of symmetry** is the line that passes through the vertex and is parallel to the y-axis. Algebraically, we can calculate the axis of symmetry by using the formula $x = \dfrac{-b}{2a}$. In the example $f(x) = x^2 + 2x - 8$, the axis of symmetry is $x = \dfrac{-2}{2(1)} = -1$. Note that the x-coordinate of the vertex and the equation for the line of symmetry have the same value.

In real-world problems, where the minimum or maximum value of the parabola represents a critical value that is essential to the solution, quadratic functions are often written in **vertex form**, rather than in general form. Vertex form, $f(x) = a(x - h)^2 + k$, highlights the parabola's vertex, which is located at (h, k). Generally, k represents the maximum or minimum y-value and h represents the x-coordinate at which the maximum or minimum y-value occurs. For example, let the function $f(x) = -5.3(x - 3)^2 + 53.7$ model the height as a function of time for a ball thrown vertically and let the units of measure be seconds and yards. The given function $f(x)$ has turning point $(3, 53.7)$. We can see the ball reaches a maximum height of 53.7 yards in 3 seconds without any calculation.

Besides what is happening at the parabola's vertex, we are also interested in its **end behavior**. Specifically, we want to know where the function is increasing or decreasing. Remember that quadratic functions open either up or down. The coefficient of the x^2 term determines the end behavior. If a is positive, the graph

Definition

A **parabola** is a u-shaped curve with specific properties.

Definition

End behavior is what happens to the graph of a function as the independent variable approaches positive or negative infinity.

opens up. If a is negative, the graph opens down. In our example, $f(x) = x^2 + 2x - 8$, the graph opens up. Keep in mind that the vertex is a minimum point when the graph opens up and a maximum point when the graph opens down.

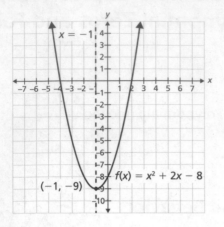

$f(x) = x^2 + 2x - 8$

$(-1, -9)$

Think It Through

Example 1

Find the axis of symmetry for the function $f(x) = x^2 - 4x - 5$.

A) $x = -2$
B) $x = 2$
C) $y = -2$
D) $y = 2$

Solution

The axis of symmetry is the vertical line that passes through the vertex and is calculated by the formula $x = \dfrac{-b}{2a}$. So, $x = \dfrac{-(-4)}{2} = 2$.

Answer: B

Example 2

Which of the following describes the vertex of the quadratic $f(x) = x^2 + 4x + 4$?

A) The turning point is (–4, 4) and it is a minimum value.
B) The turning point is (–4, 4) and it is a maximum value.
C) The turning point is (4, 36) and it is a minimum value.
D) The turning point is (4, 36) and it is a maximum value.

Solution

Since the coefficient of x^2 is positive 1, you immediately know the graph opens up and the turning point is a minimum value. This eliminates answer choices B and

D. Using the formula $x = \dfrac{-b}{2a}$, $x = \dfrac{-4}{2(1)} = -2$. This is the x-coordinate of the vertex.

Of the remaining answer choices, only A has this value.

Answer: A

Example 3

A ball tossed vertically from ground level reaches a maximum height of 7 yards after 4 seconds. Which function models this behavior?

A) $f(t) = -5.3(t-4)^2 + 7$

B) $f(t) = -5.3(t-7) + 4$

C) $f(t) = -5.3(t+4) + 7$

D) $f(t) = -5.3(t+7)^2 + 4$

Solution

The projectile motion model for functions is usually written in vertex form: $f(x) = a(x-h)^2 + k$, to highlight the maximum height, k, at time h. In this problem, the time is 4 seconds and the height is 7 yards, so substitute those values into the formula and find that $f(t) = -5.3(t-4)^2 + 7$.

Answer: A

Practice Quadratic Definitions and End Behavior

Answers begin on page 706.

1. Find the axis of symmetry for the function $f(x) = x^2 - x - 2$.

   A) $x = -1$

   B) $x = 1$

   C) $x = \dfrac{1}{2}$

   D) $x = 2$

2. Find the axis of symmetry for $f(x) = 2x^2 - 3$.

   A) $x = \dfrac{2}{3}$

   B) $x = -\dfrac{3}{2}$

   C) $x = \dfrac{2}{3}$

   D) $x = 0$

3. Identify the turning point for $f(x) = x^2 - 4x + 4$.

   A) $(0, 2)$

   B) $(0, -2)$

   C) $(2, 0)$

   D) $(-2, 0)$

4. Identify the turning point for $f(x) = 2x^2 - 2x + 1$.

   A) $\left(\dfrac{1}{2}, \dfrac{1}{2}\right)$

   B) $(1, 1)$

   C) $\left(\dfrac{-1}{2}, \dfrac{5}{2}\right)$

   D) $\left(\dfrac{-1}{2}, \dfrac{3}{2}\right)$

5. The function $f(t) = -5.3(t-2)^2 + 6$, describes a projectile's height in yards as a function of time measured in seconds. Which statement is based upon this expression?

   A) The ball reaches a maximum height of 6 yards in 2 seconds.

   B) The ball reaches a maximum height of 2 yards in 6 seconds.

   C) The ball returns to its starting height after 2 seconds.

   D) The ball returns to its starting height after 6 seconds.

1. The Sterns plan to fence off a section of their backyard, creating a rectangular enclosure, with the house acting as one side of the rectangle and with the fence material being used for the other three sides. They have 80 meters of fencing material. What is the maximum area for the Sterns' enclosure in square meters?

   A) 400 square meters

   B) 600 square meters

   C) 800 square meters

   D) 1,000 square meters

Strategy: To find the maximum area, we must first consider the perimeter of the enclosure. Since the house will be used for one side, the available 80 meters of fencing will be dedicated to 3 sides of the barrier. So, we can write the linear equation: $2w + l = 80$, and solve it for l: $l = 80 - 2w$. Now we can focus on the area. You know the formula for the area of a rectangle is $A = lw$. Substitute in $80 - 2w$ for l, and the area of the fenced-in region is $A = (80 - 2w)w$. Distribute to find $A = -2w^2 + 80w$. This equation is a quadratic function, represented by a parabola opening downward and a maximum value occurring at the vertex. The axis of symmetry is $w = \dfrac{-b}{2a} = \dfrac{-80}{2(-2)} = 20$. Thus, the turning point is $(20, A)$ with $A = -2(20)^2 + 80(20) = -800 + 1{,}600 = 800$. The maximum area is 800 square meters. Select answer choice C.

2. A small craft store knows that the higher the price they charge for an item, the fewer the items sold. They are able to produce a window decoration for $2. Unsure about the appropriate selling price, they experimented with different prices, each for the same period of time. They found the following linear relationship between s, the selling price and q, the quantity sold:

$$q = -2s + 80.$$

   Find the maximum profit the craft store will earn from selling the window decoration.

   A) $722

   B) $798

   C) $836

   D) $874

Strategy: A company's profit, P, on the sale of q items is calculated by subtracting the cost of production from the money taken in. To find the money taken in, multiply the quantity sold by the selling price. To calculate the cost of production, multiply the quantity sold by the cost to make each item. Then, $P =$ quantity $(q) \cdot$ selling price (s) – quantity $(q) \cdot$ production cost per item ($2), or $P = qs - 2q$. The question provided the linear function for q, so we can substitute that into our profit equation. Then, $P = (-2s + 80)s - 2(-2s + 80)$. Distribute and then collect the like terms to find $P = -2s^2 + 80s + 4s - 160 = -2s^2 + 84s - 160$. From the leading coefficient, we know this function opens downward and has a maximum. The turning point is $s = \dfrac{-b}{2a} = \dfrac{-84}{2(-2)} = 21$. The maximum profit is reached by selling the item for $21. The number to be sold at that price $= -2(21) + 80 = 38$. The profit would be $P = qs - 2q = 38 \cdot 21 - 38 \cdot 2 = \$722$. This is answer choice A.

As mentioned in a previous lesson, the parent function for exponential equations is $f(x) = b^x$ where $b > 0$, $b \neq 1$, and the variable x is a real number. If $b > 1$, the function increases as shown in the graph on the left. If $0 < b < 1$, the function decreases as shown in the graph on the right. Note how in both examples, the graphs approach but do not actually touch the x-axis. The line that a function approaches but never actually touches is defined as an **asymptote**. In this case, the asymptote is horizontal, but asymptotes can also be vertical. The x-axis, or $f(x) = 0$, is the horizontal asymptote for $f(x) = b^x$. The graphs of the family of functions $f(x) = b^x$ all have a y-intercept at the point (0, 1). The graphs do not cross the x-axis and therefore do not have an x-intercept.

The end behavior of exponential functions is determined by the value of b in the equation.

If $b > 1$, then	If $0 < b < 1$, then
as $x \rightarrow -\infty$, $y \rightarrow 0$.	as $x \rightarrow -\infty$, $y \rightarrow \infty$.
as $x \rightarrow \infty$, $y \rightarrow \infty$.	as $x \rightarrow \infty$, $y \rightarrow 0$.

You can observe these behaviors in the graphs below.

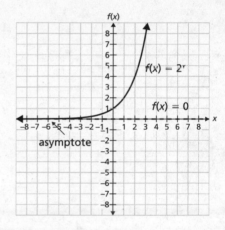 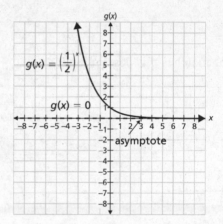

Example

In which of the following equations would you observe end behavior such that as x-values approached negative infinity, y-values would approach 0?

A) $f(x) = x^2 + 4x + \dfrac{1}{4}$

B) $f(x) = \left(\dfrac{1}{4}\right)^x$

C) $f(x) = 4^x$

D) $f(x) = \left(\dfrac{2}{3}\right)^x$

Solution

Immediately eliminate answer choice A. It is quadratic, not exponential, so its y-values do not approach 0 in its end behavior. To observe the end behavior described, the value of b in an exponential function must be greater than 1. The only possible choice is C.

Answer: C

1. Which qualities are observable on the graph of $f(x) = \left(\dfrac{1}{3}\right)^x$?

   A) The graph is increasing and has horizontal asymptote $y = \dfrac{1}{3}$.

   B) The graph is increasing and has horizontal asymptote $y = 0$.

   C) The graph is decreasing and has horizontal asymptote $y = \dfrac{1}{3}$.

   D) The graph is decreasing and has horizontal asymptote $y = 0$.

Strategy: Since the value of b is between 0 and 1, the graph will be decreasing. This eliminates answer choices A and B. All graphs derived from the parent function $f(x) = b^x$ will have a horizontal asymptote at $y = 0$. The correct answer is choice D.

2. An exponential graph has the following qualities:

   - It is increasing.

   - Horizontal asymptote at $y = 0$.

   - As $x \to \infty$, $y \to \infty$.

   Which of the following graphs matches this description?

   A)
   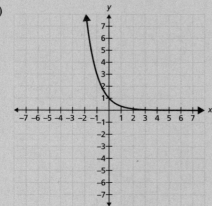

   B)
   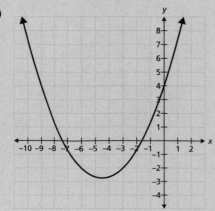

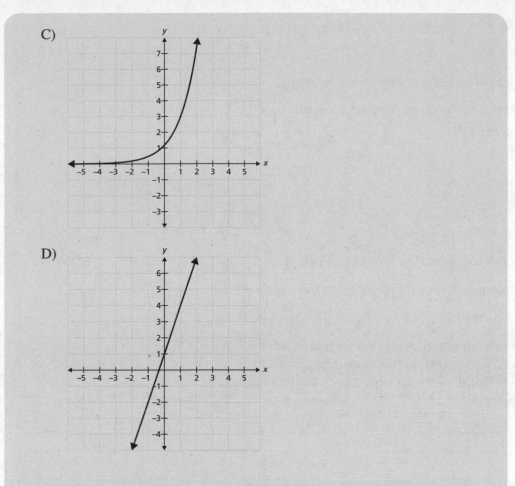

C)

D)

Strategy: Graphs B and D are not exponential, so eliminate those choices. We are looking for a graph that is increasing rather than decreasing. Of the remaining choices, C is increasing.

Relationship Between Zeros and Factors of a Polynomial Function

When a binomial expression $(x - a)$ is a factor of a polynomial $f(x)$, then $f(a) = 0$. We call the value a a root or a zero of the function. We previously made use of this relationship to factor quadratic equations. For example, the polynomial $f(x) = x^2 + 5x + 6$ has factors of $(x + 3)$ and $(x + 2)$. The roots are $x = -3$ and $x = -2$. If we evaluate $f(x)$ at $x = -3$, then $f(-3) = (-3)^2 + 5(-3) + 6 = 0$. We would observe the same result if we evaluated $f(-2)$. Generally, if we let $f(x) = k(x - a_1)(x - a_2)...(x - a_n)$ be the factored form of an nth degree polynomial, setting x equal to any of the values $a_1, a_2, ..., a_n$ results in $f(x) = 0$. We can use this information to solve certain types of questions on the SAT.

Example 1

The function f is defined by $f(x) = 2x^3 + x^2 + cx + 6$, where c is a constant.

The graph of f has three x-intercepts in the xy-plane. They are the points $\left(\frac{1}{2}, 0\right)$, $(2, 0)$, and $(p, 0)$. What is the value of c?

A) 13

B) 11

C) −11

D) −13

Solution

Begin by making sense of the information given. The points $\left(\frac{1}{2}, 0\right)$, $(2, 0)$, and $(p, 0)$ are the zeros of the polynomial. Then, using those zeros and substituting y for $f(x)$, we can rewrite the function as $y = \left(x - \frac{1}{2}\right)(x - 2)(x - p)$.

Choose one of the numeric zeros to substitute back into the original equation $f(x) = 2x^3 + x^2 + cx + 6$. The point $(2, 0)$ is easiest, so substitute 0 for y and 2 for x. Then, $0 = 2(2)^3 + 2^2 + 2c + 6$ and $0 = 16 + 4 + 2c + 6$. Collecting the like terms and isolating the variable yields $2c = -26$ and $c = -13$.

Answer: D

Example 2

The function f is defined by $f(x) = 6x^3 - 5x^2 + bx + 1$. The graph of f has three x-intercepts in the xy-plane. They are the points $\left(\frac{1}{3}, 0\right)$, $(1, 0)$, and $(-c, 0)$. What is the value of c?

Solution

We are being asked to find the value of the unknown x-intercept, c, not the unknown value of the parameter in the function. Since the zeros of f are $\frac{1}{3}$, 1, and c, we can begin by rewriting the original equation in factored form:

$f(x) = k\left(x - \frac{1}{3}\right)(x - 1)(x + c) = 6x^3 - 5x^2 + bx + 1$. Now, we know $k = 6$ since the product $k \cdot x \cdot x \cdot x = 6x^3$. We can find c, since the product of $k, -\frac{1}{3}, -1$, and

$-(-c)$ combine to produce the constant term, 1. So, $(6)\left(-\frac{1}{3}\right)(-1)(c) = 1$ and

$2(-c) = 1$. Solve and find $c = \frac{1}{2}$.

1. The function f is defined by $f(x) = x^3 - 2x^2 + cx + 2$, where c is a constant. The graph of f has three x-intercepts in the xy-plane. They are the points $(1, 0)$, $(-1, 0)$, and $(p, 0)$. What is the value of c?

   A) -2

   B) -1

   C) 1

   D) 2

Strategy: To find the value of c in the original function, you can choose one of the known numeric x-intercepts to substitute back into the equation and solve for c. The easiest point is (1, 0). Then, $0 = (1)^3 - 2(1)^2 + (1)c + 2$. Collect the like terms and solve for c to find that $c = -1$. As an alternate solution strategy, you can substitute each of the values from the answer choices in the original function until a true statement results.

2. The function f is defined by $f(x) = 3x^3 - 5x^2 + bx + 4$. The graph of f has three x-intercepts in the xy-plane. They are the points $\left(\frac{2}{3}, 0\right)$, $(2, 0)$, and $(c, 0)$. What is the value of b?

   A) -4

   B) -3

   C) 3

   D) 4

Strategy: One way we could solve this problem is to use the given x-intercepts and substitute y for $f(x)$, then rewrite the function as $y = k\left(x - \frac{2}{3}\right)(x - 2)(x - c)$.

We know $k \cdot x \cdot x \cdot x = 3x^3$; therefore $k = 3$. Then, $k \cdot \left(-\dfrac{2}{3}\right)(-2)(-c) = 4$

(the constant term). Solving for c, $4(-c) = 4$. and $c = -1$. Now, substitute

the value of c back into the original equation: $y = 3\left(x - \dfrac{2}{3}\right)(x - 2)(x + 1)$.

Multiply the two easier binomials: $y = 3\left(x^2 - x - 2\right)\left(x - \dfrac{2}{3}\right)$. Distribute the 3 and

$\left(3x^2 - 3x - 6\right)\left(x - \dfrac{2}{3}\right)$. The coefficient of $b = \left(-3 \cdot -\dfrac{2}{3}\right) + (-6 \cdot 1) = 2 - 6 = -4$.

This is answer choice A. You can also solve this problem directly by selecting the given zero (2, 0) and substituting the values back into the original function f and solving for b.

SAT-Type Questions

Answers begin on page 706.

1. Which of the following equations is represented by the graph below?

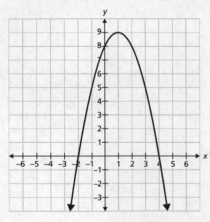

A) $f(x) = x^2 - 2x - 8$

B) $f(x) = -(x^2 - 2x - 8)$

C) $f(x) = -x^2 - 2x - 8$

D) $f(x) = x^2 + 2x - 8$

2. Which curve is the graph of the function $f(x) = -x^2 + 2x + 3$?

A)

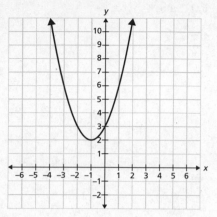

B)

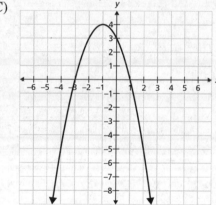

C)

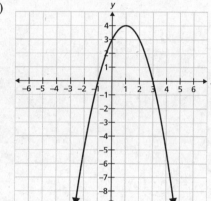

D)

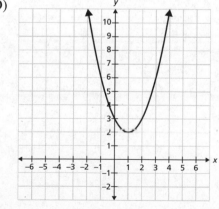

3. The function f is defined by $f(x) = 2x^3 + x^2 + cx$, where c is a constant. The graph of f has three x-intercepts in the xy-plane. They are the points $\left(\frac{1}{2}, 0\right)$, $(-1, 0)$, and $(p, 0)$. What is the value of c?

A) -3
B) -2
C) -1
D) 1

4. What equation does the graph below represent?

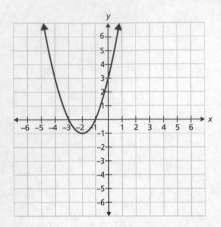

A) $f(x) = x^2 + 4x + 3$
B) $f(x) = x^2 - 4x + 3$
C) $f(x) = -x^2 + 4x + 3$
D) $f(x) = -x^2 - 4x + 3$

5. The function f is defined by $f(x) = 3x^3 - 2x^2 + cx$, where c is a constant. The graph of f has three x-intercepts in the xy-plane. They are the points $\left(-\frac{1}{3}, 0\right)$, $(1, 0)$, and $(p, 0)$. What is the value of p?

A) 1
B) $\frac{1}{3}$
C) $-\frac{1}{3}$
D) 0

6. Which equation does the parabola in the graph represent?

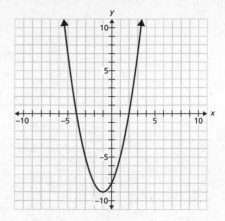

A) $f(x) = -x^2 - 2x - 8$

B) $f(x) = x^2 - 2x - 8$

C) $f(x) = -x^2 + 2x + 8$

D) $f(x) = x^2 + 2x - 8$

7. What equation does the graph below represent?

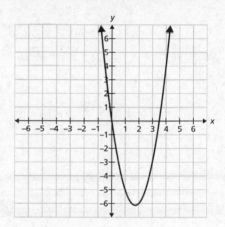

A) $f(x) = \dfrac{7}{4}x^2$

B) $f(x) = 2x^2 + 7x$

C) $f(x) = 2x^2 - 7x$

D) $f(x) = \dfrac{-4}{7}x^2$

8. The function f is defined by $f(x) = 2x^3 - x^2 + bx + 1$. The graph of f has three x-intercepts in the xy-plane. They are the points $\left(\dfrac{1}{2}, 0\right)$, $(-1, 0)$, and $(c, 0)$. What is the value of c?

A) -1

B) $-\dfrac{1}{2}$

C) $\dfrac{1}{2}$

D) 1

9. What equation does the graph below represent?

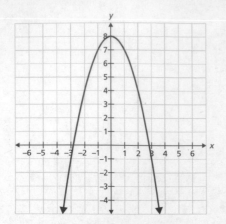

A) $f(x) = x^2 + 8x$

B) $f(x) = -x^2 - 8x$

C) $f(x) = x^2 + 8$

D) $f(x) = -x^2 + 8$

10. Which curve is the graph of the function $f(x) = -2x^2 - 6x$?

A)

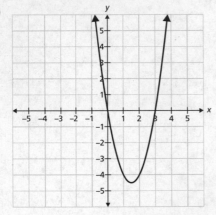

B)

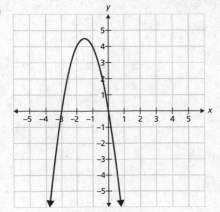

C)

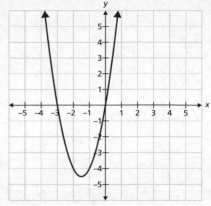

D)

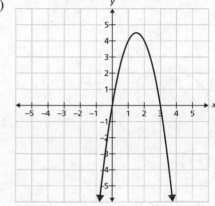

11. The function f is defined by $f(x) = 6x^3 + 5x^2 + bx - 2$. The graph of f has three x-intercepts in the xy-plane. They are the points $\left(-\dfrac{1}{2}, 0\right)$, $\left(\dfrac{2}{3}, 0\right)$, and $(c, 0)$. What is the value of c?

A) 1

B) $\dfrac{1}{2}$

C) $-\dfrac{2}{3}$

D) -1

Student-Produced Response Questions

12. The axis of symmetry for $f(x) = 2x^2 - 3x + 4$ is $x = k$. What is the value of k?

13. The function $f(t)$, which describes projectile height for a ball thrown by a strong player, as a function of time measured in seconds, obeys the equation $f(t) - 53.7 = -5.3(t-3)^2$. After how many seconds will the ball return to the height from which it was thrown?

14. The horizontal asymptote for $f(x) = 3^x + 8$ is $y = k$. What is the value of k?

15. The function f is defined by $f(x) = 3x^3 - 10x^2 + cx$, where c is a constant. The graph of f has three x-intercepts in the xy-plane. They are the points $(3,0)$, $\left(\frac{1}{3},0\right)$, and $(p,0)$. What is the value of c?

LESSON 6:

Solving Systems of Equations Involving One Linear and at Least One Higher-Order Equation

- ■ Graphic Solutions to Quadratic-Linear Systems

- ■ Algebraic Solutions to Quadratic-Linear Systems

- ■ Solutions for Higher Order Systems

· · · · · · **Explain** **Graphic Solutions to Quadratic-Linear Systems** · · · · · · ·

The graphic solution of a quadratic-linear system is the intersection or intersections of the graph of the quadratic function and the graph of the linear function. To find the intersection(s), read the x- and y-coordinates off the axes. You can check that your intersection points are correct by substituting your solutions into the original equations. Note that the solution set may consist of two points, one point, or no points as shown below.

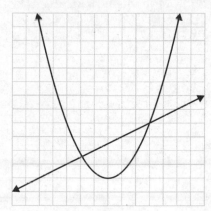

Two Solutions

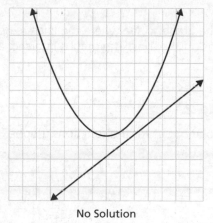

One Solution

No Solution

Example 1

Find the solution set for the functions graphed below:

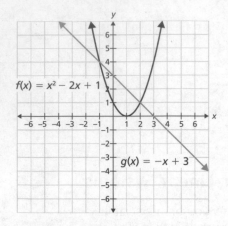

$f(x) = x^2 - 2x + 1$

$g(x) = -x + 3$

A) {(−1,4), (2,1), (1,0), (3,0)}

B) {(−1,4), (2,1)}

C) {(1,0), (3,0)}

D) {(−1,4), (2,1), (1,0), (3,0), (0,1), (0,3)}

Solution

Examine the graph to see where the line crosses the parabola, then read the coordinates off the axes. The graphs intersect at the points (−1,4) and (2,1).

Answer: B

Example 2

Find the solution set for the functions graphed below:

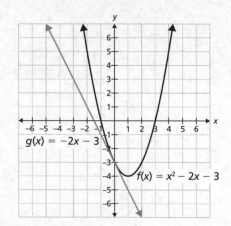

$g(x) = -2x - 3$

$f(x) = x^2 - 2x - 3$

A) No Solution

B) {(−3, 0)}

C) {(−1.5, 0), (−1,0), (3,0)}

D) {(0, −3)}

Solution

Examine the graph to see where the line crosses the parabola, then read the coordinates off the axes. The graphs intersect at (0, −3).

Answer: D

Answers begin on page 708.

1. How many coordinate pairs are in the solution set for the system shown below?

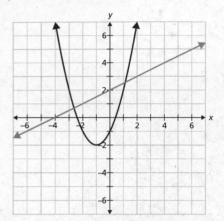

   A) 0
   B) 1
   C) 2
   D) 3

2. How many coordinate pairs are in the solution set for the system shown below?

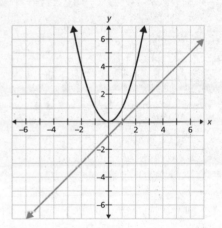

   A) 0
   B) 1
   C) 2
   D) 3

3. Find the solution set for the system of equations shown below.

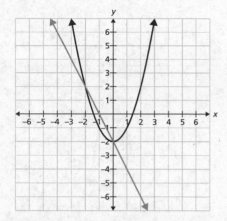

   A) $\{(-1.5,0), (-1,0), (1.5,0)\}$
   B) $\{(-2,2), (-1.5,0), (-1,0), (1.5,0), (0,-2)\}$
   C) $\{(-2,2), (0,-2)\}$
   D) $\{(-2,2), (0, 2), (2,0)\}$

1. Which of the following graphs shows the solution to the system
   $f(x) = x^2 + 2x + 3$ and $g(x) = x - 3$?

A)

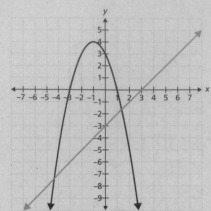

B)

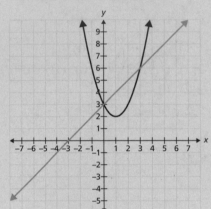

C)

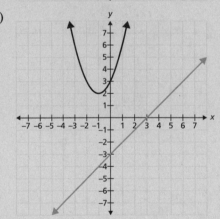

D)

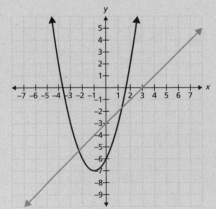

Strategy: In order to solve this problem, you must verify that the graph matches the functions in the question. It is easier to check the linear function first. We can eliminate choice B because the y-intercept is incorrect. Now examine the quadratic function. Choice A is incorrect since the graph of the quadratic should have a minimum and this graph shows a maximum. We are left with C and D. Choose an easy point from the graph of answer choice C and substitute it into the equation to see if a true statement is returned. If we pick (0, 3), then $f(x) = x^2 + 2x + 3$ and $f(0) = 0^2 + 2(0) + 3 = 3$. This is a true statement, so choose answer C.

2. The vertices of a triangle T are the origin and the solution set of the functions $f(x) = x^2 + 3x + 2$ and $g(x) = x + 2$, shown below. What is the area of triangle T?

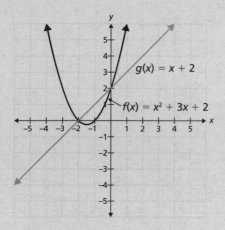

A) 2

B) 4

C) $\{(0, 2), (2, 0)\}$

D) $2\sqrt{2}$

Strategy: Begin by reading the coordinates of the solutions to the system off the given graph: $\{(0, 2), (-2, 0)\}$. Now the points of the triangle's vertices are the set $\{(0, 0), (0, 2), (-2, 0)\}$. The base of the triangle is 2, the distance from $(-2, 0)$ to $(0,0)$. The height of the triangle is 2, the distance from $(0, 2)$ to the origin. Then $A = \dfrac{b \cdot h}{2} = \dfrac{2 \cdot 2}{2} = 2$. This is answer choice A.

Explain Algebraic Solutions to Quadratic-Linear Systems

The process to find algebraic solutions to a quadratic-linear system is handled the same way as solutions to linear-linear systems. Depending on the problem, you can use the substitution method or the elimination method.

Solving quadratic-linear systems using the <u>substitution</u> method is a 4-step process.

(1) Solve the linear equation for one of the variables, x or y. Solving for either variable will work.

(2) Substitute this expression for the appropriate variable in the quadratic equation.

(3) Solve the quadratic equation.

(4) Substitute the solutions found in step 3 in the linear equation and solve.

Solving quadratic-linear systems using the <u>elimination</u> method is a 3-step process. In many cases, this method is faster than the substitution method.

(1) Add the two equations to eliminate one variable, y. You may need to add an opposite (subtract). If necessary, first write an equivalent equation for one or both of the original equations.

(2) The sum will be a quadratic equation in one variable, x. Solve it.

(3) Substitute the solutions in the original linear equation and solve.

Think It Through

For example 1 and example 2, we will solve the same question. In example 1, we will solve using the substitution method. In example 2, we will solve using the elimination method.

Example 1

Solve the following system of equations.

$$y = x^2 - 4x + 4$$
$$2y = x + 4$$

A) $\left\{\left(\dfrac{9}{4}, \dfrac{1}{2}\right)\right\}$

B) $\{(4,4)\}$

C) $\left\{\left(\dfrac{1}{2}, \dfrac{9}{4}\right), (4,4)\right\}$

D) $\left\{\left(\dfrac{9}{4}, \dfrac{1}{2}\right), (4,4)\right\}$

Solution: To use the <u>substitution</u> method, we need to solve one of the equations for one of the variables. Since the x term is squared in the quadratic equation, we will solve the linear equation for y. Then, $2y = x + 4$ and $y = \dfrac{x}{2} + 2$.

Substitute this expression for y in the quadratic equation: $\dfrac{x}{2} + 2 = x^2 - 4x + 4$

Clear the fraction by multiplying both sides by 2: $2\left(\dfrac{x}{2} + 2 = x^2 - 4x + 4\right) =$

$$x + 4 = 2x^2 - 8x + 8$$

$$0 = 2x^2 - 9x + 4$$
$$0 = (2x - 1)(x - 4)$$

Collect the like terms and factor to solve: $(2x - 1) = 0, \ (x - 4) = 0$

$$x = \dfrac{1}{2}, \ x = 4$$

Substitute both *x*-values in the linear equation to find the corresponding *y*-values:

If $x = \dfrac{1}{2}$

$2y = x + 4$

$2y = \dfrac{1}{2} + 4$

$2y = \dfrac{9}{2}$

$y = \dfrac{9}{4}$

If $x = 4$

$2y = x + 4$

$2y = 4 + 4$

$2y = 8$

$y = 4$

The solution to the system is $\left\{ \left(\dfrac{1}{2}, \dfrac{9}{4} \right), (4, 4) \right\}$.

Answer: C

Example 2

Solve the following system of equations.

$y = x^2 - 4x + 4$

$2y = x + 4$

A) $\left\{ \left(\dfrac{9}{4}, \dfrac{1}{2} \right) \right\}$

B) $\{(4, 4)\}$

C) $\left\{ \left(\dfrac{1}{2}, \dfrac{9}{4} \right), (4, 4) \right\}$

D) $\left\{ \left(\dfrac{9}{4}, \dfrac{1}{2} \right), (4, 4) \right\}$

Solution

To use the elimination method:

1. To eliminate *y*, multiply all terms in the quadratic equation by 2 and add the two equations.

$2y = 2x^2 - 8x + 8$

$\underline{-2y = \qquad - x - 4}$

$0 = 2x^2 - 9x + 4$

2. Solve the new quadratic equation.

$2x^2 - 9x + 4 = (2x - 1)(x - 4) = 0$

$2x - 1 = 0 \quad x - 4 = 0$

$x = \dfrac{1}{2} \quad x = 4$

3. Proceed as in the substitution method.

Answer: C

1. Solve the system $y = x^2 - 4$ and $y = x + 2$.

   A) $\{(3, 5)\}$

   B) $\{(3, 5), (-2, 0)\}$

   C) $\{(3, 5), (2, 0)\}$

   D) $\{(-3, -1), (-2, 0)\}$

Strategy: Note that both of the given equations are already solved for the variable y. Use the substitution method and set the equations equal to each other since they are both equal to y. Then, $x^2 - 4 = x + 2$. Now collect the like terms and factor to solve. So, $x^2 - x - 6 = 0$ and $(x - 3)(x + 2) = 0$. The x-coordinates of the solution set are 3 and −2. Use the linear equation to substitute each of the x-values back to find the y-values. Now, $y = x + 2$, $y = 3 + 2$, $y = 5$ and $y = x + 2$, $y = -2 + 2$, $y = 0$. The solution set is $\{(3, 5), (-2, 0)\}$. This is answer choice B.

2. Consider the following system:

   $$x^2 + y^2 = 416$$

   $$y = -5x$$

   If (x, y) is a solution to the system, what is the value of x^2?

   A) 4

   B) 16

   C) 26

   D) 36

Strategy: The linear equation is already solved for y. Substitute its value into the non-linear equation. Then, $x^2 + y^2 = 416$, $x^2 + (-5x)^2 = 416$ and $x^2 + 25x^2 = 416$. Collect the like terms and isolate the variable to find the value of x^2. Now, $26x^2 = 416$, $x^2 = 16$. Select answer choice B.

Explain Solutions for Higher Order Systems

A system may be made up of more than two functions or may include graphs of relations that are not functions. On the SAT, you may be presented with graphs of these systems and asked to find the number of solutions. Keep in mind that like the quadratic-linear systems, the solution set is the set of points common to all functions and relations shown.

Which of the following answer choices represents the solution(s) to the given system?

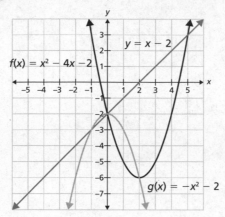

A) $\{(-1, -3), (0, -2), (5, 0)\}$

B) $\{(-1, -3), (0, -2), (5, 0), (2, -6)\}$

C) $\{(-1.5, 0), (2, 0), (4.5, 0)\}$

D) $\{(0, -2)\}$

Solution

We are looking for the point that is common to all three functions. The only such point is $(0, -2)$.

Answer: D

Model SAT Questions

1. A system of three equations and their graphs in the *xy*-plane are shown below. How many solutions does the system have?

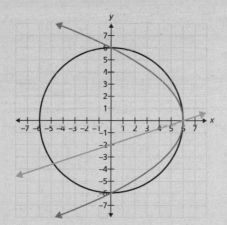

$$x^2 + y^2 = 36$$

$$y^2 + 6x = 36$$

$$y = \frac{x}{3} - 2$$

A) One

B) Two

C) Three

D) Four

2. A system of three equations and their graphs in the xy-plane are shown below. How many solutions does the system have?

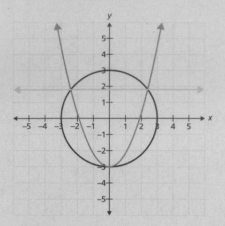

$$x^2 + y^2 = 9$$

$$5x^2 - 6y = 18$$

$$y = \frac{9}{5}$$

A) One
B) Two
C) Three
D) Four

•••• SAT-Type Questions ••••••••••••••••••••••••••••••

Answers begin on page 708.

1. Solve the system $y = -x^2 - 4x + 1$ and $y - 2x = 10$.

A) $\{(-3, 4)\}$
B) $\{(-3, 4), (3, 16)\}$
C) $\{(9, 28)\}$
D) $\{(-9, -8), (9, 28)\}$

2. Which graph shows the solution set for the system $3x + 2y = 6$ and $y = x^2 - 4x + 3$?

A)

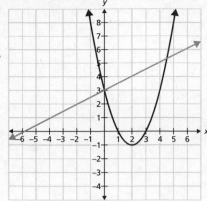

B)

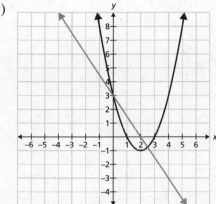

C)

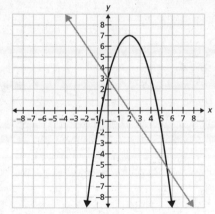

D)

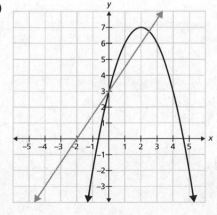

3. Solve the system $y = \frac{1}{2}x^2 + 3x - 2$ and $y = 4x - \frac{1}{2}$.

   A) $\{(3, -1)\}$
   B) $\{(3, 11.5), (1, 3.5)\}$
   C) $\{(3, 11.5), (-1, -4.5)\}$
   D) $\{(-4.5, 11.5)\}$

4. $x^2 + y^2 = 180$

   $y = -2x$

   If (x, y) is a solution to the system above, what is the value of x^2?

   A) 6
   B) 9
   C) 25
   D) 36

5. Which graph shows the solution set for the system $f(x) = x^2 - 2x$ and $g(x) = x + 4$?

   A)

   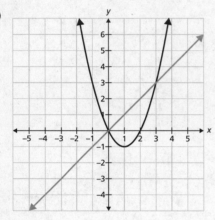

   B)

   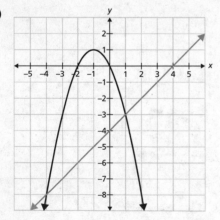

C)

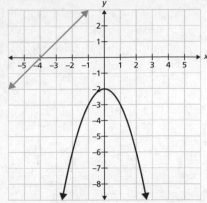

D)

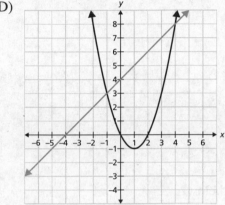

6. $x^2 + y^2 = 234$

$x + y = 18$

Find the solution set for the system above.

A) $\{(-3, 21)\}$

B) $\{(15, 3)\}$

C) $\{(15, 3), (-3, 21)\}$

D) $\{(15, 3), (3, 15)\}$

7. A system of three equations and their graphs in the *xy*-plane are shown below. How many solutions does the system have?

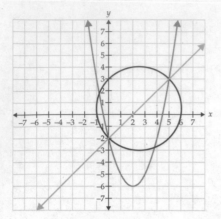

A) One

B) Two

C) Three

D) Four

Student-Produced Response Questions

8. How many coordinate pairs are in the solution set for the system shown below?

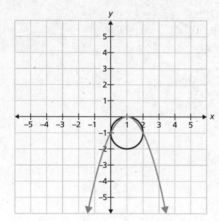

9. $x^2 + y^2 = 45$

   $y = -2x$

   If (x, y) is a solution to the system above, what is the value of y^2?

10. A system of three equations and their graphs in the xy-plane are shown below.
    How many solutions does the system have?

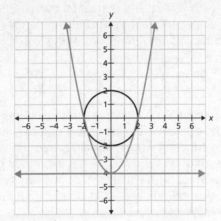

LESSON 7:

Transformation and Composition of Functions

- Transformations
- Composition of Functions
- Transformations and Composition of Functions

<hr>

Explain Transformations

In mathematics, **transformations** take the original graph of a parent function, such as $y = x$, $y = x^2$, or $y = |x|$, and translate it by moving it about the coordinate plane. Transformations can also change the shape of a graph, reflect the original parent graph, or cause any combination of these. A graph can be translated vertically or horizontally, it can be stretched or compressed, or it can be reflected over either the x- or y-axis. Graphs can also be reflected over lines drawn in the coordinate plane such as $y = x$. On the SAT, you will need to be familiar with vertical and horizontal translations, stretching and compressing of parent graphs, and reflection of parent graphs over the x-axis. Note that horizontal translations are addressed in the context of composition of functions in the last section of this lesson.

Vertical Translations:

Vertical translations move the parent graph of a function or relation up or down in the coordinate plane. If you have a constant function, say, $h(x) = n$, where the domain is the set of real numbers and the range is the set $\{n\}$, and you add that to $g(x)$, which is any function whose domain is also the set of real numbers, then you create $f(x)$, which is equal to the sum of $g(x)$ and $h(x)$. This is expressed by the equation $f(x) = g(x) + h(x)$. But remember that $h(x)$ is a constant term equal to n. So we can say that $f(x) = g(x) + n$. Note that the function $f(x)$ will also have the real numbers as its domain. For each value of x, $f(x)$ is $|n|$ more or less than $g(x)$.

Formally, the vertical translation rule is that for any function g:

- If $h(x) = n$, a constant, and $f(x) = g(x) + h(x) = g(x) + n$, then the graph of $f(x)$ is the graph of $g(x)$ translated n units in the vertical direction.

Stretching and Compressing:

Stretching or compressing alters the size. If we let $h(x) = n$ be a positive constant function and $g(x)$ is any function whose domain is the set of real numbers, then $f(x) = g(x) \cdot h(x)$ is the stretch or compression of $g(x)$. For each value of x, $f(x)$ is n times the value of $g(x)$. The graph of $f(x)$ is the graph of $g(x)$ stretched by a factor of n in the vertical direction if n is greater than 1. This is because $f(x)$ gets taller faster than $g(x)$. The graph of $f(x)$ is the graph of $g(x)$ compressed by a factor of n in the vertical direction if n is less than 1. This is because $f(x)$ gets taller slower than $g(x)$. The domain of $f(x)$ is the set of real numbers.

Formally, the stretching/compressing rule is that for any function g:

- If $h(x) = n$, a positive constant, and $f(x) = g(x) \cdot h(x) = h(x) \cdot g(x)$, then $f(x) = n \cdot g(x)$. The graph of $f(x)$ is the graph of $g(x)$ stretched by a factor of n in the vertical direction when $n > 1$ and compressed in the vertical direction by a factor of n when $0 < n < 1$.

Reflections over the *x*-axis:

A reflection is a transformation that creates a mirror image of the line or curve across a line known as the axis of reflection. In this case, the axis of reflection is the *x*-axis. If we let $h(x) = -1$, then the domain of h is the set of real numbers and the range of h is $\{-1\}$. Now let $g(x)$ be any function whose domain is the set of real numbers. Then $f(x) = g(x) \cdot h(x) = g(x) \cdot (-1) = -1 \cdot g(x)$. Since, for each value of *x*, $f(x)$ is $-1 \cdot g(x)$, $f(x)$ is the opposite of $g(x)$, and the graph of $f(x)$ is the graph of $g(x)$ reflected over the *x*-axis. The domain of $f(x)$ is the set of real numbers.

 Think It Through

Example 1

Let $g(x) = |x|$ and $h(x) = 2$. Let $f(x) = g(x) + h(x) = |x| + 2$. Which graph is a representation of $f(x)$?

A)
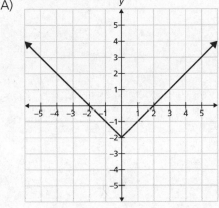

B)
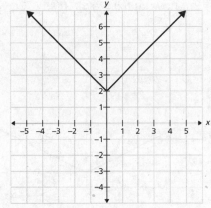

C)
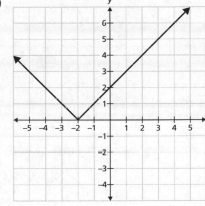

D)
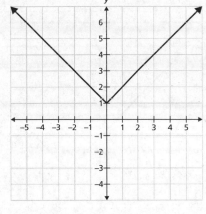

Solution

We are told that $f(x) = g(x) + h(x) = |x| + 2$. This means that the graph of $f(x)$ is the graph of $g(x)$ translated 2 positive units in the vertical direction. The graph below shows the parent graph, $g(x) = |x|$, and the translation $f(x) = |x| + 2$. Graphs A and C are translated in the wrong direction, so eliminate those answer choices. Graph D is moved 1 unit in the positive vertical direction, so it is not correct. Select answer choice B.

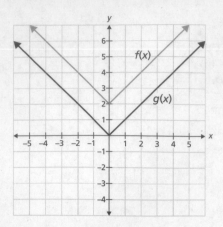

Answer: B

Example 2

Let $g(x) = |x|$ and $h(x) = 2$ as in example 1. But now let $f(x) = g(x) \cdot h(x)$.
Which graph is a representation of $f(x)$?

A)

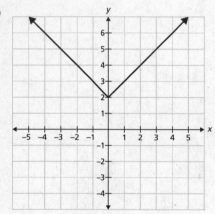

B)

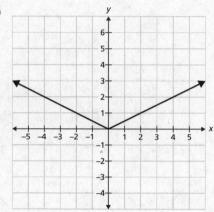

C)

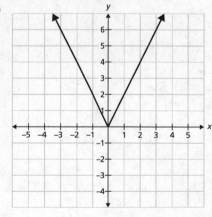

D)

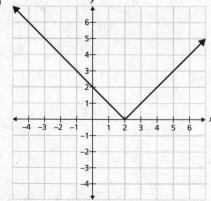

Solution

In this case, since $f(x) = g(x) \cdot h(x) = |x| \cdot 2$ or $2 \cdot |x|$, we are looking for a stretch of $g(x)$. Examine the answer choices. Graph A is a vertical translation. Graph B is a compression of $g(x) = |x|$. Graph C looks like a stretch, but check graph D to be sure. Graph D is a horizontal translation.

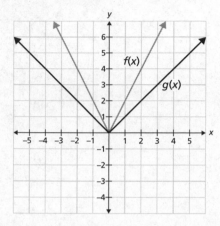

Answer: C

Example 3

Let $g(x) - |x|$ and $h(x) - 0.5$. Let $f(x) = g(x)$ $h(x)$. Which graph is a representation of $f(x)$?

A)

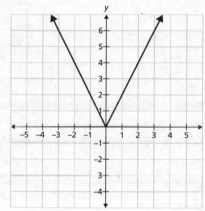

B)

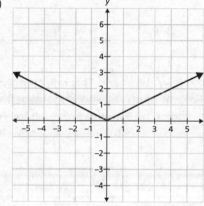

C)

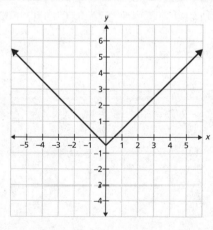

D)

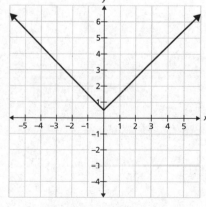

Solution

In this case, $f(x) = g(x) \cdot h(x) = |x| \cdot (0.5)$ or $(0.5) \cdot |x|$. This is a compression of $g(x)$. If we examine the answer choices, we see that Graph A is a stretch and graphs C and D are vertical translations. Answer choice B is the compression.

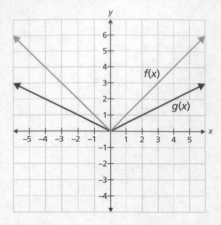

Answer: B

Example 4

Let $g(x) = |x|$ and $h(x) = -1$. Let $f(x) = g(x) \cdot h(x)$. Which coordinate pair would the graph of $f(x)$ pass through?

A) (2, 0)
B) (−2, 2)
C) (0, 2)
D) (2, −2)

Solution

The graph of $f(x)$ is the graph of $g(x)$ reflected over the *x*-axis. This reflection will change all the signs on all the *y*-values. The graph of $g(x)$ has only non-negative values for *y*, and answer choice D is the only choice with a negative value for *y*.

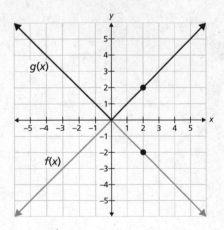

Answer: D

Answers begin on page 709.

1. Let $g(x) = x^2$ and $h(x) = -1$. Let $f(x) = g(x) + h(x) = x^2 - 1$. Which graph is a representation of $f(x)$?

A)
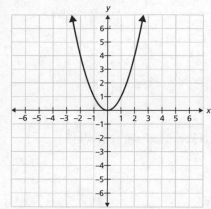

B)
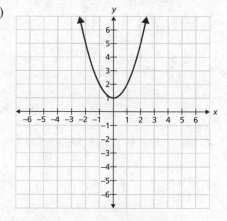

C)
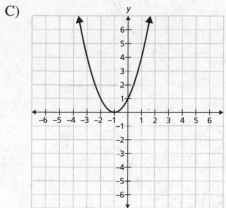

D)
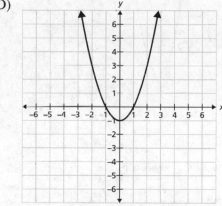

2. Let $g(x) = 2^x$ and $h(x) = 1$. Let $f(x) = g(x) + h(x) = 2^x + 1$. Which graph is a representation of $f(x)$?

A)
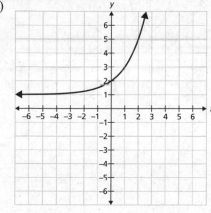

B)
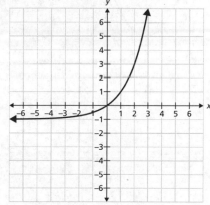

C)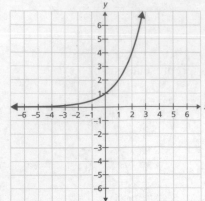

D)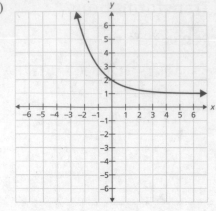

3. Let $g(x) = x^2$ and $h(x) = 0.5$. Let $f(x) = g(x) \cdot h(x) = 0.5x^2$. Which graph is a representation of $f(x)$?

A)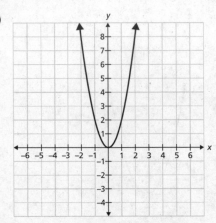

B)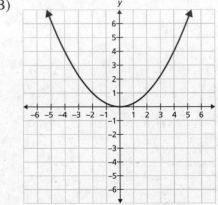

C)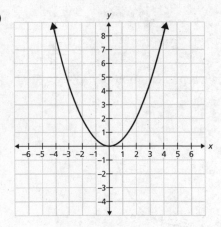

D)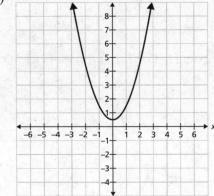

1. Let $g(x) = x^2$ and $h(x) = 4$. Let $f(x) = g(x) \cdot h(x)$. Which point is on the graph of $f(x)$?

   A) $(0, 4)$

   B) $(-1, 4)$

   C) $(4, 1)$

   D) $(1, -4)$

Strategy: If $f(x) = g(x) \cdot h(x)$, then $f(x) = 4x^2$. Now take each of the given points and substitute in the values of x to see if a true statement results. Then $f(0) = 4(0)^2$ is not equal to 4. Eliminate answer choice A. Go to answer choice B: $f(-1) = 4(-1)^2 = 4$. This is a true statement. Stop checking and select answer choice B.

2. Let $g(x) = x^2$ and $h(x) = -1$. Let $f(x) = g(x) \cdot h(x)$. Which coordinate would the graph of $f(x)$ pass through?

   A) $(-1, -1)$

   B) $(-4, -2)$

   C) $(2, -1)$

   D) $(2, 4)$

Strategy: Since $f(x) = g(x) \cdot h(x)$, $f(x) = -x^2$. This is a reflection of the parent function over the x-axis. Reflecting over the x-axis will reverse the signs of all the y-coordinates, but x-coordinates will remain the same. You can substitute in the given x-values and solve to see if a true statement results. You can also reason that the correct y-value must be negative while the x-value remains unchanged. The only answer that makes sense is choice A.

Explain Composition of Functions

Composition of functions is a process in which we combine two functions. One function is performed first and the result of the first function is substituted in place of x in the second function. For example, if we let $g(x) = x + 2$ and $h(x) = x^2$, the composite function $f(x) = $ is the set of ordered pairs $(x, f(x))$ that result from mapping x to $g(x)$ and $g(x)$ to $h(x)$. It is the set of ordered pairs $(x, f(x))$ that is the **composition** of the two functions.

The notations for composition of functions are $f(x) = h(g(x))$ or $f(x) = (h \cdot g)(x)$. The function g is applied first, followed by the function h. We evaluate the composition of functions from right to left. Keep in mind that if the left function has a restricted domain, the domain of the right function must be restricted so that its range is a subset of the domain of the left function. Note that composition of functions is not commutative. Composition is not multiplication. It is not necessarily true that $h(g(x)) = g(h(x))$. For example, if we let $g(x) = x + 2$ and $h(x) = x^2$ as we did above and defined $k(x) = g(h(x))$, then evaluating right to left, $k(x) = g(x^2) = x^2 + 2$ and is not equal to $f(x) = (x + 2)^2$.

Example 1

Let $p(x) = x + 4$ and $q(x) = \sqrt{x}$. If $f(x) = q(p(x))$, find $f(5)$.

A) 2
B) 3
C) ±3
D) $\sqrt{5} + 4$

Solution

First, create the function $f(x)$ from $q(x)$ and $p(x)$. Work from right to left; $q(p(x))$ means $q(x)$ evaluated at $p(x)$. So add 4 to x, giving $x + 4$, and then take the square root of that. This means $f(x) = q(p(x)) = \sqrt{x + 4}$ and $f(5) = q(p(5)) = \sqrt{5 + 4} = \sqrt{9} = 3$.

Answer: B

Example 2

Let $p(x) = x + 4$ and $q(x) = \sqrt{x}$ as in example 1. What restriction must be placed on $p(x)$ if the functions are defined for real numbers only?

A) The range of $p(x)$ must be non-negative.
B) The range of $p(x)$ must be positive.
C) The domain of $p(x)$ must be non-negative.
D) The domain of $p(x)$ must be positive.

Solution

For real number solutions, the domain of $q(x) = \sqrt{x}$ must be non-negative. The domain of $q(x)$ is the range of $p(x)$, which is evaluated first. Therefore, the range of $p(x)$ must be non-negative.

Answer: A

Practice Composition of Functions

Answers begin on page 709.

1. Let $p(x) = x^2 - 5x + 6$ and $q(x) = 4x$.

   If $f(x) = p(q(x))$, find $f(1)$.

   A) 5
   B) 3
   C) 2
   D) 0

2. Let $p(x) = \dfrac{2x}{x+1}$ and $q(x) = x^2 - 5$.

   If $f(x) = p(q(x))$, find $f(4)$.

   A) $\dfrac{11}{6}$
   B) 2
   C) 1
   D) $\dfrac{1}{2}$

1. Let $p(x) = x^2$ and $q(x) = 3x$. Which of the following statements is not true?

   A) $p(q(x)) = 9x^2$

   B) $q(p(x)) = 3x^2$

   C) The domains of both $p(x)$ and $q(x)$ are all real numbers.

   D) $p(q(x)) = q(p(x))$ for all real numbers.

Strategy: Begin by determining $p(q(x))$ and $q(p(x))$. We find that $p(q(x)) = 9x^2$ and $q(p(x)) = 3x^2$, so statements A and B are true. Answer choice C is also true. The compositions $p(q(x))$ and $q(p(x))$. are clearly not equal, so select answer choice D.

2. If $h(x) = \sqrt{x+10}$ and $g(x) = x^2 + 10$, find $(g \cdot h)(6)$.

   A) 26

   B) $2\sqrt{14}$

   C) $4\sqrt{14}$

   D) 216

Strategy: The notation $(g \cdot h)(6)$ means to evaluate the function $g(x)$ at $h(6)$. So $g(h(6)) = g\left(\sqrt{6+10}\right) = g\left(\sqrt{16}\right) = g(4) = 4^2 + 10 = 26$. This is answer choice A.

•••••• **Explain** **Transformations and Composition of Functions** ••••••••••

When two or more transformations are combined to form a new transformation, the result is called a composition of transformations and can be expressed by a composition of functions. Suppose that we have three functions, $p(x)$, $q(x)$, and $g(x)$. Let $p(x) = x + 2$, $q(x) = x - 2$, and $g(x) = x^2$. Then the domain of g is the set of real numbers and the graph of $f(x) = g(p(x)) = g(x + 2) = (x + 2)^2$ is a composition of transformations that is 2 units to the left of $g(x) = x^2$. The graph of $h(x) = g(q(x)) = g(x - 2) = (x - 2)^2$ is a composition of transformations that is 2 units to the right of $g(x) = x^2$. Refer to the graph below for more detail.

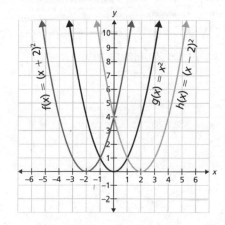

Formally, the rule is that for any function g:

- If $f(x) = g(x + a)$ for a constant a, the graph of $f(x)$ is the graph of $g(x)$ moved $|a|$ units to the left when a is positive and $|a|$ units to the right when a is negative. To shift the graph to the left a units, replace x with $x + a$. To shift the graph to the right a units, replace x with $x - a$.

Think It Through

Example

Which is the graph of $f(x) = |x + 2|$?

A)

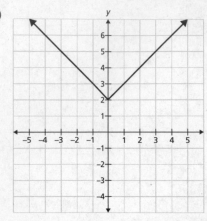

B)

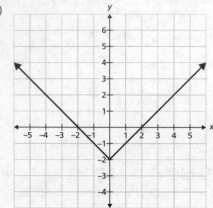

C)

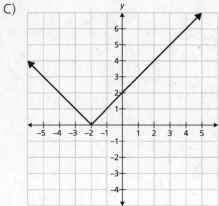

D)

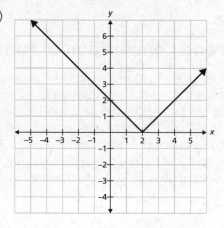

Solution

The graph of $f(x) = |x + 2|$ is a composition of transformations that lies 2 units to the left of the graph of $g(x) = |x|$. This is answer choice C.

1. The equation for $g(x)$ is $g(x) = \sqrt{x}$. The function $h(x)$ is the function $g(x)$ stretched by a factor of 3. The function $f(x)$ is the function $h(x)$ moved 1 unit to the right. What is the equation for $f(x)$?

   A) $f(x) = 3\sqrt{x-1}$

   B) $f(x) = \sqrt{3x+1}$

   C) $f(x) = \sqrt{3x-1}$

   D) $f(x) = 3\sqrt{x} + 1$

Strategy: Before answering, read the question all the way through as many times as you need to make sure you understand what you are being asked. In this case, instead of picking out the correct graph, we have a composition of transformations that is described to us, and we must determine the equation $f(x)$. We are given $g(x) = \sqrt{x}$. Then $h(x) = 3(g(x))$, so $h(x) = 3\sqrt{x}$. Now, $f(x) = h(x) - 1$, so $f(x)$ must be equal to $3\sqrt{x} - 1$. Select answer choice A.

2. The equation for $g(x)$ is $g(x) = (x-1)^2$. The function $h(x)$ is the function $g(x)$ moved 2 units to the left. The function $f(x)$ is the function $h(x)$ compressed by a factor of 0.25. What is the equation for $f(x)$?

   A) $f(x) = 0.25(x+2)^2$

   B) $f(x) = 0.25(x+1)^2$

   C) $f(x) = 0.25(x-3)^2$

   D) $f(x) = (0.25x-3)^2$

Strategy: This question is very similar to the Model SAT problem 1 above, but it is important to recognize that the given function $g(x)$ is a transformation of x^2 that is further transformed. Moving $g(x)$ 2 units to the left means that $h(x) = (x-1+2)^2$, not $(x-1)^2 + 2$. The latter is a vertical movement rather than a horizontal movement. Then $h(x) = (x+1)^2$ and $f(x) = 0.25(x+1)^2$. Select answer choice B.

Answers begin on page 709.

1. Let $p(x) = x - 2$ and $q(x) = \sqrt{x}$. If $f(x) = q(p(x))$, find $f(6)$.

   A) 2

   B) ± 2

   C) 4

   D) $-2 + \sqrt{6}$

2. If $f(x)$ is defined as $f(x) = x + 4$ and $g(x)$ is defined as $g(x) = x^2 - 2$, what is the rule for $h(x) = f(g(x))$?

   A) $h(x) = x^2 + 8x + 14$
   B) $h(x) = x^2 + 8x + 18$
   C) $h(x) = x^2$
   D) $h(x) = x^2 + 2$

3. The equation for $g(x)$ is $g(x) = |x|$. The function $h(x)$ is the function $g(x)$ compressed by a factor of 0.5. The function $f(x)$ is the function $h(x)$ moved 2 units to the left. What is the equation for $f(x)$?

   A) $f(x) = |0.5x| + 2$
   B) $f(x) = |0.5x| - 2$
   C) $f(x) = 0.5|x + 2|$
   D) $f(x) = 0.5|x - 2|$

4. If $m(x) = 2 - 4x$ and $k(x) = x^2 - 3x$, find $m(k(-1))$.

   A) 18
   B) 14
   C) −14
   D) −18

5. If $f(x)$ is defined as $f(x) = x^2 + 1$ and $g(x)$ is defined as $g(x) = x - 1$, what is the rule for $h(x) = f(g(x))$?

   A) $h(x) = x^2 + 2x + 2$
   B) $h(x) = x^2 + 2$
   C) $h(x) = x^2 - 2$
   D) $h(x) = x^2 - 2x + 2$

6. The equation for $g(x)$ is $g(x) = x^2$. The function $h(x)$ is the function $g(x)$ moved 3 units to the right. The function $f(x)$ is the function $h(x)$ stretched by a factor of 3. What is the equation for $f(x)$?

   A) $f(x) = 3(x + 3)^2$
   B) $f(x) = 3(x - 3)^2$
   C) $f(x) = 3x^2 + 3$
   D) $f(x) = 3x^2 - 3$

7. The equation for $g(x)$ is $g(x) = |x + 2|$. The function $h(x)$ is the function $g(x)$ compressed by a factor of 0.5. The function $f(x)$ is the function $h(x)$ shifted 2 units to the right. What is the equation for $f(x)$?

   A) $f(x) = |0.5x + 2|$
   B) $f(x) = |x + 2| - 0.5$
   C) $f(x) = 0.5|x|$
   D) $f(x) = |x| - 0.5$

Student-Produced Response Questions

Questions 8 and 9 refer to the graphs of $f(x)$ and $g(x)$ below.

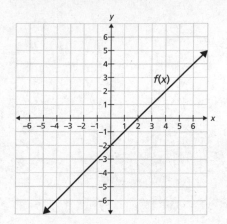
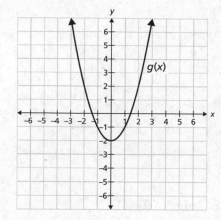

8. Evaluate $h(x) = g(f(0))$.

9. Evaluate $h(x) = f(g(-2))$.

10. If $f(x) = |x| + 3$ and $g(x) = \sqrt{x+1}$, find the value of $g(f(-5))$.

11. If $f(x) = \sqrt{x-11}$ and $g(x) = x^2$, find the value of $f(g(6))$.

12. If $f(x) = \dfrac{x-5}{2}$ and $g(x) = \sqrt{3x^2 + 4}$, find $g(f(9))$.

• • • • • • | Multiple Choice | •

Calculators Allowed

Answers begin on page 710.

1. If $x^6 = \dfrac{3}{a}$ and $x^5 = \dfrac{a^2}{6}$, then which of the following expresses x in terms of a?

    A) $\dfrac{a}{2}$

    B) $\dfrac{2}{a}$

    C) $\dfrac{a^3}{18}$

    D) $\dfrac{18}{a^3}$

2. When $\dfrac{5}{2}x^2 - \dfrac{3}{4}x + 1$ is subtracted from $\dfrac{3}{2}x^2 - \dfrac{1}{4}x - 4$, the difference is

    A) $-x^2 - x - 3$

    B) $x^2 - \dfrac{1}{2}x + 5$

    C) $x^2 - x - 3$

    D) $-x^2 + \dfrac{1}{2}x - 5$

3. If $\dfrac{16x^2}{4x-1} = \dfrac{1}{4x-1} + M$, what is the simplest algebraic expression for M?

    A) $16x^2$
    B) $4x + 1$
    C) $4x - 1$
    D) $16x^2 - 1$

4. If the sum of the two roots of a quadratic equation is -1 and their product is -12, which of the following could be the quadratic equation?

    A) $x^2 - x - 12 = 0$
    B) $x^2 - x + 12 = 0$
    C) $x^2 + x - 12 = 0$
    D) $x^2 + x + 12 = 0$

5. For how many integers is it true that the function $f(x) = -2x^2 + 6$ is positive?

    A) 2
    B) 3
    C) 4
    D) 5

6. Which of the following are the (x, y) solutions for the system of equations given below?

    $y = x^2 + x - 4$
    $y = 2x - 2$

    A) $(-2, -2), (1, 4)$
    B) $(2, -1), (2, -4)$
    C) $(2, 2), (-1, -4)$
    D) $(2, -6), (1, 0)$

7. If $y = f(x) = x^2$ is the parent function, then which of the following equations is represented by the graph shown below?

    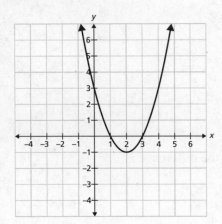

    A) $y = (x + 2)^2 - 1$
    B) $y = (x - 2)^2 + 1$
    C) $y = (x - 2)^2 - 1$
    D) $y = (x + 2)^2 + 1$

8. If the area of a square is represented by $\dfrac{1}{A}$, then which of the following represents the perimeter of the square in terms of A?

    A) $\dfrac{4}{A}$

    B) $\dfrac{A}{4}$

    C) $\sqrt{A}$

    D) $\dfrac{4\sqrt{A}}{A}$

9. The expression $\dfrac{a^2+1}{a^2-1} - \dfrac{a}{a+1}$ is equivalent to

A) $\dfrac{-1}{a+1}$

B) $\dfrac{1}{a+1}$

C) $\dfrac{1}{a-1}$

D) $\dfrac{1}{1-a}$

10. The equation $4+\sqrt{x^2-6x}=0$ has

A) 8 and −2 as its roots.

B) 8 as its only root.

C) −2 as its only root.

D) no roots.

11. A bacteria culture doubles every 30 minutes. After two and one-half hours, there were 24,000 bacteria present. What was the initial number of the bacteria count?

A) 500

B) 750

C) 1000

D) 9600

12. Which of the following quadratic equations has solutions $\dfrac{3}{2}$ and $-\dfrac{1}{4}$ and integer coefficients?

A) $8x^2 - 10x - 3 = 0$

B) $8x^2 + x - 3 - 0$

C) $8x^2 - 10x + 3 = 0$

D) $8x^2 - 14x + 3 = 0$

13. What is the solution set to the given system of equations?

$y = x^2 - 4$
$y = x + 2$

A) $\{(5,3),(0,-2)\}$

B) $\{(3,5),(-2,0)\}$

C) $\{(-3,-1),(2,4)\}$

D) $\{(-1,-3),(4,2)\}$

14. If the parent function is $y = -x^2 + 4$, then which equation represents the transformed graph as shown in the figure below?

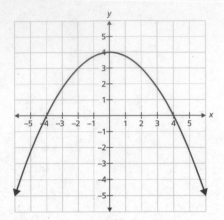

A) $y = -2x^2 + 4$

B) $y = -\left(\dfrac{1}{2}x\right)^2 + 4$

C) $y = -\dfrac{x^2}{2} + 4$

D) $y = 2x^2 + 4$

15. What value of x satisfies the equation $8^{3x+1} = 4^{2x-4}$?

A) -1

B) $-\dfrac{3}{2}$

C) $-\dfrac{11}{5}$

D) -5

16. For all values for which the fraction is defined, simplify $\dfrac{a^{-1} - b^{-1}}{b^{-2} - a^{-2}}$.

A) $\dfrac{-ab}{a+b}$

B) $\dfrac{ab}{a+b}$

C) $a - b$

D) $-b - a$

17. Which of the following represents K if $\left(5 - \dfrac{1}{x}\right)(K) = \dfrac{1}{x}$?

A) $\dfrac{1}{5x^2 - 1}$

B) $\dfrac{1}{5x - 1}$

C) $\dfrac{5}{5x - 1}$

D) $\dfrac{5x - 1}{x^2}$

18. The concentration of a certain medication in a person's bloodstream decreases exponentially. This medication loses 20% of its concentration every hour. If the initial concentration given was 3.0 mg per liter, what is the approximate time (in hours) when the concentration is reduced by 50%?

    A) 2.8 hours

    B) 3.0 hours

    C) 3.1 hours

    D) 3.3 hours

19. The graphs of $y = 3^x$ and $y = 3^{-x}$ have a common intersection with the graph of which of the following linear equations?

    A) $y = x$

    B) $x = 1$

    C) $x = 0$

    D) $y = 0$

20. Which of the following is the complete set of solutions for the given system of equations?

$$x^2 + y^2 = 25$$
$$x + y = 1$$

    A) $\{(3, -2), (4, -3)\}$

    B) $\{(4, -3), (-3, 4)\}$

    C) $\{(-2, 3), (-3, 4)\}$

    D) $\{(5, -4), (-2, 3)\}$

21. If $f(x) = 3x - 5$ and $m(x) = x + 10$, then which of the following is equivalent to $3x + 25$?

    A) $f(x) + m(x)$

    B) $f(x) - m(x)$

    C) $m(f(x))$

    D) $f(m(x))$

22. Which of the following is NOT true?

    A) $\left(2^{\sqrt{3}}\right)^{\sqrt{3}} = 8$

    B) $\left(4^{\frac{1}{\sqrt{2}}}\right)^{\sqrt{2}} = 4$

    C) $\left(10^{\sqrt{2}}\right)\left(10^{\sqrt{2}}\right) = 100$

    D) $9^{\frac{1}{\sqrt{2}}} = 3^{\sqrt{2}}$

23. Simplify: $\left[a^2 + b^2 - (a - b)^2\right]^2$.

    A) $4b^4$

    B) $4a^2b^2$

    C) $2ab$

    D) $a^2 - 2ab + b^2$

24. A math sequence is called geometric if each term is the product of some number r and the preceding term. For example, $5, 15, 45, 135, \ldots$ is a geometric sequence such that $3 \cdot 5 = 15$, $3 \cdot 15 = 45$, and $3 \cdot 45 = 135, \ldots$ where $r = 3$. What is the <u>integer</u> value of x if $2x - 1$, $4x + 1$, and $15x - 3$ is a geometric sequence?

A) 1

B) 2

C) 3

D) 4

25. If $\dfrac{36x^2}{6x+5}$ equals $\dfrac{25}{6x+5} + M$, what is M in terms of x?

A) $36x$

B) $36x - 5$

C) $6x + 5$

D) $6x - 5$

26. If the sum of the roots of the equation $2x^2 - 5x - 3 = 0$ is added to the product of the roots, the result is

A) 1

B) 4

C) $-\dfrac{1}{4}$

D) -1

27. Which of the following is a solution for the system of equations below?

$$y = -x^2$$

$$\dfrac{y+1}{x+1} = \dfrac{1}{2}$$

A) $\left(\dfrac{1}{2}, -\dfrac{1}{4}\right)$

B) $\left(\dfrac{1}{2}, \dfrac{1}{4}\right)$

C) $\left(-\dfrac{1}{2}, -\dfrac{1}{4}\right)$

D) $\left(-\dfrac{1}{2}, \dfrac{1}{4}\right)$

28. If the graph of $y = (x - 2)^2$ is shifted left 3 units and down 4 units, which of the following equations is the axis of symmetry of the transformed graph?

A) $x = -2$

B) $x = -1$

C) $x = 1$

D) $x = -5$

29. The expression $\left(\sqrt[3]{x^4}\right)\left(x^{-\frac{1}{2}}\right)$ is equivalent to

A) $\sqrt[3]{x^{-2}}$

B) $\sqrt[4]{x^3}$

C) $\sqrt[5]{x^{-4}}$

D) $\sqrt[6]{x^5}$

30. For all values of x for which the expressions are defined, $\left(1+\dfrac{1}{x}\right)\div\left(\dfrac{x+1}{x^2}\right)$ is equivalent to

A) x

B) $\dfrac{2x}{x+1}$

C) $\dfrac{x^2}{x+1}$

D) $\dfrac{(x+1)^2}{x^3}$

Student-Produced Response Questions

31. If $(x+y)^2 - (x-y)^2 = 56$ and x and y are positive integers, what is the value of xy?

32. To the nearest hundredth, what is the positive difference between the zeroes of the function $3x^2 - 6x - 1 = 0$?

33. If $x = 7$ is the equation of the axis of symmetry for the graph of $y = ax^2 - 7x - 14$, what is the value of a?

34. What is the positive x-value (to the nearest hundredth) of the point of intersection of this system of equations: $x^2 + y^2 = 16$ and $y = x$?

35. If $f(x) = x^2 - 1$ and $g(x) = 2^{x-1} - 1$, what is the value of $(g \circ f)(3)$?

36. If $a^x a^y = 1$ and $a \neq \pm 1$, then what is the value of $x + y$?

37. A type of aquatic bird known as a cormorant is flying over open water and accidentally drops a small fish from a height of 30 feet. The distance the fish is from the water as it falls can be described by the function $h(t) = -16t^2 + 30$ where t = time in seconds. A seagull spies the falling fish and flies along a straight line to intercept the fish. His line of flight is represented by the linear equation $g(t) = -8t + 15$.

PART 1

After how many seconds does the seagull catch the falling fish?

PART 2

After the seagull catches the fish, he changes his travel path to $k(t) = -2t + 12$. The cormorant chases the seagull in an attempt to try to win back the fish, descending along the path $-t^2 + 15$. How many feet above the water will the cormorant catch up to the seagull?

································ Multiple Choice ···

No Calculator Allowed

Answers begin on page 715.

1. Which of the following does <u>not</u> reduce to x?

   A) $\dfrac{x^{-3}}{x^{-4}}$

   B) $\dfrac{2x^2}{(2x)^2(2x)^{-1}}$

   C) $\dfrac{x^{-3}}{x^{-2}}$

   D) $\dfrac{x^3 y^6}{(xy)^2 y^4}$

2. Which of the following is the polynomial that when multiplied by $(2x^2 - 5x + 7)$ gives the product $6x^3 - 19x^2 + 31x - 14$?

   A) $6x - 2$

   B) $3x - 2$

   C) $3x - 3$

   D) $3x^2 - 2$

3. Which value for N satisfies the equation $\left(\sqrt{3} - 1\right) \cdot N = 1$?

   A) $\dfrac{\sqrt{3}}{2}$

   B) $\sqrt{3}$

   C) $\sqrt{3} + 2$

   D) $\dfrac{\sqrt{3} + 1}{2}$

4. A football is kicked upward and its maximum height of 65 feet occurs after 2.8 seconds. Which of the following functions models this event?

   A) $h(t) = -16(t + 2.8) + 65$

   B) $h(t) = -16(t - 2.8) + 65$

   C) $h(t) = -16(t - 2.8)^2 + 65$

   D) $h(t) = -16(t + 2.8)^2 + 65$

5. Which of the following expresses the axis of symmetry and the vertex of the function $f(x) = -x^2 + 2x + 4$?

A) $x = 1$; $(1, 5)$

B) $x = -1$; $(-1, 1)$

C) $x = 2$; $(2, 4)$

D) $x = 1$; $(1, 7)$

6. Which is the most likely solution set for the system shown in the graph below?

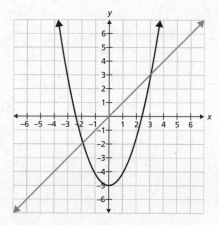

A) $\{(1.9, -2.3), (4, 4)\}$

B) $\{(-3, 0), (3, 0)\}$

C) $\{(-2.3, -1.9), (4, 3.4)\}$

D) $\{(-2.3, 1.9), (3.4, 4)\}$

7. If two points have coordinates $(x_1, y_1) = \left(\sqrt{5}, \sqrt{3}\right)$ and $(x_2, y_2) = \left(\sqrt{3}, -\sqrt{5}\right)$, and the distance, d, can be determined by the distance formula $d = \sqrt{(x_1 - x_2)^2 + (y_1 - y_2)^2}$, then which of the following expresses that distance?

A) $\sqrt{15}$

B) 4

C) $\sqrt{68}$

D) 16

8. If $a > 0$ and $b > 0$, then which of the following could be the graph of $y = ax^2 + b$?

A)

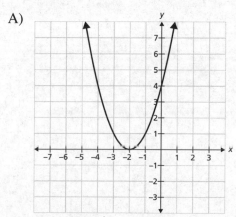

B)

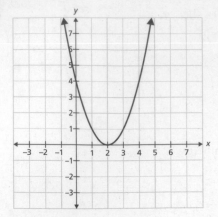

C)

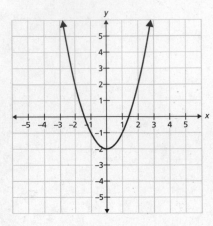

D)

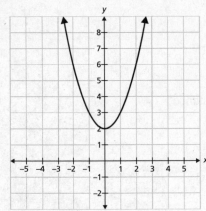

9. For all variables for which the expression is defined, simplify

$$\frac{x^2-16}{x^2-25} \div \left(\frac{x^2-16}{x^2-x-20} \cdot \frac{x+4}{x-4} \right).$$

A) $\dfrac{x+4}{x-5}$

B) $\dfrac{x-4}{x+5}$

C) $\dfrac{x+5}{x-4}$

D) $\dfrac{x-5}{x+4}$

10. If $x > 1$ and $\dfrac{p}{q} = 1 - \dfrac{1}{x}$, then $\dfrac{q}{p} =$

   A) x

   B) $x - 1$

   C) $\dfrac{x-1}{x}$

   D) $\dfrac{x}{x-1}$

11. Solve for x: $\dfrac{2x^2}{x^2-1} - \dfrac{3}{x+1} = \dfrac{x}{x-1}$

   A) $\{1\}$

   B) $\{3\}$

   C) $\{1, 3\}$

   D) $\{-3, -1\}$

12. The graph of $y = f(x)$ is shown in the figure below. If $f(x) = ax^2 + bx + c$ for constants a, b, and c, and if $abc \neq 0$, then which of the following must be true?

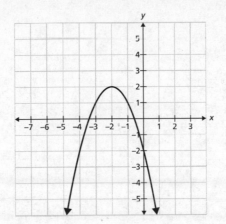

   A) $a > 0$

   B) $ac < 0$

   C) $ac > 0$

   D) $b > 0$

13. Which of the following is the (x, y) solution for the system of equations given below?

   $x^2 - y^2 = 3$
   $x + y = -1$

   A) $(3, 4)$

   B) $(-2, 1)$

   C) $(3, -4)$

   D) $(4, 3)$

14. The vertex of a parabola defined by $f(x) = x^2 - 4x + 3$ has coordinates $(2, -1)$. Which of the following are the coordinates of the vertex defined by $g(x) = f(x + 2) + 1$?

A) $(4, 0)$

B) $(0, -1)$

C) $(0, 0)$

D) $(1, 1)$

15. In simplest form, which of the following is equivalent to $3\sqrt{\dfrac{1}{m^{-2}}} + \left(\sqrt{m^{-2}}\right)^{-1}$?

A) $2m$

B) $4m$

C) $\dfrac{4}{m}$

D) $3m + 1$

Student-Produced Response Questions

16. If $xy = -5$ and $x^2 + y^2 = 22$, then $(x - y)^2 =$

17. Solve for x: $2x + \sqrt{x} - 1 = 0$.

18. Emma throws a baseball in the air, and the distance, or height in feet, that the ball is from the ground at any time t is represented by the function $h(t) = -16t^2 + 32t + 6$. At what time is the ball at its maximum height?

19. The function f is defined by $f(x) = x^3 + 0.5x^2 - cx + 3$ where c is a constant. The graph has three x-intercepts in the xy-plane. They are the points $(2, 0), (-3, 0)$ and $(p, 0)$. What is the value of c?

20. If the line $y = 4$ intersects the parabola $y = x^2 - x + 4.25$ at one point, what is the x-value of that point?

Correlation Chart

Summary SAT-Type Test—Passport to Advanced Math (Calculators Allowed)

Use the chart below to mark the questions you found difficult to determine which lessons you need to review.

Question Number	Lesson 1 (p. 281 – 297)	Lesson 2 (p. 298 – 315)	Lesson 3 (p. 316 – 326)	Lesson 4 (p. 327 – 342)	Lesson 5 (p. 343 – 358)	Lesson 6 (p. 359 – 373)	Lesson 7 (p. 374 – 388)
1							
2							
3							
4							
5							
6							
7							
8							
9							
10							
11							
12							
13							
14							
15							
16							
17							
18							
19							
20							
21							
22							
23							
24							
25							
26							
27							
28							
29							
30							
31							
32							
33							
34							
35							
36							
37a							
37b							
Total Correct	____ / 8	____ / 6	____ / 2	____ / 4	____ / 4	____ / 8	____ / 5

Correlation Chart

Summary SAT-Type Test—Passport to Advanced Math (No Calculators Allowed)

Use the chart below to mark the questions you found difficult to determine which lessons you need to review.

Question Number	Lesson 1 (p. 281 – 297)	Lesson 2 (p. 298 – 315)	Lesson 3 (p. 316 – 326)	Lesson 4 (p. 327 – 342)	Lesson 5 (p. 343 – 358)	Lesson 6 (p. 359 – 373)	Lesson 7 (p. 374 – 388)
1	□						
2		□					
3			□				
4					□		
5					□		
6						□	
7			□				
8							□
9		□					
10		□					
11		□					
12							□
13						□	
14					□		
15			□				
16				□			
17			□				
18					□		
19				□			
20						□	
Total Correct	____ / 1	____ / 4	____ / 4	____ / 2	____ / 4	____ / 3	____ / 2

CATEGORY 4
Additional Topics in Math

LESSON 1:
Using Formulas to Calculate Side Length, Area, and Volume

☐ The SAT Formula Sheet and Additional Formulas and Relationships to Know

☐ Prism Surface Area and Volume

☐ Surface Area and Volume of Other Shapes

· · · · · · **Explain** **The SAT Formula Sheet and Additional** · · · · · · · · · · · ·
Formulas and Relationships to Know

A formula sheet similar to what is shown on the next page is provided for your use during the SAT examination. You should be familiar with all of the formulas shown. Formulas that cannot be derived from information on this sheet will be provided as part of the question. You should not waste time looking for formulas that are not provided.

Definition

The **area** of a given figure, denoted A, is the amount of surface contained within the figure's boundary. Area is measured in square units.

The **volume** of a given figure, denoted V, is a measure of how much space an object occupies. Volume is measured in cubic units.

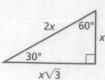

$A = \pi r^2$
$C = 2\pi r$

$A = lw$

$A = \frac{1}{2}bh$

$c^2 = a^2 + b^2$

Special Right Triangles

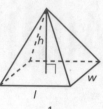

$V = lwh$

$V = \pi r^2 h$

$V = \frac{4}{3}\pi r^3$

$V = \frac{1}{3}\pi r^2 h$

$V = \frac{1}{3}lwh$

The number of degrees of arc in a circle is 360.

The number of radians of arc in a circle is 2π.

The sum of the measures in degrees of the angles of a triangle is 180.

The following formulas and relationships can be derived from given information. However, it will save you time on the SAT if you know these facts.

Equilateral Triangle

An **equilateral triangle** is a triangle in which all of the sides (s) have the same length. Also, all the angles have the same measure, namely 60°. Some special formulas for working with an equilateral triangle are shown below.

Area $= \dfrac{s^2\sqrt{3}}{4}$ Height (h) $= \dfrac{s}{2}\sqrt{3}$

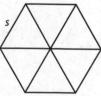

Equilateral Triangle

Regular Hexagon

A **regular hexagon** is a polygon with six equal sides and six equal angles. It is made up of six equilateral triangles (see figure below). Therefore, if a side has measurement s,

then the area of a regular hexagon is $A = 6\left(\dfrac{s^2\sqrt{3}}{4}\right) = \dfrac{3s^2\sqrt{3}}{2}$.

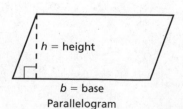

Regular Hexagon

Parallelograms

A **parallelogram** is a four-sided figure that has opposite sides parallel. The formula for finding the area of a parallelogram is $A = bh$, where b is the length of the base and h is the height of the parallelogram.

h = height

b = base
Parallelogram

408 Additional Topics in Math • Lesson 1

Trapezoids

Trapezoids are also four-sided figures, but they have only one pair of parallel sides. To find the area of a trapezoid, you must find the average length of the parallel sides and then multiply that quotient by the height. The formula is $A = h\left(\dfrac{b_1 + b_2}{2}\right)$.

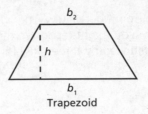
Trapezoid

Kites, Rhombi, and Squares

A **kite** is another type of four-sided figure. It possesses two distinct pairs of adjacent sides that are each equal in length. Kites are related to rhombi and squares. In fact, a **rhombus** is a particular type of kite in which all sides have the same length and a **square** is a rhombus that has all angles equal to 90°. While there are specific formulas for finding the area of each of these figures, if you know the measures of the diagonals in any of these figures, you can use this formula for finding the area of a kite, rhombus, or square:

$$A = \frac{\text{diagonal}_1 \cdot \text{diagonal}_2}{2}$$

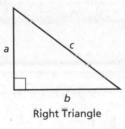

Other Relationships

Similar Figure Ratios

Recall from the lessons in Category 2 that similar figures are those that have the same shape but not necessarily the same size. For example, two equilateral triangles are similar. When figures are similar, the ratios of the lengths of their corresponding sides are proportional. Similar figures also share this type of relationship with their areas and volumes. If the ratio of any corresponding lengths for two similar figures is $\dfrac{a}{b}$, the ratio of corresponding area measures is $\dfrac{a^2}{b^2}$ and the ratio of volumes is $\dfrac{a^3}{b^3}$.

Pythagorean Triples

The Pythagorean theorem relates the lengths of the legs in a right triangle to the length of the hypotenuse. Specifically, the Pythagorean theorem states that in any right triangle, $a^2 + b^2 = c^2$, where a and b are the lengths of the legs and c is the length of the hypotenuse. While this relationship holds true for all right triangles, when all the lengths a, b, and c are integer values, the triangle is known as a Pythagorean triple. Some common Pythagorean triples are (3, 4, 5), (5, 12, 13), (8, 15, 17), and (7, 24, 25). It is helpful to know these triples on the SAT. It is also important to know that multiples of the Pythagorean triples are also triples.

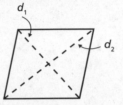
Right Triangle

Think It Through

Example 1

Assume the numbers below each give the side lengths of a right triangle. Which is a Pythagorean triple?

A) 4, 11.31, 12

B) 2, 3, $\sqrt{13}$

C) 24, 45, 51

D) $2\sqrt{85}$, 12, 22

Solution

Pythagorean triples are made up of integer values. The only answer choice with all integer values is C. Alternately, you might recognize that choice C is the known Pythagorean triple (8, 15, 17) multiplied by three: 3(8, 15, 17) = (24, 45, 51).

Answer: C

Example 2

What is the radius of a circle whose area is 64π?

Solution

In this problem, we are being asked to work backwards. We know from the given formula sheet that the area of a circle is calculated by $A = \pi r^2$. Substitute in the area from the problem to find $64\pi = \pi r^2$,

then divide both sides by π and take the square root. So $\dfrac{64\pi}{\pi} = \dfrac{\pi r^2}{\pi}$

becomes $64 = r^2$, and $\sqrt{64} = \sqrt{r^2}$ is $r = 8$. Bubble in 8 on the response grid.

Answer: 8

Example 3

A regular hexagon has an area of 64.95 square inches. What is its side length, *s*?

$\left(\text{The area of a hexagon is given by the formula } A = \dfrac{3s^2\sqrt{3}}{2}. \right)$

A)   5 inches
B)   25 inches
C)   4 inches
D)   16 inches

Solution

Again, we must work backwards. The formula we need to use was given in the

problem, so $A = \dfrac{3s^2\sqrt{3}}{2}$ is now $64.95 = \dfrac{3s^2\sqrt{3}}{2}$. Begin solving for *s*. Multiply both

sides by 2 and $129.9 = 3s^2\sqrt{3}$. Then divide both sides by $3\sqrt{3}$ to find that $24.99 = s^2$. Take the square root of 24.99 and find that $s = 4.99$, which we can round to 5 inches.

Answer: A

Example 4

Find the shaded area.

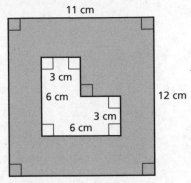

11 cm

3 cm

6 cm

3 cm

6 cm

12 cm

Note: Figure <u>not</u> drawn to scale

A) 45 cm²

B) 105 cm²

C) 27 cm²

D) 132 cm²

Solution

Begin by finding the area of the large rectangle: $11 \cdot 12 = 132$ cm². Then find the area of the smaller shape; notice that shape is two rectangles put together. The horizontal rectangle has an area of $6 \cdot 3 = 18$ cm², and the vertical rectangle has an area of $(6 - 3) \cdot 3 = 9$ cm². Then $132 - 18 - 9 = 105$ cm².

Answer: B

Model SAT Questions

1. Cube A has an edge of 2. Each edge of cube A is increased by 50%, creating a second cube B as shown below.

    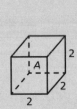
    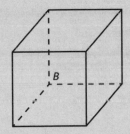

    What is the ratio of the volume of cube A to cube B? (The formula for the volume of a cube is $V = s^3$.)

    A) $\dfrac{2}{3}$

    B) $\dfrac{4}{9}$

    C) $\dfrac{7}{15}$

    D) $\dfrac{8}{27}$

Strategy: Since the length of a side in cube A is 2, its volume is $V = 2^3 = 8$ cubic units. Now determine the length of a side in cube B. Increasing 2 by 50% yields $2 + 2(0.50) = 2 + 1 = 3$. Then the volume of cube B is $3^3 = 27$ cubic units. The ratio of the volumes is $\dfrac{A}{B} = \dfrac{8}{27}$. Alternatively, we know the ratio of volumes is the cube of the ratio of sides, $\dfrac{A}{B} = \left(\dfrac{2}{3}\right)^3 = \dfrac{8}{27}$. This is answer choice D.

2. If the area of triangle A, with sides of lenghts 6, 8, and 10, is equal to the area of rectangle B, with a length of 4, what is the width of the rectangle?

Strategy: Immediately recognize that the triangle is a Pythagorean triple. Then from the formula sheet, the area of the triangle is $A = \dfrac{1}{2}bh \to \dfrac{1}{2}(6)(8) = 24$ square units. Now, the area of a rectangle is $A = lw$, so $24 = 4w$ and $w = 6$. Bubble in 6 on your answer grid.

3. If the area of a square S is the same as the area of a triangle T, with base equal to 12 and height equal to 9, then to the nearest tenth, what is the length of a side of the square?

    A) 7.3 inches

    B) 12 inches

    C) 9 inches

    D) 8.5 inches

Strategy: Start the problem by finding the area of the triangle: $A = \dfrac{1}{2}bh \to$ $\dfrac{1}{2}(12)(9) = 54$ square inches. This area is the same as the square's area. To find the length of a side of the square, use the formula for the area of a square, which is $A = s^2$. Then $54 = s^2$ and, taking the square root of 54, $s = 7.3$. This is answer choice A.

A **prism** is a solid figure that has parallel bases. The bases themselves are congruent polygons and the sides are parallelograms. The shape of the base gives the prism its name, as shown in the diagrams below. There are two broad categories of prisms: right and oblique. **Right prisms** have sides perpendicular to their bases. The sides are rectangles.

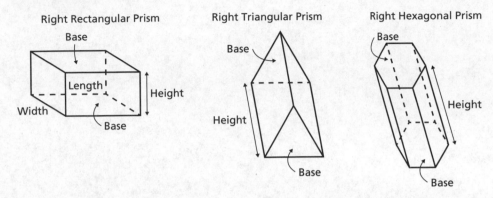

The sides in **oblique prisms** are not perpendicular to their bases. Their sides are parallelograms.

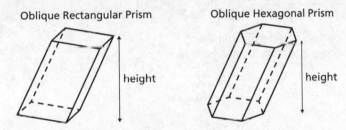

Let B be the area of the base of any prism. Then the **volume** is equal to Bh, the product of the area of the base and the height. The volume formula for the rectangular prism is specifically included on the SAT formula sheet, but it holds true for *all* prisms. The **surface area** of any prism is the sum of the areas of the sides and the areas of both bases.

Right rectangular solids have an additional property that is an extension of the Pythagorean theorem. Suppose that we have a right rectangular prism, as shown below.

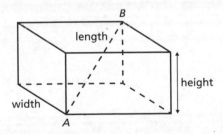

Then the length of the diagonal *AB* can be calculated by this formula:

The length of diagonal $AB = \sqrt{\text{length}^2 + \text{width}^2 + \text{height}^2}$.

Example 1

What is the length of diagonal *AB* in the figure below?

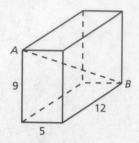

A) 18

B) $5\sqrt{10}$

C) $9\sqrt{2}$

D) 13

Solution

When finding the length of a diagonal in a rectangular prism, we use this formula: $\sqrt{\text{length}^2 + \text{width}^2 + \text{height}^2}$. So, $\overline{AB} = \sqrt{(12)^2 + (5)^2 + (9)^2}$ and $\sqrt{144 + 25 + 81} = \sqrt{250}$. The number 250 is not a perfect square. Examine the answer choices; none of them are decimals, so we need to simplify the radical. Then $\sqrt{250} = \sqrt{25} \cdot \sqrt{10}$, which becomes $5\sqrt{10}$.

Answer: B

Example 2

You want to create a wedge-shaped object as shown below. The base will have a length of 18 inches and a height of 12 inches. When standing on its base, the height of the wedge will be 2 feet. What is the volume of the wedge?

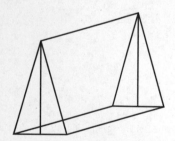

A) 3 ft³

B) 216 ft³

C) 5,184 ft³

D) 1.5 ft³

Solution

Begin by identifying the shape. The ends are congruent triangles and the faces are rectangles, so it must be a triangular prism. The formula for the volume of a prism is $V = Bh$, where *B* is the formula for the area of the base and *h* is the height of the figure. Since we will need to use two different height measurements, we'll call the height of the figure h and the height of the triangle h'. So, for this shape,

$V = \left(\dfrac{bh'}{2}\right)h$. Notice that the dimensions of the wedge are not given in consistent

units. We have the option of working in inches or feet. Since the answer choices are given in cubic feet, convert 18 inches and 12 inches to 1.5 feet and 1 foot,

respectively. Then $V = \left(\dfrac{1 \cdot 1.5}{2}\right) \cdot 2$ and $V = 1.5$ ft³. Note that you could have worked

this problem in inches and converted the product to cubic feet in the final step.

Answer: D

Example 3

All the dimensions of a certain rectangular prism are integers greater than 1. If the volume is 126 cubic inches and the height is 6 inches, what is the perimeter of the base?

A) 16 inches
B) 20 inches
C) 21 inches
D) 27 inches

Solution

The formula for the volume of a rectangular prism is $V = lwh$. With the information from the problem, we can substitute in to find that $126 = 6 \cdot lw$. Dividing both sides by 6, $21 = lw$. The number 21 has factors of 1 and 21 or 3 and 7. If the base has dimensions of 1 by 21, the perimeter of the base would be $P = 1 + 1 + 21 + 21 = 44$ inches. This is not an answer choice. If the base has dimensions of 3 by 7, the base perimeter would be $P = 3 + 3 + 7 + 7 = 20$ inches. This is answer choice B.

Answer: B

Model SAT Questions

1. A rectangular solid has a square base. The volume is 360 cubic inches and the height is 10 inches. What is the perimeter of the base?

   A) 24 inches
   B) 36 inches
   C) 40 inches
   D) 60 inches

   Strategy: Quickly realize that if the volume of the object is 360 cubic inches and the height is 10 inches, the area of the base must be $360 \div 10 = 36$ inches. You know that 36 is a perfect square and its square root is 6, which is the length of a single side of the square. The perimeter of the square must be $6 \cdot 4 = 24$ inches. Select answer choice A.

2. If a box has dimensions 3, $\sqrt{10}$, and 9, what is the length of the longest line segment that can be drawn joining two vertices?

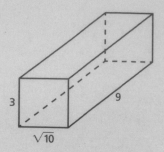

A) $\sqrt{19}$

B) $\sqrt{90}$

C) $\sqrt{91}$

D) 10

Strategy: For this problem, we must first determine where the longest line segment is. It is the diagonal m through the center of the box as shown below.

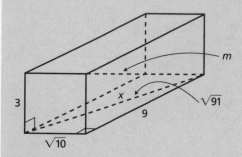

To find the length of diagonal m, we could create a second diagonal, x, across the bottom of the box. This creates a right triangle with sides 9, $\sqrt{10}$, and x. Using the Pythagorean theorem, $x^2 = \left(\sqrt{10}\right)^2 + (9)^2$ and $x^2 = 10 + 81$. Simplifying and taking the square root of both sides, $x = \sqrt{91}$. Now that we know the length of x, we can use it to find the length of m. Again applying the Pythagorean theorem, $m^2 = 3^2 + \left(\sqrt{91}\right)^2$, $m^2 = 9 + 91$, and $m = 10$. This is answer choice D. Alternately, you could solve this problem using the diagonal formula, $\overline{AB} = \sqrt{\text{length}^2 + \text{width}^2 + \text{height}^2}$.

3. A cereal box has a volume of 176 cubic inches. When it stands upright, its base has an area of 16 square inches. If a supermarket displays the box standing upright on a shelf, what is the minimum number of inches between that shelf and the one above it?

A) 11 inches

B) 16 inches

C) 8 inches

D) 24 inches

Strategy: The formula to find the volume of a rectangular prism is $V = lwh$. So, $176 = 16h$ and $h = 11$. There is a minimum of 11 inches between the two shelves; otherwise the box of cereal will not be able to stand upright. Select answer choice A.

Cylinders

A **right circular cylinder** is a solid that has two parallel circular bases that are connected by a curved surface. On the SAT, you may be asked about either the surface area or the volume of a cylinder.

Definition

The **surface area** of a solid is the measure of the total area of the surface of the solid.

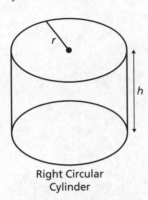

Right Circular Cylinder

If we need to find the surface area of a cylinder, we must consider the area of the bases and the area of the curved surface connecting the bases. We know that the area of a circle is calculated by $A = \pi r^2$. Since there are two circles, multiply that formula by two to find $2\pi r^2$. Now consider the curved surface. Think of it as a rectangular label we can unwrap and lie flat, and the length of the rectangular label is the height, h, of the cylinder. The width is the circumference of the circular base, $2\pi r$. Therefore, the area of the curved surface is $2\pi rh$. The surface area of the whole cylinder is the sum of the areas of its parts, so the formula for the surface area of a cylinder is $2\pi r^2 + 2\pi rh$ or $2\pi r(r + h)$.

The formula for the volume of a cylinder is included on the SAT formula sheet. The general form is $V = Bh$, the product of the area of the base and the height. Since the base of a right circular cylinder is a circle, we can rewrite the formula as $V = \pi r^2 h$.

Spheres, Cones, and Rectangular Pyramids

The formulas needed to calculate the volume of a sphere, cone, and rectangular pyramid are included on the formula sheet. You may be asked to determine the area of a hemisphere, which is a sphere that has been sliced in half. You can derive this formula by multiplying the given sphere volume formula by $\frac{1}{2}$. If you do so, the volume formula becomes $V = \frac{1}{2} \cdot \frac{4\pi r^3}{3}$, which is $\frac{2\pi r^3}{3}$. If diagrams or descriptions refer to cones or pyramids where the apex is not centered over the base, the volume formulas provided on the formula sheet are still valid. If the SAT asks you to find the surface area of any of these shapes, the formula will be provided within the context of the question.

Sphere   Cone   Rectangular Pyramid

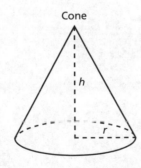
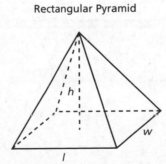

Example 1

Find the volume of a cylinder that has a base with diameter 12 and height 10.

A) 6π

B) 12π

C) 360π

D) 144π

Solution

The formula for the volume of a cylinder is $V = \pi r^2 h$. The radius is $\dfrac{\text{diameter}}{2} = \dfrac{12}{2} = 6$, so $V = \pi r^2 h = \pi \cdot 6^2 \cdot 10 = 360\pi$.

Answer: C

Example 2

The Great Pyramid of Giza has a square base with side lengths of about 252 yards each. When it was completed, the pyramid was about 160 yards tall, but over the millennia, it has eroded, and the pyramid is now only about 152 yards tall. By what percentage has the volume of the pyramid decreased due to erosion?

A) 2%

B) 6.8%

C) 5%

D) 3.9%

Strategy: This problem requires more than one calculation. First, we must determine the original volume of the pyramid. Then we must determine the volume of the pyramid as it is today. Finally, we will need to find the percentage decrease in the volume of the pyramid due to erosion. The formula for the volume of a pyramid is $V = \dfrac{1}{3}lwh$. We can rewrite this formula as $V = \dfrac{lwh}{3}$.

The original volume of the pyramid was $V = \dfrac{252 \cdot 252 \cdot 160}{3} = 3{,}386{,}880$ cubic yards. The current volume is $V = \dfrac{252 \cdot 252 \cdot 152}{3} = 3{,}217{,}536$ cubic yards. Recall from Category 2 that the formula for calculating the percentage change is

$100\left(\dfrac{\text{the difference}}{\text{the original amount}}\right)$. So the percentage change in the volume of the pyramid

is $100\left(\dfrac{3386880 - 3217536}{3386880}\right) = 5\%$. Pick answer choice C.

Answer: C

Answers begin on page 718.

1. If the volume of a cylinder is 72π and the height is 8, what is the circumference of the base?

   A) 3π

   B) 6π

   C) 9π

   D) 12π

2. If the area of one face of a cube is 16, what is the volume of the cube? (The formula for the volume of a cube is $V = s^3$.)

   A) 4

   B) 12

   C) 48

   D) 64

3. On a farm, cylindrical silos are used for storing wheat. If the circumference of a certain silo is 18π feet and the height is twice the diameter, what is the volume of wheat that can be stored in this silo?

   A) 36π ft^3

   B) 81π ft^3

   C) 324π ft^3

   D) $2{,}916\pi$ ft^3

Model SAT Questions

1. Two cylinders, A and B, have diameters 8 yards and 12 yards, respectively. The volume of B is twice the volume of A. What is the ratio of the height of A to the height of B?

   A) $\dfrac{4}{9}$

   B) $\dfrac{2}{3}$

   C) $\dfrac{8}{9}$

   D) $\dfrac{9}{8}$

Strategy: Divide each of the given diameters by 2 to find that the radius for cylinder A is 4 yards and the radius for cylinder B is 6 yards. Then area of the base for cylinder A is $4^2\pi = 16\pi$, and the area of the base for cylinder B is $6^2\pi = 36\pi$. We know the volume of cylinder B is twice the volume of cylinder A, so $\dfrac{\text{volume of cylinder B}}{\text{volume of cylinder A}}$ is $\dfrac{2}{1} = \dfrac{36\pi(\text{height of B})}{16\pi(\text{height of A})}$. Now multiply both sides of the expression $\dfrac{2}{1} = \dfrac{36\pi(\text{height of B})}{16\pi(\text{height of A})}$ by $\dfrac{16\pi}{36\pi}$. Then $\dfrac{\text{height of B}}{\text{height of A}} = \dfrac{2 \cdot 16\pi}{36\pi} = \dfrac{32}{36} = \dfrac{8}{9}$.

The height of A to the height of B is $\dfrac{9}{8}$. This is answer choice D.

2. The radius of the Sun is approximately 400,000 miles. The radius of Earth is approximately 4,000 miles. What is the ratio of the volume of the Sun to the volume of Earth?

A) $\dfrac{100}{1}$

B) $\dfrac{10,000}{1}$

C) $\dfrac{1,000,000}{1}$

D) $\dfrac{100,000,000}{1}$

Strategy: The quickest method to solve this problem is to determine the ratio of the given radii. Then the ratio of the Sun's radius to the Earth's radius is $\dfrac{400,000}{4,000} = \dfrac{100}{1}$.

Volume is a cubic measure, so simply cube the ratio and $\dfrac{100^3}{1^3} = \dfrac{1,000,000}{1}$. Select answer choice C.

3. A restaurant coffee filter is cone shaped, as shown in the illustration to the right. It has a diameter of 1 foot and a height of 10 inches. Water passes through the filter at the rate of 12 cubic inches per minute. To the nearest minute, how long will it take the filter, when completely filled with water, to empty?

Strategy: Determine the radius of the base to be 6 inches. Then the volume of the cone is $V = \dfrac{\pi r^2 h}{3} = \dfrac{\pi 6^2 \cdot 10}{3} = \dfrac{360\pi}{3} = 120\pi$ in³ ≈ 377 in³. Now use the drainage rate and determine how long it will take the filter to empty: $\dfrac{377 \text{ in}^3}{1} \cdot \dfrac{1 \text{ minute}}{12 \text{ in}^3} = 31.4$ minutes. To the nearest minute, that is 31 minutes. Bubble in 31 on the SPR grid.

Answers begin on page 718.

1. A rectangular piece of tin 10 inches by 15 inches is to be made into a box by cutting out squares that measure 2.5 inches on a side from each corner as shown below. If the sides are then bent up to form the box, what will be the volume of the box in cubic inches?

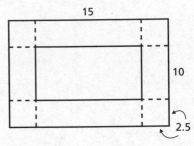

    A) 50 in³
    B) 125 in³
    C) 250 in³
    D) 375 in³

2. If the ratio of the surface area of sphere A to the surface area of sphere B is $\frac{9}{4}$, what is the ratio of the volume of sphere A to the volume of sphere B? (The formula for the surface area of a sphere is $4\pi r^2$.)

    A) $\dfrac{3}{2}$

    B) $\dfrac{27}{12}$

    C) $\dfrac{9}{8}$

    D) $\dfrac{27}{8}$

3. When the rectangle shown below revolves 360° about side a, the resulting cylinder has a volume in cubic units that can be written as

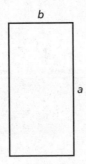

    A) πab^2
    B) $\pi a^2 b$
    C) $\pi a^2 b^2$
    D) πab

4. The rectangular solid base for an office sign is made of concrete and measures 9 feet long, 6 feet wide, and 6 inches high. How much is the cost of the concrete in the pedestal, if concrete costs $90 per cubic yard?

   A) $90
   B) $270
   C) $810
   D) $2,430

5. To determine the number of pounds of ice, N, required to reduce the temperature of water in a swimming pool by $F°$ Fahrenheit, use the formula $N = 0.31FV$, where V is the volume of the pool (in cubic feet). Ruth has a circular pool with a diameter of 16 feet, which is filled to a depth of 4 feet. Ice is sold in 5-pound bags costing $3.00 each. How much money will Ruth need to reduce the pool's temperature from 84° to 80° Fahrenheit?

   A) $30
   B) $60
   C) $300
   D) $600

6. A scout troop is packing open cardboard boxes of small toys for a holiday event. Each box has a length of 8.5 inches, a width of 6 inches, and a height of 5 inches. The boxes do not have lids. How much cardboard is needed to make each box?

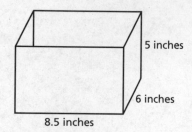

   5 inches

   6 inches

   8.5 inches

   A) 247 in²
   B) 196 in²
   C) 145 in²
   D) 81 in²

7. Kiran wants to paint the outside walls of a row of sheds that each measure 10 feet long, 8 feet wide, and 7 feet high. Each gallon of paint covers about 350 ft² of surface. How many gallons of paint will Kiran need to paint 5 sheds?

   A) 8
   B) 7
   C) 4
   D) 3

8. The child's wooden block shown below is 9 inches long, 3 inches high, and 4 inches deep. There are 3 cylindrical tunnels in the block. Each tunnel has a diameter of 2.4 inches. The density of the wood used to make this block is $\dfrac{0.02 \text{ lbs}}{\text{in}^3}$. To the nearest tenth of a pound, what is the mass of the block?

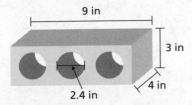

A) 0.9 lb
B) 1.0 lb
C) 1.1 lb
D) 1.2 lb

9. Which of the following expressions reflects the volume of the solid shown below?

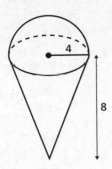

A) $4\pi \cdot 4^3 \cdot 8$

B) $\dfrac{2}{3}\pi \cdot 4^3 + \dfrac{1}{3}\pi \cdot 8 \cdot 4^2$

C) $\dfrac{\pi \cdot 4^2}{3}(2 \cdot 4 + 8)$

D) $\pi \cdot 4^3 \cdot 8 + \dfrac{4}{3} \cdot 8 \cdot 4^2$

Student-Produced Response Questions

10. The volume of a pyramid is 49 ft³. If the pyramid's height is 12 feet and the base is a square, what is the length of a side of the base in feet?

11. The base of pyramid P is a rhombus with sides that are 17 ft in length. The longer diagonal of the rhombus is 30 ft. The height is 12 ft. Find the volume of the pyramid measured in cubic feet.

12. The volume of a sphere is $12{,}348\pi$ cm³. Find the radius of the sphere, measured in centimeters.

13. Prism A and prism B are similar. The surface area of prism A is 33 ft² and the surface area of prism B is 132 ft². The height of prism B is 5 ft. Find the height of prism A, measured in feet.

14. Cylinder A and cylinder B are similar figures. If the ratio of the volume of cylinder A to the volume of cylinder B is $\dfrac{125}{64}$, what is the ratio of the height of cylinder A to the height of cylinder B?

LESSON 2:

Applying Concepts and Theorems About Lines, Angles, Triangles, and Other Polygons

- Computations Involving Angles and Lines

- Computations Involving Triangles

- Determining Lengths and Angles for Special Right Triangles

- Computing Polygon Line Lengths and Angle Measures

· · · · · **Explain** **Computations Involving Angles and Lines** · · · · · · · · · · · ·

The charts below show common vocabulary for angles and lines as well as relationships that are commonly found on the SAT. You should become familiar with and memorize these basics so you can apply them to more complex problems.

Angles are formed when lines intersect.

Angles	Description	Examples
Right Angle	is a 90° angle. The symbol for a *right angle* is a square at the vertex.	
Acute Angle	is less than 90°.	
Obtuse Angle	is greater than 90°.	
Straight Angle	is a straight line. It measures 180°.	Since $x + 130 = 180, x = 50$.
Adjacent Angles	are two angles that have the same vertex and a common side between them.	∠1 and ∠2 are adjacent angles.
Complementary Angles	are two angles whose sum is 90°. The angles need not be adjacent.	Since $y + 75 = 90, y = 15$.
Supplementary Angles	are two angles whose sum is 180°. The angles need not be adjacent.	
Vertical Angles (opposite angles)	are formed by intersecting lines. Vertical angles are equal.	$x = y$

Lines

Lines	Description	Examples
Angle Bisector	is a straight line, segment, or ray that divides an angle into two equal parts. The statement $\overline{FH}$ bisects $\angle EFG$ means that the measure of $\angle EFH$ = the measure of $\angle HFG$ or $m\angle EFH = m\angle HFG$	$\angle EFG = 70°$ and $\overline{FH}$ bisects $\angle EFG$. $m\angle EFH = m\angle HFG = 35°$.
Perpendicular Lines or Line Segments	are lines that form **right angles**. The statement $\overline{BC} \perp \overline{AC}$ means that BC is *perpendicular* to AC.	Since $\overline{BC} \perp \overline{AC}$, $m\angle C$ is 90°.
Parallel Lines	are lines that **do not intersect**. The statement $l_1 \parallel l_2$ means that line l_1 is *parallel* to line l_2. $AB = CD$ The perpendicular distance between parallel lines is always the same.	$l_3 \parallel l_4$ $\angle 1 = \angle 3 = \angle 5 = \angle 7$ $\angle 2 = \angle 4 = \angle 6 = \angle 8$ $\angle 4$ and $\angle 5$ are supplementary. $\angle 3$ and $\angle 6$ are supplementary.

In geometry, we often use symbols rather than words to denote specific relationships. Some of those symbols were explained in the charts above. On the SAT, you may also need to know these common symbol notations:

≅   This symbol means "is congruent to." Two shapes are **congruent** if they have the same shape and size.

↔   This symbol represents a line. For example, $\overleftrightarrow{DR}$ is a line containing the points D and R.

→   This symbol is for a ray. For example, $\overrightarrow{PQ}$ is a ray with endpoint P and passing through point Q.

−   This is the symbol for a line segment. In this case, $\overline{RM}$ is a line segment with endpoints R and M and containing all points in between.

Example 1

In the figure below, lines m and n are parallel. The measure of $\angle x = 55°$. What is the measure of $\angle y$?

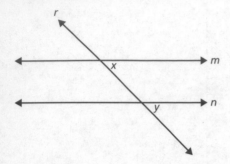

Solution

Refer to the "Lines" chart on p. 427. Since we are told that lines m and n are parallel, that makes $\angle x$ and $\angle y$ corresponding angles. By definition, corresponding angles have the same measure. Bubble in 55 on the grid.

Answer: 55

Example 2

Line *l* is a straight line. What is the measure of ∠*x*?

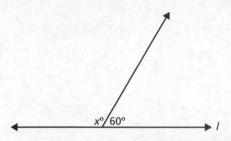

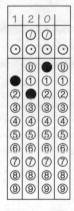

Solution

Recognize that line *l* is a straight angle. By definition, a straight angle has a measure of 180°. Thus, we can set up the equation $x + 60 = 180$, and $x = 120°$. Bubble in 120 on the grid.

Answer: 120

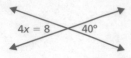
Answers begin on page 720.

1. In the figure below, what is the value of *x*?

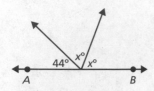

4x = 8   40°

A) 8
B) 8.5
C) 10
D) 12

2. In the figure below, $\overline{AB}$ is a straight line. What is the value of *x*?

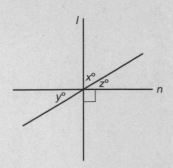

44° x° x°
A   B

A) 22
B) 20
C) 68
D) 78

3. In the figure below, $\angle x + \angle z = \angle y$. What is the value of *y*?

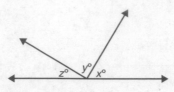

z° y° x°

A) 30
B) 45
C) 60
D) 90

4. For the two intersecting lines below, what is the value of $a + c - d$?

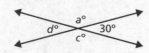

d° a° 30°
c°

A) 270
B) 300
C) 330
D) 240

· · · · **Model SAT Questions** ·

1. In the figure below, $l \perp n$. What is the measure of $\angle y$ if $\angle x$ is 60°?

l

x° z°
y°   *n*

A) 30°
B) 45°
C) 60°
D) 75°

Strategy: Begin by noticing that angles *y* and *z* are vertical angles. Then, since
$l \perp n$, the sum of angles *x* and *z* must be 90°. So $x + z = 90$ and $x = 60$,
so $60 + z = 90$, and $z = 30° = y$. Select answer choice A.

2. In the figure below, $l \parallel m$ and line n bisects $\angle ABC$. If $\angle x = 30°$, what is the value of a?

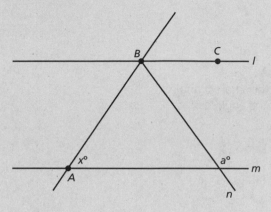

A) 45

B) 60

C) 75

D) 105

Strategy: Because lines l and m are parallel and angle x is 30 degrees, $\angle ABC$ measures 150 degrees (it is supplementary to angle x). Then, line n bisects $\angle ABC$, so angle 1 is 75°. Angle 2 is also 75° because they are alternate interior angles. Thus, angle a is 105 degrees since it is supplementary to angle 2. Answer choice D is correct. See illustration below.

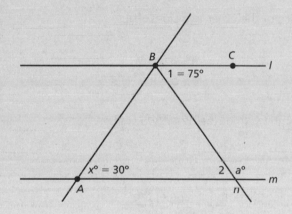

···· **Explain** **Computations Involving Triangles** · · · · · · · · · · ·

A **triangle** is a closed figure formed by three line segments. The symbolic notation $\triangle ABC$ means a triangle with vertices A, B, and C. The point where two sides of a triangle meet is called a **vertex**. All triangles have three vertices. The following triangle facts are helpful to know for the SAT.

For all triangles,

- The sum of the *interior angles* is 180°. This fact can be used to find the measure of an unknown angle.

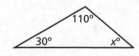

Add up all the angles. $x + 30 + 110 = 180$

Solve for x. $x + 140 = 180$

                                           $x = 40°$

- The *longest side* is opposite the *largest angle*.

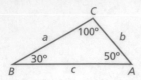

Since $\angle C$ is the largest angle, c is the longest side. For this triangle, the size order of the sides is:

$$b < a < c$$

- The *smallest angle* is opposite the *shortest side*.

Since c is the shortest side, $\angle C$ is the smallest angle. For this triangle, the size order of the angles is:

$$\angle C < \angle A < \angle B$$

- The *exterior angle* of a triangle equals the sum of the measures of the two nonadjacent interior angles.

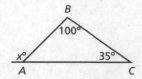

$\angle x$ is the exterior angle. $\angle B$ and $\angle C$ are the nonadjacent interior angles.

$$x = 100 + 35 = 135°$$

- The sum of *any two sides* of a triangle must be greater than the third side.

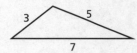

$3 + 5 > 7$	$a + b > c$
$5 + 7 > 3$	$b + c > a$
$3 + 7 > 5$	$a + c > b$

- Any side of a triangle is greater than the difference of the other two sides. Thus,

$3 > 7 - 5$	$a > c - b$
$5 > 7 - 3$	$b > c - a$
$7 > 5 - 3$	$c > b - a$

Together, the two statements above yield
the difference of the other two sides < any side < the sum of the other two sides:

$$5 - 3 < 7 < 5 + 3$$
$$b - a < c < a + b$$

- If two angles of one triangle are equal to two angles of another triangle, the third angle of each triangle is also equal, and the triangles are **similar**. Their corresponding sides are in proportion. The symbol for similar is ~.

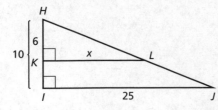

In the triangle to the left, since $\angle H$ is in both triangles, and both triangles have right angles, then $\triangle KHL \sim \triangle IHJ$.

The triangles are similar, so use a proportion of corresponding sides to find x.

$$\text{smaller triangle} \rightarrow \frac{6}{10} = \frac{x}{25} \leftarrow \text{smaller triangle}$$
$$\text{larger triangle} \rightarrow \qquad \qquad \leftarrow \text{larger triangle}$$

$$10x = 150$$
$$x = 15$$

Special Triangles

Name	Description	Example
Isosceles Triangle	• has two equal sides called legs. The third side is called the base. • has two equal angles called base angles. The third angle, which is opposite the base, is called the vertex angle.	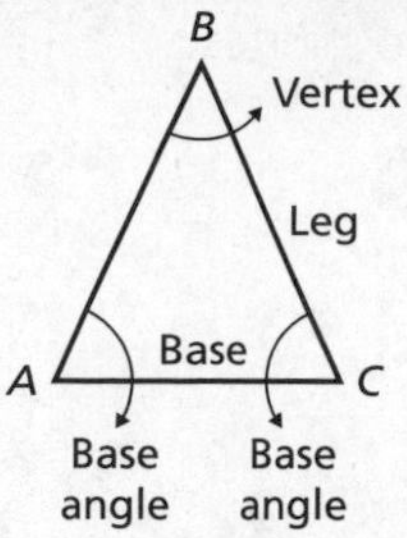 $AB = BC$ $\angle A = \angle C$
In an isosceles triangle, the altitude, drawn from the vertex angle to the base, bisects the base and the vertex angle. Note: $AB = BC$		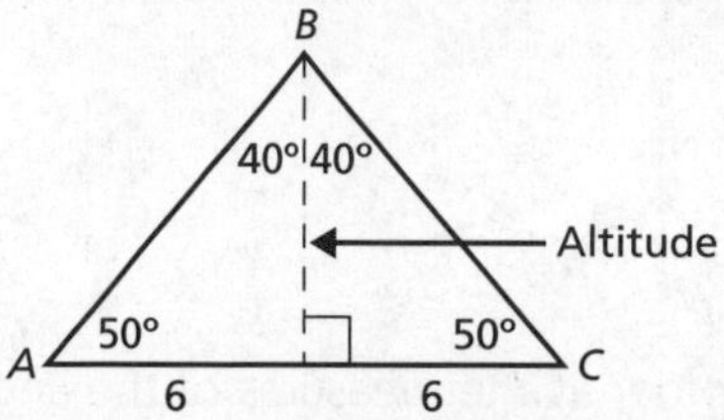
Equilateral Triangle	has all sides equal. Equilateral triangles are equiangular. All angles are 60°.	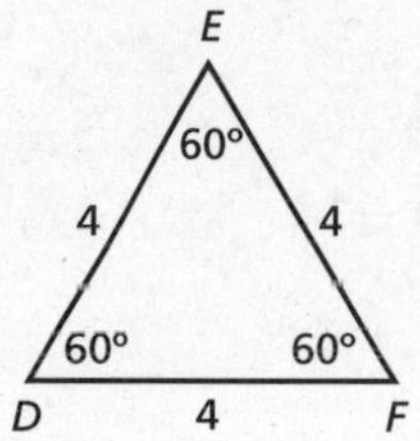
Right Triangle	has one right angle. The **Pythagorean theorem**, which is true for all right triangles, states that for any hypotenuse c and legs a and b, $a^2 + b^2 = c^2$.	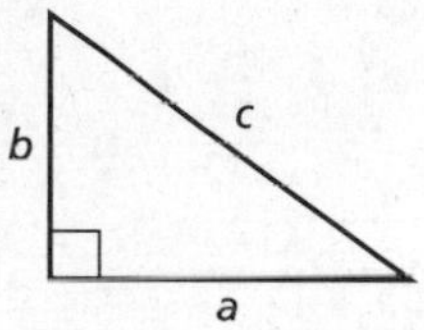 $a^2 + b^2 = c^2$

When solving geometry questions on the SAT, it is important to

1. draw a diagram to fit the facts of the problem if a diagram has not been provided.

2. examine any given diagrams for helpful clues.

3. draw additional lines or curves if needed.

4. use formulas and relationships among lines, angles, or shapes wherever necessary.

Example 1

1. List the sides of triangle below from longest to shortest.

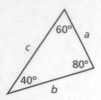

A) *b, c, a*

B) *a, b, c*

C) *b, a, c*

D) *c, b, a*

Solution

The sides will have the same relative order as the measures of the angles opposite them. So side *c* is the longest, then side *b*, then side *a*.

Answer: D

2. Find the measure of ∠*B* in the triangle below.

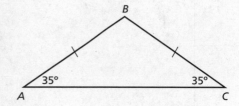

A) 110°

B) 35°

C) 30°

D) 15°

Solution

The sum of the 3 angles of a triangle is 180°. If the sum of two angles is $35 + 35 = 70°$, the third angle is $180 - 70 = 110°$.

Answer: A

Answers begin on page 720.

1. List the sides of triangle below from shortest to longest.

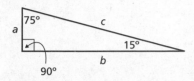

A) a, b, c
B) c, b, a
C) b, a, c
D) a, c, b

2. Find the measure of $\angle A$ in the triangle below. Note that the marks on $\overline{AB}$ and $\overline{BC}$ indicate that the line segments are equal in length.

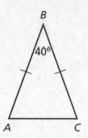

A) 140°
B) 100°
C) 70°
D) 40°

3. Find the measure of $\angle A$ in the triangle below.

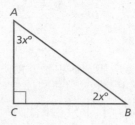

A) 18°
B) 36°
C) 54°
D) 90°

4. Find the perimeter of triangle ABC.

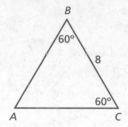

A) 24
B) 20
C) 18
D) 16

•••••• **Model SAT Questions** ••••••••••••••••••••••••••••••

1. If the ratio of the angles of a triangle is $2 : 3 : 4$, what is the degree measure of the largest angle?

A) 20°
B) 40°
C) 60°
D) 80°

Strategy: Represent the angles as $2x$, $3x$, and $4x$. We know the sum of the angles in a triangle is 180 degrees. Then $2x + 3x + 4x = 180$, $9x = 180$, and $x = 20$. But the question asks for the measure of the largest angle. So $4(20) = 80°$. This is answer choice D.

2. If 3 units and 8 units are the lengths of two sides of a triangle, what is the smallest possible integer value of the third side?

   A) 5 units

   B) 6 units

   C) 7 units

   D) 8 units

Strategy: Any side of a triangle is greater than the difference of the other two sides. Thus $8 - 3 = 5$ and the smallest possible integer value for the third side must be 6 units. Select answer choice B.

····· Explain **Determining Lengths and Angles for Special Right Triangles** ·········

In a **special right triangle**, there is some fixed feature, such as degree measure, that makes calculations on the triangle easier or for which simple formulas exist. Typically, there are two types of special right triangles found on the SAT exam: 45°–45°–90° isosceles right triangles and 30°–60°–90° right triangles.

45°–45°–90° Isosceles Right Triangle

In this type of triangle, if the length of a leg is known, then the hypotenuse can be calculated by multiplying the known leg by $\sqrt{2}$.

If the length of the hypotenuse is known, then the length of each leg can be calculated by the formula $\dfrac{\text{hypotenuse} \cdot \sqrt{2}}{2}$.

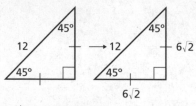

$$\text{hypotenuse} = 12$$
$$\text{leg} = \frac{1}{2}(12)\sqrt{2} = 6\sqrt{2}$$

30°–60°–90° Right Triangle

If the length of the hypotenuse is known for this special right triangle, then:

the length of the leg opposite the 30° angle $= \dfrac{\text{hypotenuse}}{2}$.

the length of the leg opposite the 60° angle $= \dfrac{\text{hypotenuse} \cdot \sqrt{3}}{2}$.

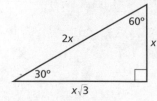

Example 1

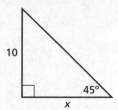

Find the value of *x* in the diagram above.

Solution

First identify the type of right triangle. This is a 45°–45°–90° isosceles right triangle. In this type of triangle, the legs are congruent, so *x* = 10. Bubble in 10 on the answer grid.

Answer: 10

Example 2

Find the value of *x* in the diagram.

A) 10
B) $5\sqrt{3}$
C) $5\sqrt{2}$
D) 5

Solution

This is a 30°–60°–90° triangle. The side opposite the 30° angle is half the length of the hypotenuse. We can use this information and determine that the length of the hypotenuse must be twice the measure of the side opposite the 30° angle. So $5 \cdot 2 = 10$. This is answer choice A.

Answer: A

Practice Determining Lengths and Angles for Special Right Triangles

Answers begin on page 720.

1. Find the value of *x* in the diagram below.

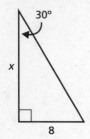

A) 8
B) $\dfrac{8}{\sqrt{3}}$
C) $8\sqrt{3}$
D) $4\sqrt{3}$

2. Find the value of *x* in the diagram below.

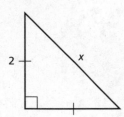

A) 2
B) $2\sqrt{2}$
C) $2\sqrt{3}$
D) $\dfrac{2}{\sqrt{2}}$

3. Find the value of *x* in the diagram below.

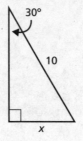

A) 5
B) $5\sqrt{2}$
C) $5\sqrt{3}$
D) 10

4. Find the value of *x* in the diagram below.

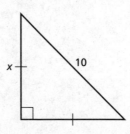

A) 5
B) $\dfrac{5}{\sqrt{2}}$
C) $5\sqrt{2}$
D) 10

1. In the triangle below, the lengths of AB, BC, and CA are equal. Point D is the mid-point between A and C. What is the length of $\overline{BD}$?

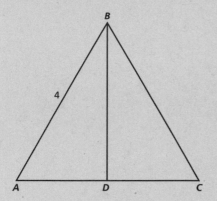

A) $\sqrt{2}$

B) $\sqrt{3}$

C) 2

D) $2\sqrt{3}$

Strategy: Because $\triangle ABC$ is equilateral, the measure of $\angle ABC$ is 60° and $\overline{BD}$ bisects $\angle ABC$.

Thus, $\triangle ABD$ is a 30° 60° 90° triangle with hypotenuse equal to 4. The leg opposite a 60° angle $= \dfrac{\text{hypotenuse} \cdot \sqrt{3}}{2}$.

So $BD = \dfrac{4 \cdot \sqrt{3}}{2}$ and $BD = 2\sqrt{3}$. Select answer choice D.

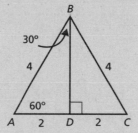

2. In the figure below, what is the length of $\overline{BD}$?

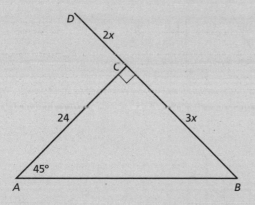

A) 16

B) 24

C) 32

D) 40

Strategy: Notice that $\triangle ABC$ is a 45°–45°–90° right isosceles triangle. In this type of triangle, the lengths of the legs are equal. So $3x = 24$ and $x = 8$. Then $2x = 2(8) = 16$. Add the lengths of the segments to find that $24 + 16 = 40$. This is answer choice D.

3. In the figure below, $\triangle ABC$ is an isosceles right triangle. What is the length of $\overline{DB}$?

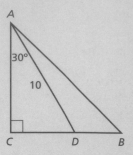

A) $5\sqrt{3} - 5$

B) 5

C) $5\sqrt{3}$

D) $10\sqrt{3} - 10$

Strategy: Begin by noting that $\triangle ACD$ is a 30°–60°–90° triangle. The length of the hypotenuse is 10 and side AC is the side opposite the 60° angle. Then the length of side AC is $\dfrac{10 \cdot \sqrt{3}}{2} = 5\sqrt{3}$. Now, because $\triangle ABC$ is isosceles, $\overline{AC} = \overline{BC}$. Side CD is the side opposite the 30° angle. So $\overline{CD} = \dfrac{10}{2} = 5$. Calculate the length of side DB as sides $BC - CD$. The length of side DB is $5\sqrt{3} - 5$, or answer choice A.

4. In the figure at right, $x = 60°$, $y = 60°$, $z = 30°$, and the length of $\overline{BD}$ is 2. What is the length of $\overline{CD}$?

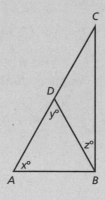

A) $\dfrac{4\sqrt{3}}{2} - 2$

B) $\dfrac{2\sqrt{3}}{3}$

C) 2

D) $\dfrac{4\sqrt{3}}{3}$

Strategy: Place all the information you know on the given figure. Since x and y both measure 60°, $\angle ABD$ must also measure 60° because the sum of the angles must be 180°. $\triangle ABD$ is equilateral, and $AB = AD = BD = 2$. $\angle ABC = 60° + z = 60° + 30° = 90°$. The measure of $\angle ACB$ is 30°. Thus, $\triangle BCD$ with two equal angles is an isosceles triangle.

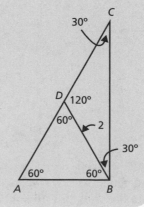

$$CD = BD = 2$$

That is answer choice C.

A **polygon** is a closed figure consisting of line segments. A polygon can have any number of sides. These are the names of some common polygons and their number of sides.

Name	Number of Sides
Triangle	3
Quadrilateral	4
Pentagon	5
Hexagon	6
Octagon	8
Decagon	10

A **regular polygon** has all sides equal and all angles equal. A regular polygon is both equilateral and equiangular.

An n-gon is a polygon with n sides. There are $n - 2$ triangles in every n-gon.

The sum of the interior angles in any triangle is 180°. Using this fact, the sum of the interior angles for an n-gon is $180(n - 2)$. If the polygon is a regular polygon, the measure of each interior angle is $\dfrac{180(n - 2)}{n}$.

Earlier in the lesson, we learned that the measure of a straight angle is 180°. Each of a polygon's exterior angles are less than 180°. The angle starts at the side of the polygon.

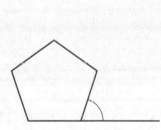 

The sum of the measures of the exterior angles of a polygon is 360°. The measure of each exterior angle of a regular polygon is $\dfrac{360}{n}$, where n is the number of sides in the polygon.

Note that at the same vertex, the interior angle and the exterior angle are supplementary.

You can save some computation time on the SAT by making use of common relationships in special quadrilaterals. The sum of the interior angles in any quadrilateral is 360°.

Name	Properties
Parallelogram	Opposite sides are parallel.
	$\overline{AB} \parallel \overline{CD}$ $\overline{BC} \parallel \overline{AD}$
	Opposite sides are equal.
	$AB = CD$ $BC = AD$
	Opposite angles are equal.
	$\angle A = \angle C$ $\angle B = \angle D$
	Consecutive angles are supplementary.
	$\angle A + \angle D = 180°$ $\angle A + \angle B = 180°$
	Diagonals bisect each other.
	$AE = EC$ $BE = DE$
Rectangle	Has all the properties of a parallelogram, plus all angles are right angles.
	$m\angle F = 90°$ $m\angle G = 90°$ $m\angle H = 90°$ $m\angle I = 90°$
	The diagonals are equal in length.
	$FH = GI$
Rhombus	Has all the properties of a parallelogram, plus all sides are equal.
	$JK = KL = LM = MJ$
	Diagonals are perpendicular.
	$\overline{JL} \perp \overline{KM}$
	Diagonals bisect the angles of the rhombus.
	$\angle KJL = \angle MJL$ $\angle JKM = \angle LKM$
	$\angle KLJ = \angle MLJ$ $\angle LMK = \angle JMK$
Square	Has all the properties of a rectangle and a rhombus.
	All angles are right angles.
	All sides are equal.
	Diagonals are equal and perpendicular.
	Diagonals bisect the angles of the square.
Trapezoid	Has only one pair of parallel sides.
	$\overline{ST} \parallel \overline{RU}$
Isosceles Trapezoid	The nonparallel sides (the legs) are equal.
	$VW = YX$
	Diagonals are congruent. $VX = YW$
	The base angles are equal.
	$\angle 1 = \angle 2$ and $\angle 3 = \angle 4$

Example 1

If the rectangle *ABCD* is divided into 24 equal squares, as shown below, what is the ratio of *AC* to *EF*? Diagonal $\overline{AC} \parallel \overline{EF}$.

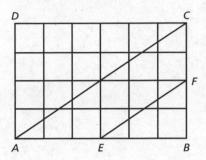

A) 1:3
B) 1:2
C) 2:1
D) 3:1

Solution

Notice that the diagonals create the similar figures $\triangle ABC$ and $\triangle EBF$. Since they are similar, the lengths of their sides are proportionate. Then $AB = 6$ units and $EB = 3$ units, and side lengths $AC : EF = AB : EB = 6:3$, or 2:1.

Answer: C

Example 2

In the figure below, $\overline{AD} \parallel \overline{BC}$. What is the degree measure of angle *x*?

A) 43
B) 53
C) 63
D) 73

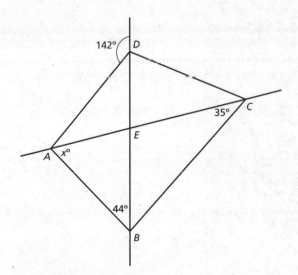

Solution

The measure of $\angle BDA$ is $180 - 142 = 38°$. The measure of $\angle EBC$ is also $38°$ because it is an alternate interior angle to $\angle BDA$. Then, in the large triangle *ABC*, $x = 180 - (35 + 44 + 38) = 180 - 117 = 63°$. Select answer choice C.

1. In the figure below, what is the length of $\overline{AB}$?

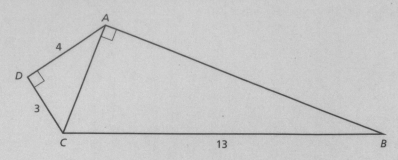

A) 5
B) 8
C) 10
D) 12

Strategy: The figure *ABCD* is a quadrilateral that is sectioned into two right triangles. Immediately identify that $\triangle ADC$ is the Pythagorean triple 3-4-5 with side $AC = 5$, and $\triangle CAB$ is the Pythagorean triple 5-12-13 with side $AB = 12$. Select answer D.

2. In the figure below, $\overline{AF} \parallel \overline{GD}$. What is the degree measure of angle x?

A) 25
B) 35
C) 45
D) 55

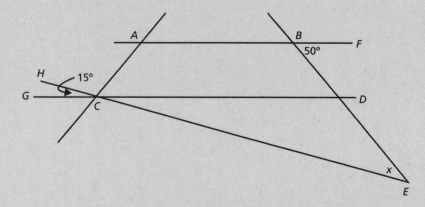

Strategy: Start with straight angle *ABF*. The measure of angle ABD is $180 - 50 = 130°$. Then, because $\overline{AF} \parallel \overline{GD}$, $m\angle ABD = \angle CDE = 130°$. Consider $\angle GCH$. It is a vertical angle with $\angle DCE$, so $m\angle GCH = \angle DCE = 15°$. Then $x = 180 - (130 + 15) = 35°$. This is answer choice B.

3. How many sides does a polygon have if the sum of its interior and exterior angles equals 200 right angles?

A) 18,000

B) 100

C) 98

D) 12

Strategy: Since the sum of the interior angles and exterior angles is the same as the measure of 200 right angles, the sum is $200 \cdot 90 = 18,000$ degrees. The sum of the exterior angles of a polygon is $360°$. Subtract 360 from the total angle measures and find that $18,000 - 360 = 17,640$. Then the sum of the interior angles is $180(n-2) = 17,640$. Solving for the variable, $n - 2 = \dfrac{17,640}{180} = 98$ and $n = 98 + 2 = 100$. Select answer choice B.

SAT-Type Questions

Answers begin on page 721.

1. If the unequal sides of a triangle are integers, and in size order are $5, x,$ and $15,$ what is the largest possible value of x?

A) 11

B) 12

C) 13

D) 14

2. In the right triangle ABC below, $m\angle ABD = 15°$ and $m\angle A = 30°$. What is the length of $\overline{DB}$?

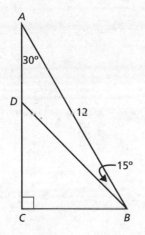

A) $6\sqrt{3}$

B) $6\sqrt{2}$

C) $6\sqrt{3} - 6$

D) $6\sqrt{2} - 6$

3. If three of the exterior angles of an equiangular polygon total 90°, how many sides does the polygon have?

   A) 6
   B) 8
   C) 12
   D) 16

4. In the figure below, the measure of ∠APD is 140°. What is the degree measure of angle x?

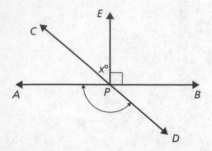

   A) 50
   B) 45
   C) 40
   D) 55

5. Lines k, l, and m intersect as shown below. What is the value of t in terms of r and s?

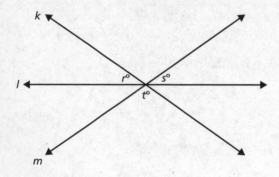

   A) s
   B) r + s
   C) 180 − (r − s)
   D) 180 − (r + s)

6. In the figure below, the lengths of $\overline{AB}$, $\overline{BC}$, and $\overline{CA}$ are equal. What is the sum of $x + y$?

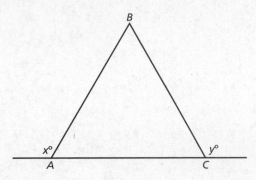

A) 60

B) 240

C) 180

D) 120

7. Triangle *ADC* below is an isosceles right triangle. What is the length of side *AC*?

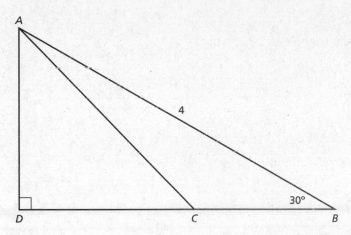

A) 1

B) $\sqrt{2}$

C) $\sqrt{3}$

D) $2\sqrt{2}$

8. The figure below is an equilateral triangle. What is the value of the altitude, h?

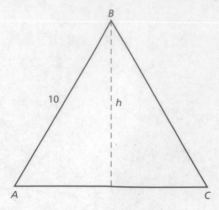

A) $5\sqrt{3}$

B) $\dfrac{5\sqrt{3}}{2}$

C) $5\sqrt{2}$

D) $\dfrac{5\sqrt{2}}{2}$

9. If the length of the hypotenuse of a $45° - 45° - 90°$ right triangle is $3\sqrt{2}$, what is the triangle's area?

A) $\dfrac{3\sqrt{2}}{2}$

B) $3\sqrt{2}$

C) 4.5

D) $4.5\sqrt{2}$

10. How many triangles can be drawn from one vertex of a convex polygon having 17 sides?

A) 12

B) 13

C) 14

D) 15

11. In the figure below, what is the value of $(c + f) - 2(a + b + d + e)$?

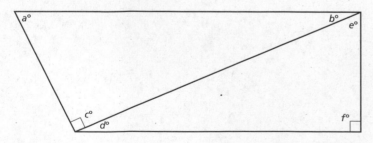

A) $0°$

B) $-90°$

C) $-180°$

D) $90°$

12. In the figure below, $j \parallel k$ and $l \parallel m$. If $x + y = 140°$, what is the value of w?

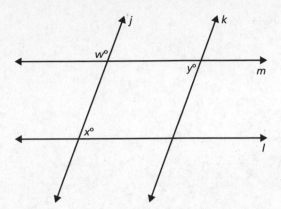

   A) 40
   B) 110
   C) 140
   D) 70

13. In the figure below, what is the value of y?

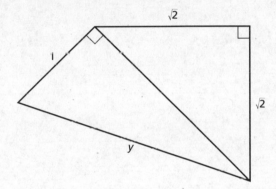

   A) 5
   B) $\sqrt{2}$
   C) $\sqrt{5}$
   D) 1

14. If the sum of the interior angles of a regular polygon equals twice the sum of its exterior angles, how many sides does it have?

   A) 3
   B) 6
   C) 8
   D) 12

15. If $x°$, $y°$, and $z°$ are measures of the angles of a triangle, then $\dfrac{x-1}{2} + \dfrac{y}{2} + \dfrac{z+1}{2} =$

   A) 90°
   B) 180°
   C) 270°
   D) 360°

16. In the isosceles right triangle *ABC* shown below, leg $\overline{AC}$ = 2.25 units. What is the length of $\overline{CD}$?

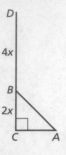

Note: Figure not drawn to scale.

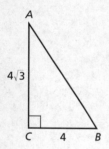

17. In the figure below, what is the measure of *AB*?

Note: Figure not drawn to scale.

18. In the figure below, triangle ACD is an equilateral triangle with $z = 30°$. The length of $CB = 3.5$ units. What is the length of $\overline{BD}$?

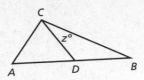

19. How many degrees are in the sum of the interior and exterior angles of a polygon having 5 sides?

20. How many sides does a polygon have if the sum of its interior and exterior angles is the same as 1,000 right angles?

Using Circle Theorems to Find Arc Lengths, Angle Measures, Chord Lengths, and Sector Areas

- **Basic Circle Terms**
- **Angles in a Circle**
- **Area of Sectors**
- **Angles Formed by Chords, Tangents, and Secants**
- **Lengths of Chords, Tangents, and Secants**
- **Intersection of Circles**

• • • • **Explain** **Basic Circle Terms** •

A **circle** is the set of points that are the same distance from a fixed point called the **center.** This distance is called the **radius.**

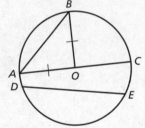

- All radii of the same circle are equal in length.
  $OA = OB = OC$

- Every triangle drawn from the center of the circle is an *isosceles* triangle, since two legs are radii. $\triangle AOB$ is isosceles.

A **chord** is a line segment that joins any two points on the circle. $\overline{AC}$ and $\overline{DE}$ are chords

A **diameter** is a chord that passes through the center of the circle. $\overline{AC}$ is a diameter.

- A diameter is the longest chord: $AC > DE$.
- The diameter is twice the radius: $AC = 2(OC)$.

An **arc** is a section of the circle, defined by two endpoints. The notation for arc AB is $\overset{\frown}{AB}$. Arcs are measured in degrees (or radians). The symbol $m\overset{\frown}{AB}$ means "the measure of arc AB."

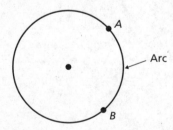

Angles in a Circle

The previous Explain section reviewed basic circle vocabulary. In this section, we review the angles in a circle and how to determine their degree measure.

- The total number of *degrees* in a circle is 360°.

- The diameter divides a circle in half. Half a circle, or **semicircle**, is 180°.

- Since there are 12 hours on a clock face, each hour

  measures $\frac{360}{12} = 30°$.

A **central angle** has its vertex at the center of the circle and its sides are radii.

$\angle AOB$ is a central angle.

$m\angle AOB = m\overset{\frown}{AB}$

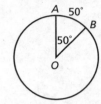

An **inscribed angle** has its vertex on the circle.

$\angle CDE$ is an inscribed angle.

$m\angle CDE = \frac{1}{2}\overset{\frown}{CE}$

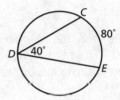

A special case of the inscribed angle is the angle inscribed in half a circle. An angle inscribed in a semicircle is a right angle.

Example: In circle O, $m\overset{\frown}{AB} = 100°$. What is the value of x? of y? of z?

$$m\overset{\frown}{AD} = 80°, \text{ and } m\overset{\frown}{BCD} = 180°.$$

$$m\angle x = \frac{1}{2} \cdot 80° \qquad m\angle y = \frac{1}{2} \cdot 100° \qquad m\angle z = \frac{1}{2} \cdot 180°$$
$$= 40° \qquad\qquad = 50° \qquad\qquad = 90°$$

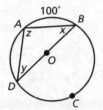

Thus $\triangle DAB$ is a right triangle, and chord DB is a diameter as well as the hypotenuse of the right triangle.

Note: The circle's diameter is always the hypotenuse of an inscribed right triangle.

Area of Sectors

A **sector of a circle** is a region defined by two radii and the arc they intercept.

The ratio of the area of a sector to the area of its circle is the same as the ratio of the central angle C to 360°.

$$\frac{\text{sector area}}{\pi r^2} = \frac{\text{central angle}}{360°}$$

Solving for sector area, sector area $= \left(\dfrac{\text{central angle}}{360°}\right)\pi r^2$.

Example 1

In the figure below, what is the value of *a*?

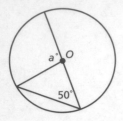

Note: Figure not drawn to scale.

A) 80°
B) 100°
C) 120°
D) 140°

Solution

Since the sides of the triangle are radii, the triangle is isosceles, and the base angles are each 50°. The third angle is 180 − (50 + 50) = 80°. Write this information on the figure.

Then *a* = 180 − 80 = 100°

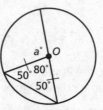

Answer: B

Example 2

The radius of circle C, shown below, is 10 cm. To the nearest tenth, what is the area of the unshaded sector in cm²?

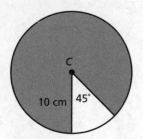

Solution

Use the formula for the area of a sector. Then sector

$$\text{area} = \left(\frac{\text{central angle}}{360°}\right)\pi r^2 = \frac{45}{360}\cdot\pi\cdot10^2 \approx 39.3°.$$

Example 3

In the figure below, what is the measure of ∠*ONC*?

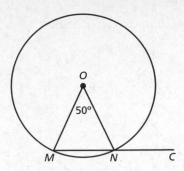

A) 50°
B) 65°
C) 100°
D) 115°

Solution

Since two legs of the triangle are radii of the circle, the triangle is isosceles. Since $m\angle MON = 50°$, the sum of the two equal base angles is $180 - 50 = 130$. Each angle is $\frac{130}{2} = 65$. The supplement of 65 is 115°.

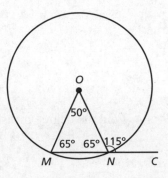

Answer: D

· · · · · · Practice **Basic Circle Terms/Angles in a Circle/ Areas of Sectors**

Answers begin on page 723.

1. In circle O, below, what is the degree measure of a?

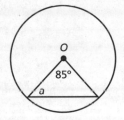

A) 10°

B) $47\frac{1}{2}°$

C) $62\frac{1}{2}°$

D) 85°

2. In the following circle, what is the degree measure of x?

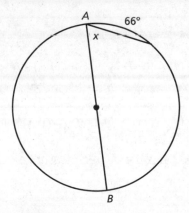

A) 57°
B) 114°
C) 65°
D) 180°

3. The radius of the circle below is 8 inches. To the nearest square inch, what is the area of the shaded sector of the circle below?

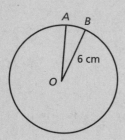

290°

A) 170 in²

B) 162 in²

C) 139 in²

D) 39 in²

4. Find the measure of ∠ADB in the circle below.

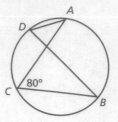

A) 20°

B) 40°

C) 80°

D) 160°

1. The sector area defined by $\overarc{AB}$ is π. Find the degree measure of ∠AOB.

6 cm

A) 1

B) 10

C) 6

D) 60

Strategy: Remember that the ratio of the area of a sector to the area of its circle is the same as the ratio of the central angle C to 360°: $\dfrac{\text{sector area}}{\pi r^2} = \dfrac{\text{central angle}}{360°}$.

Substituting given values, $\dfrac{\pi}{\pi \cdot 6^2} = \dfrac{\angle AOB}{360}$. Then $\dfrac{1}{36} = \dfrac{\angle AOB}{360}$. Cross-multiply to see that $36 \cdot (\angle AOB) = 360$. Thus the degree measure of $\angle AOB = 10$. The correct answer is choice B.

A **tangent** to a circle is a line, ray, or line segment that is drawn outside the circle and intersects the circle at exactly one point.

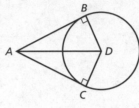

- Line $\overleftrightarrow{AC}$ is tangent to circle O at point A.

- At a given point on a circle, only one line can be drawn that is tangent to the circle.

- The radius drawn to the point of tangency is **perpendicular** to the tangent line. $\overline{OA} \perp \overline{AC}$

- Tangents drawn to a circle from the same exterior point are equal in length.

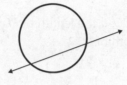

In the figure to the left, $\overline{AB}$ and $\overline{AC}$ are tangent to circle D at points B and C, respectively, so that $AB = AC$, and triangles ABD and ACD are congruent right triangles.

A **secant** to a circle is a line that intersects the circle in two points as shown.

The measure of an angle formed by one tangent and one secant is half the measure of the intercepted arc.

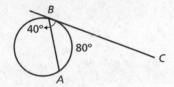

$$m\angle ABC = 40° \leftrightarrow m\widehat{BA} = 80°$$

The measure of an angle formed by two chords intersecting within a circle is equal to the average of their intercepted arcs.

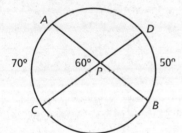

$$m\angle APC = \frac{1}{2}\left(m\widehat{AC} + m\widehat{DB}\right)$$

The measure of an angle formed by two secants, two tangents, or a secant and a tangent is equal to $\frac{1}{2}$ of the difference between the measures of the intercepted arcs.

The following illustrations show different presentations of this theorem.

1)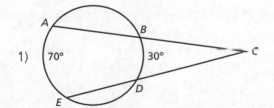

$$m\angle ACE = \frac{1}{2}(70 - 30) = \frac{1}{2}(40) = 20°$$

2)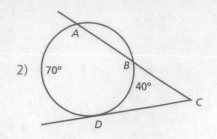

$$m\angle ACD = \frac{1}{2}(70-40) = \frac{1}{2}(30) = 15°$$

3)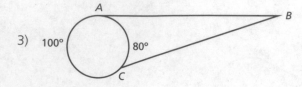

$$m\angle ABC = \frac{1}{2}(100-80) = \frac{1}{2}(20) = 10°$$

Think It Through

Example 1

In the figure below, chord $\overline{PR} \perp \overline{OQ}$. If the length of $\overline{PR}$ is 24 and the length of segment OS is 9, what is the length of $\overline{OT}$?

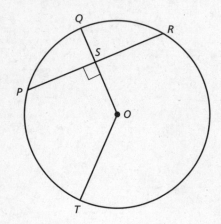

A) $\sqrt{63}$

B) 15

C) 21

D) $\sqrt{657}$

Solution

Draw in radius OP, whose length will equal the length of radius $\overline{OT}$. Find the length of OP. Since $PR \perp OQ$, OQ bisects PS at S. Therefore, PS is 12. Now use the Pythagorean theorem and $\overline{OP} = \sqrt{12^2 + 9^2} = \sqrt{225} = 15 = OT$.

Answer: B

Example 2

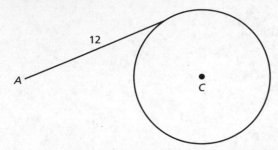

Given the figure above, if the radius of circle *C* is 5 and the tangent from exterior point *A* is 12, what is the length of segment *AC* (not drawn)?

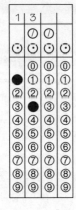

Solution

Draw the radius perpendicular to the point of tangency and label the lengths given. Then draw in line segment $\overline{AC}$. Since the radius and the tangent are perpendicular, we can use the Pythagorean theorem to solve for the length *AC*. So $5^2 + 12^2 = (AC)^2$, $25 + 144 = (AC)^2$, and $169 = (AC)^2$. Then $AC = 13$. Bubble in 13 on the answer grid.

Answer: 13

Example 3

Mt. Everest is approximately 8,000 meters high. The Earth's radius is approximately 6,400 kilometers. What is the approximate distance to the horizon from the top of Mt. Everest?

A) 102,464 km

B) 51,232 km

C) 320 km

D) 160 km

Solution

Begin by converting 8,800 meters to 8 kilometers. Draw a diagram.

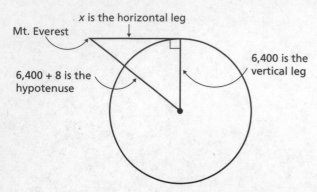

It is now easy to see that we need to use the Pythagorean theorem to solve the problem. So $x^2 + 6,400^2 = 6,408^2$. Solving for the variable, $x \approx \sqrt{6,408^2 - 6,400^2} \approx 320$ km.

Answer: C

Example 4

In circle O, secant $\overline{PBC}$ and tangent $\overline{PA}$ are drawn.

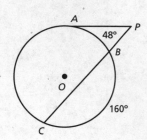

If $m\widehat{AB} = 48°$ and $m\widehat{BC} = 160°$, what is the degree measure of $\angle P$?

A) 52

B) 76

C) 100

D) 104

Solution

The degree measure of $\angle P = \dfrac{1}{2}\left(m\widehat{AC} - m\widehat{AB}\right)$. Since a circle has 360°,

$m\widehat{AC} = 360 - (48 + 160)$ which simplifies to $360 - 208 = 152°$. Substitute this

value into the formula to see that the measure of $\angle P = \dfrac{1}{2}(152 - 48) = \dfrac{1}{2}(104) = 52°$.

Answer: A

1.

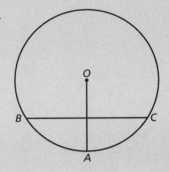

In the figure above, chord $\overline{BC}$ bisects $\overline{OA}$, and $\overline{BC} \perp \overline{OA}$. If the radius of the circle O is 12, what is the length of chord $\overline{BC}$?

A) $3\sqrt{3}$

B) 63

C) $8\sqrt{3}$

D) $12\sqrt{3}$

Strategy:

Method 1: Draw radii OB and OC. Mark each length as 12. Mark the intersection of OA and BC as point D. Since OA is also 12, and BC bisects OA, OD is 6. The triangles formed are right triangles ($BC \perp OA$ is given). You should recognize the triangles as 30°–60°–90° right triangles because a leg is $\dfrac{1}{2}$ hypotenuse. The other leg is $\dfrac{1}{2}$ hypotenuse ·

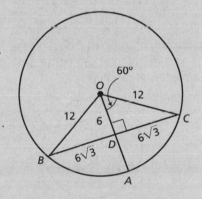

$\sqrt{3}$ or $\dfrac{1}{2}(12)\sqrt{3} = 6\sqrt{3}$. The length of chord BC is

the sum of the lengths of these two "other" legs. $6\sqrt{3} + 6\sqrt{3} = 12\sqrt{3}$.

Method 2: If you didn't recognize the special triangle, then you could have used the Pythagorean Theorem to find the unknown leg; that is, $6^2 + x^2 = 12^2$, $36 + x^2 = 144$, and $x^2 = 108$. Then $x = \sqrt{108} = \sqrt{36 \cdot 3} = 6\sqrt{3}$. Again, $6\sqrt{3} + 6\sqrt{3} = 12\sqrt{3}$.

2. In circle O, chords $\overline{AB}$ and $\overline{CD}$ intersect at point E.

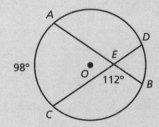

If $m\overset{\frown}{AC} = 98°$ and $m\angle CEB = 112°$, what is $m\overset{\frown}{DB}$?

A) $38°$

B) $49°$

C) $68°$

D) $83°$

Explain Lengths of Chords, Tangents, and Secants

Just as we can use theorems and relationships to determine arc and angle measures, we can also make use of chord, tangent, and secant relationships to determine their measures. The following are commonly tested on the SAT.

- If two chords intersect within a circle, the product of the segments of one chord equals the product of the segments of the other chord.

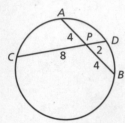

$$AP \cdot PB = CP \cdot PD$$
$$4 \cdot 4 = 8 \cdot 2$$

- If two secants to a circle meet at a common point P outside the circle, the product of the whole length of secant 1 and its external segment equals the product of the whole length of secant 2 and its external segment.

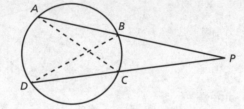

$PA \cdot PB = PD \cdot PC$

Whole $\cdot$ External = Whole $\cdot$ External

- If one tangent and one secant meet at a common point P outside the circle, the product of the whole length of the secant and its external segment equals the square of the length of the tangent.

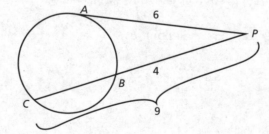

$PC \cdot PB = (PA)^2$

Whole $\cdot$ External = Tangent^2

- If two tangents to a circle are drawn from a common point, the lengths of the tangents are equal.

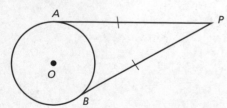

$$PA = PB$$

462 Additional Topics in Math • Lesson 3

Explain   Intersection of Circles

If two circles intersect at two points, the line connecting their centers is the perpendicular bisector of their common chord.

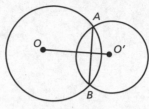

$\overline{OO'}$ cuts $\overline{AB}$ into 2 congruent parts,

$\overline{OO'}$ is called the **line of centers** for the circles.

Think It Through

Example 1

Examine the illustration below. Circle O is inscribed in $\triangle MNP$ with tangent points A, B, and C. If $MN = 12$, $MP = 14$, and $NB = 7$, find the perimeter of the triangle.

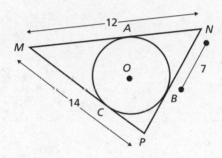

A) 46

B) 38

C) 40

D) 42

Solution

Since tangents from the same point are equal in length, $NB = NA = 7$. Then $MA = MN - NA$, and $MA = 12 - 7 = 5$. Because $MA = 5$, $MC = 5$. Now, $CP = MP - MC$, and $CP = 14 - 5 = 9$. Since $CP = 9$, $BP = 9$. Finally, the perimeter of $\triangle MNP = 12 + 14 + 7 + 9 = 42$.

Answer: D

Example 2

In the following figure, tangent $\overline{PA}$ and secant $\overline{PCB}$ are drawn to the circle. $PA = 6$ and $PC = 4$. Find PB.

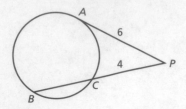

Note: Figure not drawn to scale.

A) $\dfrac{3}{2}$

B) 5

C) 6

D) 9

Solution

In the figure, tangent PA and secant PCB meet at a common point, P, outside the circle. So, to determine the length of PB, use the relationship whole · external = tangent². Then $PB \cdot 4 = 6^2$ and $PB = \dfrac{36}{4} = 9$.

Answer: D

· · · · · **Practice** **Lengths of Chords, Tangents, and Secants/Intersection of Circles** · · · · · · · · · · · · ·

Answers begin on page 723.

1. In the circle, secant $\overline{ADB}$ and tangent $\overline{AC}$ are drawn from external point A.

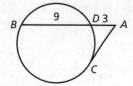

If $AD = 3$ and $DB = 9$, what is the length of $\overline{AC}$?

A) $\sqrt{6}$

B) $3\sqrt{3}$

C) 6

D) 27

2. In the circle, secants $\overline{PA}$ and $\overline{PD}$ are drawn from point P.

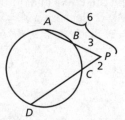

If $PB = 3$, $PA = 6$, and $PC = 2$, what is the length of $\overline{PD}$?

A) 7

B) 9

C) 11

D) 16

1. In the figure below, chords $\overline{AC}$ and $\overline{BD}$ intersect in the circle at point E. What is the length of chord $\overline{AC}$?

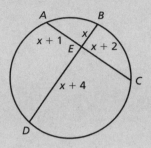

A) 3

B) 4

C) 6

D) 7

Strategy: Segments AC and BD are both chords, and the product of the segments of each chord are equal. So $AE \cdot EC = BE \cdot ED$, and $(x+1)(x+2) = x(x+4)$. FOIL on the left-hand side and distribute on the right-hand side to see that $x^2 + 3x + 2 = x^2 + 4x$. Subtract x^2 from each side and solve for the unknown: $3x + 2 = 4x$, and then $x = 2$. Now the length of $\overline{AC}$ is $x + 1 + x + 2$. Substituting 2 for x, $2 + 1 + 2 + 2 = 7$. Answer choice D is correct.

Example 2

Secants $\overline{ABP}$ and $\overline{DCP}$ are drawn to the circle below. Find the sum of the lengths of the secants.

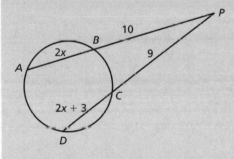

A) 18

B) 30

C) 34

D) 54

Solution

The lengths of two secants that meet at point outside the circle have the relationship whole $\cdot$ external = whole $\cdot$ external. So $(2x + 10) \cdot 10 = (2x + 3 + 9) \cdot 9$. Simplifying, $20x + 100 = 18x + 108$. Then $2x = 8$ and $x = 4$. The length of secant $ABP = 2(4) + 10 = 18$, and the length of segment $DCP = 2(4) + 3 + 9 = 20$. The sum of the secants is $18 + 20 = 38$. Select answer choice C.

Answers begin on page 723.

1. Circles O and O' share common chord $\overline{AB}$. If the length of $\overline{OA} = 13$ and the length of $\overline{OE} = 12$, find the length of $\overline{AB}$.

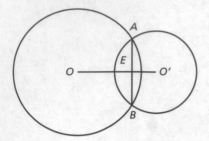

   A) 4
   B) 7
   C) 10
   D) 14

2. If the radius of the circle below is 5 units, what is the length of the side of the square?

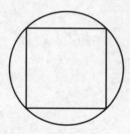

   A) 5
   B) $5\sqrt{2}$
   C) $5\sqrt{3}$
   D) 10

3. The sector area defined by $\overset{\frown}{AB}$ is 14π. Find the radius of circle O.

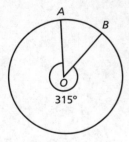

   A) 64
   B) 32
   C) 16
   D) 4

4. In the figure below, $\overline{AB}$ and $\overline{AC}$ are tangents to the circle.

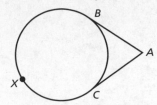

If $m\widehat{BXC} = 250°$, what is $m\angle BAC$?

A) 55

B) 70

C) 90

D) 110

5. Chords $\overline{AC}$ and $\overline{BD}$ intersect in the circle at point E. What is the length of chord $\overline{BD}$?

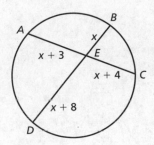

A) 12

B) 20

C) 31

D) 32

6. Segment $\overline{MN}$ passes through the centers of each tangent circle in the figure below. The radius of each circle is twice the radius of the circle to its left.

What is $\dfrac{ON}{MN}$?

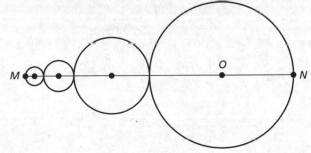

A) $\dfrac{4}{15}$

B) $\dfrac{1}{8}$

C) $\dfrac{1}{5}$

D) $\dfrac{1}{10}$

7. Circles O and O' intersect at two distinct points. The maximum number of common tangents the two circles may have is

A) 1

B) 2

C) 3

D) 4

8. In the circle below, chord $\overline{CD}$ intersects chord $\overline{AB}$ at E.

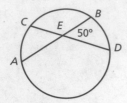

If $m\angle BED = 50°$, what is the sum of $m\widehat{BC}$ and $m\widehat{DA}$?

A) 50°

B) 100°

C) 260°

D) 130°

9. In the figure below, $\overline{RS}$ is tangent to circle O. If $\overline{PO}$ is 5 and $\overline{QR}$ is 8, what is the value of $\overline{RS}$?

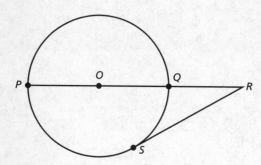

A) 5

B) 12

C) $\sqrt{39}$

D) $\sqrt{8}$

10. Given: $\overline{PA}$ and $\overline{PB}$ are tangent to circle O at points A and B, respectively.

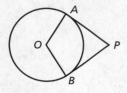

Which of the following is *always* true?

A) $m\angle P - m\angle AOB$

B) $m\angle P > m\angle AOB$

C) $m\angle P + m\angle AOB - 90°$

D) $m\angle P + m\angle AOB - 180°$

11. In circle O, chord $\overline{CD}$ is perpendicular to diameter $\overline{AOB}$ at point E.

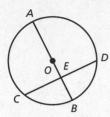

If $OD = 17$ and $CD = 30$, what is the length of $\overline{EB}$?

A) 8

B) 9

C) 10

D) 15

12. Two chords intersect inside a circle. The lengths of the segments of the first chord are 6 and 15, and the full length of the second chord is 23. The lengths of the segments of the second chord could be:

A) 5 and 18

B) 3 and 20

C) 11.5 and 11.5

D) 10 and 13

Student-Produced Response Questions

13. Circle O is inscribed in $\triangle ACE$ as shown below. If $AB = 6$ inches, $BC = 5$ inches, and $DE = 7$ inches, what is the perimeter of $\triangle ACE$, in inches?

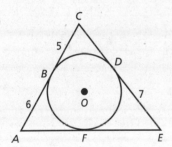

14. $\overline{PA}$ and $\overline{PB}$ are tangents drawn to circle O from point P. The measure of $\angle AOP$ is 40°. What is $m\angle APB$?

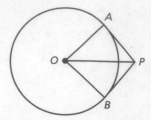

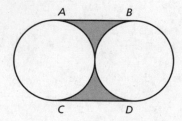

15. The two congruent circles in the figure below each have a radius of 5.

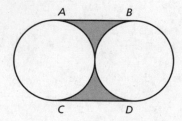

If $\overline{AB}$ and $\overline{CD}$ are tangent to the circles as shown, what is the area of the shaded region to the nearest tenth?

16. In circle O, secant $\overline{PC}$ and tangent $\overline{PA}$ are drawn.

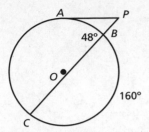

If $m\widehat{AB} = 48°$ and $m\widehat{BC} = 160°$, what is $m\angle P$?

17. In circle O, chords $\overline{AB}$ and $\overline{CD}$ intersect at E.

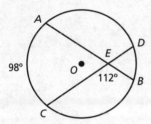

If $m\widehat{AC} = 98°$ and $m\angle CEB = 112°$, what is $m\widehat{BD}$?

18. In the figure below, $\overrightarrow{AB}$ and $\overrightarrow{AC}$ are tangents to the circle.

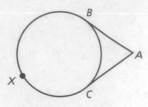

If $m\overarc{BXC} = 250°$, what is $m\angle BAC$?

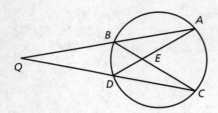

19. In the given circle, secants $\overline{QBA}$ and $\overline{QDC}$ are drawn from external point Q. Chords $\overline{AD}$ and $\overline{CB}$ intersect at point E.

If $m\angle ABC = 40°$ and $m\angle DCB = 20°$, what is $m\angle AEC$?

20. In a circle, chords $\overline{AB}$ and $\overline{CD}$ intersect at point E. Point E is the midpoint of chord $\overline{CD}$, $AE = 4$, and $BE = 16$. What is the length of chord CD?

LESSON 4:

Derivation and Application of Trigonometric Ratios and the Pythagorean Theorem; Solving Right Triangles

- **Derivation and Application of Trigonometric Ratios**

- **The Pythagorean Theorem**

This lesson reviews strategies for solving right triangle mathematics problems. As you work through the problems in this lesson, remember that if the problem is strictly limited to the lengths of sides of the right triangle, use the Pythagorean theorem. If a problem includes information about angles or asks for information about angles, use trigonometric ratios.

Explain Derivation and Application of Trigonometric Ratios

For any right triangle, we can define certain ratios for the acute angles in the triangle. These ratios of trigonometry allow us to find a missing angle or missing side when given some information about the triangle. The trigonometric ratios we are concerned with here are **sine**, **cosine**, and **tangent**.

The following chart of definitions and formulas refers to the right triangle ABC where $m\angle C = 90°$.

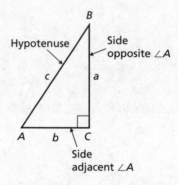

Definition	Formulas
The **sine** of an acute angle equals the length of the leg opposite the angle divided by the hypotenuse.	$\sin \angle A = \dfrac{\text{leg opposite } \angle A}{\text{hypotenuse}} = \dfrac{a}{c}$ $\sin \angle B = \dfrac{\text{leg opposite } \angle B}{\text{hypotenuse}} = \dfrac{b}{c}$
The **cosine** of an acute angle equals the length of the leg adjacent the angle divided by the hypotenuse.	$\cos \angle A = \dfrac{\text{leg adjacent to } \angle A}{\text{hypotenuse}} = \dfrac{b}{c}$ $\cos \angle B = \dfrac{\text{leg adjacent to } \angle B}{\text{hypotenuse}} = \dfrac{a}{c}$
The **tangent** of an acute angle equals the length of the leg opposite the angle divided by the leg adjacent to the angle.	$\tan \angle A = \dfrac{\text{leg opposite } \angle A}{\text{leg adjacent to } \angle A} = \dfrac{a}{b}$ $\tan \angle B = \dfrac{\text{leg opposite } \angle B}{\text{leg adjacent to } \angle B} = \dfrac{b}{a}$

$$\mathbf{S}in = \frac{Opp}{Hyp} \qquad \mathbf{C}os = \frac{Adj}{Hyp} \qquad and \ \mathbf{T}an = \frac{Opp}{Adj}.$$

<u>Note</u>: Remember these trigonometric ratios with **"SOH-CAH-TOA."**

There are a number of formulas that show the relationships among the trigonometric functions. Use the table to verify these for yourself.

- $\sin \angle A = \cos \angle B$
- $\sin \angle B = \cos \angle A$
- $\tan \angle A = \dfrac{\sin \angle A}{\cos \angle A}$
- $\tan \angle B = \dfrac{\sin \angle B}{\cos \angle B}$

Since the value of the trig ratio depends only on the angle and not the size of the right triangle, consider the following three overlapping right triangles. They all share a common acute angle, $\angle A$. Since all three triangles ($\triangle ABC$, $\triangle ADE$, $\triangle AFG$) are similar, the corresponding sides are proportional.

Therefore, $\dfrac{BC}{AB} = \dfrac{DE}{AD} = \dfrac{FG}{AF} = \sin \angle A$. This relationship is true for $\cos \angle A$ and $\tan \angle A$.

<u>Reminders</u>:

1. The value of the trigonometric ratio does not depend on the size of the right triangle.
2. The value of a trigonometric ratio depends only on the measure of the angle.
3. Trigonometric ratios are **not functions** of the 90° right angle.
4. The product of $\tan \angle A \cdot \tan \angle B = 1$. See above where $\tan \angle A = \dfrac{a}{b}$ and $\tan \angle B = \dfrac{b}{a}$, so that $\dfrac{a}{b} \cdot \dfrac{b}{a} = 1$.

<u>Note</u>: When you use a calculator to find trigonometric functions, first be sure that the calculator is in degree mode.

Think It Through

Example

If equilateral $\triangle ABC$ has a side of 6.8 feet, what is the length, to the nearest tenth, of an altitude drawn to any side?

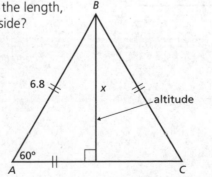

Solution

We need to find the length of the altitude marked x. It is opposite $\angle A$, so we can use the sine function to solve. Then $\sin 60° = \dfrac{x}{6.8}$. Cross-multiply to find that $6.8 \cdot \sin 60° = x$ and $x = 5.88$. Rounding to the nearest tenth, $x = 5.9$ inches. Note that this problem also could have been solved by utilizing 30°–60°–90° triangle relationships.

Answer: 5.9

Practice Derivation and Application of Trigonometric Ratios

Answers begin on page 726.

1. In triangle ABC, $m\angle A = 30°$, and the length of the hypotenuse is 7 feet. What is the length of side BC?

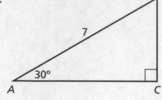

2. In the figure given, what is the value of side x to the nearest tenth?

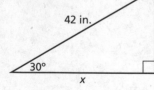

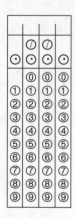

3. The triangle below illustrates the flight of a fighter jet that takes off at an angle of 45° with the ground. When the altitude of the plane is 28,000 feet, what is the distance, d, in miles (to the nearest tenth), that the plane has flown? (5,280 feet = 1 mile)

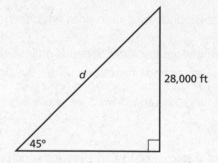

1. If a tree, shown below, casts a 12-foot shadow when the sun is at a 60° angle with the ground, which of the following equations gives the height, x, in feet, of the tree?

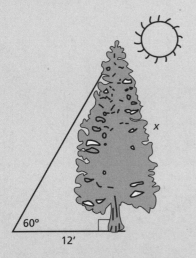

A) $12 \cos 60° = x$

B) $12 \sin 60° = x$

C) $12 \cos 30° = x$

D) $12 \tan 60° = x$

Strategy: Since the hypotenuse is not known or involved in this problem, the correct trigonometric function must be the tangent. Using the angle given, the correct equation is $\tan 60° = \dfrac{x}{12}$, or $12 \tan 60° = x$.

2 In the figure below, $\triangle ABD$ is an isosceles right triangle. If $AB = 10\sqrt{2}$ and $m\angle BCD = 30°$, what is the length of segment DC?

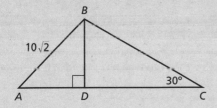

A) $5\sqrt{6}$

B) 10

C) $10\sqrt{2}$

D) $10\sqrt{3}$

Strategy: First, using special right triangle data, the sides of an isosceles right triangle are known as leg-leg-leg $\sqrt{2}$, or (in this case) $10-10-10\sqrt{2}$. This means that $AD = BD = 10$.

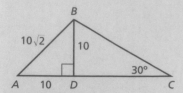

Then using trigonometry, $\tan 30° = \dfrac{\text{opposite leg}}{\text{adjacent}} = \dfrac{10}{DC}$

$DC (\tan 30°) = 10$

$DC = \dfrac{10}{\tan 30°} = \dfrac{10}{0.5774} = 17.32$

Checking the calculated answer against the answer choices, we find that A, B, and C are too small. But $10\sqrt{3} = 17.32$. Select answer choice D.

3. If $\sin x = \cos (x + 20)$, what is the value of x?

Solution

The unknown values x and $x + 20$ must be complementary angles. Add the values and set them equal to 90°. Then $x + x + 20 = 90$, $2x + 20 = 90$, $2x = 70$, and $x = 35$. Bubble in 35 on the answer grid.

We have referenced the Pythagorean theorem in several previous lessons and problems.
In Lesson 1 of this category, the formula was listed as one to memorize:

For any right triangle, *ABC*, with right angle *C* and acute angles *A* and *B*,
hypotenuse *c*, and legs *a* and *b*,

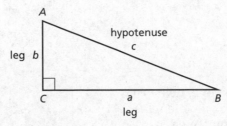

$$c^2 = a^2 + b^2 \text{ or } c = \sqrt{a^2 + b^2}$$

Make sure you have memorized the following Pythagorean triples:

3, 4, 5   5, 12, 13   7, 24, 25   8, 15, 17

Problems may contain multiples of the triples:

6, 8, 10   10, 24, 26   14, 48, 50   16, 30, 34

Knowing these common triples and their multiples will save you time on the SAT.

····· **Think It Through** ··

Example

Which of the following number sets represents the side lengths of a right triangle?

A) 1, 2, 3
B) 1.5, 2, 2.5
C) 3.5, 4.5. 5.5
D) 5, 6, 7

Solution

Eliminate choices A and D as they are not triples. Multiply the remaining choices by
2 to transform them into integers until you find a triple. Answer choice B becomes
$2(1.5, 2, 2.5) \rightarrow 3, 4, 5$. Stop checking and select answer choice B.

Answer: B

····· **Practice** **The Pythagorean Theorem** ·····························

Answers begin on page 726.

1. Two college roommates, Howie and Manuel, leave
    their math class at the same time. Howie travels
    south at 30 miles per hour and Manuel travels
    west at 40 miles per hour. How far apart are the
    roommates at the end of one hour?

    A) 50 miles
    B) 60 miles
    C) 70 miles
    D) 80 miles

2. If a right triangle has sides of lengths $x + 9, x + 2$,
    and $x + 10$, where $x + 10$ is the hypotenuse, find the
    value of x.

    A) 3
    B) 5
    C) 12
    D) 13

1. If the hypotenuse of a triangle is 4 inches more than one leg and 2 inches more than the other leg, then what is the perimeter of the triangle?

    A) 4 inches

    B) 10 inches

    C) 24 inches

    D) 48 inches

Strategy: Use the Pythagorean theorem to determine the lengths of the triangle's sides. Let x represent the hypotenuse. Then the legs can be represented by $x - 2$ and $x - 4$.

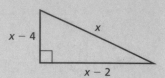

Then, $c^2 = a^2 + b^2$, so substituting in the values, $x^2 = (x-4)^2 + (x-2)^2$.

$x^2 = (x^2 - 8x + 16) + (x^2 - 4x + 4)$	Expand the binomials.
$x^2 = 2x^2 - 12x + 20$	Combine like terms.
$0 = x^2 - 12x + 20$	Subtract x^2 from each side.
$0 = (x - 10)(x - 2)$	Factor.
$x - 10 = 0 \qquad x - 2 = 0$	
$x = 10 \qquad$ or $\qquad x = 2$	Solve.

The value cannot be $x = 2$, because then the side lengths are 0 and –2. Reject this value. Then $x = 10$ and the side lengths are 10 inches, 8 inches, and 6 inches. The perimeter is 24 inches. Select answer choice C.

2. The semicircle below has a radius of r inches, and chord $\overline{CD}$ is parallel to the diameter $\overline{AB}$. If the length of $\overline{CD}$ is $\dfrac{1}{2}$ of the length of $\overline{AB}$, what is the distance between the chord and the diameter in terms of r?

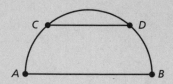

    A) $r\sqrt{3}$

    B) $\dfrac{r}{2}\sqrt{3}$

    C) $\dfrac{r}{2}$

    D) $\dfrac{r}{2}\sqrt{2}$

Strategy: Draw a line from the center of length $\overline{AB}$ to the center of length $\overline{CD}$ and label it x. We know that since x is the distance from $\overline{AB}$ to $\overline{CD}$, $\overline{OE}$ is perpendicular to $\overline{CD}$ and bisects $\overline{CD}$. The length of $\overline{CD}$ is half the length of $\overline{AB}$, or $\frac{1}{2} \cdot (2r) = r$. Then $ED = \frac{r}{2}$.

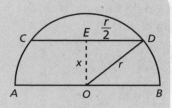

Then using the Pythagorean theorem, $x^2 + \left(\frac{r}{2}\right)^2 = r^2$. Isolate the x^2 term on one side of the equation and $x^2 = r^2 - \left(\frac{r}{2}\right)^2$. Combine the like terms by creating a common denominator: $\frac{4r^2}{4} - \frac{1r^2}{4} = \frac{3}{4}r^2$. Now take the square root of both sides and $x = \sqrt{\frac{3}{4}r^2} = \frac{r}{2}\sqrt{3}$. Select answer choice B.

· · · · · · **SAT-Type Questions** ·

Answers begin on page 726.

1. If the length of an altitude of an equilateral triangle is $5\sqrt{3}$, then the length of a side of the triangle is

    A) 4
    B) 5
    C) $5\sqrt{3}$
    D) 10

2. Triangle ABC is inscribed in circle O so that side AB of the triangle is the diameter of the circle and $m\angle CAB$ is $30°$. If the radius of the circle is 4, what the measure of $\angle COB$?

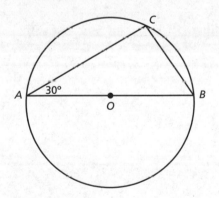

    A) $30°$
    B) $45°$
    C) $60°$
    D) $90°$

3. In the figure below, $\triangle ABC$ is a right triangle. If $\sin \angle A = \dfrac{1}{2}$ and the length of side AB is 6, what is the length of side AC?

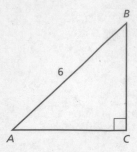

A) $\dfrac{3\sqrt{3}}{3}$

B) $3\sqrt{3}$

C) 3

D) $3\sqrt{2}$

4. To the nearest tenth of an inch, find the perimeter of a rectangle whose diagonal is 25 inches and whose width is 16 inches.

A) 19.2 inches

B) 29.2 inches

C) 70.4 inches

D) 60.2 inches

5. In an isosceles triangle, each of the equal sides is 26 cm long. The base is 20 cm long. Find the area of the triangle.

A) 12 cm²

B) 24 cm²

C) 240 cm²

D) 480 cm²

6. The legs of a right triangle have a ratio of 5:12. If the hypotenuse is 65 feet long, what is the length of the shorter leg?

A) 13 feet

B) 25 feet

C) 60 feet

D) 125 feet

7. In the figure below, arc *QRC* is a quarter of a circle with center at *A*. If *AB* is 8 and the measure of ∠*BAC* is 30°, then, to the nearest tenth, segment *AR* =

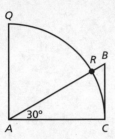

   A) 6.9
   B) 5.6
   C) 6
   D) 4

8. In the figure below, if $\sin n° + \sin n° = 1$, then $x° =$

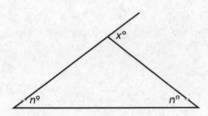

   A) 90
   B) 60
   C) 45
   D) 30

9. In the figure below, $\sin B - \sin A =$

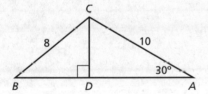

   A) $\dfrac{1}{8}$

   B) $\dfrac{1}{2}$

   C) $\dfrac{5}{8}$

   D) $\dfrac{2}{3}$

10. The semicircle below has a radius of r, and chord $\overline{CD}$ is parallel to the diameter $\overline{AB}$. If the distance between the chord and the diameter is $\dfrac{\sqrt{5}}{3}r$, what is the length of the chord $\overline{CD}$ in terms of r?

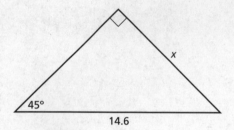

A) $\dfrac{4}{3}r$

B) $\dfrac{2}{3}r$

C) $\dfrac{2}{9}r^2$

D) $\dfrac{4}{9}r^2$

Student-Produced Response Questions

11. In the figure below, what is the length of side x to the nearest tenth?

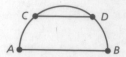

12. In $\triangle ABC$, $\angle C$ is a right angle. If $\sin \angle A = \dfrac{3}{4}$, what is the tan $\angle B$ to the nearest thousandth?

13. In $\triangle DFG$, $\angle G$ is a right angle and $\tan \angle D = \dfrac{5}{7}$. What is the cos $\angle F$ to the nearest thousandth?

14. In $\triangle RST$, $\angle T$ is a right angle and $\cos \angle R = \dfrac{4}{9}$. To the nearest thousandth, find the cos $\angle S$.

15. If the length of the altitude of equilateral $\triangle ABC$ is $12\sqrt{3}$, what is the perimeter of the triangle?

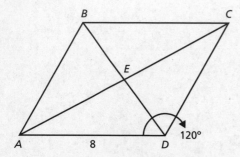

16. In the given figure, rhombus $ABCD$, $\angle ADC = 120°$, $AD = 8$, and the diagonals intersect at E. What is the length of segment ED?

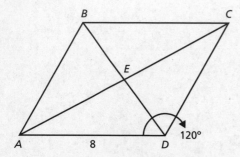

17. In triangle ABC, $\angle A = 30°$, $\angle B = 60°$, and $BC = 4$. What is the length of AC to the nearest hundredth?

18. A ladder is leaning against a house with the top of the ladder 104 inches off the ground. The base of the ladder is 40 inches from the side of the house. How many inches long is the ladder? Round your answer to the nearest whole nu

19. What is the length of the missing side x of the triangle to the nearest tenth?

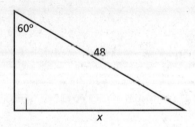

20. Find the length of the missing side *x* of the triangle to the nearest tenth.

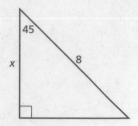

⊙	⊘ ⊙	⊘ ⊙	⊙
	⓪	⓪	⓪
①	①	①	①
②	②	②	②
③	③	③	③
④	④	④	④
⑤	⑤	⑤	⑤
⑥	⑥	⑥	⑥
⑦	⑦	⑦	⑦
⑧	⑧	⑧	⑧
⑨	⑨	⑨	⑨

LESSON 5:

Degree and Radian Measure, Trigonometric Functions, and the Unit Circle

- **Degrees, Radians, and Arc Lengths**

- **The Unit Circle and Trigonometric Functions with Radian Measure**

• • • • • • **Explain**   **Degrees, Radians, and Arc Lengths** •

A **radian** is the measure of a central angle that intercepts an arc equal in length to the radius of the circle.

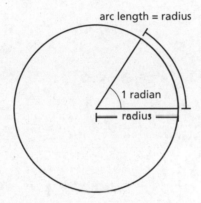

For a circle with radius r, let θ be the measure of a central angle, in radians, and let s be the measure of the intercepted arc. Then

$$\theta = \frac{s}{r}$$

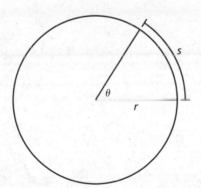

The circumference of a circle is the length of one complete rotation of a circle's radius and its formula is $C = 2\pi r$. Consider one complete rotation to be s. Then, substituting that information into the formula above, we have

$$\theta = \frac{2\pi r}{r} = 2\pi$$

Therefore, a complete rotation, which we know is 360°, is also 2π radians. A half rotation is π radians.

$360° = 2\pi$ radians.

Divide both sides by 2: $180° = \pi$ radians.

The above relationship shows that we can easily convert between degree measure and radian measure. To convert between degrees and radians, use the same techniques we used for measurement conversions. If you are careful to include labels and see that they cancel correctly, the process is straightforward.

To convert from d degrees to r radians: $d \text{ degrees} \cdot \dfrac{\pi \text{ radians}}{180 \text{ degrees}} = r \text{ radians}.$

To convert from r radians to d degrees: $r \text{ radians} \cdot \dfrac{180 \text{ degrees}}{\pi \text{ radians}} = d \text{ degrees}.$

Think It Through

Example 1

Convert 40° to radians.

A) $\dfrac{\pi}{3}$ radians

B) $\dfrac{\pi}{9}$ radians

C) $\dfrac{4}{9}\pi$ radians

D) $\dfrac{2}{9}\pi$ radians

Solution

We are converting from degrees to radians, so use

$d \text{ degrees} \cdot \dfrac{\pi \text{ radians}}{180 \text{ degrees}} = r \text{ radians}.$ Then

$40 \text{ degrees} \cdot \dfrac{\pi \text{ radians}}{180 \text{ degrees}} = \dfrac{40\pi}{180} \text{ radians} = \dfrac{2}{9}\pi \text{ radians}.$

Answer: D

Example 2

Express $\dfrac{4\pi}{3}$ radians in degree measure.

A) 240 degrees

B) 240 π degrees

C) 480 degrees

D) 480 π degrees

Solution

We are converting from radians to degrees, so use

$r \text{ radians} \cdot \dfrac{180 \text{ degrees}}{\pi \text{ radians}} = d \text{ degrees}.$ Then

$\dfrac{4\pi}{3} \text{ radians} \cdot \dfrac{\overset{60}{\cancel{180}} \text{ degrees}}{\pi \text{ radians}} = 240 \text{ degrees}.$

Answer: A

Example 3

Circle O has a radius of 10 inches. What is the length, in inches, of the arc subtended by a central angle measuring 2 radians?

A) 0.2 inches

B) 5 inches

C) 10 inches

D) 20 inches

Solution

We know the measure of any central angle is $\theta = \dfrac{s}{r}$. So $2 = \dfrac{s}{10}$ and $s = 20$ inches.

Answer: D

> **Definition**
>
> In mathematics, **subtended** means "opposite from."

···· **Practice** **Degrees, Radians, and Arc Lengths** ··········

Answers begin on page 729.

1. Express 270° in radian measure.

    A) $-\dfrac{3\pi}{2}$ radians

    B) $\dfrac{4\pi}{3}$ radians

    C) $\dfrac{4\pi}{3}$ radians

    D) $\dfrac{3\pi}{2}$ radians

2. Express $\dfrac{5}{6}\pi$ radians in degree measure.

    A) 120 degrees

    B) 150 degrees

    C) 150π degrees

    D) 180π degrees

···· **Model SAT Questions** ··················

1. Find the length of the radius of a circle in which a central angle of 3 radians intercepts an arc of 6 meters.

    A) 2 meters

    B) $\dfrac{1}{2}$ meter

    C) 18 meters

    D) 2π meters

    Strategy: We know that $\theta = \dfrac{s}{r}$. Substituting in the known values, $3 = \dfrac{6}{r}$ and $r = 2$ meters. This is answer choice A.

$\cdots\cdots$ **Explain** **The Unit Circle and Trigonometric** $\cdots\cdots\cdots\cdots\cdots\cdots\cdots$
Functions with Radian Measure

A unit circle is a circle whose center is at the origin of the *xy*-plane and whose radius is 1 unit.

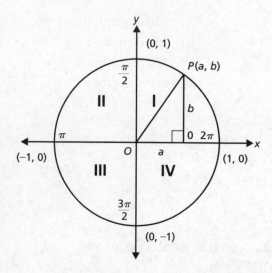

Let point *P* start at the coordinate (1,0) and move counterclockwise along the unit circle. The measure of the angle formed by the *x*-axis and the **terminal side**, $\overrightarrow{OP}$, starts at 0 and increases until it reaches 2π (one complete rotation). If *P* were to move clockwise around the unit circle, the angle measurements would start at 0 and be negative, ending at -2π (one complete rotation). As point *P* moves around the unit circle, both the angle measure and the (*a*, *b*) coordinates of *P* change. As pictured above, the hypotenuse of the right triangle formed is always 1 unit. Since the distance from *P* to the origin remains 1 unit, use the Pythagorean theorem to see that $\sqrt{a^2 + b^2} = 1$. Because the unit circle makes use of a right-angled triangle, we can use trigonometric ratios:

$$\sin\theta = \frac{\text{opposite}}{\text{hypotenuse}} = \frac{b}{1} = b$$

$$\cos\theta = \frac{\text{adjacent}}{\text{hypotenuse}} = \frac{a}{1} = a$$

$$\tan\theta = \frac{\text{opposite}}{\text{adjacent}} = \frac{b}{a}$$

In the unit circle, $\cos\theta$ is the *x*-coordinate and $\sin\theta$ is the *y*-coordinate of the point *P*.

Look at the point $P(a, b)$ in the first quadrant. The angle, θ, formed by $\overrightarrow{OP}$ and the positive x-axis is an acute angle. Now consider a point $P'(-a, b)$ in quadrant II. An acute angle can be formed by using the negative x-axis and creating ray $\overrightarrow{OP'}$. The acute angle formed has measure $\pi - \theta$. We can also form acute angles with the x-axis and rays from the origin to points in quadrant III and quadrant IV. We will use these **reference angles** to find trigonometric function values of angles in the other quadrants.

Angle Measure	Quadrant	Reference Angle
$0 < \theta < \dfrac{\pi}{2}$	I	θ
$\dfrac{\pi}{2} < \theta < \pi$	II	$\pi - \theta$
$\pi < \theta < \dfrac{3\pi}{2}$	III	$\theta - \pi$
$\dfrac{3\pi}{2} < \theta < 2\pi$	IV	$2\pi - \theta$

The illustration below is a reminder showing the sign of the trigonometric functions in each quadrant.

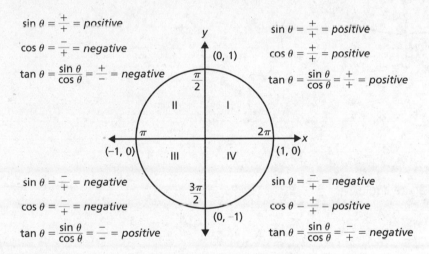

$$\sin \theta = \frac{+}{+} = positive \qquad\qquad \sin \theta = \frac{+}{+} = positive$$
$$\cos \theta = \frac{-}{+} = negative \qquad\qquad \cos \theta = \frac{+}{+} = positive$$
$$\tan \theta = \frac{\sin \theta}{\cos \theta} = \frac{+}{-} = negative \qquad \tan \theta = \frac{\sin \theta}{\cos \theta} = \frac{+}{+} = positive$$

$$\sin \theta = \frac{-}{+} = negative \qquad\qquad \sin \theta = \frac{-}{+} = negative$$
$$\cos \theta = \frac{-}{+} = negative \qquad\qquad \cos \theta = \frac{+}{+} = positive$$
$$\tan \theta = \frac{\sin \theta}{\cos \theta} = \frac{-}{-} = positive \qquad \tan \theta = \frac{\sin \theta}{\cos \theta} = \frac{-}{+} = negative$$

Additionally,

$\cot \theta = \dfrac{1}{\tan \theta}$, so cotangent and tangent have the same signs in each quadrant.

$\sec \theta = \dfrac{1}{\cos \theta}$, so secant and cosine have the same signs in each quadrant.

$\csc \theta = \dfrac{1}{\sin \theta}$, so cosecant and sine have the same signs in each quadrant.

Remember that each angle measure has an (*a*, *b*) coordinate associated with it. As stated previously, cos θ is the *x*-coordinate and sin θ is the *y*-coordinate of the point. Also, an angle is in what is called **standard position** if its vertex is located at the origin and one ray is on the positive *x*-axis.

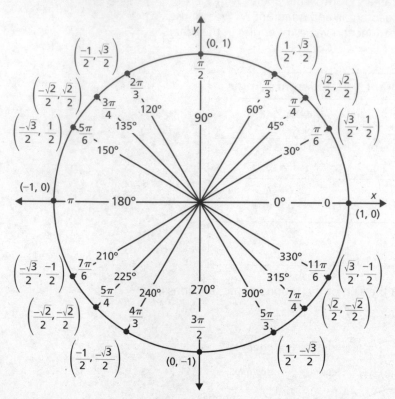

• • • **Think It Through** •

Example 1

Express $\sin \dfrac{5\pi}{4}$ as a function of a positive acute angle.

A) $\sin\left(\dfrac{\pi}{4}\right)$

B) $-\sin\left(\dfrac{\pi}{4}\right)$

C) $\sin\left(\dfrac{4\pi}{5}\right)$

D) $-\sin\left(\dfrac{4\pi}{5}\right)$

Solution

Refer to the table above. The measure $\dfrac{5\pi}{4}$ is larger than π and smaller than $\dfrac{3\pi}{2}$.

The angle is in quadrant III, where sine is negative. Apply the quadrant III reference

angle formula. Then $\sin\dfrac{5\pi}{4} = -\sin\left(\dfrac{5\pi}{4} - \pi\right) = -\sin\left(\dfrac{\pi}{4}\right)$.

Answer: B

Example 2

Express $\cos\dfrac{5\pi}{3}$ as a function of a positive acute angle.

A) $\cos\left(\dfrac{\pi}{3}\right)$

B) $-\cos\left(\dfrac{\pi}{3}\right)$

C) $\sin\left(\dfrac{\pi}{3}\right)$

D) $-\sin\left(\dfrac{\pi}{3}\right)$

Solution

Refer to the table above. $\dfrac{5\pi}{3}$ is larger than $\dfrac{3\pi}{2}$ and smaller than 2π. The angle

is in quadrant IV, where cosine is positive. Apply the quadrant IV reference angle

formula. Then $\cos\dfrac{5\pi}{3} = \cos\left(2\pi - \dfrac{5\pi}{3}\right) = \cos\left(\dfrac{\pi}{3}\right)$.

Answer: A

· · · · · · · **Practice** **The Unit Circle and Trigonometric Functions with Radian Measure**

Answers begin on page 729.

1. Express $\sin\left(\dfrac{6\pi}{5}\right)$ as a function of a positive acute angle.

   A) $-\cos\left(\dfrac{\pi}{5}\right)$

   B) $\cos\left(\dfrac{\pi}{5}\right)$

   C) $-\sin\left(\dfrac{\pi}{5}\right)$

   D) $\sin\left(\dfrac{\pi}{5}\right)$

2. Express $\cos\left(\dfrac{11\pi}{6}\right)$ as a function of a positive acute angle.

   A) $-\cos\left(\dfrac{5\pi}{6}\right)$

   B) $\cos\left(\dfrac{5\pi}{6}\right)$

   C) $-\cos\left(\dfrac{\pi}{6}\right)$

   D) $\cos\left(\dfrac{\pi}{6}\right)$

1. If $\sin x = \dfrac{\sqrt{2}}{2}$ and $\cos x = -\dfrac{\sqrt{2}}{2}$, then $x =$

    A) $\dfrac{\pi}{4}$

    B) $\dfrac{3\pi}{4}$

    C) $\dfrac{5\pi}{4}$

    D) $\dfrac{7\pi}{4}$

Strategy: Look at the signs on the trigonometric functions. Since sine is positive and cosine is negative, angle x must lie in quadrant II. Examining the answer choices, $\dfrac{3\pi}{4}$ is the only choice in quadrant II. Select answer B.

2. It is given that $\sin\theta = a$, where θ is the radian measure of an angle between 0 and $\dfrac{\pi}{2}$. If $\sin x = -a$, which of the following could be the value of x?

    A) $2\pi - \theta$

    B) $\pi - \theta$

    C) $\theta + 2\pi$

    D) $2\theta + \pi$

Strategy: The terminal side of angle θ lies in quadrant I. The measure $\sin\theta = a$ will be the y-coordinate of the point P where its terminal side intersects the unit circle. If $\sin x = -a$, then when the angle with radian measure x is placed in standard position, its terminal side will intersect the unit circle at a point with y-coordinate equal to $-a$. There are two such points on the unit circle: the reflection of P across the x-axis, which would correspond to an angle with radian measure $-\theta$ or $2\pi - \theta$, and the reflection of P through the origin, which would correspond to $\pi + \theta$. The choice that meets the description is A.

SAT-Type Questions

Answers begin on page 730.

1. If $\csc x < 0$ and $\cos x > 0$, which might be the value of x?

    A) $\dfrac{\pi}{6}$

    B) $\dfrac{2\pi}{3}$

    C) π

    D) $\dfrac{11\pi}{6}$

2. If the minute hand of a clock measures 6 inches, how long is the arc traced by this hand from 2:00 to 2:15?

   A) 3 inches

   B) 3π inches

   C) $\dfrac{\pi}{3}$ inches

   D) $\dfrac{2\pi}{3}$ inches

3. An angle of measure $\dfrac{2\pi}{3}$ radians lies in which quadrant?

   A) I

   B) II

   C) III

   D) IV

4. If $\tan x < 0$ and $\sin x > 0$, which might be the value of x?

   A) $\dfrac{3\pi}{4}$

   B) $\dfrac{\pi}{4}$

   C) $\dfrac{7\pi}{6}$

   D) $\dfrac{11\pi}{6}$

5. It is given that $\cos x = a$, where x is the radian measure of an angle that lies between $\dfrac{\pi}{2}$ and π. If $\cos y = -a$, which of the following could be the value of y?

   A) $2\pi + x$

   B) $x - \pi$

   C) $\pi - x$

   D) $2\pi - x$

6. If $\cot x > 0$ and $\sec x > 0$, what might be the value of x?

   A) $\dfrac{\pi}{3}$

   B) $\dfrac{2\pi}{3}$

   C) $\dfrac{4\pi}{3}$

   D) $\dfrac{5\pi}{3}$

7. In what quadrant does an angle whose measure is $\frac{4\pi}{3}$ lie?

A) I

B) II

C) III

D) IV

8. Latitude for a given location represents the measure of a central angle with the vertex at the center of the earth, its initial side passing through a point on the equator and its terminal point passing through the given location. City B is directly north of City A. The latitude of City A is 30° north, and the latitude of City B is 75° north. The radius of the earth is approximately 6,400 miles. Find the approximate distance between the two cities along the circumference of the earth.

A) 4,700 miles

B) 4,800 miles

C) 4.900 miles

D) 5,000 miles

9. It is given that $\cos x = a$, where x is the radian measure of an angle between $\frac{3\pi}{2}$ and 2π. If $\cos y = -a$, which of the following are the possible values of y?

A) $x + \pi$ and $\pi - x$

B) $x - \pi$ and $2\pi - x$

C) $x - \pi$ and $\pi - x$

D) $x + \pi$ and $\pi - x$

10. It is given that $\sin \theta = a$, where a is the radian measure of an angle, and $\pi < \theta < \frac{3\pi}{2}$. If $\sin \beta = -a$, which of the following are the possible values of β?

A) $\theta - \pi$ and $2\pi - \theta$

B) $\theta - \pi$ and $\pi - \theta$

C) $\theta + \pi$ and $2\pi - \theta$

D) $\theta + \pi$ and $\pi - \theta$

11. In standard position, an angle of $\frac{4\pi}{3}$ radians has the same terminal angle as

A) 60 degrees

B) 120 degrees

C) 300 degrees

D) 240 degrees

Student-Produced Response Questions

12. Express $\dfrac{3\pi}{4}$ radians in degree measure less than 360°.

13. Express $-\dfrac{5\pi}{6}$ radians in positive degree measure.

14. Find the length, in meters, of the radius of a circle in which a central angle of 4 radians intercepts an arc of 5 meters.

15. A weight suspended from a brace makes an angle of 6 radians as its center travels 6 feet. What is the length of the rope, in feet, connecting the weight to the brace?

16. A pendulum 4 feet long travels 10 feet in one direction each swing. What is the angle measure of the swing, as measured in radians?

17. In standard position, an angle of $\dfrac{5\pi}{3}$ radians has the same terminal angle as what degree measure?

18. A wheel whose radius measures 18 inches is rotated. If a point on the circumference of the wheel moves through an arc of 10 inches, what is the measure, in radians, of the angle through which a spoke of a wheel travels?

19. In standard position, an angle of $-\dfrac{\pi}{3}$ radians has the same terminal angle as what degree measure?

Explain **Circle Definitions and Equations**

A circle is defined as the locus (or set) of all points equidistant from a fixed point called the center. Just as we can write equations that describe lines and curves in the xy-plane, we can also write equations to describe any given circle of radius r. The equation of a circle is closely related to the distance formula, $d = \sqrt{(x_1 - x_2)^2 + (y_1 - y_2)^2}$. In fact, the equation of a circle and the distance formula are inseparable. Consider these two cases:

Case 1: A circle, radius r, with center at the origin, (0, 0)

To write an equation that describes all the points $P(x, y)$ in the xy-coordinate plane that lie a distance r from the origin, we substitute the following information into the distance formula as follows: $d = r$ and $(x_2, y_2) = (0,0)$. Then $r = \sqrt{(x-0)^2 + (y-0)^2} = \sqrt{x^2 + y^2}$

Now, square both sides of the equation and we have $r^2 = x^2 + y^2$. This is the standard equation for a circle with center at the origin.

Case 2: A circle, radius r, with center (h, k) *not* at the origin

In this case, writing an equation that describes all the points $P(x, y)$ that lie a distance r from the origin, we allow $d = r$ and $(x_2, y_2) = (h, k)$ in the distance formula. Then $r = \sqrt{(x-h)^2 + (y-k)^2}$ and, squaring both sides, $r^2 = (x - h)^2 + (y - k)^2$. This is the general equation for any circle with any center. Notice that the circle described by the equation $(x - h)^2 + (y - k)^2 = r^2$ is simply a translation of the circle $x^2 + y^2 = r^2$ by h horizontal units and k vertical units.

Think It Through

Example 1

Write the equation of a circle with its center at the origin and that passes through the point (–6, 1).

A) $(x+6)^2 + (y-1)^2 = 37$
B) $x^2 + y^2 = \sqrt{37}$
C) $x^2 + y^2 = 37$
D) $(x-6)^2 + (y+1)^2 = 37$

Solution

The center is located at the origin, so the circle's equation will have a general form $r^2 = x^2 + y^2$. Use the origin and the given points to determine the radius. Then $r^2 = (-6-0)^2 + (1-0)^2$ and $r^2 = 36 + 1 = 37$. So the equation that describes this circle is $x^2 + y^2 = 37$.

Answer: C

Example 2

Which of the following is the equation of a circle whose center has coordinates (5, –3) and whose radius has a length of 6?

A) $(x + 5)^2 + (y - 3)^2 = 36$
B) $(x - 5)^2 + (y + 3)^2 = 36$
C) $(x + 5)^2 + (y - 3)^2 = 6$
D) $(x - 5)^2 + (y + 3)^2 = 6$

Solution

The general equation of the form $(x - h)^2 + (y - k)^2 = r^2$ shows us that $r^2 = 6^2 = 36$, so choices C and D are wrong. Since the center is (5, –3), this means $h = 5$ and $k = -3$. By substitution, $(x - 5)^2 + (y - (-3))^2 = 6^2$ is equivalent to $(x - 5)^2 + (y + 3)^2 = 36$, or choice B.

Answer: B

Example 3

Which point lies on the circle described by the equation $x^2 + y^2 = 49$?

A) (0, 0)
B) (3, 4)
C) (–4, 3)
D) (0, 7)

Solution

To determine the correct point, we will simply substitute the (x, y) pairs into the given circle equation until we find one that returns a true statement. Obviously, choice A is incorrect because $0^2 + 0^2 \neq 49$. Choice B: $3^2 + 4^2 = 9 + 16 = 25$, not 49. For the same reason, choice C is wrong. Thus choice D, $0^2 + 7^2 = 49$, is correct.
Answer: D

Practice Circle Definitions and Equations

Answers begin on page 731.

1. A circle centered at the origin passes through the point (2, 4). Write the equation of the circle.

   A) $x^2 + y^2 = 20$
   B) $x^2 + y^2 = 400$
   C) $(x - 2)^2 + (y - 4)^2 = 20$
   D) $(x - 2)^2 + (y - 4)^2 = 400$

2. The equation of a circle is $(x - 8)^2 + (y + 11)^2 = 25$. Find the length of radius and the coordinates of the center.

   A) radius 25, center (8, –11)
   B) radius 25, center (–8, 11)
   C) radius 5, center (–8, 11)
   D) radius 5, center (8, –11)

Model SAT Questions

1. A circle centered at the point (–1, 2) passes through the point (4, –3). Which choice is the equation of the circle?

   A) $(x + 1)^2 + (y - 2)^2 = 25$
   B) $(x + 1)^2 + (y + 2)^2 = 25$
   C) $(x - 1)^2 + (y - 2)^2 = 50$
   D) $(x + 1)^2 + (y - 2)^2 = 50$

Strategy: Use the distance formula to find r^2. Then $r^2 = (x_2 - x_1)^2 + (y_2 - y_1)^2$ becomes $(4-(-1))^2 + (-3-2)^2$. Simplifying, $5^2 + (-5)^2 = 25 + 25 = 50$. We are told the center is $(-1, 2)$. Putting it all together, the equation of the circle is $(x + 1)^2 + (y - 2)^2 = 50$. This is answer choice D.

2. Write the equation of the circle whose diameter is defined by the endpoints $(2, 1)$ and $(4, -5)$.

   A) $(x - 3)^2 + (y + 2)^2 = 10$

   B) $(x - 3)^2 + (y + 2)^2 = \sqrt{10}$

   C) $(x + 3)^2 + (y - 2)^2 = 10$

   D) $(x - 3)^2 + (y + 2)^2 = 100$

Strategy: Remember that the center of a circle is the midpoint of its diameter. To solve this problem, we first need to find the coordinates of the midpoint, M. Recall from Category 1, Lesson 6, that the midpoint formula is

$$M = \left(\frac{x_1 + x_2}{2}, \frac{y_1 + y_2}{2}\right) = \left(\frac{2+4}{2}, \frac{1+(-5)}{2}\right) = (3, -2).$$

We can use this information, along with the coordinates of either endpoint, to calculate the radius of the circle. If we use the endpoint $(2, 1)$, then the radius^2 is $r^2 = (3-2)^2 + (-2-1)^2$ and $r^2 = 10$. Now, using the general form for the equation of a circle with the center $(3, -2)$ and $r^2 = 10$, this circle is described by the equation $(x - 3)^2 + (y + 2)^2 = 10$. Select answer choice A.

SAT-Type Questions

Answers begin on page 731.

1. Which of the following points does <u>not</u> lie on the circle whose equation is $(x - 3)^2 + (y - 2)^2 = 100$?

   A) $(-7, 2)$

   B) $(3, -8)$

   C) $(3, 12)$

   D) $(13, 1)$

2. Which two points are on the circle defined by $(x + 2)^2 + (y - 5)^2 = 16$?

   A) $(-2, 5)$ and $(2, -5)$

   B) $(-2, 1)$ and $(2, 5)$

   C) $(-2, 5)$ and $(-2, -5)$

   D) $(-2, -5)$ and $(2, 5)$

3. Write an equation of a circle if the endpoints of the diameter of the circle are $(0, 3)$ and $(0, -4)$.

   A) $x^2 + \left(y - \dfrac{7}{2}\right)^2 = \dfrac{1}{4}$

   B) $x^2 + \left(y + \dfrac{1}{2}\right)^2 = \dfrac{49}{4}$

C) $x^2 + \left(y + \dfrac{1}{4}\right)^2 = \dfrac{7}{2}$

D) $x^2 + \left(y - \dfrac{1}{2}\right)^2 = \dfrac{1}{4}$

4. Find the circumference of a circle whose equation is $2x^2 + 2y^2 = 72$.

   A) 36π
   B) 12π
   C) 72π
   D) 144π

5. A circle with center $(3, -3)$ is tangent to the x-axis. Find the equation of the circle.

   A) $(x-3)^2 + (y+3)^2 = 3$
   B) $(x-3)^2 + (y+3)^2 = 9$
   C) $(x+3)^2 + (y-3)^2 = 3$
   D) $(x+3)^2 + (y-3)^2 = 9$

Student-Produced Response Questions

6. What is the radius of a circle with diameter endpoints $(-2, 5)$ and $(4, -3)$?

7. What is the diameter of a circle having the equation $\sqrt{(x-0.5)^2 + (y+7.5)^2} = 1.44$?

LESSON 7:

Simplifying and Performing Arithmetic Operations on Complex Numbers

☐ **Simplification of Imaginary Monomial Expressions**

☐ **Arithmetic Operations on Complex Numbers**

Explain **Simplification of Imaginary Monomial Expressions**

An equation such as $x = \sqrt{-4}$ has no solution in the real number system. A solution does exist in the system of **imaginary numbers**. The imaginary unit, i, has the value $\sqrt{-1}$. We traditionally write imaginary numbers with i to the right of the whole number and to the left of a radical expression. Thus $\sqrt{-4} = \sqrt{4} \cdot \sqrt{-1} = 4i$, and $\sqrt{-20} = \sqrt{4} \cdot \sqrt{5} \cdot \sqrt{-1} = 4\sqrt{5}i = 4i\sqrt{5}$.

> **Definition**
>
> An **imaginary number** is one that returns a negative result when squared.

The powers of i form an important pattern:

$i^0 = 1$

$i^1 = i$

$i^2 = \left(\sqrt{-1}\right)^2 = -1$

$i^3 = i^2 \cdot i = (-1)i = -i$

Then $i^4 = (i^2)(i^2) = (-1)(-1) = 1$ and the pattern repeats.

Extend the pattern to any positive integer n:

$i^0 = 1$	$i^4 = 1$	$i^{4n} = 1$
$i^1 = i$	$i^5 = i$	$i^{4n+1} = i$
$i^2 = -1$	$i^6 = -1$	$i^{4n+2} = -1$
$i^3 = -i$	$i^7 = -i$	$i^{4n+3} = -i$

Simplify powers of i the same way you simplify powers of numbers and variables. When adding and subtracting, simplify and combine like terms. Be cautious when subtracting signed numbers. When multiply and dividing, remember the rule for the product of powers of the same base. To multiply, add the powers and to divide, subtract the powers.

Think It Through

Example 1

The sum of $6i^{10}$ and $10i^{24}$ is

A) 4

B) 16

C) −4

D) −16

Solution

Simplify the powers of i first. Looking at the repeating pattern, $i^{10} = i^{4n+2} = -1$ and $i^{24} = i^{4n} = 1$. So $6i^{10} + 10i^{24} = 6(-1) + 10(1) = -6 + 10 = 4$.

Answer: A

Example 2

Simplify $(10i^{15})^2$

A) 100

B) 100i

C) −100

D) −100i

Solution

Begin by distributing the power outside the parentheses to the term inside the parentheses. Don't forget to distribute to the number: $(10i^{15})^2 = 10^2 i^{15 \cdot 2} = 100i^{30}$. Continue to simplify so that i is raised to a power between 0 and 3 inclusive. Then $100i^{30} = 100i^{4(7)+2} = 100i^2 = 100(-1) = -100$.

Answer: C

Example 3

Express $8\sqrt{\dfrac{-3}{8}}$ in terms of i in simplest form.

A) $2\sqrt{6}$

B) $2i\sqrt{6}$

C) $\dfrac{i\sqrt{6}}{2}$

D) $\dfrac{i\sqrt{6}}{4}$

Solution

Rewrite the problem as $8\left(\dfrac{\sqrt{-1}\sqrt{3}}{\sqrt{4}\sqrt{2}}\right)$. Now begin simplifying. So $8\left(\dfrac{\sqrt{-1}\sqrt{3}}{\sqrt{4}\sqrt{2}}\right)$ becomes $8\left(\dfrac{i\sqrt{3}}{2\sqrt{2}}\right) = \dfrac{8}{2}\left(\dfrac{i\sqrt{3}}{\sqrt{2}}\right)$. Finishing, $4\left(\dfrac{i\sqrt{3}}{\sqrt{2}}\right) = \dfrac{4\sqrt{2}}{\sqrt{2}}\left(\dfrac{i\sqrt{3}}{\sqrt{2}}\right) = 2i\sqrt{6}$. Alternately, you could first rationalize the denominator under the radical and then simplify:

$8\sqrt{\dfrac{-3 \cdot 2}{8 \cdot 2}} = 8\sqrt{\dfrac{-3 \cdot 2}{16}} = \dfrac{8}{4}\sqrt{-6} = 2\sqrt{-1} \cdot \sqrt{6} = 2i\sqrt{6}$.

Answer: B

Example 4

Which of the following is not equal to the other three?

A) i^{15}

B) i^{17}

C) i^{31}

D) i^{39}

Solution

Completely simplify each expression using the repeating pattern previously explained. Then:

$i^{15} = i^{4(3)+3} = -i$

$i^{17} = i^{17 = 4(4)+1} = i$

$i^{31} = i^{4(7)+3} = -i$

$i^{39} = i^{4(9)+3} = -i$

Answer: B

Answers begin on page 732.

Practice Simplification of Imaginary Monomial Expressions

1. Simplify $\sqrt{-49}$ in terms of i.

   A) -7

   B) $-7i$

   C) $7i$

   D) $7\sqrt{i}$

2. Simplify $\sqrt{-18}$ in terms of i.

   A) $i\sqrt{9}$

   B) $9i\sqrt{2}$

   C) $i\sqrt{18}$

   D) $3i\sqrt{2}$

3. Simplify $4\sqrt{-16}$ in terms of i.

   A) $-16i$

   B) $-4i$

   C) $16i$

   D) $-16i$

4. Simplify $3\sqrt{-12}$ in terms of i.

   A) $36i\sqrt{3}$

   B) $18i\sqrt{3}$

   C) $12i\sqrt{3}$

   D) $6i\sqrt{3}$

5. Simplify i^{11}.

   A) 1

   B) i

   C) -1

   D) $-i$

Model SAT Questions

1. If $x^{25} = 2048 + 2048i$ and $x^{23} = 1024 + 1024i$, then x^2 is

   A) $-2i$

   B) $2i$

   C) -2

   D) 2

Strategy: Use the rules of exponents to rewrite the problem. Since $x^{25} = x^{23}(x^2)$, $2048 + 2048i = (1024 + 1024i)(x^2)$. Now, divide both sides by $(1024 + 1024i)$, we have $\dfrac{2048+2048i}{1024+1024i} = \dfrac{(\cancel{1024+1024i})\left(x^2\right)}{(\cancel{1024+1024i})}$. Factor to see $\dfrac{2048\cancel{(1+i)}}{1024\cancel{(1+i)}} = x^2$ and $2 = x^2$. Answer choice D is correct.

2. If $i^{x+2} + i^x + i^{x-2} = i$, then x could be

    A) 0
    B) 1
    C) 2
    D) 3

Strategy: Notice the powers on the first and second terms; they differ by 2. By the pattern of i terms, their sum will always equal 0. Concentrate on the third term: $i^{x-2} = i^1$ becomes $x - 2 = 1$, and $x = 3$. The correct answer choice is D.

· · · · · · · **Explain** **Arithmetic Operations on Complex Numbers** · · · · · · · · · · · · ·

A **complex number** is any number that can be expressed in the form $a + bi$, where a and b are real numbers and $i = \sqrt{-1}$. The number a is the real component of the complex number and the number bi is the complex component. The **conjugate** of a complex number $a + bi$ is $a - bi$. When you multiply a complex number by its conjugate, the product is a real number. Just as you find with the difference of squares, $(a + bi)(a - bi) = a^2 - (bi)^2 = a^2 - b^2i^2 = a^2 - b^2(-1) = a^2 + b^2$.

When adding and subtracting complex numbers, think of the number as a binomial. The real components are like terms and the complex components are like terms and you must combine those like terms. When multiplying complex numbers, use the box method or FOIL, which is the distribution of multiplication over addition and/or subtraction. To divide complex numbers, write the problem in fractional form. Complex expressions in simplest form have real number denominators. Make the denominator real by multiplying the numerator and the denominator by the complex conjugate of the denominator. (Remember that a complex number multiplied by its conjugate will result in a real number.)

· · · · · · **Think It Through** ·

Example 1

Simplify: $(8 + 8i)^2 - (1 + 8i)^2$.

A) $112i - 63$
B) $112i + 63$
C) $144i - 63$
D) $144i + 63$

Solution

Use FOIL or the box method to expand the squared binomial expressions. Then $(8 + 8i)^2 = (8 + 8i)(8 + 8i) = 64 + 64i + 64i + 64(-1) = 64 + 64i + 64i - 64 = 128i$, and $(1 + 8i)^2 = (1 + 8i)(1 + 8i) = 1 + 8i + 8i + 64(-1) = 16i - 63$. Subtract the two simplified binomials and find $128i - 16i + 63 = 112i + 63$.

Answer: B

Example 2

If the average of $3 + 2i$, $1 + 3i$, and x is $2 + i$, then x equals

A) $-2 - 4i$

B) $2 - 2i$

C) $2 + 2i$

D) $-2 + 2i$

Solution

The average of the three values is $2 + i$, so $\dfrac{3 + 2i + 1 + 3i + x}{3} = 2 + i$. Combine like terms and multiply both sides by 3 to clear the denominator: $4 + 5i + x = 3(2 + i)$. Distribute and collect the like terms to see $x = 2 - 2i$.

Answer: B

Practice Arithmetic Operations on Complex Numbers

Answers begin on page 732.

1. Express $(3 + 2i)(4 - i)$ in $a + bi$ form.

    A) $14 + 5i$

    B) $10 + 5i$

    C) $14 + 3i$

    D) $10 + 5i$

2. Express $(3 - 2i) - (4 - i)$ in $a + bi$ form.

    A) $1 - i$

    B) $-1 - i$

    C) $1 + i$

    D) $-1 + i$

3. Express in $a + bi$ form: $(3 - 2i)^2$.

    A) $11 - 12i$

    B) $5 - 12i$

    C) $11 - 7i$

    D) $7 - 7i$

4. Express in $a + bi$ form: $i(3 + i) - 5i$.

    A) $-2 + 2i$

    B) $-2 - 2i$

    C) $-1 - 2i$

    D) $-1 + 2i$

Model SAT Questions

1. If $(x + 5i)$ is a factor of $2x^2 + kx + 15$, then $k =$

    A) $-7i$

    B) $3i$

    C) $7i$

    D) $13i$

Strategy: We know one binomial factor and need to find the second binomial. The product of the real components x and a is $2x^2$. Then $a = \dfrac{2x^2}{x} = 2x$. We know the product of the imaginary components $5i$ and bi is 15. So $5i \cdot bi = 5bi^2$, but $i^2 = -1$, so $5b(-1) = -5b$. Then $-5b = 15$ and $b = -3$. The other factor is $2x - 3i$. Multiply the two binomials: $(x + 5i)(2x - 3i) = 2x^2 - 3xi + 10xi - 15i^2 = 2x^2 + 7xi + 15$. The value of $k = 7i$.

2. Divide $4 + 2i$ by $3 - i$.

A) $\dfrac{5}{4}(1+i)$

B) $\dfrac{5}{4}(1-i)$

C) $1-i$

D) $1+i$

Strategy: To divide by a complex number, write the problem in fractional form and then make the denominator real by multiplying both the numerator and the denominator by the conjugate of the denominator. Then $\dfrac{4+2i}{3-i} \cdot \dfrac{3+i}{3+i} =$

$\dfrac{12+4i+6i+2i^2}{9-i^2}$. Simplify: $\dfrac{12+10i-2}{9-(-1)} = \dfrac{10+10i}{10} = \dfrac{10(1+i)}{10} = 1+i.$

· · · · · **SAT-Type Questions** ·

Answers begin on page 732.

1. $(2 + 2i)^2 - (1 + 2i)^2$ equals

A) 1

B) $1 + 4i$

C) $3 + 4i$

D) $1 + 8i$

2. $i^3 + i(2 - i)$ is equal to

A) $1 + i$

B) $1 - i$

C) $-1 + 3i$

D) $1 + 3i$

3. If the average of $4 + i$, $1 + 2i$, and x is $1 + i$, then x equals

A) $-2 + 4i$

B) -2

C) $2 - 4i$

D) $3 + 3i$

4. The given number $\left[\left((1+i)i+1\right)i\right]i+1$ is equivalent to

A) 0

B) $1 - i$

C) 1

D) $1 + i$

5. If $i = \sqrt{-1}$, then $(1 + i)^2$ is equal to

A) $2 - 2i$

B) $2i$

C) $-2 + 2i$

D) $2 + 2i$

6. If $f(x) = 2x^2$ and $g(x) = \dfrac{ix}{2}$, then $g(f(2i))$ is

A) 4

B) -4

C) $4i$

D) $-4i$

7. Simplify: $(2-i)\left(\dfrac{2}{5} + \dfrac{1}{5}i\right)$.

A) $1 - \dfrac{4}{5}i$

B) $\dfrac{4}{5} - \dfrac{1}{5}i$

C) $1 + \dfrac{4}{5}i$

D) 1

8. Divide: $\dfrac{1 + \sqrt{-4}}{2 + \sqrt{-9}}$.

A) $\dfrac{8 + i}{13}$

B) $\dfrac{-4 + i}{13}$

C) $\dfrac{4 - i}{5}$

D) $\dfrac{8 + 1}{5}$

9. Simplify: $\dfrac{4 - 3i}{3i}$.

A) $\dfrac{4i + 3}{3}$

B) $\dfrac{-4i - 3}{3}$

C) $-1 + \dfrac{4i}{3}$

D) $-1 - \dfrac{4i}{3}$

10. The expression $\dfrac{1}{7-4i}$ is equivalent to

A) $\dfrac{7+4i}{33}$

B) $\dfrac{7-4i}{33}$

C) $\dfrac{7+4i}{65}$

D) $\dfrac{7-4i}{65}$

Student-Produced Response Questions

11. What is the product of $5 + 2i$ and its conjugate?

12. What is the product of $3 - 3i$ and its conjugate?

Calculators Allowed

Answers begin on page 733.

1. Suppose the length of each edge of a cube is increased by 25%. Which of the following is the closest approximation to the percent increase in the volume of the cube?

   A) 25%

   B) 50%

   C) 95%

   D) 100%

2. In the figure below (not drawn to scale), $AB = 7$ and $BC = 4$. Point D (not shown) lies on $\overline{AC}$ between A and C such that $\overline{BD} \perp \overline{AC}$. Which of the following could be the length of $\overline{BD}$?

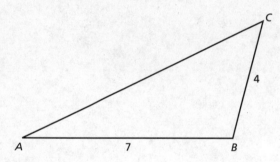

   A) 3

   B) 4

   C) 5

   D) 6

3. In the figure below, $\overline{PA}$ and $\overline{PB}$ are tangent to circle O at points A and B respectively. If radii $\overline{OA}$ and $\overline{OB}$ are drawn, then which of the following is always true?

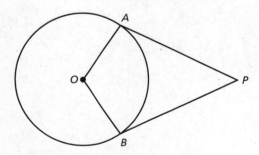

   A) $m\angle P = m\angle AOB$

   B) $m\angle P > m\angle AOB$

   C) $m\angle P + m\angle AOB = 90°$

   D) $m\angle P + m\angle AOB = 180°$

4. In $\triangle DEG$, the altitude $EF = 12$ and $DE = 15$. Which of the following points can be found on side DE?

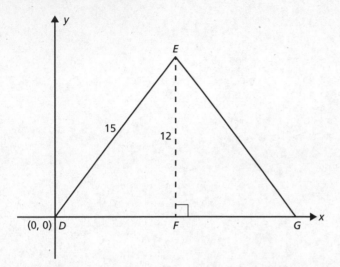

A) $(3, 3)$

B) $(3, 6)$

C) $(6, 8)$

D) $(8, 10)$

5. In radian measure, what is the acute angle determined by the hands of a clock at 4:30?

A) $\dfrac{\pi}{2}$

B) $\dfrac{\pi}{3}$

C) $\dfrac{\pi}{4}$

D) $\dfrac{\pi}{6}$

6. The equation of the circle whose center is $(-2, 3)$ and whose radius is 2 is which of the following?

A) $x^2 + y^2 - 4x + 6y + 9 = 0$

B) $x^2 + y^2 - 4x - 6y + 9 = 0$

C) $x^2 + y^2 + 4x + 6y + 9 = 0$

D) $x^2 + y^2 + 4x - 6y + 9 = 0$

7. If a and b are real numbers and $(a + b) + 7i = 11 + ai$, what is the value of b?

A) 4

B) 7

C) 11

D) $7 + 4i$

8. In the figure below, a sphere of radius 13 is intersected by a plane. If the center of the sphere is 12 units from the plane, what is the circumference of the circle formed by the intersection of the sphere and the plane?

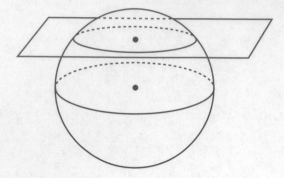

A) 10π

B) 25π

C) 144π

D) 169π

9. What is the absolute value of the difference in degree measures between an interior angle and an exterior angle of a regular octagon?

A) $45°$

B) $90°$

C) $135°$

D) $180°$

10. In the figure below, quadrilateral $ABCD$ is inscribed in circle O. If $m\angle A = 3x - 5$ and $m\angle C = 2x + 10$, what is the measure of $\angle A$?

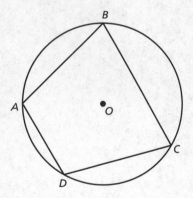

A) $40°$

B) $80°$

C) $100°$

D) $106°$

11. In the figure below, if $BC = CD$, then which of the following could be the value of $\tan \angle A$?

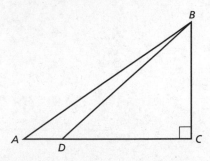

A) 0

B) 0.8511

C) 1

D) 2

12. The central angle of a circle of radius 8 intercepts an arc of length $\dfrac{16\pi}{3}$. What is the degree measure of that angle?

A) 30°

B) 60°

C) 120°

D) 150°

13. If point O is the center of the circle below and the coordinates of point A are $(8, 6)$, what is the area of the shaded region?

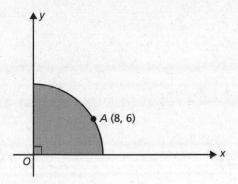

A) 10π

B) 25π

C) 50π

D) 100π

14. Which of the following expressions is equal to zero?

A) $i^2 \cdot i^2$

B) $i^2 + i^2$

C) $i^4 \cdot i^2$

D) $i^4 + i^2$

15. In the figure below, if ΔI is similar to ΔII, then what is the area of ΔII?

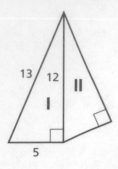

A) 25.6

B) 30.0

C) 35.2

D) 51.1

16. In the given figure, the hypotenuse of isosceles right triangle ACB is 10 cm. If three semicircles are drawn, one on each side, what is the sum of the areas of the shaded regions?

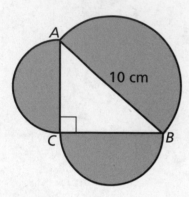

A) 12.5π

B) 25π

C) 37.5π

D) 50π

17. In circle O (shown below), chord $\overline{CD}$ is perpendicular to diameter $\overline{AOB}$ at E. If $OD = 17$ and $CD = 30$, what is the length of $\overline{EB}$?

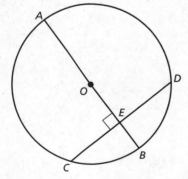

A) 8

B) 9

C) 10

D) 15

18. In the figure below, if $\triangle OAB$ is an equilateral triangle, then the x-intercept of $\overline{AB}$ is

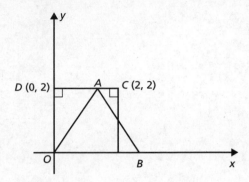

A) 4

B) $4 - 2\sqrt{3}$

C) $\dfrac{2}{\sqrt{3}}$

D) $\dfrac{4}{\sqrt{3}}$

19. In the given figure, if the length of diameter $\overline{AC}$ is 1, then the perimeter of quadrilateral $ABCD$ can be expressed as

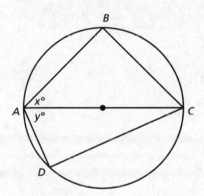

A) $(\sin x°)(\cos x°) + (\sin y°)(\cos y°)$

B) $\sin x° + \cos x° + \sin y° + \cos y°$

C) $\tan x° + \tan y°$

D) $\sin (x + y)° + \cos (x + y)°$

20. Which of the following coordinates is the center of the circle described by the equation $x^2 + y^2 - 6x + 2y - 6 = 0$?

A) $(3, 1)$

B) $(3, -1)$

C) $(-3, -1)$

D) $(-3, 1)$

21. The expression $(1 + i)^5$ is equivalent to

A) $4 - 4i$

B) $-4 - 4i$

C) $4 + 4i$

D) $-4 + 4i$

22. If a rectangle $ABCD$, 4 cm by 10 cm (shown below), is rotated about its sides, first $\overline{AB}$ and then $\overline{AD}$, two different size cylinders are formed. What is the positive difference in the volumes of these two cylinders?

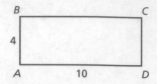

A) $240\,\pi$ cm²

B) $560\,\pi$ cm²

C) $720\,\pi$ cm²

D) $960\,\pi$ cm²

23. In the figure below, $\overline{AE}$ and $\overline{BC}$ are both perpendicular to $\overline{EC}$, and $\overline{BD} \perp \overline{AD}$. If $x = y$, the length of $\overline{BD} = 6$, and the length of $\overline{AD}$ is 8, what is the length of $\overline{EC}$?

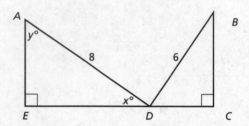

A) $7\sqrt{2}$

B) $7\sqrt{3}$

C) $10\sqrt{3}$

D) $14\sqrt{2}$

24. $\overline{AB}$ is tangent to circle O at point E in the figure below. If $\overline{CE}$, $\overline{ED}$, and $\overline{DC}$ are chords and $m\angle AED = 136°$, what is the measure of $\angle C$?

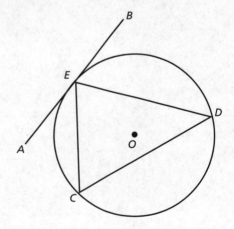

A) 22°

B) 44°

C) 68°

D) 88°

25. A ship at sea is heading toward a coastline formed by a vertical cliff $\overline{BC}$, which is 80 meters high (shown below). At point A, the angle of elevation from the ship to point B is 10 degrees. A little while later, the ship travels to point D, and the angle of elevation increases to 20 degrees. To the nearest meter, what is the distance between the two sightings?

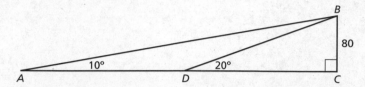

A) 220 meters

B) 234 meters

C) 454 meters

D) 674 meters

26. In the figure below, the center of circle O is at the origin, radius $OB = 1$, and $m\angle AOB = 30°$. What are the coordinates of point B?

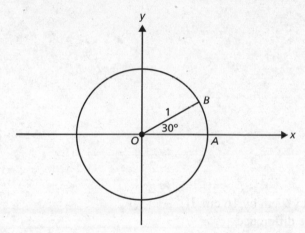

A) $\left(\dfrac{1}{2}, \dfrac{\sqrt{3}}{2}\right)$

B) $\left(\dfrac{\sqrt{2}}{2}, \dfrac{\sqrt{2}}{2}\right)$

C) $\left(\dfrac{\sqrt{3}}{2}, \dfrac{1}{2}\right)$

D) $(1, 1)$

27. If isosceles $\triangle ABC$ is inscribed in circle O, and $\overline{AC}$ is the diameter of circle O with endpoints A $(2, 4)$ and C $(4, 2)$, then the shaded area is equal to

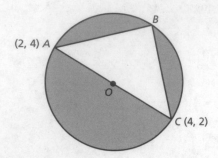

A) $\pi - 1$

B) $2\pi - 2$

C) $4\pi - 2$

D) $4\pi - 4$

28. The expression $\dfrac{5}{4-3i}$ is equivalent to

A) $\dfrac{20+15i}{7}$

B) $\dfrac{4+3i}{5}$

C) $\dfrac{20-15i}{7}$

D) $\dfrac{7i}{5}$

29. A rectangular solid block of aluminum has dimensions 2 cm by 2 cm by 16 cm. If the aluminum is melted down and recast as a cube, what is the difference (in square units) in the surface area between the rectangular solid and the cube?

A) 0 cm²

B) 40 cm²

C) 64 cm²

D) 72 cm²

30. In parallelogram $ABCD$ below, the side lengths are 8 inches and 10 inches and the $m\angle D = 150°$. If this parallelogram has an area equal to the area of a rectangle with a width of x and a length of $2x$, what is the value of x?

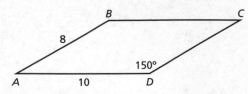

A) $2\sqrt{5}$ in

B) $2\sqrt{10}$ in

C) 8 in

D) 20 in

31. In the given figure, $\overline{EA}$ is tangent to circle O at point A, and secant $\overline{ED}$ intersects circle O at C and D. Diameter $\overline{AB}$ intersects $\overline{ED}$ at F. If the $m\angle E = 26°$ and $m\overset{\frown}{AD} = 108°$, what is the $m\angle ABC$?

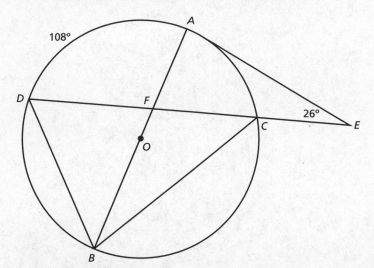

32. Given the rectangle $ABCD$, with $\tan \angle x = \dfrac{3}{4}$ and $\tan \angle y = \dfrac{1}{6}$, the area of the shaded region is what fraction of the area of the rectangle?

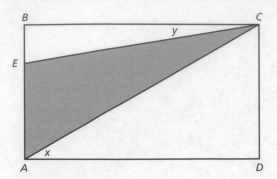

33. In a circle with a radius of 2.5 cm, a central angle has a measure of 5 radians. What is the length, in centimeters, of the arc intercepted by that central angle?

34. A sleeve of 3 tennis balls is sold in a tightly packed cylindrical container wherein the tennis balls touch the top, sides, and bottom of the can. If the radius of one tennis ball is r, what is the total number of sleeves that can be shipped in a box $4r$ by $6r$ by $12r$?

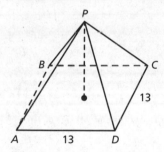

35. A circle centered at the origin passes through the point $(4, 6)$. To the nearest hundredth, what is the radius of that circle?

36. The base of pyramid P (shown below) is a rhombus $ABCD$ with each side measuring 13 fcet. The longer diagonal $\overline{AC}$ of the rhombus is 24 feet in length, and the height of the pyramid is 15 feet. Find the volume of this prism in cubic feet.

In the figure below (not drawn to scale) two segments, tangent $\overline{AB}$ and secant $\overline{AT}$, are drawn to circle O. The measure of arcs $\overparen{BR}$, $\overparen{RT}$, and $\overparen{TB}$ are in the ratio of $1 : 3 : 5$. The length of segment $\overline{RT} = 12$ inches and $AR = 5$ inches.

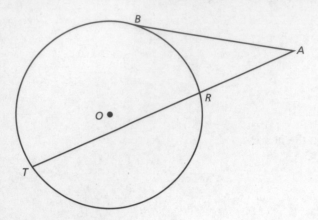

37. What is the measure of $\angle A$ in degrees?

38. What is the length of $\overline{AB}$ to the nearest tenth of an inch?

No Calculator Allowed

Answers begin on page 738.

1. If the radius of a sphere is r, then the ratio of the surface area to the volume of the sphere is

    A) 3π

    B) πr

    C) $\dfrac{\pi}{r}$

    D) $\dfrac{3}{r}$

2. If $\overline{BD}$ is an altitude of right triangle ABC, which of the segment lengths should replace the k in the proportion $\dfrac{AD}{BD} = \dfrac{AB}{k}$?

    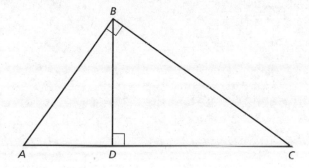

    A) AD

    B) DC

    C) BC

    D) BD

3. In circle O (shown below) with diameter $\overline{AC}$, which of the following is equal to x?

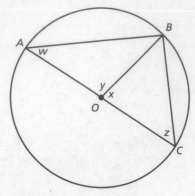

A) $\dfrac{y}{2}$

B) z

C) $2w$

D) $y - 90$

4. Which of the following is the value of the product $\sin (45) \cdot \cos (30) \cdot \tan (60)$?

A) $\dfrac{3\sqrt{2}}{4}$

B) $\dfrac{2\sqrt{3}}{3}$

C) $\dfrac{\sqrt{2}}{4}$

D) $\dfrac{3}{4}$

5. The value of $\sin (-240°)$ is

A) $-\dfrac{\sqrt{3}}{2}$

B) -0.5

C) 0.5

D) $\dfrac{\sqrt{3}}{2}$

6. The circle whose equation is $(x + 1)^2 + (y + 3)^2 = 9$ is tangent to

A) the y-axis only

B) the x-axis only

C) both axis

D) neither axes

7. Simplify: $\left(3 - \sqrt{-49}\right) - 2(2 - 2i)^2$

A) $3 - 9i$

B) $3 - 23i$

C) $3 + 9i$

D) $11 + 9i$

8. If the surface areas of the three faces of a rectangular solid are a, b, and c square centimeters, respectively, which of the following represents the volume of the solid in cubic centimeters?

A) abc

B) $\sqrt{abc}$

C) $a^2b^2c^2$

D) $(abc)^3$

9. In the figure below, the lengths of the legs of right triangle ABC are 5 and 12. Arc Cy is drawn with A as the center and 5 as the radius. Arc Cx is drawn with B as the center and 12 as the radius. What is the length of xy?

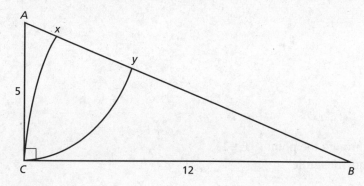

A) 2.4

B) 3.5

C) 3

D) 4

10. Two chords intersect inside a circle. If the lengths of the segments of the first chord are 6 and 15 and the full length of the second chord is 23, then the lengths of the segments of the second chord are

A) 3 and 20

B) 5 and 18

C) 11.5 and 11.5

D) 10 and 13

11. From the top of a building, the angle of depression with a point on the ground is 35°. The point is 50 yards from the base of the building. Which of the following can be used to determine the height, x, of the building?

A) $x = \dfrac{50}{\tan 35°}$

B) $x = \dfrac{50}{\tan 55°}$

C) $x = 50\,(\tan 55°)$

D) $x = 50\,(\cot 35°)$

12. Using the given figure, the expression $\dfrac{\sin A + \sin B}{\cos A}$ equals

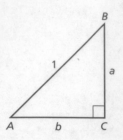

A) $a + b$

B) $1 + \dfrac{b}{a}$

C) $\dfrac{a}{b} + 1$

D) $\dfrac{a + b}{2}$

13. If a given circle has a center of $(-5, 3)$ and passes through the point $(-1, -1)$, which of the following is the equation that represents the circle?

A) $(x + 5)^2 + (y - 3)^2 = 32$
B) $(x - 5)^2 + (y + 3)^2 = 32$
C) $(x + 1)^2 + (y - 7)^2 = 32$
D) $(x - 1)^2 + (y + 7)^2 = 32$

14. The multiplicative identity for the set of complex numbers is which of the following?

A) $1 + 0i$
B) $1 + 1i$
C) $0 + 1i$
D) $0 + 0i$

15. A rectangular milk container measures 4 in by 4 in by 9 in. If a full container of milk must be poured into a larger empty cylindrical container with a diameter of 6 inches, what will be the height (h) of the milk, assuming none of it is spilled?

A) $\dfrac{4}{\pi}$ in^3

B) $\dfrac{9}{\pi}$ in^3

C) $\dfrac{16}{\pi}$ in^3

D) $\dfrac{36}{\pi}$ in^3

16. If the lengths of two sides of a triangle are 11 and 4, what is the difference between the largest and smallest possible integer perimeters?

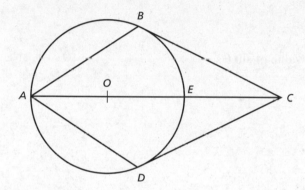

17. Examine the figure below. $\overline{CB}$ and $\overline{CD}$ are tangents to circle O, $\overline{CA}$ is a secant, and $m\overset{\frown}{AB} = m\overset{\frown}{AD}$. If $m\overset{\frown}{AB} = 110°$, what is the degree measure of $\angle ADC$?

18. In the triangle PQR shown below, with $PQ = 10$, $QR = 6$, altitude $\overline{QM}$ drawn, and $m\angle PQM = 60°$, what is the value of $(\sin R - \sin P)^2$?

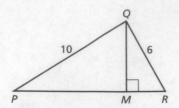

19. If $\cos \theta = -\dfrac{\sqrt{3}}{2}$ and θ is not in the third quadrant, what is the value of $\sin \theta$?

20. Points A, B, C, and D are the centers of four faces of the given cube. If the volume of the cube is 1,000 cubic units, what is the area of quadrilateral $ABCD$?

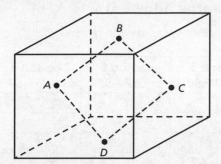

Correlation Chart

Summary SAT-Type Test—Additional Topics in Math (Calculator Allowed)

Use the chart below to mark the questions you found difficult to determine which lessons you need to review.

Question Number	Lesson 1 (p. 407 – 425)	Lesson 2 (p. 426 – 451)	Lesson 3 (p. 452 – 473)	Lesson 4 (p. 474 – 488)	Lesson 5 (p. 489 – 501)	Lesson 6 (p. 502 – 505)	Lesson 7 (p. 506 – 513)
1	☐						
2		☐					
3			☐				
4		☐					
5					☐		
6					☐		
7							☐
8	☐						
9		☐					
10			☐				
11				☐			
12		☐					
13			☐				
14							☐
15	☐						
16		☐					
17	☐						
18				☐			
19				☐			
20						☐	
21							☐
22	☐						
23		☐					
24			☐				
25				☐			
26		☐					
27					☐		
28							☐
29	☐						
30	☐						
31			☐				
32					☐		
33			☐				
34			☐				
35						☐	
36			☐				
37			☐				
38	☐						
Total Correct	____ / 8	____ / 6	____ / 10	____ / 4	____ / 4	____ / 2	____ / 4

Correlation Chart

Summary SAT-Type Test—Additional Topics in Math (No Calculator Allowed)

Use the chart below to mark the questions you found difficult to determine which lessons you need to review.

Question Number	Lesson 1 (p. 407 – 425)	Lesson 2 (p. 426 – 451)	Lesson 3 (p. 452 – 473)	Lesson 4 (p. 474 – 488)	Lesson 5 (p. 489 – 501)	Lesson 6 (p. 502 – 505)	Lesson 7 (p. 506 – 513)
1							
2							
3							
4							
5							
6							
7							
8							
9							
10							
11							
12							
13							
14							
15							
16							
17							
18							
19							
20							
Total Correct	____ / 4	____ / 2	____ / 3	____ / 1	____ / 6	____ / 2	____ / 2

SAT Math Model Exams

Now that you have completed the lessons and other practice material in this book, you are ready to try the full-length SAT Math Model Exams. We suggest that you review the information in the Introduction, pages 4 – 7, before you take any of these exams. Those pages provide essential reminders to prepare you for taking the complete SAT Math Test.

These four SAT Math Model Exams match the new SAT in format, types of questions, sequence of difficulty, and timing. When you take these tests, you should do so under conditions as similar as possible to the actual test conditions.

- Complete each of the exams in one sitting, with a break of 3 to 5 minutes between each section.

- Time yourself according to the guidelines of each section.

- Work as quickly as possible and don't waste time on difficult problems.

- Remember that it is advantageous to answer every question on each section of the test. Make an educated guess if you don't know the answer for sure.

After you complete each SAT Math Model Exam:

- Use the answer key with complete solutions that follows each SAT Math Model Exam to check your answers.

- Study the solutions for any questions you have missed.

- Use the correlation charts to determine error trends and identify your areas of strengths and weaknesses.

    The correlation charts show the category and lesson where you can find explanatory text and similar questions. Circle or highlight any questions you missed. Go back and review that information before taking another SAT Math Model Exam.

- Determine your estimated SAT score by using the Score Conversion Chart on p. 40.

- Compare each of the scores you earn to your Diagnostic Test score to gauge your improvement over the course of the book.

This is a great opportunity to see what you know well and what you still need to practice before you take the real SAT. If you would like additional practice, the following link will take you to the official College Board site and four full-length practice tests for the new SAT:

https://collegereadiness.collegeboard.org/sat/practice/full-length-practice-tests

Good luck!

Answer Sheet

SAT Math Model Exam

Use a No. 2 pencil. Fill in the circle completely. If you erase, erase completely.
Incomplete erasures may be read as answers.

No Calculator

1 Ⓐ Ⓑ Ⓒ Ⓓ   6 Ⓐ Ⓑ Ⓒ Ⓓ   11 Ⓐ Ⓑ Ⓒ Ⓓ
2 Ⓐ Ⓑ Ⓒ Ⓓ   7 Ⓐ Ⓑ Ⓒ Ⓓ   12 Ⓐ Ⓑ Ⓒ Ⓓ
3 Ⓐ Ⓑ Ⓒ Ⓓ   8 Ⓐ Ⓑ Ⓒ Ⓓ   13 Ⓐ Ⓑ Ⓒ Ⓓ
4 Ⓐ Ⓑ Ⓒ Ⓓ   9 Ⓐ Ⓑ Ⓒ Ⓓ   14 Ⓐ Ⓑ Ⓒ Ⓓ
5 Ⓐ Ⓑ Ⓒ Ⓓ   10 Ⓐ Ⓑ Ⓒ Ⓓ   15 Ⓐ Ⓑ Ⓒ Ⓓ

16 | **17** | **18** | **19** | **20**

(grid-in bubble grids for questions 16, 17, 18, 19, and 20)

Calculator

1 Ⓐ Ⓑ Ⓒ Ⓓ   7 Ⓐ Ⓑ Ⓒ Ⓓ   13 Ⓐ Ⓑ Ⓒ Ⓓ   19 Ⓐ Ⓑ Ⓒ Ⓓ   25 Ⓐ Ⓑ Ⓒ Ⓓ
2 Ⓐ Ⓑ Ⓒ Ⓓ   8 Ⓐ Ⓑ Ⓒ Ⓓ   14 Ⓐ Ⓑ Ⓒ Ⓓ   20 Ⓐ Ⓑ Ⓒ Ⓓ   26 Ⓐ Ⓑ Ⓒ Ⓓ
3 Ⓐ Ⓑ Ⓒ Ⓓ   9 Ⓐ Ⓑ Ⓒ Ⓓ   15 Ⓐ Ⓑ Ⓒ Ⓓ   21 Ⓐ Ⓑ Ⓒ Ⓓ   27 Ⓐ Ⓑ Ⓒ Ⓓ
4 Ⓐ Ⓑ Ⓒ Ⓓ   10 Ⓐ Ⓑ Ⓒ Ⓓ   16 Ⓐ Ⓑ Ⓒ Ⓓ   22 Ⓐ Ⓑ Ⓒ Ⓓ   28 Ⓐ Ⓑ Ⓒ Ⓓ
5 Ⓐ Ⓑ Ⓒ Ⓓ   11 Ⓐ Ⓑ Ⓒ Ⓓ   17 Ⓐ Ⓑ Ⓒ Ⓓ   23 Ⓐ Ⓑ Ⓒ Ⓓ   29 Ⓐ Ⓑ Ⓒ Ⓓ
6 Ⓐ Ⓑ Ⓒ Ⓓ   12 Ⓐ Ⓑ Ⓒ Ⓓ   18 Ⓐ Ⓑ Ⓒ Ⓓ   24 Ⓐ Ⓑ Ⓒ Ⓓ   30 Ⓐ Ⓑ Ⓒ Ⓓ

31

	/	/	
⊙	⊙	⊙	⊙
	⓪	⓪	⓪
①	①	①	①
②	②	②	②
③	③	③	③
④	④	④	④
⑤	⑤	⑤	⑤
⑥	⑥	⑥	⑥
⑦	⑦	⑦	⑦
⑧	⑧	⑧	⑧
⑨	⑨	⑨	⑨

32

	/	/	
⊙	⊙	⊙	⊙
	⓪	⓪	⓪
①	①	①	①
②	②	②	②
③	③	③	③
④	④	④	④
⑤	⑤	⑤	⑤
⑥	⑥	⑥	⑥
⑦	⑦	⑦	⑦
⑧	⑧	⑧	⑧
⑨	⑨	⑨	⑨

33

	/	/	
⊙	⊙	⊙	⊙
	⓪	⓪	⓪
①	①	①	①
②	②	②	②
③	③	③	③
④	④	④	④
⑤	⑤	⑤	⑤
⑥	⑥	⑥	⑥
⑦	⑦	⑦	⑦
⑧	⑧	⑧	⑧
⑨	⑨	⑨	⑨

34

	/	/	
⊙	⊙	⊙	⊙
	⓪	⓪	⓪
①	①	①	①
②	②	②	②
③	③	③	③
④	④	④	④
⑤	⑤	⑤	⑤
⑥	⑥	⑥	⑥
⑦	⑦	⑦	⑦
⑧	⑧	⑧	⑧
⑨	⑨	⑨	⑨

35

	/	/	
⊙	⊙	⊙	⊙
	⓪	⓪	⓪
①	①	①	①
②	②	②	②
③	③	③	③
④	④	④	④
⑤	⑤	⑤	⑤
⑥	⑥	⑥	⑥
⑦	⑦	⑦	⑦
⑧	⑧	⑧	⑧
⑨	⑨	⑨	⑨

36

	/	/	
⊙	⊙	⊙	⊙
	⓪	⓪	⓪
①	①	①	①
②	②	②	②
③	③	③	③
④	④	④	④
⑤	⑤	⑤	⑤
⑥	⑥	⑥	⑥
⑦	⑦	⑦	⑦
⑧	⑧	⑧	⑧
⑨	⑨	⑨	⑨

37

	/	/	
⊙	⊙	⊙	⊙
	⓪	⓪	⓪
①	①	①	①
②	②	②	②
③	③	③	③
④	④	④	④
⑤	⑤	⑤	⑤
⑥	⑥	⑥	⑥
⑦	⑦	⑦	⑦
⑧	⑧	⑧	⑧
⑨	⑨	⑨	⑨

38

	/	/	
⊙	⊙	⊙	⊙
	⓪	⓪	⓪
①	①	①	①
②	②	②	②
③	③	③	③
④	④	④	④
⑤	⑤	⑤	⑤
⑥	⑥	⑥	⑥
⑦	⑦	⑦	⑦
⑧	⑧	⑧	⑧
⑨	⑨	⑨	⑨

SAT Model Exam 1

Use the No Calculator section of your answer sheet to answer the questions in this section.

Directions

For questions 1–15, calculate the answer to each problem and choose the best option from the choices given. Bubble in the corresponding circle on your answer sheet. For the remaining questions, solve the problem and enter your answer in the grid on your answer sheet. Refer to the directions before question 16 on how to enter your answers in the grid.

Notes

1. The use of a calculator is <u>not</u> permitted on this test section.
2. All variables and expressions represent real numbers unless otherwise indicated.
3. Figures provided are drawn to scale unless otherwise noted.
4. All figures lie in a plane unless otherwise noted.
5. Unless otherwise noted, the domain of a given function f is the set of all real numbers x for which $f(x)$ is a real number.

Reference

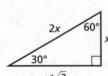

$A = \pi r^2$
$C = 2\pi r$

$A = lw$

$A = \frac{1}{2}bh$

$c^2 = a^2 + b^2$

Special Right Triangles

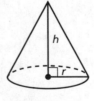
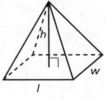

$V = lwh$

$V = \pi r^2 h$

$V = \frac{4}{3}\pi r^3$

$V = \frac{1}{3}\pi r^2 h$

$V = \frac{1}{3}lwh$

The number of degrees of arc in a circle is 360.
The number of radians of arc in a circle is 2π.
The sum of the measures in degrees of the angles of a triangle is 180.

CONTINUE

1

A circle in the *xy*-coordinate plane has center $(-3, 2)$ and radius 4 units. Which of the following equations represents this circle?

A) $(x + 3)^2 - (y + 2)^2 = 16$

B) $(x + 3)^2 + (y - 2)^2 = 16$

C) $(x - 3)^2 + (y - 2)^2 = 16$

D) $(x - 3)^2 - (y + 2)^2 = 16$

2

A certain bacterial cell replication triples its population every 4 days. If the original cell culture starts with a half-dozen cells, which of the following expressions gives the population of the culture after 32 days?

A) $6 \cdot 3^8$

B) $6 \cdot 8^3$

C) $6 \cdot 3^4$

D) $6 \cdot 4$

3

In lowest terms, the product
$$\frac{m^2 - 2mn + n^2}{m + n} \cdot \frac{m + n}{m^2 - mn} \text{ is equivalent to}$$

A) $\dfrac{m - n}{m}$

B) $\dfrac{m + n}{m}$

C) $\dfrac{m}{m - n}$

D) $\dfrac{m - n}{m + n}$

4

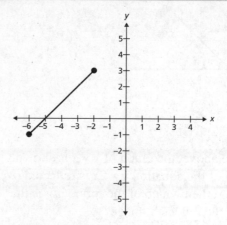

What is the equation of the line that runs parallel to the above line segment if the line passes through the point $(5, -4)$?

A) $y - 9x = 1$

B) $9x - y = 1$

C) $x - y = 9$

D) $y - x = -9$

If $i^{x+2} + i^x + i^{x-2} = 1$, then what is the value of x?
(Note: $i = \sqrt{-1}$)

A) 0

B) 1

C) 2

D) 3

If $g(x) = x^2 - x$, then $g(a - 1) =$

A) $a^2 - a - 1$

B) $a^2 - a + 1$

C) $a^2 - a + 2$

D) $a^2 - 3a + 2$

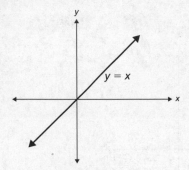

In the figure above, the graph of $y = x$ is shown. If the graph of the equation $y = 2x$ is reflected over the line $y = x$, then which of the following is the equation of the reflected image?

A) $y = 2x$

B) $y = \dfrac{x}{2}$

C) $y = 2$

D) $y = -\dfrac{x}{2}$

If $g(x) = 2x - 4$ and f is the function defined such that $f(g(x)) = x$, then $f(x) =$

A) $-2x + 4$

B) $x - 2$

C) $-\dfrac{1}{2}x - 2$

D) $\dfrac{1}{2}x + 2$

CONTINUE

No Calculator Allowed

If $(x - 3)(x + 1) = 0$, then which of the following could be the solution to $2x + 5$?

A) 5

B) 11

C) 7

D) −1

For all real numbers x, $g(x) = ax^2 + bx + c$, $g(0) = 1$, and $g(1) = 3$. What is the value of $a + b$?

A) 2

B) 1

C) 0

D) −2

Georgia is a college student working two part-time jobs. She has up to a total of 20 hours per week to dedicate to working. One of Georgia's jobs pays her $9.50 per hour and the other job pays $10.25 per hour. Suppose that Geogia needs to earn at least $600 per month to cover her expenses. Which of the following systems of inequalities could help her decide how many hours she must work per month at each job if x is the number of hours she works at job #1 and y is the number of hours she works at job #2? (Assume there are four weeks in one month.)

A) $\begin{cases} x - y \le 80 \\ 9.50x + 10.25y \ge 600 \end{cases}$

B) $\begin{cases} x + y \ge 80 \\ 9.50x + 10.25y \le 600 \end{cases}$

C) $\begin{cases} x + y \le 80 \\ 9.50x + 10.25y \ge 600 \end{cases}$

D) $\begin{cases} x - y \le 80 \\ 9.50x + 10.25y \le 600 \end{cases}$

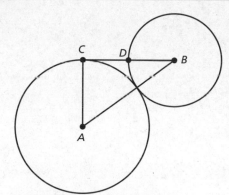

The two circles in the figure above are externally tangent. The circle with center A has a radius of 5 and the circle with center B has a radius of 2. If segment $\overline{BC}$ is tangent to the larger circle at C and intersects the smaller circle at D, what is the length of segment $\overline{CD}$?

A) 3

B) $2\sqrt{6}$

C) $\sqrt{6} - 2$

D) $2\sqrt{6} - 2$

CONTINUE

If each system of equations below is sketched on the same set of axes, which system will have more than one point of intersection?

A) $\begin{cases} x+y=0 \\ x-y=0 \end{cases}$

B) $\begin{cases} x+y=6 \\ x^2+y^2=36 \end{cases}$

C) $\begin{cases} y=-x^2 \\ x=-2 \end{cases}$

D) $\begin{cases} y=x^2 \\ y=0 \end{cases}$

14

Cable wires for television are measured to a thickness that cannot exceed a range of 3.05 cm to 3.15 cm. Which of the following absolute value inequalities can be used to determine the acceptable thickness of a given cable wire?

A) $|n-3.1| \le 0.05$

B) $|n+0.05| \ge 3.1$

C) $|n+3.1| \ge 0.05$

D) $|n-3.1| \ge 0.05$

Solve $I = \dfrac{PN}{RN+A}$ for N.

A) $N = IA(P - IR)$

B) $N = \dfrac{IA}{IR - P}$

C) $N = IR(IA - P)$

D) $N = \dfrac{IA}{P - IR}$

CONTINUE

No Calculator Allowed

For the remaining questions, solve the problem and enter your answer in the answer grid. Instructions for entering your answer in the grid are described below.

1. It is not required that you write your answer in the boxes at the top of the grid, but it is suggested.

2. Do not mark more than one circle in each column.

3. There are no negative answers in this portion of the test.

4. If the problem has more than 1 correct answer, grid only 1 of those answers.

5. Grid fractions as proper or improper fractions only.

6. Decimal answers must fill the entire grid.

Examples

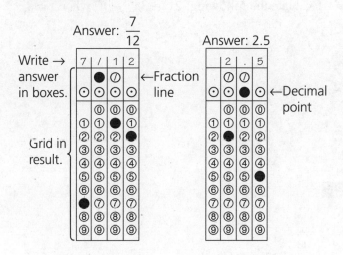

Answer: $\frac{7}{12}$

Write answer in boxes. ←Fraction line

Grid in result.

Answer: 2.5 ←Decimal point

Acceptable ways to grid $\frac{2}{3}$ are:

Answer: 201 – either position is correct

CONTINUE

16

According to Boyle's law, the volume V, of a gas at a constant temperature varies inversely with the pressure, P, applied to it. If the volume of a gas is 120 cubic inches when the pressure is 30 pounds per square inch, what is the volume, in cubic inches, when the pressure is 40 pounds per square inch?

17

Solve for x: $3x - \dfrac{2}{3}(5x - 6) = 2$.

18

If $xy = -3$ and $(x - y)^2 = 33$, then what is the value of $x^2 + y^2$?

19

Evaluate the following: $2x^0 - 3x^{-\frac{2}{3}} + 1^x$ when $x = 8$

20

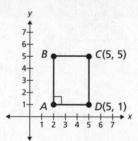

Given rectangle $ABCD$ in the xy-coordinate system, if the diagonal $\overline{AC}$ is drawn and the point $P(x, 4)$ lies on that diagonal, what is the value of x?

STOP

**If you finish before time is called, you may check your work on this section only.
Do not turn to any other section.**

No Calculator Allowed

SAT Model Exam 1

55 MINUTES, 38 QUESTIONS

CALCULATOR ALLOWED

Use the Calculator section of your answer sheet to answer the questions in this section.

Directions

For questions 1–30, calculate the answer to each problem and choose the best option from the choices given. Bubble in the corresponding circle on your answer sheet. For the remaining questions, solve the problem and enter your answer in the grid on your answer sheet. Refer to the directions before question 31 on how to enter your answers in the grid.

Notes

1. The use of a calculator is permitted on this test section.
2. All variables and expressions represent real numbers unless otherwise indicated.
3. Figures provided are drawn to scale unless otherwise noted.
4. All figures lie in a plane unless otherwise noted.
5. Unless otherwise noted, the domain of a given function f is the set of all real numbers x for which $f(x)$ is a real number.

Reference

$A = \pi r^2$
$C = 2\pi r$

$A = lw$

$A = \frac{1}{2}bh$

$c^2 = a^2 + b^2$

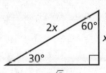

Special Right Triangles

$V = lwh$

$V = \pi r^2 h$

$V = \frac{4}{3}\pi r^3$

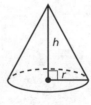

$V = \frac{1}{3}\pi r^2 h$

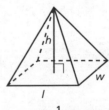

$V = \frac{1}{3}lwh$

The number of degrees of arc in a circle is 360.

The number of radians of arc in a circle is 2π.

The sum of the measures in degrees of the angles of a triangle is 180.

CONTINUE →

If y varies inversely as x, which of the following is the equation of variation for $y = \dfrac{2}{3}$ and $x = \dfrac{9}{2}$?

A) $y = \dfrac{2}{3}x$

B) $y = 3x$

C) $y = \dfrac{3}{x}$

D) $y = 2x$

2

If a group of data consists of the numbers 6, 6.5, 8.5, 6, and 8, which of the following is true?

A) median < mean

B) median = mean

C) median < mode

D) median = mode

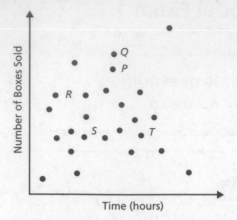

Students sold boxes of cookies to raise money for a local charity. They logged the number of hours they worked as well as the number of boxes they sold. In math class, they plotted the time each student worked against the number of boxes sold. The plot is shown above. Of the points labeled P, Q, R, S, T, which one corresponds to the most cookies sold per hour?

A) P

B) Q

C) R

D) T

Sabah invests $10,000. He puts some in 3% municipal bonds and he invests the rest at 5% in rental properties. Which of the following expressions would identify the sum of money invested at 3% that would produce $60 more income than the other investment?

A) $0.05(10{,}000 - x) = 0.03x + 60$

B) $0.03x = 0.05(10{,}000 - x) + 60$

C) $0.03x - 60 = 0.05(10{,}000) - x$

D) $0.05x = 0.03(10{,}000 - x) + 60$

CONTINUE

Calculator Allowed

If $ax - a > 2a$ and $x - 1 < -2$, then

A) $a = 1$

B) $a = -1$

C) $a > 0$

D) $a < 0$

Which of the following is the equation of a line perpendicular to the line $y + 1 = 4x$ if the perpendicular line has the same y-intercept as the line $2x + 3y = 6$?

A) $4x + y = 2$

B) $4x - y = 8$

C) $x + 4y = 8$

D) $-x + 4y = 2$

To estimate the total number of deer in a wildlife preserve, staff members capture 112 deer and tag them before releasing them. Two weeks later 218 deer living on the preserve are caught; of these, 78 of them are tagged. About how many deer are living in this wildlife preserve?

A) 313 deer

B) 295 deer

C) 335 deer

D) 305 deer

Scores	Frequency
91–100	3
81–90	11
71–80	8
61–70	6
51–60	1
41–50	1

The table above shows the distribution of scores of 30 students on a given test. In which interval does the median fall?

A) 61–70

B) 71–80

C) 81–90

D) 91–100

CONTINUE

9

In the given system of linear equations, $\frac{1}{3}x - \frac{1}{6}y = 3$ and $kx - 5y = 30$, k is a constant. If the system has no solution, what is the value of k?

A) $\dfrac{1}{3}$

B) 2

C) 10

D) 20

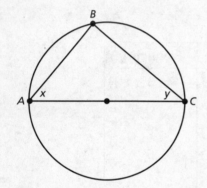

In the given figure, $\overline{AC}$ is the diameter of the circle, B is a point on the circle and $\cos x = \dfrac{2}{3}$. What is $\cos y$?

A) $\dfrac{\sqrt{5}}{5}$

B) $\dfrac{\sqrt{5}}{3}$

C) $\dfrac{2\sqrt{5}}{5}$

D) $\dfrac{3\sqrt{5}}{5}$

A survey of the town of Banner Hill found a mean of 3.2 people per household and a mean of 2.8 cell phones per household. If 80,000 people live in Banner Hill, how many cell phones are in the town?

A) 25,000

B) 70,000

C) 91,000

D) 224,000

$$y^2 - 2x^2 = 7$$
$$2x - y = 1$$

If (x, y) is a solution to the system of equations above, what is one possible value of $x + y$?

A) -4

B) -2

C) 2

D) 3

CONTINUE

Calculator Allowed

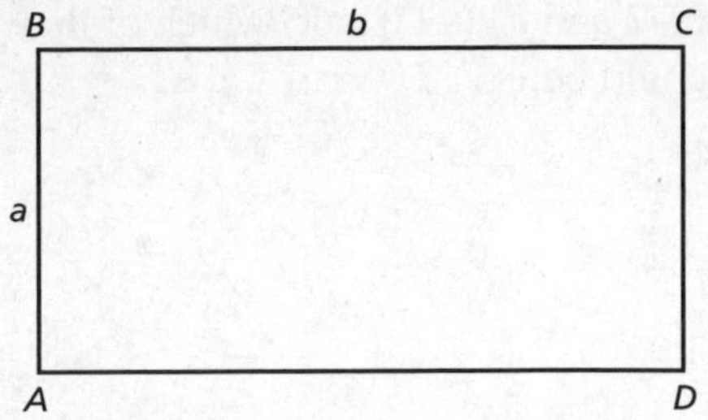

In the figure above, if the perimeter of rectangle

$ABCD$ is equal to P and $a = \dfrac{3}{4}b$, what is the value

of b in terms of P?

A) $\dfrac{7P}{2}$

B) $\dfrac{2P}{7}$

C) $\dfrac{P}{7}$

D) $\dfrac{P}{14}$

What is the radian measure of an angle formed by the minute hand and the hour hand when a clock reads 8:30?

A) $\dfrac{5\pi}{24}$

B) $\dfrac{\pi}{6}$

C) $\dfrac{5\pi}{12}$

D) $\dfrac{\pi}{3}$

A college basketball team had a ratio of wins to losses of 3:1. After the team won 8 games in a row, its ratio of wins to losses became 5:1. How many games did the team win prior to winning 8 games in a row?

A) 4

B) 8

C) 12

D) 16

If points $A(0, 0)$, $B(N, 1)$, and $C(2, N)$ are collinear, what is the value of N?

A) $\dfrac{1}{2}$

B) 1

C) 2

D) $\sqrt{2}$

CONTINUE

If 5 and −3 are both zeros of the polynomial function $m(x)$, then a factor of $m(x)$ is

A) $x^2 - 15$

B) $x^2 - 2x - 15$

C) $x^2 + 15$

D) $x^2 + 2x - 15$

In a school of 1,000 students, 225 are seniors and 250 students are enrolled in a math class. Of the students enrolled in a math class, 50 are seniors. What is the probability that a randomly chosen student is a senior enrolled in a math class?

A) $\dfrac{2}{9}$

B) $\dfrac{1}{4}$

C) $\dfrac{1}{5}$

D) $\dfrac{1}{20}$

If $f(x) = 2x + 7$ and $f(g(-1)) = 15$ which of the following could be $g(x)$?

A) $-x + 4$

B) $x^2 + 4$

C) $3x + 7$

D) $2x^2 + 1$

In 2005, 30 percent of the 200 apartments in a certain small town were redesigned for the handicapped. By 2006, the total number of apartments had increased by 25% and now 40% of the apartments were for the handicapped. What was the percent increase of redesigned handicapped apartments during this period?

A) 10.2%

B) $33\dfrac{1}{3}\%$

C) 40%

D) $66\dfrac{2}{3}\%$

CONTINUE

Calculator Allowed

The equation $\sqrt{y+5} = 7 - y$ has

A) only one real root.

B) two positive real roots.

C) one positive root and one negative root.

D) no real roots.

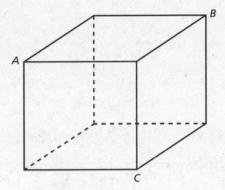

The measure of each edge of the cube above is 1 unit. If the three vertices, A, B, and C, were joined to form a triangle, what would be the area of the triangle ABC?

A) $\dfrac{\sqrt{3}}{2}$

B) $\dfrac{\sqrt{2}}{2}$

C) $\dfrac{\sqrt{6}}{4}$

D) $\dfrac{\sqrt{3}}{4}$

If a is a positive integer and $3^a + 3^{a+1} = n$, what is 3^{a+2} in terms of n?

A) $3n$

B) $\dfrac{9n}{2}$

C) $\dfrac{9n}{4}$

D) $\dfrac{3n}{4}$

The distance a spring stretches varies directly with the force applied to the spring. If a force of 140 newtons stretches a spring 5 cm, how much will a force of 212 newtons stretch the same spring?

A) 28 cm

B) 7.6 cm

C) 15.2 cm

D) 9.1 cm

CONTINUE

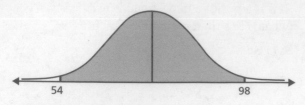

54   98

In the diagram above, the shaded area represents approximately 95% of the scores on a standardized test. If these scores ranged from 54 to 98, what is the standard deviation?

A) 11
B) 22
C) 44
D) 76

Which of the following does <u>not</u> represent or define a function?

A) $y = 4x$
B) $y = |x|$
C) $\{(2, 2), (3, 2)\}$
D) $\{(2, 2), (2, 3)\}$

If $x + y = a$ and $x - y = b$, then y is equal to

A) $\dfrac{a+b}{2}$

B) $\dfrac{a-b}{2}$

C) $\dfrac{b-a}{2}$

D) $a - b$

Time in years, x	0	1	2	3	4	5	6
Paired Songbird Population, y	5	10	20	40	80	160	320

Which of the following equations best models the data in the table above?

A) $y = 2x + 5$
B) $y = 2^x$
C) $y = 2x$
D) $y = 5(2^x)$

CONTINUE

Calculator Allowed

29

On a standardized test, the distribution of scores is normal with a mean of 75 and a standard deviation of 5.8. Suppose Lorena earned a score of 82 on the test. Her score ranks

A) lower than 1 standard deviation above the mean.

B) exactly one standard deviation above the mean.

C) higher than one standard deviation above the mean but lower than two standard deviations above the mean.

D) higher than 2 standard deviations above the mean.

30

The graph of $g(x) = -x^2$ is shifted 3 units left and 1 unit up. If this new graph is $f(x)$, then what is the value of $f(-1.5)$?

A) −2.25

B) −1.25

C) 1.25

D) 3.25

CONTINUE

For the remaining questions, solve the problem and enter your answer in the answer grid. Instructions for entering your answer in the grid are described below.

1. It is not required that you write your answer in the boxes at the top of the grid, but it is suggested.

2. Do not mark more than one circle in each column.

3. There are no negative answers in this portion of the test.

4. If the problem has more than 1 correct answer, grid only 1 of those answers.

5. Grid fractions as proper or improper fractions only.

6. Decimal answers must fill the entire grid.

Examples

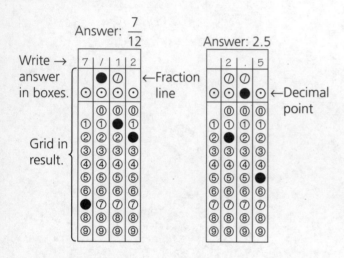

Acceptable ways to grid $\frac{2}{3}$ are:

Answer: 201 – either position is correct

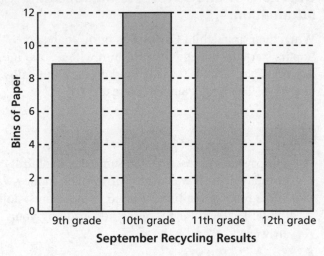

31

September Recycling Results

Star High School recycles white paper. The amount of white paper recycled for each grade level is shown in the chart above. The school goal is to recycle 50 bins of paper each month. What percent of the school goal was achieved in September?

An integer data set has 5 data points such that the mean and mode are each equal to the median. If four of the five points are 9, 12, 12, and 16, what is the fifth data point?

A line segment has endpoints $\left(-\dfrac{9}{4}, 1\right)$ and $(3, -1)$. Find the product of the line segment's midpoint coordinates.

If $(3, -5)$ and $\left(k, -\dfrac{1}{5}\right)$ are ordered pairs of coordinates for the equation $y = mx^2$, what is the positive value of k?

CONTINUE

Questions 35 and 36 refer to the following information.

The number of students, S, at Storrs High School who will catch the flu through week w of school is modeled by the function $S(w) = \dfrac{900w^2 + 20}{w^2 + 2}$.

35

According to the model, how many students will catch the flu through week 3?

36

What is the percent increase of flu victims from week 3 to week 5?

Questions 37 and 38 refer to the following information.

When their grandchild Carlos was born, Juan and Sophia started a college fund for him with a $500 initial deposit. They add $500 to the fund on each of Carlos' birthdays. The fund's annual interest is 6%.

37

Carlos started preschool the same day his third birthday deposit was made. How much money was in the fund at that time? Round to the nearest dollar. (Note: Disregard the $ sign when gridding your answer.)

38

After the interest deposit on Carlos' 4th birthday, his college fund had a balance of $2,318.55. On that day, Juan and Sophia decided to move all the money in that account to a new account that pays 4% interest for each half year. They deposited the full $2,318.55 and an additional $500 into the new account on that day. Juan and Sophia continued to deposit $500 into the account on each of Carlos' birthdays. What is the difference between the amount in the new account on Carlos' sixth birthday and the amount that would have been in the old account on that date? Round to the nearest dollar. (Note: Disregard the $ sign when gridding your answer.)

STOP

If you finish before time is called, you may check your work on this section only.
Do not turn to any other section.

Calculator Allowed

SAT Model Exam 1 Answer Key

No Calculator Test

1. (B)   The center-radius form for a circle is $(x-h)^2+(y-k)^2=r^2$.
Substitute in the values for the center and radius of the circle; then,
$(x-(-3))^2+(y-2)^2=4^2$ which becomes $(x+3)^2+(y-2)^2=16$.

2. (A)   The initial number of cells is 6. This number triples every 4 days; in
32 days, the number of bacteria will have tripled $32 \div 4 = 8$ times. Put
this information into the general exponential formula and you get $6 \cdot 3^8$.

3. (A)   Factor each numerator and denominator, then cancel the common factors.
So, $\dfrac{m^2-2mn+n^2}{m+n} \cdot \dfrac{m+n}{m^2-mn} = \dfrac{(m-n)(m-n)}{m+n} \cdot \dfrac{m+n}{m(m-n)} = \dfrac{m-n}{m}$.

4. (D)   Determine the slope of the line segment using the coordinates of the
endpoints and the slope formula. Then $\dfrac{-1-3}{-6-(-2)} = \dfrac{-4}{-4} = 1$. The line parallel
to line segment will also have a slope of $m = 1$. Now use the point-slope
formula to generate the equation of the line. So $y - (-4) = 1(x - 5)$ and
$y = x - 9$. None of the answer choices are presented in this form, so collect
all the terms with variables on the left-hand side of the equation to see
that $y - x = -9$.

5. (C)   Begin by rewriting $i^{x+2} + i^x + i^{x-2} = 1$ using rules of exponents. Then
$i^x \cdot i^2 + i^x + \dfrac{i^x}{i^2} = 1$. Factor out ^{x}. Then $i^x \left(i^2 + 1 + \dfrac{1}{i^2} \right) = 1$. We know that
$i^2 = -1$, so $i^x \left(-1 + 1 + \dfrac{1}{-1} \right) = 1$. Now simplify: $i^x \left(\dfrac{1}{-1} \right) = 1$ and $i^x = -1$.
The solution must be $x = 2$.

6. (B)   When $y = 2x$ is reflected across the line $y = x$, interchange x and y in the
original equation and solve again for y. Then, $x = 2y$ and $y = \dfrac{x}{2}$.

7. (D)   Since $g(x) = x^2 - x$, then $g(a - 1) = (a - 1)^2 - (a - 1)$. Simplifying,
$g(a - 1) = a^2 - 2a + 1 - a + 1$ and $a^2 - 3a + 2$.

8. (D)   For this question, we can either test each of the given answer choices
to see which one produces the correct answer for $f(x)$, or we can
interchange x and y in the equation $y = 2x - 4$ and solve again for y.
Doing so, $x = 2y - 4$ and $x + 4 = 2y$. Then $y = \dfrac{1}{2}x + 2$.

9. (B)   Since $(x - 3)(x + 1) < 0$, $x = 3$ or $x = -1$. Test each possible solution
in $2x + 5$. If $x = 3$, then $2(3) + 5 = 11$. If $x = -1$, then $2(-1) + 5 = 3$.
Select answer choice B.

10. (C)   Georgia can dedicate up to 20 hours per week to work. This means she
can work up to 80 hours per month. We represent this as $x + y \le 80$. This
eliminates answer choices A, B, and D. That leaves only answer choice C.
As a check: Between her two jobs, Georgia must earn at least $600, so
$9.50x + 10.25y \ge 600$.

11. (A)   Since $g(0) = 1$, $a(0)^2 + b(0) + c = 1$ and $c = 1$. Then, $g(1) = 3$ means that
$a(1)^2 + b(1) + 1 = 3$, which simplifies to $a + b = 2$.

12. (D)   Triangle ACB is a right triangle since a radius drawn to a tangent forms a right angle at point C. Then, the length of leg $\overline{AC} = 5$ and the length of hypotenuse $\overline{AB}$ is equal to the sum of the radii, which is $5 + 2 = 7$. Calculate the length of leg $\overline{CDB}$ using the Pythagorean theorem: $5^2 + (CDB)^2 = 7^2$. Then, $(CDB)^2 = 49 - 25$, $(CDB)^2 = 24$, and $CDB = \sqrt{24}$. Simplifying the root, $CDB = 2\sqrt{6}$. The length of segment $\overline{CD}$ is then $2\sqrt{6} - 2$.

13. (B)   Immediately eliminate answer choices A and D. Choice A is a pair of linear equations that will have only 1 intersection point. Choice D is the intersection of the parabola with the x-axis at the parabola's vertex. Choice C can also be eliminated as a parabola and a vertical line will also have only 1 intersection. The answer must be choice B; this circle and line will have two intersection points.

14. (A)   The midpoint of the acceptable range of measurement is 3.10 cm. This may vary by no more than 0.05, so allowing n to be the measure of the thickness of any given cable wire, $|n - 3.1| \leq 0.05$.

15. (D)   We need to manipulate the equation so that it is solved for N rather than I. Begin by multiplying both sides by the quantity $RN + A$ so that $I(RN + A) = PN$. Distribute so that $IRN + IA = PN$ and then collect all the terms with an N on the left-hand side of the equation: $IRN - PN = -IA$. Factor out the N and $N(IR - P) = -IA$. Finish by dividing both sides by $(IR - P)$ and eliminate the negative sign on $-IA$ to see that $N = \dfrac{IA}{P - IR}$.

16. (90)   For an inverse variation problem, we must first determine the constant of proportionality, k, using the formula $y = \dfrac{k}{x}$. Then, $120 = \dfrac{k}{30}$ and $k = 3{,}600$. Now we can calculate the volume of gas at 40 pounds per square inch pressure: $y = \dfrac{3600}{40} = 90$ cubic inches.

17. (6)   Begin by distributing through the parenthesis so that $3x - \dfrac{2}{3}(5x - 6) = 2$ becomes $3x - \dfrac{10x}{3} + 4 = 2$. Now, collect the like terms and create a common denominator for the left-hand side: $\dfrac{9x}{3} - \dfrac{10x}{3} = -2$. Solve for x in any of a variety of ways to see that $x = 6$.

18. (27)   Using FOIL, $(x - y)^2$ becomes $x^2 - 2xy + y^2 = 33$. Substitute in for xy and $x^2 - 2xy + y^2 = 33$ is now $x^2 - 2(-3) + y^2 = 33$. Then, $x^2 + y^2 = 33 - 6$ and $x^2 + y^2 = 27$.

19. $\left(2.25 \text{ or } \dfrac{9}{4}\right)$ Substitute 8 for all the values of x and calculate. Then, $2x^0 - 3x^{-\frac{2}{3}} + 1^x$ is $2(8)^0 - 3(8)^{-\frac{2}{3}} + 1^8$. Simplifying, $2(1) - 3\left(\dfrac{1}{\sqrt[3]{8^2}}\right) + 1$ and $2 - \dfrac{3}{4} + 1 = 2.25$ or $\dfrac{9}{4}$.

20. $\left(4.25 \text{ or } \dfrac{17}{4}\right)$ Diagonal $\overline{AC}$ has endpoints $(2, 1)$ and $(5, 5)$. Since point P is on the diagonal, the slope of $\overline{AC}$ must be the same as the slope of $\overline{AP}$. Then, $\dfrac{1 - 5}{2 - 5} = \dfrac{1 - 4}{2 - x}$. Simplifying, $\dfrac{-4}{-3} = \dfrac{-3}{2 - x}$. Cross multiply and $-8 + 4x = 9$ and $x = \dfrac{17}{4}$ or 4.25.

Calculator Test

1. (C)   We express inverse variation using the equation $y = \dfrac{k}{x}$. Substitute the given x and y values so that $\dfrac{2}{3} = \dfrac{k}{\frac{9}{2}}$. To make the math a bit easier we'll change $\dfrac{9}{2}$ to its equivalent decimal, 4.5: $\dfrac{2}{3} = \dfrac{k}{4.5}$. Cross-multiplying, $9 = 3k$ and $k = 3$. Expressing this as the variation equation, $y = \dfrac{3}{x}$.

2. (A)   Quickly calculate the mean, median, and mode for the given data set. The mode is 6, the median is 6.5, and the mean is 7. The median is less than the mean.

3. (C)   The point R is shows the highest number of boxes sold with the least amount of time spent. This is the most logical choice.

4. (B)   Label one investment x and the other $(10{,}000 - x)$. Now consider the situation. The 3% investment is producing $60 more than the 5% investment. Thus, if we add $60 to the 5% investment then the two investments should be equal. That is exactly what choice B presents.

5. (D)   Subtract $2a$ from both sides of $ax - a > 2a$ so that $ax - 3a > 0$. Now factor and see that $a(x - 3) > 0$. It is given that $x - 1 < -2$. Simplifying, $x < -1$. Thus $(x - 3)$ is a negative sum. For $a(x - 3) > 0$ to be true means that a must also be negative also, so $a < 0$.

6. (C)   Solve $y + 1 = 4x$ for y, we have $y = 4x - 1$. A line perpendicular to this line would have a slope of $-\dfrac{1}{4}$. Solve $2x + 3y = 6$ for y, we have $3y = -2x + 6$. Manipulate the equation so it is in slope-intercept form and $y = -\dfrac{2}{3}x + 2$. The y-intercept is 2. The new equation is $y = -\dfrac{1}{4}x + 2$. But that is not one of the choices. Multiply through by 4 and we have $4y = -x + 8$ or $x + 4y = 8$.

7. (A)   The most direct way to solve this problem is to set up a proportion with the number of tagged deer over the total population. Then $\dfrac{78}{218} = \dfrac{112}{x}$ and, cross-multiplying, $78x = 24416$, $x \approx 313$ deer.

8. (B)   The median can be found where the 15th and 16th scores reside. Score numbers 15–22 are in the interval 71–80.

9. (C)   Since there is no solution to the system, the lines must be parallel. Lines that are parallel have the same slope. Manipulate the equation $\dfrac{1}{3}x - \dfrac{1}{6}y = 3$ into slope-intercept form: $y = 2x - 18$. Do the same for the second equation: $y = \dfrac{k}{5}x - 6$. Now set the slopes equal to each other and solve for k. Then $2 = \dfrac{k}{5}$ and by cross-multiplication, $k = 10$.

10. (B)   The triangle ABC inscribed in the half circle is a right triangle with a right angle at point B. By the Pythagorean theorem, (side AB)^2 + (side BC)^2 = (hypotenuse AC)^2. Since $\cos x = \dfrac{2}{3}$, we have $(AB)^2 + 2^2 = 3^2$, $(AB)^2 = 9 - 4 = 5$, and $(AB) = \sqrt{5}$. Thus, $\cos y = \dfrac{\sqrt{5}}{3}$. Alternately, the triangle ABC has a right angle at point B. We know that $\cos y = \sin x$. Then $\sin^2 x + \cos^2 x = 1$ and $\sin x = \sqrt{1 - \cos^2 x} = \sqrt{1 - \left(\dfrac{2}{3}\right)^2}$ which becomes $\sqrt{\dfrac{5}{9}} = \dfrac{\sqrt{5}}{3}$. So, $\cos x = \dfrac{\sqrt{5}}{3}$.

11. (B)   First determine the number of household in the town: $\dfrac{80000}{3.2} = 25{,}000$.

Then multiply the number of households by the number of cell phone per household. So, $25000(2.8) = 70{,}000$ cell phones.

12. (A)   Solve the linear equation $2x - y = 1$ for y, so that $y = 2x - 1$. Substitute this equation in for y in the second equation. Now, $(2x - 1)^2 - 2x^2 = 7$ and $4x^2 - 4x + 1 - 2x^2 = 7$. Simplifying, $2x^2 - 4x - 6 = 0$. Divide through by 2 and factor to see that $x^2 - 2x - 3 = 0$ and $(x - 3)(x + 1) = 0$. Then, $x = 3$ or $x = -1$. If $x = 3$, then $2(3) - y = 1$ and $y = 5$. If $x = -1$, then $2(-1) - y = 1$ and $y = -3$. The coordinate solution pairs are $(x, y) = (3, 5)$ and $(x, y) = (-1, -3)$. The possible sums are 8 or -4.

13. (B)   The formula for the perimeter of a rectangle is $2l + 2w$. In this case, the side measurements are a and b, so $2a + 2b = P$. Substituting for a we have $2\left(\dfrac{3}{4}b\right) + 2b = P$. Then, $\dfrac{3}{2}b + 2b = P$ and $\dfrac{7}{2}b = P$. Solve this equation for b and $b = \dfrac{2P}{7}$.

14. (C)   At 8:30, the minute hand points to the 6 and the hour hand is between 8 and 9. Since 360° divided by 12 = 30°, each hour is a 30° arc. There are 2 and one-half arcs from the minute hand to the hour hand, so $2.5(30) = 75°$. Now convert 75° to radian measure, and we have $\dfrac{75}{1}\left(\dfrac{\pi}{180}\right) = \dfrac{5\pi}{12}$ radians.

15. (C)   Assign a variable to represent the unknown number of games played. Then, the first ratio becomes $3x : 1x$. Then, $3x + 8 =$ the new total of wins and $\dfrac{3x + 8}{x} = \dfrac{5}{1}$, the new relationship of wins to losses. Solving, $5x = 3x + 8$, $2x = 8$ and $x = 4$. Hence, $3x$ or $3(4) = 12$ is the number of games originally won.

16. (D)   The slopes from points A to B to C must be the same if the points are collinear. Thus, $\dfrac{1 - 0}{N - 0} = \dfrac{N - 1}{2 - N}$. Cross multiply and find that $2 - N = N(N - 1)$ and $2 - N = N^2 - N$. Collect the like terms and solve for N to see that $2 = N^2$ and $N = \sqrt{2}$.

17. (B)   Since two zeros are 5 and -3, set $x = 5$ and $x = -3$ and begin working backwards to build the factor. Then, $x - 5 = 0$ and $x + 3 = 0$. The product of $(x - 5)(x + 3) = x^2 - 2x - 15$, which is one of the factors of the polynomial function $m(x)$.

18. (A) Using the rule for conditional probability, $\dfrac{P(A) \cdot P(B)}{P(A)}$, the probability of selecting a senior, $P(A)$, is $\dfrac{225}{1000}$ and the probability of selecting a senior taking math, $P(B)$, is $\dfrac{50}{225}$. Thus, $\dfrac{P(A) \cdot P(B)}{P(A)} = \dfrac{\frac{225}{1000} \cdot \frac{50}{225}}{\frac{225}{1000}} = \dfrac{50}{225} = \dfrac{2}{9}$.

19. (C) Given that $f(x) = 2x + 7$ and $f(g(-1)) = 15$, solve $2x + 7 = 15$ to find that $2x = 8$ and $x = 4$. That means $g(-1)$ must equal 4. Only the expression $3x + 7 = 3(-1) + 7 = -3 + 7 = 4$.

20. (D) First calculate 30% of 200 = 60 redesigned apartments. Then, 25% of 200 = 50 new units so that 200 + 50 = 250 total apartments. Thus, 40% of 250 = 100 apartments for handicapped, an increase of 40 from the past year. The percent increase is $\dfrac{40}{60} = \dfrac{2}{3}$ or $66\dfrac{2}{3}\%$.

21. (A) Square both sides of $\sqrt{y+5} = 7 - y$ so that $\left(\sqrt{y+5}\right)^2 = (7-y)^2$ and $y + 5 = 49 - 14y + y^2$. Collect the like terms and then factor to see that $0 = y^2 - 15y + 44$ and $(y-4)(y-11) = 0$ Solve for y: $y = 4$ or $y = 11$. Check both solutions in the original equation to make sure neither is extraneous. Only $y = 4$ works.

22. (A) Segments $\overline{AB}$, $\overline{BC}$, and $\overline{AC}$ are all diagonals of the square sides of the given cube. The measure of each diagonal is $\sqrt{2}$ and triangle ABC is equilateral. Using the formula for the area of an equilateral triangle and substituting $\sqrt{2}$ for S, $\dfrac{S^2\sqrt{3}}{4} = \dfrac{\left(\sqrt{2}\right)^2 \sqrt{3}}{4} = \dfrac{2\sqrt{3}}{4} = \dfrac{\sqrt{3}}{2}$.

23. (C) Consider that $3^a + 3^{a+1} = n$ can be rewritten as $3^a + 3^a\left(3^1\right) = n$. Then we can factor out the 3^a term to see that $3^a(1+3) = n$ and $3^a = \dfrac{n}{4}$. Now, to write 3^{a+2} in terms of n, consider 3^{a+2} is $3^a\left(3^2\right)$. Substitute in $3^a = \dfrac{n}{4}$ and find that $\dfrac{n}{4} \cdot 3^2 = \dfrac{9n}{4}$.

24. (B) Use the formula $y = kx$ to determine k, the constant of proportionality. Then $5 = 140k$ and $k = \dfrac{1}{28}$. Now the distance the spring will stretch with a force of 212 newtons is $\left(\dfrac{1}{28}\right)(212) \approx 7.6$ cm.

25. (A) Since the distribution covers 95% of the scores, this includes two standard deviations above the mean and two standard deviations below the mean. Find the difference between the two scores and divide by four: $\dfrac{98-54}{4} = 11$.

26. (D)   A function is defined as having only one output, y, for each input, x. Answer choice D has two values of y, 2 and 3, for one value of x, 2.

27. (B)   There are multiple ways to solve this problem. We can start by summing the two given equations and by the elimination method, $x = \dfrac{a+b}{2}$. Substitute that value back into either equation. So, $x + y = a$ becomes $\dfrac{a+b}{2} + y = a$. Isolate y and combine the like terms to find that $y = a - \left(\dfrac{a+b}{2}\right) \to \dfrac{2a - a - b}{2} = \dfrac{a-b}{2}$.

28. (D)   Examine the values. For each 1-unit increase in x, there is a factor-of-2-unit increase in y. The ratio of growth in y is constant, so this is an exponential function. Eliminate answer choices A and C. Answer choice B is incorrect because $2^0 = 1$, not 5. Select choice D.

29. (C)   Since the mean is 75 and the standard deviation is 5.8, a score of $75 + 5.8 = 80.8$ is one standard deviation above the mean and a score of $75 + 2(5.8) = 86.6$ is two standard deviations above the mean. Therefore, a score of 82 is between 1 and 2 standard deviations above the mean.

30. (B)   The transformation changes $g(x)$ into $g(x + 3) + 1$ which becomes $f(x)$. Then, $f(x) = -(x + 3)^2 + 1$. So, $f(-1.5) = -(-1.5 + 3)^2 + 1 = -1.25$.

31. (80)   Read the amount of white paper recycled by each grade off the bar graph: $9 + 12 + 10 + 9 = 40$ bins. Then, $\dfrac{40}{50} = 0.80 = 80\%$. When gridding in the answer, we ignore the percent sign.

32. (0)   Use the midpoint formula to see that the coordinates of the midpoint are given by $\left(\dfrac{-\frac{9}{4}+3}{2}, \dfrac{1+(-1)}{2}\right) = \left(\dfrac{3}{8}, 0\right)$. The product of the coordinates is 0.

33. (11)   Since the 4 known data points are 9, 12, 12, and 16, the median can only be 12, no matter the value of the 5th integer. Let x be the value of the unknown integer. Then, the mean is $\dfrac{9 + 12 + 12 + 16 + x}{5} = 12$ and $49 + x = 60$. Solve for x and $x = 11$. The data set is now 9, 11, 12, 12, 16 and its mode is 12.

34. $\left(\dfrac{3}{5}\right)$ First determine the value of m by substituting $(3, -5)$ for (x, y) in the equation $y = mx^2$. Then, $-5 = m \cdot (3)^2$ and $-\dfrac{5}{9} = m$. Now use the value of m and the other coordinate pair to calculate k. So, $-\dfrac{1}{5} = -\dfrac{5}{9}k^2$; multiply both sides by $-\dfrac{9}{5}$ and $k^2 = \dfrac{9}{25}$. Then, $k = \dfrac{3}{5}$.

35. (738)   Substitute in 3 for w in the given function. Then, $S(3) = \dfrac{900 \cdot (3)^2 + 20}{(3)^2 + 2} = \dfrac{8120}{11} \approx 738$ students.

36. (13)   Determine the number of students who have caught the flu in week 5. So, $S(5) = \dfrac{900 \cdot (5)^2 + 20}{(5)^2 + 2} = \dfrac{22520}{27} \approx 834$ students. Now calculate the percentage increase: $100\left(\dfrac{834 - 738}{738}\right) \approx 13\%$. When gridding in the answer, we ignore the percent sign.

37. (2187)   The initial deposit was $500. On Carlos' first birthday, the interest for the first year and another $500 is deposited. So the account has $500(1.06) + $500 = $1,030 in it. On his second birthday, the interest for the second year is deposited along with another $500: $1030(1.06) + $500 = $1,591.80. On his third birthday the interest for the third year and another $500 deposit means the account balance is $1591.80(1.06) + $500 = $2187.31. Rounded to the nearest dollar, this is $2,187.

38. (141)   First calculate the amount of money that would have been in the old account on Carlos' sixth birthday. The amount given for his 4th birthday includes the interest but not Juan and Sophia's regular deposit, so $2318.55 + $500 = $2,818.55. On his fifth birthday, the amount would have been $2,818.55(1.06) + $500 = $3487.66, and on his sixth birthday, the amount would have been $3487.66(1.06) + $500 = $4,196.92. In the new account, interest is earned every six months. These calculations are easiest to keep track of in a table:

Carlos' Age	Interest Calculation	Juan/Sophia Deposit	Account Balance
4 years	$0	$500	$2,818.55
4 years, 6 months	$2,818.55(1.04)	$0	$2931.29
5 years	$2,931.29(1.04)	$500	$3548.54
5 years, 6 months	$3,548.54(1.04)	$0	$3690.49
6 years	$3,690.49(1.04)	$500	$4338.10

The difference between the two accounts is $4,338.10 − $4,196.92 = $141.18. Grid in 141.

Correlation Chart

SAT Math Model Exam 1—No Calculator Allowed

Use the chart below to mark the questions you found difficult to determine which lessons you need to review.

(The No Calculator section of the SAT Math Exam will not contain items from Category 2, Problem Solving and Data Analysis.)

Question Number	Heart of Algebra	Problem Solving & Data Analysis	Passport To Advanced Math	Additional Topics in Math	Pages to Study
1				Lesson 6	502 – 505
2			Lesson 3		316 – 326
3			Lesson 2		298 – 315
4	Lesson 6				120 – 138
5				Lesson 7	506 – 513
6			Lesson 7		374 – 388
7			Lesson 7		374 – 388
8			Lesson 7		374 – 388
9			Lesson 5		343 – 358
10	Lesson 4				98 – 111
11			Lesson 4		327 – 342
12				Lesson 3	452 – 473
13	Lesson 4				98 – 111
14	Lesson 2				57 – 80
15	Lesson 2				57 – 80
16	Lesson 5				112 – 119
17	Lesson 2				57 – 80
18			Lesson 4		327 – 342
19			Lesson 1		281 – 297
20	Lesson 3				81 – 97
Total Correct	＿＿ / 8		＿＿ / 9	＿＿ / 3	NA

Correlation Chart

SAT Math Model Exam 1—Calculator Allowed

Use the chart below to mark the questions you found difficult to determine which lessons you need to review.

Question Number	Heart of Algebra	Problem Solving & Data Analysis	Passport to Advanced Math	Additional Topics in Math	Pages to Study
1	Lesson 5				112 – 119
2		Lesson 6			231 – 245
3		Lesson 3			188 – 200
4	Lesson 1				43 – 56
5	Lesson 4				98 – 111
6	Lesson 3				81 – 97
7		Lesson 1			157 – 176
8		Lesson 6			231 – 245
9	Lesson 4				98 – 111
10				Lesson 4	474 – 488
11	Lesson 2				57 – 80
12			Lesson 6		359 – 373
13	Lesson 2				57 – 80
14				Lesson 5	489 – 501
15		Lesson 1			157 – 176
16	Lesson 3				81 – 97
17			Lesson 4		327 – 342
18		Lesson 5			215 – 230
19			Lesson 7		374 – 388
20		Lesson 1			157 – 176
21			Lesson 3		316 – 326
22				Lesson 1	407 – 425
23	Lesson 4				98 – 111
24	Lesson 5				112 – 119
25		Lesson 6			231 – 245
26	Lesson 3				81 – 97
27	Lesson 4				98 – 111
28		Lesson 3			188 – 200
29		Lesson 6			231 – 245
30			Lesson 7		374 – 388
31		Lesson 1			157 – 176
32	Lesson 6				120 – 138
33		Lesson 6			231 – 245
34			Lesson 4		327 – 342
35			Lesson 2		298 – 315
36		Lesson 1			157 – 176
37		Lesson 1			157 – 176
38		Lesson 1			157 – 176
Total Correct	_____ / 13	_____ / 15	_____ / 7	_____ / 3	NA

25 MINUTES, 20 QUESTIONS

NO CALCULATOR ALLOWED

Use the No Calculator section of your answer sheet to answer the questions in this section.

Directions

For questions 1–15, calculate the answer to each problem and choose the best option from the choices given. Bubble in the corresponding circle on your answer sheet. For the remaining questions, solve the problem and enter your answer in the grid on your answer sheet. Refer to the directions before question 16 on how to enter your answers in the grid.

Notes

1. The use of a calculator is <u>not</u> permitted on this test section.
2. All variables and expressions represent real numbers unless otherwise indicated.
3. Figures provided are drawn to scale unless otherwise noted.
4. All figures lie in a plane unless otherwise noted.
5. Unless otherwise noted, the domain of a given function f is the set of all real numbers x for which $f(x)$ is a real number.

Reference

$A = \pi r^2$
$C = 2\pi r$

$A = lw$

$A = \frac{1}{2}bh$

$c^2 = a^2 + b^2$

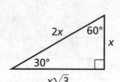

Special Right Triangles

$V = lwh$

$V = \pi r^2 h$

$V = \frac{4}{3}\pi r^3$

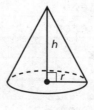
$V = \frac{1}{3}\pi r^2 h$

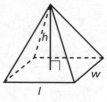
$V = \frac{1}{3}lwh$

The number of degrees of arc in a circle is 360.
The number of radians of arc in a circle is 2π.
The sum of the measures in degrees of the angles of a triangle is 180.

CONTINUE

1

The sum of $6 - 5i$, the additive inverse of $5 - 7i$, and the conjugate of $-3 - 2i$ corresponds to a point in which quadrant? (Note: $i = \sqrt{-1}$)

A) I

B) II

C) III

D) IV

2

In terms of m, how many hours will it take to travel $m + 50$ miles at an average speed of 50 miles per hour?

A) $m + 1$ hours

B) $\dfrac{1}{m+1}$ hours

C) $\dfrac{50}{m+50}$ hours

D) $\dfrac{m+50}{50}$ hours

3

If x varies inversely as the square of y and if $x = 3$ when $y = -1$, what is the value of x when $y = 3$?

A) -3

B) $\dfrac{1}{3}$

C) 3

D) 27

4

If $\dfrac{1}{x} = \dfrac{1}{a} + \dfrac{1}{b}$, then x is equivalent to

A) $a + b$

B) $\dfrac{ab}{a+b}$

C) $\dfrac{a+b}{ab}$

D) $\dfrac{2ab}{a+b}$

CONTINUE

5

$x = y - 4$

$4y - 3x = 14$

For the system of equations listed above, what is the sum $x + y$?

A) 8

B) −10

C) 0

D) 6

C)

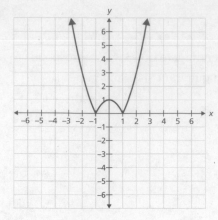

D)

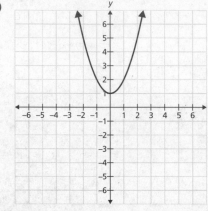

6

The graph of $y = |x^2 - 1|$ is best represented by which of the following?

A)

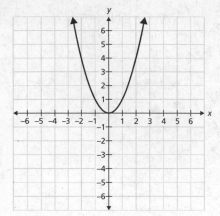

B)

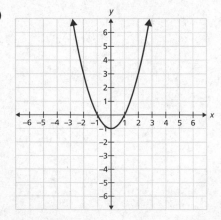

7

What is the result when the fraction $\dfrac{3}{\sqrt{3x^2 a}}$ is rationalized?

A) $\dfrac{\sqrt{3a}}{ax}$

B) $\dfrac{1}{x\sqrt{a}}$

C) $\dfrac{\sqrt{a}}{ax}$

D) $\dfrac{\sqrt{3}}{x}$

CONTINUE

No Calculator Allowed

$(x + 1)^2 + (y - 3)^2 = 9$

$y = (x + 1)^2 - 1$

How many points are there in the solution to the system of equations listed above?

A) 0

B) 1

C) 2

D) 4

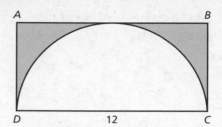

If a half-circle is inscribed in rectangle *ABCD*, as shown above, which of the following represents the area of the shaded region?

A) $144\pi - 72$

B) $72 - 72\pi$

C) $72 - 36\pi$

D) $72 - 18\pi$

Which of the following represent the simplified quotient of $\dfrac{a^{-1} - 1}{a - 1}$?

A) -1

B) $\dfrac{1}{a^2}$

C) $-\dfrac{1}{a}$

D) $\dfrac{1}{(a-1)^2}$

The minimum point on the graph of $y = h(x)$ is $(-1, -4)$. What is the minimum point on the graph of the equation $y = h(x) + 7$?

A) $(-1, 3)$

B) $(6, -4)$

C) $(-1, 11)$

D) $(-8, -4)$

CONTINUE

If $f(x) = 3x - 1$ and $f(g(x)) = x$, which of the following functions is $g(x)$?

A) $g(x) = -3x + 1$

B) $g(x) = 3x - 1$

C) $g(x) = \dfrac{x-1}{3}$

D) $g(x) = \dfrac{x+1}{3}$

If $a^5 - a^3 \neq 0$, which of the following is equal to $\dfrac{a^5 + 2a^4 + a^3}{a^5 - a^3}$?

A) $2a^4$

B) $\dfrac{a+1}{a-1}$

C) $2a + 1$

D) $\dfrac{a+2}{a-1}$

If $a^x = c^y$ and $c^m = a^z$, then which of the following expressions about the exponents is true?

A) $xm = yz$

B) $\dfrac{x}{m} = \dfrac{y}{z}$

C) $x + m = y + z$

D) $x - m = y - z$

15

Suppose the linear function h has a slope of $m = -6$, passes through the point $(2, 3)$, and crosses the y-axis at the point $(0, y)$. Which of the following is the value of y?

A) $y = 10$

B) $y = 12$

C) $y = 15$

D) $y = 14$

CONTINUE

No Calculator Allowed

For the remaining questions, solve the problem and enter your answer in the answer grid. Instructions for entering your answer in the grid are described below.

1. It is not required that you write your answer in the boxes at the top of the grid, but it is suggested.

2. Do not mark more than one circle in each column.

3. There are no negative answers in this portion of the test.

4. If the problem has more than 1 correct answer, grid only 1 of those answers.

5. Grid fractions as proper or improper fractions only.

6. Decimal answers must fill the entire grid.

Examples

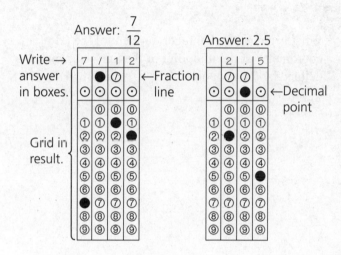

Acceptable ways to grid $\frac{2}{3}$ are:

Answer: 201 – either position is correct

CONTINUE

What is the slope of the line perpendicular to $\frac{3}{4}x + 9y = 12$?

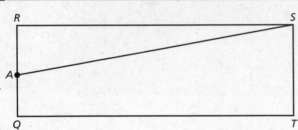

In rectangle $QRST$, above, A is the midpoint of $\overline{QR}$. If the area of quadrilateral $QAST$ is $\frac{2}{5}$ square units, what is the area of rectangle $QRST$?

If $f(x) = |2x - 15|$, for how many integer values of x is it true that $f(x) < x$?

What is the positive integer quotient of the (x, y) coordinates of the midpoint of the line segment defined by the endpoints $A(6, 10)$ and $B(8, 4)$?

$ax - y = 5$

$x + by = 0$

If $(x, y) = (-3, 1)$ is a solution for the above system of equations, what is the value of $a + b$?

STOP

**If you finish before time is called, you may check your work on this section only.
Do not turn to any other section.**

No Calculator Allowed

55 MINUTES, 38 QUESTIONS

CALCULATOR ALLOWED

Use the Calculator section of your answer sheet to answer the questions in this section.

Directions

For questions 1–30, calculate the answer to each problem and choose the best option from the choices given. Bubble in the corresponding circle on your answer sheet. For the remaining questions, solve the problem and enter your answer in the grid on your answer sheet. Refer to the directions before question 31 on how to enter your answers in the grid.

Notes

1. The use of a calculator is permitted on this test section.
2. All variables and expressions represent real numbers unless otherwise indicated.
3. Figures provided are drawn to scale unless otherwise noted.
4. All figures lie in a plane unless otherwise noted.
5. Unless otherwise noted, the domain of a given function f is the set of all real numbers x for which $f(x)$ is a real number.

Reference

$A = \pi r^2$
$C = 2\pi r$

$A = lw$

$A = \frac{1}{2}bh$

$c^2 = a^2 + b^2$

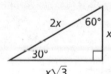

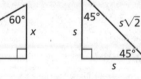

Special Right Triangles

$V = lwh$

$V = \pi r^2 h$

$V = \frac{4}{3}\pi r^3$

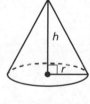

$V = \frac{1}{3}\pi r^2 h$

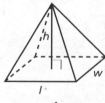

$V = \frac{1}{3}lwh$

The number of degrees of arc in a circle is 360.
The number of radians of arc in a circle is 2π.
The sum of the measures in degrees of the angles of a triangle is 180.

CONTINUE

1

If $B = A - 7$ then $(A - B)^2 + 8 =$

A) 7

B) 15

C) 49

D) 57

3

Mei, a professional softball pitcher, recorded 9, 7, 16, 8, 12, 10, and 8 strikeouts, respectively, in seven consecutive games. If m represents the median of these strikeouts and a represents the arithmetic mean, then what is the value of $-(m - a)^2$?

A) -2

B) -1

C) 0

D) 1

2

A florist bought x orchids at d dollars each and sold them at n dollars each. Which of the following expressions represents the profit the florist made?

A) $x(d - n)$

B) $x(n - d)$

C) $d(x - n)$

D) $x(d + n)$

4

If $(3x - 4)(7x - 2) = 21x^2 + kx + 8$ for all real numbers x, then the value of k is

A) -34

B) -22

C) 22

D) 34

CONTINUE

Calculator Allowed

If $|2x - 3| = 5$, which of the following is a possible value of x^2?

A) 4

B) 16

C) −1

D) −16

A suitable nighttime temperature range in degrees Fahrenheit, F, for a gardenia is 50 $\leq F \leq 77$. The conversion formula for representing degrees in Celsius, C, is $C = \dfrac{5}{9}(F - 32)$. Which of the following is the corresponding nighttime temperature range in degrees Celsius for gardenias?

A) $0 \leq C \leq 15$

B) $5 \leq C \leq 20$

C) $10 \leq C \leq 25$

D) $15 \leq C \leq 30$

An equation for a circle in the xy-coordinate plane is given as $(x - 9)^2 + y^2 = 21$. What are the coordinates of the center of the circle and the radius of the circle?

A) Center $(-9, 0)$, Radius 10.5

B) Center $(9, 0)$, Radius 10.5

C) Center $(9, 0)$, Radius $\sqrt{21}$

D) Center $(-9, 0)$, Radius $\sqrt{21}$

A manufacturer sells sets of golf clubs to a retail sports store for 25 percent more than they cost to produce. The retail store sells a set of those clubs to a customer for a 30 percent profit. The price the customer paid for the clubs was what percent greater than the cost of production?

A) 50%

B) 55%

C) 60%

D) 62.5%

CONTINUE

A rectangular block of a certain type of metal weighs 1,950 grams. If the dimensions of the block are 8 cm by 6 cm by 5 cm, what is the density of the metal? $\left(density = \dfrac{mass}{volume} \right)$

A) 8.125 g/cm³
B) 468,000 g/cm³
C) 0.123 g/cm³
D) 46,800 g/cm³

The frequency table below shows the class scores on a biology quiz. Which interval contains the median score?

Intervals	Frequency
90–99	5
80–89	9
70–79	10
60–69	4
50–59	2

A) 60–69
B) 70–79
C) 80–89
D) 90–99

Which of the given functions represents the following data table?

x	f(x)
1	$\dfrac{1}{2}$
2	$\dfrac{1}{4}$
3	$\dfrac{1}{8}$
4	$\dfrac{1}{16}$

A) $f(x) = 2x + 1$
B) $f(x) = 2^x$
C) $f(x) = \left(\dfrac{1}{2} \right)^x$
D) $f(x) = \left(\dfrac{3}{2} \right)^x$

CONTINUE

Calculator Allowed

12

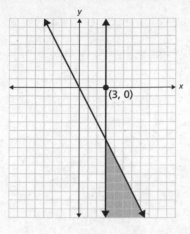

Which of the following systems of inequalities is represented by the shaded region of the graph above?

A) $y \le -2x$ and $x \le 3$

B) $y \le -2x$ and $x \ge 3$

C) $y \ge -2x$ and $x \ge 3$

D) $y \ge -2x$ and $x \le 3$

14

A solution is made by mixing an x amount of concentrate with water. Approximately how many liters (x) of this concentrate should be mixed with 5 liters of water so that 32 percent of the solution is concentrate?

A) 0.68

B) 1.6

C) 2.28

D) 2.35

13

If y varies directly as x, and $y = \pi$ when $x = 120$, what is the value of y when $x = 360$?

A) $\dfrac{1}{3}$

B) $\dfrac{\pi}{3}$

C) 3

D) 3π

15

If θ is an acute angle of a right triangle and $\cos \theta = \dfrac{a}{b}$, where $a > 0$ and $b > 0$ and $a \ne b$, then $\tan \theta =$

A) $\dfrac{\sqrt{b^2 - a^2}}{a}$

B) $\dfrac{b - a}{a}$

C) $\dfrac{a}{\sqrt{b^2 - a^2}}$

D) $\dfrac{b}{\sqrt{b^2 - a^2}}$

CONTINUE

16

A researcher wants to know the potential effect of consuming at least 50 ounces of soda per day. Which technique would be best for her data collection?

A) Survey a sample of people who report drinking some soda each day.

B) Observation of a sample of people who report drinking more than 50 ounces of soda per day.

C) Experiment in which half the participants are allowed to drink only soda until they have consumed at least 50 ounces, regardless of their typical soda consumption.

D) Experiment in which half of the participants are not allowed to drink any soda, regardless of their typical soda consumption.

If $\left(2+\dfrac{1}{x}\right)k=\dfrac{1}{x}$, which of the following represents k?

A) -2

B) $\dfrac{1}{2}$

C) $\dfrac{1}{2x+1}$

D) $\dfrac{2}{2x+1}$

The formula for the volume of a cone is $V=\dfrac{1}{3}\pi r^2 h$.

Which of the following is the expression for the radius, r?

A) $3\sqrt{\dfrac{V}{\pi h}}$

B) $\dfrac{1}{3}\sqrt{\dfrac{V}{\pi h}}$

C) $\sqrt{\dfrac{3V}{\pi h}}$

D) $\sqrt{\dfrac{V}{3\pi h}}$

The minimum stopping distance for a moving car is calculated to be directly proportional to the square of the car's speed. If a certain car has a stopping distance of 44 feet when traveling at 30 mph, what will be the stopping distance for the same car traveling at 45 mph?

A) 31 feet

B) 66 feet

C) 99 feet

D) 97 feet

CONTINUE

Calculator Allowed

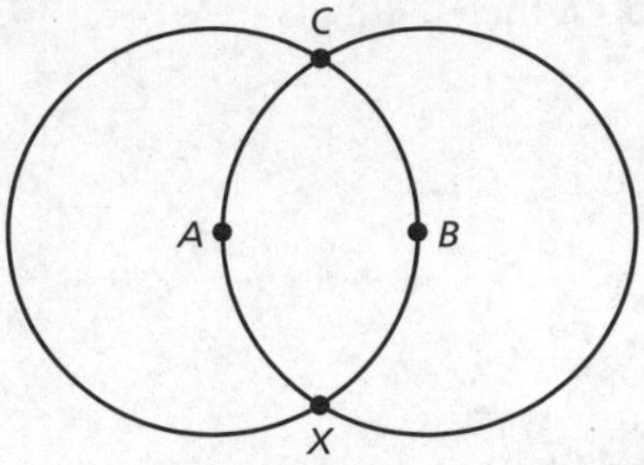

In the given figure A and B are the centers of two congruent circles that intersect at points C and X. If arc CBX has a length of 2π, what is the area of the circle with center at A?

A) 36π

B) 9π

C) 6π

D) 4π

On a scale drawing, 1 inch represents 3 feet. Suppose that the area of a built room is 180 ft². If the length of the built room is 15 feet, what is the width of the room on the scale drawing?

A) 12 inches

B) 5 inches

C) 4 inches

D) 9 inches

The volume of a mixture of sand, gravel, and cement are in the ratio of 2 to 1 to 3. If 1 cubic foot of each item weighs 30, 40, and 20 pounds, respectively, what is the ratio of the weights of sand to gravel to cement in this mixture?

A) 3:1:2

B) 3:2:3

C) 2:1:3

D) 3:1:3

An amateur golfer calculated his scoring average for the 5-month season. If his data is normally distributed, about how many of his 60 games were within one standard deviation of the mean?

A) 19

B) 20

C) 39

D) 41

CONTINUE

If $f(x) = -x + 1$ and $g(x) = -x^2 + 1$, then what are all the values of x for which is it true that $f(g(x)) = g(f(x))$?

A) $\{0, 1\}$

B) $\{0, 2\}$

C) $\{-1, 2\}$

D) $\{0, 1, 2\}$

If $5^a - 5^{a-1} = 2{,}500$, then a equals

A) 3

B) 4

C) 5

D) 6

If $x - \dfrac{1}{x} = 1$, then what is the value of $x^2 + \dfrac{1}{x^2}$?

A) -2

B) -1

C) 1

D) 3

Zora is developing a nutrition plan for a patient. Calories from food eaten for breakfast and lunch can be no more than a total of 950 calories and breakfast must comprise at least 300 calories. If b = the number of calories consumed at breakfast, and l = the number of calories consumed at lunch, which of the following systems describes these constraints?

A) $\begin{cases} b + l \leq 950 \\ b \geq 300 \end{cases}$

B) $\begin{cases} b + l \leq 950 \\ b \leq 300 \end{cases}$

C) $\begin{cases} b - l \leq 950 \\ b \geq 300 \end{cases}$

D) $\begin{cases} b - l \leq 950 \\ b \leq 300 \end{cases}$

CONTINUE

Calculator Allowed

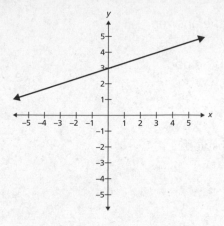

Which of the following functions generated the graph above?

A) $f(x) = 3x + 1$

B) $f(x) = \dfrac{1}{3}x + 3$

C) $f(x) = \left(\dfrac{1}{3}\right)^x$

D) $f(x) = 3x + \dfrac{1}{3}$

For what value of k does the equation
$x^2 - 9 = k(x - 3)$ have $x = 3$ as its <u>only</u> root?

A) 0 only

B) 3 only

C) 6 only

D) all real values

If $f(x) = 2x + \dfrac{1}{x}$ and $x \neq 0$, which of the following would be equal to $f(-x)$?

A) $-f(-x)$

B) $f(x)$

C) $-\dfrac{1}{f(x)}$

D) $-f(x)$

CONTINUE

For the remaining questions, solve the problem and enter your answer in the answer grid. Instructions for entering your answer in the grid are described below.

1. It is not required that you write your answer in the boxes at the top of the grid, but it is suggested.

2. Do not mark more than one circle in each column.

3. There are no negative answers in this portion of the test.

4. If the problem has more than 1 correct answer, grid only 1 of those answers.

5. Grid fractions as proper or improper fractions only.

6. Decimal answers must fill the entire grid.

• • • • **Examples** •

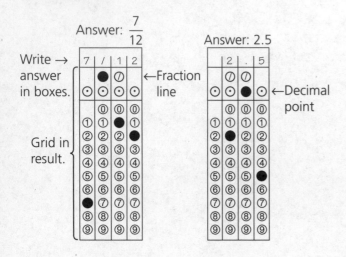

Answer: $\frac{7}{12}$

Write → answer in boxes.

←Fraction line

Grid in result.

Answer: 2.5

←Decimal point

Acceptable ways to grid $\frac{2}{3}$ are:

Answer: 201 – either position is correct

Calculator Allowed

31

According to recent currency exchange rates, 1 US dollar can purchase 14.9 Mexican pesos or 62.2 Indian rupees. Using this information, determine how many Indian rupees can be purchased with 1 Mexican peso. Round to the nearest hundredth.

33

When the function $g(x) = \left(x - \dfrac{1}{2} \right)^2$ is graphed on the xy-coordinate plane, the x-intercept is $(n, 0)$ and the y-intercept is $(0, b)$. What is the value of the product nb?

32

The small, wealthy town of Luxuria has a school population of 900 children. Of the 175 children in elementary school, 100 children receive an allowance. What is the probability that a randomly chosen student who attends the elementary school receives an allowance?

34

A pool is being filled at a constant rate of 4 gallons per minute. At 12:00 noon, it is $\dfrac{6}{25}$ full and at 3:30 pm, the pool is 40% full. How many gallons of water does the pool hold when full?

CONTINUE

If the graphs of the equations $4y - 2x = 7$ and $ax + 5y = 10$ are perpendicular to each other, what is the numerical value of a?

Suppose the distance between two points in the xy-plane is 6, and that the two points are $(1, 3)$ and $(x, 5)$. What is the value of x? Round your answer to the nearest integer.

CONTINUE

Calculator Allowed

Questions 37 and 38 refer to the following information.

Brooklynn and her friend, Thanos, recently traveled to Brazil while the exchange rate was 1 Brazilian real = 0.36 US dollar.

37

While in Brazil, Brooklynn used her credit card to purchase a leather coat costing 540 Brazilian Reals. Her credit card company charges a small percentage fee for purchases made in currencies other than US dollars. When Brooklynn returned home, her bank statement showed a final charge for the coat of $201.69. What percent fee did the credit card company charge for Brooklynn's Brazilian purchase?

Brooklynn's travel partner, Thanos, exchanged 500 US dollars for Brazilian reals in advance at his bank. The bank charged a 4% conversion rate to convert US dollars to Brazilian reals before he left and a 3% conversion rate to convert Brazilian reals back to US dollars. When Thanos returned home and exchanged his remaining reals, the bank gave him $257. What was the cost, to the nearest real, of the cash purchases Thanos made while in Brazil?

STOP

If you finish before time is called, you may check your work on this section only.
Do not turn to any other section.

SAT Model Exam 2 Answer Key

No Calculator Test

1. (B)   The additive inverse of $5 - 7i$ is $-5 + 7i$ and the conjugate of $-3 - 2i$ is $-3 + 2i$. Then the sum of the expressions is $6 + 5i + (-5 + 7i) + (-3 + 2i) = 6 + 5i - 5 + 7i - 3 + 2i$. Collect the like terms and the sum is $-2 + 14i$. This point is located in quadrant II.

2. (D)   Using the formula $d = rt$, $(m + 50) = 50t$. Solving for t in terms of m yields $t = \dfrac{m+50}{50}$ hours.

3. (B)   Translate the given statement so that $xy^2 = 3(-1)^2$ which is $x(3)^2$. Simplify and $3 = 9x$. Solve for the variable to see that $x = \dfrac{1}{3}$.

4. (B)   There are several ways to solve this problem. The quickest is to multiply every term in the equation by the common denominator abx. The result is $ab = bx + ax$. Factor x out of the right-hand side and $ab = x(b + a)$. Solve for $x = \dfrac{ab}{a+b}$.

5. (C)   Substitute $y - 4$ for x in the second equation. Then $4y - 3(y - 4) = 14$. Distribute and collect the like terms to see that $4y - 3y + 12 = 14$ and $y = 2$. Use the y-value and the first equation to solve for $x = 2 - 4 = -2$. The sum of -2 and 2 is 0.

6. (C)   The graph of $y = x^2 - 1$ is a parabola with vertex at $(0, -1)$. In this case, we are graphing the absolute value of $x^2 - 1$, so there are no negative y-values. This means that the bottom of the parabola folds up and the turning point is now at $(0, 1)$.

7. (A)   Before rationalizing the denominator, simplify the given fraction so that $\dfrac{3}{\sqrt{3x^2a}}$ becomes $\dfrac{3}{x\sqrt{3a}}$. Now multiply the numerator and the denominator of the fraction by the term in the denominator and $\dfrac{3}{x\sqrt{3a}} = \dfrac{3 \cdot x\sqrt{3a}}{x\sqrt{3a} \cdot x\sqrt{3a}} = \dfrac{3x\sqrt{3a}}{3x^2a}$. Cancel the like terms to see that $\dfrac{\cancel{3}x\sqrt{3a}}{\cancel{3}x^{\cancel{2}^1}a} = \dfrac{\sqrt{3a}}{ax}$.

8. (D)   Use your knowledge of the general forms of a circle and a parabola to draw a quick sketch of the equations. The circle equation has center at $(-1, 3)$ and radius $= 3$. The parabola opens up with a minimum at the vertex $(-1, -1)$.

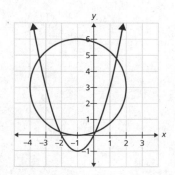

9. (C) Rewrite the fraction $\dfrac{a^{-1}-1}{a-1}$ as $\dfrac{\frac{1}{a}-1}{a-1}$, which translates into $\left(\dfrac{1}{a}-1\right)\div(a-1)$.

Create a common denominator in the first set of parenthesis and use the rules of dividing fractions to find $\dfrac{1-a}{a}\cdot\dfrac{1}{a-1}$. Multiply the fractions and factor a negative 1 out of the numerator. Then cancel the like terms and

simplify: $\dfrac{1-a}{a}\cdot\dfrac{1}{a-1}=\dfrac{-1(a-1)}{a(a-1)}=\dfrac{-1}{a}$.

10. (D) The diameter of the circle is 12 so the radius is 6. This means that the width of the rectangle is also 6, so the area of the rectangle is $6(12)=72$.

Now subtract half the area of the circle or $\dfrac{\pi r^2}{2}=\dfrac{36\pi}{2}=18\pi$. The area of the shaded region is $72-18\pi$.

11. (A) The minimum point on $h(x)$ is $(-1, -4)$, which means the equation for $h(x)=(x+1)^2-4$. Adding 7 to that function will translate the entire parabola up 7 units, so $h(x)+7=(x+1)^2-4+7$ which is $(x+1)^2+3$. The new minimum is at $(-1, 3)$.

12. (D) For this question, we can either substitute each of the given functions into $f(x)$ to find that $f(g(x))$, or recognize that $f\left(f^{-1}(x)\right)=x$, so we are looking for $g(x)=f^{-1}(x)$. The quickest way to find the inverse function is to interchange x and y in $f(x)$ and resolve for y. Then, $x=3y-1$, $x+1=3y$ and $y=\dfrac{x+1}{3}$.

13. (A) Consider that we can rewrite $c^m=a^z$ as $\left(c^m\right)^{\frac{1}{m}}=\left(a^z\right)^{\frac{1}{m}}$. Then $c=a^{\frac{z}{m}}$. Now

substitute this value for c in the other equation so that $a^x=\left(a^{\frac{z}{m}}\right)^y$ which

becomes $a^x=a^{\frac{yz}{m}}$. The bases are equal to each other, so we can set the

exponents equal to each other and $x=\dfrac{yz}{m}$. Multiply both sides by m and

$xm=yz$.

14. (B) Factor the original expression fully. Then,

$\dfrac{a^5+2a^4+a^3}{a^5-a^3}-\dfrac{a^3\left(a^2+2a+1\right)}{a^3\left(a^2-1\right)}=\dfrac{a^3(a+1)(a+1)}{a^3(a+1)(a-1)}$. Now cancel the like terms

and find that $\dfrac{a^3(a+1)(a+1)}{a^3(a+1)(a-1)}=\dfrac{a+1}{a-1}$.

15. (C) Use point-slope formula, $y-y_1=m(x-x_1)$, where $m=-6$ and $(x_1, y_1)=(2, 3)$ to determine the missing value. So $y-3=-6(x-2)$ becomes $y-3=-6x+12$. Solve for y and $y=-6x+15$. The y-intercept is $y=15$.

16. (12) Solve the given equation for y. Then $\frac{3}{4}x + 9y = 12$ becomes

$9y = -\frac{3}{4}x + 12$ and $y = -\frac{1}{12}x + \frac{4}{3}$. This line has a slope of $m = -\frac{1}{12}$ and a line perpendicular to this will have a negative reciprocal slope of 12.

17. $\left(\frac{8}{15}\right)$ Begin by drawing segment $\overline{AX}$ such that X is the midpoint of side $\overline{ST}$. Also draw segment $\overline{QX}$ so the rectangle is divided into 4 parts of equal area. The area of $QAST$, $\frac{2}{5}$,

is $\frac{3}{4}$ of the area of the rectangle $QRST$. We can write $\frac{3}{4}$ (Area $QRST$) $= \frac{2}{5}$

and solve for the area. Then the area of rectangle $QRST$ is $\frac{2}{5}\left(\frac{4}{3}\right) = \frac{8}{15}$.

18. (9) For $f(x) < x$, we need to calculate $|2x - 15| < x$ which means solving both $2x - 15 < x$ and $2x - 15 > -x$. Then, for $2x - 15 < x$, $2x < x + 15$ and $x < 15$. For $2x - 15 > -x$, $2x > 15 - x$, and $x > 5$. The solution set lies in the range $5 < x < 15$ and there are 9 integer values in that range.

19. (1) Find the midpoint of (6, 10) and (8, 4) $= \left(\frac{6+8}{2}, \frac{10+4}{2}\right)$ which is (7, 7).

The quotient $\frac{7}{7} = 1$.

20. (1) Substitute $(-3, 1)$ for (x, y) in the given system and we have $-3a - 1 = 5$ and $-3 + b = 0$. So $-3a = 6$ and $a = -2$ in the first equation and $b = 3$ in the second equation. Then, $a + b = -2 + 3 = 1$.

Calculator Test

1. (D) Look at the problem's algebraic structure. Since $B = A - 7$, it follows that $7 = A - B$. By substitution, the value of $(A - B)^2 + 8 = 7^2 + 8$ which is $49 + 8 = 57$.

2. (B) The cost of the orchids is dx, and the income is nx. The difference is the profit: $nx - dx$ or, by factoring, $x(n - d)$.

3. (B) The strikeouts in numerical order are 7, 8, 8, 9, 10, 12, and 16. The median is 9 and the mean is 10. The value of $-(m - a)^2$ is $-(9 - 10)^2$ or $-(-1)^2 = -1$.

4. (A) FOIL the left-hand side of the equation. Then, $(3x - 4)(7x - 2) = 21x^2 + kx + 8$, becomes $21x^2 - 6x - 28x + 8 = 21x^2 + kx + 8$. Simplify and collect the like terms to see that $-34x = kx$, so that $k = -34$.

5. (B) Solve the given absolute value. Remember that you must solve two equations: $2x - 3 = 5$ and $2x - 3 = -5$. For $2x - 3 = 5$, $2x = 8$, and $x = 4$. For $2x - 3 = -5$, $2x = -2$, and $x = -1$. If $x = 4$, $x^2 = (4)^2 = 16$. If $x = -1$, $x^2 = (-1)^2 = 1$. Select choice B.

6. (C) The general equation for a circle is $(x - h)^2 + (y - k)^2 = r^2$ where (h, k) is the location of center and r is the radius. The center is at (9, 0), so immediately eliminate answer choices A and D as they have the wrong coordinates for the circle's center. Then, determine the radius of the circle to be $r^2 = 21$ so that $r = \sqrt{21}$.

7. (C) Substitute the endpoints of the given Fahrenheit range into the formula $C = \frac{5}{9}(F - 32)$ to determine the endpoints for the Celsius range. Then, for $F = 50$, $C = \frac{5}{9}(50 - 32) = \frac{5}{9}(18) = 10$ and for $F = 77$, $C = \frac{5}{9}(77 - 32) = \frac{5}{9}(45) = 25$.

8. (D) Choose a friendly number, say $100, as the amount it cost the manufacturer to produce the clubs. Then, a 25% mark-up means the retail store pays $125 for the clubs, and the customer pays $125(1.30) = $162.50. The total difference between manufacturer and customer cost is 62.50, so the percent paid over production cost is the fraction $\frac{62.50}{100} = 0.6250$ or 62.5%.

9. (A) First determine the volume of the rectangular block by multiplying its dimensions together: $(8)(6)(5) = 240$ cubic centimeters. Then use the density formula density $= \frac{\text{mass}}{\text{volume}} = \frac{1950}{240} = 8.125$ g/cm³.

10. (B) The frequency sum is 30 so the median value is the average of the 15th and 16th scores. Counting from the 50–59 range up, both the 15th and 16th scores are in the interval 70–79.

11. (C) The dependent values are decreasing in a constant ratio, so this is an exponential function. Eliminate answer choice A because it is linear. Substitute x-values into each of the remaining choices to determine the correct equation. If $x = 1$, choice B yields 2, choice C is $\frac{1}{2}$ and choice D is $\frac{3}{2}$. Choice C is correct.

12. (B) Quickly see that one of the inequalities must be $x \geq 3$ because the shading is to the right of that line. Then, since the shading is below the other line, the other inequality must be $y \leq 2x$.

13. (D) First determine the constant of proportionality, k, using the formula $y = xk$: $\pi = 120k$ and $k = \frac{\pi}{120}$. Then $y = \frac{\pi}{120} \cdot \frac{360}{1} = 3\pi$.

14. (D) Set up a proportion to solve this problem. The total amount of the solution is $5 + x$, of which, 32% is x, so $\frac{32}{100} = \frac{x}{x+5}$. Cross multiply and we have $32(x + 5) = 100x$. Distribute and collect the like terms to find that $32x + 160 = 100x$ and $160 = 68x$. Solve for the unknown and $x = 2.3529$ or approximately 2.35.

15. (A) Quickly draw a sketch of the situation based on the known information. Take care to label the sketch correctly so $\cos \theta = \frac{a}{b}$. Then, to find $\tan \theta$, we need to identify the side opposite angle θ. Using the Pythagorean theorem, we write $a^2 + x^2 = b^2$ and solve for x. Thus, $x^2 = b^2 - a^2$ and $x = \sqrt{b^2 - a^2}$. So, the tangent $\theta = \frac{\sqrt{b^2 - a^2}}{a}$.

16. (B)   Answer choices C and D are unethical. You cannot force people to consume soda nor deprive them of it for the purpose of an experiment. A survey of those who drink some soda each day will contain participants who drink less than 50 ounces of per day, so we may not obtain the desired results. Answer choice B is best.

17. (C)   Divide both sides by $\left(2+\dfrac{1}{x}\right)$. Then, $k = \dfrac{1}{x} \div \left(2+\dfrac{1}{x}\right)$. Create a common denominator within the parenthesis, then find the reciprocal of the divisor fraction and multiply it by the dividend. So, $\dfrac{1}{x} \div \left(\dfrac{2x+1}{x}\right)$ becomes $\dfrac{1}{x} \cdot \left(\dfrac{x}{2x+1}\right)$. Cancel the common factors as shown and $k = \dfrac{1}{2x+1}$.

18. (C)   Given that $V = \dfrac{1}{3}\pi r^2 h$, then $3V = \pi r^2 h$ and $r^2 = \dfrac{3V}{\pi h}$. Thus, $r = \sqrt{\dfrac{3V}{\pi h}}$.

19. (C)   Translate "... minimum stopping distance for a moving car is ... directly proportional to the square of the car's speed," to $y = x^2 k$. Solve for k: $44 = 30^2 k$, $k = \dfrac{11}{225}$. Then the minimum stopping distance for the car traveling at 45 mph is $y = \dfrac{11}{225} \cdot 45^2 = 99$ feet.

20. (B)   Connect the given points to form radii $\overline{AC}, \overline{AB}, \overline{AX}, \overline{BX},$ and $\overline{BC}$. Now, triangles ACB and AXB are both equilateral triangles since all the radii are of equal length. Then, $m\angle CBX = 120°$ and the length of $\overset{\frown}{CBX} = 2\pi$. There are three such arcs in circle A, so its circumference is three times the length of $\overset{\frown}{CBX}$, or $3(2\pi) = 6\pi$. Thus, $2\pi r = 6\pi$, $r = 3$, and the area of circle A is $\pi r^2 = \pi(3)^2 = 9\pi$.

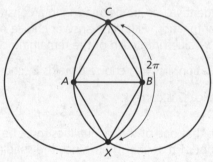

21. (C)   Since the area of the real room is 180 ft² and its length is 15 feet, we know the real width of the room is $\dfrac{180}{15} = 12$ feet. We are given that 1 inch = 3 feet, so $\dfrac{12}{3} = 4$ inches.

22. (B)   Sand: gravel: cement is 2:1:3 by volume. If 1 cubic foot of each item weighs 30, 40, and 20 pounds, respectively, then 2(30):1(40):3(20) becomes 60:40:60. Reduced, we have 6:4:6 or 3:2:3.

23. (D)   The percentage of scores that will be within one standard deviation of the mean, both above and below, is 34.1% + 34.1% = 68.2%. Thus, 68.2% of 60 games = 40.92 or approximately 41 games.

24. (A)   Begin by determining the required compositions. So, $f(g(x)) = f(-x^2 + 1) = -(-x^2 + 1) + 1 = x^2 - 1 + 1 = x^2$. On the other hand, $g(f(x)) = g(-x + 1) = -(-x + 1)^2 + 1 = -(x^2 - 2x + 1) + 1 = -x^2 + 2x - 1 + 1 = -x^2 - 2x$. Setting $f(g(x)) = g(f(x))$, we have $x^2 = -x^2 + 2x$ and $2x^2 - 2x = 0$. Dividing by 2, we have $x^2 - x = 0$. Solving, $x(x - 1) = 0$ and $x = 0$, or $x = 1$.

25. (D) Given that $x - \dfrac{1}{x} = 1$ we can square both sides of the equation so that $\left(x - \dfrac{1}{x}\right)^2 = 1^2$. Then, the equation becomes $x^2 - 2 + \dfrac{1}{x^2} = 1$. Collect the like terms to see that $x^2 + \dfrac{1}{x^2} = 3$.

26. (C) Rewrite the equation using the rules of exponents so that $5^a - 5^{a-1} = 2{,}500$ becomes $5^a - \dfrac{5^a}{5^1} = 2{,}500$. Now factor out 5^a to see that $5^a\left(1 - \dfrac{1}{5}\right) = 2{,}500$.

Simplify and isolate the term with the variable: $5^a = 2{,}500\left(\dfrac{5}{4}\right)$ and $5^a = 3{,}125$. Since $5^5 = 3{,}125$, $a = 5$.

27. (A) Represent the total amount of calories from breakfast and lunch as $b + l \le 950$. The constraint of breakfast comprising at least 300 calories is $b \ge 300$. This system is answer choice A.

28. (B) Immediately eliminate answer choice C as it is an exponential function but the graph is linear. The y-intercept is $y = 3$, so the only correct choice is B.

29. (C) Rearrange the given equation to $x^2 - kx + 3k - 9 = 0$. If $x = 3$ is the only root, then the equation must be equivalent to $(x - 3)^2 = x^2 - 6x + 9 = 0$. Comparing this to the given equation, we see that only $k = 6$ makes them equivalent.

30. (D) Since $f(x) = 2x + \dfrac{1}{x}$, that means $f(-x) = 2(-x) + \dfrac{1}{-x}$, which simplifies to $-2x + \left(-\dfrac{1}{x}\right)$. That is answer choice D.

31. (4.17) Both the exchange rates are given in terms of 1 US dollar, so we can set 14.9 pesos = 62.2 rupees. We want the rate of rupees to 1 peso, so divide both sides by 14.9. The result is about 4.17.

32. $\left(\dfrac{4}{7} \text{ or } 57\right)$ Let $P(A)$ be the probability that a student is in elementary school. Then $P(A) = \dfrac{175}{900} = \dfrac{7}{36}$. Let $P(B)$ be the probability that the student is in elementary school and receiving an allowance. So, $P(B) = \dfrac{100}{175} = \dfrac{4}{7}$.

Using $\dfrac{P(A) \cdot P(B)}{P(A)} = \dfrac{\frac{7}{36} \cdot \frac{4}{7}}{\frac{7}{36}} = \dfrac{4}{7}$ or about 57%.

33. $\left(\dfrac{1}{8} \text{ or } .125\right)$ Since the x-intercept is $(n, 0)$, the coordinate n can be found by solving $0 = \left(n - \dfrac{1}{2}\right)^2$. Then, $0 = n - \dfrac{1}{2}$ and $n = \dfrac{1}{2}$. Similarly, the b coordinate of the y-intercept is calculated by solving $b = \left(0 - \dfrac{1}{2}\right)^2$ and $b = \dfrac{1}{4}$.

The product $nb = \dfrac{1}{2} \cdot \dfrac{1}{4} = \dfrac{1}{8}$ or 0.125.

34. (5250)   Note that the fill rate is given in gallons per minute. Convert the time from 12:00 noon to 3:30pm from hours to minutes. Then, in 210 minutes, the pool has gained $210(4) = 840$ gallons of water. Let the variable P = the amount of water in the pool when it is full and convert $\frac{6}{25}$ into a decimal $= 0.24$. So $0.24P + 840 = 0.40P$. Combine the like terms and $840 = 0.16P$. Divide both sides by 0.16, and $P = 5{,}250$ gallons.

35. (10)   Begin by solving each of the given equations for the variable term y. Then $4y - 2x = 7$ becomes $y = \frac{2}{4}x + \frac{7}{4}$ and $ax + 5y = 10$ becomes $y = -\frac{a}{5}x + 2$. We are told the lines are perpendicular to each other, so that means their slopes are negative reciprocals. In the first equation, we know the slope is $\frac{2}{4}$ and its negative reciprocal is $-\frac{4}{2} = -2$. So, $-2 = -\frac{a}{5}$ and $a = 10$.

36. (7)   Substitute the given information into the distance formula and solve for the value of x. Then $6 = \sqrt{(x-1)^2 + (5-3)^2}$. Simplify under the radical and square both sides so that $6 = \sqrt{(x-1)^2 + 4}$ becomes $36 = (x-1)^2 + 4$. Isolate x by subtracting 4 and taking the square root of both sides and $\sqrt{32} = x - 1$. So $x = \sqrt{32} + 1 \approx 6.667$, which rounds to 7.

37. (3.75)   Since the coat cost 540 Brazilian reals, set up a proportion to determine its cost in US dollars. Then, $\frac{540 \ \text{real}}{1} \cdot \frac{0.36 \ \text{dollar}}{1 \ \text{real}} = \$194.40$. Now let f = the fee charged by Brooklynn's bank and $(\$194.40)(1 + f) = \$201.69$. Solving for f, $1 + f = \frac{201.69}{194.40}$, and $f = 1.0375 - 1 = 0.0375$. This is the fee expressed as a decimal. Multiply the fee by 100 to convert it to a percent.

38. (641)   When Thanos exchanged his US dollars for Brazilian reals, he received $\frac{500 \ \text{dollars}}{1} \cdot \frac{1 \ \text{real}}{0.36 \ \text{dollars}} \cdot \frac{(1-0.04)}{1} = 1{,}333.33$ reals. Note that the $\frac{(1-0.04)}{1}$ represents the fee Thanos had to pay the bank. Let x = the number of reals Thanos had upon return to the United States. Then, $\frac{x \ \text{real}}{1} \cdot \frac{0.36 \ \text{dollar}}{1 \ \text{real}} \cdot \frac{(1-0.03)}{1} = \$257$ and $x = \frac{257 \cdot 0.97}{0.36} = 692.47$ reals. Thanos spent $1333.33 - 692.47 = 640.86$ reals, which we round to \$641.

Correlation Chart

SAT Math Model Exam 2—No Calculator Allowed

Use the chart below to mark the questions you found difficult to determine which lessons you need to review.

(The No Calculator section of the SAT Math Exam will not contain items from Problem Solving and Data Analysis category.)

Question Number	Heart of Algebra	Problem Solving & Data Analysis	Passport To Advanced Math	Additional Topics in Math	Pages to Study
1				Lesson 7	506 – 513
2	Lesson 1				43 – 56
3	Lesson 5				112 – 119
4			Lesson 3		316 – 326
5	Lesson 4				98 – 111
6			Lesson 4		327 – 342
7			Lesson 3		316 – 326
8			Lesson 6		359 – 373
9			Lesson 1		281 – 297
10				Lesson 1	407 – 425
11			Lesson 7		374 – 388
12			Lesson 7		374 – 388
13			Lesson I		281 – 297
14			Lesson 1		281 – 297
15	Lesson 3				81 – 97
16	Lesson 4				98 – 111
17				Lesson 1	407 – 425
18	Lesson 1				43 – 56
19	Lesson 6				120 – 138
20	Lesson 4				98 – 111
Total Correct	_____ / 8		_____ / 9	_____ / 3	NA

Correlation Chart

SAT Math Model Exam 2—Calculator Allowed

Use the chart below to mark the questions you found difficult to determine which lessons you need to review.

Question Number	Heart of Algebra	Problem Solving & Data Analysis	Passport to Advanced Math	Additional Topics in Math	Pages to Study
1	Lesson 1				43 – 56
2	Lesson 1				43 – 56
3		Lesson 6			231 – 245
4			Lesson 4		327 – 342
5	Lesson 2				57 – 80
6				Lesson 6	502 – 505
7	Lesson 2				57 – 80
8		Lesson 1			157 – 176
9		Lesson 2			177 – 187
10		Lesson 6			231 – 245
11		Lesson 4			201 – 214
12	Lesson 4				98 – 111
13	Lesson 5				112 – 119
14		Lesson 1			157 – 176
15				Lesson 4	474 – 488
16		Lesson 8			252 – 264
17			Lesson 3		316 – 326
18	Lesson 2				57 – 80
19	Lesson 5				112 – 119
20				Lesson 3	452 – 473
21		Lesson 2			177 – 187
22		Lesson 1			157 – 176
23		Lesson 7			246 – 251
24			Lesson 7		374 – 388
25			Lesson 2		298 – 315
26			Lesson 1		281 – 297
27	Lesson 4				98 – 111
28	Lesson 6				120 – 138
29			Lesson 4		327 – 342
30	Lesson 3				81 – 97
31		Lesson 1			157 – 176
32		Lesson 5			215 – 230
33			Lesson 4		327 – 342
34		Lesson 1			157 – 176
35	Lesson 3				81 – 97
36	Lesson 6				120 – 138
37		Lesson 1			157 – 176
38		Lesson 1			157 – 176
Total Correct	_____ / 13	_____ / 15	_____ / 7	_____ / 3	NA

FULL-LENGTH SAT-TYPE MATH PRACTICE TEST

SAT Model Exam 3

25 MINUTES, 20 QUESTIONS
NO CALCULATOR ALLOWED

Use the No Calculator section of your answer sheet to answer the questions in this section.

· · · · · **Directions** ·

For questions 1–15, calculate the answer to each problem and choose the best option from the choices given. Bubble in the corresponding circle on your answer sheet. For the remaining questions, solve the problem and enter your answer in the grid on your answer sheet. Refer to the directions before question 16 on how to enter your answers in the grid.

· · · · · · **Notes** ·

1. The use of a calculator is <u>not</u> permitted on this test section.
2. All variables and expressions represent real numbers unless otherwise indicated.
3. Figures provided are drawn to scale unless otherwise noted.
4. All figures lie in a plane unless otherwise noted.
5. Unless otherwise noted, the domain of a given function f is the set of all real numbers x for which $f(x)$ is a real number.

· · · · · · **Reference** ·

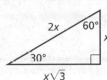

$A = \pi r^2$ $\quad$ $A = lw$ $\quad$ $A = \frac{1}{2}bh$ $\quad$ $c^2 = a^2 + b^2$ $\quad$ Special Right Triangles
$C = 2\pi r$

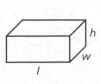

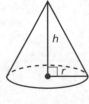
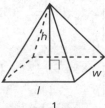

$V = lwh$ $\quad$ $V = \pi r^2 h$ $\quad$ $V = \frac{4}{3}\pi r^3$ $\quad$ $V = \frac{1}{3}\pi r^2 h$ $\quad$ $V = \frac{1}{3}lwh$

The number of degrees of arc in a circle is 360.
The number of radians of arc in a circle is 2π.
The sum of the measures in degrees of the angles of a triangle is 180.

CONTINUE ▶

1

If $ab = 1$, then b must be the reciprocal of a. Which of the following represents the mean of a and its reciprocal?

A) $\dfrac{a+1}{2a}$

B) $\dfrac{a^2+1}{a}$

C) $\dfrac{a^2+1}{2a}$

D) $\dfrac{a^2+2}{2a}$

2

Apostolis is making a beaded dress to enter in a design competition. He must buy the beads to fulfill the pattern, but he can spend no more than $125 of this part of the project. Packages of blue beads contain 10 beads per package and cost $0.85 whereas the packages of yellow beads contain 15 beads per package and cost $1.15 per package. Apostolis needs at least 425 beads. If b represents the number of blue beads and y represents the number of yellow beads, which of the following systems best describes these constraints?

A) $\begin{cases} 0.85b + 1.15y \leq 125 \\ b + y = 425 \end{cases}$

B) $\begin{cases} \dfrac{0.85b}{10} + \dfrac{1.15y}{15} \leq 125 \\ b + y \geq 425 \end{cases}$

C) $\begin{cases} \dfrac{0.85b}{10} + \dfrac{1.15y}{15} \leq 125 \\ b - y \geq 425 \end{cases}$

D) $\begin{cases} 0.85b + 1.15y \geq 125 \\ b + y \leq 425 \end{cases}$

3

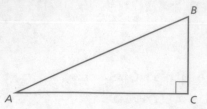

In right triangle ABC, if $\sin A = m$, then the value of $(\sin A)(\cos A)(\tan A)$ is equal to

A) $\dfrac{1}{m}$

B) 1

C) m

D) m^2

4

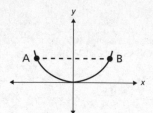

The graph of $y = x^2$ is the parabola shown above. If the y-coordinate of A and the y-coordinate of B are each 7, what is the length of $\overline{AB}$?

A) 14

B) 7

C) $2\sqrt{7}$

D) $\sqrt{7}$

CONTINUE

No Calculator Allowed

If 6 apples cost a cents and 4 peaches cost p cents, then what is the cost of two apples and two peaches in terms of a and p?

A) $\dfrac{6a+4p}{10}$

B) $\dfrac{3ap}{5}$

C) $\dfrac{2a+3p}{6}$

D) $\dfrac{3a+2p}{6}$

If $f(x) = \dfrac{x-1}{2}$ and $h(x) = 2x + 1$, then

$f(h(x)) - (h(f(x))) =$

A) 0

B) 2

C) 3

D) 5

Completely simplify: $\dfrac{x^2 - 2x - 3}{x^2 - 3x + 2} \cdot \dfrac{x^2 - 4}{x^2 - x - 6}$.

A) -1

B) 1

C) $\dfrac{x-1}{x+1}$

D) $\dfrac{x+1}{x-1}$

If the numerator n and the denominator d of a common fraction are each increased by the same amount, x, the resulting fraction is equal to the reciprocal of the original fraction. Which of the following is the completely simplified expression for x in terms of n and d?

A) $d + n$

B) $-d - n$

C) $n - d$

D) $d - n$

CONTINUE

If $x = 1 + \dfrac{1}{2} + \dfrac{1}{4} + \dfrac{1}{8}$ and $a = 1 + \dfrac{1}{2}x$, then a is how much larger than x?

A) $\dfrac{1}{48}$

B) $\dfrac{1}{16}$

C) $\dfrac{3}{16}$

D) $\dfrac{15}{16}$

Which of the following graphs shows the solution to $f(x) = \dfrac{1}{2}x^2 - 2x + 1$ and $g(x) = x$?

A)

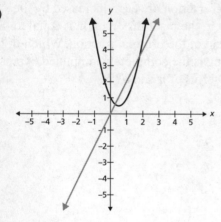

B)

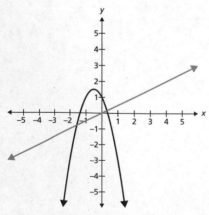

C)

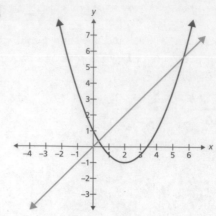

D)

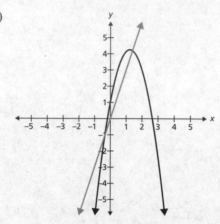

What is the area of the triangle formed by the graph of the two equations $y = |x|$ and $y = 5$?

A) 50 square units

B) 25 square units

C) 20 square units

D) 12.5 square units

CONTINUE

No Calculator Allowed

Simplify $(2 - i)\left(\dfrac{2}{5} + \dfrac{1}{5}i\right)$.

$\left(\text{Note: } i = \sqrt{-1}.\right)$

A) $1 - \dfrac{3}{5}i$

B) $\dfrac{4}{5} - \dfrac{1}{5}i$

C) $1 + \dfrac{4}{5}i$

D) 1

Simplify $\dfrac{3 - \sqrt{2}}{2 - \sqrt{2}}$.

A) $2 + \sqrt{2}$

B) $\dfrac{1}{2 - \sqrt{2}}$

C) $\dfrac{4 + \sqrt{2}}{2}$

D) $\dfrac{2 + \sqrt{2}}{2}$

x	f(x)
1	1.5
a	9
b	a + 7

Using the given table and the function f defined as $f(x) = \dfrac{5x - 2}{2}$, what is the value of b?

A) 11

B) 4.8

C) 4

D) 2.4

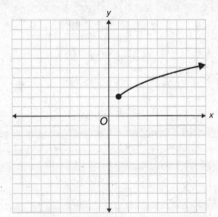

15

If the parent function of a graph is $y = f(x) = \sqrt{x}$, which of the following is the equation for the graph of the function shown above?

A) $y = \sqrt{x + 1} + 2$

B) $y - 1 = \sqrt{x} + 2$

C) $y + 2 = \sqrt{x - 1}$

D) $y - 2 = \sqrt{x - 1}$

CONTINUE

For the remaining questions, solve the problem and enter your answer in the answer grid. Instructions for entering your answer in the grid are described below.

1. It is not required that you write your answer in the boxes at the top of the grid, but it is suggested.

2. Do not mark more than one circle in each column.

3. There are no negative answers in this portion of the test.

4. If the problem has more than 1 correct answer, grid only 1 of those answers.

5. Grid fractions as proper or improper fractions only.

6. Decimal answers must fill the entire grid.

••••• **Examples** ••

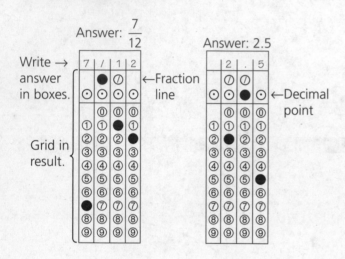

Write → answer in boxes.

Grid in result.

Answer: $\frac{7}{12}$ ←Fraction line

Answer: 2.5 ←Decimal point

Acceptable ways to grid $\frac{2}{3}$ are:

Answer: 201 – either position is correct

CONTINUE →

16

What value of x will satisfy this equation:
$\sqrt{2x} + 4 = x$?

17

Simplify: $9\sqrt{3x^9} - 3x^4\sqrt{27x}$.

18

The intensity, H, of heat radiation (also called thermal energy) on a surface varies inversely as the square of the distance d from the heat source to the surface. If $H = 2.7$ when $d = 4$, what is the value of H when $d = 3$?

19

Solve for x: $\dfrac{3}{x} + \dfrac{6}{x-1} = \dfrac{x+13}{x^2-x}$.

20

Find the y-coordinate of the endpoint B of $\overline{AB}$ if A is $(-3, -4)$ and the midpoint M is $(4, 3)$.

STOP

**If you finish before time is called, you may check your work on this section only.
Do not turn to any other section.**

55 MINUTES, 38 QUESTIONS

CALCULATOR ALLOWED

Use the Calculator section of your answer sheet to answer the questions in this section.

Directions

For questions 1–30, calculate the answer to each problem and choose the best option from the choices given. Bubble in the corresponding circle on your answer sheet. For the remaining questions, solve the problem and enter your answer in the grid on your answer sheet. Refer to the directions before question 31 on how to enter your answers in the grid.

Notes

1. The use of a calculator is permitted on this test section.
2. All variables and expressions represent real numbers unless otherwise indicated.
3. Figures provided are drawn to scale unless otherwise noted.
4. All figures lie in a plane unless otherwise noted.
5. Unless otherwise noted, the domain of a given function f is the set of all real numbers x for which $f(x)$ is a real number.

Reference

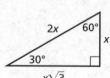

$A = \pi r^2$ $A = lw$ $A = \frac{1}{2}bh$ $c^2 = a^2 + b^2$ Special Right Triangles

$C = 2\pi r$

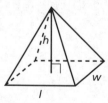

$V = lwh$ $V = \pi r^2 h$ $V = \frac{4}{3}\pi r^3$ $V = \frac{1}{3}\pi r^2 h$ $V = \frac{1}{3}lwh$

The number of degrees of arc in a circle is 360.

The number of radians of arc in a circle is 2π.

The sum of the measures in degrees of the angles of a triangle is 180.

CONTINUE

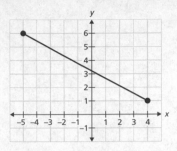

1

If a line perpendicular to the segment shown above was drawn through the segment's midpoint, which of the following answer choices is the equation of that line?

A) $22 - 5y = 9x$

B) $-5y - 9x = 22$

C) $5y = 9x + 22$

D) $-9x - 22 = 5y$

What is the solution set for a in the equation $|-a| = -a$?

A) All real numbers

B) only $\{-1, 0\}$

C) $\{a \geq 0\}$

D) $\{a \leq 0\}$

The quadratic equation $x^2 + m^2 x + 2m = 0$ has exactly one real solution for x. If m is a nonzero integer, what is the value of m?

A) 2

B) $2\sqrt{2}$

C) 4

D) 8

A city public works department wants to collect information about the community feeling regarding the speed at which road repairs are progressing. Which sample would provide the least bias?

A) People using a neighborhood park on a weekday morning.

B) Shoppers exiting a community grocery store.

C) Parents of local elementary school children.

D) Seniors at a community center event.

CONTINUE

Atif gets 23 miles to the gallon on the highway when he drives at the rate of 60 mph. His gas tank holds 18 gallons of gas at the beginning of his trip north to Maine and he travels on the highway at the average speed of 60 mph. Which of the following functions, f, models the number of gallons of gas remaining in Atif's tank h hours after the trip begins?

A) $f(h) = 18 - \dfrac{60}{23h}$

B) $f(h) = 18 - \dfrac{60h}{23}$

C) $f(h) = \dfrac{23h - 18}{60}$

D) $f(h) = 18 - \dfrac{23h}{60}$

The fraction $\dfrac{x^{-1}}{x^{-1} + y^{-1}}$ is equivalent to

A) $\dfrac{x}{x+y}$

B) $\dfrac{y}{x+y}$

C) $\dfrac{x+y}{x}$

D) $\dfrac{x+y}{y}$

If $x = \dfrac{y+a}{y-a}$, then $y =$

A) $\dfrac{x-1}{a-ax}$

B) $\dfrac{a+ax}{x-1}$

C) $\dfrac{a-ax}{x+1}$

D) $\dfrac{a+ax}{x+1}$

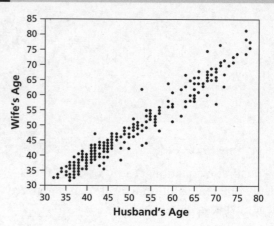

The scatterplot above reflects the ages of husband/wife couples entering a theater performance. Which of the following is the best interpretation of the collected data?

A) Husbands are always older than wives.

B) Wives are always older than husbands.

C) Usually a husband is older than his wife.

D) If a husband is younger than 50, his wife is the same age.

Calculator Allowed

CONTINUE

If Simon is paid time and a half for all hours worked in excess of 40 hours a week and he averaged 9.5 hours a day for a 5-day week, by approximately what percent are his regular wages for the week increased?

A) 11.25%

B) 18.75%

C) 24%

D) 28%

$4x + 5y = 7$
$8x + by = 3$

The given system of equations has a solution for all values of b except when $b =$

A) −10

B) −4

C) 0

D) 10

Tane travels from town A to town B at a uniform rate of x miles per hour and returns over the same route at y mph. In terms of x and y, what is Tane's average speed for the entire trip?

A) $\dfrac{2xy}{x+y}$

B) $\dfrac{x+y}{2}$

C) $\dfrac{xy}{x+y}$

D) $\dfrac{2(x+y)}{xy}$

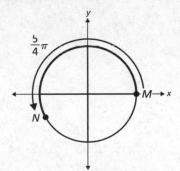

12

In the figure above, the major arc $\overarc{MN}$ has a radian measure of $\dfrac{5}{4}\pi$. What are the coordinates of point N?

A) $\left(\dfrac{\sqrt{2}}{2}, \dfrac{\sqrt{2}}{2} \right)$

B) $\left(-\dfrac{\sqrt{3}}{2}, -\dfrac{1}{2} \right)$

C) $\left(-\dfrac{\sqrt{2}}{2}, \dfrac{\sqrt{2}}{2} \right)$

D) $\left(-\dfrac{\sqrt{2}}{2}, -\dfrac{\sqrt{2}}{2} \right)$

CONTINUE

Questions 13 and 14 refer to the following information.

Student	Allergic	Non-Allergic	Total
Male	15	8	23
Female	10	7	17
Total	25	15	40

The table above shows the results of a recent survey of students in an elementary school regarding their allergies to tree and grass pollen.

13

Suppose a student is randomly selected from the school. What is the probability the selected student is not allergic to tree and grass pollen given that the student is male?

A) $\dfrac{7}{23}$

B) $\dfrac{8}{23}$

C) $\dfrac{15}{23}$

D) $\dfrac{23}{40}$

14

Which of the following is the most probable random selection?

A) Selecting a student who is allergic given that the student is a female.

B) Selecting a female given that the person selected is allergic.

C) Selecting a student who is allergic given that the student is male.

D) Selecting a male student given that the person selected is allergic.

15

If a given line r passes through the points $(3, 9)$ and $(-1, 1)$, then the x-intercept of line r is

A) $-\dfrac{3}{2}$

B) $-\dfrac{2}{3}$

C) 2

D) 3

16

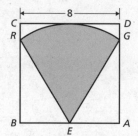

Given the square $ABCD$ with a side length of 8, what is the area of the inscribed sector ERG?

A) 16π

B) 32π

C) $\dfrac{64\pi}{3}$

D) $\dfrac{32\pi}{3}$

CONTINUE

Calculator Allowed

17

If $\dfrac{9x^2}{3x+1} = \dfrac{1}{3x+1} + K$, then which of the following represents K?

A) $9x^2$

B) $3x - 1$

C) $3x + 1$

D) $9x^2 - 1$

18

A commercial retailer conducted a survey regarding the type of packaging one of their products is sold in. The survey reported with 95% confidence that 63% of consumers surveyed preferred package A. The margin of error was 4.2 percentage points. Which statement best describes the desires of all consumers who purchase this product?

A) We can be 63% confident that between 91.8% and 99.2% of all consumers will prefer package A.

B) We can be 95% confident that exactly 63% of all consumers will prefer package A.

C) We can be 95% confident that between 58.8% and 67.2% of all consumers will prefer package A.

D) We can be 63% confident that at least 95% of all consumers will prefer package A.

19

If the lengths of two sides of a triangle measure 10 and 13, while the third side has a length of x, then which of the following best represents the range of possible integer perimeters P of this triangle?

A) $3 < P < 23$

B) $26 < P < 46$

C) $27 < P < 45$

D) $27 \le P \le 45$

20

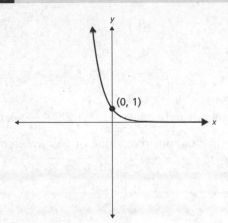

Which of the following best describes the graph above?

A) Exponential, decreasing, y-intercept = 1.

B) Linear, increasing, slope = 2, y-intercept = 1.

C) Exponential, increasing, y-intercept = 1.

D) Linear, decreasing, slope = 2, y-intercept = 1.

CONTINUE

21

Gail has taken n tests and has an average of 80. Which of the following represents the score, x, that she must earn on her next test to raise her average to 83?

A) $n + 83$

B) $3n + 80$

C) $3n + 83$

D) $80n + 3$

22

If the function p is defined as $p(x) = -28 + \dfrac{x^2}{9}$ and $p(3y) = 12y$ then the positive value of y is which of the following?

A) 2

B) 4

C) 7

D) 14

Questions 23 and 24 refer to the following information.

Team Name	Wins	Losses
Larks	8	4
Jays	10	2
Hawks	4	8
Cardinals	2	10

The chart above shows the current standings of a girls' summer softball league, where each team has played 12 games and has the record indicated. Each team still has 12 games left to play. There have been no tie games.

23

What is the least number of additional games that the Hawks have to win in order to have more wins than losses for the season?

A) 7

B) 8

C) 9

D) 13

24

If the Jays win 8 of their remaining 12 games, how many of their remaining 12 games will the Larks have to win in order to have $\dfrac{5}{6}$ as many wins as the Jays for the season?

A) 5

B) 6

C) 7

D) 15

CONTINUE

Calculator Allowed

25

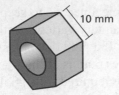

10 mm

Given a regular hexagonal nut with edges of length 10 mm, as shown above, what is the height, h, of the hexagonal nut?

A) $4\sqrt{3}$

B) $5\sqrt{2}$

C) $5\sqrt{3}$

D) $10\sqrt{3}$

26

Simplify the given expression into an equivalent expression with a rational denominator: $\dfrac{\sqrt{12}-\sqrt{6}}{\sqrt{12}}$.

A) $\dfrac{2-\sqrt{2}}{2}$

B) $\dfrac{1}{2}$

C) $\dfrac{\sqrt{12}+\sqrt{6}}{12}$

D) $\dfrac{2+\sqrt{2}}{2}$

27

Last month, 38,860 residents of Lakewood County and 46,204 residents of Rockland County voted on Referendum A. From the two counties, a total of 63,798 residents voted yes. If the same percentage of voters in each county voted yes, how many of the residents of Lakewood County voted yes?

A) 17,594

B) 24,938

C) 29,145

D) 34,653

28

x	y
1	1
2	4
4	16

In the table above, some values are given for the variables x and y. Based on the table, which of the following answer choices is directly proportional to y?

A) $\sqrt{x}$

B) x

C) $2x$

D) x^2

CONTINUE

If the graph of $x^2 + y^2 = 16$ and the graph of $y = b$ are drawn on the same set of axes, the graphs will not intersect if

A) $b = 4$

B) $b > 4$

C) $2 < b < 4$

D) $0 < b < 2$

The amount of a certain chemical needed to keep a backyard swimming pool sanitary varies directly with the capacity of the pool. If a pool that holds 8,000 gallons of water requires 6 units of the chemical, how many units are required for a pool with a capacity of 10,000 gallons?

A) 7.5 units

B) 4.2 units

C) 8 units

D) 9.1 units

CONTINUE ➡

Calculator Allowed

For the remaining questions, solve the problem and enter your answer in the answer grid. Instructions for entering your answer in the grid are described below.

1. It is not required that you write your answer in the boxes at the top of the grid, but it is suggested.

2. Do not mark more than one circle in each column.

3. There are no negative answers in this portion of the test.

4. If the problem has more than 1 correct answer, grid only 1 of those answers.

5. Grid fractions as mixed numbers only.

6. Decimal answers must fill the entire grid.

Examples

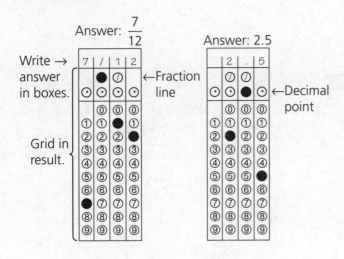

Answer: $\frac{7}{12}$

Write → answer in boxes.

←Fraction line

Answer: 2.5

←Decimal point

Grid in result.

Acceptable ways to grid $\frac{2}{3}$ are:

Answer: 201 – either position is correct

If $0 \le x \le 4$ and $-4 \le y \le 5$, what is the smallest possible value for $\dfrac{16}{|x-y|}$?

In a survey of 10 high school seniors, two measurements were taken: left foot length and height (both in centimeters). After entering the data pairs and using linear regression to determine the line of best fit, the following screen appeared on the calculator:

Lin Reg
$y = ax + b$
$a = 4.8308732354$
$b = 43.82208582$
$r^2 = 0.9556128231$
$r = 0.9775545116$

Using the information given, if a senior's left foot length was 24.8 cm, what height, in centimeters, does the linear regression predict?

Abbie has 3 more apps on her phone than Kishan, and Rayen has one more app than Abbie. If the combined number of apps that the three of them have is greater than 70 but less than 76, how many apps does Kishan have?

If h and k are constants and $x^2 + kx + 9$ factors into $(x + 1)(x + h)$, what is the value of k?

CONTINUE

Calculator Allowed

35

$$\frac{1}{5}x + \frac{1}{2}y = 10$$

$$ax + 2y = 8$$

When graphed, the system of equations above forms perpendicular lines. What is the value of a^2?

36

If $f(x) = |5x - 19|$, what is one possible integer value of n for which $f(n) < n$?

Questions 37 and 38 refer to the following information.

Median Sales Prices of New One-Family Homes

Region	1980	2000
West	$35,000	$152,000
Midwest	$36,500	$130,000
South	$32,500	$110,000
Northeast	$40,500	$190,000

The table above shows the median sales price of new one-family homes in four regions of the United States in 1980 and in 2000. The growth factor in home prices over the given 20-year period has been exponential and is determined by the fraction $\left(\dfrac{\text{price in the year 2000}}{\text{price in 1980}} \right)^{\frac{1}{20}}$.

The exponential function is $f(x) = $ (price in 1980, in thousands) $\cdot$ (growth factor)^x, where x represents the number of years since the first listing of median prices in 1980.

37

To the nearest hundredth, what is the growth factor in the Northeast?

38

Suppose a home purchased in Florida (south region) in 1980 cost $32,500. Now suppose that same home were transferred to California (west region) in 2015. What would be the expected median price (in thousands) of such a new home in California in the year 2015?

SAT Model Exam 3 Answer Key

No Calculator Test

1. (C)   The reciprocal of a is $\dfrac{1}{a}$. The arithmetic mean of these two terms is $\dfrac{a+\dfrac{1}{a}}{2}$.

Simplifying by creating a common denominator within the parenthesis,

$\left(\dfrac{a^2+1}{a}\right) \div \dfrac{2}{1}$. Using fraction rules, $\left(\dfrac{a^2+1}{a}\right) \cdot \dfrac{1}{2} = \dfrac{a^2+1}{2a}$.

2. (B)   Apostolis needs at least 425 beads. Since b represents the number of blue beads and y represents the number of yellow beads, the total number of beads needed is $b + y \geq 425$. This eliminates answer choices A, C and D.

3. (D)   Since $\sin A = m$, the length of the side opposite $\angle A = m$ and the length of the hypotenuse is 1. By the Pythagorean theorem, the length, x, of the side adjacent to $\angle A$ is found by $x^2 + m^2 = 1$, so that $x^2 = 1 - m^2$, and $x = \sqrt{1-m^2}$. Then $(\sin A)(\cos A)(\tan A) =$

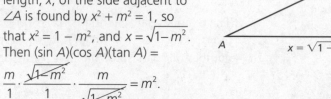

$\dfrac{m}{1} \cdot \dfrac{\sqrt{1-m^2}}{1} \cdot \dfrac{m}{\sqrt{1-m^2}} = m^2$.

4. (C)   Substitute 7 for y in $y = x^2$, so that $7 = x^2$ and $\pm\sqrt{7} = x$. The coordinate for point A is $\left(-\sqrt{7}, 7\right)$ and for point B it is $\left(\sqrt{7}, 7\right)$. The distance from point A to point B is $2\sqrt{7}$.

5. (C)   Using the relationships given in the problem, the cost of one apple is $\dfrac{a}{6}$ and the cost of one peach is $\dfrac{p}{4}$. Then, the cost of 2 apples is $\dfrac{2a}{6}$ and the cost of 2 peaches is $\dfrac{2p}{4}$. The sum of $\dfrac{2a}{6}$ and $\dfrac{2p}{4}$ is $\dfrac{2a}{6} + \dfrac{2p}{4} = \dfrac{a}{3} + \dfrac{p}{2}$ which is $\dfrac{2a+3p}{6}$.

6. (D)   Fully factor both numerators and denominators and then cancel the common factors to find that $\dfrac{x^2-2x-3}{x^2-3x+2} \cdot \dfrac{x^2-4}{x^2-x-6} =$

$\dfrac{(x-3)(x+1)}{(x-1)(x-2)} \cdot \dfrac{(x-2)(x+2)}{(x-3)(x+2)} = \dfrac{x+1}{x-1}$.

7. (A)   The compositions $f(h(x)) - (h(f(x)))$ translate to $f(2x+1) - h\left(\dfrac{x-1}{2}\right) =$

$\dfrac{2x+1-1}{2} - 2\left(\dfrac{x-1}{2}\right) + 1 = x - x = 0$.

8. (B) Translating the words into an algebraic equation, we have $\dfrac{n+x}{d+x} = \dfrac{d}{n}$.

Now cross-multiply and distribute so that $n(n + x) = d(d + x)$ and $n^2 + nx = d^2 + dx$. Rearrange the equation, $nx - dx = d^2 - n^2$, and factor out the common term, $x(n - d) = (d - n)(d + n)$. Then,

$$x = \frac{-1(\cancel{d - n})(d+n)}{(\cancel{n - d})} = (-1)(d + n) = -d - n.$$

9. (B) There are several ways to solve this problem, but one of the quicker

methods is to change the denominators to 8, so that $x = \dfrac{8}{8} + \dfrac{4}{8} + \dfrac{2}{8} + \dfrac{1}{8} = \dfrac{15}{8}$

or $\dfrac{30}{16}$. Do the same for a and substitute the value of x into the equation.

Then, $\dfrac{8}{8} + \dfrac{1}{2}\left(\dfrac{15}{8}\right) = \dfrac{16}{16} + \dfrac{15}{16} = \dfrac{31}{16}$. So, a is $\dfrac{1}{16}$ larger than x.

10. (C) We can eliminate B and D because the parabolas open down rather than up as indicated by the given parabolic equation. Now examine the linear equation on graph A. For the given equation $g(x) = x$, the line should run through the points $(0, 0)$, $(1, 1)$, $(2, 2)$, etc. While this line does move through $(0, 0)$, it does not touch $(1, 1)$, $(2, 2)$ and so on. This cannot be the correct graph. Select choice C.

11. (B) Draw a quick sketch of the functions; now it is clear that the inverted triangle has a base of 10 and height of 5, so that $\dfrac{1}{2}(10)(5) = 25$ square units.

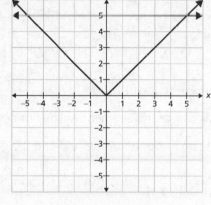

12. (D) Rewrite the expression as

$\left(\dfrac{2-i}{1}\right)\left(\dfrac{2+i}{5}\right) = \left(\dfrac{(2-i)(2+i)}{5}\right)$. Now

FOIL the numerator and $\dfrac{4 - i^2}{5}$, but

$i^2 = -1$, so $\dfrac{4 - (-1)}{5} = \dfrac{5}{5} = 1$.

13. (C) To simplify $\dfrac{3 - \sqrt{2}}{2 - \sqrt{2}}$, multiply the numerator and denominator

by the denominator's conjugate. Then, $\left(\dfrac{3 - \sqrt{2}}{2 - \sqrt{2}}\right)\left(\dfrac{2 + \sqrt{2}}{2 + \sqrt{2}}\right) =$

$\dfrac{6 + 3\sqrt{2} - 2\sqrt{2} - 2}{4 - 2} = \dfrac{4 + \sqrt{2}}{2}$.

14. (B) Begin by solving for a since b is defined in terms of $a + 7$. So, $f(a)$

becomes $\dfrac{5a - 2}{2} = 9$, $5a - 2 = 18$, $5a = 20$, and $a = 4$. Then, $a + 7 = 11$, so

$f(b) = \dfrac{5b - 2}{2} = 11$. Solving for b in $\dfrac{5b - 2}{2} = 11$, we find $5b - 2 = 22$, $5b = 24$, and $b = 4.8$.

15. (D) Looking at the graph, the parent function has been shifted 1 unit to the right and shifted up 2 units. This results in the equation $y = \sqrt{x - 1} + 2$, which can also be written as $y - 2 = \sqrt{x - 1}$.

16. (8)   Given that $\sqrt{2x} + 4 = x$, we rewrite the equation as $\sqrt{2x} = x - 4$ and then square both sides so that $2x = x^2 - 8x + 16$ or $0 = x^2 - 10x + 16$. Factoring the resulting trinomial, $(x - 8)(x - 2) = 0$. Now set each factor to 0 so that $x = 8$ or $x = 2$. Check each solution to see if one or both are extraneous. So $\sqrt{2(8)} + 4 = 8$ and $4 + 4 = 8$. This is a solution. Then checking 2, $\sqrt{2(2)} + 4 = 2$ or $6 \neq 2$. The solution $x = 2$ is extraneous. Bubble in 8 on the answer grid.

17. (0)   Recall that you cannot add or subtract terms containing radicals unless the radical terms are like. So, $9\sqrt{3x^9} - 3x^4\sqrt{27x}$ becomes $9\sqrt{x^8 \cdot 3 \cdot x} - 3x^4\sqrt{9 \cdot 3 \cdot x}$. Simplify and $9x^4\sqrt{3x} - 3x^4(3)\sqrt{3x} = 9x^4\sqrt{3x} - 9x^4\sqrt{3x} = 0$.

18. (4.8)   The inverse variation here is $H = \dfrac{k}{d^2}$ which we can rewrite as $Hd^2 = k$. Then, substituting what we know, $(2.7)(4)^2 = H(3^2)$. Simplifying and solving for H yields $43.2 = 9H$ and $H = 4.8$.

19. (2)   To solve this problem, multiply through by the least common denominator $x(x - 1)$. Then, $3(x - 1) + 6x = x + 13$. Simplifying, $3x - 3 + 6x = x + 13$ and $8x = 16$. Thus, $x = 2$.

20. (10)   Only considering the y-coordinates, a move from A $(x, -4)$ to M $(x, 3)$ adds 7 units. Add 7 units to the midpoint coordinate and you arrive at B $(x, 10)$.

Calculator Test

1. (C)   First determine the midpoint of the line segment: $\left(\dfrac{-5+4}{2}, \dfrac{6+1}{2}\right) = \left(-\dfrac{1}{2}, \dfrac{7}{2}\right)$.

Now find the line segment's slope as $m = \dfrac{1-6}{4-(-5)} = -\dfrac{5}{9}$. The slope of the line perpendicular to this segment will have a negative reciprocal slope of $\dfrac{9}{5}$. Use the point-slope formula and find the equation of the line.

So $y - \dfrac{7}{2} = \dfrac{9}{5}\left(x - \left(-\dfrac{1}{2}\right)\right)$. Simplifying and moving into slope-intercept form,

$y = \dfrac{9}{5}x + \dfrac{22}{5}$; notice that none of the answer choices are in this form,

but if we multiply through by 5, we arrive at answer choice C.

2. (A)   Since there is only one real solution to the quadratic equation $x^2 + m^2x + 2m = 0$, we can use the discriminant, $b^2 - 4ac = 0$, to determine the value of m. Then, $\left(m^2\right)^2 - 4(1)(2m) = 0$, so that $m^4 - 8m = 0$ and $m(m^3 - 8)$. Thus, $m = 0$, which we reject since we're looking for a nonzero integer, and $m^3 - 8 = 0$. Then $m^3 = 8$ and $m = 2$.

3. (D)   Since the result of $|-a|$ is positive or zero, for $-a$ to be positive, a must be negative or zero; hence, $\{a \leq 0\}$.

4. (B)   People using a neighborhood park on a weekday morning only represent a small, specific portion of those who drive on the city roads, as do parents of local elementary school children, and seniors at a community center. The best option to capture segments of the entire population is shoppers exiting a community grocery store.

5. (B)

Begin with the relationship $d = rt$. Then, $d = 60$ mph $\cdot$ (h hours). If we divide the distance, $60h$, by 23 miles/gallon, we should know then how many gallons were used so far. Then subtracting $\dfrac{60h}{23}$ from 18 should tell us how many gallons are left h hours after the trip began.

6. (B)

If we rewrite $\dfrac{x^{-1}}{x^{-1} + y^{-1}}$ as $\dfrac{\dfrac{1}{x}}{\dfrac{1}{x} + \dfrac{1}{y}}$ and multiply every term by the common denominator of xy then we have $\dfrac{xy\dfrac{1}{x}}{xy\dfrac{1}{x} + xy\dfrac{1}{y}} = \dfrac{y}{x+y}$.

7. (B)

To begin solving for y, cross-multiply the given equation, $x = \dfrac{y+a}{y-a}$ to see that $xy - ax = y + a$. Since we're solving for y, rewrite the equation as $xy - y = a + ax$ and factor the left-hand side: $y(x - 1) = a + ax$. Then divide both sides by $x - 1$ so that $y = \dfrac{a+ax}{x-1}$.

8. (C)

Answers A and B are given in absolutes by use of the term "always" so eliminate those choices. Answer choice D is not evidenced by the scatterplot. Answer choice C is the only one that makes sense.

9. (D)

First determine the number of hours Simon worked as 5(9.5 hours) = 47.5 hours for the week, which is 7.5 hours in overtime. For calculating purposes, let us assume he earns $10 an hour. In a regular week Simon earns ($10)(40) = $400. In this week, Simon will earn $400 plus ($15)(7.5) = $112.50. The approximate percentage increase in Simon's weekly wages is $100 \cdot \left(\dfrac{112.50}{400} \right) \approx 28\%$.

10. (D)

Given the two equations $4x + 5y = 7$ and $8x + by = 3$, if the lines are parallel then there are no solutions. Solving for y in $4x + 5y = 7$ we have $y = -\dfrac{4}{5}x + \dfrac{7}{5}$, so the slope here is $-\dfrac{4}{5}$. Solving $8x + by = 3$ for y, we have $y = -\dfrac{8}{b}x + \dfrac{y}{b}$. Set the slopes equal to each other and solve: $-\dfrac{4}{5} = -\dfrac{8}{b}$ or $\dfrac{4}{5} = \dfrac{8}{b}$ so that $4b = 40$ and $b = 10$.

11. (A)

Use the formula $d = vt$. Since the distance, d, is the same in both directions, we can write $d = x\,(t_1)$ and $d = y\,(t_2)$, where t_1 and t_2 are the different times. In general, using $d = vt$, the average speed (v_{avg}) is found by dividing the total distance (d_{tot}) by the total time (t_{tot}), or $v_{avg} = \dfrac{d_{tot}}{t_{tot}}$. Hence, we have $v_{avg} = \dfrac{\text{total distance}}{\text{total time}} = \dfrac{d+d}{t_1+t_2}$. Taking each of the earlier statements, $d = x\,(t_1)$ and $d = y(t_2)$, we can solve for t_1 and t_2. Then $t_1 = \dfrac{d}{x}$ and $t_2 = \dfrac{d}{y}$. Substituting in $v_{avg} = \dfrac{d+d}{t_1+t_2} = \dfrac{2d}{\dfrac{d}{x}+\dfrac{d}{y}}$. Multiplying numerator and denominator by xy, we have $v_{avg} = \dfrac{2dxy}{dy+dx} = \dfrac{2d\,xy}{d(y+x)} = \dfrac{2xy}{x+y}$.

12. (D)   The degree measure for $\frac{5}{4}\pi$ is 225° and point N is in the 3rd quadrant.

Its coordinates are (cos θ, sin θ) or (cos 225°, sin 225°) $= \left(-\dfrac{\sqrt{2}}{2}, -\dfrac{\sqrt{2}}{2}\right)$.

13. (B)   The conditional probability of a randomly selected student not having an allergy given that student is a male is $\dfrac{8}{23}$.

14. (C)   Conditional probability is the probability that some event A will occur given that some event B has already occurred. To solve this question, calculate each of the conditional probabilities. For answer choice A, $\dfrac{10}{17} = 58.8\%$, for answer choice B, the probability is $\dfrac{10}{25} = 40\%$, for choice C it is $\dfrac{15}{23} = 65.2\%$, and for answer choice D, the probability is $\dfrac{15}{25} = 60\%$.

The most probable random selection is given by answer choice C.

15. (A)   First determine the slope of the line that contains the given points. Then $m = \dfrac{9-1}{3-(-1)} = \dfrac{8}{4} = 2$. Using the point (3, 9) and substituting in to $y = mx + b$, we have $9 = 2(3) + b$ and $b = 3$. The line is $y = 2x + 3$. The x-intercept occurs when $y = 0$, so $0 = 2x + 3$ means that $x = -\dfrac{3}{2}$.

16. (D)   Recognize that the sector is from a circle with radius equal to the length of a side of the square. Then, $BE = 4$ so that in right triangle RBE, the length of the hypotenuse $\overline{RE} = 8$, $m\angle BRE = 30°$ and $m\angle BER = 60°$. Also, $m\angle AEG = 60°$. Thus the central angle of the sector is 60° and the area of the sector is equal to $\dfrac{60}{360}\pi r^2 = \dfrac{1}{6}\pi 8^2$ or $\dfrac{64\pi}{6} = \dfrac{32\pi}{3}$.

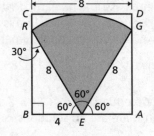

17. (B)   To find K in this equation multiply each term by the common denominator $(3x + 1)$ to see that $(3x+1)\cdot\left(\dfrac{9x^2}{3x+1} = \dfrac{1}{3x+1} + K\right)$ becomes $9x^2 = 1 + K(3x + 1)$. Now isolate K by subtracting 1, dividing both sides by $3x + 1$, and factoring. Then, $K = \dfrac{9x^2 - 1}{3x+1} = \dfrac{(3x+1)(3x-1)}{3x+1} = 3x - 1$.

18. (C)   Immediately reject answer choices A and D as they have the wrong confidence level. Answer choice B has the correct confidence level but we cannot say that exactly 63% of consumers will prefer package A because there is a margin of error. The best option is C.

19. (D)   The length of the third side is between the sum and the difference of the two given sides such that difference $< x <$ sum. Thus, $3 < x < 23$; however, as an integer, the third side's length is between 4 and 22 and the range of the integer perimeter is $23 + 4 < P < 23 + 22$, so $27 < P < 45$.

20. (A)   The graph shows a curve rather than a line, so eliminate answer choices B and D. The graph is decreasing rather than increasing and the y-intercept is located at (0, 1).

21. (C)   The total of all of Gail's scores is $80n$ and $(80n + x)$ is the total score with the next test score, x, added in. The formula that we can use to find x in terms of n is $\dfrac{\text{sum of all scores}}{\text{the number of scores}}$ which is $\dfrac{80n+x}{n+1} = 83$. Solving for x, $80n + x = 83n + 83$, and $x = 3n + 83$.

22. (D)   Rewrite as $p(3y) = -28 + \dfrac{(3y)^2}{9} = 12y$. Then, $-28 + \dfrac{\cancel{9}y^2}{\cancel{9}} = 12y$ and $-28 + y^2 = 12y$. Rearranging terms, we have $y^2 - 12y - 28 = 0$. Factoring, $(y - 14)(y + 2) = 0$, so that $y = 14$ or $y = -2$. Since we want the positive value, $y = 14$.

23. (C)   Since there are 24 games in total, any of the teams need to have 13 wins to have more wins than losses. The Hawks already have 4 wins, so they need at least 9 more out of the 12 possible.

24. (C)   The Jays have won 10 games already so if they win 8 more, they will have 18 wins for the season. Then $\dfrac{5}{6}$ of 18 = 15 games. Since the Larks already have 8 wins, they need 7 more.

25. (D)   The diagonals of a regular hexagon divide it into six equilateral triangles. We can calculate the height of one of these triangles and double the result to answer 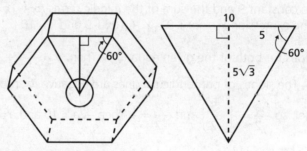 this question. Since all the edges are of length 10 mm, if we draw in a perpendicular to the base, as is shown in the figure above right, we create a right triangle. The height of this triangle is $\dfrac{\text{hypotenuse} \cdot \sqrt{3}}{2} = \dfrac{10 \cdot \sqrt{3}}{2} = 5\sqrt{3}$. Therefore, the height of the nut, h, is $2 \cdot 5\sqrt{3} = 10\sqrt{3}$.

26. (A)   To rationalize the fraction, multiply both the numerator and the denominator by $\dfrac{\sqrt{12}}{\sqrt{12}}$. Then, $\dfrac{\sqrt{12} - \sqrt{6}}{\sqrt{12}} \cdot \dfrac{\sqrt{12}}{\sqrt{12}}$ is $\dfrac{12 - \sqrt{72}}{12}$ and since $\sqrt{72} = \sqrt{36 \cdot 2} = 6\sqrt{2}$, we have $\dfrac{12 - 6\sqrt{2}}{12} = \dfrac{2 - \sqrt{2}}{2}$.

27. (C)   Let x = the fraction of voters from the two counties who voted yes. Then $38{,}860x + 46{,}204x = 63{,}798$ and $85{,}064x = 63{,}798$ and $x = 0.75$ or $x\% = 75\%$. Thus, 75% of Lakewood County residents, or $38{,}860(0.75) = 29{,}145$ voted yes.

28. (D)   Trying each relationship of $\dfrac{\sqrt{x}}{y}, \dfrac{x}{y}, \dfrac{2x}{y}$, and $\dfrac{x^2}{y}$ only $\dfrac{x^2}{y}$ has the same result, 1, for all given x-values.

29. (B)   The graph of the equation $x^2 + y^2 = 16$ is a circle with center at (0, 0) and radius of 4. Of the answer choices, only $b > 4$ will result in no solution to the system.

30. (A)   Immediately eliminate answer choice B as there should be more than 6 units needed for 10,000 gallons. Set up a direct proportion to solve: $\dfrac{8000}{6} = \dfrac{10000}{x}$, $8000x = 60000$, and $x = 7.5$ units.

31. (2)   The smallest possible value for the fraction $\dfrac{16}{|x-y|}$ occurs when the denominator is the largest it can be. In this case, the largest denominator we can make is $|4-(-4)| = 8$. Then, $16 \div 8 = 2$.

32. (164)   The linear regression equation is defined by $ax + b$ with a and b equal to the values listed. Substitute 24.8 for x and calculate $y = 4.83(24.8) + 43.82 = 119.784 + 43.82 = 163.604$, or approximately 164 cm.

33. (22)   Let $A =$ the number of apps Abbie has, $K =$ the number of apps Kishan has, and $R =$ the number of apps Rayen has. Then $A - 3 = K$, $A + 1 = R$ and $70 < A + K + R < 76$. Substituting for the variables, $70 < A + (A - 3) + (A + 1) < 76$. Simplifying, $70 < 3A - 2 < 76$, $72 < 3A < 78$, and $24 < A < 26$. Therefore, Abbie has 25 apps and Kishan has $25 - 3 = 22$ apps.

34. (10)   Algebraically, since $(x + 1)(x + h) = x^2 + hx + 1x + h = x^2 + kx + 9$ then h is equal to the constant 9 and the sum of the middle terms $hx + 1x = 9x + 1x = 10x$. The expression $x^2 + kx + 9$ is $x^2 + 10x + 9$ and $k = 10$.

35. (25)   Find the slopes for both of the given equations. Then, $y = -\dfrac{2}{5}x + 20$ and $y = -\dfrac{ax}{2} + 4$. The slopes of perpendicular lines are negative reciprocals of each other, so $-\dfrac{a}{2} = -\left(-\dfrac{5}{2}\right)$ and $-\dfrac{a}{2} = \dfrac{5}{2}$. Then $-2a = 10$ and $a = -5$, so $a^2 = 25$.

36. (4)   Substitute $f(n)$ for $f(x)$ and then $f(n) = |5n - 19|$. We must determine when this expression is less than n, so remove the absolute value signs and solve the two equations $5n - 19 < n$ and $5n - 19 > -n$. So $4n < 19$ and $n < 4.75$. For $5n - 19 > -n$, we get $6n > 19$ and $n > 3\dfrac{1}{6}$. The only integer value between $3\dfrac{1}{6} < n < 4.75$ is 4.

37. (1.08)   Use the given fraction $\left(\dfrac{\text{price in the year 2000}}{\text{price in 1980}}\right)^{\frac{1}{20}}$ and the data from the chart regarding median new home prices in the Northeast. Then $\left(\dfrac{190000}{40500}\right)^{\frac{1}{20}} \approx 1.08$.

38. (422)   First determine the growth rate for a home in the West region. So, $\left(\dfrac{152000}{35000}\right)^{\frac{1}{20}} \approx 1.076$. Then use the exponential function $f(x) = (\text{price in 1980, in thousands}) \cdot (\text{growth factor})^x$ with 32.5 as the price in 1980, 1.076 as the growth factor, and $x = 35$ to calculate the price of the home in California in 2015. So, $f(35) = 32.5(1.076)^{35} \approx 422.000$ or 422 thousand dollars.

Correlation Chart

SAT Math Model Exam 3—No Calculator Allowed

Use the chart below to mark the questions you found difficult to determine which lessons you need to review.

(*The No Calculator section of the SAT Math Exam will not contain items from Problem Solving and Data Analysis category.*)

Question Number	Heart of Algebra	Problem Solving & Data Analysis	Passport To Advanced Math	Additional Topics in Math	Pages to Study
1	Lesson 1				43 – 56
2	Lesson 4				98 – 111
3				Lesson 4	474 – 488
4			Lesson 4		327 – 342
5	Lesson 2				57 – 80
6			Lesson 2		298 – 315
7			Lesson 7		374 – 388
8	Lesson 2				57 – 80
9	Lesson 2				57 – 80
10			Lesson 6		359 – 373
11				Lesson 1	407 – 425
12				Lesson 7	506 – 513
13			Lesson 1		281 – 297
14	Lesson 3				81 – 97
15			Lesson 7		374 – 388
16			Lesson 3		316 – 326
17			Lesson 1		281 – 297
18	Lesson 5				112 – 119
19			Lesson 3		316 – 326
20	Lesson 6				120 – 138
Total Correct	_____ / 8		_____ / 9	_____ / 3	NA

Correlation Chart

SAT Math Model Exam 3—Calculator Allowed

Use the chart below to mark the questions you found difficult to determine which lessons you need to review.

Question Number	Heart of Algebra	Problem Solving & Data Analysis	Passport to Advanced Math	Additional Topics in Math	Pages to Study
1	Lesson 6				120 – 138
2			Lesson 4		327 – 342
3	Lesson 1				43 – 56
4		Lesson 8			252 – 264
5	Lesson 2				57 – 80
6			Lesson 1		281 – 297
7	Lesson 1				43 – 56
8		Lesson 3			188 – 200
9		Lesson 1			157 – 176
10	Lesson 4				98 – 111
11		Lesson 2			177 – 187
12				Lesson 5	489 – 501
13		Lesson 5			215 – 230
14		Lesson 5			215 – 230
15	Lesson 2				57 – 80
16				Lesson 3	452 – 473
17			Lesson 4		327 – 342
18		Lesson 7			246 – 251
19	Lesson 1				43 – 56
20		Lesson 4			201 – 214
21		Lesson 6			231 – 245
22			Lesson 7		374 – 388
23		Lesson 1			157 – 176
24		Lesson 1			157 – 176
25				Lesson 1	407 – 425
26			Lesson 1		281 – 297
27		Lesson 1			157 – 176
28	Lesson 5				112 – 119
29			Lesson 6		359 – 373
30	Lesson 5				112 – 119
31	Lesson 1				43 – 56
32		Lesson 3			188 – 200
33	Lesson 4				98 – 111
34			Lesson 5		343 – 358
35	Lesson 2				57 – 80
36	Lesson 1				43 – 56
37			Lesson 4		327 – 342
38			Lesson 4		327 – 342
Total Correct	_____ / 13	_____ / 13	_____ / 9	_____ / 3	NA

25 MINUTES, 20 QUESTIONS

NO CALCULATOR ALLOWED

Use the No Calculator section of your answer sheet to answer the questions in this section.

Directions

For questions 1–15, calculate the answer to each problem and choose the best option from the choices given. Bubble in the corresponding circle on your answer sheet. For the remaining questions, solve the problem and enter your answer in the grid on your answer sheet. Refer to the directions before question 16 on how to enter your answers in the grid.

Notes

1. The use of a calculator is <u>not</u> permitted on this test section.
2. All variables and expressions represent real numbers unless otherwise indicated.
3. Figures provided are drawn to scale unless otherwise noted.
4. All figures lie in a plane unless otherwise noted.
5. Unless otherwise noted, the domain of a given function f is the set of all real numbers x for which $f(x)$ is a real number.

Reference

$A = \pi r^2$
$C = 2\pi r$

$A = lw$

$A = \frac{1}{2}bh$

$c^2 = a^2 + b^2$

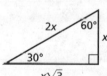

Special Right Triangles

$V = lwh$

$V = \pi r^2 h$

$V = \frac{4}{3}\pi r^3$

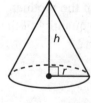

$V = \frac{1}{3}\pi r^2 h$

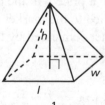

$V = \frac{1}{3}lwh$

The number of degrees of arc in a circle is 360.
The number of radians of arc in a circle is 2π.
The sum of the measures in degrees of the angles of a triangle is 180.

CONTINUE

Questions 1 and 2 refer to the following information.

$$S(p) = \frac{1}{2}p + 80$$

$$D(p) = 255 - 2p$$

The amount of a product supplied by a company and how much the public demands of that product are functions of the price of that product. The functions shown above are the estimated supply and demand for a certain product. The function $S(p)$ gives the quantity of a product supplied to the market when the price is p dollars, and the function $D(p)$ gives the quantity of the product demanded by the market when the price is p dollars.

1

How will the quantity of the product supplied to the market change if the price of the product is decreased by \$10?

A) The quantity supplied will decrease by 5.

B) The quantity supplied will increase by 5.

C) The quantity supplied will increase by 10.

D) The quantity supplied will decrease by 10.

2

At what price will the quantity of the product supplied to the market equal the quantity of the product demanded by the market?

A) \$150

B) \$95

C) \$175

D) \$70

3

If $x = 3 - 2i$, then $x^2 =$

A) $5 + 12i$

B) $13 - 12i$

C) $5 - 12i$

D) $13 + 12i$

4

Simplify: $\dfrac{1-a}{a-3} \div \dfrac{a^4-1}{12a-36}$.

A) $\dfrac{12(1-a)}{a^2+1}$

B) $\dfrac{-12}{(a+1)(a^2+1)}$

C) $\dfrac{12}{a+1}$

D) $\dfrac{1-a}{a-3}$

CONTINUE

No Calculator Allowed

5

Which of the following is the result when the product $(w-3)(w-1)$ is subtracted from $(w-1)^2$?

A) $2(w-1)$

B) $4(w-1)$

C) $w(w-1)$

D) $-2(w-1)$

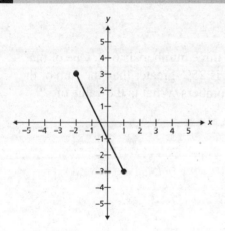

What is the slope of the line segment shown above?

A) Undefined

B) -1

C) 0

D) -2

Using the slope-intercept form $y = mx + b$, which of the following equations is equivalent to $y - 3 = \dfrac{2}{5}(x - 8)$?

A) $y = \dfrac{2}{5}x + 5$

B) $y = \dfrac{2}{5}x - \dfrac{1}{5}$

C) $y = \dfrac{2}{5}x + \dfrac{1}{5}$

D) $y = \dfrac{2}{3}x - \dfrac{31}{5}$

The expression $\sqrt[3]{x+1}\left(\sqrt{x+1}\right)$ is equivalent to

A) $(x+1)^{1/6}$

B) $(x+1)^{5/6}$

C) $(x+1)^{6/5}$

D) $(x+1)^{3/2}$

CONTINUE

If $f(x) = x^3 - 1$ and $g(x) = x^2$, what is the minimum value of $f(g(x))$ if the domain for x is $-1 \leq x \leq 1$?

A) -3

B) -2

C) -1

D) 0

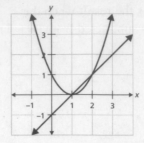

The graphs of the equations $y = (x-1)^2$ and $y = x - 1$ are shown above on the xy-coordinate plane. What real values of x satisfy the inequality $(x - 1)^2 < (x - 1)$?

A) No real values

B) $x < 1$ and $x > 2$

C) $1 \leq x \leq 2$

D) $1 < x < 2$

What is the sum of the roots of $x^2 - 8x + 16 = 0$?

A) -8

B) -4

C) -2

D) 8

The sum of three numbers is 612. One of the numbers, x, is 25% greater than the sum of the other two numbers. What is the value of x?

A) 340

B) 300

C) 226

D) 324

CONTINUE

No Calculator Allowed

13

$(x-4)^2 + y^2 = 9$

$y = (x-4)^2 - 3$

How many points of intersection can be found in the graphs of the system of equations given above?

A) 1

B) 2

C) 3

D) 4

14

Which of the following equations represents a line that is perpendicular to the line with equation $y = -\dfrac{2}{3}x + 8$?

A) $3x - 2y = 3$

B) $2y - 3x = 18$

C) $2y + 18x = 3$

D) $2y + 3x = 18$

15

Several friends wanted to rent a summer beach house for \$3,200. When 2 more people joined the group, each person's share was reduced by \$80. If n represents the number of people in the original group, which of the following equations could be used to find n?

A) $\dfrac{3200}{n} = 80$

B) $\dfrac{3200}{n+2} = 80$

C) $\dfrac{3200}{n+2} = 3200 - 80n$

D) $\dfrac{3200}{n+2} = \dfrac{3200}{n} - 80$

CONTINUE

For the remaining questions, solve the problem and enter your answer in the answer grid. Instructions for entering your answer in the grid are described below.

1. It is not required that you write your answer in the boxes at the top of the grid, but it is suggested.

2. Do not mark more than one circle in each column.

3. There are no negative answers in this portion of the test.

4. If the problem has more than 1 correct answer, grid only 1 of those answers.

5. Grid fractions as proper or improper fractions only.

6. Decimal answers must fill the entire grid.

Examples

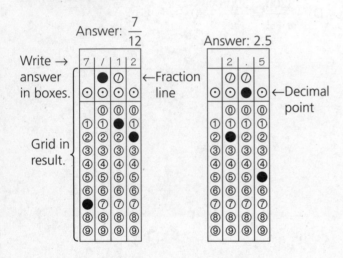

Answer: $\frac{7}{12}$

Write answer in boxes. ←Fraction line

Grid in result.

Answer: 2.5 ←Decimal point

Acceptable ways to grid $\frac{2}{3}$ are:

Answer: 201 – either position is correct

CONTINUE

It is given that A varies directly as the product of x and y and inversely as the square of m. When $x = 4$, $y = 2$, and $m = \dfrac{1}{2}$, the value of A is 8. What is the value of k, the constant of proportionality?

If $\sqrt{3 + \sqrt{N}} = 4$, then $N =$

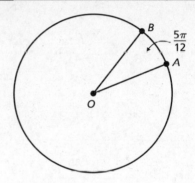

The area of sector AOB of circle O is $\dfrac{5\pi}{12}$ square units.

If the radius of the circle is 10 units, what is the degree measure of the central angle?

In the given equation $ax^k = x^{k+1}$, where a, k, and x are all positive integers greater than 1, what is the value of $\dfrac{a - x}{k}$?

The area of equilateral $\triangle PQR$, shown above, is $\dfrac{10}{7}$ square units. Point A is the midpoint of side $\overline{PR}$, point B is the midpoint of side $\overline{PQ}$, and point C is the midpoint of side $\overline{QR}$. What is the area of parallelogram $ABQC$?

STOP

If you finish before time is called, you may check your work on this section only.
Do not turn to any other section.

55 MINUTES, 38 QUESTIONS

CALCULATOR ALLOWED

Use the Calculator section of your answer sheet to answer the questions in this section.

Directions

For questions 1–30, calculate the answer to each problem and choose the best option from the choices given. Bubble in the corresponding circle on your answer sheet. For the remaining questions, solve the problem and enter your answer in the grid on your answer sheet. Refer to the directions before question 31 on how to enter your answers in the grid.

Notes

1. The use of a calculator is permitted on this test section.
2. All variables and expressions represent real numbers unless otherwise indicated.
3. Figures provided are drawn to scale unless otherwise noted.
4. All figures lie in a plane unless otherwise noted.
5. Unless otherwise noted, the domain of a given function f is the set of all real numbers x for which $f(x)$ is a real number.

Reference

$A = \pi r^2$
$C = 2\pi r$

$A = lw$

$A = \frac{1}{2}bh$

$c^2 = a^2 + b^2$

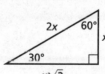

Special Right Triangles

$V = lwh$

$V = \pi r^2 h$

$V = \frac{4}{3}\pi r^3$

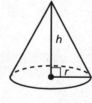

$V = \frac{1}{3}\pi r^2 h$

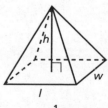

$V = \frac{1}{3}lwh$

The number of degrees of arc in a circle is 360.
The number of radians of arc in a circle is 2π.
The sum of the measures in degrees of the angles of a triangle is 180.

CONTINUE

Calculator Allowed

The solution set of the inequality $|2x - 1| < 9$ is

A) $\{-4 < x < 5\}$

B) $\{x < -4 \text{ or } x > 5\}$

C) $\{x < 5\}$

D) $\{x < -4\}$

Sterling silver is made of an alloy of silver and copper in the ratio of 37:3. If the mass of a sterling silver ingot is 600 grams, how much silver in grams does it contain?

A) 48.65 g

B) 200 g

C) 450 g

D) 555 g

Karima's average golf driving distance increased by 10% from 2012 to 2013 and by 20% from 2013 to 2014. By what percent did her driving distance increase from 2012 to 2014?

A) 15%

B) 30%

C) 32%

D) 40%

Which of the following represents N if

$$\left(2 + \frac{1}{x}\right)(N) = \frac{1}{x}?$$

A) $-\dfrac{1}{2}$

B) $\dfrac{1}{2x+1}$

C) $\dfrac{2}{2x+1}$

D) $\dfrac{2x+1}{x}$

CONTINUE

Calculator Allowed

Questions 5 and 6 refer to the following information.

Gender/Flavor	Vanilla	Chocolate	Other	Total
Female	8	7	1	16
Male	10	5	9	24
Total	18	12	10	40

The above two-way frequency table reflects the results of a survey regarding gender and ice cream flavor preference.

5

Of those surveyed, what percent are males who prefer chocolate ice cream?

A) 12.5%
B) 20.8%
C) 33.3%
D) 41.6%

6

By how many percentage points is the percent of all those surveyed who prefer vanilla greater than the percent of those who prefer all other flavors?

A) 5
B) 20
C) 25
D) 45

Zina traveled 210 miles on a car trip. She traveled 60 miles on local roads at the speed of x mph and 150 miles on the highway at a speed 30 mph faster than on the local roads. If the trip took 4 hours, which equation can be used to find both rates of speed for Zina's trip?

A) $\dfrac{60}{x} + \dfrac{150}{x+30} = 4$ hours

B) $\dfrac{x}{60} + \dfrac{x+30}{150} = 4$ hours

C) $\dfrac{60}{x+30} + \dfrac{150}{x} = 4$ hours

D) $\dfrac{x}{x+30} - \dfrac{60}{150} = 4$ hours

8

Suppose a line segment has endpoints $A(2, 5)$ and $B(x, y)$. If the midpoint of this segment, M, has coordinates of $(x + A, y - 2A)$, what are the coordinates of B?

A) $\left(7, \dfrac{1}{3}\right)$

B) $(4, 3)$

C) $\left(\dfrac{1}{2}, 8\right)$

D) $(-3, 5)$

CONTINUE

If a line contains the points $(2, 2)$ and $(-2, -1)$, then the x-intercept must be

A) $\dfrac{4}{3}$

B) $\dfrac{3}{4}$

C) $-\dfrac{2}{3}$

D) $-\dfrac{3}{2}$

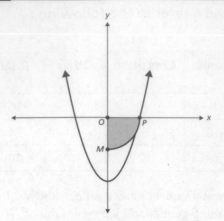

In the given figure, $\overarc{MP}$ is the arc of a circle with center O. The area of sector MOP is π. If the point P lies on the graph of the parabola $y = x^2 - a$, where a is a constant, what is the numerical value of a?

A) -4

B) -2

C) 2

D) 4

If $\dfrac{1}{5}$ of the tomato plants in Richard's garden represent $\dfrac{1}{10}$ of all the vegetable plants in his garden, what is the ratio of the tomato plants to plants that are not tomato plants?

A) 1:10

B) 2:5

C) 1:2

D) 1:1

In a math class with 20 students, the grades on a recent quiz ranged from 0 to 10, inclusive. The average grade of the first 12 quiz papers the teacher marked was 7.5. If x is the average grade for the class on this quiz, then which of the following could be the possible grade range?

A) $4 \le x \le 8.5$

B) $4 \le x \le 7.5$

C) $3.5 \le x \le 7.5$

D) $5 \le x \le 8.50$

CONTINUE

Calculator Allowed

A research study was conducted to determine if a certain treatment is successful in reducing hair loss in men. From a large population of adult males with varying stages of hair loss, 500 participants were selected at random. Half of the participants were randomly assigned to receive the treatment and half of the participants received a placebo treatment. The resulting data showed that participants who received the treatment had moderately improved hair growth compared to those who received the placebo treatment. Based on the design and results of the study, which of the following is an appropriate conclusion?

A) The treatment improves hair growth in males better than all other available treatments.

B) The treatment is likely to improve the hair growth of males who experience hair loss.

C) The treatment will improve the hair growth of any male who takes it.

D) The treatment will cause a substantial improvement in hair growth for males.

B)

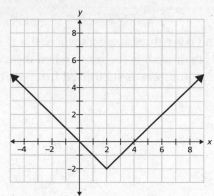

C)

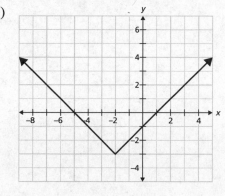

D)

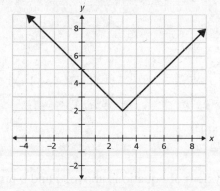

Which of the following would be the graphic transformation of $y = f(x) = |x|$ by the equation $y + 3 = |x + 2|$?

A)

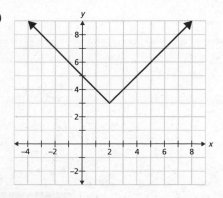

CONTINUE

Calculator Allowed

If a, b, and c are three integers where $b = a + 5$ and $c = b - 1$, then what is the result when the average of the three numbers is subtracted from the median?

A) 2

B) 1

C) 0

D) −1

$$ax + by = 10$$
$$2x + 4y = 30$$

In the system of equations above, a and b are constants. If the system has infinitely many solutions, what is the value of ab?

A) $\dfrac{8}{9}$

B) $\dfrac{2}{3}$

C) $\dfrac{4}{3}$

D) $\dfrac{2}{9}$

17

At the Purity Bottling Company, machine F fills bottles with spring water and machine A accepts the bottles only if the number of fluid ounces in each bottle is between $7\dfrac{3}{4}$ and $8\dfrac{1}{4}$ fluid ounces.

If machine A accepts a bottle containing x fluid ounces, which of the following describes all acceptable values of x?

A) $|x - 8| = \dfrac{1}{4}$

B) $|x - 8| \leq \dfrac{1}{4}$

C) $|x - 8| \geq \dfrac{1}{4}$

D) $|x + 8| = \dfrac{1}{4}$

If two points on a line have (x, y) coordinates of $(N, 0)$, and $(3, -4)$, and the slope of the line is N, what is the value of N?

A) −2

B) −1

C) 1

D) 2

CONTINUE

Calculator Allowed

The vertex of a parabola defined by $f(x) = x^2 - 4x + 3$ has coordinates $(2, -1)$. Which of the following are the coordinates of the vertex defined by $g(x) = f(x - 2) - 2$?

A) $(4, 1)$

B) $(0, -3)$

C) $(4, -3)$

D) $(0, -3)$

A large collection of coins contains American pennies, nickels, and dimes. Yannic wants to estimate the proportion of the collection that is nickels by taking several large samples of the collection. Which of the following statements about Yannic's sampling method is true?

A) It is important that all of his samples are the same size.

B) All samples of the same size will have the same proportion of nickels.

C) The larger the sample, the larger the margin of error.

D) The larger the sample, the smaller the margin of error.

If $x = 7^a$ and $a = b + 1$, what is $\frac{x}{7}$ in terms of b?

A) $b + 1$

B) $7b$

C) $7b + 1$

D) 7^b

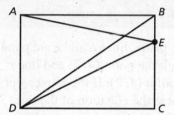

In the rectangle above, if $\tan \angle BAE = \frac{1}{5}$ and $\tan \angle EDC = \frac{1}{2}$, what is $\tan \angle ABD$?

A) 0.50

B) 0.40

C) 0.70

D) 0.90

CONTINUE

If it takes 10 people 9 hours to complete a certain job, how many hours will it take 4 people to do $\frac{1}{5}$ of the job?

A) 4 hours

B) 4.5 hours

C) 5 hours

D) 5.5 hours

In the xy-coordinate plane, lines a and r are parallel. Line a passes through the point $(4, 7)$ and line r passes through the point $(4, 2)$. If the y-intercept for line r is -2, what is the equation of the line perpendicular to line a that also intersects line a on the y-axis?

A) $y = -x + 1$

B) $y = -x + 3$

C) $y = x + 3$

D) $y = -\frac{3}{2}x + 3$

25

The function f is defined by $f(x) = x^3 - 1.5x^2 - 11.5x + c$, where c is a constant. The graph of f has three x-intercepts in the xy-plane. They are the points $\left(\frac{1}{2}, 0\right)$, $(-3, 0)$, and $(p, 0)$. What is the value of c?

A) -21

B) -6

C) 6

D) 21

$$\frac{1}{2}x + \frac{2}{3}y \leq 6$$

$$2x + \frac{1}{2}y \geq 4$$

For the system of inequalities above, which of the given coordinates are members of the solution set?

A) $(4, 1)$

B) $(8, 5)$

C) $(0, 0)$

D) There is no solution to this inequality system.

CONTINUE

Calculator Allowed

Line k in the xy-plane contains coordinates from each of quadrants I, III, and IV, but no points from quadrant II. Which of the following must be true?

A) The slope of line k is undefined.
B) The slope of line k is zero.
C) The slope of line k is positive.
D) The slope of line k is negative.

The scores on a special Chemistry make-up exam were 75, 75, 85, 90, and 100. Which statement about these scores is true?

A) mode > median
B) mode > mean
C) mean < median
D) mean = median

An investment opportunity allowed Osamu to place $15,000 in a mutual fund that was valued at $18,000 after 2 years. To the nearest tenth, what was the annual percent rate of return, r, on his investment?

A) 20%
B) 17.7%
C) 10.9%
D) 9.5%

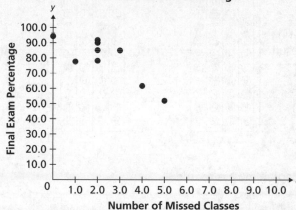

30

Number of Missed Classes versus Final Exam Percentage

Mr. Dorfei created a scatterplot, shown above, of the number of classes missed by each of his students and the score each student earned on the final exam. If a line of best fit were drawn through the scatterplot, which of the following statements would best describe the line?

A) Positive slope greater than 1.
B) Negative slope of less than −1.
C) Positive slope of less than 1.
D) Negative slope of greater than −1.

CONTINUE

For the remaining questions, solve the problem and enter your answer in the answer grid. Instructions for entering your answer in the grid are described below.

1. It is not required that you write your answer in the boxes at the top of the grid, but it is suggested.

2. Do not mark more than one circle in each column.

3. There are no negative answers in this portion of the test.

4. If the problem has more than 1 correct answer, grid only 1 of those answers.

5. Grid fractions as proper or improper fractions only.

6. Decimal answers must fill the entire grid.

Examples

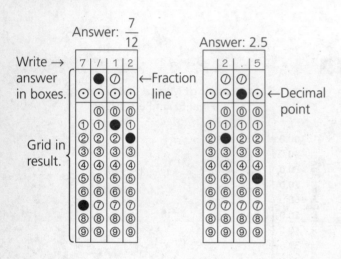

Answer: $\frac{7}{12}$

Write answer in boxes. ←Fraction line

Answer: 2.5 ←Decimal point

Grid in result.

Acceptable ways to grid $\frac{2}{3}$ are:

Answer: 201 – either position is correct

If $-\dfrac{7}{5} < -4x + 3 < -\dfrac{5}{4}$ what is one possible value of $8x - 6$?

The equation $P(I) = -12(I^2) + 120(I)$ represents the available power P, in watts, of a 120 volt circuit with resistance of 12 ohms when a current I, in amperes, is flowing through the circuit. What is the maximum power, in watts, that can be delivered by this circuit?

A scientist recorded the growth of two colonies of bacteria in two Petri dishes. After the initial placement ($t = 0$), the scientist measured and recorded the area covered by the bacteria every hour. The data were fit by a smooth curve as shown below, where each curve represents the area of a dish covered by bacteria as a function of time, in hours.

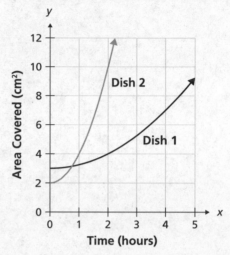

At the measurement for hour 2, the area covered by the bacteria in Dish 2 was what percent greater than the area covered by bacteria in Dish 1?

34

A large container of ice cream is a right circular cylinder. The base of the cylinder has a diameter of 6 inches and the cylinder's height is 8 inches. If a scoop of ice cream is a sphere with a diameter of 2.4 inches, determine (to the nearest integer) how many full scoops of ice cream are in the container.

CONTINUE

35

The density of gold is 19.282 grams per cm³. A cylindrical shaped container half filled with water has a base with radius 2 cm. When a piece of gold was dropped into the cylinder, the water rose 0.5 cm. To the nearest gram, what is the gold's mass? $\left(\text{Density} = \dfrac{\text{mass}}{\text{volume}} \right)$

36

What is a solution for $\dfrac{1}{2} + \dfrac{2}{x-2} = \dfrac{5}{x-1}$?

Questions 37 and 38 refer to the following information.

A sports survey of students at North Midville College had the following results:

I.   66% of those surveyed like baseball,
     48% like football, and
     38% like golf.

II. Furthermore,
     30% like baseball and football,
     22% like baseball and golf, and
     28% like football and golf.

III. Lastly,
     12% of those surveyed like all three sports.

Suppose a random student is chosen.

37

To the nearest tenth, what is the probability that the student chosen likes football given that they like baseball?

38

To the nearest tenth, what is the probability that the student chosen likes baseball and golf given that they like baseball?

STOP

If you finish before time is called, you may check your work on this section only.
Do not turn to any other section.

SAT Model Exam 4 Answer Key

No Calculator Test

1. **(A)** If the price of the product is decreased by \$10, the supply function becomes $S(p-10) = \frac{1}{2}(p-10)+80$. Simplifying, $S(p-10)$ is $\frac{1}{2}p+75$ which shows that $S(p-10)$ is $S(p) - 5$.

2. **(D)** Supply will equal demand when the equations are equal. Solve $\frac{1}{2}p+80 = 255-2p$ for p. Then $2.5p = 175$ and $p = \$70$.

3. **(C)** Square the complex expression and $(3-2i)^2$ is $(3-2i)(3-2i) = 9 - 12i + 4i^2$ Remember that $i^2 = -1$ and then $9 - 12i - 4 = 5 - 12i$.

4. **(B)** Begin by rewriting the division of fractions: $\dfrac{1-a}{a-3} \div \dfrac{a^4-1}{12a-36} =$ $\dfrac{1-a}{a-3} \cdot \dfrac{12a-36}{a^4-1}$. Now completely factor each numerator and denominator and cancel the like terms. Then $\dfrac{1-a}{a-3} \cdot \dfrac{12a-36}{a^4-1} = \dfrac{1-a}{a-3} \cdot \dfrac{12(a-3)}{(a-1)(a+1)(a^2+1)}$, which can be further simplified: $\dfrac{12(1-a)(-1)}{(a-1)(a+1)(a^2+1)} = \dfrac{-12}{(a+1)(a^2+1)}$.

5. **(A)** Set up the subtraction of the binomials: $(w-1)^2 - [(w-3)(w-1)]$. Then expand to find $w^2 - 2w+1 - [w^2 - 4w+3]$. Distribute the negative sign through the brackets and $w^2 - 2w+1 - w^2 + 4w - 3 = 2w - 2$. None of the answer choices match, so factor out the common term and the answer is $2(w - 1)$.

6. **(D)** Use the endpoints of the line segment and the slope formula. Then $\dfrac{-3-3}{1-(-2)} = \dfrac{-6}{3} = -2$.

7. **(B)** Given $y - 3 = \frac{2}{5}(x-8)$, we can distribute the fraction $\frac{2}{5}$ through the parentheses so that $y = 3 + \frac{2}{5}x - \frac{2}{5}(8)$ which becomes $\frac{2}{5}x - \frac{16}{5} + \frac{15}{5}$ and simplifies to $y = \frac{2}{5}x - \frac{1}{5}$.

8. **(D)** The expression $\sqrt[3]{x+1}\left(\sqrt{x+1}\right)$ can be rewritten using the exponent rule for the product of like bases: $(x+1)^{\frac{1}{3}}(x+1)^{\frac{1}{2}}$. Simplifying, $(x+1)^{\frac{1}{3}+\frac{1}{2}} = (x+1)^{\frac{5}{6}}$.

9. **(C)** Determine the composition $f(g(x)) = (x^2)^3 - 1 = x^6 - 1$. The domain is restricted to $-1 \le x \le 1$. Looking at the endpoints, -1 and 1, either raised to the sixth power will result in 1, and $1 - 1 = 0$. If $x = 0$, the other integer value in the domain, $f(g(0)) = (0)6 - 1 = -1$. This is the minimum value of $f(g(x))$.

10. **(D)** Factor the given polynomial $x^2 - 8x + 16 = 0$ into the binomials $(x-4)(x-4) = 0$. Then 4 is a double root and $4 + 4 = 8$.

11. **(D)** The values of x for which the inequality $(x-1)^2 < (x-1)$ is true can be read from the graph where the parabola $y = (x-1)^2$ is beneath the linear graph of $y = x - 1$. That occurs where $x > 1$ and $x < 2$, which can be written as the compound inequality $1 < x < 2$.

12. (A) Let x be one of the numbers that sums to 612 and let y and z be the other two numbers. Then $x + y + z = 612$. We know that x is 25% greater than the sum of y and z so $1.25(y + z) = x$ and $y + z = \dfrac{x}{1.25}$. Substitute this value for $y + z$ in $x + y + z = 612$. Then $x + \dfrac{x}{1.25} = 612$. Simplifying, $\dfrac{1.25x + x}{1.25} = 612$ which becomes $2.25x = 765$, and $x = 340$.

13. (C) The two equations are a circle with center $(4, 0)$ and radius 3, and a parabola with vertex at $(4, -3)$. A quick sketch would show that there are three intersections.

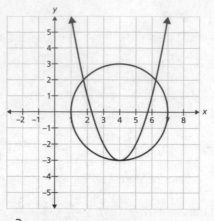

14. (B) Perpendicular lines have negative reciprocal slopes. The slope of the given equation is $-\dfrac{2}{3}$, so the perpendicular slope will be $\dfrac{3}{2}$. We don't know the y-intercept of the perpendicular line, but we can say that the equation will be of the form $y = \dfrac{3}{2}x + c$, where c is a constant.

Multiplying through by 2, $2y = 3x + 2c$ and $2y - 3x = 2c$. Answer choice B has this form.

15. (D) Since n = the original number of people, then $\dfrac{3200}{n}$ is the expression we can use to represent the original cost per person. Then, $\dfrac{3200}{n+2}$ is the new cost per person. The new cost per person = the old cost per person $- 80$ which is $\dfrac{3200}{n+2} = \dfrac{3200}{n} - 80$.

16. $\left(\dfrac{1}{4}\right)$ Let k = the constant of proportionality. According to the given statement,

$A = k\dfrac{xy}{m^2}$, so that $8 = k\left(\dfrac{4 \cdot 2}{\left(\dfrac{1}{2}\right)^2}\right)$ which simplifies into $k\left(\dfrac{8}{\dfrac{1}{4}}\right) = k(8)(4)$.

So $8 = 32k$, and $k = \dfrac{8}{32} = \dfrac{1}{4}$.

17. $\left(\dfrac{3}{2} \text{ or } 1.5\right)$ Since the radius of the circle is 10, the area of circle O is $\pi(10^2) = 100\pi$. Now determine what part of 100π the area of sector AOB is. Then

$\dfrac{\dfrac{5}{12}\pi}{100\pi} = \dfrac{5}{12} \cdot \dfrac{1}{100} = \dfrac{1}{240}$. The sector is $\dfrac{1}{240}$ of the circle. There are 360° in a

circle so $\dfrac{1}{240}$ of 360° $= \dfrac{36}{24} = \dfrac{3}{2} = 1.5°$

18. (169)　Given that $\sqrt{3+\sqrt{N}} = 4$, square both sides so that $\left(\sqrt{3+\sqrt{N}}\right)^2 = 4^2$. We now have $3+\sqrt{N} = 16$ or $\sqrt{N} = 13$. Again, squaring both sides, we arrive at $N = 169$.

19. (0)　Since $ax^k = x^{k+1}$, where a, k, and x are all positive integers greater than 1, rewrite the equation by solving for a. We find that $a = \dfrac{x^{k+1}}{x^k}$, which simplifies to $x^{k+1-k} = x$. So $a = x$ and $\dfrac{a-x}{k} = \dfrac{a-a}{k} = \dfrac{0}{k} = 0$.

20. $\left(\dfrac{5}{7}\right)$　Draw in segment $\overline{BC}$ to create 4 congruent equilateral triangles.

Parallelogram $ABQC$ is $\dfrac{2}{4} = \dfrac{1}{2}$ the number of triangles formed.

Thus, parallelogram $ABQC$ is $\dfrac{1}{2}$ of the given area $\dfrac{10}{7}$ square units.

Hence, $\dfrac{1}{2} \cdot \dfrac{10}{7} = \dfrac{5}{7}$ square units.

Calculator Test

1. (A)　Split the given inequality into two expressions: $2x - 1 < 9$ and $2x - 1 > -9$. Solving each we find that if $2x - 1 < 9$ then $2x < 10$ and $x < 5$. If $2x - 1 > -9$, then $2x > -8$, and $x > -4$. Thus, the solution set is $\{-4 < x < 5\}$.

2. (C)　If we select a friendly number, such as 100 yards, as Karima's initial driving distance, then $100(1.10) = 110$ yards is her distance at the end of 2012. Karima starts 2013 driving an average distance of 110 yards and ends the year driving the ball $110(1.20) = 132$ yards. To find the percentage increase from 2012, $100 \cdot \left(\dfrac{32 \text{ yards}}{100 \text{ yards}}\right) = 32\%$ increase.

3. (D)　Silver to copper is in the ratio of 37:3, so that 37:40 is the ratio of silver to the entire alloy. Write the proportion $\dfrac{37}{40} = \dfrac{x}{600}$ to determine the solution. Cross-multiplying, $40x = 37(600)$. Solving, we find that $x = 555$ g.

4. (B)　Begin simplifying the equation by summing the terms in the parentheses to $\left(\dfrac{2x}{x} + \dfrac{1}{x}\right) = \dfrac{2x+1}{x}$ and then $\dfrac{2x+1}{x}(N) = \dfrac{1}{x}$. Multiply both sides of the equation by the reciprocal of $\dfrac{2x+1}{x}$ so that $N = \dfrac{1}{x}\left(\dfrac{x}{2x+1}\right)$ which becomes $\dfrac{1}{2x+1}$.

5. (A)　Of those surveyed, there are 5 males out of a total of 40 people surveyed who prefer chocolate ice cream, so $\dfrac{5}{40} = 0.125 = 12.5\%$.

6. (B)　The percent of males and females who prefer vanilla ice cream is $\dfrac{18}{40} = 0.45 = 45\%$. The percent of males and females who prefer all other flavors is $\dfrac{10}{40} = 0.25 = 25\%$. Their difference is $45 - 25 = 20$ percentage points.

7. (A) Set up the equation using the simple formula $d = rt$. Since the two traveling times are not equal, we label them t_1 and t_2. We do know that the sum of the times is 4 hours so, $t_1 = \dfrac{\text{Distance}}{\text{Rate}} = \dfrac{60}{x}$ and $t_2 = \dfrac{150}{x+30}$. Putting it all together, $\dfrac{60}{x} + \dfrac{150}{x+30} = 4$ hours.

8. (C) Use the midpoint formula to determine the coordinates of each midpoint in terms of A. Then $\dfrac{2+x}{2} = x + A$ and $\dfrac{5+y}{2} = y - 2A$. Solving the first equation for A yields $2 + x = 2(x + A)$, $2 + x = 2x + 2A$, and $\dfrac{2-x}{2} = A$. Tackling the second equation, $5 + y = 2(y - 2A)$, $5 + y = 2y - 4A$, and $\dfrac{y-5}{4} = A$. Since the coordinates of the midpoints are both equal to A, set the equations equal to each other: $\dfrac{2-x}{2} = \dfrac{y-5}{4}$. Cross-multiplying, $4(2 - x) = 2(y - 5)$, $8 - 4x = 2y - 10$, and $y + 2x = 9$. Substitute each of the given coordinates into the equation to see which one produces a true statement. Only answer choice C works.

9. (C) Begin by finding the slope of the line. Then $m = \dfrac{2-(-1)}{2-(-2)} = \dfrac{3}{4}$. Pick one of the given points to determine the equation of the line; point-slope form will give you the equation directly. So, using $m = \dfrac{3}{4}$ and the point $(-2, -1)$, the equation is $y + 1 = \dfrac{3}{4}(x + 2)$. Simplifying, $y = \dfrac{3x}{4} + \dfrac{6}{4} - 1$ which becomes $y = \dfrac{3x}{4} + \dfrac{1}{2}$. The x-intercept occurs when $y = 0$; so solve $0 = \dfrac{3x}{4} + \dfrac{1}{2}$ to see that $0 = 3x + 2$ and $\dfrac{-2}{3} = x$.

10. (D) Chose a friendly number; say 20, for the number of tomato plants. If 20 is $\dfrac{1}{5}$ of all the tomato plants, then there are 100 tomato plants. Since those 20 tomato plants represent $\dfrac{1}{10}$ of all the vegetable plants, there are 200 plants in the garden. Of those 200, there are 100 that are not tomato plants. So the requested ratio is $\dfrac{\text{tomato plants}}{\text{not tomato plants}} = \dfrac{100}{100} = 1{:}1$.

11. (D) Since the area of sector MOP is π, the area of the full circle is 4π. Incorporating the formula for the area of a circle, $\pi r^2 = 4\pi$, the radius of O is 2. Since $r = 2$, $\overline{OP} = 2$. The (x, y) coordinates of point P must be $(2, 0)$, which we can substitute into the equation $y = x^2 - a$, so that $0 = 2^2 - a$ and $a = 4$.

12. (A) If the other 8 students earned a score of 0, then $\dfrac{12(7.5)+8(0)}{20} = 4.5$ is the lowest possible average. If the other 8 students earned a score of 10, then $\dfrac{12(7.5)+8(10)}{20} = 8.5$ is the highest possible average. Thus, the extreme grade range is $4.5 \leq x \leq 8.5$, but this is not one of the answer choices. The only choice that includes this range is D, $5.00 \leq x \leq 8.50$.

13. (B) In this study, the population is well defined, the participants were selected at random, and they were randomly assigned to treatment groups. Thus, we can generalize the results of the study to the population studied, namely males experiencing hair loss. This eliminates choice C as not all males experience hair loss. Of the remaining choices, only B makes sense. We cannot make a statement about other treatments available, nor can we say the treatment causes a substantial improvement in hair growth.

14. (C) Solve $y + 3 = |x + 2|$ for y, and we have $y = |x + 2| - 3$. This means that the graph of $y = f(x) = |x|$ translates 2 units to the left and 3 units down.

15. (B) We are given that $c = b - 1$ and $b = a + 5$, so $c = a + 5 - 1$ or $a + 4$. Put the numbers in order: a, $c = a + 4$, and $b = a + 5$ where c (or $a + 4$) is the median. Find the average such that $\dfrac{a + b + c}{3} = \dfrac{a + a + 5 + a + 4}{3}$ which becomes $\dfrac{3a + 9}{3} = a + 3$. Subtract the average from the median and find that $a + 4 - (a + 3)$ is $a + 4 - a - 3 = 1$.

16. (A) For a system of linear equations to have an infinite number of solutions, the two equations must be equivalent. Multiply the second equation through by 3 so that $3ax + 3by = 30$. Now that both equations are equal to 30, we can equate the coefficients. So $3a = 2$ and $3b = 4$, $a = \dfrac{2}{3}$, $b = \dfrac{4}{3}$. The product ab is then $\dfrac{8}{9}$.

17. (B) Using the average and difference approach, the average of $7\dfrac{3}{4}$ fl. oz. and $8\dfrac{1}{4}$ fl. oz. is 8 fl. oz. and the difference between $8\dfrac{1}{4}$ and 8 and between 8 and $7\dfrac{3}{4}$ is $\dfrac{1}{4}$. Hence, the machine will accept bottles containing $|x - 8| \leq \dfrac{1}{4}$ fl. oz.

18. (B) Use the given information in the slope formula to determine the value of N. Then $\dfrac{-4 - 0}{3 - N} = N$. Cross-multiply and $-4 = N(3 - N)$. Distribute and collect all the terms on the left-hand side of the equation so that $-4 = 3N - N^2$ becomes $N^2 - 3N - 4 = 0$. Factor so that $(N - 4)(N + 1) = 0$ and $N = 4$ or $N = -1$. Neither is an extraneous solution. $N = -1$ is answer choice B.

19. (C) Since the vertex coordinates of f are $(2, -1)$, $g(x) = f(x - 2) - 2$ will move the vertex to the right 2 units and down 2 units which is $(2 + 2, -1 - 2) = (4, -3)$.

20. (D) All other factors remaining equal, the larger the sample size, the smaller the margin of error.

21. (D) Rewrite $x = 7^a$ as 7^{b+1} using the given information. Then $x = 7^{b+1} = 7^1 \cdot 7^b = 7 \cdot 7^b$. Divide both sides by 7 and find that $\dfrac{x}{7} = 7^b$.

22. (C) Give the fractions $\frac{1}{5}$ and $\frac{1}{2}$ a common denominator. Then $\frac{1}{5}$ and $\frac{1}{2}$ become $\frac{2}{10}$ and $\frac{5}{10}$, respectively. Use this information to label the sides with the corresponding lengths. Since $\tan \angle BAE = \frac{1}{5} = \frac{2}{10}$, $BE = 2$, $AB = 10$. The $\tan \angle EDC = \frac{1}{2} = \frac{5}{10}$ means that $EC = 5$ and $DC = 10$. Hence, $\tan \angle ABD = \frac{7}{10}$. None of the answers are in fractional form, so convert $\frac{7}{10}$ to a decimal, which is 0.70.

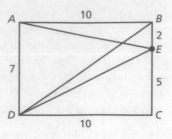

23. (B) Consider that 10 people working 9 hours on a project constitutes $10 \cdot 9 = 90$ work hours. To divide 90 work-hours among only four people means that it will take $90 \div 4 = 22.5$ hours to complete the same task. Calculate $\frac{1}{5}$ of $22.5 = 4.5$ hours.

24. (B) The line r passes through the point (4, 2) and the y-intercept (0, –2). This means the slope is $m = \frac{2-(-2)}{4-0} = \frac{4}{4} = 1$. Using the form $y = mx + b$, the equation for line r is $y = 1x - 2$. Line a has the same slope as line r since they are parallel. Line a passes through the point (4, 7), so its equation is $y - 7 = 1(x - 4)$ which simplifies to $y = x + 3$. The slope of a line perpendicular to a will have a value that is equal to the negative reciprocal of 1, which is –1. The equation of the line perpendicular to a and passing through the same y-intercept as line a is $y = -x + 3$.

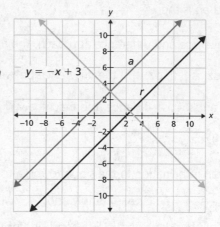

25. (C) Given the x-intercepts, which are the zeros of the function, we can substitute y for $f(x)$, and we can choose one of the numeric zeros to work with. The easiest is (–3, 0), so we substitute 0 for y and –3 for x in the given function. Then $0 = (-3)^3 - 1.5(-3)^2 - 11.5(-3) + c$. Simplifying, $0 = -27 - 13.5 + 34.5 + c$ and $0 = -6 + c$ which becomes $c = 6$.

26. (A) There are several ways we could solve this problem. The quickest is to substitute the given (x, y) coordinates into each inequality to see if two true statements result. If $x = 4$ and $y = 1$, $\frac{1}{2}x + \frac{2}{3}y \le 6$ becomes $\frac{1}{2}(4) + \frac{2}{3}(1) \le 6$, which simplifies to $2 + \frac{2}{3}$ which is less than 6, so this statement is true. Substituting into $2x + \frac{1}{2}y \ge 4$, $2(4) + \frac{1}{2}(1) \ge 4$, and $8\frac{1}{2}$ is greater than 4, so this statement is also true. Stop here and pick A.

27. (D)   A line running through three quadrants of the xy-plane must have either positive or negative slope, so eliminate answer choices A and B. A positively sloping line does not necessarily run through quadrant II.

28. (D)   Calculate the mean, median, and mode. The mean is 85, the median is 85, and the mode is 75.

29. (D)   Using an exponential growth model, substitute $15,000 as the initial value, r as the growth rate, 2 as the time, and $18,000 as the future value. Then $18,000 = 15,000 \left(1+r\right)^2$. Start solving for r by dividing both sides of the equation by 15,000 to see that $1.2 = (1 + r)^2$. Take the square root of both sides, $\sqrt{1.2} = \sqrt{\left(1+r\right)^2}$, and $1 + r = 1.095$. Thus, $r = 0.095$ which is 9.5%.

30. (B)   If a line of best fit were drawn, it would be negatively sloped. Moving along the line from left to right, the y-coordinate decreases much faster than the x-coordinate increases, so the slope would be less than -1.

31. ($2.50 < 8x -$ Notice that $8x - 6$ is $-2(-4x + 3)$. If we multiply every term of
     $6 < 2.80$) $-\dfrac{7}{5} < -4x + 3 < -\dfrac{5}{4}$ by (-2) we can write $\dfrac{14}{5} > 8x - 6 > \dfrac{10}{4}$ which is $2.80 > 8x - 6 > 2.50$. So $8x - 6$ can have any decimal value between, but not including, 2.50 and 2.80.

32. (300)   Look at the structure of the given equation; it is a parabola, so the maximum power occurs at the vertex. Solving for the vertex, $I = -\dfrac{b}{2a} = -\dfrac{-120}{2(-12)} = \dfrac{-120}{-24} = 5$ amperes. When $I = 5$, $P(I) = -12(5)^2 + 120(5)$ which simplifies to $-300 + 600 = 300$ watts.

33. (150)   At hour 2, the bacteria in dish 2 cover 10 cm² and the bacteria in dish 1 cover 4 cm². The difference between these two measurement is 6 cm² and so we calculate $\dfrac{6\ cm^2}{4\ cm^2} = 1.5$ which means the area of the bacteria in dish 2 is 150% greater than the area of the bacteria in dish 1.

34. (31)   To solve this problem, we need to divide the volume of the cylinder by the volume of the spherical scoop. Using your SAT formula sheet and substituting the values for this problem, $\dfrac{\pi\left(3^2\right)(8)}{\frac{4}{3}\pi(1.2)^3}$. Simplifying, $\dfrac{72\,\pi}{2.304\,\pi} = 31.25$ which we round to 31 full scoops.

35. (121)   Find the volume of water displacement in cm³. So $\pi(2^2) \cdot 0.5 = 2\pi$ cm³. Thus, 2π cm³ · 19.282 grams/cm³ = 121.152 grams which we round to 121 grams.

36. (3 or 6)   Eliminate the denominators by multiplying through by the least common denominator, $2(x - 2)(x - 1)$. Then $\dfrac{1}{2} + \dfrac{2}{x-2} = \dfrac{5}{x-1}$ becomes $(x - 2)(x - 1) + 2(2)(x - 1) = 5(2)(x - 2)$. Simplifying and collecting the like terms gives $x^2 - 3x + 2 + 4x - 4 = 10x - 20$ and $x^2 + x - 2 = 10x - 20$. Move all the terms to the left-hand side of the equation and then factor

$x^2 - 9x + 18 = 0$ which is $(x - 3)(x - 6) = 0$. The solutions are $x = 3$ or $x = 6$. Check to make sure neither is extraneous and then bubble in either 3 or 6 on your SPR grid.

37. (45.5)   Pick 100 as a friendly size of the student body. We are given that 66% of the student body, 66 students, say they like baseball, and of that group, 30% of the student body, 30 students, like both football and baseball. So the probability that a randomly chosen student from among those who like baseball also likes football is $\dfrac{30}{66} = \dfrac{5}{11} \approx 45.5\%$.

38. (33.3)   Again, pick 100 as a friendly size of the student body. We are given that 66% of the student body, 66 students, like baseball. We are also given that 22% of the student body, 22 students, like both baseball and golf. That means 22 out of the 66 students who like baseball also like golf. So the probability that a randomly chosen student from among those who like baseball also likes golf is $\dfrac{22}{66} = \dfrac{1}{3} \approx 33.3\%$.

Correlation Chart

SAT Math Model Exam 4—No Calculator Allowed

Use the chart below to mark the questions you found difficult to determine which lessons you need to review.

(The No Calculator section of the SAT Math Exam will not contain items from Problem Solving and Data Analysis category.)

Question Number	Heart of Algebra	Problem Solving & Data Analysis	Passport To Advanced Math	Additional Topics in Math	Pages to Study
1	Lesson 4				98 – 111
2	Lesson 4				98 – 111
3				Lesson 7	506 – 513
4			Lesson 2		298 – 315
5			Lesson 2		298 – 315
6	Lesson 6				120 – 138
7	Lesson 3				81 – 97
8			Lesson 1		281 – 297
9			Lesson 7		374 – 388
10			Lesson 4		327 – 342
11			Lesson 6		359 – 373
12	Lesson 2				57 – 80
13			Lesson 6		359 – 373
14	Lesson 3				81 – 97
15	Lesson 2				57 – 80
16	Lesson 5				112 – 119
17				Lesson 3	452 – 473
18			Lesson 3		316 – 326
19			Lesson 1		281 – 297
20				Lesson 1	407 – 425
Total Correct	_____ / 8		_____ / 9	_____ / 3	NA

Correlation Chart

SAT Math Model Exam 4—Calculator Allowed

Use the chart below to mark the questions you found difficult to determine which lessons you need to review.

Question Number	Heart of Algebra	Problem Solving & Data Analysis	Passport to Advanced Math	Additional Topics in Math	Pages to Study
1	Lesson 2				57 – 80
2		Lesson 1			157 – 176
3		Lesson 1			157 – 176
4	Lesson 2				57 – 80
5		Lesson 5			215 – 230
6		Lesson 5			215 – 230
7			Lesson 4		327 – 342
8	Lesson 6				120 – 138
9	Lesson 3				81 – 97
10		Lesson 1			157 – 176
11				Lesson 3	452 – 473
12		Lesson 1			157 – 176
13		Lesson 8			252 – 264
14			Lesson 7		374 – 388
15		Lesson 1			157 – 176
16	Lesson 4				98 – 111
17	Lesson 2				57 – 80
18	Lesson 3				81 – 97
19			Lesson 7		374 – 388
20		Lesson 7			246 – 251
21			Lesson 1		281 – 297
22				Lesson 4	474 – 488
23	Lesson 5				112 – 119
24	Lesson 3				81 – 97
25			Lesson 5		343 – 358
26	Lesson 4				98 – 111
27	Lesson 3				81 – 97
28		Lesson 6			231 – 245
29			Lesson 4		327 – 342
30		Lesson 3			188 – 200
31	Lesson 2				57 – 80
32			Lesson 5		343 – 358
33		Lesson 4			201 – 214
34				Lesson 1	407 – 425
35		Lesson 2			177 – 187
36	Lesson 2				57 – 80
37		Lesson 5			215 – 230
38		Lesson 5			215 – 230
Total Correct	_____ / 13	_____ / 15	_____ / 7	_____ / 3	NA

Category 1: Heart of Algebra

Lesson 1: Representing Relationships Between Quantities and Creating Algebraic Expressions

Practice: Simplifying and Evaluating Algebraic Expressions (page 44)

1. (A)   Rewrite the problem so the like terms are grouped together.
Then $2x^3 - 4x + 8 - x^3 + 5x - 15$ becomes $2x^3 - x^3 - 4x + 5x + 8 - 15$.
Now combine like terms and the simplified expression is $x^3 + x - 7$.

2. (D)   Distribute -2 through the parentheses to see that $-2(3y - 1) + y + 1 = -6y + 2 + y + 1$. Now collect the like terms and $-6y + y + 2 + 1 = -5y + 3$.

3. (D)   Substitute the given values for a, b, and c. Then, $(a + b)^2 (a - c)$ is $(-1 + (-2))^2(-1 - 1)$. Simplify within the parentheses and $(-3)^2(-2) = 9(-2) = -18$.

4. (A)   Substitute the given values for a, b, and c. Then, $a - c(b + c)$ is $1 - (-1)(2 + (-1))$. Simplify within the parentheses and $1 - (-1)(1) = 1 - (-1) = 1 + 1 = 2$.

5. (D)   The length of PR is $x + y + x - y = 2x$. Since $x = 15$, $2(15) = 30$.

6. (B)   We must rewrite $4c$ as $2(2c)$ in order to use the information given.
Then, $(4 - 4c)^2 = (4 - 2(2c))^2$ becomes $(4 - 2(-1)) = (6)^2 = 36$.

7. (C)   Rewrite the problem as $9x - 15 - (10x - 7)$. Distribute the negative sign through the parentheses to obtain $9x - 15 - 10x + 7$ and combine like terms to see that the answer is $-x - 8$.

8. (B)   Distribute the 5 through the first set of parentheses and the negative sign through the second set of parentheses. Then, $5(x + y) - (5x - y)$ is $5x + 5y - 5x + y = 6y$.

Practice: Formulas and Absolute Value (page 48)

1. (2)   The area of a kite is given by the formula $A = \dfrac{d_1 \cdot d_2}{2}$. Substitute in the lengths of the diagonals and $\dfrac{\sqrt{2} \cdot \sqrt{8}}{2} = \dfrac{\sqrt{16}}{2} = \dfrac{4}{2} = 2$.

2. (C)   To solve this problem, first simplify the given absolute value expression into $\dfrac{|-6|}{-2} - \dfrac{|4 - 7|}{6} = \dfrac{6}{-2} - \dfrac{3}{6} = -3 - \dfrac{1}{2} = -3\dfrac{1}{2}$. Now the task is to determine which of the answer choices gives the same result. Clearly A is incorrect because as $4|3 - 1|$ will not yield $\dfrac{1}{2}$. Answer choice B will simplify into $-\dfrac{1}{2} + 3 \neq -3\dfrac{1}{2}$.

Move to answer choice C. The expression $\dfrac{-|2 - 4|}{4} + \dfrac{-3|2 - 5|}{3}$ becomes

$\dfrac{-|-2|}{4} + \dfrac{-3|-3|}{3} = \dfrac{-2}{4} + \dfrac{-3(3)}{3} = -\dfrac{1}{2} + (-3) = -3\dfrac{1}{2}$.

Practice: Representing Relationships Using Algebraic Language (page 50)

1. (C)   The square root of a number n is $\sqrt{n}$. The number n squared is n^2. Their difference is $\sqrt{n} - n^2$.

2. (B)   The sum of a and b is $a + b$. The product of a and b is ab. The sum decreased by the product is $a + b - ab$.

3. (B)   The product of m and n is mn. Three times their difference is $3(m - n)$.

Divide the two terms and the answer is $\dfrac{mn}{3(m-n)}$.

4. (A)   Three times the difference of a and b is $3(a - b)$. Twice the sum of a and b

is $2(a + b)$. Their division is $\dfrac{3(a-b)}{2(a+b)}$.

Practice: Finding Equivalent Expressions (page 52)

1. (C)   Begin by distributing the negative sign through the parentheses. Then $m^2n - 4m^2 + 3mn^2 - (-m^2n + 3mn^2 - 2m^2)$ becomes $m^2n - 4m^2 + 3mn^2 + m^2n - 3mn^2 + 2m^2$. Combine like terms for $2m^2n - 2m^2$.

2. (D)   Rewrite the original quotient $\dfrac{3x^2y + 6xy - 9xy^2}{3}$ as the sum of fractions so

that $\dfrac{3x^2y}{3} + \dfrac{6xy}{3} - \dfrac{9xy^2}{3}$. Now simplify each term to find $x^2y + 2xy - 3xy^2$.

SAT-Type Questions (page 52)

1. (D)   Immediately eliminate answer choices A and B as any number raised to an even power will be positive. You can substitute in and solve to see that $(ab)^c$ is $((2)(-3))^4 = (-6)^4 = 1{,}296$ or reason that the answer must be greater than 1.

2. (C)   There are no integer numbers between -1 and 0, so pick an easy

fraction for w, such as $-\dfrac{1}{2}$, and substitute in for w^2 and w^3. Then

$w^2 = \left(-\dfrac{1}{2}\right)^2 = \dfrac{1}{4}$ and $w^3 = \left(-\dfrac{1}{2}\right)^3 = -\dfrac{1}{8}$. Therefore, $w^3 < w < w^2$.

3. (C)   Select an odd integer for k, say 5, and substitute that number in for k. Then $3(5) = 15$, an odd number, and $5^3 = 125$, which is also odd. But $k^2 + 1 = 5^2 + 1 = 26$, which is even. Choose answer choice C.

4. (B)   We can substitute in each of the given values for the variables, but it is faster to think through the formula. Given $V = \pi r^2 h$, the product rh must be less than 24 because we have to square r before multiplying it by h. Eliminate answer choices C and D. Then, $2^2 = 4$ and $(4)(3) = 12$. The answer must be B, $\pi(2)^2(6) = 4(6)\pi = 24\pi$.

5. (B)   Sum the given segments. Then $2x + 4 + 8 + 10 - x = x + 22$.

6. (A)   First sum the expressions $x + 3$ and $5 - x$, which is 8. Then subtract $8 - (3 - 2x) = 8 - 3 + 2x = 5 + 2x$.

7. (B)   Convert 12% on sales of d dollars into a decimal term: $0.12d$. Add Anton's basic salary of \$800. He earns $800 + 0.12d$ dollars per week.

8. (A)   Change the room tax from a percent to a decimal so that 8.25% is now 0.0825. Add 1 to the decimal to represent 100% of the cost of the room plus the tax, so 1.0825. Then, for each night, the room and parking costs are $125.99 \cdot 1.0825 + 10$ dollars. For n nights, multiply by n.

9. (B)   Simplify the expression by distributing the 3 through the first set of parentheses and the negative sign through the second set of parenthesis. Then combine the like terms. So $3x + 3y - 3x + y$ is $4y$. Substitute -1 for y and $4(-1) = -4$.

10. (B)   Note that in this expression only the variable y is being raised to the power z. Then $(-3)(2)^3 = (-3)(8) = -24$.

11. (D) We are looking for an expression that does not equal 0 when $x = -2$. Immediately eliminate answer choice A as 0 divided by any number (other than 0) is 0. If you square -2, it is 4 and $4 - 4 = 0$. For C, $(-2) + (-(-2)) = -2 + 2 = 0$. The answer must be D, as $-2 - 2 = -4$.

12. (B) Consider that $\frac{x-y}{x}$ can be rewritten as $\frac{x}{x} - \frac{y}{x} = 1 - \frac{y}{x}$. Since $\frac{x}{y} = m$,

$\frac{y}{x} = \frac{1}{m}$. Putting it all together, $1 - \frac{y}{x} = 1 - \frac{1}{m}$ which is the same as

$\frac{m}{m} - \frac{1}{m} = \frac{m-1}{m}$.

13. (A) The total the three friends contributed was $3x$. So, $3x - d$ is the difference between the money collected and the actual price of the present. The leftover money needs to be divided into 3 equal parts, so the refund is $\frac{3x-d}{3}$.

14. (C) Solve the two inequalities $x - 5 < 4$ and $x - 5 > -4$. Then, $x < 9$ and $x > 1$, so the solutions are between $1 < x < 9$. The only answer choice between these values is 4.

15. $\left(\frac{2}{10} \text{ or } \frac{1}{5} \text{ or } 0.2\right)$ Substitute the values for a and b into the given expression and find that $\frac{6-4}{6+4} = \frac{2}{10}$. Remember that on the SAT, gridded answers may be unsimplified fractions, simplified fractions, or decimals.

16. (1) Substitute $w = 3$, $x = 4$, $y = -3$, and $z = -4$ into the expression to find $\frac{4-3}{-3-(-4)} = \frac{1}{-3+4} = \frac{1}{1} = 1$.

17. $\left(\frac{1}{4} \text{ or } 0.25\right)$ Substitute $j = 2$, $k = -2$, $m = 1$ and $n = -1$. Then $\left(\frac{1}{2}\right)^{(-2)(-1)} = \left(\frac{1}{2}\right)^2 = \frac{1}{4}$.

18. (27) Substitute $p = 3$, $q = 3$, $r = 5$, and $s = 4$ to see that $\left(\frac{5+4}{3}\right)^3 = \left(\frac{9}{3}\right)^3 = 3^3 = 27$.

Lesson 2: Creating and Solving Linear Equations and Inequalities; Literal Equations and More on Absolute Value

Practice: Creating and Solving Equations (page 61)

1. (B) Distribute the negative sign through the parentheses to see that $4x - (7 - 2x) = 1 + 2x + 8$ becomes $4x - 7 + 2x = 1 + 2x + 8$. Then combine the like terms on each side of the equation: $6x - 7 = 2x + 9$. Solving for the variable, $4x = 16$ and $x = 4$.

2. (5) Multiply each term in the parentheses on the left-hand side of the equation by the fraction $\frac{1}{3}$ and simplify the right-hand side. Then $\frac{1}{3}(6a - 15) = (a - 2) + 2$ is $2a - 5 = a$. Collect the like terms and $a = 5$.

3. (24)   Work with the decimals as they are or multiply the equation through by 100 to move all the decimal points two places to the right. If we do so, the equation becomes $4(12) + 1m = 2(12 + m)$. Distribute and begin collecting like terms: $48 + m = 24 + 2m$, $-m = -24$, and $m = 24$.

4. (C)   Examine the terms of the original equation and the terms in the answer choices. If we remove a common factor of 6 from $24p = 54q + 36$ by dividing each term by 6, we arrive at $4p = 9q + 6$.

5. (D)   Ibragim can already process 65 slides per hour. Each week he increases this total by 2 slides per hour. In w weeks, Ibragim will be able to process $65 + 2w$ slides per hour.

Practice: Absolute Value Equations (page 66)

1. (D)   Set up two equations to solve: $x + 4.3 = 9$ and $x + 4.3 = -9$. Then $x = 4.7$ and $x = -13.3$. Checking both solutions in the original equation, true statements result.

2. (A)   Set up two equations to solve: $x - 2 = 3$ and $x - 2 = -3$. Then $x = 5$ and $x = -1$. Checking both solutions in the original equation, true statements result.

Practice: Creating and Solving Linear Inequalities (page 70)

1. (C)   Begin by adding 8 to both sides. Then $3x < 9$ and by division, $x < 3$.

2. (A)   Subtract 1 from each side and the inequality becomes $-5x > -10$. Remember that dividing by a negative number across the inequality sign reverses the direction of the sign. Then $x < 2$.

3. (C)   Work with all three parts of the compound inequality at the same time. Begin by subtracting 3 and $1 < 2a + 3 < 7$ is $-2 < 2a < 4$. Divide through by 2 to see that $-1 < a < 2$.

Practice: Solving Absolute Value Inequalities (page 73)

1. (A)   Read the solution set from the number line; we are looking for the inequality that yields $-5 < x < 1$. This eliminates answer choices B and D. Then for answer choice A, solve $2x + 4 < 6$, into $2x < 2$, and $x < 1$. Solve $2x + 4 > -6$, $2x > -10$, and $x > -5$. This is the solution graphed.

2. (D)   Read the solution set from the number line; it is $x \le 1$ or $x \ge 3$.

3. (D)   The inequality $|x| < 5$ is the same as $x < 5$ and $x > -5$. This can be written as the compound inequality $-5 < x < 5$.

4. (D)   The inequality $|x + 3| > 6$ is the same as $x + 3 > 6$ or $x + 3 < -6$. Solving each of the inequalities, $x > 3$ or $x < -9$.

SAT-Type Questions (page 74)

1. (B)   Given that $33mn + 10 = 38mn$, subtract $33mn$ from both sides so that $10 = 5mn$ and $mn = 2$. Then $-\frac{3}{2}mn = -\frac{3}{2}(2) = -3$.

2. (A)   Cross multiply so that $\frac{7x + 9n}{5} = x$ becomes $7x + 9n = 5x$. Combine the like terms and $2x = -9n$. Twice $2x = 4x$, so twice $(-9n) = -18n$.

3. (B)   Begin by multiplying each term of $\frac{5x}{3} - \frac{3x}{2} - x = 5$ by the least common denominator of 6 to eliminate the fractions. Then, $2(5x) - 3(3x) - 6x = 6(5)$ and $10x - 9x - 6x = 30$. Solving, $-5x = 30$, and $x = -6$. The value of $x + x^2$ is $(-6) + (-6)^2 = -6 + 36 = 30$.

4. (C) To solve $|-5x - 5| = 45$, we must solve both $-5x - 5 = 45$ and $-5x - 5 = -45$. For $-5x - 5 = 45$, $-5x = 50$, and $x = -10$. For $-5x - 5 = -45$, $-5x = -40$, and $x = 8$. The sum of -10 and 8 is -2.

5. (D) Scan the answer choices. Eliminate B and C as unreasonable. Try choice A; $-x - 6 = 18$ becomes $x = -24$. This is not the solution we are looking for. Quickly check choice D to make sure it is right. Then $|-12 - 6| = |-18| = 18$, and $|24 - 6| = |18| = 18$.

6. (A) Solve each part of the compound inequality. Then $\frac{x}{2} > 2$ is $x > 4$ and $-3(x - 2) > 0$ becomes $-3x + 6 > 0$. Solving for x, $-3x > -6$ leads to $x < 2$.

7. (C) Write the two inequalities: 6 more than x is less than 9 becomes $x + 6 < 9$ and 3 less than x is greater than 7 is $x - 3 > 7$. Now solve each of the inequalities. For $x + 6 < 9$, $x < 3$ and for $x - 3 > 7$, $x > 10$. The solution set is $x < 3$ or $x > 10$. The only answer choice between 3 and 10 is C.

8. (A) Begin by solving $\left|\frac{3}{4}x + 2\right| - 1 > 3$ by isolating the absolute value on the left-hand side of the inequality. Then $\left|\frac{3}{4}x + 2\right| > 4$. Set up and solve two inequalities: $\frac{3}{4}x + 2 > 4$ or $\frac{3}{4}x + 2 < -4$. For $\frac{3}{4}x + 2 > 4$, $\frac{3}{4}x > 2$, and $x > \frac{8}{3}$. For $\frac{3}{4}x + 2 < -4$, $\frac{3}{4}x < -6$ and $x < -8$.

9. (B) There are multiple solution strategies for this problem. The most straightforward is to collect the like terms on each side of the equal sign. Then $\frac{1}{2}k - 4 = -1 + 2k$ is $\frac{1}{2}k - 2k = -1 + 4$. Simplifying, $-\frac{3}{2}k = 3$ and $k = \frac{-3 \cdot 2}{3} = -2$. So $k^{-k} = (-2)^{-(-2)} = (-2)^2 = 4$.

10. (C) Cross multiply $\frac{ax}{w - a} = 1$ so that $ax = w - a$. Rearrange, $ax + a = w$, and then factor out the common term a so $a(x + 1) = w$. Solving for a, $a = \frac{w}{x + 1}$.

11. (C) Solve $\frac{1}{2}b = r$ for b. Then, $b = 2r$. Substitute the values for b and c in $a = bc$. So $a = (2r)(8r)$ and $a = 16r^2$. Solve this equation for r to find that $r^2 = \frac{a}{16}$ and $r = \frac{\sqrt{a}}{4}$.

12. (B) Solve the two inequalities $\frac{1 - 5x}{3} \geq 7$ or $\frac{1 - 5x}{3} \leq -7$. For $\frac{1 - 5x}{3} \geq 7$, cross-multiply and $1 - 5x \leq 21$, $-5x \leq 20$, and $x \geq -4$. Then $\frac{1 - 5x}{3} \leq -7$ is $1 - 5x \leq -21$ and $-5x \leq -22$. So $x \geq 4.4$.

13. (D) You can move through the algebraic manipulations to solve this question, or notice that this problem is of the form $|x| \geq k$. The solution to this type of inequality must be of the form $x \geq k$ or $x \leq -k$. The only possible solution is D.

14. (B) Solve each piece of the inequality to find that $x > -2$ and $x > -4$. Since $x > -2$ is encompassed in the solution set $x > -4$, the solution is B.

15. (A) Immediately eliminate answer choice D as it clearly has a solution. As we scan the other choices, we are looking for an equation where the variables will completely cancel each other and leave us with a false statement. Expanding answer choice A, $2x + 4 = 2x + 8$. If we collect the like terms, the variables will cancel and leave $4 = 8$, which is a false statement.

16. (D) To solve $\left|\dfrac{k}{3} + 6\right| = 4$, we must solve both $\dfrac{k}{3} + 6 = 4$ and $\dfrac{k}{3} + 6 = -4$. Then, for $\dfrac{k}{3} + 6 = 4$, $\dfrac{k}{3} = -2$, and $k = 3(-2) = -6$. For $\dfrac{k}{3} + 6 = -4$, $\dfrac{k}{3} = -10$, and $k = 3(-10) = -30$. The product of $(-6)(-30) = 180$.

17. (D) To find the smaller solution of $\left|18 - \dfrac{x}{4}\right| = 4$, we must solve both $18 - \dfrac{x}{4} = 4$ and $18 - \dfrac{x}{4} = -4$. For $18 - \dfrac{x}{4} = 4$, $-\dfrac{x}{4} = -14$, and $x = 56$. Then, $18 - \dfrac{x}{4} = -4$ becomes $-\dfrac{x}{4} = -22$, and $x = 88$. The smaller solution is 56.

18. (D) Cross-multiply so that $a(1 - x) = x$. Distribute on the left-hand side and $a - ax = x$. Add ax to the right-hand side so that $a = x + ax$. Factor and divide: $a = x(1 + a)$ and $x = \dfrac{a}{a+1}$.

19. (B) Multiply both sides of $\dfrac{x^2}{6} = 4p$ by 6. Then $x^2 = 24p$. Reason that $12p$ is half of $24p$, so $12p = \dfrac{x^2}{2}$.

20. (D) To calculate the positive difference of the solutions, solve $2 + \dfrac{p}{3} = 5$ and $2 + \dfrac{p}{3} = -5$. Then, for $2 + \dfrac{p}{3} = 5$, $\dfrac{p}{3} = 3$, and $p = 9$. For $2 + \dfrac{p}{3} = -5$, $\dfrac{p}{3} = -7$ and $p = -21$. The positive difference is $9 - (-21) = 30$.

21. (A) To solve this problem directly, set up and solve $\dfrac{3 - x}{5} \geq 4$ and $\dfrac{3 - x}{5} \leq -4$. Then $\dfrac{3 - x}{5} \geq 4$ is $3 - x \geq 20$. Subtracting 3 and dividing by -1, $x \leq -17$.

To solve $\dfrac{3 - x}{5} \leq -4$, multiply both sides by 5 and $3 - x \leq -20$. Then $-x \leq -23$ and $x \geq 23$. Since x cannot be less than -17 *and* greater than 23, select answer choice A.

22. (A) Set up the two equations and solve. Then $\dfrac{2}{3}a + 14 < 2$ and $\dfrac{2}{3}a + 14 > -2$.

Solving $\dfrac{2}{3}a + 14 < 2$, $\dfrac{2}{3}a < -12$, and $a < -18$. For $\dfrac{2}{3}a + 14 > -2$, $\dfrac{2}{3}a > -16$, and $a > -24$.

23. (C) For an equation to produce infinitely many solutions, both sides must be completely equal. Quickly scan the choices. Answer choices A and B cannot be made equal. Expand answer choice C and $4x - 10 = 4x - 8 - 2$ becomes $4x - 10 = 4x - 10$. Stop here and choose C.

24. (C) Solve each of the given inequalities. Then $4x \geq -x + 5$ becomes $5x \geq 5$ and $x \geq 1$. You can continue solving, or look at the answer choices and realize the only correct solution is C.

25. (C) Do a bit of manipulation to see that $-x \geq 4$ is really $x \leq -4$. This eliminates answer choices A and B. Then, $2x - 1 \geq 7$ is $2x \geq 8$ and $x \geq 4$.

26. (25) Either by trial and error or from knowledge of perfect cubes, determine that $7^3 = 343$, so $b = 3$. Then $8(3) + 1 = 25$.

27. (6) Multiply the equation by the least common denominator, 6, and

$$6\left(\frac{5m}{2} - 12 = \frac{m}{3} + 1\right) = 15m - 72 = 2m + 6.$$ Collect the like terms and

simplify so that $13m = 78$. Then $m = 6$.

28. (6.4) Begin by distributing 0.25 through the parentheses on the left-hand side. So $0.25(a + 32) = 3.2 + a$ becomes $0.25a + 8 = 3.2 + a$. Collect the like terms and $4.8 = 0.75a$; $a = 6.4$.

29. (34) There are 7 days in a week, so $7w + 3 = 241$ days. Solving for w, $7w = 238$ days and $w = 34$ weeks.

30. (0) Translate the words into algebraic symbols: "When 5 times the number y is added to 14, the result is 4," means $5y + 14 = 4$. The phrase "3 times y is added to 6" translates to $3y + 6$. Solve $5y + 14 = 4$ for y and $5y = -10$, $y = -2$. Then $3y + 6$ becomes $3(-2) + 6 = 0$.

Lesson 3: Linear Functions

Practice: Creating, Evaluating, and Interpreting Linear Functions (page 83)

1. (19) $f(7) = 2(7) + 5 \Rightarrow 14 + 5 = 19$.

2. (5) $f(0) = 2(0) + 5 = 5$.

3. (0) $f(-2.5) = 2(-2.5) + 5 \Rightarrow -5 + 5 = 0$.

4. (B) Each row of flowers contains x plants. Since there are 5 rows of flowers, there are $5x$ flowers in the rectangular array. The four additional flowers are added to $5x$, so the total number of flowers is $f(x) = 5x + 4$.

5. (D) Since n represents the total number of copies sold, $3n$ is the profit made from the book sales. The \$3 represents the profit to the publisher from the sale of each copy. The \$3,000 amount is subtracted from the total profit, so it is the amount of money the company spent preparing the books for sale.

Practice: Slope, Parallel Lines, and Perpendicular Lines (page 90)

1. (B) Examine the graph. The line runs through the points $(-2, 3)$ and $(3, -1)$; use these points in the slope formula. Let (x_1, y_1) be $(-2, 3)$ and let (x_2, y_2) be $(3, -1)$. Then $m = \frac{y_2 - y_1}{x_2 - x_1}$ is $\frac{-1-3}{3-(-2)}$ and $m = -\frac{4}{5}$.

2. (0) Again we will need to use the formula for slope, $m = \frac{y_2 - y_1}{x_2 - x_1}$. Let (x_1, y_1) be $(-3, 4)$ and let (x_2, y_2) be $(4, 4)$. So, $m = \frac{4-4}{4-(-3)}$. You can quickly see that $m = 0$.

3. (0) Here we know the value of the slope and we need to solve for a such that $m = -2$. Let (x_1, y_1) be $(-2, 6)$ and let (x_2, y_2) be $(1, -3a)$ and $\frac{-3a-6}{1-(-2)} = -2$. Then $\frac{-3a-6}{3} = -2$, $-3a - 6 = -6$, and $a = 0$.

4. $\left(\dfrac{4}{3}\right)$ Substitute the given point into the formula for the equation of the line and $m\left(\dfrac{1}{3}\right) + 4(4) = 17$ becomes $m\left(\dfrac{1}{3}\right) = 1$, and $m = 3$. Rearrange the given formula so that $4y = -3x + 17$ and $y = -\dfrac{3}{4}x + \dfrac{17}{4}$. The slope of this line is $-\dfrac{3}{4}$ and the slope of the line perpendicular to it will have a slope that is the negative reciprocal of $-\dfrac{3}{4}$ which is $\dfrac{4}{3}$.

5. (B) You can run the given points through the slope formula or mentally compute the denominator of the slope to be $1 - 1 = 0$. The slope of this line is undefined.

SAT-Type Questions (page 92)

1. (B) Begin by solving the given equation for y to determine the slope. Then, $6y = 4x - 3$ becomes $y = \dfrac{2}{3}x - \dfrac{1}{2}$. The slope of this line is $m = \dfrac{2}{3}$ and the slope of the line perpendicular to this one will have slope $m = -\dfrac{3}{2}$. Examine the answer choices to see which will have this slope. If we divide answer choice B through by 2, we get $y = -\dfrac{3}{2} + \dfrac{k}{2}$.

2. (B) The requested value is $f(-9) - f(0) = 2(-9) + 5 - (2(0) + 5)$. Simplifying, $-18 + 5 - 5 = -18$.

3. (C) When $x = 0$, $f(x) = 1$. This eliminates answer choices B and D. Choose any of the remaining $(x, f(x))$ pairs to test choices A and C. If $x = 1$, answer choice A is $f(1) = -1 + 1 = 0$ which is not equal to -1. The correct choice must be C, but quickly check to make sure: $f(1) = -2(1) + 1 = -2 + 1$ which is -1.

4. (C) The number of miles Isaac drives in h hours is represented by $50h$. Then, $\dfrac{50h}{25}$ is the number of gallons used at the rate of 25 miles per gallon. He had 19 gallons in his tank at the beginning of the trip, so subtract $\dfrac{50h}{25}$ from 19 to find the number of gallons remaining.

5. (A) Parallel lines have the same slope, so begin by determining the slope of the given equation. Divide all the terms by 5 and $y = 5.10x - 21$. The slope is $m = 5.10$ and it is easy to see that answer choice A has the same slope when you divide through by 10.

6. (D) We will need to use the formula for slope, $m = \dfrac{y_2 - y_1}{x_2 - x_1}$. Let (x_1, y_1) be (r, s) and let (x_2, y_2) be $(-s, -r)$. So, $m = \dfrac{-r - s}{-s - r}$. You can quickly see that $m = 1$.

7. (A) Since $h(x) = f(2x - 3)$, $h(4) = f(2 \cdot 4 - 3) = f(5)$. Read the value of $f(5)$ from the given chart and the answer is -2.

8. (B) The variable cost associated with membership depends on the number of people in the family; each costs \$10. Express this as $10p$. Add in the \$30 parking permit and the function is $f(p) = 10p + 30$.

9. (C) Subtract $3x$ from each side so the equation is in slope-intercept form; $y = -3x + 1$. Linear equations with negative slopes run through both quadrants II and IV for sure. There is only one answer choice listing both quadrants II and IV.

10. (B) One way to express the function is $P(x) = \$100 - x\%(100)$. We know that $P(x) = \$80$. Then, $80 = 100 - x\%(100)$. Solving for x, $-20 = -x\%(100)$ and $20 = x\%(100)$. So, $x\% = \dfrac{20}{100} = 20\%$, so that $x = 20$.

11. (D) The opposite sides of the rectangle are parallel and the adjacent sides are perpendicular. Remember that the product of a number and its negative reciprocal is -1. Then, the slope of $\overline{AB}$ times the slope of $\overline{BC} = -1$, and the slope of $\overline{CD}$ times the slope of $\overline{DA}$ is also -1. So, the product of the slopes is $(-1)(-1) = 1$.

12. (A) To break even means to set the function equal to zero. So, $0 = 4x - 80$, $4x = 80$, and $x = 20$.

13. (D) Since $P(x) = 7x - (5x + b)$, $250 = 7(300) - [5(300) + b]$. Solving, we write $250 = 2100 - (1500 + b)$ and $250 = 2100 - 1500 - b$. Thus, $250 = 600 - b$, and $b = 350$.

14. (C) Lines that are perpendicular have negative reciprocal slopes and the product of a number and its negative reciprocal is -1.

15. (D) Consider that 100% of the cost of producing the frame can be represented as the decimal 1.00. Then the cost, C, + 60% of C + 6%(C + 60% of C) is Cilla's income each week. This becomes $1C + 0.60C + 0.06(1C + 0.60C)$. Simplifying, $1.60C + 0.06(1.6C) = 1.60C + 0.096C$ which becomes $1.696C$. Recall that $C = f(n)$ so the income is represented by $1.696f(n)$.

16. (24) Using the given function, $2t(2) - t(2)$ is $2(5 \cdot 2 + 14) - (5 \cdot 2 + 14)$. Simplifying, $2(10 + 14) - (10 + 14)$ becomes $2(24) - 24 = 24$.

17. (9652) Substitute the relevant numbers for $C(t) = p + ant$. Then, $C(3) = 29{,}000 + (\$3.85)(832)(3)$ and $29000 + 9609.60 = \$38{,}609.96$. This is the total cost for the car over the three-year period. Four students are sharing the car, so the cost to each student is $\dfrac{38609.96}{4} = \$9652.40$. Round the answer to the nearest dollar.

18. (3) By definition parallel lines have the same slope. The slope of line n is 3, so the slope of line r must also be $m = 3$.

19. (24) Use the given function and $6 = \dfrac{1}{12}a + 4$. Solving for a, $2 = \dfrac{1}{12}a$, and $a = 24$.

20. (15) Write the linear function that models this context. Let $p =$ the number of premium movies Isla rented during that month and $f(p) = 0.85p + 10.99$. Then, $23.74 = 0.85p + 10.99$. Solving for p, $12.75 = 0.85p$, and $p = 15$.

Lesson 4: Systems of Equations and Systems of Inequalities

Practice: Solving Systems of Linear Equations in Two Variables (page 101)

1. (D) Begin by substituting $2x$ for y in the second equation. Then $x + 2x = 9$, $3x = 9$, and $x = 3$. Now substitute $x = 3$ in the first equation: $y = 2(3) = 6$.

2. (B) Substitute $2x$ for y in the second equation. Then $3x + 2(2x) = 28$, $3x + 4x = 28$, $7x = 28$, and $x = 4$. Substitute $x = 4$ in the first equation so that $y = 2(4) = 8$.

3. (A) The equations have y terms with opposite signs. Add to eliminate y:

$$x + y = 5$$
$$\underline{2x - y = 7}$$
$$3x \quad\;\; = 12 \text{ and } x = 4.$$ Substitute this value into the first equation and $4 + y = 5$, $y = 1$.

4. (D)   The equations have y terms with opposite signs. Add to eliminate y:

$x - 3y = 1$
$\underline{2x + 3y = 20}$
$3x = 21$ and $x = 7$. Substitute this value into the first equation and $7 - 3y = 1$. Then $-3y = -6$ and $y = 2$.

5. (A)   Both equations have 3 as the coefficient for y. Subtracting the first equation from the second eliminates the y-terms and preserves positive numbers. Then,

$4x + 3y = 3$
$\underline{-2x - 3y = -2}$
$2x = 1$ and $x = \dfrac{1}{2}$. Substitute this value into the first equation to see

that $2\left(\dfrac{1}{2}\right) + 3y = 2$, $1 + 3y = 2$, and $3y = 1$. Then $y = \dfrac{1}{3}$.

Practice: Solving Systems of Linear Inequalities in Two Variables (page 105)

1. (D)   Substitute the given ordered pairs into both inequalities stopping when you find an ordered pair that makes both inequalities true. Answer choices A, B, and C fail in at least one inequality. For choice D, $y \geq 2x + 10$, becomes $40 \geq 2(10) + 10$, which is $40 \geq 30$, a true statement. Then, $y \geq 4x$ is $40 \geq 4(10)$ or $40 \geq 40$, which is also true.

2. (C)   You can solve this question in the same manner we solved question #1 or you can graph the inequalities on your graphing calculator. Only choice C is true for both coordinate pairs. Note that this solution strategy would have worked for question #1 as well.

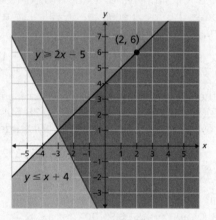

3. (B)   Look at the shading on the graph. The vertical line has shading to the right of $x = 3$, so the inequality that created that graph is $x \geq 3$. This eliminates answer choices A and D. The shading on the other inequality is below the line so the other inequality must be $y \leq -2x$.

4. (C)   Use the first given inequality to determine which xy-coordinate might be the correct answer by summing the coordinates and checking if the sum is less than 3. This eliminates answer choices A and B. Then, for choice C, substitute the coordinates into the second given equation and $x - 3y > 10$ becomes $-0.5 - 3(-5) = -0.5 + 15 > 10$.

5. (D)   In quadrant IV, values of x are positive and values of y are negative. You can verify this by graphing the inequalities on your calculator.

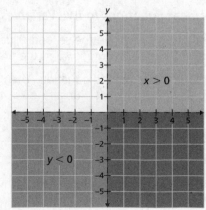

6. (C)   The solution to the given system of inequalities is found by the substitution method. Set the two inequalities equal to each other and solve for x. Then, $x + 1 = -2x - 11$, $3x = -12$, and $x = -4$. Substituting this value into either $x + 1$ or $-2x - 11$, $y = -3$. Since both inequalities include a $\geq$ sign, -3 is the minimum possible value of b. Use your calculator to verify.

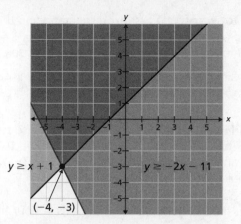

$y \geq x + 1$ $y \geq -2x - 11$

$(-4, -3)$

SAT-Type Questions (page 107)

1. (B)   This system is most easily solved using substitution. Solve $x + 3y = 0$ for x so that $x = -3y$. Then, $2(-3y) + 5y = 3$. Simplifying, $-6y + 5y = 3$ and $y = -3$. There is only one (x, y) coordinate pair with $y = -3$.

2. (A)   Recall from Lesson 3 that we can use point-slope form to write a linear equation. Then the equation of the first line is $y - 7 = 3(x - 1)$. Simplifying a bit, $y = 3x + 4$. Now determine the second equation.

The slope is $m = \dfrac{5-2}{2-(-4)} = \dfrac{1}{2}$. Using point-slope form again, $y - 5 = \dfrac{1}{2}(x - 2)$

and $y = \dfrac{1}{2}x + 4$. Notice that the y-intercepts of both equations are $b = 4$.

The point of intersection must be $(0, 4)$ and $0 + 4 = 4$.

3. (C)   The number of yards of brown cloth required is $2.5x + 6y$. The company has 352 yards of brown cloth, so $2.5x + 6y \leq 352$. You can stop here, since choice C is the only choice that lists this inequality. If you worked with the plastic tubing constraints first, the number of yards of plastic tubing required is $4x + 2y$. The company has 460 yards of plastic tubing, so that inequality is $4x + 2y \leq 460$.

4. (A)   The upper graph has a slope of 1, a y-intercept of 2 and it is a "$y <$" graph. So its inequality is $y < x + 2$. The lower graph has a slope of 1 and a y-intercept of -1. It is a "$y >$" graph so its inequality is $y > x - 1$.

5. (C)   Write a system of equations that models the context. Since $x =$ the larger number and $y =$ the smaller number, $x = y + 4$ and $2x = 3y + 3$. The first equation expresses x in terms of y, so substitute $y + 4$ for x in the second equation. Then, $2(y + 4) = 3y + 3$. Distributing and collecting the like terms, $2y + 8 = 3y + 3$ and $y = 5$. The x-value is $x = 5 + 4 = 9$.

6. (A)   Generate a pair of equations that model the problem. Let $t =$ the price of a pound of tomatoes and let $p =$ the price of a pound of potatoes. Then the system is:

$3t + 5p = 8.80$
$7t + 6p = 15.15$

There is no quick way to solve this system by hand. Use the elimination method and multiply the first equation by -6 and the second equation by 5:

$-18t - 30p = -52.80$
$35t + 30p = 75.75$

Sum the equations to find $17t = 22.95$. Divide both sides by 17 and $t = \$1.35$. Then, $3(1.35) + 5p = 8.80$. Solving for p, $4.05 + 5p = 8.80$, $5p = 4.75$, and $p = \$0.95$. The positive difference between the prices is $t - p = \$0.40$.

7. (B)   Distribute to simplify the first expression and find that $4x + 4 = 2y$. Look at the second equation. If we double it, we find $4x + 4 = 2y$. Both equations are the same so there are an infinite number of solutions.

8. (B)   Create a pair of equations that model the problem:

$2l + 2w = 320$

$l = 3w - 8$

The second equation expresses l in terms of w, so substitute it into the first equation. Then, $2(3w - 8) + 2w = 320$ and $6w - 16 + 2w = 320$. Combine like terms and simplify to find that $8w = 336$, $w = 42$. There is only one answer choice with $w = 42$.

9. (D)   Remember that 45 minutes is the same as $\frac{3}{4}$ hour, so one of the inequalities is $\frac{c}{2} + \frac{3}{4}t \le 8$. The amount of flour required for the cookies is $2c$ and the amount of flour required for tarts is t, which means $2c + t \le 20$.

10. (A)   Simplify the second equation by distributing 6 through the parentheses. Then $6(x + 6) = 4y$ becomes $6x + 36 = 4y$. Consider the first equation. If we double it, we find $6x + 12 = 4y$. The variables in both equations have the same coefficients but their constants are different so there are no solutions.

11. (50) The largest value of $\frac{x}{y}$ will have the greatest numerator and the smallest denominator, so $\frac{0.5}{0.01} = 50$.

12. (10) Solve the system of inequalities as if they were a system of equations. Then $3x - 2 = \frac{3}{2}x + 4$ and, multiplying through by 2, $6x - 4 = 3x + 8$.

Collect the like terms and solve for x to see that $x = 4$. Then, using $y = 3x - 2$, $y = 3(4) - 2 = 10$.

13. (432) Write a system of equations to model this context. Let $x =$ the first number and let $y =$ the second number. Then

$x - y = 24$

$\underline{x + y = 48}$

Clearly, we can solve this system by addition. Then $2x = 72$ and $x = 36$. The variable $y = 48 - 36 = 12$ and the product of these two numbers is $36 \cdot 12 = 432$.

14. (2)   Multiply the second equation by 2 and add to eliminate the variable y. Then,

$$\begin{aligned}4x + y &= 12 \\ \underline{+ (4x - y = \ 4)} \\ 8x \quad\ \ &= 16\end{aligned}$$

Divide both sides by 8 and $x = 2$.

15. (35) Create a system of equations that models this context. Let $x =$ the number of questions on the test worth 2 points and let $y =$ the number of questions on the test worth 3 points. Then,

$x + y = 50$

$2x + 3y = 115$

Manipulate $x + y = 50$ into $y = 50 - x$ and substitute that expression into the second equation. So $2x + 3(50 - x) = 115$. Distribute and collect the like terms so that $2x + 150 - 3x = 115$ and $-x = -35$. Divide by -1 to see that $x = 35$.

Lesson 5: Direct and Inverse Variation

Practice: Direct and Inverse Variation Equations and Computation (page 115)

1. (36) Set up the direct variation as $\dfrac{0.5}{6} = \dfrac{3}{x}$ and then cross-multiply to see that $0.5x = 18$. Divide both sides by 0.5 and $x = 36$.

2. (12) Consider the relationship $y = \dfrac{k}{x}$. Multiplying both sides by x, $xy = k$.

   Extending to this problem, $hb = k$ and $8(9) = k$. This means that $k = 72$. Then $6b = 72$ and $b = 12$.

3. (9.6) Applying the same principle as in question #2, $12(8) = k$ and $k = 96$. Then $10x = 96$ so $x = 9.6$.

4. (13.5) The direct variation proportion is $\dfrac{4}{9} = \dfrac{6}{b}$. Cross-multiply and $4b = 54$ so that $b = 13.5$.

5. (27) Pay close attention to the wording of this problem; x varies directly as the square of y. So, $\dfrac{12}{4^2} = \dfrac{x}{6^2}$, $16x = 12 \cdot 36 = 432$ and $x = \dfrac{432}{16} = 27$.

6. (5) Here we're being asked to find the constant of variation rather than the missing piece of the proportion. Since a varies directly as the square of x, $\dfrac{45}{3^2} = \dfrac{45}{9} = 5$.

SAT-Type Questions (page 117)

1. (B) In direct variation the ratio between the two variables is constant. In choice A, for every 1-unit increase in x, there is a 5-unit increase in y, so it is direct variation. In choice B, for every half unit decrease in A, there is a $\dfrac{1}{2}$-unit decrease in B, except for the pair $1, \dfrac{1}{3}$. Since the ratio is not constant, the table does not represent direct variation.

2. (D) The formula for inverse variation is $y = \dfrac{k}{x} \Rightarrow xy = k$. In this scenario, $k = \$450$ and x and y are represented by r and n, respectively. Then, $rn = 450$.

3. (C) Think this problem through. If 4 workers take 3 hours to complete a job, doubling the amount of workers will halve the amount of time it takes to complete the task. Half of 3 hours is 1.5 hours.

4. (B) This is a direct variation problem, so set up the proportion $\dfrac{4 \text{ essays}}{1.25 \text{ hours}} = \dfrac{100 \text{ essays}}{x}$ and solve for x. Cross-multiply to see that $4x = 100(1.25)$, $4x = 125$, and $x = 31.25$ hours.

5. (C) Remember that inverse variation is represented as $y = \dfrac{k}{x} \Rightarrow xy = k$. Examine the answer choices. Answer C, $xy = 8$, is of this form.

6. (D) In direct variation, the ratio between the two variables is constant. Look at the values in each table. The only table with a constant ratio is D.

7. (C) Set up the direct proportion $\dfrac{44}{30^2} = \dfrac{x}{45^2}$ and solve. Then $x = \dfrac{44(45)^2}{30^2} = 99$ feet.

8. (72.5)   Set up the direct proportion, $\dfrac{50 \text{ kg}}{6 \text{ cm}} = \dfrac{x}{8.7 \text{ cm}}$, and solve. Then $6x = 50(8.7)$ and $x = 72.5$ kg.

9. (2335)   To solve this problem set up the proportion $\dfrac{\$5{,}253}{\left((1.8)^2 \text{ carats}\right)} = \dfrac{x}{\left((1.2)^2 \text{ carats}\right)}$.

Then $1.44(5253) = 3.24x$, $7564.32 = 3.24x$, and $x = \$2{,}334.67$ which becomes $\$2{,}335$ when rounded to the nearest dollar.

10. (0.081)   Set up the direct variation proportion $\dfrac{0.00027 \text{ ohms}}{1 \text{ foot}} = \dfrac{x}{300 \text{ feet}}$ so that $x = 300(0.00027) = 0.081$ ohms.

Lesson 6: Understanding and Interpreting the Algebraic Connections Between Linear Equations and Their Graphical Representations

Practice: The xy-Plane; Distance and Midpoint Formulas (page 122)

1. (5)   Utilize the distance formula. Let $(x_1, y_1) = (1, -1)$ and let $(x_2, y_2) = (4, -5)$.

Then $d = \sqrt{(4-1)^2 + ((-5)-(-1))^2}$ which becomes $\sqrt{3^2 + (-4)^2}$. Simplifying, $\sqrt{9+16} = 5$.

2. (13)   Again, we need to utilize the distance formula. Let $(x_1, y_1) = (-14, -1)$ and let $(x_2, y_2) = (-2, -6)$. Then $d = \sqrt{((-2)-(-14))^2 + ((-6)-(-1))^2}$ which becomes $\sqrt{12^2 + (-5)^2}$. Simplifying, $\sqrt{144+25} = 13$.

3. (B)   Using the midpoint formula, $\left(\dfrac{-4+4}{2}, \dfrac{4+0}{2}\right) = (0, 2)$.

4. (C)   Consider the distance between endpoint A and the midpoint M. Counting up from 1 to 3 is 2 units. Then, two units past 3 is 5, so the x-coordinate is 5. For the y-coordinate, counting down from 3 to 0 is 3 units. Three units smaller than 0 is -3. The endpoint B has coordinates of $(5, -3)$.

Practice: More on Functions; Other Graphical Representations (page 130)

1. (C)   Draw or imagine a vertical line drawn on each of the given graphs. The only answer choice where the vertical line passes through the graph once is C.

2. (B)   Since the whole function, including the y-intercept, is shifting down, the only thing changing about the linear function is the value of b. Therefore, to shift down a units, the equation of h is $h(x) = mx + b - a$.

3. (C)   The graph has a negative slope, so immediately eliminate answer choices A and D. The coordinate of the x-intercept should be of the form $(0, y)$; eliminate answer choice B. The correct choice is C.

4. (C)   Draw or imagine a vertical line drawn on each of the given graphs. The only answer choice where the vertical line passes through the graph more than once is C.

1. (A)   The *x*-coordinate of the midpoint is the average of the *x*-coordinates of the endpoints. Then, $\frac{(-5)+3}{2} = -1$, and since the *y*-coordinates are both –2, the *y*-coordinate of the midpoint is also –2. The midpoint is (–1, –2).

2. (C)   Looking at the graph, the *S*-intercept is (0, 50). Leda is not charging $50 per bracelet because the label on the vertical axis states "Sunk Cost." The number of bracelets sold is given along the horizontal axis, so also eliminate choice B. Answer choice C makes sense with the labeling of the *S*-axis and the title of the graph.

3. (A)   We know the *S*-intercept is (0, 50), so neither of answer choices C or D is correct. Examining the graph, we can use the points (0, 50) and (5, 15) to determine the slope of the graph to be $m = \frac{15-50}{5-0} = -7$. Alternately, we know by its appearance that the slope of this line must be negative, so either way, the correct answer choice is A.

4. (A)   There are a number of ways to solve this problem. Using the given graph, we can see that Leda will begin making a profit shortly after the sale of her 7th bracelet. If she sells 8 more, she will earn about $55. Alternately, we can use the solution to problem #3, and see that $S = 50 - 7(15)$ which is –$55. The equation from question #3 tells us Leda's cost; this solution is negative because it is the amount over her cost and it represents her profit.

5. (B)   Draw in or imagine a vertical line running through each of the given graphs. The vertical line will intersect answer choice B in two places, so B fails the vertical line test and it is not a function.

6. (B)   Utilize the distance formula. Then the distance, *d*, between the two points is $d = \sqrt{(7-4)^2 + (6-2)^2}$. Simplifying, $\sqrt{3^2 + 4^2} = \sqrt{25} = 5$.

7. (D)   One-to-one functions must pass both the vertical and the horizontal line tests. Draw in or imagine a vertical line on each of the given graphs. They all pass the vertical line test. Move to the horizontal line test. Answer choices A, B, and C fail. Only choice D is a one-to-one function.

8. (C)   Quickly calculate the slope of the line segment as $m = \frac{-3-1}{5-1} = -1$.

The slope of the line perpendicular to this will have slope $m = 1$. We don't know which of the endpoints the equation will be perpendicular to, but that's not a problem. Scan the answer choices and find that B and D have the incorrect slope value. Of the remaining choices, A has a *y*-intercept of –2, while the two possible *y*-intercepts for the lines described in the problem are 0 and a value clearly less than –2, as we see from the graph. That eliminates A. Answer choice C is correct.

9. (A)   Consider what you know about linear functions that have negative reciprocal slopes. Function *g* must be perpendicular to function *h*, and the functions will intersect at a point (*x*, *y*). Functions that are perpendicular are not parallel. The only incorrect statement is answer choice A.

10. (B)   Draw in or imagine a vertical line running through each of the given graphs. The vertical line will intersect answer choice B in two places, so it fails the vertical line test and it is not a function.

11. (21)   The midpoint of (1, 2) and (6, 10) is $\left(\dfrac{1+6}{2}, \dfrac{2+10}{2}\right) = \left(\dfrac{7}{2}, 6\right)$.

Multiplying, $\dfrac{7}{2} \cdot 6 = 21$.

12. (9)   The difference between the x-coordinates of the midpoint, (2, −5), and the given endpoint, (−5, 2), is 7. Adding 7 to the x-coordinate of the midpoint will yield the x-coordinate of the other endpoint.

13. ($1.2 < y < 1.5$)   The slope from point A to point B is $m = \dfrac{y-0}{1-(-2)}$, which simplifies to $\dfrac{y}{3}$.

Then $0.4 < \dfrac{y}{3} < 0.5$ and, multiplying all terms by 3, we find $1.2 < y < 1.5$.

Any value in this range is an acceptable answer.

Summary SAT-Type Test

Multiple Choice (page 139)

Calculator Allowed

1. (B)   There are a couple of ways to solve this problem. The simplest is to use the

slope formula, $\dfrac{y_2 - y_1}{y_2 - x_1}$, so that $\dfrac{3-y}{2-5} = -\dfrac{7}{6}$. Simplify and cross-multiply to find that $6(3 - y) = -7(-3)$, which becomes $18 - 6y = 21$. Solve for y and find that $-6y = 3$, $y = -0.5$. Alternately, you can determine the equation of the line defined by the given point and slope and then substitute in (5, y) to solve for y.

2. (D)   Use mathematical logic to solve this problem. Since $\dfrac{a}{b} > 1$, a and b must have the same sign and $|a| > |b|$. Because $|a| > |b|$, we know the fraction $\dfrac{b}{a}$ must be less than 1.

3. (D)   Begin solving $|-n - 2| + 3 = 2$. Subtracting 3 from both sides to isolate the absolute value yields $|-n - 2| = -1$. Remember that the absolute value of a number cannot be negative. Thus there is no value of n that makes this statement true.

4. (C)   Quickly plot the given points. The possible points for (k, 4) are (1, 4), (2, 4), (3, 4), or (4, 4). Notice that if you plot (3, 4), the graph will fail the vertical line test at $x = 3$. Hence, the correct choice C, $k = 3$.

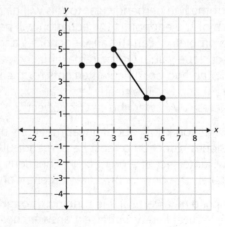

5. (C)   Let c = the number of child desserts sold and let a = the number of adult desserts sold. The system $a + c = 160$ and $3c + 6a = 816$ is a system that represents this situation. This system can be solved many different ways. If you solve the first equation for c, then $c = 160 - a$. Substitute this value into the second equation becomes $6a + 3(160 - a) = 816$. Distribute and simplify to see that $6a + 480 - 3a = 816$ and $3a = 336$. Divide through by 3 and $a = 112$ desserts.

6. (B) Rewrite the second inequality as $2x - b < y$. Then we can write the compound inequality $2x - b < y < 2x - a$ and simplify it to $2x - b < 2x - a$. Now subtract $2x$ from each side and $-b < -a$. This is not one of the answer choices, so multiply both sides by -1, changing the signs and reversing the inequality. This results in $b > a$.

7. (D) We can substitute in each of the given values or mentally sum and square the coordinates of each of the given ordered pairs. For choices A through C, the coordinates sum to 3 or -3 and either of these sums squared is 9. The sum of 1 and -5 is -4, $(-4)^2 = 16$ and $16 > 11$.

8. (D) Substitute in $\dfrac{1}{3}$ for x so that $\dfrac{1}{x} + \dfrac{1}{x-1}$ becomes $\dfrac{1}{\frac{1}{3}} + \dfrac{1}{\frac{1}{3}-1}$. Simplifying,

$3 + \dfrac{1}{-\frac{2}{3}}$ is $3 - \dfrac{3}{2} = 1.5$.

9. (C) Since $\dfrac{1}{4}x + \dfrac{1}{5}y = 3$, we can multiply each term by 20 because that is the least common multiple of 4 and 5, so $5x + 4y = 60$. Notice that the left-hand side of this equation has the same value as the numerator of the fraction. Then by substitution, $\dfrac{5x + 4y}{12} = \dfrac{60}{12} = 5$.

10. (A) We can represent the weight of x boxes each weighing 30 pounds as $30x$. The weight of y boxes each weighing 55 pounds is $55y$. The combined weight of the boxes is $30x + 55y$, which must be $\leq 2{,}000$. The total number of boxes is $x + y$, which must be ≤ 60.

11. (C) Since $6x = 14$, $x = \dfrac{14}{6} = \dfrac{7}{3}$. The value of $9x^2$ is $9 \cdot \left(\dfrac{7}{3}\right)^2 = \cancel{9} \cdot \left(\dfrac{49}{\cancel{9}}\right) = 49$.

12. (B) Simplify $4x - y = 2y + 8$ into $4x - 3y = 8$. Manipulate $x + 6y = 5$ into $y = \left(\dfrac{5 - x}{6}\right)$. Then $4x - 3\left(\dfrac{5 - x}{6}\right) = 8$, which simplifies to $4x - \cancel{3}\left(\dfrac{5 - x}{\cancel{6}^2}\right) = 8$

and $8x - 5 + x = 16$. Collect the like terms and

$9x = 21$, $x = \dfrac{21}{9} = \dfrac{7}{3}$.

13. (B) The total income is the initial \$10,000 plus m months at \$1,000, which can be represented as $1{,}000m$. The phrase "at least" translates as the symbol $\geq$ (greater than or equal to). Putting it all together, the inequality is $10{,}000 + 1{,}000m \geq 25{,}000$.

14. (A) Since Bobby is now b years old, he was x years old $(b - x)$ years ago. If Adrian is a years old now, she was $a - (b - x)$ years old exactly $(b - x)$ years ago. Thus, the solution is $a - (b - x)$, which simplifies to $a - b + x$.

15. (D) Use your calculator to graph the inequalities and find no solution to either inequality in quadrant IV. The overlapping sectors for the graphs can be seen in each of the remaining quadrants.

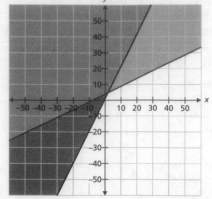

16. (A) For a line to exist only in quadrants II and III, it must be parallel to the y-axis. Lines that are parallel to the y-axis have undefined slopes. The slope of l is therefore undefined.

17. (C) Let $z = 2$. Then for the choices A, B, and D, the expression is greater than 0. For choice C, however, the expression becomes $|2 - 1| - 1 = 0$. Alternately, reason that whatever the value of the absolute value for choices A, B, and D, adding one will result in an expression > 0. If the absolute value of the expression in choice C is equal to 1, this expression will have a value of zero.

18. (C) Determine the slope of line a using the given points $(1, 4)$ and $(2, 7)$.

Then the slope m is $\dfrac{4-7}{1-2} = \dfrac{-3}{-1} = 3$. Use the point-slope formula to find

the equation: $y - 4 = 3(x - 1)$. Simplifying, $y = 3x + 1$.

19. (B) Translate the words into equations: $n = 2a - 18$ and $a = n + 3$. Substitute the second equation into the first and $n = 2(n + 3) - 18$. Solving for n, $n = 2n + 6 - 18$ and $-n = -12$ which becomes $n = 12$.

20. (B) Create a system of equations using the given points and the equation. Then $5 = 2a(1) + b$ and $11 = 2a(3) + b$. Simplifying, $5 = 2a + b$ and $11 = 6a + b$. Now subtract and

$$11 = 6a + b$$
$$\underline{-5 = -2a - b}$$
$6 = 4a$ and $a = \dfrac{6}{4} = \dfrac{3}{2}$. Substitute $\dfrac{3}{2}$ for a in $5 = 2a + b$ and we have

$5 = \cancel{2}\left(\dfrac{3}{\cancel{2}}\right) + b$ so that $b = 2$. Since $a = \dfrac{3}{2}$ and $b = 2$, $ab = \left(\dfrac{3}{\cancel{2}}\right) \cdot \cancel{2} = 3$.

21. (C) Either b_e or b_a can be the larger value as long as the positive difference between the two values is less than or equal to 12.

22. (B) Let m = the length of the string and let f = the frequency in hertz. Then since the relation is an inverse relation, $m_1 \cdot f_1 = m_2 \cdot f_2$, $m \cdot 78 = 6 \cdot 117$,

becomes $m = \dfrac{6(117)}{78}$, which simplifies to 9 inches.

23. (C) Solving $ar^n - rx = 0$ for x yields $ar^n = rx$ and $x = \dfrac{ar^n}{r}$.

24. (A) Examine the answer choices. Notice that none of them include the

variable t, so solve $V = gt$ for t which is $t = \dfrac{V}{g}$. Substitute this into the other

given equation so that $S = \dfrac{1}{2} \cdot \dfrac{g}{1} \cdot \left(\dfrac{V}{g}\right)^2$. Simplify $S = \dfrac{1}{2} \cdot \dfrac{\cancel{g}}{1} \cdot \dfrac{V^2}{g^{\cancel{2}1}}$ which is $\dfrac{V^2}{2g}$.

25. (C) Translate the words into a mathematical equation. $I \cdot d^2 = k$,

and $I = \dfrac{k}{d^2}$.

26. (A)   Consider point A and the midpoint. To move from $x = 6$ to $x = 2$, we need to subtract 4. Subtract 4 again to find the x-coordinate of point B. Then $x = -2$. To move from $y = -6$ to $y = -1$, we add 5. Add 5 again and $y = 4$. The coordinates of B are $(-2, 4)$.

27. (B)   Solve $2x - \dfrac{15x}{2} = -11$ for x. So $4x - 15x = -22$, and $-11x = -22$. Thus $x = 2$. Substitute $x = 2$ into $y = \dfrac{-3x}{2}$, so $y = \dfrac{-3(2)}{2} = -3$. The sum $2x + y = 2(2) + -3 = 1$.

28. (C)   Solving $3x + y = 5$ for y, we have $y = -3x + 5$ and the slope of this line is -3. Since $y = mx + b$ is perpendicular to $3x + y = 5$, the slope we are looking for is the negative reciprocal of -3, so $m = \dfrac{1}{3}$.

29. (D)   Find the value of y in the system of equalities:

$y = -10x + 2000$

$y = 40x$

Then $40x = -10x + 2000$, $50x = 2000$, and $x = 40$. Substitute this value into one of the equalities; $y = 40(40) = 1{,}600$. Since the given system shows $\leq$, the maximum value is 1,600.

30. (D)   The graph has a positive slope, so immediately eliminate answer choices B and C. Choice A has an incorrect y-intercept.

Student-Produced Response Questions (page 145)

Calculator Allowed

31. (10)   Look at the structure of the given equations and add both:

$2x + y = -3$

$\underline{x + 2y = 18}$

$3x + 3y = 15$

Divide through by 3 to find $x + y = 5$; now multiply by 2 and $2x + 2y = 10$.

32. (1.25)   Consider that 12 people working for 5 hours is $12 \cdot 5 = 60$ work hours. If 4 more people were hired, those 60 hours would be divided among 16 people rather than 12 people. So $\dfrac{60}{16}$ is 3.75 hours for the same job to be completed. Be careful! The question asks for how much less time, so subtract 3.75 from 5 to arrive at 1.25 hours less.

33. $(6.75 < x < 10)$ Examine the given inequality and the expression we are asked to solve. Notice that $9x - 6 = -3(-3x + 2)$ so multiply the entire inequality by -3. Then $-\dfrac{10}{3} < -3x + 2 < -\dfrac{9}{4}$ becomes $-3\left(-\dfrac{10}{3} < -3x + 2 < -\dfrac{9}{4}\right)$, which is $10 > 9x - 6 > \dfrac{27}{4}$. The solution to this question is any value between 6.75 and 10.

34. (2 or 3)   If Olja walks 8 dogs per morning, it will take her $\dfrac{24}{8} = 3$ mornings to walk 24 dogs. If she walks 12 dogs per morning, it will take her $\dfrac{24}{12} = 2$ mornings to walk 24 dogs. Either 2 or 3 is a correct answer for this question.

35. $\left(\dfrac{8}{5}\right)$

Use the endpoints of the line segment to determine its slope. Then $m = \dfrac{6-1}{0-8} = -\dfrac{5}{8}$. The slope of the line perpendicular to this segment, regardless of the point it runs through, will be the negative reciprocal of $-\dfrac{5}{8}$ which is $\dfrac{8}{5}$.

36. (1)

By substitution, $\dfrac{\frac{1}{4}}{\left(\frac{1}{3}\right)^2} = \dfrac{\frac{9}{4}}{x^2}$ so that, after cross-multiplying,

$\dfrac{1}{4}(x^2) = \left(\dfrac{1}{3}\right)^2 \cdot \dfrac{9}{4}$. Simplifying, $\dfrac{x^2}{4} = \dfrac{1}{\cancel{9}} \cdot \dfrac{\cancel{9}}{4}$ which is $\dfrac{x^2}{4} = \dfrac{1}{4}$ and $4x^2 = 4$, $x^2 = 1$ and $x = \pm 1$. The problem asks for the positive value, so grid in 1 on your bubble sheet.

37. (9)

Let x be the number of videos each cousin downloads. Melanija's fee is $10.50 + 3.50x$ dollars; Nassim's fee is $25.00 + 2.00x$. For Melanija's expenses to be less than Nassim's, the following inequality must be true: $10.50 + 3.50x < 25.00 + 2.00x$. Solving for x, $1.5x < 14.5$, divide both sides by 1.5 and find that $x < 9.\overline{6}$. The greatest integer value of x is 9.

38. (10)

Again, let x be the number of videos each cousin downloads. During June, Melanija's fee is $5.25 + 3.50x$ dollars. Nassim's fee is $25.00 + 2.00(x - 2)$ dollars. This simplifies to $25 + 2x - 4 = 21 + 2x$. Set Melanij'a fee less than Nassim's and solve. Then $5.25 + 3.5x < 21 + 2x$ becomes $1.5x < 15.75$. Divide and find $x < 10.5$. The greatest integer value of x is 10.

Summary SAT-Type Test

Multiple Choice (page 149)

No Calculator Allowed

1. (D)

Since $6 - x > 0$ then $6 > x$ and $5x + 2 > -8$ becomes $5x > -10$, and $x > -2$. Thus, $-2 < x < 6$. The only listed value that is not in this range is -2.

2. (D)

The only example of an equation that is not a direct variation is $xy = k$, which is an example of an inverse variation.

3. (B)

You can use the slope formula to solve this problem. A point lying on the line must have coordinates that obey the rule $\dfrac{y - (-1)}{x - 0} = \dfrac{y + 1}{x} = \dfrac{1}{3}$. Substitute the given points to determine that only choice B produces a true statement: $\dfrac{1 + 1}{6} = \dfrac{2}{6} = \dfrac{1}{3}$.

4. (D)

Translate the words, "a number n such that one-third of its square root is 3," into an algebraic sentence: $\dfrac{1}{3}\sqrt{n} = 3$. Examine the answer choices. We need to solve for n. Multiply both sides by 3 and $\sqrt{n} = 9$. Finish by squaring both sides and $n = 81$.

5. (B)

Choose values in the solution set and substitute them into I, II, and III to see which produce true statements. If $x = 4$, $4^2 > 3$ is true. The absolute value of 4 is also larger than 3, as is 4^3. If $x = -4$, $4^2 > 3$ is still true and $|-4| > 3$. But $(-4)^3 = -64$, which is not greater than 3. Only statements I and II are true.

6. (D) Recognize that this is a linear equation with y-intercept 28 and slope $m = -4$. Since h is the number of hours Dr. Jeffrey has worked, the coefficient -4 tells us that Dr. Jeffrey sees 4 patients each hour. As a side note, the y-intercept 28 means that Dr. Jeffrey sees 28 patients per day.

7. (C) Represent the amount Rita earns as $8r$ dollars and the amount Carlos earns as $6c$ dollars. Sum the terms to find the amount they earned together: $8r + 6c$ dollars.

8. (A) Since the system has no solution, the lines are parallel. Begin by solving for y in $\frac{1}{4}x - \frac{1}{2}y = 8$. Multiply through by 4 to eliminate the fractions and $x - 2y = 32$. Then $-2y = -x + 32$ and $y = \frac{1}{2}x - 16$. The slope of this equation is $\frac{1}{2}$. Solve the equation $ax - 3y = 10$ for y to find $y = \frac{ax}{3} - \frac{10}{3}$. Now set the slopes equal to each other and solve for a. So $\frac{a}{3} = \frac{1}{2}$, $2a = 3$ and $a = \frac{3}{2}$.

9. (D) Use the values in the table to determine the slope of each relation. The slope of (a) is $\frac{6-4}{-3-0} = \frac{2}{-3}$, so $m_a = -\frac{2}{3}$. The slope of (b) is $\frac{2-1}{5-6} = \frac{1}{-1} = -1$, so $m_b = -1$. The product $m_a \cdot m_b = -\frac{2}{3} \cdot (-1) = \frac{2}{3}$.

10. (C) In this problem $x^2y = k$, so we can substitute any of the given coordinate points for x and y to determine the value of k. Then using $(2, 3)$, we have $2^2(3) = k$ and $12 = k$. Using the same equation, $x^2y = k$, and the point $(6, n)$, we have $6^2(n) = 12$ which becomes $36n = 12$. Dividing by 36, we have $n = \frac{12}{36} = \frac{1}{3}$.

11. (A) Imagine or draw a vertical line through each of the graphs. The vertical line will intersect graph A in two places, so it fails the vertical line test and it is not a representation of a function.

12. (A) Begin by simplifying the numerators of each fraction. Then $\frac{4(k+3)-5}{6} = \frac{12-(3-k)}{9}$ becomes $\frac{4k+12-5}{6} = \frac{12-3+k}{9}$ and $\frac{4k+7}{6} = \frac{9+k}{9}$. Now cross-multiply so that $6(9 + k) = 9(4k + 7)$. Distribute and collect the like terms: $54 + 6k = 36k + 63$ and $30k = -9$. Divide both sides by 30 and simplify the resulting fraction. Then $k = -\frac{9}{30} = -\frac{3}{10}$.

13. (C) Pay close attention to the wording of the question. A 4.6-mile trip will cost the same as a 5-mile trip. A 2.8-mile trip will cost the same as a 3-mile trip. You can either substitute $m = 5$ and then $m = 3$ into the given equation and then subtract the resulting cost, C, or you can reason that the difference in cost is $(5 - 3)(2.5) = 2(2.5) = \$5.00$, since the equation tells you that the cost per mile is $2.50.

14. (A)   Collect all the y-terms on the left-hand side of the equation so that $3x - y = y + 8$ becomes $3x - 2y = 8$. Solve $x + 4y = 5$ for x and $x = 5 - 4y$. Substitute this expression into the first equation for x and $3(5 - 4y) - 2y = 8$. Distribute, collect like the terms, and solve for y: $15 - 12y - 2y = 8$, $15 - 14y = 8$, $-14y = -7$, $y = \dfrac{1}{2}$. Then $x = 5 - 4\left(\dfrac{1}{2}\right) = 3$. The product $xy = \dfrac{1}{2}(3) = 1.5$.

15. (B)   Set up the direct variation $\dfrac{x}{2n+1} = \dfrac{6}{2(4)+1}$, which becomes $\dfrac{x}{2n+1} = \dfrac{2}{3}$.

To determine the value of n when $x = 18$, solve $\dfrac{18}{2n+1} = \dfrac{2}{3}$. Cross-multiply and find that $2(2n + 1) = 54$. Distributing, $4n + 2 = 54$, $4n = 52$, and $n = 13$.

Student-Produced Response Questions (page 153)

No Calculator Allowed

16. (48)   Notice the structure of the equation and the expression. Take the given equation and multiply through by 6. Then $\dfrac{1}{3}x + \dfrac{1}{2}y = 8$ becomes $2x + 3y = 48$.

17. (Any of the values 4, 12, 20, 28, 36, 44, 52, or 60)   Represent the income from the number of cookie plates sold as $5c$ and the income from the number of brownie plates sold as $8b$. Then $5c + 8b = 500$. We know that $b \geq 25$. If $b = 25$, then $5c + 8(25) = 500$ becomes $5c = 300$, and $c = 60$ cookie plates. If $b = 30$, then $5c + 8(30) = 500$ yields $c = 52$ cookie plates. Following the pattern, if $b = 35$, $c = 44$. Generalize the pattern that is emerging. If n = the total number of cookie plates sold, then the solution set is described by the inequality $4 + 8n \leq 60$. Note that if b is not a multiple of 5, the number of cookie plates yielded is fractional. We cannot sell a fraction of a cookie plate.

18. (3)   Subtract the first equation from the second:

$$4x + y = 5$$
$$\underline{-(x + y = -4)}$$
$$3x = 9$$

Divide both sides by 3 and find $x = 3$.

19. (4.5)   Use the coordinates of R (3, 1) and M (5, 5) to find the slope of the diagonal connecting the points.

Then the slope m is $\dfrac{1-5}{3-5} = \dfrac{-4}{-2} = 2$.

Now use the point-slope formula to determine the equation of the diagonal: $y - 5 = 2(x - 5)$. Simplifying, $y - 5 = 2x - 10$ and $y = 2x - 5$. Substitute in the coordinates $(x, 4)$ and $4 = 2x - 5$, $9 = 2x$, and $x = 4.5$.

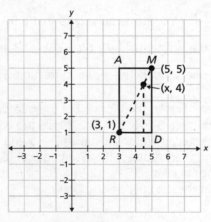

20. (10)   Substitute the given points into the distance formula and completely simplify. Then $d = \sqrt{(x_2 - x_1)^2 + (y_2 - y_1)^2} = \sqrt{(5+3)^2 + (-2-4)^2} = \sqrt{8^2 + 6^2} = \sqrt{64 + 36} = \sqrt{100} = 10$.

Category 2: Problem Solving and Data Analysis

Lesson 1: Solving Problems Using Ratios, Proportions, and Percent

Practice: Ratio and Proportion (page 160)

1. (C) $\dfrac{a}{b} = \dfrac{3}{4}$ and $\dfrac{c}{b} = \dfrac{9}{10}$. Invert the second proportion: $\dfrac{b}{c} = \dfrac{10}{9}$. Then

           $\dfrac{a}{b} \cdot \dfrac{b}{c} = \dfrac{3}{4} \cdot \dfrac{10}{9}$ and $\dfrac{a}{c} = \dfrac{5}{6}$.

2. (C)   In any proportion, the product of the means = the product of the extremes. $y{:}7 = 5{:}3$ tells you $(7)(5) = (y)(3)$. Look at the answers to find one where the same product pairs appear. Choice C works. The means here are y and 3. The extremes are 5 and 7.

3. (C) $\dfrac{3x}{5} = \dfrac{6y}{4}$ Cross-multiply. $12x = 30y$. To get the expression $\dfrac{x}{y}$ on the left,

           divide both sides by $12y$. $\dfrac{12x}{12y} = \dfrac{30y}{12y} = \dfrac{30}{12} = \dfrac{5}{2}$. So $\dfrac{x}{y} = \dfrac{5}{2}$.

4. (A) $\dfrac{7}{3} = \dfrac{R}{1}$ $\left(\text{since both fractions} = \dfrac{1}{m}\right)$. Flip both fractions. $\dfrac{3}{7} = \dfrac{1}{R}$.

5. (D) $\dfrac{7}{10} = \dfrac{b}{1}$ $\left(\text{since both fractions} = \dfrac{1}{a}\right)$. Flip both fractions. $\dfrac{10}{7} = \dfrac{1}{b}$.

6. (A)   If s stickers can be bought for c cents, $100s$ stickers can be bought for

           c dollars. Set up a proportion. $\dfrac{100s}{c \text{ dollars}} = \dfrac{x \text{ stickers}}{d \text{ dollars}}$. Cross-multiply.

           $cx = 100sd$. Divide both sides by c: $\dfrac{cx}{c} = \dfrac{100sd}{c}$ or $x = \dfrac{100sd}{c}$.

Practice: Percents I (page 162)

1. 63	4. 24	7. 150%	10. 18
2. 18%	5. 35%	8. 4,000	11. 1.6
3. 350	6. 160	9. 250	12. 2%

Practice: Percents II (page 164)

1. (D)   For this problem you could set up a proportion: $\dfrac{8}{100} = \dfrac{8}{N}$. Immediately you

           see $N = 100$. Alternately, you could use an equation: $8 = 0.08N$. $N = \dfrac{8}{0.08}$.

           Use a calculator to find that $N = 100$, or multiply both the numerator and denominator by 100, making an easy division problem.

           $\dfrac{8(100)}{(0.08)(100)} = \dfrac{800}{8} = 100$

2. (B)   20% of the 60 girls $= 0.20 \cdot 60 = 12$. 40% of the 30 boys $= 0.40 \cdot 30 = 12$. So, 24 campers out of 90 campers passed the ropes course test.

           $\dfrac{24}{90} = 0.26\overline{6} = 26\dfrac{2}{3}\%$

3. (C)   Substitute in values. For example, if Gohar has \$90, then Jasmyn must have \$120. The difference is \$30. The task is now to find out what percent

           30 is of 120. So, $\dfrac{30}{120} = \dfrac{1}{4} = 25\%$.

4. (B)   Rewrite 150% of J as $1\frac{1}{2}J = \frac{1}{2}K$. You might notice here that K is 3 times

as large as J. If not rewrite again as $\frac{3}{2}J = \frac{1}{2}K$. Multiply both sides of the

equation by 2 to clear the denominator, and then $3J = K$. Divide both

sides by $3K$. Thus, $\frac{3J}{3K} = \frac{K}{3K}$, or $\frac{J}{K} = \frac{1}{3}$.

5. (A)   <u>Method 1:</u> 30% of the males attended the game. 30% of 50% of the
students are males who attended. $(0.30)(0.50) = (0.15) = 15\%$.

<u>Method 2:</u> Just substitute in a friendly number of students. For example,
if there are 100 students, then 50% of the students, or 50 students, are
male. 30% of the 50 males, or $(0.30)(0.50) = 15$ male students attended
the game. 15 is 15% of 100.

Practice: Percents III (page 172)

1. (28%)   Begin by finding the difference between the new stock price and the old
stock price. Then divide that difference by the stock price and multiply the

quotient by 100 to convert it to a percent: $100\left(\frac{18 - 25}{25}\right) = -28\%$ equals

28% decrease.

2. ($71.20)   Find 20% of $89. Subtract the discount from the original price:
$89 - (89 \cdot 0.20) = \$71.20$. Alternately, consider that the person buying
a coat at a 20% discount is paying 80% of the original price. You could
multiply the original price by 0.80 to find the discount price directly:
$89 \cdot 0.80 = \$71.20$

3. (100%)   To find the percentage increase, determine the difference between the
price the Pollitts paid for their home and the price they sold it for. Divide
that difference by the price the Pollitts paid and multiply the quotient by

100 to convert it to a percent: $100\left(\frac{340000 - 170000}{170000}\right) = 100\%$.

4. ($81)   Use the formula $I = Prt$. Remember that 6 months is half a year. Then,
$I = (2700)(0.06)(0.5) = \$81$.

5. ($30)   If the sale price of $25.50 represents 15% off the original price, then it is
85% of the original price. Set up a proportion to solve for the missing

original price: $\frac{85}{100} = \frac{25.50}{x}$. Cross-multiply to find $85x = 2550$ and

divide to see that $x = \$30$.

SAT-Type Questions (page 173)

1. (A)   This is a percent change problem. Begin by determining how much weight
Raven has lost: $120 - 110 = 10$ pounds. Divide this difference by Raven's
starting weight and multiply by 100 to make the answer a percent:
$100(10 \div 120) = 8.3\%$, so answer A is correct.

2. (C)   Solve this problem proportionally: $\frac{1.78}{1} = \frac{w}{3}$. Then, $w = 5.3$, which is
answer choice C.

3. (B)   We aren't given Berko's hourly wage, so choose a number that is easy to
work with. Let's say he makes $10/hour; then, 36 hours of work yields
$360 and 40 hours of work yields $360 + 4(10 + 5) = \$420$. Berko earns
$60 extra dollars when working 40 hours. Calculate his percent increase:

$100(60 \div 360) = 16.667 = 16\frac{2}{3}\%$.

4. (B) Notice that the U.S. flag ratio is 10:19 and that 10 is a little more than half of 19. The flag for Honduras is a 1:2 ratio, which is exactly half and closer to the U.S. flag ratio than the other answer choices.

5. (D) Let A = Andrew's hourly wage, B = Bob's hourly wage, and C = Chuck's hourly wage. Then, $\dfrac{A}{B} = \dfrac{2}{3}$, $\dfrac{B}{C} = \dfrac{9}{4}$, and $\dfrac{A}{\cancel{B}} \cdot \dfrac{\cancel{B}}{C} = \dfrac{A}{C} = \dfrac{3}{2}$. But we know that Andrew worked twice as many hours as Bob, so $\dfrac{2A}{C} = \dfrac{\cancel{2} \cdot 3}{\cancel{2}} = \dfrac{3}{1}$. Then $\dfrac{3}{1} = \dfrac{600}{x}$ and $x = \$200$.

6. (D) Mental math tells you that $72 is the cost of the comic book plus 20%. Remember, though, that the dealer wants to offer his customers a discount of 10% on the item, so the marked cost must be more than $72. Thus, you can eliminate choices A and B. Try choice D since it is a whole dollar amount. Subtracting 10% from $80 leaves you with $72, which is 20% over cost. There is no need to calculate with answer C; the correct answer is D.

7. (15) Meike purchased a $10 item that was not included with his 20% off coupon, and he purchased $28.75 of merchandise that can be reduced by 20%. Thus, Meike purchased $38.75 of supplies without the discount. Calculate 20% off $28.75: $(0.20)(28.75) = \$5.75$. This is the difference between the amount Meike would have paid and the amount he did pay. Use the percent change formula to determine the percent saved on all the supplies: $100\left(\dfrac{5.75}{38.75}\right) = 14.838$. Round to the nearest whole percent, which is 15%.

8. (1544) First, determine the amount of interest that Unice will pay using the $I = Prt$ formula: $I = (2400)(0.06)(1) = \$144$. Add the interest to the principal amount to determine the total amount Unice will owe on her loan: $2400 + 144 = \$2,544$. But she paid off $1,000 during the year, so subtract that from her balance: $2544 - 1000 = \$1,544$. This is the amount Unice will pay at the end of the year.

9. (90) Determine the cost of the watch with the discount: $(120)(0.90) = \$108$. This price allows the merchant a 20% profit, so to find the cost of the watch, divide 108 by 1.20, which represents the wholesale cost of the watch plus the 20%. Then, $108 \div 1.20 = \$90$.

10. (28) Assume Selena will be successful after x additional shots. Then $(x + 4) = 0.6(x + 15)$. Distributing through the parentheses, $x + 4 = 0.6x + 9$. Simplifying: $0.4x = 5$, and $x = \dfrac{5}{0.4} = 12.5$. Selena needs at least 13 additional shots and has already attempted 15. Sum $13 + 15 = 28$.

Lesson 2: Solving Measurement, Unit Rate, and Density Problems

Practice: Measurement & Scale Drawings (page 180)

1. (C) There are 12 inches in 1 foot, so $3 \cdot 12 = 36$.

2. (B) There are 3 feet in 1 yard, and from the previous problem, you know there are 36 inches in 3 feet. Thus, $10 \cdot 36 = 360$.

3. (A) Since there are 3 feet in 1 yard, then there are 3^2 feet^2 in 1^2 yard^2.

So, $\dfrac{45 \; \cancel{\text{feet}^2}}{1} \cdot \dfrac{1 \; \text{yard}^2}{9 \; \cancel{\text{feet}^2}} = 5 \; \text{yards}^2$.

4. (2.93)   Use the conversions chart on page 177 to assist you.

$$\frac{2 \text{ miles}}{1 \text{ hour}} \cdot \frac{5280 \text{ feet}}{1 \text{ mile}} \cdot \frac{1 \text{ hour}}{60 \text{ minutes}} \cdot \frac{1 \text{ minute}}{60 \text{ seconds}} = 2.93 \text{ feet per second.}$$

5. (B)   The problem information is given in feet and yards, but the answers are given in inches and feet. You know that 1 yard is 36 inches, so

$$\frac{1440 \text{ feet}}{1 \text{ yard}} = \frac{1440 \text{ feet}}{36 \text{ inches}} = \frac{40 \text{ feet}}{1 \text{ inch}}.$$

Practice: Unit Rates (page 183)

1. (4)   If Lugus can walk 6 km in 3 hours, he can walk $6 \div 3 = 2$ km in 1 hour. Then, $8 \div 2 = 4$ hours.

2. (12.5)   A rate of 10 books in 5 weeks is 2 books per week. Divide 25 by 2 to find that it will take Michael 12.5 weeks to read 25 books.

3. (D)   A rate of $15 for 4 people is $15 \div 4 = \$3.75$ per person. Multiply the rate by the number of people to find that it will cost $37.50.

4. (C)   Divide the population by the land area to find the smallest population density.

Practice: Density (page 184)

1. (B) $\text{Density} = \dfrac{\text{mass}}{\text{volume}} = \dfrac{306 \text{ grams}}{22.5 \text{ mL}} = 13.6 \text{ g/mL.}$

2. (D)   Using the density formula, set up a proportion to solve for the missing

mass: $\dfrac{0.789}{1} = \dfrac{m}{200.0}$. Cross-multiply to find that $m = 157.8$ grams.

SAT-Type Questions (page 185)

1. (D)   Begin by converting the length of the actual playground from yards to

feet. There are 3 feet in 1 yard, so $\dfrac{50 \text{ yards}}{1} \cdot \dfrac{3 \text{ feet}}{1 \text{ yard}} = 150$ feet. The

model has a scale factor of 1 inch = 10 feet. Use this to convert the actual

playground to the scale model: $\dfrac{150 \text{ feet}}{1} \cdot \dfrac{1 \text{ inch}}{10 \text{ feet}} = \dfrac{150}{10} = 15$ inches.

2. (D)   Change pounds to ounces. $2\dfrac{1}{2} \cdot 16 = 40$ ounces. $40 \cdot \$5.50 = \$220$.

3. (B)   Find the volume of the lead cube by solving $6^3 = 216$ cm^3. Then, use

a proportion to find the cube's mass: $\dfrac{11.39 \text{ grams}}{1 \text{ cm}^3} = \dfrac{x \text{ grams}}{216 \text{ cm}^3}$.

Cross-multiply and divide to find that $x = 11.39 \cdot 216 = 2460.24$ grams.

4. (A)   10% of the 500-liter tank is 50 liters. 50 liters $\div 1,000 = 0.050$ kiloliters. The rate of flow is thus 0.050 kiloliters per minute. Since there are 60 minutes in an hour, the rate of flow is $0.050 \cdot 60$ kiloliters per hour, or 3 kiloliters per hour.

5. (D)   Juanita makes 10 centerpieces in 15 minutes, or 10 centerpieces in $\dfrac{1}{4}$ hour.

$$\frac{10 \text{ centerpieces}}{\frac{1}{4} \text{ hour}} = \frac{960 \text{ centerpieces}}{x \text{ hours}}, \text{ and } x = \frac{\frac{1}{4} \cdot 960}{10} = \frac{240}{10} = 24.$$

6. (D)   Population density = $\dfrac{\text{Total Population}}{\text{Land Area}}$. Divide each population by its

corresponding land area to find that Malta has the lowest population density.

7. (B)   6 ft. = 6 · 12 in. = 72 in. Carl is 72 + 4 = 76 inches tall. $\dfrac{3}{4} \cdot (76 \text{ inches}) =$

57 inches. The difference in heights is 76 − 57 = 19 inches = 1 ft. 7 in.

8. (A)   Since density is measured in grams per cubic centimeter, it is best to start

by finding the volume in cubic centimeters: $\dfrac{0.00373 \text{ g}}{1 \text{ cm}^3} = \dfrac{9 \times 10^2}{x \text{ cm}^3}$.

Cross-multiply and divide. Find that x is approximately 241286.
Since 1 cm = 0.01 meters, 1 cm^3 = (0.01)^3 m^3. Then 241,286 · 0.01^3
is 0.241286, or 2.413 · 10^{-1} m^3.

9. (C)   In a regular 8-hour shift they would pave 1.5 × 5,280 feet or 7,920 feet.

However, they worked 2 hours, or $\dfrac{1}{4}$ of their shift. $\dfrac{1}{4} \times \dfrac{7,920}{1} = 1{,}980$ feet.

10. (A)   The formula for the volume of the cylinder is $V = Bh$. Use this

to solve for the height of the cylinder: $h = \dfrac{V}{B} = \dfrac{240\pi}{60\pi} = 4$. Then,

height is a linear measure and volume is a cubic measure, so

$\dfrac{(\text{height of the model})^3}{(\text{height of the structure})^3} = \dfrac{\text{volume of the model}}{\text{volume of the structure}}$. Expressing the height

of the model as 1 foot and putting in the numbers, $\dfrac{1^3}{4^3} = \dfrac{x}{240\pi}$.

Cross-multiply and divide to find that $x = \dfrac{1^3 \cdot 240\pi}{4^3} = 3.75\pi$ ft^3.

11. (19)   Each 4-inch layer of bricks except the last must be covered in a one-inch
layer of cement, making a 5-inch layer. The final layer is a 4-inch layer
of bricks. Seven feet 10 inches = 7 · 12 + 10 inches = 84 + 10 inches =
94 inches. The number of 5-inch brick-cement layers is the integer
quotient of 94 ÷ 5, or 18. The remainder is 4 inches, just enough for
the 19th layer of bricks only.

12. (4)   Add the waste from each table:

3 quarts	1 pint
4 quarts	
2 quarts	
3 quarts	1 pint
12 quarts	2 pints, or 13 quarts.

$\dfrac{13 \text{ quarts}}{4 \text{ quarts}} = 3$ gallons (3 containers) and 1 quart remaining (1 more container).

Alyssa would need at least 4 containers.

Lesson 3: Describing and Interpreting Scatterplots

SAT-Type Questions (page 196)

1. (B) The data is linear with a negative slope, and the *y*-intercept is positive. The only equation fitting these criteria is $y = -2x + 5$, choice B.

2. (A) Scatterplots are not meant as exact predictions, so the statement given in answer choice A is invalid.

3. (D) The graph does not mimic linear behavior, eliminating choice A and choice B. The graph is not a precise predictor, eliminating choice C, so choice D describes the scatterplot.

4. (D) As is true for all lines, a line of best fit has a constant slope, choice D.

5. (D) Choose consecutive data points that are easy to read and compare rates of growth. The ratios of consecutive month sales values are not constant and are increasing. This is characteristic of quadratic growth.

6. (C) Find approximate ratios of successive pairs of values: $\frac{27}{9} = 3$, $\frac{9}{3} = 3$, $\frac{3}{1} = 3$.

   You see that the ratios are constant and the values are decreasing. Thus, the behavior is exponential decline, choice C.

7. (2) Reading from the graph, there were two people whose height was more than 10 cm taller than predicted by the line of best fit.

8. (85) Predict from the line of best fit. The expected score for a student who studies for 4 hours is 85.

Lesson 4: Comparing Linear Growth with Exponential Growth

SAT-Type Questions (page 209)

1. (D) The given function is linear as are all the graphs. Additionally, the *y*-intercept of the given function is −1, and all the graphs except choice B have this *y*-intercept value. Thus, we need to look at the slope of the line to help determine the correct answer. The slope is positive, increasing from the lower left to the upper right. Only A and D have this feature. In option A, the graph crosses the *x*-axis at $x = 1$, so check to see if the function has $(1, 0)$ as a solution: $f(1) = 0.5(1) - 1 = 0.5 - 1 = -0.5$. The function does not produce the needed solution, so the correct answer must be choice D.

2. (C) Option 1 is an example of exponential growth. For any number *n* of baskets, the payment is $0.01(2)^{n-1}$. Then for $n = 15$, $0.01(2)^{14} = \$163.84$.

3. (B) Option 2 is linear growth. Flavio does not receive additional salary for the first 4 baskets he picks. He receives \$10 for each of the remaining 11 baskets and \$10 for agreeing to work, so $11 \cdot \$10 + \$10 = 12 \cdot \$10 = \$120$.

4. (D) The values of $f(x)$ are decreasing, so the answer is either B or D. Check to see if the behavior is linear or exponential. The *x*-values shown are equally spaced. The differences between their corresponding $f(x)$ values are not the same, so the behavior is not linear. You could stop here and choose choice D. To check, look at the ratios of dependent variable values for pairs of independent variable values differing by 5.7 units.

   Then, $\frac{f(5.7)}{f(0)} = \frac{50}{100} = \frac{1}{2}$, $\frac{f(11.4)}{f(5.7)} = \frac{25}{50} = \frac{1}{2}$. Stop here. Choose choice D.

5. (D)   The ratios of successive balances over equal intervals of time are constant, showing exponential growth.

6. (B)   By quick inspection, the function is not linear, so test answer choices A and B.

A. $f(x) = 3^x - 4 \rightarrow f(4) = 3^4 - 4 = 77 \neq 17$, so choice A fails.

B. $f(x) = 2^x + 1 \rightarrow f(4) = 2^4 + 1 = 17$ and $f(6) = 2^6 + 1 = 65$.

Choice B works.

7. (C)   The graphs are not identical, so the heights of both plants were not the same throughout the study. Eliminate choice A. At the end of 4 weeks, the height of both plants was the same. Eliminate choice B. For the second 4 weeks, $\frac{y_2 - y_1}{x_2 - x_1}$ is greater for Plant A for any (x_1, x_2) interval shown. Choice C is correct. You should stop here. Since the rate of growth from time 0 to time 4 is the same for both plants, choice D is not correct.

8. (B)   At the measurement for hour 2, the bacteria in Dish 1 covered 4 cm² and the bacteria in Dish 2 covered 10 cm². Quickly note that 4 is 40% of 10.

9. (C)   The given function is exponential in form, so eliminate answer choices A and B. The function we are looking for is increasing, so the answer must be choice C.

10. (57)   Since each row's number is 6 more than the prior row, this pattern is linear growth and the rate of change, or slope, is 6. To find a $y = mx + b$ equation to fit the pattern, substitute into the general formula to find b. Choose any row. If you choose row 1, $3 = 6(1) + b$ and $b - 3 - 6 - -3$. Thus, the formula is $y = 6x - 3$. Use this formula to solve for the number of beads in row 10: $6(10) - 3 = 57$.

11. (512)   Since each day's bonus is double the previous day's, the pattern is exponential. As the table shows, the bonus for the nth day is 2^{n-1}. The bonus for the 10th day is $2^9 = \$512$.

Lesson 5: Summarizing Categorical Data and Relative Frequencies; Calculating Conditional Probability

SAT-Type Questions (page 224)

1. (C)   Start the problem by completing the table.

	Historical Fiction	Mystery	Fantasy	Total
Female	$88 - 50 = 38$	40	42	120
Male	50	25	$47 - 42 = 5$	$200 - 120 = 80$
Total	88	$40 + 25 = 65$	47	$88 + 65 + 47 = 200$

The marginal relative frequency for fantasy preference is $\frac{47}{200}$, so eliminate choice A. The marginal relative frequency for males is $\frac{80}{200} = \frac{2}{5}$.

This is choice C.

2. (B)   Start the problem by completing the table.

	In School Band	Not in School Band	Total
On Math Team	40	20	40 + 20 = 60
Not on Math Team	10	80	10 + 80 = 90
Total	40 + 10 = 50	20 + 80 = 100	100 + 50 = 150

The relative frequency of math team members is $\frac{60}{150} = 0.40$. The row

conditional probabilities for math team are $\frac{40}{60}$ (in school band) and

$\frac{20}{60}$ (not in school band), which are significantly different. Math team

membership and school band membership are associated.

3. (C)   Quick mental math tells you that passing the assessment is associated with use of the review sheet for this teacher's students. The marginal frequency of students not using the review sheet is 22.

4. (B)   A quick check shows that the categorical variables are independent,

since $\frac{24}{60} = 0.40$, and $\frac{50}{125} = 0.40$. Therefore, decisions about bag choice

are not dependent on purchase of pet food. This limits the correct answer

choices to B or D. The conditional probability for shoppers buying pet food

using disposable bags is $\frac{36}{60} = 0.60$, and the conditional relative frequency

for shoppers not buying pet food using disposable bags is $\frac{75}{125} = 0.60$.

Stop here; answer choice B is correct.

5. (D)   Find the marginal frequency for females who want more days of street cleaning, and then subtract the joint frequency for females who want fewer days of street cleaning. Fully reduce the resulting answer.

$\frac{140}{300} - \frac{60}{300} = \frac{80}{300} = \frac{8}{30} = \frac{4}{15}$.

6. (A)   Complete the table, calculating the "Start 1 hour later/Did not have an after school job" cell first.

	Keep start time	Start 1 hour later	Total
Had an after- school job	150 − 30 = 120	350 − 270 = 80	200
Did not have an after-school job	30	300 − 30 = 270	300
Total	500 − 350 = 150	350	200 + 300 = 500

Mental math tells you the categorical variables are associated. If you compare the first two columns, you see that among students wanting to keep the current start time, the majority had an after-school job. Among the students wanting to start an hour later, the majority did not have an after-school job. Thus, the only possible answer choices are A or C. The conditional relative frequency for students having a job after school who want to start school one hour later is $\frac{80}{200} = \frac{2}{5}$. This is answer choice A.

7. (A)   Start the problem by completing the table.

	Brown Eyes	Blue Eyes	Total
Over 65 Inches	$100 - 80 = 20$	4	24
65 Inches or Shorter	80	$20 - 4 = 16$	$80 + 16 = 96$
Total	$120 - 20 = 100$	20	$24 + 96 = 120$

Check row or column conditional relative frequencies. Brown eyes and over 65 inches: $\frac{20}{100} = 0.20$. Blue eyes and over 65 inches: $\frac{4}{20} = 0.20$. Since the row/column conditional relative frequencies are equal, the categories are independent, choice A.

8. (B)   Gender and sports preference are independent as $\frac{45}{60}$ and $\frac{60}{80}$ are both equal to 0.75. So, fact # 2 is correct and answer choices A and C are eliminated. Check fact #3 next. The conditional relative frequency for boys to prefer relay races is $\frac{20}{80}$, or 0.25. Fact # 3 is correct. Do not check fact #4 since there is no choice selecting 3 facts.

9. (C)   Percents are as follows: grade 9: $\frac{82}{250} = 32.8\%$. Grade 10: don't waste time computing; if you compare the raw numbers ffor grade 10 to the raw numbers for grade 9, you see that the numerator is smaller and the denominator is larger. So, you know the percentage for grade 9 is larger than the percentage for grade 10. Then, grade 11 is $\frac{95}{240} \approx 40\%$. The percentage for grade 12 is clearly smaller than grade 11, so don't bother to calculate.

10. (A)   Mental math will tell you that the variables are associated. If you compare the first two columns, you will see that among patients wanting weekend hours, the majority were males. Among the patients wanting weekday evening hours, the majority were females. This eliminates answer choices B and D. Then, the marginal probability for weekend preference is $\frac{200}{350} \approx 0.57$. Choice A matches both of these facts.

11. (150)   Read this information directly from the table.

12. (60)   Read this information directly from the table.

13. $\left(\frac{1}{2} \text{ or } 0.50\right)$ $\frac{60}{120} = \frac{1}{2}$ or 0.50.

14. $\left(\frac{1}{4} \text{ or } 0.25\right)$ $\frac{75}{300} = \frac{1}{4}$ or 0.25.

Lesson 6: Working with Measures of Center and Spread

Practice: Measures of Spread (page 237)

1. (A) Call the unknown fraction x. Then, the three fractions are $\frac{5}{12}$, $\frac{1}{2} = \frac{6}{12}$, and x. Since the mean and median are the same number, the difference between the first number and the median $\left(\frac{1}{12}\right)$ is the same as the difference between the median and the missing number. Then, $\frac{6}{12} + \frac{1}{12} = \frac{7}{12}$.

2. (B) The graph for New York, NY, shows skewed data. Spread of skewed data cannot be measured using standard deviation.

3. (C) $[(2m + 3) + (3m - 1) + (7m - 5)] \div 3 = (12m - 3) \div 3 = 4m - 1$

4. (D) Standard deviation is only appropriate for data symmetric about the mean.

5. (C) Given that the circle graph shows 100% of the boys on the sports teams, we can assume there are 100 athletes. Then, $25(70) + 30(72) + 25(71) + 20(71) = 7105$. Divide the sum by the number of boys on the teams: $7105 \div 100 = 71.05$.

6. (B) The range is $4 - 0 = 4$.

7. (B) The number of data values is $4 + 3 + 5 + 1 + 1 = 14$. The median is the average of the 7th and 8th values: $(1 + 2) \div 2 = 1.5$.

SAT-Type Questions (page 241)

1. (A) The number of test scores is not given. Make a small, easy-to-handle set. For example, assume the old set is 73, 73, and 73. Then, adding a score of 75 to the set will raise the mean score.

2. (B) The sum of A and B is $2(10) = 20$. The sum of X, Y, and Z is $3(20) = 60$. The sum of A, B, X, Y, and Z is $20 + 60 = 80$. The average is sum $\div$ number $= 80 \div 5 = 16$.

3. (D) Range is measured differently than standard deviation. We have no information about size or range or mean. A smaller standard deviation implies less variation.

4. (D) The sum of the first 15 scores is $15(70) = 1050$. The sum of the set of 16 scores is $16(71) = 1136$. The last score was $1136 - 1050 = 86$.

5. (C) The sum of the four integers is $4(12) = 48$. Consider the integers less than the largest integer. Their smallest sum is $2 + 4 + 6 = 12$. Then, the largest integer could only be $48 - 12 = 36$.

6. (A) The sum of the 5 test scores is $5(85) = 425$. The sum of the 3 known scores is $80 + 78 + 91 = 249$. Subtract the two sums to find the sum of the remaining 2 scores: $425 - 249 = 176$. Then, the mean is $176 \div 2 = 88$.

7. (B) Let B = Baby Bear's weight. Then, Papa Bear's weight is $7B + 20$. We know their average weight is 330 pounds, so $\frac{B + 7B + 20 + 330}{3} = 330$ and $8B + 350 = 990$. Solving for B, $B = \frac{990 - 350}{8}$ and $B = 80$ pounds. This is Baby Bear's weight. Papa Bear weighs $7(80) + 20 = 580$ pounds.

8. (B)   Since the mean and the median are the same value in set A, the data is symmetric. The data in set B is right skewed. The mean will have a more pronounced change than the median.

9. (C)   Start by converting the largest and the smallest values in the data set to inches. $5'7'' = 5 \cdot 12 + 7 = 67$ inches and $4'10'' = 4 \cdot 12 + 10 = 58$ inches. Subtract the two values: $67 - 58 = 9$.

10. (C)   There are 100 values in the data set, and the data is approximately normal. The middle value is between $5'2''$ and $5'3''$. Counting down 32 data values gets us to $5'1''$. Counting up 32 data values gets us to $5'4''$.

11. (80)   To determine the median, find the total number of students in the class. Add the frequencies for each bar.

$$4 + 8 + 6 + 10 + 3 = 31 \text{ students}$$

The middle student is the 16th student, who can be found in the bar that represents those who received a grade of 80. Thus, the median is 80.

12. (80)   Before Nia took the test, there were 13 scores and the median score was 80 (the 7th test score). After Nia took the test, there were 14 scores, but the median did not change. So, the median, still 80, was then the mean of the 7th test score and the 8th test score. Nia's score must also be 80, so listing the scores in size order would leave the original 80 in the 7th position and place Nia's 80 in the 8th position.

13. (550)   The average number of stamps bought in the first four years is $\frac{300 + 250 + 400 + 150}{4} = 275$. If the average for all 6 years is also 275, the sum of all the stamps purchased is $6(275) = 1,650$ and the number bought in the last two years is $1,650 - 1,100 = 550$.

14. (53)   The average of three scores is twice the median equals $2(12) = 24$. Thus, the sum of the scores is $3(24) = 72$. The lowest score is 7 and the middle score (median) is 12, so the highest score is $72 - (7 + 12) = 72 - 19 = 53$.

15. (94)   The sum of the first 8 scores is $8 \cdot 85 = 680$. The sum of the scores including Valentino's is $9 \cdot 86 = 774$. Subtract the two sums to find Valentino's score: $774 - 680 = 94$.

Lesson 7: Making Inferences About Population Parameters Based on Sample Data

SAT-Type Questions (page 250)

1. (C)   Statistics is the study of numerical data.

2. (A)   Answer choice A is the only choice showing a 90% confidence level. To be sure the other information is correct, calculating 75% with a 5% margin of error gets the prediction to between 70% and 80% of the population.

3. (C)   The confidence level is 90%, so eliminate answer choices B and D. Three-quarters is 75%, so calculating $75\% \pm 4\%$ gives us $75 - 4 = 71\%$ to $75 + 4 = 79\%$. This is answer choice C.

4. (C)   A lower confidence level results in a lower margin of error.

5. (A)   An increased sample size, with all other factors being the same will decrease the confidence interval.

6. (C)   An increased sample size, with all other factors being the same will decrease the margin of error.

7. (D)   The larger the sample size, the smaller the margin of error, if all other
          factors are the same.

8. (B)   If he picked the biggest packs of books, the sample size would be bigger
          and the margin of error would be smaller.

Lesson 8: Data Collection, Justifying Conclusions, and Making Inferences

Practice: Analyzing Data Collection Methods (page 255)

1. (B)   The researchers gathered their data from pre-existing groups; this is an
          observational study.

2. (B)   By definition, the purpose of sampling is to choose a fair representation
          of a group a researcher wishes to study.

3. (D)   The high school principal used a systematic random sample method to
          choose his participants, and the parents/guardians of all students in the
          school had an equal chance of being selected. This means his sample was
          large, unbiased, and represented the entire population. This is answer
          choice D.

4. (D)   Because all the members of the population were surveyed, the athletic
          director conducted a census.

Practice: Justifying Conclusions (page 257)

1. (D)   Clearly, tenth grade students do not represent the entire town population,
          so eliminate choice A. If you only ask women, men are excluded. Eliminate
          choice B. Going to the beach is a leisure activity and not one in which
          everyone may participate, so answer choice D is the best selection.

2. (B)   Cell phone use being linked to lung cancer might indicate a lurking
          variable of using the phone on smoking breaks, so answer choice A is not
          correct. The age of a respondent could be a lurking variable in linking ice
          cream flavors to grade in school. An increase in your life span has nothing
          to do with the number of cars in your household. Answer choice B is
          correct.

3. (C)   Answer choices A and B lack anonymity. Customers are more likely to give
          a favorable review of food when speaking to the chef, and employees are
          more likely to give a positive review of their job when talking to their boss.
          Answer choice D does not provide all the information about the tax and is
          printed on biased letterhead.

SAT-Type Questions (page 261)

1. (C)   Sample data is not a precise copy of population data. Choice C reflects a
          comparison evident in the chart.

2. (B)   Although the actual quantities of white catfish and pirate perch are not
          known, the data tells us the quantities are similar.

3. (B)   Larger samples produce more accurate results.

4. (B)   Since 300 students requested the earlier start, 500 requested the change
          to a later start. $\frac{500}{800} = 0.625$, and then $0.625(3600) = 2,250$.

5. (1000) The chart shows that 6 out of the 40 respondents exercise for periods of
          at least 30 minutes, at least 5 days each week. $\frac{8}{40} \cdot 5000 = 1,000$.

6. (270)   Of the 30 families responding, 3, or 10% said they would buy chocolate chip cookies. Assume 10% of the entire population of 2,700 would buy chocolate chip cookies. So, 10% of 2,700 = 270.

7. (9450)   From the 30 families surveyed, 60 boxes would be purchased. Thus, 30 families would spend $30 \cdot \$3.50 = \$105$. Set up a proportion to find out the money earned from the entire population based on the sample:

$\dfrac{30}{2,700} = \dfrac{\$105}{x}$. Cross-multiply and divide to find that $x = (105 \cdot 2,700) \div 30 = \$9,450$.

Summary SAT-Type Test

Multiple Choice (page 265)

1. (D)   Use mental math to eliminate Pennsylvania and Connecticut. Then,

New York $= \dfrac{20114}{31094} = 0.6469$, which is approximately 65% and

Rhode Island $= \dfrac{8004}{11735} = 0.6821$, which is approximately 68%. Rhode Island has the largest percentage.

2. (B)   They are independent because the conditional frequencies, column by column, are nearly the same.

3. (C)   The description tells you the behavior is exponential growth because the ratio of populations (2) for each pair of consecutive equal time intervals (of 20 years) is constant. The y-intercept is 20 because the initial population at time 0 is 20.

4. (B)   This study does not require manipulation of treatment plans, so eliminate experiment. An observation or intuition would lead to researcher inference. A survey would lead to the best data.

5. (C)   Start by finding the actual width of the room. Set up a proportion:

$\dfrac{5}{44} = \dfrac{3}{x}$, then cross-multiply and divide to find that $x = \dfrac{3 \cdot 44}{5} = 26.4$ ft,

and the actual area of the living room is $44 \cdot 26.4 = 1161.6$ ft². No answer matches. Notice the unit labeling of the answer choices and change the unit from ft² to yd². Divide the area of the living room measured in square feet by $3 \cdot 3$ or 9 square feet in one square yard and $1161.6 \div 9 = 129.0\overline{6}$ yd².

6. (C)   Since 2 standard deviations covers about 47.5% above and 47.5% below the mean, and 70 is 2 standard deviations above the mean, choice C is correct.

7. (B)   Increasing the sample size reduces the margin of error.

8. (A)   Although not strong, there is a negative linear correlation between the time these 40 students spent playing video games and their midterm grades.

9. (C)   Set up a proportion: $\dfrac{\$1.16}{1\,\text{Euro}} = \dfrac{x\,\text{dollars}}{43.45\,\text{Euros}}$. Cross-multiply to solve for the unknown $x = 1.16 \cdot 43.45 = \$50.402$. Finally, divide the total by 4 to find the cost for each friend: $50.402 \div 4 = \$12.6005$. Round to the nearest penny.

10. (D) Set up a proportion where the missing height is

$$x: \frac{38 \text{ grams}}{1 \text{ cm}^3} = \frac{456 \text{ grams}}{3 \text{ cm} \cdot 2 \text{ cm} \cdot x \text{ cm}}. \text{ Simplify: } \frac{38 \text{ grams}}{1 \text{ cm}^3} = \frac{456 \text{ grams}}{6x \text{ cm}^3}.$$

Then, cross-multiply and divide to find that $228x = 456$ and $x = 2$ cm.

11. (B) The function $g(t)$ models exponential decay where 500 mg is the initial weight of the bacteria, and 0.5 tells us the amount of bacteria is cut in half for every unit of time.

12. (B) The successive pairs of independent variable values are decreasing at a constant ratio, showing exponential decay.

13. (C) Since 95% of normally distributed data lies within 2 standard deviations of the mean, choice C is correct.

14. (B) This model fits the definition of systematic random sample, where members are chosen according to a rule.

15. (C) There are four data points above the line of best fit.

16. (D) The marginal frequency for travel is 10, and the total is 123. Remember that the relative marginal frequency is $\dfrac{\text{marginal frequency}}{\text{total}} = \dfrac{10}{123}$.

17. (C) Since three-quarters is the same as 75% and the margin of error is 4%, the confidence interval is from $(75 - 4)\%$ to $(75 + 4)\%$, or 71% to 79%. We are told the confidence level is 95%.

18. (B) Charlie donated 10% of $150, or $15. He spent $20 on a CD and $2 \cdot \$20 = \$40$ on his brother. He still had $\$150 - \$15 - \$20 - \$40 = \$75$. He saved $\dfrac{\$75}{3} = \$25$. The ratio of savings to donations is $25:15 = 5:3$.

19. (D) The population for this study is all the eligible voters in the town.

20. (C) The mode is 75, the score with the highest frequency. Since there are 28 scores, the median is the mean of the 14th and 15th scores, which are 80 and 85. The mean of 80 and 85 is 82.5.

21. (A) The only choice that shows symmetry about a minimum or maximum value is choice A.

22. (A) Of the 195 women surveyed, 45 selected football. So, $\dfrac{45}{195} = \dfrac{3}{13}$.

23. (C) Two positive standard deviations from the mean covers about 47.5% of the data, and 150 is 2 standard deviations from the mean, 120.

24. (C) Use the sample to calculate the sample proportion of students taking the bus in the morning: $\dfrac{15}{60}$, or 25%. Then, 25% of 800 = 200.

25. (B) Set up a proportion to find the number of weeks needed to collect 1,200 cans: $\dfrac{560 \text{ cans}}{4 \text{ weeks}} = \dfrac{1,200 \text{ cans}}{x \text{ weeks}}$. Cross-multiply and divide to find that $x = 8.6$ weeks. Therefore, $8.6 - 4 = 4.6$ additional weeks are needed for 1,200 cans and, using the answer choices, 5 weeks are needed for more than 1,200 cans.

26. (A)   Note that the given rate is in words per minute, but the answers are expressed in words per hour. Then, $\dfrac{x \text{ words}}{m \text{ minutes}} \cdot \dfrac{60 \text{ minutes}}{1 \text{ hour}} = \dfrac{\frac{60x}{m} \text{ words}}{1 \text{ hour}}$ or $\dfrac{60x}{m}$ words per hour. Now, find the number of hours it will take to read y words. We'll call that number of hours h. So, $\dfrac{\frac{60x}{m} \text{ words}}{1 \text{ hour}} = \dfrac{y \text{ words}}{h \text{ hours}}$. Cross-multiply to solve for y: $\dfrac{60xh}{m} = y$, then multiply both sides by $\dfrac{m}{60x}$ to solve for h: $h = \dfrac{ym}{60x}$.

27. (B)   The graph we are looking for is exponential, not linear, so eliminate answer choices A and D. Look at the y-intercept. Only answer choice B has an intercept of $\dfrac{3}{2}$.

28. (B)   The number of boys not choosing Romance is $3 + 6 = 9$. Since there are 12 boys, $\dfrac{9}{12} = \dfrac{3}{4}$.

29. (C)   The 30th score is the median and it is 6.

30. (A)   The margin of error extends the possible proportion from $\dfrac{118}{250}$, or 47.2%, to 47.2% + 4% or 51.2%.

Student-Produced Response Questions (page 274)

31. $\left(\dfrac{3}{8} \text{ or } .375\right)$ Start by completing the table.

	Rocky Road	Peanut Brittle	Mocha Fudge	Mint Chip	Total
Male	5	5	6	4	20
Female	3	8	0	1	12
Total	8	13	6	5	32

We are given that the student likes Rocky Road, so that marginal frequency is 8. The number of females in this group choosing Rocky Road is 3. Then, $\dfrac{3}{8} = 0.375$.

32. (600)   Since 5 students out of the 25 asked requested tennis more than 1 day per week, the proportion is: $\dfrac{5}{25} = \dfrac{1}{5}$. Then, $\dfrac{1}{5}$ of 3,000 = 600.

33. (243)   The pattern shows a constant ratio of $\left(\dfrac{3}{1}\right)$ from term to term. So, $\dfrac{x}{81} = \dfrac{3}{1}$. Cross-multiply and divide to find that $x = 3 \cdot 81 = 243$.

34. (153)   First, find the volume of 15 grams of benzene: $\dfrac{0.8786\text{ grams}}{1\text{ cm}^3} = \dfrac{15\text{ grams}}{x\text{ cm}^3}$,

and $x = 15 \div 0.8786 = 17.07$ cm³. Now, find out the mass of copper that

can fit in 17.07 cm³: $\dfrac{8.96\text{ g}}{1\text{ cm}^3} = \dfrac{x\text{ g}}{17.07\text{ cm}^3}$. Cross-multiply and divide to

find that $x = 8.96 \cdot 17.07 = 152.9$ g. Round your answer to 153.

35. (32)   Kohen's compensation increases exponentially, doubling with every
10 papers. For the first 10, he earns $0.50(2)^{1-1} = 0.50(2)^0 = \$0.50$. For the
second 10 papers, he earns $0.50(2)^{2-1} = 0.50(2)^1 = \$1.00$. Generalize this
pattern: for $10n$ papers, he earns $0.50(2)^{n-1}$. Thus, for 70 papers, he will
earn $0.50(2)^{7-1} = 0.50(2)^6 = \$32$.

36. (8)   Counting the dots above the line of best fit, there is 1 dot for each of ages
1, 4, 5, 6, 7, and 8, and 2 dots above the line for age 3.

37. PART 1

  (96)   We need to convert the gallons-per-minute measurement into cubic

feet per hour: $\dfrac{12\ \cancel{\text{gallons}}}{1\ \cancel{\text{minute}}} \times \dfrac{1\text{ ft}^3}{7.48\ \cancel{\text{gallons}}} \times \dfrac{60\ \cancel{\text{minutes}}}{1\text{ hour}} = 96.3\text{ ft}^3/\text{hour}.$

Rounded to the nearest cubic foot, the answer is 96.

37. PART 2

  (4)   To complete this part of the problem, determine how many gallons
Mr. Bourne will drain each hour with a setting of 90 ft³ per hour.

$\dfrac{90\ \cancel{\text{ft}^3}}{1\text{ hour}} \cdot \dfrac{7.48\text{ gallons}}{1\ \cancel{\text{ft}^3}} = 673.2$ gallons/hour. Now determine how many

hours are needed to fully drain the pool: $\dfrac{15{,}000\text{ gallons}}{x} = \dfrac{673.2\text{ gallons}}{1\text{ hour}}$

and $x = 22.28$ hours. But Mr. Bourne can only run the drainage pump
for 6 hours each day, so divide the 22.28 hours by 6 and round up.

Category 3: Passport to Advanced Math

Lesson 1: Creating Equivalent Expressions Involving Rational Exponents and Radicals

Practice: Integer Exponents and Rules for Operations (page 284)

1. (D)   Use the rule for changing an expression with a negative exponent to a unit fraction. Then, $2^{-3} = \dfrac{1}{2^3} = \dfrac{1}{8}$ and $2^{-2} = \dfrac{1}{2^2} = \dfrac{1}{4}$. Finish the problem by summing the fractions: $\dfrac{1}{8} + \dfrac{1}{4} = \dfrac{1}{8} + \dfrac{2}{8} = \dfrac{3}{8}$.

2. (C)   Use the rule for multiplication of like bases with different exponents: $3^3 \cdot 3^2 = 3^{3+2} = 3^5 = 243$.

3. (B)   Use the rule for addition, which states that the powers must be simplified before adding. So, $4^2 + 4^3 = 16 + 64 = 80$.

4. (C)   Begin by carrying the exponent outside the parentheses in both the numerator and the denominator to the respective parts. Then, $\dfrac{\left(-9a^2b^2\right)^2}{\left(3a^3b\right)^3} = \dfrac{81a^4b^4}{27a^9b^3}$. Simplify using the rules of exponents to find that $\dfrac{3a^{-5}b}{1} = \dfrac{3b}{a^5}$.

5. (B)   Since the bases are alike, we can use the division rule: $\dfrac{5^4}{5^2} = 5^{4-2} = 5^2 = 25$.

6. (D)   We must use the rule for raising a power to a power. Then, $\left(3^3\right)^2 = 3^{3 \cdot 2} = 3^6 = 729$.

7. (D)   To answer this question, we need to remember that any number raised to the 0 power is 1 (except the number 0). Then, $10^0 \cdot 10^3 = 1 \cdot 10^3 = 1,000$.

Practice: Radicals and Fractional Exponents (page 288)

1. (C) $125^{\frac{2}{3}} = \left(125^{\frac{1}{3}}\right)^2 = 5^2 = 25$.

2. (A) $16^{\frac{3}{4}} = \left(16^{\frac{1}{4}}\right)^3 = 2^3 = 8$.

3. (D) $\sqrt{24x^4yz^5} = \sqrt{4x^4z^4 \cdot 6yz} = \sqrt{4x^4z^4} \cdot \sqrt{6yz} = 2x^2z^2\sqrt{6yz}$.

4. (B) $\sqrt{\dfrac{a^2b^6}{c^2}} = \dfrac{\sqrt{a^2b^6}}{\sqrt{c^2}} = \dfrac{ab^3}{c}$.

Practice: Operations on Terms with Radicals (page 291)

1. (C) $3\sqrt{48} + 11\sqrt{75} = 3\sqrt{16} \cdot \sqrt{3} + 11\sqrt{25} \cdot \sqrt{3} = 3 \cdot 4\sqrt{3} + 11 \cdot 5\sqrt{3} = 12\sqrt{3} + 55\sqrt{3} = 67\sqrt{3}$.

2. (A) $\sqrt{96} - \sqrt{54} = \sqrt{16} \cdot \sqrt{6} - \sqrt{9} \cdot \sqrt{6} = 4\sqrt{6} - 3\sqrt{6} = \sqrt{6}$.

3. (D) $\sqrt{3m} \cdot \sqrt{8m} = \sqrt{24m^2} = \sqrt{4m^2 \cdot 6} = 2m\sqrt{6}$.

4. (B) $\sqrt{14m^4} \div \sqrt{6m^2} = \dfrac{\sqrt{14m^4}}{\sqrt{6m^2}} = \sqrt{\dfrac{14m^4}{6m^2}} = \sqrt{\dfrac{7m^2}{3}} = \sqrt{\dfrac{7m^2 \cdot 3}{3 \cdot 3}} = \sqrt{\dfrac{21m^2}{9}} = \dfrac{m}{3}\sqrt{21}$.

1. (D)   Rewrite the problem using the rule $\sqrt[n]{\dfrac{a}{b}} = \dfrac{\sqrt[n]{a}}{\sqrt[n]{b}}$. Then, $\sqrt[3]{\dfrac{a^4 b^3}{16c^4}} = \dfrac{\sqrt[3]{a^4 b^3}}{\sqrt[3]{16c^4}} =$

$\dfrac{\sqrt[3]{a^3 b^3 \cdot a}}{\sqrt[3]{8c^3 \cdot 2c}} = \dfrac{ab\sqrt[3]{a}}{2c\sqrt[3]{2c}}$. Now rationalize the denominator by multiplying

both numerator and denominator by $\sqrt[3]{4c^2}$. Multiplying by this factor will

completely eliminate the radical in the denominator. So, $\dfrac{ab\sqrt[3]{a} \cdot \sqrt[3]{4c^2}}{2c\sqrt[3]{2c} \cdot \sqrt[3]{4c^2}} =$

$\dfrac{ab\sqrt[3]{4ac^2}}{2c\sqrt[3]{8c^3}} = \dfrac{ab\sqrt[3]{4ac^2}}{2c \cdot 2c} = \dfrac{ab\sqrt[3]{4ac^2}}{4c^2}$.

2. (D)   Completely simplify the radicals: $3a\sqrt{6a^9} + 3\sqrt{54a^{11}} =$

$3a\sqrt{6a \cdot a^8} + 3\sqrt{9 \cdot 6 \cdot a^{10} \cdot a} = 3a^5\sqrt{6a} + 9a^5\sqrt{6a} = 12a^5\sqrt{6a}$.

3. (A)   Using radical simplification: $\dfrac{2}{3}\sqrt{\dfrac{128a^4 b}{8a^5}} = \dfrac{2}{3}\sqrt{\dfrac{16b}{a}} = \dfrac{2}{3}\dfrac{\sqrt{16} \cdot \sqrt{b} \cdot \sqrt{a}}{\sqrt{a} \cdot \sqrt{a}} =$

$\dfrac{2 \cdot 4\sqrt{ab}}{3\sqrt{a^2}} = \dfrac{8\sqrt{ab}}{3a}$.

4. (A)   The expression can be rewritten $-(4)^2 x^3 x^2$. Use the multiplication rule to find $-16x^5$.

5. (C)   Look at just the exponents and use the multiplication rule. Then, $3x + 7 = 31$, $3x = 24$, and $x = 8$.

6. (B)   Use radical simplification: $\sqrt[3]{54x^4 y^3 z^8} = \sqrt[3]{27x^3 y^3 z^6 \cdot 2xz^2} =$

$\sqrt[3]{27x^3 y^3 z^6} \cdot \sqrt[3]{2xz^2} = 3xyz^2 \sqrt[3]{2xz^2}$.

7. (A)   Completely simplify the radicals to find: $9\sqrt{3m^9} - 3m^4\sqrt{27m} =$

$9\sqrt{3m^8 \cdot m} - 3m^4\sqrt{9 \cdot 3m} = 9m^4\sqrt{3m} - 9m^4\sqrt{3m} = 0$.

8. (B)   Using radical simplification: $2y^3\sqrt{18x^5} + 2\sqrt{18x^5 y^6} - 2x\sqrt{12x} =$

$2y^3\sqrt{9 \cdot 2 \cdot x^4 \cdot x} + 2\sqrt{9 \cdot 2 \cdot x^4 \cdot x \cdot y^6} - 2x\sqrt{4 \cdot 3x} =$

$6x^2 y^3\sqrt{2x} + 6x^2 y^3\sqrt{2x} - 4x\sqrt{3x} = 12x^2 y^3\sqrt{2x} - 4x\sqrt{3x}$.

9. (C)   Fully simplify underneath each radical and then rationalize the

denominator. So, $\dfrac{\sqrt{5x^4 y^9}}{\sqrt{32x^7 y^{22}}} = \sqrt{\dfrac{5x^4 y^9}{32x^7 y^{22}}} = \sqrt{\dfrac{5}{16 \cdot 2 \cdot x^2 \cdot x \cdot y^{12} \cdot y}} =$

$\dfrac{1}{4xy^6}\sqrt{\dfrac{5}{2xy}} = \dfrac{1}{4xy^6}\sqrt{\dfrac{5 \cdot 2xy}{2xy \cdot 2xy}} = \dfrac{1}{8x^2 y^7}\sqrt{10xy} = \dfrac{\sqrt{10xy}}{8x^2 y^7}$.

10. (C)   Use the rule for division of like bases with different exponents and

then finish simplifying by removing the negative exponents: $\dfrac{-6x^5 z^2}{2x^2 z^3} =$

$-3x^3 z^{-1} = \dfrac{-3x^3}{z}$.

11. (B)   Begin underneath the radical by using the rule for division of like bases

with different exponents: $\sqrt[3]{\dfrac{16a^4 d^3}{3a}} = \sqrt[3]{\dfrac{16a^3 d^3}{3}}$. Then, use radical

simplification to find $\dfrac{\sqrt[3]{16a^3 d^3}}{\sqrt[3]{3}} = \dfrac{\sqrt[3]{8a^3 d^3} \cdot \sqrt[3]{2}}{\sqrt[3]{3}} = \dfrac{2ad\sqrt[3]{2}}{\sqrt[3]{3}} = \dfrac{2ad\sqrt[3]{2} \cdot \sqrt[3]{9}}{\sqrt[3]{3} \cdot \sqrt[3]{9}} =$

$\dfrac{2ad\sqrt[3]{18}}{\sqrt[3]{27}} = \dfrac{2ad\sqrt[3]{18}}{3}$.

12. (B)   Simplify the numerator and denominator separately. The numerator becomes $\left(a^2b^{-1}\right)^3 = a^6b^{-3}$, and the denominator becomes $\left(a^3b^2\right)^2 = a^6b^4$.

Put the pieces back together to find: $\dfrac{(a^2b^{-1})^3}{(a^3b^2)^2} = \dfrac{a^6b^{-3}}{a^6b^4} = \dfrac{1}{b^3b^4} = \dfrac{1}{b^7}$.

13. (D)   Simplifying the radical we find that $\sqrt{\dfrac{2x^2z}{3a^2b}} = \dfrac{\sqrt{2x^2z}}{\sqrt{3a^2b}} = \dfrac{\sqrt{x^2}\cdot\sqrt{2z}}{\sqrt{a^2}\cdot\sqrt{3b}} = \dfrac{x\sqrt{2z}}{a\sqrt{3b}}$.

Note that none of the answer choices contain a radical sign in the denominator, so you must rationalize it: $\dfrac{x\sqrt{2z}\cdot\sqrt{3b}}{a\sqrt{3b}\cdot\sqrt{3b}} = \dfrac{x\sqrt{6zb}}{a\sqrt{9b^2}} = \dfrac{x\sqrt{6zb}}{3ab}$.

14. (A)   Use the power to a power rule: $\dfrac{2\left(x^{-2}y^{-2}\right)^2}{4x^{-4}} = \dfrac{2\left(x^{-4}y^{-4}\right)}{4x^{-4}}$. Continue

simplifying to see that $\dfrac{2x^{-4}2y^{-4}}{4x^{-4}} = \dfrac{1}{2y^4}$.

15. (4)   Using the power to a power rule, $2(3x + 2) = 28$, $3x + 2 = 14$, $3x = 12$, $x = 4$.

16. $\left(\dfrac{5}{16}\right)$ Simplify the exponential numbers and then add the fractions: $\dfrac{1}{4^2} + \dfrac{1}{2^2} = $
$\dfrac{1}{16} + \dfrac{1}{4} = \dfrac{1}{16} + \dfrac{4}{16} = \dfrac{5}{16}$.

17. (36)   Simplify using the division of like bases with different exponents rule:
$\dfrac{6^6}{6^4} = 6^2 = 36$.

18. $\left(\dfrac{4}{9}\right)$ Simplify using the negative exponents rule. Then add the resulting

fractions: $3^{-1} + 3^{-2} = \dfrac{1}{3} + \dfrac{1}{9} = \dfrac{3}{9} + \dfrac{1}{9} = \dfrac{4}{9}$.

Lesson 2: Operating on Polynomial and Rational Expressions

Practice: Simplifying Rational Expressions (page 299)

1. (D)   Fully factor the denominator and set the expression equal to 0. Then, $x(x - 6) = 0$ and $x = 0$ or $x = 6$.

2. (A)   Factor the greatest common factor out of the numerator and factor the perfect square binomial in the denominator. Then cancel the common

factors: $\dfrac{10 - 2x}{x^2 - 25} = \dfrac{2(5 - x)}{(x - 5)(x + 5)} = \dfrac{-2(x - 5)}{(x + 5)(x - 5)} = \dfrac{-2}{x + 5}$.

3. (B)   Removing the greatest common factor from the numerator leaves you with a perfect square binomial to factor. The denominator also has a common factor of x to remove, and then you can factor the trinomial that

is left and cancel the common factors: $\dfrac{x^3 - 16x}{x^3 + 12x^2 + 32x} = \dfrac{x(x^2 - 16)}{x(x^2 + 12x + 32)} = $
$\dfrac{x(x + 4)(x - 4)}{x(x + 4)(x + 8)} = \dfrac{x - 4}{x + 8}$.

Practice: Adding and Subtracting Polynomial Expressions with Rational Coefficients (page 301)

1. (C)   Use the commutative property and then combine like terms:
$$\left(\frac{5}{2}x^2+\frac{3}{2}x-5\right)+\left(\frac{x^2}{2}-\frac{7}{2}x-2\right)=\left(\frac{5}{2}+\frac{1}{2}\right)x^2+\left(\frac{3}{2}-\frac{7}{2}\right)x-7=3x^2-2x-7.$$

2. (B)   Use the commutative property and then combine like terms:
$$(-1.2x^2+3.4x-1.6)+(2.3x^2-4.1x-1.2)=(-1.2+2.3)x^2+(3.4-4.1)x+$$
$$(-1.6-1.2)=1.1x^2-0.7x-2.8.$$

3. (D)   Begin by using the distributive property on the second set of parentheses. Then use the commutative property to combine like terms:
$$(7.1x^2-6.4x+1.9)-(-2.3x^2+3.8x-1)=7.1x^2-6.4x+1.9+2.3x^2-3.8x+1=$$
$$(7.1+2.3)x^2+(-6.4-3.8)x+(1+1.9)=9.4x^2-10.2x+2.9.$$

4. (A)   Begin by using the distributive property on the second set of parentheses. Then use the commutative property to combine like terms:
$$(2.1x^2+4)-(2.8x^2+3x-1.3)=(2.1-2.8)x^2-3x+5.3=-0.7x^2-3x+5.3.$$

5. (A)   Work on the set of nested parentheses first. Remove the inner parentheses, as there are no like terms that can be combined within them, and use the distributive property: $7.1x^2-3.2-[x-(2.5x^2+1)]=$ $7.1x^2-3.2-[x-2.5x^2-1]$. Now distribute the negative sign that is outside the bracket: $7.1x^2-3.2-x+2.5x^2+1$. Finally, combine like terms: $(7.1+2.5)x^2-x-2.2=9.6x^2-x-2.2.$

Practice: Dividing Polynomial Expressions with Rational Coefficients (page 304)

1. (C)   You can rewrite this problem as three separate fractions and then simplify (similar to the Think It Through problem on page 303), or you could notice that each term in the numerator is divisible by 3: $\dfrac{3x^2+6x+9}{3}=x^2+2x+3.$

2. (B)   The fastest way to complete this problem is to rewrite it as three separate fractions and then simplify the coefficients and the exponents. So,
$$\frac{12x^4-3x^2+6x}{3x}=\frac{12x^4}{3x}+\frac{-3x^2}{3x}+\frac{6x}{3x}=4x^3-x+2.$$

Practice: Adding and Subtracting Rational Expressions (page 307)

1. (B)   Combine the numerators: $\dfrac{m^2}{m^2-m}-\dfrac{3m-2}{m^2-m}=\dfrac{m^2-3m+2}{m^2-m}$. Factor and simplify: $\dfrac{(m-1)(m-2)}{m(m-1)}=\dfrac{m-2}{m}.$

2. (D)   Combine the numerators: $\dfrac{3}{a^2-a-6}-\dfrac{a}{a^2-a-6}=\dfrac{3-a}{a^2-a-6}$. Factor and simplify: $\dfrac{3-a}{a^2-a-6}=\dfrac{3-a}{(a-3)(a+2)}$. Now note that $(3-a)=-(a-3)$. Rewrite the numerator and simplify: $\dfrac{-(a-3)}{(a-3)(a+2)}=\dfrac{-1}{a+2}.$

3. (A)   Combine the numerators: $\dfrac{d^2+2d}{2d+10}+\dfrac{4d+5}{2d+10}=\dfrac{d^2+6d+5}{2d+10}$. Factor and simplify: $\dfrac{d^2+6d+5}{2d+10}=\dfrac{(d+1)(d+5)}{2(d+5)}=\dfrac{d+1}{2}.$

4. (C) Combine the numerators to find $\dfrac{k^3 - k^2 - 2k}{2k^2 - 4k} + \dfrac{k^3 + k^2 - 6k}{2k^2 - 4k} = \dfrac{2k^3 - 8k}{2k^2 - 4k}$.

Factor and simplify both the numerator and the denominator: $\dfrac{2k^3 - 8k}{2k^2 - 4k} =$

$\dfrac{2k(k^2 - 4)}{2k(k - 2)} = \dfrac{2k\cancel{(k-2)}(k+2)}{2k\cancel{(k-2)}} = k + 2$.

Practice: Multiplying and Dividing Rational Expressions (page 310)

1. (C) Begin this problem by rewriting it and factoring the numerical coefficients.

Then, $\dfrac{3a^3}{14b^2} \cdot \dfrac{7b^4}{6a} = \dfrac{\cancel{3} \cdot \cancel{7} \cdot a^3 b^4}{2 \cdot \cancel{7} \cdot 2 \cdot \cancel{3} \cdot a \cdot b^2}$. Cancel the like terms and subtract

the exponents on the like bases to find that the answer is $\dfrac{a^2 b^2}{4}$.

2. (A) Fully factor the numerator of the first fraction, then cross-cancel the like

terms, multiply, and simplify: $\dfrac{x^2 - 4}{2} \cdot \dfrac{4x}{x + 2} = \dfrac{\cancel{(x+2)}(x-2)}{2} \cdot \dfrac{4x}{\cancel{x+2}} = 2x(x-2)$.

3. (D) Multiply the dividend, $\dfrac{8x^3 z^2}{3y^3}$, by the reciprocal of the divisor, $\dfrac{3y}{4xz}$. Then,

$\dfrac{8x^3 z^2}{3y^3} \cdot \dfrac{3y}{4xz} = \dfrac{\cancel{8}^2 x^{\cancel{3}2} z^2}{\cancel{3}y^{\cancel{3}2}} \cdot \dfrac{\cancel{3}y}{\cancel{4}\cancel{x}z} = \dfrac{2x^2 z}{y^2}$.

SAT-Type Questions (page 311)

1. (D) Factor completely and cancel the common factors. So,

$\dfrac{x^2 - x - 12}{x^2 + x - 20} \cdot \dfrac{x^2 + 11x + 30}{x^3 + 9x^2 + 18x} = \dfrac{\cancel{(x-4)}\cancel{(x+3)}}{\cancel{(x-4)}\cancel{(x+5)}} \cdot \dfrac{\cancel{(x+5)}\cancel{(x+6)}}{x\cancel{(x+3)}\cancel{(x+6)}} = \dfrac{1}{x}$.

2. (C) The unknown polynomial must be of the form $ax + b$ because the greatest exponent in the product, 3, is one degree more than the greatest exponent in the known factor. Go back to the general form $ax + b$. You know $a \cdot 2 = 4$, so $a = 2$. Now look at the constant term: $b \cdot 1 = -2$, so $b = -2$. The polynomial is $2x - 2$.

3. (A) Since none of the answer choices show a remainder, the simplest technique is to test each answer choice by multiplying it with the divisor. Stop when the product is $x^3 + 2x^2 - 2x - 4$. You could also use long division of polynomials to solve this problem.

4. (A) Begin by rewriting the denominators in factored form. Then,

$\dfrac{6}{x^2 + 4x + 3} + \dfrac{3}{x^2 + 7x + 12} = \dfrac{6}{(x+3)(x+1)} + \dfrac{3}{(x+3)(x+4)}$. Create a

common denominator, $(x + 1)(x + 3)(x + 4)$, and use that denominator

to create equivalent fractions: $\dfrac{6(x+4)}{(x+3)(x+1)(x+4)} + \dfrac{3(x+1)}{(x+3)(x+1)(x+4)}$.

Distribute, then combine the numerators and simplify, if possible.

So, $\dfrac{6x + 24}{(x+3)(x+1)(x+4)} + \dfrac{3x + 3}{(x+3)(x+1)(x+4)} = \dfrac{9x + 27}{(x+3)(x+1)(x+4)} =$

$\dfrac{9\cancel{(x+3)}}{\cancel{(x+3)}(x+1)(x+4)} = \dfrac{9}{(x+1)(x+4)} = \dfrac{9}{x^2 + 5x + 4}$.

5. (B)   Remember that you can make any number or expression a fraction by putting it over the number 1. So, $\dfrac{z^3 - 36z}{3z - 18} \div (z^2 - 2z - 48) =$ $\dfrac{z^3 - 36z}{3z - 18} \div \dfrac{z^2 - 2z - 48}{1}$. Now, multiply the dividend by the reciprocal of the divisor, factor, and simplify: $\dfrac{z^3 - 36z}{3z - 18} \cdot \dfrac{1}{z^2 - 2z - 48} =$ $\dfrac{z(z+6)(z-6)}{3(z-6)} \cdot \dfrac{1}{(z-8)(z+6)} = \dfrac{z}{3(z-8)}$.

6. (D)   Remember that the equation will be valid as long as the denominator is not 0, so we need to find the values of m that will result in a 0 denominator. Note that the problem presented is division of fractions, so we need to begin by multiplying the dividend by the reciprocal of the divisor: $\dfrac{m^2 + 4m + 3}{6m + 6} \div \dfrac{m^2 + 3m}{6m} = \dfrac{m^2 + 4m + 3}{6m + 6} \cdot \dfrac{6m}{m^2 + 3m}$. Now set each denominator binomial equal to 0 to find that m cannot be any of the values 0, −1, or −3.

7. (A)   Factor completely and simplify by canceling common factors. Then, $\dfrac{7 - x}{x^3 - 49x} \cdot \dfrac{x^2 + 10x + 21}{3 + x} = \dfrac{7 - x}{x(x+7)(x-7)} \cdot \dfrac{(x+7)(x+3)}{3+x}$. Note that $x + 3 = 3 + x$ by the commutative law of addition. You are left with $\dfrac{7 - x}{x(x - 7)}$. Rewrite $7 - x$ as $-1(x - 7)$ and $\dfrac{-(x-7)}{x(x-7)} = \dfrac{-1}{x}$ or $-\dfrac{1}{x}$.

8. (B)   Create a chart of the terms to easily keep track of them and to lessen your chance of making a multiplication error:

	x^2	$-2.5x$	1
$1.5x$	$1.5x^3$	$-3.75x^2$	$1.5x$
-1	$-x^2$	$2.5x$	-1

Then, combine the like terms to find that:
$1.5x^3 + (-1 - 3.75)x^2 + (2.5 + 1.5)x - 1 = 1.5x^3 - 4.75x^2 + 4x - 1$.

9. (A)   Create a chart of the terms to easily keep track of them and to lessen your chance of making a multiplication error. Recall that multiplication of fractions does not require a common denominator.

	$\frac{1}{2}x^2$	$\frac{1}{4}x$	1
$\frac{2}{3}x$	$\frac{1}{3}x^3$	$\frac{1}{6}x^2$	$\frac{2}{3}x$
$\frac{1}{3}$	$\frac{1}{6}x^2$	$\frac{1}{12}x$	$\frac{1}{3}$

Then, combine the like terms to find that: $\dfrac{1}{3}x^3 + \left(\dfrac{1}{6} + \dfrac{1}{6}\right)x^2 + \left(\dfrac{2}{3} + \dfrac{1}{12}\right)x + \dfrac{1}{3} =$ $\dfrac{1}{3}x^3 + \dfrac{1}{3}x^2 + \dfrac{3}{4}x + \dfrac{1}{3}$.

10. (C) Think through the problem. You know that $\frac{1}{3}x$ must be multiplied by another fraction to result in $\frac{1}{6}x^2$. Of the answer choices available, only $\frac{1}{2}x$ makes sense. This eliminates answer choices B and D. Check the remaining choices: $\left(\frac{1}{2}x+\frac{1}{3}\right)\left(\frac{1}{3}x-\frac{2}{3}\right)=\frac{1}{6}x^2-\frac{2}{9}x-\frac{2}{9}$. Stop checking and select choice C.

11. (B) You know the formula for the area of a rectangle is length times width. Then, the formula for the width of the rectangle is $w=\frac{A}{l}=\frac{4x+4}{2x+4}\div\frac{x+1}{x+2}$ or $\frac{4x+4}{2x+4}\cdot\frac{x+2}{x+1}=\frac{4\cancel{(x+1)}}{2\cancel{(x+2)}}\cdot\frac{\cancel{x+2}}{\cancel{x+1}}=2$.

12. (C) Set up and carry out long division of polynomials:

$$
\begin{array}{r}
x^2-2x+4+\dfrac{2}{x-1} \\[4pt]
x-1\overline{\smash{)}\,x^3-3x^2+6x-2} \\
-\left(x^3-x^2\right) \\ \hline
-2x^2+6x \\
-(-2x+2x) \\ \hline
4x-2 \\
-(4x-4) \\ \hline
2
\end{array}
$$

13. (B) Rewrite the terms in factored form: $\frac{x-3}{x^2-1}+\frac{3}{x-1}-\frac{4}{2x+2}=$ $\frac{x-3}{(x+1)(x-1)}+\frac{3}{x-1}-\frac{4}{2(x+1)}$. Create a common denominator, $2(x+1)(x-1)$, and use the common denominator to make equivalent fractions: $\frac{2(x-3)}{2(x+1)(x-1)}+\frac{3\cdot2(x+1)}{2(x+1)(x-1)}-\frac{4(x-1)}{2(x+1)(x-1)}$. Then distribute, combine like terms, and simplify to find $\frac{2x-6+6x+6-4x+4}{2(x+1)(x-1)}=$ $\frac{4x+4}{2(x+1)(x-1)}=\frac{4\cancel{(x+1)}}{2\cancel{(x+1)}(x-1)}=\frac{2}{x-1}$.

14. (C) Rewrite the terms in factored form to see that $\frac{x}{x^2+9x+18}-\frac{3}{x^2+3x}=$ $\frac{x}{(x+3)(x+6)}-\frac{3}{x(x+3)}$. Now, create a common denominator, $x(x+3)(x+6)$, and equivalent fractions: $\frac{x^2}{x(x+3)(x+6)}-\frac{3(x+6)}{x(x+3)(x+6)}=$ $\frac{x^2-3x-18}{x(x+3)(x+6)}$. Finally, factor the numerator and completely simplify: $\frac{(x-6)\cancel{(x+3)}}{x\cancel{(x+3)}(x+6)}=\frac{x-6}{x(x+6)}$.

15. (D) Rewrite the terms in factored form: $\dfrac{1}{a^2-a-6}-\dfrac{1}{2a^2-7a+3}=$

$\dfrac{1}{(a-3)(a+2)}-\dfrac{1}{(2a-1)(a-3)}$. Create a common denominator,

$(a-3)(a+2)(2a-1)$, and equivalent fractions: $\dfrac{2a-1}{(a-3)(a+2)(2a-1)}-$

$\dfrac{a+2}{(2a-1)(a-3)(a+2)}=\dfrac{a-3}{(a-3)(a+2)(2a-1)}$. Finish by canceling the

common factors and FOILing the denominator: $\dfrac{\cancel{a-3}}{\cancel{(a-3)}(a+2)(2a-1)}=$

$\dfrac{1}{(a+2)(2a-1)}=\dfrac{1}{2a^2+3a-2}$.

16. (B) Remember that $(2-x)=-1\cdot(x-2)$, so rewrite the problem as

$\dfrac{-1}{x-2}+\dfrac{2}{x-2}=\dfrac{1}{x-2}$.

17. (A) Begin by factoring all the numerators and denominators. Then,

$\dfrac{x^2-9}{3-x}\cdot\dfrac{4x+16}{x^2+7x+12}=\dfrac{(x+3)(x-3)}{3-x}\cdot\dfrac{4(x+4)}{(x+3)(x+4)}=$

$\dfrac{-\cancel{(x+3)}\,\cancel{(x-3)}}{\cancel{x-3}}\cdot\dfrac{4\cancel{(x+4)}}{\cancel{(x+3)}\,\cancel{(x+4)}}=-4$.

18. (D) As usual, begin by rewriting the terms in factored form, then create the common denominator and the equivalent fractions. Distribute and completely simplify as needed. For this problem: $\dfrac{x}{x^2-4x+3}-\dfrac{x}{x^2+2x-3}=$

$\dfrac{x}{(x-3)(x-1)}-\dfrac{x}{(x+3)(x-1)}=\dfrac{x(x+3)}{(x-3)(x+3)(x-1)}-\dfrac{x(x-3)}{(x-3)(x+3)(x-1)}=$

$\dfrac{x^2+3x-x^2+3x}{(x-3)(x+3)(x-1)}=\dfrac{6x}{(x+3)(x-3)(x-1)}$.

19. (C) Rewrite all the terms in factored form. Then, $\dfrac{1}{x}+\dfrac{1}{x-2}-\dfrac{2}{x^2-2x}=$

$\dfrac{1}{x}+\dfrac{1}{x-2}-\dfrac{2}{x(x-2)}$. Create a common denominator, $x(x-2)$,

and equivalent fractions. Then completely simplify. So,

$\dfrac{x-2}{x(x-2)}+\dfrac{x}{x(x-2)}-\dfrac{2}{x(x-2)}=\dfrac{2x-4}{x(x-2)}=\dfrac{2\cancel{(x-2)}}{x\cancel{(x-2)}}=\dfrac{2}{x}$.

20. (A) Rewrite the terms in factored form, create a common denominator and equivalent fractions, then completely simplify: $\dfrac{2}{a^2-4}-\dfrac{1}{a^2+2a}=$

$\dfrac{2}{(a+2)(a-2)}-\dfrac{1}{a(a+2)}=\dfrac{2a}{a(a+2)(a-2)}-\dfrac{a-2}{a(a+2)(a-2)}=\dfrac{a+2}{a\cancel{(a+2)}(a-2)}=$

$\dfrac{1}{a(a-2)}=\dfrac{1}{a^2-2a}$.

Lesson 3: Solving Radical and Rational Equations

Practice: Solving Radical Equations (page 317)

1. (4) Square both sides of the equation to eliminate the square root signs: $\sqrt{3m+4} = 2\sqrt{m}$ is $\left(\sqrt{3m+4}\right)^2 = \left(2\sqrt{m}\right)^2 = 3m+4 = 4m$. Now combine the like terms and isolate the variable to find that $m = 4$.

2. (5) Square both sides of the equation to eliminate the square root signs. Don't forget to square the 4 that is sitting outside the root sign. So, $4\sqrt{2x-6} = \sqrt{13x-1}$ is $\left(4\sqrt{2x-6}\right)^2 = \left(\sqrt{13x-1}\right)^2 = 16(2x-6) = 13x-1$. Distribute, combine like terms, and isolate the variable to find: $32x - 96 = 13x - 1$, $19x = 95$, $x = 5$.

3. (3) Square both sides of the equation to eliminate the square root signs. Don't forget to square the 2 that is sitting outside the root sign. So, $\sqrt{13+x} = 2\sqrt{1+x}$ is $\left(\sqrt{13+x}\right)^2 = \left(2\sqrt{1+x}\right)^2 = 13+x = 4(1+x)$. Distribute, combine like terms, and isolate the variable to find: $13 + x = 4 + 4x$, $3x = 9$, $x = 3$.

4. (3) Square both sides of the equation to eliminate the square root signs. Don't forget to square the 2 that is sitting outside the root sign. So, $2\sqrt{8x+1} = \sqrt{33x+1}$ is $\left(2\sqrt{8x+1}\right)^2 = \left(\sqrt{33x+1}\right)^2 = 4(8x+1) = 33x+1$. Distribute, combine like terms, and isolate the variable to find: $32x + 4 = 33x + 1$, $x = 3$.

Practice: Solving Rational Equations (page 321)

1. (A) Multiply through by the common denominator, a, to eliminate the denominator: $9 - \dfrac{2}{a} = 5$, $\dfrac{a}{1}\left(9 - \dfrac{2}{a}\right) = \dfrac{a}{1}(5)$, $9a - 2 = 5a$, $4a = 2$, $a = \dfrac{1}{2}$. Alternately, you could subtract 9 from both sides and then use cross-multiplication to solve for the unknown. If you do, $9 - \dfrac{2}{a} = 5$, $\dfrac{-2}{a} = \dfrac{-4}{1}$, $-4a = -2$, and $a = \dfrac{1}{2}$.

2. (D) Eliminate the denominator by multiplying through by $10x$. Then, $\dfrac{10x}{1}\left(\dfrac{3}{x} + \dfrac{1}{2}\right) = \dfrac{10x}{1}\left(\dfrac{11}{5x}\right)$, $\dfrac{30x}{x} + \dfrac{10x}{2} = \dfrac{110x}{5x}$, $30 + 5x = 22$, $5x = -8$, $x = -\dfrac{8}{5}$.

3. (B) Here we have two fractions set equal to each other, so we can use proportional reasoning to solve. Cross-multiply to find that $2x^2 + x = 6$. Now write the equation in standard form: $2x^2 + x - 6 = 0$. Factor and then solve for each unknown. So, $(2x-3)(x+2) = 0$ and $x = -2$ or $x = \dfrac{3}{2}$. Checking back in the original equation, both solutions work.

4. (C) Again, we have two fractions set equal to each other, so we can use proportional reasoning to solve. Cross-multiply to find that $(m+3)(m-1) = 32$. Expand and set equal to 0: $m^2 - m + 3m - 3 = 32$, $m^2 + 2m - 35 = 0$. Factor and solve for each unknown. So, $(m+7)(m-5) = 0$. Then $m = -7$ or $m = 5$. Checking back in the original equation, both solutions work.

1. (A)   Start the problem by squaring both sides. Then, $\sqrt{6b+4} = 20$ becomes $\left(\sqrt{6b+4}\right)^2 = 20^2$, and $6b+4 = 400$. Subtract 4 from both sides and divide by 6 to find that $b = 66$.

2. (A)   The fastest solution method for this problem is to substitute in the values given in the answer choices to see which one(s) produce true statements. Both $x = 3$ and $x = 6$ work. Alternately, you could multiply both sides of the equation by the least common denominator, $2(x-1)(x-2)$, and solve.

3. (C)   Although you can calculate the answer, examine the answer choices. If you substitute either of $x = 2$ or $x = -2$ into the original equation, you will obtain a zero denominator. Thus, the correct answer from the given choices is no solution.

4. (D)   Square both sides of the equation to find $\left(\sqrt{3x+3}\right)^2 = \left(3\sqrt{x-1}\right)^2$ and $3x+3 = 9(x-1)$. Distribute, collect like terms, and solve for x: $3x+3 = 9x-9$, $-6x+3 = -9$, $-6x = -12$, and $x = 2$. After checking to make sure the solution is valid, square the value to find $x^2 = 4$.

5. (B)   Factor the right-hand side of the equation. Then, $\dfrac{2}{p+3} + \dfrac{4}{p} = \dfrac{6}{2(p+3)}$. Multiply both sides by the least common denominator, $2(p)(p+3)$, and simplify and find $4p + 8p + 24 = 6p$. Collect the like terms and solve for the variable: $6p = -24$ and $p = -4$. Check to make sure this is a valid solution.

6. (D)   Start by squaring both sides of the equation: $\left(2\sqrt{6x}\right)^2 = \left(\sqrt{4x^2}\right)^2$. Then, $4(6x) = 4x^2$, $24x = 4x^2$, $6x = x^2$, and $0 = x^2 - 6x$. Factor and solve for x to find that $x = 0$ and $x = 6$. Quickly check to make sure neither answer is an extraneous solution, and then select answer choice D.

7. (C)   Factor and rewrite to clearly see the least common denominator: $\dfrac{2b}{5+b} + \dfrac{1}{b-5} = \dfrac{10}{(b+5)(b-5)}$. Now multiply through by the least common denominator to find $2b^2 - 10b + b + 5 = 10$. Continue to simplify and factor. Then, $2b^2 - 9b - 5 = 0$, $(2b+1)(b-5) = 0$, and $b = -\dfrac{1}{2}$ or $b = 5$. Notice the denominators in the original equation. If $b = 5$, we obtain a 0 denominator, so reject $b = 5$ as extraneous and select answer choice C.

8. (B)   Multiply through by the least common denominator, $x(x+5)(x-5)$. Then, $x(x-5)(x+5)\left(\dfrac{4}{x-5} - \dfrac{2}{x+5} = \dfrac{2}{x}\right)$, and $4x(x+5) - 2x(x-5) = 2(x+5)(x-5)$. Distribute, combine the like terms, and solve for x to find: $4x^2 + 20x - 2x^2 + 10x = 2x^2 - 50$, $30x = -50$, and $x = -\dfrac{5}{3}$. Check and confirm that this is a valid solution, and then select answer choice B.

9. (12)   Begin by dividing both sides of the equation by 3. Then, $\sqrt{2x+1} = 5$. Now square both sides and solve for the variable: $\left(\sqrt{2x+1}\right)^2 = 5^2$, $2x+1 = 25$, $2x = 24$, $x = 12$.

10. (2)   Notice that the two fractions have the same denominator and multiply through by that expression. Then you obtain $2x+3 = x+5$. Solve for x to see that $x+3 = 5$ and $x = 2$.

11. (5)   Square both sides of the equation. Then, $20x = 4(4x+5)$. Distribute, collect like terms, and solve for x to see that: $20x = 16x + 20$, $4x = 20$, and $x = 5$.

12. (3)   Rewrite the equation so that $\sqrt{x}$ is alone. So, $\sqrt{x} = x - 6$. Now square both sides and see that $\left(\sqrt{x}\right)^2 = (x-6)^2$ or $x = (x-6)^2$. Expand and find $x^2 - 13x + 36 = 0$. Factor the trinomial and solve: $x = 9$ or $x = 4$. Check the solutions in the original equation to see which one is extraneous. Since $x = 4$ fails in the check, find the square root of $9 = 3$ and bubble in 3 as the answer.

13. (12)   As usual, square both sides of the equation to eliminate the radical signs. Then, $\left(5\sqrt{5x-1}\right)^2 = \left(7\sqrt{2x+5}\right)^2$, $25(5x-1) = 49(2x+5)$, $125x - 25 = 98x + 245$. Collect the like terms and solve for x to find that $27x = 270$, and $x = 10$. The question asks for $x + 2$, so $10 + 2 = 12$.

14. (5)   Begin by noticing that the fraction on the right-hand side of the equation can be simplified. Factor that denominator and see $\dfrac{4x+3}{x-6} - \dfrac{(x-4)}{x-6} = \dfrac{\overset{22}{\cancel{44}}}{\cancel{2}(x-6)}$. Multiply both sides by $(x-6)$ to eliminate the fractions. Then, $4x + 3 - x + 4 = 22$, $3x + 7 = 22$, $3x = 15$, $x = 5$. Check to see that this is a valid solution.

Lesson 4: Creating, Analyzing, Interpreting, and Solving Nonlinear Equations

Practice: Solving Quadratic Equations (page 329)

1. (C)   The leading coefficient of this quadratic is 1, so attempt to factor. Note that 15 and 2 multiply together for 30 and can be summed to produce -13. Then, $(x - 15)(x + 2) = 0$ and $x = 15$ or $x = -2$.

2. (B)   Before we can factor or use the quadratic formula, the trinomial must be set equal to 0. Start by subtracting 6 from both sides of the equation to see that $x^2 + 5x - 6 = 0$. Now factor and solve: $(x+6)(x-1) = 0$, and $x = -6$ or $x = 1$.

3. (B)   For this type of problem you must work backwards. If the roots are $x = 3$ and $x = 4$, then the binomial factors must be $(x-3)$ and $(x-4)$. Multiply the binomials to find $x^2 - 7x + 12 = 0$.

4. (A)   Again, work backwards. The trinomial must have $(x+8)$ and $(x-2)$ as factors since its zeros are $x = -8$ and $x = 2$. Multiply the binomials and find $x^2 + 6x - 16 = 0$.

Practice: Creating, Analyzing, and Interpreting Quadratic Equations (page 333)

1. (A)   Determine the form of the equations. They are all set up so they are equal to the time the trip took. Then, we are looking for addends in the form $\dfrac{\text{distance}}{\text{rate}}$. Choice A is correct since 1 mile is associated with a speed of x mph and 12 miles is associated with $x + 25$ mph.

2. (D)   Consider that the entire job is completed in 8 days. Therefore, $\dfrac{1}{8}$ of the job is completed in 1 day. The addends show the portion each team will complete in 1 day. Luke and Sead would complete $\dfrac{1}{x}$ in one day. Luke would complete half that amount, or $\dfrac{1}{2x}$.

3. (A)   Rewrite the numerator of $\dfrac{25x^2}{5x-1}$ to create a term that is both divisible

by $5x + 1$ and is the difference of squares. Then, $\dfrac{(25x^2-1)+1}{5x-1}=$

$\dfrac{\cancel{(5x-1)}(5x+1)+1}{\cancel{5x-1}}=5x+1+\dfrac{1}{5x-1}$.

4. (C)   Examine the answer choices. You know you are looking for a quadratic
in the general form $f(x)=a(x-h)^2+k$, where the football will have a
maximum height k at time h. Answer choice C is the only correct choice.

Practice: Creating, Analyzing, and Interpreting Exponential Equations (page 336)

1. (A)   To find the amount that the investment grows each quarter, take the
annual rate, 6%, and divide it by four since there are four quarters in

a year. Then, $\dfrac{6\%}{4}=1.5\%$ and the duration of this investment is $3 \cdot 4 =$

12 quarters. Using the exponential growth model, substitute $2,000 for
the initial investment, 0.015 as the growth rate r, and 12 as the time.
So, $A = 2,000(1.015)^{12} = \$2,391.24$.

2. (B)   To solve this problem, you can either substitute each answer choice into
the expression $A = 1.5(.75)^t$, and stop when the result is approximately
0.75, or, on your graphing calculator, enter $Y_1 = 1.5(.75)^x$ and $Y_2 = 0.75$.
Then go to [second] [trace] and select 5:intersect. Press enter through
the First Curve?, Second Curve?, and Guess prompts. You will see
X=2.4468085 and Y=.75. The closest x answer choice is B, which is
2.4 hours. Note that these calculator instructions are for the TI 83/84.

SAT-Type Questions (page 337)

1. (C)   Cross-multiply to find $(x+2)(x+3)=2$. Expand and collect like terms:
$x^2+5x+6=2$. Set the trinomial equal to 0, factor, and solve. So,
$x^2+5x+4=0$, $(x+1)(x+4)=0$, $x+1=0$ or $x+4=0$. The solution set
is $\{-1, -4\}$. Quickly check to make sure neither answer will make the
equation undefined, and then select answer choice C.

2. (C)   Here we want the differences in the average speeds. The distance 250
is associated with t, and the distance 240 is associated with $t+1$. Their
difference is 10. This is answer choice C.

3. (D)   Long division with polynomials or working backwards are
possible techniques to solve this problem. A quicker solution
involves creating a numerator that has $x-1$ as a factor. Then,

$\dfrac{(x^2-3x-2)+2}{x-1}=\dfrac{\cancel{(x-1)}(x-2)+2}{\cancel{x-1}}=x-2+\dfrac{2}{x-1}$.

4. (B)   Multiply through by the LCD, $(x+2)(x+3)$. Then

$\dfrac{5(x+2)\cancel{(x+3)}}{\cancel{x+3}}+\dfrac{5\cancel{(x+2)}\cancel{(x+3)}}{\cancel{(x+2)}\cancel{(x+3)}}=(x+2)(x+3)$. Cancel the

like binomial factors, distribute, and then combine the like terms
to find: $5x+10+5=x^2+5x+6$, and $x^2=9$. So, $x=\pm 3$.
Reject $x = -3$ because it is an extraneous solution.

5. (C)   Multiply through by the LCD, $(x-2)(x+2)$. Then,

$\dfrac{x(x+2)(x-2)}{x-2}+\dfrac{(x+2)(x-2)}{x+2}=\dfrac{(x+6)(x+2)(x-2)}{x^2-4}$. Distribute and combine

the like terms to find: $x^2+2x+x-2=x+6$, and $x^2+2x-8=0$. Now,
$(x+4)(x-2)=0$ and $x=-4$ or $x=2$. But we reject $x=2$ because it is an
extraneous solution.

6. (A) Recognize this as an exponential growth problem. The initial rate is $2,000 and the growth rate is $\dfrac{0.05}{2} = 0.025$ for 6 periods. Then, $A = 2000(1.025)^6 = \$2,319.39$.

7. (B) Rewrite the numerator of $\dfrac{81x^2}{9x+1}$ to create a term that is both divisible by $9x + 1$ and is the difference of squares. Then, $\dfrac{81x^2}{9x+1} = \dfrac{(81x^2-1)+1}{9x+1} = \dfrac{\cancel{(9x+1)}(9x-1)+1}{\cancel{9x+1}} = 9x-1+\dfrac{1}{9x+1}$.

8. (A) The addends reflect how the 1.5 hours of travel time is divided. Remember that time $= \dfrac{\text{distance}}{\text{rate}}$. Examining the answer choices, only A is correct since 2 miles is associated with a speed of x mph and 4 miles is associated with $x + 5$ mph.

9. (B) Begin this problem by calculating the growth factor, b. You know that in 2010 there were 240 donations and in 2011, one year later, there were 288 donations. So, $b = \dfrac{288}{240} = 1.2$. So, in 2014, 3 years after 2011, there were $288(1.2)^3 = 497.664$ donations.

10. (A) Remember that when two fractions are set equal to each other, you can cross-multiply. So, $(x-1)(x+1) = 48$. FOIL to find $x^2-1=48$, then $x^2=49$ and $x = \pm 7$. Quickly check to make sure both solutions are valid, then select answer choice A.

11. (D) Like number 10, we can begin this problem by cross-multiplying. Then, $(3x+4)(3x-4)=9$, $9x^2-16=9$, and $9x^2-25=0$. Factor the difference of squares to find $(3x+5)(3x-5)=0$. Then $3x+5=0$ or $3x-5=0$. The solution set is $\left\{\dfrac{5}{3}, -\dfrac{5}{3}\right\}$.

12. (B) The units in this problem are in miles and minutes. We know that the addends are rates. Thus, 10 miles per hour is 10 miles per 60 minutes, which is $\dfrac{1}{6}$ mile per minute. This eliminates answer choices C and D. We know we are looking for the difference in rates, so the only possible correct answer is choice B.

13. (A) Start by cross-multiplying. So, $(5x+2)(5x-2)=32$. FOIL, collect the like terms, and then factor the difference of perfect squares: $25x^2 - 4 = 32$, $25x^2 - 36 = 0$, and $(5x+6)(5x-6) = 0$. Now, $5x+6=0$ or $5x-6=0$. The solution set is $\left\{\dfrac{6}{5}, -\dfrac{6}{5}\right\}$.

14. (B) The addends need to show the parts of the $1\dfrac{1}{2}$ hours $\left(\dfrac{3}{2} \text{ hours}\right)$ Ruth drove. Since time is $\dfrac{\text{distance}}{\text{rate}}$, answer choice B is correct. Remember that you can distribute 60 to show $\dfrac{60}{x}$ as the speed for the first part of the trip and $\dfrac{60}{x+5}$ as the speed for the second part of the trip.

15. (2 or 8) Cross-multiply to find $(x-4)(x-6)=8$. Expand by FOILing, then collect the like terms. So, $x^2-10x+24=8$ and $x^2-10x+16=0$. Now factor and solve: $(x-2)(x-8)=0$. Solutions are 2 and 8.

16. (6)   Remember that time = $\dfrac{\text{distance}}{\text{rate}}$. Now, let x be Margie's walking

speed. Then her skating speed is $x + 4$. The park is 3 miles from her

house. So, $\dfrac{3}{x} + \dfrac{3}{x+4} = 2$. Multiply through by the LCD $x(x+4)$ to find

that $3(x+4) + 3x = 2x(x+4)$. Distribute and then collect like terms:
$3x + 12 + 3x = 2x^2 + 8x$, $2x^2 + 2x - 12 = 0$. Divide through by 2 and see
that $x^2 + x - 6 = 0$. Factor and solve: $(x+3)(x-2) = 0$, $x = 2$ and $x = -3$.
Reject $x = -3$ as an extraneous solution. Margie's skating speed is $2 + 4 =$
6 miles per hour.

17. (1.05)   In this function, n is the growth factor, $1 + 0.05 = 1.05$.

18. (92.2)   Recognize this as an exponential decay problem. The decay rate is
20% and the initial value is 225. The time is 4. So, $A = 225(1 - 0.2)^4 =$
$225(0.8)^4 = 92.2$ gallons.

Lesson 5: The Meaning of the Terms in Nonlinear Expressions; Relationships Between the Polynomial Zeros and Factors

Practice: Quadratic Definitions and End Behavior (page 345)

1. (C)   For the function $f(x) = x^2 - x - 2$, $a = 1$ and $b = -1$. Using the formula for

the axis of symmetry, $x = \dfrac{-b}{2a} = \dfrac{-(-1)}{2(1)} = \dfrac{1}{2}$.

2. (D)   For the function $f(x) = 2x^2 - 3$, $a = 2$ and $b = 0$. Using the formula for the

axis of symmetry, $x = \dfrac{-b}{2a} = \dfrac{-0}{2(4)} = 0$.

3. (C)   For the function $f(x) = x^2 - 4x + 4$, $a = 1$ and $b = -4$. The x-coordinate

will have the value $\dfrac{-b}{2a} = \dfrac{-(-4)}{2(1)} = 2$. Substituting into $f(x) = x^2 - 4x + 4$,

$f(2) = 2^2 - 4(2) + 4 = 0$. The turning point is $(2, 0)$.

4. (A)   For the function $f(x) = 2x^2 - 2x + 1$, $a = 2$ and $b = -2$. The x-coordinate

will have the value $\dfrac{-b}{2a} = \dfrac{-(-2)}{2(2)} = \dfrac{1}{2}$. Substituting into $f(x) = 2x^2 - 2x + 1$,

$f\left(\dfrac{1}{2}\right) = 2\left(\dfrac{1}{2}\right)^2 - 2\left(\dfrac{1}{2}\right) + 1 = \dfrac{1}{2} - 1 + 1 = \dfrac{1}{2}$. The turning point is $\left(\dfrac{1}{2}, \dfrac{1}{2}\right)$.

5. (A)   The turning point of $f(x) = a(x-h)^2 + k$ is (h, k). In this case, the turning
point is $(-(-2), 6) = (2, 6)$. At 2 seconds the ball reaches a maximum height
of 6 yards.

SAT-Type Questions (page 352)

1. (B)   The graph has a maximum, so limit your viable choices to B and C. Since

$\dfrac{-b}{2a} > 0$, the coefficients a and b will have opposite signs. Of the two, only

answer choice B passes through the turning point $(1, 9)$.

2. (B)   The graph will open down since the coefficient of the x^2 term is negative.
This eliminates answer choices A and D. Calculate the x-coordinate of the

vertex: $x = \dfrac{-b}{2a} = \dfrac{-2}{2(-1)} = 1$. Answer choice B has an x-coordinate of 1 at
the vertex.

3. (C) Using the given the x–intercepts and substituting y for $f(x)$, we can rewrite the function as $y = \left(x - \dfrac{1}{2}\right)(x + 1)(x - p)$. The intercepts show us the zeros of the function: $\dfrac{1}{2}$, -1, and p. Now we can choose one of the numeric zeros and substitute those values into the function f. The coordinate pair $(-1, 0)$ is easiest. Then, $0 = 2(-1)^3 + (-1)^2 + c(-1)$, and $-2 + 1 - c = 0$. Solving for c, we find that $c = -1$.

4. (A) The graph opens up, therefore $a > 0$. This limits your choices to A and B. The axis of symmetry is $x = \dfrac{-b}{2a} = -2$. Because $\dfrac{-b}{2a}$ is a negative number, both a and b have the same sign. Only choice A fits both criteria.

5. (D) Written in factored form, $f(x) = k\left(x + \dfrac{1}{3}\right)(x - 1)(x - p)$. The product of k, $\dfrac{1}{3}$, -1, and $(-p) = 0$. Since k is a non-zero number, $p = 0$.

6. (D) The graph opens up so limit your focus to answer choices B and D. The axis of symmetry is $x = \dfrac{-b}{2a} = -1$. Cross-multiply and find $-b = -2a$ or $b = 2a$. Thus a and b have the same sign. Only Choice D meets these requirements.

7. (C) Calculate the axis of symmetry, $x = \dfrac{-b}{2a} = \dfrac{7}{4}$. Then, $\dfrac{b}{2a} = \dfrac{-7}{4}$ and $\dfrac{b}{a} = \dfrac{-7}{2}$. Choice C fits this criterion.

8. (D) Since the zeros of f are $\dfrac{1}{2}$, -1, and c, rewriting in the function in factored form yields $f(x) = k\left(x - \dfrac{1}{2}\right)(x + 1)(x - c) = 2x^3 - x^2 + bx + 1$. We know $k = 2$ since the product $k \cdot x \cdot x \cdot x = 2x^3$. We can find c, since $(k)\left(-\dfrac{1}{2}\right)(1)(-c) = 1$ (the constant term). Recall that $k = 2$. So, $(2)\left(-\dfrac{1}{2}\right)(1)(-c) = 1$ and $c = 1$.

9. (D) The graph opens down so limit choices to B and D, where $a < 0$. Since the axis of symmetry is $x = 0$, you know that $b = 0$. Choice D fits these criteria.

10. (B) The graph opens down since $a < 0$ so limit your choices to B and D. The axis of symmetry is $x = \dfrac{-b}{2a} = \dfrac{-(-6)}{2(-2)} = -\dfrac{6}{4} = -\dfrac{3}{2}$. Select choice B.

11. (D) Since the zeros of f are $-\dfrac{1}{2}$, $\dfrac{2}{3}$, and c, rewriting the original function in factored form gives us $f(x) = k\left(x + \dfrac{1}{2}\right)\left(x - \dfrac{2}{3}\right)(x - c) = 6x^3 + 5x^2 + bx - 2$. We know $k = 6$ since the product $k \cdot x \cdot x \cdot x = 6x^3$. We can find c, since the product (the constant term). Recall that $k = 6$. Therefore, $(6)\left(\dfrac{1}{2}\right)\left(-\dfrac{2}{3}\right)(-c) = -2$. Solve and find $c = -1$.

12. $\left(0.75 \text{ or } \dfrac{3}{4}\right)$ We know the formula for the axis of symmetry is $x = \dfrac{-b}{2a}$. If we substitute the values from the function into the formula, we find $x = \dfrac{-(-3)}{2(2)} = \dfrac{3}{4}$ or 0.75.

13. (6)   Rearrange the equation so the function is in vertex form: $f(t) = -5.3(t-3)^2 + 53.7$. The ball's initial height is $f(0) = (-5.3 \cdot 9) + 53.7 = 6$ yards. From the vertex form you can see it takes 3 seconds for the ball to reach its maximum height of $f(3) = 53.7$ yards. Due to the symmetry of a parabola, we are assured the ball will return to its initial height of 6 yards in 3 more seconds, 6 seconds after it is thrown.

14. (8)   This graph, $f(x) = 3^x + 8$, is an 8-unit positive vertical shift of $f(x) = 3^x$. Thus, $k = 0 + 8 = 8$.

15. (3)   Given the x-intercepts and substituting y for $f(x)$, we can rewrite the function as $y = k(x-3)\left(x - \dfrac{1}{3}\right)(x-p)$. The intercepts show us the zeros of the function: 3, $\dfrac{1}{3}$, and p. Choose one of the numeric zeros. The whole number 3 is easiest to work with. Substitute 0 for y and 3 for x to see that $0 = 3(3)^3 - 10(3)^2 + c(3)$. Simplify and rearrange and solve for c. Then, $3c = 9$ and $c = 3$.

Lesson 6: Solving Systems of Equations Involving One Linear and at Least One Higher-Order Equation

Practice: Graphic Solutions to Quadratic-Linear Systems (page 361)

1. (C)   The parabola and line intersect in 2 locations.

2. (A)   The parabola and line have no common points.

3. (C)   Examine the graph to see where the line crosses the parabola, then read the coordinates off the axes. The functions intersect at $(-2, 2)$ and $(0, -2)$.

SAT-Type Questions (page 368)

1. (A)   Rewrite the linear equation as $y = 2x + 10$. Now set the two equations equal to each other: $-x^2 - 4x + 1 = 2x + 10$. Combine the like terms and multiply through by -1 to change the sign on the leading coefficient, and find $x^2 + 6x + 9 = 0$. Factor and solve to see $(x+3)(x+3) = 0$. Then $x = -3$ is a root. Substitute $x = -3$ into $y = 2x + 10$ and find $y = 4$.

2. (B)   Notice that $y = x^2 - 4x + 3$ has a minimum value, so eliminate answer choices C and D. Focusing on choices A and B, the linear equation $3x + 2y = 6$ has slope $m = -\dfrac{3}{2}$. Choice B is the only remaining option with a negative slope.

3. (C)   Begin by setting the two equations equal to each other: $\dfrac{1}{2}x^2 + 3x - 2 = 4x - \dfrac{1}{2}$. Clear fractions by multiplying through by 2 to see that $x^2 + 6x - 4 = 8x - 1$. Now combine terms and find $x^2 - 2x - 3 = 0$. Factor and solve to get $(x-3)(x+1) = 0$, $x = 3$, $x = -1$. Substitute each of the x-values into the linear equation and determine the solutions to be $(3, 11.5)$ and $(-1, -4.5)$.

4. (D)   Substitute $-2x$ for y in the first equation. Now, $x^2 + (-2x)^2 = 180$, $x^2 + 4x^2 = 180$, $5x^2 = 180$, and $x^2 = 36$.

5. (D)   By looking at the given equations, we can determine that the parabola should open up and the line should have a y-intercept of $(0, 4)$.

6. (D) Solve the linear equation for y. Then substitute $18 - x$ for y in the first equation. Now, $x^2 + (18 - x)^2 = 234$. Distribute and collect the like terms on one side of the equation to see that $x^2 + 324 - 36x + x^2 = 234$ and $2x^2 - 36x + 90 = 0$. Divide through by 2 to make factoring easier: $x^2 - 18x + 45 = 0$. Factor and solve: $(x - 15)(x - 3) = 0$, $x = 15$, $x = 3$. Substitute each of the x-values into the linear equation and determine the solutions to be $\{(15, 3), (3, 15)\}$.

7. (B) We can determine the solutions from the graph without knowing the equations that created the graph. There are two points common to all three: $(0, -2)$ and $(5, 3)$.

8. (3) The graphs intersect at $(0, -1)$, $(1, 0)$, and $(2, -1)$.

9. (36) Substitute $-2x$ for y in the first equation. Now, $x^2 + (-2x)^2 = 45$, $5x^2 = 45$, and $x^2 = 9$. Then, $y^2 = 45 - 9 = 36$.

10. (0) Examine the graph. Although the circle and the parabola intersect, as do the line and the parabola, there is no point shared by the circle, parabola, and line.

Lesson 7: Transformation and Composition of Functions

Practice: Transformations (page 379)

1. (D) $f(x)$ is a vertical shift of $g(x) = x^2$ one unit down.

2. (A) $f(x)$ is a vertical shift of $g(x) = 2^x$ one unit up. The graph is increasing, so eliminate answer choice D. Shifting $g(x)$ one unit up moves the y-intercept from $(0, 1)$ to $(0, 2)$ as in choice A.

3. (C) $f(x)$ is a compression of $g(x) = x^2$. The point $(0,0)$ remains on the graph, eliminating answer choice D. Choice A shows stretching. Try choices B and C. Choice B fails the test at $(2, 1)$. Select answer choice C.

Practice: Composition of Functions (page 382)

1. (C) First create the function $f(x)$ from $q(x)$ and $p(x)$. Work from right to left; $p(q(x))$ means $q(x)$ evaluated at $p(x)$. Then, $f(x) = (4x)^2 - 5(4x) + 6$. Simplify and find $f(x) = 16x^2 - 20x + 6$, and $f(1) = 16(1)^2 - 20(1) + 6 = 2$.

2. (A) Again, we must first create the function $f(x)$. Work from right to left; $p(q(x))$ means $q(x)$ evaluated at $p(x)$. So, $f(x) = \dfrac{2(x^2 - 5)}{(x^2 - 5) + 1} = \dfrac{2x^2 - 10}{x^2 - 4}$. Now, $f(4) = \dfrac{2(4)^2 - 10}{(4)^2 - 4} = \dfrac{22}{12} = \dfrac{11}{6}$.

SAT-Type Questions (page 385)

1. (A) If $f(x) = q(p(x))$, then $f(6) = \sqrt{6 - 2} = \sqrt{4} = 2$.

2. (D) Since $h(x) = f(g(x))$, $h(x) = f(x^2 - 2) = x^2 - 2 + 4 = x^2 + 2$.

3. (C) Start by transforming $g(x)$ into $h(x)$. Then $h(x) = 0.5|x|$. Now transform $h(x)$ into $f(x)$. So, $f(x) = 0.5|x + 2|$.

4. (C) The composition $m(k(-1)) = m((-1)^2 - 3(-1)) = m(1 + 3) = m(4) = 2 - 4(4) = -14$.

5. (D) The function $h(x)$ is a composition of $f(x)$ and $g(x)$. So, $h(x) = f(x - 1) = (x - 1)^2 + 1 = x^2 - 2x + 1 + 1 = x^2 - 2x + 2$.

6. (B)   Transforming $g(x)$ into $h(x)$ yields $h(x) = (x-3)^2$. Then $f(x) = 3(x-3)^2$.

7. (C)   If we start with $g(x) = |x+2|$, then $h(x) = 0.5|x+2|$, and
$f(x) = 0.5|x+2-2| = 0.5|x|$.

8. (2)   First determine the equations of the graphs. Calculate the slope and y-intercept of $f(x)$ to find that $f(x) = x - 2$. Then the graph of $g(x)$ is the graph of x^2 translated two units down. So, $g(x) = x^2 - 2$. Now, $f(0) = -2$ and $g(-2) = (-2)^2 - 2 = 4 - 2 = 2$.

9. (0)   Note that in this problem, we're being asked for $f(g)$ rather than $g(f)$ as in the previous problem. Thus, $g(-2) = (-2)^2 - 2 = 2$ and $f(2) = 2 - 2 = 0$.

10. (3)   Begin by evaluating $f(-5) = |-5| + 3 = 5 + 3 = 8$. Then, $g(8) = \sqrt{8+1} = \sqrt{9} = 3$.

11. (5)   Start the problem by evaluating the inner function at the given value. Then, $g(6) = 6^2 = 36$ and $f(x) = \sqrt{36-11} = \sqrt{25} = 5$.

12. (4)   The inner function evaluated at 9 yields $f(9) = \dfrac{9-5}{2} = \dfrac{4}{2} = 2$. Then,
$g(2) = \sqrt{3 \cdot 2^2 + 4} = \sqrt{3 \cdot 4 + 4} = \sqrt{12 + 4} = \sqrt{16} = 4$.

Summary SAT-Type Test

Multiple Choice (page 389)

Calculator Allowed

1. (D)   We can use the rules of exponents to express x^6 as $x \cdot x^5$. Then,
$x^6 = x \cdot x^5 = \dfrac{3}{a}$, and we know that $x^5 = \dfrac{a^2}{6}$. Thus, $x \cdot \dfrac{a^2}{6} = \dfrac{3}{a}$ and
$x = \dfrac{3}{a} \cdot \dfrac{6}{a^2} = \dfrac{18}{a^3}$.

2. (D)   Express the problem mathematically: $\dfrac{3}{2}x^2 - \dfrac{1}{4}x - 4 - \left[\dfrac{5}{2}x^2 - \dfrac{3}{4}x + 1\right]$.

Then distribute the negative sign through the second set of brackets and combine the like terms. Doing so, you find that $\dfrac{3}{2}x^2 - \dfrac{1}{4}x - 4 - \dfrac{5}{2}x^2 + \dfrac{3}{4}x - 1 = -x^2 + \dfrac{1}{2}x - 5$.

3. (B)   Multiply each term in the equation by the common denominator $(4x - 1)$, to cancel out the fractions. Now, $16x^2 = 1 + M(4x - 1)$. Solve this equation for M by dividing both sides by $(4x - 1)$, then factor and cancel like terms:
$M = \dfrac{16x^2 - 1}{4x - 1}$ and $M = \dfrac{\cancel{(4x-1)}(4x+1)}{\cancel{4x-1}} = 4x + 1$.

4. (C)   Consider the factors of 12. They are 1, 2, 3, 4, 6, and 12. Of those, only 3 and 4 have a potential difference of -1 if the 4 were negative and the 3 positive; those two factors also have a product of -12. Then you know that $x = -4$ and $x = 3$. Working backwards to create the quadratic equation, $(x + 4)(x - 3) = 0$ and $x^2 + x - 12 = 0$. This is answer choice C.

5. (B)   For the function to have a positive output, it must have a y-value greater than 0. Begin by setting the given function, $y = -2x^2 + 6$, equal to zero. Then, $0 = -2x^2 + 6$ and $2x^2 = 6$. Solve by dividing both sides by 2 and taking the square root to find that $x = \pm\sqrt{3}$. As a decimal, $\pm\sqrt{3} = \pm1.732$. There are three integers, $\{-1, 0, 1\}$, between those values. You can also see this by graphing the equation on your calculator:

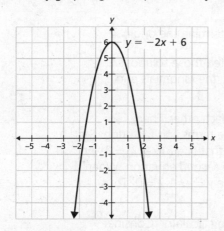

6. (C)   Substitute $2x - 2$ for y in the first equation so that $2x - 2 = x^2 + x - 4$ and $x^2 - x - 2 = 0$. Factoring, $(x - 2)(x + 1) = 0$ and $x = 2$ or $x = -1$. Substitute these values back into the second equation. If $x = 2$, then $y = 2(2) - 2 = 2$. If $x = -1$, then $y = 2(-1) - 2 = -4$. Thus, the solutions are $(2, 2)$, $(-1, -4)$.

7. (C)   The translation of the parent parabola is a shift to the right 2 units and down 1 unit. Thus, $y = x^2$ is now $y = (x - 2)^2 - 1$.

8. (D)   If the area of a square is $s^2 = \dfrac{1}{A}$, then the length of a side, s, of the square must be $\sqrt{\dfrac{1}{A}}$. The perimeter of the square is then $4 \cdot \sqrt{\dfrac{1}{A}}$. But none of the answer choices match this expression. Rationalize the denominator to find $\dfrac{4}{\sqrt{A}} \cdot \dfrac{\sqrt{A}}{\sqrt{A}} = \dfrac{4\sqrt{A}}{A}$.

9. (C)   Multiply the second fraction by $\dfrac{a-1}{a-1}$ to make a common denominator.

Now, $\dfrac{a^2+1}{a^2-1} - \left(\dfrac{a}{a+1} \cdot \dfrac{(a-1)}{(a-1)} \right) = \dfrac{a^2+1}{a^2-1} - \dfrac{a^2-a}{a^2-1} = \dfrac{a^2+1-a^2+a}{a^2-1}$. Simplifying,

we have $\dfrac{\cancel{a+1}}{(a-1)\cancel{(a+1)}} = \dfrac{1}{a-1}$.

10. (D)   Subtract 4 from both sides so that $4 + \sqrt{x^2 - 6x} = 0$ is now $\sqrt{x^2 - 6x} = -4$. Square both sides and set the equation equal to 0 to see that $x^2 - 6x = 16$ and $x^2 - 6x - 16 = 0$. Factor: $(x - 8)(x + 2) = 0$ and $x = 8$ or $x = -2$. Check your solutions. If $x = 8$, then $4 + \sqrt{64 - 48} = 4 + \sqrt{16} \neq 0$, and if $x = -2$, $4 + \sqrt{4 - 6(-2)} = 4 + \sqrt{16} \neq 0$. Neither solution works.

11. (B) Begin by determining how many doubling periods have passed. If we convert 2.5 hours into 150 minutes, and divide by 30, we know there were 5 doubling periods. Then use the general equation of an exponential function to determine the initial number of bacteria present. So, $y = ab^x$, and $24000 = a(2)^{\frac{150\text{min}}{30\text{min}}}$. Simplifying, $24000 = a(2)^5$ and $24000 = a(32)$. Divide both sides by 32: $a = 750$.

12. (A) Set $x = \dfrac{3}{2}$ and $x = -\dfrac{1}{4}$ and work backwards to determine the original quadratic equation. Then, the binomials that created those solutions must have been $(2x - 3) = 0$ and $(4x + 1) = 0$. FOIL the binomials and $8x^2 - 10x - 3 = 0$.

13. (B) Since $y = y$, set the two given equations equal to each other. Then, $x^2 - 4 = x + 2$. Now solve for x by collecting the like terms and factoring. So, $x^2 - x - 4 - 2 = 0$ and $x^2 - x - 6 = 0$. Factor to see that $(x - 3)(x + 2) = 0$ and $x = 3$ or $x = -2$. Substitute these values for x in the second equation. When $x = 3$ we have $y = 3 + 2 = 5$ and for $x = -2$ we have $y = -2 + 2 = 0$. Thus, the coordinate pairs (x, y) are $(3, 5)$ and $(-2, 0)$.

14. (B) Graph the given parent function on your graphing calculator. Consider that the graph in the question is compressed in the vertical direction by a factor of $\dfrac{1}{2}$, but not translated vertically or horizontally. Thus, the correct equation is $y = -\left(\dfrac{1}{2}x\right)^2 + 4$.

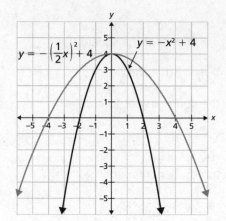

15. (C) If the bases were both the same number, we could use the rules of exponents to solve for the unknown. Both 8 and 4 are powers of 2, so rewrite the problem as $\left(2^3\right)^{3x+1} = \left(2^2\right)^{2x-4}$ and $2^{9x+3} = 2^{4x-8}$. Now set the exponents equal to each other: $9x + 3 = 4x - 8$ and $5x = -11$. So $x = -\dfrac{11}{5}$.

16. (A) Notice the negative exponents on all the bases. We can rewrite $\dfrac{a^{-1} - b^{-1}}{b^{-2} - a^{-2}}$ as $\dfrac{\dfrac{1}{a} - \dfrac{1}{b}}{\dfrac{1}{b^2} - \dfrac{1}{a^2}}$ using the rules of exponents. The simplest way to solve from this point is to multiply all four terms by $a^2 b^2$, which is the common denominator for all the terms, and then $\dfrac{ab^2 - a^2 b}{a^2 - b^2} = \dfrac{ab\,(a - b)(-1)}{(a - b)(a + b)} = \dfrac{-ab}{a + b}$.

17. (B) Simplify the expression in the parentheses first: $\left(5-\dfrac{1}{x}\right)(K)=\dfrac{1}{x}$ is $\left(\dfrac{5x}{x}-\dfrac{1}{x}\right)(K)=\left(\dfrac{5x-1}{x}\right)(K)=\dfrac{1}{x}$. Multiply both sides by the reciprocal of K's coefficient and $K=\dfrac{1}{x}\cdot\dfrac{x}{5x-1}=\dfrac{1}{5x-1}$.

18. (C) First determine the equation that models the given exponential decay. The general form is $y=ab^x$. Then, $1.5=3.0\,(1-0.20)^x$ where x is the number of hours. Simplifying, we write $1.5=3(0.80)^x$ and $0.5=(0.80)^x$. Now check each answer choice: (A) $(0.80)^{2.8}=0.535$; (B) $(0.80)^{3.0}=0.512$; (C) $(0.80)^{3.1}=0.501$; and (D) $(0.80)^{3.3}=0.479$. Answer choice C yields a true statement. Note that this problem could also be solved by taking the log of both sides after determining the simplified form of the equation.

19. (C) Both exponential graphs pass through the y-axis at $y=1$, when $x=0$. This is easiest to see if you use your graphing calculator:

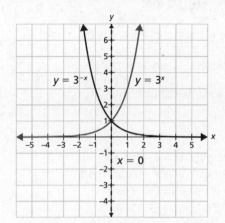

20. (B) Solve for y in the linear equation and substitute that expression in for y in $x^2+y^2=25$. Since $y=1-x$, we have $x^2+(1-x)^2=25$ and $x^2+(1-x-x+x^2)$ becomes $2x^2-2x+1=25$. Combining the like terms and dividing through by the common factor yields $2x^2-2x-24=0$ and $x^2-x-12=0$. Factor and solve. Then $(x-4)(x+3)=0$ and $x=4$ or $x=-3$. The only pairings that have these x-values are in choice B.

21. (D) Quickly notice that neither adding nor subtracting the two functions will yield the correct constant term. Move to choice C and find that $m(f(x))=3x-5+10$, which is not correct. But, choice D works: $f(m(x))=f(x+10)=3(x+10)-5=3x+30-5=3x+25$.

22. (C) Answer choice C, $\left(10^{\sqrt{2}}\right)\left(10^{\sqrt{2}}\right)=100$, should be $10^{\sqrt{2}+\sqrt{2}}=10^{2\sqrt{2}}=10^{2.8284}$, approximately 673.6, not 100.

23. (B) The expression $\left[a^2+b^2-(a-b)^2\right]^2$ can be simplified within the parentheses first: $\left[a^2+b^2-(a^2-2ab+b^2)\right]^2=\left[a^2+b^2-a^2+2ab-b^2\right]^2$. Combine the like terms and find that $(2ab)^2=4a^2b^2$.

24. (B) Using the given example, if $\dfrac{15}{5}=3=\dfrac{45}{15}=3$, then by analogy, $\dfrac{4x+1}{2x-1}=\dfrac{15x-3}{4x+1}$. Cross-multiply to see that $(4x+1)(4x+1)=(2x-1)(15x-3)$, and $16x^2+8x+1=30x^2-6x-15x+3$. Collect the like terms and factor to solve. Then, $0=14x^2-29x+2$ and $0=(14x-1)(x-2)$. Thus, $x=\dfrac{1}{14}$ or $x=2$.

25. (D) Translate the words into a mathematical equation: $\dfrac{36x^2}{6x+5} = \dfrac{25}{6x+5} + M$.

Subtract so the M is isolated on the right-hand side of the equation. Then, $\dfrac{36x^2}{6x+5} - \dfrac{25}{6x+5} = M$. The denominators are alike. Combine the fractions and see that the numerator is the difference of two perfect squares. Factor and cancel the like terms. Then, $\dfrac{(6x-5)\cancel{(6x+5)}}{\cancel{6x+5}} = M$.

26.(A) Begin by factoring the given quadratic. Then, $2x^2 - 5x - 3 = 0$ becomes $(2x + 1)(x - 3) = 0$. The roots are $x = -\dfrac{1}{2}$ and $x = 3$. The sum of the roots $= \dfrac{5}{2}$ and the product is $\dfrac{-3}{2}$. Thus, $\dfrac{5}{2} + \dfrac{-3}{2} = \dfrac{2}{2} = 1$.

27. (A) Substitute $-x^2$ for y in the fractional equation, $\dfrac{y+1}{x+1} = \dfrac{1}{2}$, so that $\dfrac{-x^2+1}{x+1} = \dfrac{1}{2}$. Cross-multiply and solve: $-2x^2 + 2 = x + 1$ and $2x^2 + x - 1 = 0$. Factoring, $(2x - 1)(x + 1) = 0$ and $x = \dfrac{1}{2}$ or $x = -1$. Reject -1 since it makes the denominator of the fractional equation equal to 0. Substitute $x = \dfrac{1}{2}$ in $y = -x^2$, and $y = -\left(\dfrac{1}{2}\right)^2 = -\dfrac{1}{4}$.

28. (B) Since the parabola $y = (x - 2)^2$ is given in vertex form $f(x) = a(x - h)^2 + k$, the vertex is $(h, k) = (2, 0)$, and the old axis of symmetry was $x = 2$. Shifting left 3 units and down 4 units, the new vertex is $(-1, -4)$ and the axis of symmetry is $x = -1$.

29.(D) The expression $\left(\sqrt[3]{x^4}\right)\left(x^{-\frac{1}{2}}\right)$ is the same as $x^{\frac{4}{3}} \cdot x^{-\frac{1}{2}}$. Since the bases are the same, we can use the rules of exponents to simplify. Then $x^{\frac{4}{3}} \cdot x^{-\frac{1}{2}} = x^{\frac{4}{3}+\left(-\frac{1}{2}\right)} = x^{\frac{5}{6}}$. Rewriting, we have $x^{\frac{5}{6}} = \sqrt[6]{x^5}$.

30. (A) The expression $\left(1 + \dfrac{1}{x}\right) \div \left(\dfrac{x+1}{x^2}\right)$ can be rewritten as $\left(\dfrac{x}{x} + \dfrac{1}{x}\right) \cdot \left(\dfrac{x^2}{x+1}\right)$.

Applying multiplication of fraction rules, we see that $\left(\dfrac{\cancel{x+1}}{x}\right) \cdot \left(\dfrac{x^2}{\cancel{x+1}}\right) = \dfrac{x^2}{x} = x$.

Student-Produced Response Questions (page 395)

Calculator Allowed

31. (14) Expand the binomials on the left-hand side of the equation to see that $(x + y)^2 - (x - y)^2 = 56$ becomes $x^2 + 2xy + y^2 - (x^2 - 2xy + y^2)$. Distribute the negative sign through the parentheses and combine the like terms. Then, $x^2 + 2xy + y^2 - x^2 + 2xy - y^2$ is $4xy = 56$. Divide both sides by 4 and $xy = 14$.

32. (2.31)   The given quadratic is not factorable. Use the quadratic formula and

$$x = \frac{-(-6) \pm \sqrt{(-6)^2 - 4(3)(-1)}}{2(3)} = \frac{6 \pm \sqrt{36 + 12}}{6} = \frac{6 \pm \sqrt{48}}{6} = \frac{6 \pm 4\sqrt{3}}{6}.$$ Reduce

further to see that we have $\frac{3 \pm 2\sqrt{3}}{3}$. The decimal equivalent is $\frac{3 + 2\sqrt{3}}{3} =$

2.1547 and $\frac{3 - 2\sqrt{3}}{3} = -0.1547$. The positive difference is 2.1547 −

(−0.1547) = 2.3094, or 2.31 to the nearest hundredth.

33. $\left(\frac{1}{2} \text{ or } 0.5\right)$ For $y = ax^2 - 7x - 14$ the axis of symmetry is $x = -\frac{b}{2a} = \frac{-(-7)}{2a} = \frac{7}{2a}$. Then,

$\frac{7}{2a} = 7$, $14a = 7$, and $a = \frac{7}{14}$, or $\frac{1}{2}$, or 0.5.

34. (2.83)   Using the given linear equation, replace y with x in the non-linear equation. Then, $x^2 + x^2 = 16$ and $2x^2 = 16$. Solve for x and find that $x^2 = 8$, $x = \sqrt{8} = 2.828 = 2.83$ (to the nearest hundredth).

35. (127)   You can solve this problem by evaluating $g(f(3))$. First, evaluate $f(3) = 3^2 - 1 =$ 8. Then, $g(8) = 2^{8-1} - 1 = 2^7 - 1 = 128 - 1 = 127$.

36. (0)   If $a^x a^y = 1$, then $a^{x+y} = 1 = a^0$. Thus, $x + y = 0$.

37. PART 1

$\left(\frac{5}{4} \text{ or } 1.25\right)$ Since the seagull can catch the fish only if both the seagull and the fish are at the same height at the same time, set the equations equal to each other and solve for t. Thus, $-8t + 15 = -16t^2 + 30$ and $16t^2 - 8t + 15 - 30 = 0$ or $16t^2 - 8t - 15 = 0$. Now factor and find that $(4t + 3)(4t - 5) = 0$ so that $4t + 3 = 0$ or $4t - 5 = 0$. Solving, $t = -\frac{4}{3}$ or $t = \frac{5}{4}$. Time cannot be

negative, so only $t = \frac{5}{4}$ seconds makes sense. Note that you can grid in

either $\frac{5}{4}$ or 1.25.

PART 2

(6)   Again, we need to set the equations equal to each other to determine the time at which the birds meet. Then we will be able to use that answer to determine their height above the water. So, $-2t + 12 = -t^2 + 15$ and $t^2 - 2t + 12 - 15 = 0$ is $t^2 - 2t - 3 = 0$. Factor to see that $(t - 3)(t + 1) = 0$ and $t = 3$ or $t = -1$. Of these, only $t = 3$ makes sense. Then, if $k(t) = -2t + 12$, $k(3) = -2(3) + 12 = 6$. The birds are 6 feet above the water when they meet.

Summary SAT-Type Test

Multiple Choice (page 398)

No Calculator Allowed

1. (C)   The expression $\frac{x^{-3}}{x^{-2}} = \frac{x^2}{x^3} = \frac{1}{x}$.

2. (B)   Only answer choices B and C are viable because they both begin with $3x$, and $3x(2x^2) = 6x^3$ (the leading term of the product). Notice that $(-2)(7) = -14$, so that $(2x^2 - 5x + 7)(3x - 2) = 6x^3 - 19x^2 + 31x - 14$. Select answer choice B.

3. (D) To solve $\left(\sqrt{3}-1\right)N=1$ for N, we divide by $\left(\sqrt{3}-1\right)$ so that $N=\dfrac{1}{\sqrt{3}-1}$. Then we must rationalize the denominator, so multiply both numerator and denominator by the conjugate $\sqrt{3}+1$. Now, $N=\dfrac{1}{\sqrt{3}-1}\cdot\dfrac{\sqrt{3}+1}{\sqrt{3}+1}$ and $N=\dfrac{\sqrt{3}+1}{3-1}=\dfrac{\sqrt{3}+1}{2}$.

4. (C) Projectile motion in vertex form is modeled by the general equation $f(x)=a(x-h)^2+k$ where h is the time at which the maximum height k is reached. Hence, if $h=2.8$ and $k=65$, the equation is $h(t)=-16(t-2.8)^2+65$.

5. (A) The vertex is found using the formula for the axis of symmetry, $x=\dfrac{-b}{2a}$. In this case, $x=-\dfrac{2}{2(-1)}=1$. Substituting the x-value into the given equation $y=f(x)=-x^2+2x+4$, we have $-(1)^2+2(1)+4=-1+2+4=5$. The coordinates of the vertex are $(1, 5)$.

6. (C) You can use your knowledge of transformations to determine the equation of the curve and the equation of the line, or you could notice the quadrants in which the intersections occur. There is one intersection in the first quadrant and one in the third quadrant. All the coordinate pairs in the first quadrant will be $(+, +)$. All the pairs in the third quadrant will be $(-, -)$. The only answer choice that fits this pattern is C.

7. (B) Using the distance formula, $d=\sqrt{(x_1-x_2)^2+(y_1-y_2)^2}$, and substituting in the given values for $(x_1, y_1)=\left(\sqrt{5},\sqrt{3}\right)$ and $(x_2, y_2)=\left(\sqrt{3},-\sqrt{5}\right)$, we can write $d=\sqrt{\left(\sqrt{5}-\sqrt{3}\right)^2+\left(\sqrt{3}-\left(-\sqrt{5}\right)\right)^2}=\sqrt{5-2\sqrt{15}+3+\left(\sqrt{3}+\sqrt{5}\right)^2}$. Continuing, $\sqrt{8-2\sqrt{15}+3+2\sqrt{15}+5}=\sqrt{16}=4$.

8. (D) Since $a>0$, the parabola opens upward, and since $b>0$, the parabola is shifted vertically upward.

9. (B) Given $\dfrac{x^2-16}{x^2-25}\div\left(\dfrac{x^2-16}{x^2-x-20}\cdot\dfrac{x+4}{x-4}\right)$ we first factor carefully within the parentheses: $\left(\dfrac{x^2-16}{x^2-x-20}\cdot\dfrac{x+4}{x-4}\right)=\left(\dfrac{(x-4)(x+4)}{(x-5)(x+4)}\cdot\dfrac{x+4}{x-4}\right)=\dfrac{x+4}{x-5}$.

Now use the reciprocal of that fraction and multiply it by the dividend: $\dfrac{x^2-16}{x^2-25}\cdot\dfrac{x-5}{x+4}=\dfrac{(x-4)(x+4)}{(x-5)(x+5)}\cdot\dfrac{x-5}{x+4}=\dfrac{x-4}{x+5}$.

10. (D) If $\dfrac{p}{q}=1-\dfrac{1}{x}$, then $\dfrac{p}{q}=\dfrac{x}{x}-\dfrac{1}{x}=\dfrac{x-1}{x}$ and $\dfrac{q}{p}=\dfrac{x}{x-1}$.

11. (B) To solve this equation, multiply all terms by the least common denominator (x^2-1). Thus, $(x^2-1)\cdot\left(\dfrac{2x^2}{x^2-1}-\dfrac{3}{x+1}=\dfrac{x}{x-1}\right)$. Simplifying, we have $2x^2-3(x-1)=x(x+1)$, and then $2x^2-3x+3=x^2+x$. Continuing, $x^2-4x+3=0$ and $(x-3)(x-1)=0$ so that $x=3$ or $x=1$. However, $x=1$ is an extraneous root: it turns the denominators into 0. We reject that root, and the solution is $x=3$.

12. (C) If $x=0$, then c equals a negative number on the y-axis. Because the graph opens downward, the coefficient of x^2, which is a, is also negative. Since a and c are negative, then $ac>0$ since the product of two negatives is a positive.

13. (B)   Solve for y in $x + y = -1$ so that $y = -x - 1$. Substitute that equation for y in the non-linear equation, and you have $x^2 - (-x - 1)^2 = 3$. Expand and then distribute to see that $x^2 - (x^2 + 2x + 1) = 3$ and $x^2 - x^2 - 2x - 1 = 3$. Collect the like terms and solve for x: $-2x = 4$ and $x = -2$. There is only one answer choice with -2 in the x position.

14. (C)   The new function $g(x) = f(x + 2) + 1$ means to translate the original $f(x)$ function left 2 units and shift up 1 unit. Change $f(x)$ from general form to vertex form to see that $f(x) = (x - 2)^2 - 1$, then translate. Hence, the vertex $(2, -1)$ has moved to $(2 - 2, -1 + 1) = (0, 0)$.

15. (B)   The expression $3\sqrt{\dfrac{1}{m^{-2}}} + \left(\sqrt{m^{-2}}\right)^{-1} = 3\sqrt{m^2} + \left(\sqrt{\dfrac{1}{m^2}}\right)^{-1} = 3m + \left(\dfrac{1}{m}\right)^{-1} =$

$3m + \left(\dfrac{1}{m^{-1}}\right) = 3m + m = 4m.$

Student-Produced Response Questions (page 725)

No Calculator Allowed

16. (32)   Begin by expanding $(x - y)^2$ into $x^2 - 2xy + y^2$. Notice how you have the expressions $x^2 + y^2$ and xy embedded within the expanded expression. Rearrange to see it better: $x^2 + y^2 - 2xy$. Now, substitute in 22 for $x^2 + y^2$ and -5 for xy, and then $x^2 + y^2 - 2xy = 22 + (-2)(-5) = 22 + 10 = 32$.

17. $\left(\dfrac{1}{4} \text{ or } 0.25\right)$ In $2x + \sqrt{x} - 1 = 0$, we start by isolating the radical on one side of the equation. Then, $\sqrt{x} = 1 - 2x$. Now square both sides and find $x = (1 - 2x)^2 = 4x^2 - 4x + 1$. Collect the like terms and factor to solve. So, $0 = 4x^2 - 5x + 1$ and $0 = (4x - 1)(x - 1)$. If $4x - 1 = 0$, then $x = \dfrac{1}{4} = 0.25$, and if $x - 1 = 0$,

then $x = 1$. Check the solution in the original equation. If $x = 1$, then $2(1) + \sqrt{1} - 1 = 2 + 1 - 1 = 2 \neq 0$. This is an extraneous root. Now check $x = 0.25$. If $x = 0.25$, then $2(0.25) + \sqrt{0.25} - 1 = 0$, which is true.

18. (1)   The graph of a quadratic equation of this form ($y = ax^2 + bx + c$) is a parabola. The maximum height of the ball is at the t-value of the vertex of the parabola. To find the (t, h) vertex of the function $h(t) = -16t^2 + 32t + 6$,

we use the formula $t = -\dfrac{b}{2a}$ where $b = 32$ and $a = -16$. Thus,

$t = -\dfrac{b}{2a} = -\dfrac{32}{2(-16)} = \dfrac{32}{32} = 1.$

19. (6.5)   Given the x-intercepts and substituting y for $f(x)$, we can rewrite the function as $y = (x - 2)(x + 3)(x - p)$. The intercepts show us the zeros of the function, namely, 2, -3, and p. Choose one of the numeric zeros. The whole number 2 is easiest to work with. Substitute 0 for y and 2 for x in the function $f(x)$. Then, $0 = (2)^3 + 0.5(2)^2 - 2c + 3$ and $0 = 8 + 2 - 2c + 3$. Solving for c, $0 = 13 - 2c$, and $2c = 13$, so that $c = 6.5$.

20. $\left(\dfrac{1}{2} \text{ or } 0.5\right)$ If the horizontal line $y = 4$ intersects the parabola at one point, then that point must be the vertex of the parabola. Hence, we could find the axis of symmetry by $x = -\dfrac{b}{2a} = -\dfrac{-1}{2} = \dfrac{1}{2}$, so the x-value is $\dfrac{1}{2}$, or 0.5. Alternatively, we could substitute 4 for y in the given equation and solve for x. That

method produces this equation, $0 = x^2 - x + 0.25$, and factors into $0 = \left(x - \dfrac{1}{2}\right)\left(x - \dfrac{1}{2}\right)$ and, again, $x = \dfrac{1}{2}$.

Category 4: Additional Topics in Math

Lesson 1: Using Formulas to Calculate Side Length, Area, and Volume

Practice: Surface Area and Volume of Other Shapes (page 419)

1. (B)   The formula for the volume of a cylinder is $V = Bh$. We can solve this formula for B and substitute in given values to find that $B = \dfrac{V}{h} = \dfrac{72\pi}{8} = 9\pi$.

Since this figure is a cylinder, $B = \pi r^2$ and $r^2 = 9\pi$. Then $r^2 = 9$ and $r = 3$. Use the radius to find the circumference of the base: $2\pi r = 2\pi \cdot 3 = 6\pi$.

2. (D)   If the area of one face is 16, then the square of the length of a single side is $s^2 = 16$. Take the square root of 16 and the length of a side is 4. Then use the formula for the volume of a cube and $V = 4^3 = 64$.

3. (D)   If the circumference of the base is 18π, then the diameter of the base is 18 feet since circumference $= \pi d = 18\pi$. The height of the silo is twice the diameter, so $h = 2(18) = 36$ feet. Now use the formula for the volume of a cylinder and $V = \pi(9)^2 \cdot 36 = 2{,}916\pi$ ft³.

SAT-Type Questions (page 421)

1. (B)   Since the corner square cutouts are 2.5 in by 2.5 in, the bottom of the box will be 5 inches by 10 inches once the sides are folded up. Then the height is 2.5 inches, so since $V = lwh$, substitute in the values and $5 \cdot 10 \cdot 2.5 = 125$ cubic inches.

2. (D)   We know the ratio of the two surface areas. Since area is a square measurement, take the square root of the ratio to determine the ratio of linear measures. Then $\dfrac{\sqrt{9}}{\sqrt{4}} = \dfrac{3}{2}$. Now cube the linear measurement to determine the volume measurement and $\dfrac{3^3}{2^3} = \dfrac{27}{8}$.

3. (A)   The radius of the cylinder base is b and the height is a. Substituting these values into the formula $V = \pi r^2 h$, the volume is $V = \pi a b^2$.

4. (A)   The question gives us measurements in feet and inches, but we need to know how many cubic yards of concrete are used. There are 3 feet in 1 yard and 36 inches in 1 yard, so convert all the measurements prior to finding the volume. Then 9 feet = 3 yards, 6 feet = 2 yards, and 6 inches $= \dfrac{1}{6}$ yard. Then the volume of a rectangular solid is $V = lwh$ and $3 \cdot 2 \cdot \dfrac{1}{6} = 1$ cubic yard. This will cost $90.

5. (D)   First determine the volume of water in the pool, which is a circular cylinder. So $V = \pi r^2 h$, and $\pi \cdot 8^2 \cdot 4 = 256\pi$ ft³. Then the number of pounds of ice needed to reduce the pool temperature 4 degrees is $N = 0.31 \cdot 4 \cdot 256\pi = 997.27$. The ice is sold in 5-pound bags, which means Ruth will need $\dfrac{997.27}{5} = 199.5 \approx 200$ bags of ice. The bags are $3 each, and $3 \cdot 200 = 600$.

6. (B)   To know how much cardboard is needed to make each box, we must determine its surface area. Each box has 5 sides, 2 sides measuring 8.5 by 5, 2 sides measuring 6 by 5, and 1 side measuring 6 by 8.5. So $2(8.5 \cdot 5) + 2(6 \cdot 5) + 6 \cdot 8.5 = 196$ in².

7. (C)   Since each shed has 2 walls that measure 10 by 7 and 2 walls that measure 8 by 7, the area to be painted on each shed is $2(8 \cdot 7 + 10 \cdot 7) = 252$ square feet. All together, the 5 sheds have $5 \cdot 252 = 1260$ ft² of surface to paint. Then $\frac{1260 \text{ ft}^2}{350 \text{ ft}^2} = 3.6$ gallons of paint, which must be rounded to 4 gallons.

8. (C)   The volume of the block before considering the cylindrical cutouts is $V = 9 \cdot 4 \cdot 3 = 108$ in³. Now find the volume of the cylinders. The radius of each is 1.2 inches and then the volume of each tunnel is $V = \pi r^2 h$, and $\pi (1.2)^2 \cdot 4 \approx 18.1$. There are three cylinders, so subtracting their volume, the block is $108 - 3(18.1) = 53.7$ in³. Finish by calculating the mass of the block. Set up a proportion: $\frac{x \text{ lbs}}{53.7 \text{ in}^3} = \frac{0.02 \text{ lbs}}{1 \text{ in}^3}$, and $x = 0.02 \cdot 53.7 = 1.074$ lbs. Examine the answer choices. The closest is choice C.

9. (B)   The solid is a cone with a hemisphere on top. The volume of the hemisphere is half the volume of a sphere, so $V = \frac{1}{2} \cdot \frac{4}{3} \pi r^3$, which simplifies to $\frac{2}{3} \pi r^3$. The volume of the cone is $V = \frac{1}{3} \pi r^2 h$. Substituting the given values, the volume of the solid is $\frac{2}{3} \pi \cdot 4^3 + \frac{1}{3} \pi \cdot 8 \cdot 4^2$.

10. (3.5)   The formula for the volume of a pyramid is $V = \frac{lwh}{3}$. Since the base is a square with side s, rewrite the formula to reflect this: $V = \frac{s \cdot s \cdot h}{3}$, or $V = \frac{s^2 h}{3}$. Substitute in the values and $49 = \frac{s^2 \cdot 12}{3}$. Solving for the variable, $s^2 = \frac{3 \cdot 49}{12} = 12.25$. Take the square root of 12.25 and $s = 3.5$ ft.

11. (960)   To calculate the area of the rhombus, divide it into 4 right triangles. Half the given diagonal is 15. Use your knowledge of either Pythagorean triples or the Pythagorean theorem to determine that the missing side of the triangles is 8 feet. Then either find the area of one triangle and multiply by 4 or, knowing the diagonals are 30 feet and 16 feet, use the formula $A = \frac{d_1 \cdot d_2}{2} = \frac{30 \cdot 16}{2} = 240$ ft². Now use the formula for the volume of a pyramid, and the volume is $V = \frac{240 \cdot 12}{3} = 960$ ft³.

12. (21)   The formula for the volume of a sphere is $V = \frac{4 \pi r^3}{3}$. Substitute in the given values and find $12{,}348\pi = \frac{4 \cdot \pi \cdot r^3}{3}$. Divide both sides by π and get $12{,}348 = \frac{4r^3}{3}$. Now multiply 12,348 by $\frac{3}{4}$ to eliminate the fraction. Then $r^3 = 9261$ and, taking the cube root of each side, $r = 21$ cm.

13. (2.5)   When figures are similar, the ratios of their corresponding parts are proportional. Use this fact to help you solve this problem. So $\frac{\text{surface area of prism B}}{\text{surface area of prism A}} = \frac{132}{33} = \frac{4}{1}$. Area is a square measurement. Take the square root of the numerator and denominator to find the linear relationship. Then the ratio of the heights is $\frac{\sqrt{4}}{\sqrt{1}} = \frac{2}{1}$. The height of prism A is half of 5 feet, or 2.5 feet.

14. $\left(\dfrac{5}{4}\right)$ Exploit the relationship among similar figures to answer this question.

So if the ratio of the volumes, which are cubic measurements, is $\dfrac{125}{64}$, then

the ratio of the heights, which are linear measurements, is $\sqrt[3]{\dfrac{125}{64}} = \dfrac{5}{4}$.

Lesson 2: Applying Concepts and Theorems About Lines, Angles, Triangles, and Other Polygons

Practice: Computations Involving Angles and Lines (page 430)

1. (D)   The two marked angles are vertical angles (refer to the "Angles" chart if needed). By definition, vertical angles have equal measure, so $4x - 8 = 40$. Solving for x, $4x = 48$, and $x = 12$.

2. (C)   Line AB forms a straight angle. By definition, $x + x + 44 = 180$. Solving for x, $2x + 44 = 180$, $2x = 136$, and $x = 68$.

3. (D)   Angles x, y, and z form a straight angle, and $x + y + z = 180$. But $x + z = y$, so substitute this information into the first equation. Then $y + y = 180$, $2y = 180$, and $y = 90$.

4. (A)   Both $\angle a$ and $\angle c$ are supplementary to the 30° angle, so they each measure 150°. Then $\angle d$ and the 30° angle are vertical angles, thus they both measure 30°. So $a + c - d = 150 + 150 - 30 = 270°$.

Practice: Computations Involving Triangles (page 435)

1. (A)   The sides have the same relative order as the angles opposite them. Since $15 < 75 < 90$, $a < b < c$.

2. (B)   We know from the markings that we have an isosceles triangle, so $\angle A = \angle C = x$. Then $x + x + 40 = 180$, $2x = 140$, and $x = 70$.

3. (C)   Since the measure of $\angle C$ is 90, the sum of $\angle A$ and $\angle B$ must be $180 - 90 = 90$. Then $3x + 2x = 90$, $5x = 90$, and $x = 18$. But $\angle A$ is $3x$, so $3(18) = 54°$.

4. (A)   Since 2 angles in the triangle measure 60 degrees, the third angle must also be 60 degrees because their sum is 180. We know that equiangular triangles are equilateral, so all the sides are 8 units. The perimeter is $8 \cdot 3 = 24$.

Practice: Determining Lengths and Angles for Special Right Triangles (page 438)

1. (C)   Side x is opposite the 60° angle. Its value will be $\dfrac{\text{hypotenuse} \cdot \sqrt{3}}{2}$.

The other leg, opposite the 30° angle, has length $\dfrac{\text{hypotenuse}}{2} = 8$. Then

the length of the hypotenuse must be $2 \cdot 8$, which is 16. Now, calculate the

length of side x and simplify: $\dfrac{16 \cdot \sqrt{3}}{2} = 8\sqrt{3}$.

2. (B)   The markings on the illustration indicate the triangle is an isosceles right triangle. Each of the unmarked angles are 45°. So the length of the hypotenuse is $\text{leg} \cdot \sqrt{2} = 2\sqrt{2}$.

3. (A)   The length of the side opposite the 30° angle in a 30°–60°–90° triangle is $\dfrac{\text{hypotenuse}}{2}$. So $\dfrac{10}{2} = 5$.

4. (C)   The leg of a 45°–45°–90° triangle is $\dfrac{\text{hypotenuse} \cdot \sqrt{2}}{2}$. Then $\dfrac{10 \cdot \sqrt{2}}{2} = 5\sqrt{2}$.

1. (D) The sum of any two sides of a triangle must be greater than the length of the remaining side. Thus, $10 + 5 = 15$, so the greatest possible integer value for the third side is 14.

2. (B) The measure of $\angle ABC$ must be 60° because the measures of the other angles of $\triangle ABC$ are 30° and 90°. The length of side BC is $\frac{\text{hypotenuse}}{2}$ or $\frac{12}{2} = 6$. Since $\angle ABD$ measures 15°, the measure of $\angle CBD$ is $60° - 15° = 45°$. $\triangle BCD$ is thus a 45°–45°–90° right triangle. The length of the hypotenuse is $\text{leg} \cdot \sqrt{2}$, so the length of BD is $6\sqrt{2}$.

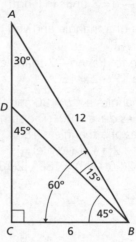

3. (C) Each exterior angle measures $\frac{90}{3} = 30°$. The sum of the exterior angles of a polygon is 360°, so $\frac{360}{30} = 12$ sides.

4. (A) Notice that $\angle APD$ is a vertical angle with $\angle CPB$. So $m\angle x + \angle EPB = 140°$, $x + 90 = 140$, and $x = 50°$.

5. (D) Angle t has the measurement as $\angle a$ marked in the diagram (vertical angles). Since $\angle r$, $\angle a$, and $\angle s$ form a straight angle, their sum is 180°. Replace $\angle a$ with $\angle t$. Again, the sum of the three angles is 180°. So $r + s + t = 180$, or $t = 180 - (r + s)$.

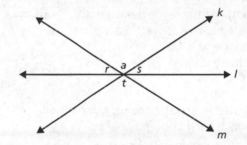

6. (B) Equilateral triangles are also equiangular. All the interior angles in the triangle measure 60°, and exterior angles x and y are supplementary to their respective interior angles. So $180 - 60 = 120°$, and $120 \cdot 2 = 240°$.

7. (D) Since leg AD is the side opposite a 30° angle, the length of AD must be $\frac{1}{2}$ (hypotenuse) $= \frac{1}{2}(4) = 2$. The length of side AC, the hypotenuse of the isosceles right triangle ADC, is $\text{leg} \cdot \sqrt{2} = 2\sqrt{2}$.

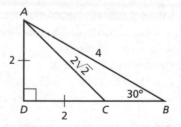

8. (A) Because $\triangle ABC$ is equilateral, the measure of each angle is 60°, and the altitude h bisects $\angle ABC$ and divides the triangle into two 30°–60°–90° right triangles. The altitude is the side opposite $\angle A$. Its length is $\frac{1}{2} \cdot \text{hypotenuse} \cdot \sqrt{3}$, which is $\frac{1}{2}(10)\sqrt{3} = 5\sqrt{3}$.

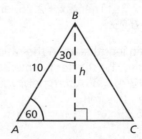

9. (C) Since the triangle is a 45°–45°–90° isosceles right triangle, use the formula $\dfrac{\text{hypotenuse} \cdot \sqrt{2}}{2}$ to determine the length of the legs. Then each leg is $\dfrac{3\sqrt{2} \cdot \sqrt{2}}{2} = \dfrac{3 \cdot 2}{2} = 3$ units in length. Substitute these values into the formula for the area of a triangle and you have $\dfrac{3 \cdot 3}{2} = 4.5$ units.

10. (D) It is possible to draw $n - 2$ triangles from any one vertex. This polygon has 17 sides, so $17 - 2 = 15$.

11. (C) The sum of angles $a + b = 90$ and the sum of angles $d + e = 90$. (The sum of the angles of a triangle is 180.) Then $(c + f) - 2(a + b + d + e) = (90 + 90) - 2(90 + 90) = 180 - 2(180) = -180$.

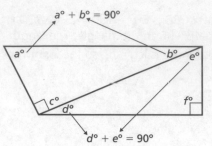

12. (B) Since the opposite sides of the figure are parallel, the figure is a parallelogram. $\angle y = \angle x$ (opposite angles are equal), $x + y = 140°$ (given), and by substituting, $x + x = 140°$, or $x = 70°$. $\angle a$, drawn in the diagram, has the same measure as $\angle x$ (alternate interior angles). So $a = x = 70°$ and $a + w = 180°$ (supplementary angles). $70° + w = 180°$, so $w = 110°$.

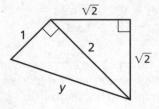

Parallelogram

13. (C) Use the Pythagorean relationship twice. The diagonal is the hypotenuse of an isosceles right triangle with legs $= \sqrt{2}$. Hypotenuse $= \text{leg} \cdot \sqrt{2} = \sqrt{2} \cdot \sqrt{2} = 2$. Now use the diagonal as the leg of the leftmost right triangle: $y^2 = 1^2 + 2^2 = 1 + 4 = 5$. Then $y = \sqrt{5}$.

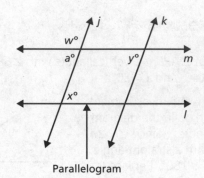

14. (B) The sum of the interior angles of the polygon must be $2(360) = 720°$. Then $180(n - 2) = 720$. Solving for the number of sides, $n - 2 = 4$, and $n = 6$.

15. (A) Sum the expressions to find that $\dfrac{x - 1 + y + z + 1}{2} = \dfrac{x + y + z}{2}$. Then the interior angles of a triangle sum to 180 degrees, so $\dfrac{180}{2} = 90°$.

16. (6.75) In an isosceles right triangle, the lengths of the legs are equal. So $BC = AC = 2.25$. Then $2x = 2.25$, and $x = 1.125$. Then $CD = 6x = 6(1.125) = 6.75$.

17. (8) Since the leg lengths are in the ratio $\sqrt{3} : 1$, the figure ABC is a 30°–60°–90° right triangle. The shorter leg measures half the length of the hypotenuse. Thus, $AB = 2(4) = 8$. Alternately, you could solve this problem via the Pythagorean theorem.

18. (2.02) Since triangle ACD is equilateral, $AD = AC = CD$ and all angles measure 60°. Then $m\angle ACB = 60 + 30 = 90°$. The large triangle ABC is a 30°–60°–90° right triangle. Since $m\angle A = 60°$ and $m\angle B = 30°$ we know that side $CB = 3.5$ units and it is $\dfrac{\sqrt{3}}{2}$ times the hypotenuse AB. So $AB = 2 \cdot \dfrac{3.5}{\sqrt{3}}$. $AD = AC$ equals half the hypotenuse, which is $\dfrac{3.5}{\sqrt{3}}$. $BD = AB - AD = 2 \cdot \dfrac{3.5}{\sqrt{3}} - \dfrac{3.5}{\sqrt{3}} = \dfrac{3.5\sqrt{3}}{3}$ units.

19. (900) The sum of the interior angles is $(5 - 2)(180) = 3(180) = 540°$. The sum of the exterior angles is 360°. Then $540 + 360 = 900°$.

20. (500) 1,000 right angles is $1{,}000 \cdot (90) = 90{,}000$. The sum of the exterior angles is 360° and sum of the interior angles is $90{,}000 - 360 = 89{,}640°$. Then $180(n - 2) = 89{,}640$. Solving for the variable, $n - 2 = \dfrac{89{,}640}{180} = 498$, and $n = 498 + 2 = 500$.

Lesson 3: Using Circle Theorems to Find Arc Lengths, Angle Measures, Chord Lengths, and Sector Areas

Practice: Basic Circle Terms/ Angles in a Circle/ Areas of Sectors (page 455)

1. (B) Since two legs of the triangle are radii of the circle, the triangle is isosceles. Since the angle formed by the two radii is 85°, the sum of the two equal base angles is $180 - 85 = 95$. Each base angle is $\dfrac{95}{2} = 47\dfrac{1}{2} = a$.

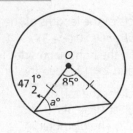

2. (A) First determine the measure of $\overset{\frown}{AB}$. There are 360° in a circle, so $360 - 180 - 66 = 114°$. Then x is an inscribed angle, so its measure is $\dfrac{1}{2}$ its intercepted arc. Divide 114 by 2 and $x = 57°$.

3. (B) A circle's sector area $= \left(\dfrac{\text{central angle}}{360°}\right)\pi r^2$. Substituting, $\left(\dfrac{290}{360}\right)\pi \cdot 8^2 \approx 162\,\text{in}^2$.

4. (C) The endpoints of $\angle ACB$ and $\angle ADB$ are the same. Therefore, they are each halves of the same intercepted arc and are congruent.

Practice: Lengths of Chords, Tangents, and Secants/ Intersection of Circles (page 464)

1. (C) Use the relationship for a secant and a tangent meeting at an external point to solve this problem. Then whole · external = tangent². Then $12 \cdot 3 = AC^2$, $36 = AC^2$, and $AC = 6$.

2. (B) Segments PA and PD are both secants, so whole · external = whole · external. Substituting in the known information, $6 \cdot 3 = (2 + CD) \cdot 2$. Now divide both sides by 2 and see that $9 = 2 + CD$. Then $CD = 7$ and $PD = 7 + 2 = 9$.

SAT-Type Questions (page 466)

1. (C) Segment OO' is the perpendicular bisector of $\overline{AB}$. Draw in segments OA and OE and you see that $\triangle AOE$ is a right triangle. Use the Pythagorean theorem to find the missing length. So $13^2 = 12^2 + AE^2$, and $AE = 5$. Then $AB = 2 \cdot 5 = 10$.

2. (B)   Always connect points that are given. Connect the center of the circle to a corner of the square to make a radius of 5. Do the same thing in the next consecutive corner, and you will have an isosceles right triangle. The sides of this triangle will follow the leg, leg, leg$\sqrt{2}$ sequence; thus 5, 5, 5$\sqrt{2}$, and 5 $\sqrt{2}$ is the side of the square. Alternately, use the Pythagorean Theorem $5^2 + 5^2 = x^2$ and solve for x.

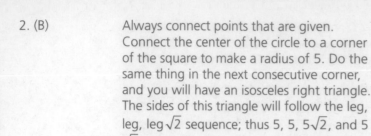

3. (D)   We know the sector area and are looking to solve for the radius. Use the proportional relationship: $\dfrac{\text{sector area}}{\pi r^2} = \dfrac{\text{central angle}}{360°}$. Substituting in the known values and canceling like terms, $\dfrac{14\cancel{\pi}}{\cancel{\pi}r^2} = \dfrac{315}{360}$ becomes $315r^2 = 14 \cdot 360$. Solve for r to see that $r^2 = \dfrac{14 \cdot 360}{315} = 16$, and $r = 4$.

4. (B)   Since the $m\overset{\frown}{BXC} = 250°$, $m\overset{\frown}{BC} = 360 - 250 = 110°$. Then
$$m\angle BAC = \frac{1}{2}(250 - 110) = \frac{1}{2}(140) = 70°.$$

5. (D)   The products of the lengths of the segments of each chord are equal: $AE \cdot EC = BE \cdot ED$. So $(x+3)(x+4) = (x)(x+8)$. FOIL on the left-hand side and distribute on the right-hand side. Then $x^2 + 7x + 12 = x^2 + 8x$. Solve for the unknown and $x = 12$. Then the length of segment $BD = 12 + 12 + 8 = 32$.

6. (A)   Substitute 1 for the radius of the smallest circle. Its diameter is 2. The diameter of the second circle is 4. The diameter of the third circle is 8. The diameter of the fourth circle is 16. Therefore, MN is $2 + 4 + 8 + 16 = 30$. ON, the radius of the fourth circle, is $\frac{1}{2}(16) = 8$. $\dfrac{ON}{MN} = \dfrac{8}{30} = \dfrac{4}{15}$.

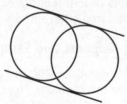

7. (B)   The best way to solve this problem is to draw a sketch. If the circles intersect at two points, the maximum number of common tangents is 2.

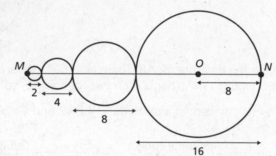

8. (C)   The measure of $\angle BED$ is equal to $\dfrac{m\overset{\frown}{AC} + m\overset{\frown}{BD}}{2}$.

Therefore, $m\overset{\frown}{AC} + m\overset{\frown}{BD} = 100°$ and $m\overset{\frown}{BC} + m\overset{\frown}{DA} = 360 - 100 = 260°$.

9. (B)   Complete triangle OSR, making $\angle OSR$ a right angle. Since PO is 5, QO is 5, and SO is 5, segment OR is now 13. Recognizing and using the Pythagorean triple of 5, 12, 13, segment $RS = 12$. Otherwise, use the Pythagorean Theorem: $13^2 = 5^2 + SR^2$, $169 - 25 = SR^2$, $144 = SR^2$, and $SR = 12$.

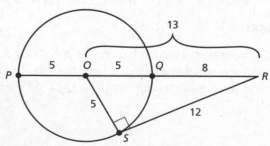

10. (D)   Since both $\angle OAP$ and $\angle OBP$ are right angles and the sum of the interior angles of quadrilaterals is 360, $m\angle P + m\angle AOB = 180°$.

11. (B)   Since chord $\overline{CD}$ is perpendicular to diameter $\overline{AB}$, the chord is bisected by the diameter and ΔOED is a right triangle. The legs of this triangle are $\overline{OE}$ and $\overline{ED}$. The hypotenuse is $\overline{OD}$. Let $x = OE$ and $ED = \dfrac{30}{2} = 15$. Then recognize from Pythagorean triples that $x^2 + 15^2 = 17^2$ results in $x = 8$.

Now, OB is a radius, so $OB = OD = 17$. Finally, $EB = 17 - 8 = 9$.

12. (A)   The products of the lengths of each chord segment must be the same. The first chord's product is $6 \cdot 15 = 90$. For the second chord, you are looking for two numbers that sum to 23 and have a product of 90. There are multiple ways to find this number pair. The simplest is to list the factors of 90 and find that $5 \cdot 18 = 90$ and $5 + 18 = 23$.

13. (36)   Segments drawn from the same external point to a point of tangency on the circle are congruent. Therefore, $CD = 5$, $EF = 7$, and $FA = 6$. The perimeter is $5 + 5 + 6 + 6 + 7 + 7 = 36$.

14. (100)   Since $AP = BP$ and $\overline{OP}$ is common to both triangles and both radii are congruent, the triangles are congruent by SSS and $m\angle BOP = 40$. Then $m\angle OAP = m\angle OBP = 90°$, and $m\angle APB = 360 - (40 + 40 + 90 + 90) = 100°$.

15. (21.5)   Draw in the diameters AC and BD. Then you have the square $ABCD$ and each side has the length of 2 radii = 10. The shaded region is the square minus 2 semi-circles, each with radius 5 or 1 circle with radius 5. So the shaded area is $10^2 - \pi 5^2 \approx 21.5$.

16. (52)   Start by finding the measure of $\overparen{AC} = 360 - (48 + 160) = 152°$. Then the measure of $\angle P = \dfrac{1}{2}(152 - 48) = 52°$.

17. (38)   Determine the measure of $\angle AEC = 180 - 112 = 68°$. Then $68 = \dfrac{98 + m\overparen{BD}}{2}$.

Multiply both sides by 2 to find that $136 = 98 + m\overparen{BD}$. Solve: $m\overparen{BD} = 38°$.

18. (70)   The measure of $\overparen{BC} = 360 - 250 = 110°$. Then you can calculate the measure of $\angle BAC = \dfrac{250 - 110}{2} = 70°$.

19. (60)   Consider the figure. You know that the measure of $\overparen{AC} = 2 \cdot m\angle ABC = 80°$. Then the measure of $\overparen{BD} = 2 \cdot m\angle DCB = 40°$. Now the measure of $\angle AEC = \dfrac{80 + 40}{2} = 60°$.

20. (16)   Sketch a picture to fully understand the description. The products of the chord segment lengths are equal. Then $x \cdot x = 4 \cdot 16$, and $x^2 = 64$. Solving for the unknown, $x = 8$. The question asks for the length of chord CD, so $2x = 16$.

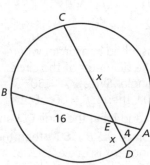

Lesson 4: Derivation and Application of Trigonometric Ratios and the Pythagorean Theorem; Solving Right Triangles

Practice: Derivation and Application of Trigonometric Ratios (page 476)

1. (3.5) Triangle leg BC is opposite $\angle A$, so use the sine function. Then $\sin 30° = \dfrac{BC}{7}$, and $BC = 7 \cdot \sin 30°$. The length of $BC = 3.5$ feet.

2. (36.4) Use the fact that the cosine of an angle is equal to $\dfrac{\text{adjacent leg}}{\text{hypotenuse}}$. Thus, $\cos 30° = \dfrac{x}{42}$, and $0.8660 = \dfrac{x}{42}$. Then $42(0.8660) = x$, and $x = 36.37$, or 36.4 inches to the nearest tenth. Alternately, you can solve this problem in the same manner as number 1 above.

3. (7.5) Use the sine function to solve for d. Then $\sin 45° = \dfrac{28000}{d}$, and $d = \dfrac{28000}{\sin 45°}$, which is 39,597.98 feet. But the problem asks for the distance in miles, so divide 39,597.98 by 5,280 to find 7.49 miles. Round to the nearest tenth and the answer is 7.5 miles.

Practice: The Pythagorean Theorem (page 479)

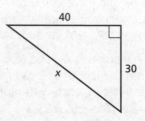

1. (A) Sketch a picture to create a right triangle. At the end of one hour, Howie has traveled 30 miles and Manuel has traveled 40 miles. Notice this is a 3, 4, 5 triangle that has been multiplied by 10. Thus, the roommates are 50 miles apart.

2. (A) Use the Pythagorean theorem with the quantity $x + 10$ as c. Then $(x+10)^2 = (x+9)^2 + (x+2)^2$. Expand the binomials and $x^2 + 20x + 100 = x^2 + 18x + 81 + x^2 + 4x + 4$. Combine like terms and set the equation equal to 0: $x^2 + 2x - 15 = 0$. Factor and solve: $(x+5)(x-3) = 0$. Then $x = -5$ and $x = 3$, but length cannot be negative so reject $x = -5$.

SAT-Type Questions (page 481)

1. (D) Draw the figure and label the parts. Notice that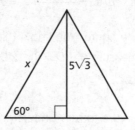

$\sin 60° = \dfrac{5\sqrt{3}}{x}$, or $x(\sin 60°) = 5\sqrt{3}$, and $x = \dfrac{5\sqrt{3}}{\sin 60°}$.

Thus, $x = \dfrac{5\sqrt{3}}{\frac{\sqrt{3}}{2}} = \dfrac{5\sqrt{3} \cdot 2}{\sqrt{3}} = 5 \cdot 2 = 10$.

2. (C) A triangle inscribed in a circle, where one side is the diameter of the circle, is a right triangle. Since $\angle A = 30°$ and $\angle C = 90°$, then $\angle B = 60°$. Draw segment CO and label the radii $\overline{CO}$ and $\overline{BO}$ 4 each. Since $m\angle B = 60°$, then the other base angle of isosceles $\triangle COB$, namely $\angle BCO$ is also 60°, which means the third angle, $\angle COB$ is 60° as well.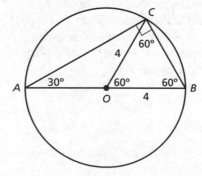

3. (B)   Since $m\angle A = 30°$, the $\cos \angle A = \dfrac{AC}{6}$. Then $\cos 30° = \dfrac{AC}{6}$, and

$6 \cos 30° = AC$. The $\cos 30°$ is $\dfrac{\sqrt{3}}{2}$, and $6 \cdot \dfrac{\sqrt{3}}{2} = 3\sqrt{3}$.

4. (C)   Sketch a picture of the rectangle and see that the diagonal creates a right triangle. Then use the Pythagorean theorem to determine the missing length. So $c^2 = a^2 + b^2$, $25^2 = 16^2 + b^2$, $625 = 256 + b^2$, $b^2 = 369$, and $b = \sqrt{369} \approx 19.21$. The question asks for the perimeter of the rectangle, so it is $\approx 2(19.21) + 2(16) \approx 70.4$.

5. (C)   Sketch an isosceles triangle and place an altitude from the apex to the base. Then you have two right triangles with hypotenuse length 26 and leg lengths 10 and x. Use the Pythagorean theorem to solve for the unknown, or recognize the triangle is a multiple of the 5, 12, 13 Pythagorean triple. The missing leg of the triangle is 24. Then the area of the triangle is $A = \dfrac{bh}{2} = \dfrac{20 \cdot 24}{2} = 240$ cm^2.

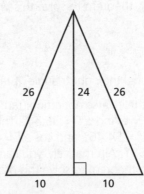

6. (B)   The lengths of the legs must be $5x$ and $12x$. Use the Pythagorean theorem and $(5x)^2 + (12x)^2 = 65^2$. Then $25x^2 + 144x^2 = 4225$, and $169x^2 = 4225$.

Solving for the unknown, $x^2 = \dfrac{4225}{169} = 25$, and $x = 5$. The shorter leg is

$5 \cdot 5 = 25$ feet in length. Alternately, recognize this is a multiple of a 5–12–13 Pythagorean triple.

7. (A)   Realize that length AR = length AC since both segments are radii. Then $\cos$

$30° = \dfrac{AC}{8}$, and $8 \cdot \cos 30° = 6.9$.

8. (B) $\sin n° + \sin n° = 1$, or $2 \cdot \sin n° = 1$, and $\sin n° = \dfrac{1}{2}$. Using the inverse

operation $(\sin^{-1})$, $n = 30°$. The exterior angle $x = n + n = 60°$.

9. (A)   Fill in the missing measurements in the given figure. Side CD is opposite the

$30°$ angle, so $CD = \dfrac{1}{2}$(hypotenuse) $= \dfrac{1}{2}(10) = 5$.

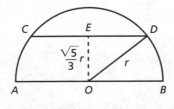

Then $\sin B - \sin A = \dfrac{5}{8} - \dfrac{1}{2} = \dfrac{5}{8} - \dfrac{4}{8} = \dfrac{1}{8}$.

10. (A)   Point O is the center of diameter $\overline{AB}$. Segment $\overline{OE}$ is perpendicular to $\overline{CD}$ and to $\overline{AB}$, and it bisects $\overline{CD}$. We can find ED using the Pythagorean theorem and doubling that

value. Let $x = ED$ and then $\left(\dfrac{\sqrt{5}}{3}r\right)^2 + x^2 = r^2$.

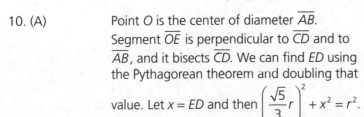

Isolate x^2 to see that $x^2 - r^2 - \left(\dfrac{\sqrt{5}}{3}r\right)^2 = r^2 - \dfrac{5}{9}r^2 = \dfrac{4}{9}r^2$

Then $x = \sqrt{\dfrac{4}{9}r^2} = \dfrac{2}{3}r$. Finally, $CD = 2ED = $

$2x = 2\left(\dfrac{2}{3}r\right) = \dfrac{4}{3}r$.

11. (10.3) Use the sine ratio. Then $\sin 45° = \dfrac{x}{14.6}$, and $14.6 \cdot \sin 45° = x \approx 10.3$. You can also use the Pythagorean theorem to solve this problem.

12. (0.882) Draw and label the right triangle. If $\sin \angle A = \dfrac{3}{4}$, then using the inverse operation ($\sin^{-1}$) to solve for sine, we find $\angle A = 48.59°$. Thus $\angle B = 90° - 48.59° = 41.41°$, and $\tan 41.41 = 0.8819$, or 0.882 to the nearest thousandth. Alternatively, you can use the Pythagorean theorem to solve this problem.

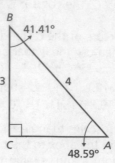

13. (.581) Draw and label the right triangle. If $\tan \angle D = \dfrac{5}{7}$, then using the inverse operation ($\tan^{-1}$) to solve for tangent, we find $\angle D = 35.54°$. Thus $\angle F = 90° - 35.54° = 54.46°$, and $\cos \angle F = \cos 54.46° = 0.581$. Alternatively, you can use the Pythagorean theorem to solve this problem.

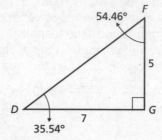

14. (0.896) Draw and label the right triangle. If $\cos \angle R = \dfrac{4}{9}$ then using the inverse operation ($\cos^{-1}$) to solve for cosine, we find $\angle R = 63.61°$, so that $\angle S = 90° - 63.61° = 26.39°$, and $\cos \angle S = 0.8958$, or 0.896 to the nearest thousandth.

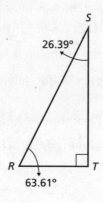

15. (72) Draw and label the equilateral triangle and the right triangle, filling in the angles.

To find a side of $\triangle ABC$, use

$\sin \angle A = \dfrac{12\sqrt{3}}{AB}$ or $\sin 60° = \dfrac{12\sqrt{3}}{AB}$.

Then $\dfrac{\sqrt{3}}{2} = \dfrac{12\sqrt{3}}{AB}$

$AB\sqrt{3} = (2)(12\sqrt{3})$

$AB\sqrt{3} = 24\sqrt{3}$

$AB = 24$.

The perimeter of $\triangle ABC = 24 + 24 + 24 = 72$.

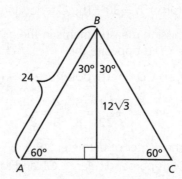

16. (4)   Label the figure, noting that the diagonals of the rhombus are perpendicular and form right triangles. Use $\cos 60° = \dfrac{ED}{8}$, or $8 \cdot \cos 60° = ED$. $ED = 8 \cdot 0.5 = 4$.

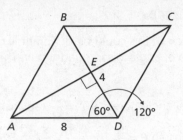

17. (6.93)   Draw the figure and label the parts. Then $\tan 60° = \dfrac{x}{4}$, and $4 \tan 60° = x$. $4 \cdot 1.732 = x$. $x = 6.928 \approx 6.93$ to the nearest hundredth.

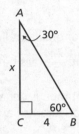

18. (111)   The ladder, house, and ground make a right triangle. The ladder is the hypotenuse. The distance from the base of the ladder to the house is a leg. The distance from the ground to where the ladder is leaning on the house is also a leg. We use the Pythagorean theorem to find the length of the ladder c. Then $c^2 = 40^2 + 104^2 \Rightarrow c = \sqrt{40^2 + 104^2} \approx 111$ inches.

19. (41.6)   The 60° angle is opposite the unknown side, so use the sine ratio. Then $\sin 60° = \dfrac{x}{48}$, and $48 \cdot \sin 60° = x = 41.6$.

20. (5.7)   The 45° angle is adjacent to the unknown side. So $\cos 45° = \dfrac{x}{8}$, and $8 \cdot \cos 45° = x = 5.7$.

Lesson 5: Degree and Radian Measure, Trigonometric Functions, and the Unit Circle

Practice: Degrees, Radians, and Arc Lengths (page 491)

1. (D) $270 \; \text{degrees} \cdot \dfrac{\pi \; \text{radians}}{180 \; \text{degrees}} = \dfrac{3\pi}{2} \; \text{radians}$.

2. (B) $\dfrac{5}{6}\pi \; \text{radians} \cdot \dfrac{180 \; \text{degrees}}{\pi \; \text{radians}} = 150 \; \text{degrees}$.

Practice: The Unit Circle and Trigonometric Functions with Radian Measure (page 495)

1. (C)   The measure of $\dfrac{6\pi}{5}$ is larger than π but smaller than $\dfrac{3\pi}{2}$. So the angle is in quadrant III, where sine is negative. Then $\sin\left(\dfrac{6\pi}{5}\right) = -\sin\left(\dfrac{6\pi}{5} - \pi\right) = -\sin\left(\dfrac{\pi}{5}\right)$.

2. (D)   The measure of $\dfrac{11\pi}{6}$ is greater than $\dfrac{3\pi}{2}$ but less than 2π. The angle is in quadrant IV, where cosine is positive. Then $\cos\dfrac{11\pi}{6} = \cos\left(2\pi - \dfrac{11\pi}{6}\right) = \cos\left(\dfrac{\pi}{6}\right)$.

1. (D)   Since $\csc x < 0$, this could be quadrant III or IV; $\cos x > 0$ in quadrants I and IV. Therefore, angle x is in quadrant IV. The only appropriate answer choice is D.

2. (B)   The central angle here is $90° = \dfrac{\pi}{2}$ radians. The radius is 6 inches. So use the relationship $\theta = \dfrac{s}{r}$. Then $\dfrac{\pi}{2} = \dfrac{s}{6}$, and $2s = 6\pi$, so $s = 3\pi$.

3. (B)   The edges of quadrant II are marked by $\dfrac{\pi}{2}$ radians and π radians. The measure $\dfrac{2\pi}{3}$ falls between these borders.

4. (A)   The tangent ratio is negative in quadrants II and IV. The sine ratio is positive in quadrants I and II. Therefore, angle x is in quadrant II. Choose answer choice A.

5. (C)   Angle x lies in quadrant II; therefore, $a < 0$ and $-a > 0$. Angle y falls in either quadrant I or quadrant IV. The value of angle y in quadrant I would be $\pi - x$, which is answer choice C, and the value in quadrant IV would be $\pi + x$, which is not an answer choice.

6. (A)   We are looking for the quadrant where both cotangent and secant are positive. Cotangent is positive in quadrant I and III. Secant is positive in quadrants I and IV. Thus angle x must be in quadrant I. The only angle measure from quadrant I is $\dfrac{\pi}{3}$.

7. (C)   The borders of quadrant III are π radians and $\dfrac{3\pi}{2}$ radians. The measure $\dfrac{4\pi}{3}$ falls between these borders.

8. (D)   We are given that City A's latitude is 30° north and City B's latitude is 75° north. Then the central angle that represents the distance between the two cities is 45°. Use the relationship $\theta = \dfrac{s}{r}$. Then $\dfrac{\pi}{4} = \dfrac{s}{6,400}$, and $4s = 6,400\pi$. Solving for the variable, $s = 1,600\pi \approx 5,026.55$ miles. The closest choice is choice A.

9. (C)   The measure of angle x is in quadrant IV. Therefore, $a > 0$ and $-a < 0$. The reference angle is $2\pi - x$. Then angle y falls in either quadrant II or quadrant III. The value of the angle in quadrant II would be $\pi - (2\pi - x) = x - \pi$, and the value in quadrant III would be $\pi + (2\pi - x) = 3\pi - x = \pi - x$.

10. (A)   Angle θ lies in quadrant III; therefore, $a < 0$ and $-a > 0$. So β is in quadrant I or quadrant II. The reference angle for θ is $\theta - \pi$, the angle in quadrant I. The value in quadrant II is $\pi - (\theta - \pi) = 2\pi - \theta$.

11. (D) $\dfrac{4\pi}{3}$ radians $\cdot \dfrac{180 \text{ degrees}}{\pi \text{ radians}} = 240$ degrees.

12. (135)   Convert radians to degrees: $\dfrac{3\pi}{4}$ radians $\cdot \dfrac{180 \text{ degrees}}{\pi \text{ radians}} = 135°$.

13. (210)   Begin by converting radians to degrees. Then $-\dfrac{5\pi}{6}$ radians $\cdot \dfrac{180 \text{ degrees}}{\pi \text{ radians}} = -150°$ degrees. But the question asks us to express this as a positive degree measure, so $360° - 150° = 210°$.

14. $\left(\dfrac{5}{4} \text{ or } 1.25\right)$ Use the relationship $\theta = \dfrac{s}{r}$. Substitute in the known values and $4 = \dfrac{5}{r}$,

$4r = 5$, and $r = \dfrac{5}{4}$, or 1.25.

15. (1)   This problem is very similar to #14. Use the same relationship, $\theta = \dfrac{s}{r}$,

and $6 = \dfrac{6}{r}$. Solve for the unknown and $r = 1$.

16. $\left(2.5 \text{ or } \dfrac{10}{4} \text{ or } \dfrac{5}{2}\right)$ Using the same relationship as the previous 2 problems, $\theta = \dfrac{s}{r}$, and

then $\theta = \dfrac{10}{4} = 2.5$ radians.

17. (300)   Convert radians to degrees: $\dfrac{5\pi}{3}$ radians $\cdot \dfrac{180 \text{ degrees}}{\pi \text{ radians}} = 300$ degrees.

18. $\left(\dfrac{5}{9}\right)$ Since $\theta = \dfrac{s}{r}$, $\theta = \dfrac{10}{18} = \dfrac{5}{9}$.

19. (300)   Convert radians to degrees: $-\dfrac{\pi}{3}$ radians $\cdot \dfrac{180 \text{ degrees}}{\pi \text{ radians}} = -60$ degrees.

Convert to standard position to see $360° - 60° = 300°$.

Lesson 6: Circles in the Coordinate Plane

Practice: Circle Definitions and Equations (page 503)

1. (A)   First we need to find the radius. Since the center of the circle is at the origin, we use the equation $r^2 = x^2 + y^2$. Substitute (2, 4) for (x, y) so that $r^2 = 2^2 + 4^2 = 20$. Then the equation of the circle is $x^2 + y^2 = 20$.

2. (D)   The given equation is of the general form $(x - h)^2 + (y - k)^2 = r^2$. The center is located at (h, k) and the radius is $\sqrt{r}$. So $-h = -8$ and $h = 8$. Similarly, $-k = 11$ and $k = -11$. Since $r^2 = 25$, $r = \sqrt{25} = 5$ The radius of the circle is 5 and the center is at $(8, -11)$.

SAT-Type Questions (page 504)

1. (D)   Substitute each of the coordinate pairs into the given equation to see which produces a false statement. Choice D fails because $(13 - 3)^2 + (-1 - 2)^2 \neq 100$.

2. (B)   Again, we need to substitute each of the coordinate pairs into the given equation, but this time we are looking for a true statement. Answer choice B produces $(-2 + 2)^2 + (1 - 5)^2 = 0 + (-4)^2 = 16$, and $(2 + 2)^2 + (5 - 5)^2 = 4^2 + 0 = 16$. These are both true statements. The other coordinate pairs contain at least one incorrect point.

3. (B)   Use the midpoint formula to determine the center of the circle. Then

$M = \left(\dfrac{0+0}{2}, \dfrac{3+(-4)}{2}\right)$, and $M = \left(0, -\dfrac{1}{2}\right)$. Calculate the radius using the

coordinates of the center and one point. So $(0-0)^2 + \left(3 - \left(-\dfrac{1}{2}\right)\right)^2 = r^2$,

and $r^2 = \dfrac{49}{4}$. The equation of the circle is $x^2 + \left(y + \dfrac{1}{2}\right)^2 = \dfrac{49}{4}$.

4. (B)   Divide through by 2 to remove the common factor: $x^2 + y^2 = 36$. Now it is easy to see that the circle's radius is 6 and the diameter is 12. Then the formula for the circumference of a circle is $C = \pi d$, and $C = 12\pi$.

5. (B)   The point of tangency on the x-axis is (3, 0). Then the radius is 3 and $r^2 = 9$. The equation is $(x - 3)^2 + (y + 3)^2 = 9$.

6. (5)   The diameter is $\sqrt{(4-(-2))^2 + (-3-5)^2} = \sqrt{6^2 + (-8)^2} = \sqrt{36 + 64} =$
$\sqrt{100} = 10$. Divide this quantity by 2 and the radius is $\frac{10}{2} = 5$. Alternately, this problem could be solved by finding the center through the midpoint formula and then substituting the center and an endpoint into the general circle equation to solve for r^2.

7. (2.88)   Square both sides of the equation to bring it into the standard form: $(x - 0.5)^2 + (y + 7.5)^2 = 1.44^2$. The radius is therefore 1.44, and the diameter is $2 \cdot 1.44 = 2.88$.

Lesson 7: Simplifying and Performing Arithmetic Operations on Complex Numbers

Practice: Simplification of Imaginary Monomial Expressions (page 508)

1. (C)   Rewrite as $\sqrt{-49} = \sqrt{49} \cdot \sqrt{-1} = 7i$.

2. (D)   Rewrite as $\sqrt{-18} = \sqrt{9} \cdot \sqrt{2} \cdot \sqrt{-1} = 3i\sqrt{2}$.

3. (C)   Rewrite as $4\sqrt{-16} = 4\sqrt{16} \cdot \sqrt{-1} = 4 \cdot 4i = 16i$.

4. (D)   Rewrite as $3\sqrt{-12} = 3\sqrt{4} \cdot \sqrt{3} \cdot \sqrt{-1} = 3 \cdot 2 \cdot \sqrt{3} \cdot i = 6i\sqrt{3}$.

5. (D)   Rewrite as $i^{11} = i^{2 \cdot 4 + 3} = i^3 = -i$.

Practice: Arithmetic Operations on Complex Numbers (page 510)

1. (A)   FOIL and $(3 + 2i)(4 - i) = 12 - 3i + 8i - 2i^2$. Remember that $i^2 = -1$. Then $12 + 5i - 2(-1) = 14 + 5i$.

2. (B)   Distribute the negative sign through the second set of parentheses. Then $(3 - 2i) - (4 - i) = 3 - 2i - 4 + i = -1 - i$.

3. (B)   Square the binomial: $(3 - 2i)^2 = (3 - 2i)(3 - 2i) = 9 - 6i - 6i + 2i^2$. Remember that $i^2 = -1$, and $9 - 12i - 4 = 5 - 12i$.

4. (C)   Distribute i through the parenthesis and then combine the like terms: $i(3 + i) - 5i = 3i + i^2 - 5i = -1 - 2i$.

SAT-Type Questions (page 511)

1. (C)   Expand the two binomials: $(2 + 2i)^2 - (1 + 2i)^2 = (2 + 2i)(2 + 2i) - [(1 + 2i)(1 + 2i)] = 4 + 4i + 4i + 4i^2 - (1 + 2i + 2i + 4i^2)$. Distribute the negative sign through the second set of parentheses and then combine the like terms: $4 + 4i + 4i + 4i^2 - 1 - 2i - 2i - 4i^2 = 3 + 4i$.

2. (A)   Distribute the i through the parentheses and simplify. Then $i^3 + i(2 - i) = i^3 + 2i - i^2 = -i + 2i + 1 = 1 + i$.

3. (B)   The average of the three values is $1 + i$, so $\dfrac{4 + i + 1 + 2i + x}{3} = 1 + i$.

Combine like terms and multiply both sides by 3 to clear the denominator: $5 + 3i + x = 3(1 + i)$. Distribute and collect the like terms to see $x = -2$.

4. (B)   Distribute from the inner parentheses outward and combine the like terms. Then $\left[\left((1+i)i+1\right)i\right]i+1=[(i+i^2+1)i]i+1=[i^2+i^3+i]i+1=i^3+i^4+i^2+1=$ $-i+1-1+1=1-i$.

5. (B)   FOIL the binomial and combine the like terms. Then $(1+i)^2=1+2i+i^2=$ $1+2i-1=2i$.

6. (D)   Evaluate $2i$ in the function f to see that $f(2i)=2(2i)^2=2(4i^2)=8i^2=$ $8(-1)=-8$. Now $g(-8)=\dfrac{i(-8)}{2}=-4i$.

7. (D)   FOIL the binomials and $(2-i)\left(\dfrac{2}{5}+\dfrac{1}{5}i\right)=\dfrac{4}{5}+\dfrac{2}{5}i-\dfrac{2}{5}i-\dfrac{i^2}{5}$. The middle two terms cancel each other out. Then $i^2=-1$, so $=\dfrac{4}{5}+\dfrac{1}{5}=1$.

8. (A)   Express the negative roots with i. Then $\dfrac{1+\sqrt{-4}}{2+\sqrt{-9}}=\dfrac{1+\sqrt{-1}\sqrt{4}}{2+\sqrt{-1}\sqrt{9}}=\dfrac{1+2i}{2+3i}$. Now multiply the numerator and denominator by the conjugate of the denominator. So $\dfrac{1+2i}{2+3i}\cdot\dfrac{2-3i}{2-3i}=\dfrac{2-3i+4i-6i^2}{4-9i^2}$. Simplify and collect the like terms to find $\dfrac{2+i-6(-1)}{4-9(-1)}=\dfrac{8+i}{13}$.

9. (B)   We must make the denominator real. Multiply both numerator and denominator by the conjugate of the denominator. Then $\dfrac{4-3i}{3i}\cdot\dfrac{-3i}{-3i}=$ $\dfrac{-12i+9i^2}{-9i^2}=\dfrac{-12i-9}{9}=\dfrac{-4i-3}{3}$.

10. (C)   We must make the denominator real. Multiply both numerator and denominator by the conjugate of the denominator. Then $\dfrac{1}{7-4i}\cdot\dfrac{7+4i}{7+4i}=$ $\dfrac{7+4i}{49+28i-28i-16i^2}=\dfrac{7+4i}{49+16}=\dfrac{7+4i}{65}$.

11. (29)   The conjugate of $5+2i$ is $5-2i$, so $(5+2i)(5-2i)=25-4i^2=25+4=29$.

12. (18)   The conjugate of $3-3i$ is $3+3i$, so $(3-3i)(3+3i)=9-9i^2=9+9=18$.

Summary SAT-Type Test

Multiple Choice (page 514)

Calculator Allowed

1. (C)   Choose a friendly number for the initial edge length, say 8. Then 25% of 8 is 2, so the new edge is 10. Then the old volume of the cube is $8^3=512$, and the new volume of the cube is $10^3=1,000$. The increase is 488 cubic units. The percent increase is $\dfrac{488}{512}=0.953=95.3\%$, or approximately 95%.

2. (A)   This makes $\overline{BC}$ the hypotenuse of $\triangle BDC$ and thus $BD<4$. Choice C is the only possible answer.

3. (D)   Radii drawn to the point of tangency form right angles. Since a quadrilateral has 360° and the sum of $m\angle A$ and $m\angle B$ is 180°, the $m\angle P+m\angle AOB=180°$.

4. (C) Recognize that ΔDEF is a multiple of a 3–4–5 right triangle such that side $DF = 9$. The slope of $DE = \dfrac{12}{9} = \dfrac{4}{3}$. Similarly, the point (6, 8) results in a slope $\dfrac{8}{6} = \dfrac{4}{3}$ and lies on segment DE.

5. (C) At 4:30, the minute hand is pointing at the number 6 and the hour hand is pointing to the middle of the arc between the 4 and the 5. Since each hour span on a clock is $\dfrac{1}{12}$ of 360°, or 30°, the degree distance at 4:30 is that of 1 and $\dfrac{1}{2}$ arcs, which is $30 + 15 = 45°$. Converting 45 degrees into radian measure, we write $\cancel{45} \cdot \dfrac{\pi}{\cancel{180}_4} = \dfrac{\pi}{4}$.

6. (D) The standard form of a circle is $(x - h)^2 + (y - k)^2 = r^2$, where (h, k) is the center of the circle and r is the radius. Then the standard form equation for the circle is $(x + 2)^2 + (y - 3)^2 = 2^2$. Expanding, $x^2 + 4x + 4 + y^2 - 6y + 9 = 4$. Subtract 4 from both sides and collect the like terms, and we have $x^2 + y^2 + 4x - 6y + 9 = 0$.

7. (A) Keep in mind we can make an equivalence between the real and imaginary parts, so that $a + b = 11$, and $a = 7$ from the $7i = ai$. Hence $7 + b = 11$ and $b = 4$.

8. (A) The radius of 13 is the hypotenuse of a right triangle with a vertical side length of 12, and the length of the other leg is 5. This is the radius of the smaller circle in the intercepted plane. The circumference is 10π.

9. (B) A regular octagon has $180(n - 2)$ degrees in its angles, so the total is $180(8 - 2) = 1{,}080°$. Then each interior angle has $\dfrac{1080}{8} = 135°$. The supplement of 135° is 45°, so $135° - 45° = 90°$.

10. (C) The $m\angle A = \dfrac{1}{2}m\overset{\frown}{BCD}$ and $m\angle C = \dfrac{1}{2}m\overset{\frown}{DAB}$ because they are inscribed angles. Now, $m\angle A + m\angle C = \dfrac{1}{2}m\overset{\frown}{BCD} + \dfrac{1}{2}m\overset{\frown}{DAB}$. By factoring, $\dfrac{1}{2}\left(m\overset{\frown}{BCD} + m\overset{\frown}{DAB}\right) = \dfrac{1}{2}(360°) = 180°$. Substitute in the algebraic expressions for the angle measures and $3x - 5 + 2x + 10 = 180$. Collect the like terms to see that $5x + 5 = 180$, and solve for $x = \dfrac{180 - 5}{5} = 35°$. Then $m\angle A = 3(35) - 5 = 100°$.

11. (B) Since $BC = DC$ and $AC > DC$, length AC must be greater than length BC. So $\tan \angle A = \dfrac{BC}{AC} < 1$. Choice B is the only possible answer.

12. (C) We can find the radian measure of the central angle by determining the ratio of the arc length to the circle's radius. So $\dfrac{\dfrac{16\pi}{3}}{8} = \dfrac{16\pi}{3} \cdot \dfrac{1}{8}$, which is $\dfrac{16\pi}{24} = \dfrac{2\pi}{3}$. Convert the radian measure to degrees and $\dfrac{2(180)}{3} = 120°$.

13. (B)   Use the given point to form a right triangle with sides of lengths 8, 6, and 10 such that the radius $OA = 10$. Then the area of a circle of radius 10 is 100π. One-fourth of that area, or 25π, is the area of the shaded region.

14. (D)   Immediately eliminate answer choices A and C; there is no power of $i = 0$, so no product involving only powers of i will equal 0. Check answer choice B: $i^2 + i^2 = (-1) + (-1) = -2$. Check answer choice D: $i^4 + i^2 = 1 + (-1) = 0$.

15. (A)   Begin by calculating the area of $\Delta I = \dfrac{(5)(12)}{2} = 30$ square units. Then

by definition, the ratio of the areas of two similar figures is the ratio of the square of any two corresponding parts. The length of the hypotenuse of ΔI is 13 and the length of the hypotenuse of ΔII is 12.

Use this information and the area of ΔI to see that $\dfrac{30}{\text{Area } \Delta II} = \dfrac{13^2}{12^2}$.

Cross-multiply and $4{,}320 = \text{Area } \Delta II \cdot 169$. Then the area of

$\Delta II = \dfrac{4320}{169} \approx 25.6$ square units.

16. (B)   The lengths of the three sides of the isosceles triangle are $5\sqrt{2}$, $5\sqrt{2}$, and 10. Each of the shaded areas is a half-circle, and the largest

half-circle has an area of $\dfrac{\pi 5^2}{2} = \dfrac{25\pi}{2} = 12.5\pi$. The two smaller half-

circles comprise one circle of radius $\dfrac{5\sqrt{2}}{2}$. The area of that circle is

$\pi \left(\dfrac{5\sqrt{2}}{2} \right)^2 = \pi \dfrac{25(2)}{4} = \pi \dfrac{50}{4} = 12.5\pi$. The sum of the shaded

areas $= 12.5\pi + 12.5\pi = 25\pi$.

17. (B)   Chord $\overline{CD}$, of length 30, is bisected by the diameter $\overline{AB}$ at point E, so that $ED = 15$. Then the right triangle OED is a Pythagorean triple of 8, 15, 17. Segment $OE = 8$. Since the length of radius $\overline{OD} = 17$, radius $\overline{OB}$ is also of length 17 and $OB - OE = EB$, or $17 - 8 = 9$.

18. (D)   Using trigonometry or the Pythagorean theorem, we can find the length of side $\overline{OA}$. Since ΔOAB is an equilateral triangle with a height of 2, the

length of $\overline{OA}$ is equal to the length of side $\overline{OB} = \dfrac{4}{\sqrt{3}}$. The x-intercept of

$\overline{AB}$ is at $\dfrac{4}{\sqrt{3}}$.

19. (B)   An angle inscribed in half a circle has a measure of 90°, so $\angle B$ and $\angle D$ are

right angles. The $\sin x = \dfrac{BC}{1} = BC$, $\sin y = \dfrac{DC}{1} = DC$, $\cos x = \dfrac{AB}{1} = AB$,

and $\cos y = \dfrac{AD}{1} = AD$. The perimeter of the quadrilateral is given by the

sum $BC + AB + DC + AD$, So $\sin x° + \cos x° + \sin y° + \cos y°$.

20. (B)   Since $x^2 + y^2 - 6x + 2y - 6 = 0$, then $x^2 + y^2 - 6x + 2y = 6$. We have to complete the square for $x^2 - 6x$ and $y^2 + 2y$. That gives $x^2 - 6x + 9 + y^2 + 2y + 1 = 6 + 9 + 1$. Factor into $(x - 3)^2 + (y + 1)^2 = 16$, and the circle's center is at $(3, -1)$.

21. (B)   Expand $(1 + i)^5$ into $(1 + i)(1 + i)(1 + i)(1 + i)(1 + i)$ and regroup as $((1 + i)(1 + i)) \cdot ((1 + i)(1 + i))(1 + i)$. Then $((1 + i)(1 + i))$ is $1 + 2i - 1 = 2i$. So $(2i)(2i)(1 + i) = 4i^2(1 + i) = -4(1 + i) = -4 - 4i$.

22. (A) The volume of the cylinder formed by rotating about the side of length 10 is $\pi r^2 h = \pi(4^2)10 = 160\pi$ cm^3. Rotating about the side of length 4, we have a volume of $\pi(10^2)4 = 400\pi$ cm^3. The positive difference is $400\pi - 160\pi = 240\pi$ cm^2.

23. (A) Since $x = y$, both $\angle x$ and $\angle y$ have measures of 45° and $\triangle AED$ is an isosceles right triangle. Then since $\overline{BD} \perp \overline{AD}$, $\angle CDB$ must have a measure of 45°. So $\triangle BCD$ is another isosceles right triangle. The length of the side opposite a 45° angle in an isosceles right triangle is $\frac{1}{2}$(hypotenuse)$\cdot \sqrt{2}$.

Hence $ED = \frac{1}{2}\cdot 8 \cdot \sqrt{2} = 4\sqrt{2}$ and, similarly, $DC = 3\sqrt{2}$. The length of $\overline{EC}$ is $4\sqrt{2} + 3\sqrt{2} = 7\sqrt{2}$.

24. (B) Since $m\angle AED = 136°$, the measure of its supplement, $\angle BED$, is 44°. This is half the measure of the intercepted arc $\overset{\frown}{ED} = 88°$. Then the $m\angle ECD$ is $\frac{1}{2}(88) = 44°$.

25. (B) To find the distance between the two sightings, we need to calculate the lengths DC and AC. So $\tan 20° = \frac{80}{DC}$, and $DC = \frac{80}{\tan(20)} \approx 219.8$ meters.

Then $\tan 10° = \frac{80}{AC}$, and $AC = \frac{80}{\tan(10)} \approx 453.7$ meters. The distance AD is $453.7 - 219.8$, or about 234 meters.

26. (C) Draw in a perpendicular line from point B to the x-axis to make a right triangle. The length of the side opposite the 30° angle is half the length of the hypotenuse $= \frac{1}{2}$ and the side opposite the 60° angle $= \frac{\text{hypotenuse}\cdot\sqrt{3}}{2}$ $= \frac{\sqrt{3}}{2}$. The (x, y) coordinates are $\left(\frac{\sqrt{3}}{2}, \frac{1}{2}\right)$.

27. (B) Since ABC is an isosceles triangle, using the given coordinates, the length of the sides must be $AB = 2$, $BC = 2$, and the hypotenuse $AC = 2\sqrt{2}$. The shaded area equals the area of the circle – the area of the right triangle. That is, πr^2 or $\pi\left(\sqrt{2}\right)^2 - 2$, or $2\pi - 2$.

28. (B) We must rationalize the denominator by multiplying both the numerator and denominator by the conjugate of $4 - 3i$. Then $\frac{5}{4-3i}\cdot\frac{4+3i}{4+3i}$ is $\frac{20+15i}{25} = \frac{4+3i}{5}$.

29. (B) The surface area of the rectangular solid is calculated by determining the sum of the areas of all the sides. There will be two sides that measure 2 cm by 2 cm and 4 sides that measure 2 cm by 16 cm, so $(2)(2)(2) + (4)(2)(16) = 136$ cm^2. The volume of the rectangular solid is 64 cubic cm, which can be recast as a cube 4 cm on a side since $\sqrt[3]{64} = 4$. The surface area of the cube will be $(6)(4)(4) = 96$ cm^2. The difference in the surface area measurements is $136 - 96 = 40$ cm^2.

30. (A) Consecutive angles are supplementary, so $m\angle A = 30°$. Draw in a perpendicular line from point B to $\overline{AD}$ so you can calculate the height of the parallelogram. The side opposite a 30° angle is one-half the length of the hypotenuse, so the height of the parallelogram is half of $8 = 4$ inches, and the area of the parallelogram is $10 \cdot 4 = 40$ square inches. Then the area of the associated rectangle is $x(2x) = 40$ and $2x^2 = 40$. So $x^2 = 20$ and $x = \sqrt{20} = 2\sqrt{5}$ in.

Calculator Allowed

31. (28) The measure of angle E is 26° and is the same measure as $\frac{1}{2}$ of the difference

of the intercepted arcs. Then $26 = \frac{1}{2}\left(108 - m\widehat{AC}\right), 52 = 108 - m\widehat{AC}$, and

$m\widehat{AC} = 56°$. Finally, $m\angle ABC = \frac{1}{2}m\widehat{AC} = \frac{1}{2}\cdot 56 = 28°$.

32. $\left(\dfrac{7}{18}\right)$ We are given that $\tan \angle x = \dfrac{CD}{AD} = \dfrac{3}{4}$ and $\tan \angle y = \dfrac{BE}{BC} = \dfrac{1}{6}$. Opposite

sides of a rectangle must be equal in length. For AD to equal BC, we give the fractions their least common denominator, which is 12. Now, we can

change the ratios to $\dfrac{3(3)}{3(4)} = \dfrac{9}{12}$ and $\dfrac{2(1)}{2(6)} = \dfrac{2}{12}$. Now $AD = 12$, $CD = 9$,

and $BC = 6(2) = 12$. We also know that $BE = 1(2) = 2$. Now, $CD = AB$, so $AB = 9$ and $AE = 9 - 2 = 7$. The area of shaded $\triangle AEC$ is given by

$\dfrac{1}{2} \cdot 7 \cdot 12 = 42$ square units, and the area of $ABCD = 9(12) = 108$ square

units. Then $\dfrac{\text{Area } \triangle AEC}{\text{Area } ABCD} = \dfrac{42}{108} = \dfrac{7}{18}$.

33. (12.5) Radius · radian measure = length of the intercepted arc, so $(2.5)(5) = 12.5$ cm.

34. (12) This is not a straight-forward volume problem. Any one sleeve, while it is cylindrical, has a diameter of $2r$ and a height of $6r$, so it will need a rectangular prism space of $2r$ by $2r$ by $6r$. The larger shipping box, with dimensions $4r$ by $6r$ by $12r$, divided by the needed space of $2r$ by $2r$ by $6r$

yields $\dfrac{4r(6r)(12r)}{2r(2r)(6r)} = \dfrac{288r^3}{24r^3} = 12$ sleeves. We can visualize that there are six

rows of two sleeves each, or a total of 12 sleeves of tennis balls.

35. (7.21) A circle centered at the origin will have the form $x^2 + y^2 = r^2$. Use the given point, $4^2 + 6^2 = r^2$. Solve for r to see that $16 + 36 = r^2$, $52 = r^2$, and

$r = \sqrt{52} \approx 7.21$.

36. (600) The diagonals of a rhombus bisect each other so that 4 smaller right triangles are formed with sides 5, 12, and 13. The shorter diagonal is of

length 10, so the area of the base is $\dfrac{1}{2}(D_1)(D_2) = \dfrac{1}{2}(10)(24) = 120$ ft³. Then

the volume of the pyramid is $\dfrac{1}{3}$(base)(height) $= \dfrac{1}{3}(120)(15) = 600$ ft³.

37. (80) The measures of the arcs of the circle can be found by using the given ratios: $1x + 3x + 5x = 360°$. Then $9x = 360$, and $x = 40°$.
So $m\widehat{BR} = 40°$, $m\widehat{RT} = 3x = (3)(40) = 120°$, and $m\widehat{TB} = 5x = 200°$.
The measure of $\angle A$ is one-half of the difference of the measures of

the intercepted arcs $m\widehat{TB} - m\widehat{BR}$, so $\dfrac{1}{2}(200 - 40) = 80°$.

38. (9.2) Remember that the square of the length of the tangent line is equal to the product of the lengths of the secant and the external segment. Note that

$AT = RT + AR = 12 + 5 = 17$ inches. So $\left(\overline{AB}\right)^2 = \overline{AT} \cdot \overline{AR}$. Then

$\left(\overline{AB}\right)^2 = 17 \cdot 5$, and $\overline{AB} = \sqrt{85} \approx 9.2$ inches.

1. (D)   The ratio of surface area to volume of a sphere is $\dfrac{4\pi r^2}{\frac{4}{3}\pi r^3}$, and it reduces to $\dfrac{3}{r}$.

2. (C)   The given proportion, $\dfrac{AD}{BD} = \dfrac{AB}{k}$, is the ratio of

$\dfrac{AD \text{ (short leg of rt } \triangle ABD)}{BD \text{ (long leg of rt } \triangle ABD)} = \dfrac{AB \text{ (short leg of rt } \triangle ABC)}{BC \text{ (long leg of rt } \triangle ABC)}$. Therefore, $k = BC$.

3. (C)   The $m\angle x = m\widehat{BC}$ and the $m\angle w = \dfrac{1}{2}\,m\widehat{BC}$, which is $\dfrac{1}{2}\,m\angle x$. So $x = 2w$.

4. (A)   The product $\sin(45) \cdot \cos(30) \cdot \tan(60) = \dfrac{\sqrt{2}}{2} \cdot \dfrac{\sqrt{3}}{2} \cdot \sqrt{3} = \dfrac{\sqrt{2 \cdot 3 \cdot 3}}{4} = \dfrac{3\sqrt{2}}{4}$.

5. (D)   The angle $-240°$ is found by moving $240°$ clockwise into quadrant II. Its sine is equal to the sine of the positive angle $120°$, which equals the sine of the positive angle $60°$, which is $\dfrac{\sqrt{3}}{2}$.

6. (B)   The standard form of a circle is $(x - h)^2 + (y - h)^2 = r^2$. The center of the circle is at (h, k) and the radius is r. Since the equation is $(x + 1)^2 + (y + 3)^2 = 9$, (h, k) must be $(-1, -3)$, and the radius is $\sqrt{9} = 3$. Plotting the point $(-1, -3)$ as the center and extending a radius of 3 units from that center indicates a tangential intersection of the circle with the x-axis at point $(-1, 0)$.

7. (C)   Simplifying the complex number expression $(3 - \sqrt{-49}) - 2(2 - 2i)^2$ means paying attention to the i-forms. Thus, $(3 - \sqrt{-49}) = (3 - \sqrt{-1}\sqrt{49}) = 3 - 7i$. Expanding $-2(2 - 2i)^2$, it becomes $-2(4 - 8i + 4i^2) = -8 + 16i - 8i^2 = 16i$. Putting these parts together, we have $3 - 7i + 16i = 3 + 9i$.

8. (B)   Assuming we don't have the needed formula memorized, choose friendly numbers for the dimensions, say 2, 3, and 5. Draw and label a rectangular solid and identify the sides and the area surfaces. Then the volume is $2 \cdot 3 \cdot 5 = 30$ cubic cm. Which of the given answers provides 30? Keep in mind that $a = 6$, $b = 15$, and $c = 10$. Answer choice A, abc, yields an answer of 900. Answer choice B: $\sqrt{abc} = \sqrt{6 \cdot 15 \cdot 10} = 30$.

9. (D)   Since $\overline{xy}$ is included in both $\overline{Ay}$ and $\overline{Bx}$, its length must be subtracted out when the segment lengths are combined to find the length of $\overline{AB}$, which is $\sqrt{5^2 + 12^2} = 13$. Then $AB = Ay + Bx - xy$, so $13 = 5 + 12 - xy$. Thus $13 = 17 - xy$ and $xy = 4$.

10. (B)   The products of the segments of intersecting chords are equal. Since $6 \cdot 15 = 90$, we are looking for a number pair that sums to 23 and has a product of 90. Only choice B fits this need.

11. (B)   The angle of depression is $35°$ and the adjacent angle, or complementary angle, has a measure of $55°$. Using the tangent function, the height can be found two ways: $\tan(35) = \dfrac{x}{50}$, which, in solving for x, becomes $x = 50(\tan(35))$; or $\tan(55) = \dfrac{50}{x}$, which, in solving for x, becomes $x = \dfrac{50}{\tan(55)}$.

12. (C)   First determine the trigonometric ratios as defined by the given triangle.

Then $\sin A = \dfrac{a}{1} = a$, $\sin B = \dfrac{b}{1} = b$, and $\cos A = \dfrac{b}{1} = b$. By substitution,

$\dfrac{\sin A + \sin B}{\cos A}$ becomes $\dfrac{a+b}{b} = \dfrac{a}{b} + \dfrac{b}{b} = \dfrac{a}{b} + 1$.

13. (A)   The standard form of a circle is $(x - h)^2 + (y - k)^2 = r^2$. Substitute in the coordinates for the center and the given point to determine the square of the radius. Then $(-1 + 5)^2 + (-1 - 3)^2 = r^2$, and $16 + 16 = r^2 = 32$. So the equation of the circle is $(x + 5)^2 + (y - 3)^2 = 32$. Alternately, the standard form of a circle is $(x - h)^2 + (y - k)^2 = r^2$. We are given that the center is $(h, k) = (-5, 3)$, so the equation becomes $(x + 5)^2 + (y - 3)^2 = r^2$. Only choice A has this form, so it is the correct choice.

14. (A)   The multiplicative identity returns the original expression; it is multiplication by 1. For the complex numbers, it must be answer choice A since multiplying a number by any of the other choice would change the original expression.

15. (C)   For this question, the volume of milk remains unchanged. So $4 \cdot 4 \cdot 9 = \pi(3^2)h$, and 144 cu in $= 9h\pi$. All the answer choices are given in terms of π, so the height $h = \dfrac{144}{9\pi} = \dfrac{16}{\pi}$ cubic inches.

Student-Produced Response Questions (page 531)

No Calculator Allowed

16. (6)   The length of the third side, x, can be represented by the inequality $7 < x < 15$, where the limits are the difference and sum of the given side lengths. The largest integer length for x would be 14 and the smallest would be 8. Thus $4 + 11 + 14 = 29$ is the larger perimeter, and $4 + 11 + 8 = 23$ is the smaller perimeter. The difference is $29 - 23 = 6$.

17. (125)   Since $\overset{\frown}{AB} = \overset{\frown}{AD}$ and $m\overset{\frown}{AB} = 110°$, $m\overset{\frown}{AD}$ is also $= 110°$. The measure of $\overset{\frown}{BED} = (360 - 220) = 140°$. The $m\angle ADC$, which is formed by the tangent $\overline{CD}$ and the chord $\overline{AD}$, is $\dfrac{1}{2}\left(m\overset{\frown}{ABD}\right) = \dfrac{1}{2}(110 + 140) = \dfrac{1}{2}(250) = 125°$.

18. $\left(\dfrac{1}{9}\right)$ Since $m\angle PQM = 60°$, $m\angle P = 30°$, and side $QM = 5$. Then the $\sin P = \dfrac{5}{10} = \dfrac{1}{2}$ and $\sin R = \dfrac{5}{6}$, and $(\sin R - \sin P)^2 = \left(\dfrac{5}{6} - \dfrac{1}{2}\right)^2 = \left(\dfrac{1}{3}\right)^2 = \dfrac{1}{9}$.

19. $\left(\dfrac{1}{2} \text{ or } 0.5\right)$ The negative value of the cosine that we are given tells us that the angle is in the second or third quadrant, with a reference angle of 30°. We are told that the angle is not in the third quadrant, so we are left with the second quadrant, where the sine is positive. The answer is $\sin \theta = \sin 30° = \dfrac{1}{2}$ or 0.5.

20. (50)   Since the volume of the cube is 1,000 cubic units, then the length of an edge of the cube is $\sqrt[3]{1000} = 10$ units. Quadrilateral $ABCD$ is a square embedded in the cube. The length of each diagonal $\overline{AC}$ and $\overline{BD}$ of the square $ABCD$ is equal to the length of an edge, which is 10 units. Then the area of a square is equal to $\dfrac{\text{product of the diagonals}}{2} = \dfrac{10 \cdot 10}{2} = 50$ square units.